CAMBRIDGE CLASSICAL TEXTS AND
COMMENTARIES

EDITORS
J. DIGGLE   SIR KENNETH DOVER   E. W. HANDLEY
H. D. JOCELYN   M. D. REEVE

14B

POSIDONIUS

Volume II

THE COMMENTARY

150.00 (2 vol. set)

POSIDONIUS

II. THE COMMENTARY:
(ii) Fragments 150–293

I. G. KIDD
*Emeritus Professor of Greek,
University of St Andrews*

CAMBRIDGE UNIVERSITY PRESS

CAMBRIDGE

NEW YORK   NEW ROCHELLE
MELBOURNE   SYDNEY

Published by the Press Syndicate of the University of Cambridge
The Pitt Building, Trumpington Street, Cambridge CB2 1RP
32 East 57th Street, New York, NY 10022, USA
10 Stamford Road, Oakleigh, Melbourne 3166, Australia

© Cambridge University Press 1988

First published 1988

Printed in Great Britain at
The Alden Press, Oxford

British Library cataloguing in publication data
Posidonius.
Posidonius. – (Cambridge classical texts
and commentaries).
Vol. 2, The commentary
1. Greek literature
I. Title II. Kidd, I.G.
888'.0108 PA4399.P2

Library of Congress cataloguing in publication data
Posidonius.
(Cambridge classical texts and commentaries, 13–)
Greek and Latin text; pref. and introd. in English.
Includes bibliographical references.
contents: v. 1. The fragments – v. 2. The
Commentary: i. Testimonia and fragments 1–149;
ii. Fragments 150–293.
I. Edelstein, Ludwig, 1902–1965, ed. II. Kidd, I. G.,
ed. III. Series: Cambridge classical texts and
commentaries; 13, etc.
PA399.P2 1972 188 77-145609

ISBN 0 521 35499 4 THE SET
ISBN 0 521 35498 6 II (ii)

AL

CONTENTS

Preface   *page* ix

VOLUME II(i): TESTIMONIA AND FRAGMENTS 1-149

PART I: TESTIMONIA

T1–72	Life and influence	3
T73–107	Characteristics of his philosophy	58
T108–15	Dubia	90

PART II: FRAGMENTS AND TITLES OF NAMED BOOKS

F1–3		99
F4–28	Physics	102
F29–41	Ethics	151
F42–5	Logic	189
F46–83	Sciences and History	205
F84–6	Dubia	336

PART III: FRAGMENTS NOT ASSIGNED TO BOOKS

F87–91	Divisions and Content of Philosophy	349
F92–149	Physics	368

VOLUME II(ii): FRAGMENTS 150-293

PART III: FRAGMENTS NOT ASSIGNED TO BOOKS (*cont.*)

F150–87	Ethics	553
F188–94	Logic	684
F195–251	Sciences	699
F252–91	History	861
F292–3	Miscellaneous	983

References   989

Indices   1009

CONTENTS

Index of passages cited or discussed — 1010
Index of proper names — 1036
Subject index — 1047

ETHICS

F150a, b Galen, *De Placitis* IV.421,
pp. 396.15–397.8 M, 284.33–286.7 De Lacy;
Galen, *De Placitis* V.471, p. 451.5–13 M,
328.21–7 De Lacy

CONTENT

F150a: Posidonius, who admired Plato's doctrines on the πάθη and the δυνάμεις of the soul, said that instruction on the virtues and on the end is tied to this, and that in short all the doctrines of ethical philosophy are bound as if by a single cord to the knowledge of the powers (δυνάμεις) of the soul.

F150b exemplifies this with another quotation from Posidonius: 'Once the cause of the emotions was seen, it broke the absurdity (of the Chrysippean explanation of the τέλος), showed the sources of distortion in choice and avoidance (of good and evil), distinguished the methods of training, and made clear the problems concerning the impulse (ὁρμῆς) that rises from emotion (πάθους).'

CONTEXT

F150a: comm. on F165.75–102.
F150b: comm. on F187.37ff.

COMMENT

F150a reiterates the claim made by the quotation from near the beginning of Περὶ παθῶν, Bk 1, given in F30. F30 listed

553

COMMENTARY: F150

good and evil, ends and virtues as being dependent on the correct study of πάθη; F150a repeats virtues and end, but explicitly widens to the whole of ethical philosophy. More importantly, it clarifies what F30 meant by the correct examination of πάθη, namely that the key of moral philosophy lies in knowledge of the δυνάμεις of the soul. Psychology is indeed both the fundamental point of difference between Posidonius and Chrysippus, and the core of investigation in all Posidonius' explanations of the problems of ethics. F150b gives one illustration of this in different subdivisions of ethics (Frs. 161, 168, 162, 187, 174, 166; and for divisions of ethics, 89).

There was probably a difference in methodology between Posidonius and Chrysippus. Chrysippus appears to have approached the fundamental problems of psychology and ethics from metaphysics, or Stoic 'physical philosophy' (Plu. *De SR* ch. 9 = *SVF* III.68). Posidonius would not have rejected this (F18), but in practice recognised the importance of observed fact in behaviour as a relevant factor, and this was especially crucial in the problem of πάθη (e.g. F169, *init.*).

Is F150a.6–10 merely a reworded interpretation by Galen of the quotation in F30? If so, all other evidence indicates that the interpretation is undoubtedly correct. But the striking elaboration of the simile, ὥσπερ ἐκ μιᾶς μηρίνθου δεδέσθαι, probably shows that Galen is following another statement of Posidonius. The comm. on T105 illustrates Posidonius' fondness for similes. μήρινθος is not common as a metaphor (but see Plu. *Mor.* 333C). The *De Placitis* gives the impression that Posidonius was rather repetitive and discursive in Περὶ παθῶν.

For F150a.1–6, cf. T97.

F150b.3–4. ὀραθεῖσα *HL*; ὁρατοῖς *HL*. When Galen repeats this section of the quotation a few lines later, the codices have εὑρεθεῖσα and αἱρετοῖς, see F161.1–2. ὁρατοῖς, F150b.4, is nonsense. The Aldine corrected to ὀρεκτοῖς (ὀρεκτοῖς ed. Basil.). This looks like a guess, and Müller was

COMMENTARY: F151

right to restore αἱρετοῖς, which I now read, and which is the normal Stoic twin for φευκτοῖς, referring to choice and avoidance of good and evil (F161). Müller also corrected ὁραθεῖσα to εὑρεθεῖσα, but this seems less probable, since ὁραθεῖσα could help to explain the copying mistake ὁρατοῖς, and ancient authors did not always feel obliged to requote exactly.

F151 Galen, *De Placitis* v.478, pp. 458.9–459.5 M, p. 334.24–33 De Lacy

CONTENT

In relation to other theories on emotions (πάθη), Posidonius is classified by Galen with Plato (and Cleanthes) against Chrysippus (and probably Zeno). Posidonius added Pythagoras.

CONTEXT

At the end of *De Plac.* Bk IV, Galen declared his intention of continuing in Bk V with criticism directed against Chrysippus' inconsistent statements on emotions (T61), using Posidonius. The direct attack on Chrysippus in Bk V lasts until p. 334.15 De Lacy. At this point Galen excuses himself from examining Zeno's position, since Chrysippus is his main target (p. 334.16–23). F151 follows, and then at p. 336.16 he turns to Plato.

COMMENT

See T91 commentary.

1f See above. Galen's plan was to vindicate Plato and Hippocrates by singling out Chrysippus alone of the Stoics for

555

COMMENTARY: F151

attack (cf. *De Plac.* 234.12ff De L), using the help of Posidonius for this.

2–8 The context is the explanation of emotions and their relation to rationality. The worst analysis (7) in Galen's view is that of Chrysippus, who thought that emotions were rational and a kind of judgement (κρίσις) (Frs. 34, 152). The best is the psychology of Plato and Hippocrates, who regarded emotions as stemming from distinct irrational faculties or factors. Posidonius and Cleanthes (and Galen) sided with the latter. Galen indicates that there is room for doubt about Zeno's position (T91), as to whether he meant the same as Chrysippus (2), or followed Plato's principles and starting points (ἀρχαῖς), roughly the same (παραπλησίως) as Cleanthes and Posidonius (3–5), or, as Galen believes (ὅπερ ἐγὼ πείθομαι, 5f), adopted an intermediate position, thinking that emotions supervene (ἐπιγίνεσθαι) on judgements (5–8) (Frs. 34, 152).

For these relationships in general: T91–102, Frs. 142–6.

9–11 Posidonius said that Pythagoras' doctrine resembled the Platonic view (of psychology), an inference from written works of some of Pythagoras' pupils, since no work of Pythagoras himself had survived to our times. This is interesting on three counts.

(i) It reveals, as elsewhere, Posidonius' interest in the history of ideas, probably expressed in initial doxographic accounts, one of which no doubt occurred in *On Emotions*: F31 comm. *B*, F165 comm. on 164–72.

(ii) Posidonius' special interest in Pythagoras and Pythagoreans (T91, T95). The revival of interest in Pythagoreanism was marked in the 1st c. B.C. (see e.g. Dillon, *The Middle Platonists* 117ff). It may well have received a major impetus from Posidonius.

(iii) Galen is careful to distinguish himself from Posidonius here. This is also true of the remarks on Zeno above; because while Galen here admits room for doubt concerning Zeno's position, there is no sign of this in Posidonius (F34, F152).

COMMENTARY: F152

F152 Galen, *De Placitis* v.429, p. 405.5-14 M, p. 292.17-25 De Lacy

CONTENT

Posidonius opposed Chrysippus' view (given in *On Emotions*, Bk I) that emotions were judgements of a kind (κρίσεις τινας) of the rational (τοῦ λογιστικοῦ), and Zeno's that they were contractions and expansions, risings and fallings of the spirit supervening on judgement. He praised and approved of Plato's doctrine. Posidonius pointed out that emotions were certain motions (κινήσεις τινας) of distinct irrational powers, given the name by Plato of desiderative (ἐπιθυμητικήν) and spirited (θυμοειδῆ).

CONTEXT

F163, Context (a). At the beginning of *De Plac.* v (292.4ff), Galen refers to his criticism in Bk IV of Chrysippus' position that the emotional and rational elements are situated in one place (the heart) and are the work of a single faculty (δύναμις), before he proceeds to a more detailed attack on Chrysippean inconsistencies at 294.26ff. F152 recalls the discussion in Bk IV given in F34. The link is also indicated in F157.

COMMENT

1-3 For Posidonius' argument against Chrysippus on emotion and judgement, see F34.

3-5 The reference to Zeno also echoes the passage in F34.4ff, *q.v.* The description of emotion by the terms συστολὰς ... ταπεινώσεις τῆς ψυχῆς (4f) is common Stoic practice, accepted by Chrysippus and probably by Posidonius (F34. *A*. 2, 3), and there is no reason for doubting that they go back to Zeno. The words are used in Greek with physical, medical and emotional reference.

συστολή is used of the contraction of organs such as the heart (LSJ, *s.v.*); of contraction of souls in pain (Plu. *Mor.* 564B); it is the opposite of διάχυσις in reference to feelings (e.g. Plu. *Mor.* 450A = *SVF* III.468; cf. also [τὴν ψυχήν] ποτὲ μὲν εἰς ἡδονὰς καὶ διαχύσεις ἄγεσθαι, ποτὲ δὲ εἰς οἴκτους καὶ συστολάς Ptol. *Harm.* 3.7). It occurs in the Stoic definition of λύπη as ἄλογος συστολή, *SVF* III.391; D.L. VII. 111 (*SVF* III.412).

διάχυσις: Müller correctly added δια, omitted by haplography after καί, cf. F34.8, and Plu. *Mor.* 450A (*SVF* III.468), where again it is opposed to συστολή. In the Hipp. Corpus (e.g. Hipp. *Vict.* 2.60) it denotes medical 'diffusion'. It is used of relaxation of mind in Plu. *Mor.* 1092D = Epicurus F410 Us. (cf. *De Plac.* 240.1–10 De L), and of merriment or cheerful expression in Plu. *Cat. Mi.* 46, *Dem.* 25.

ἔπαρσις: of medical rising or swelling, e.g. Hipp. *Coac.* 85; of sexual erection, Arist. *HA* 572b; it can refer to mental elation or exaltation. It is opposed to ταπείνωσις here and in F34, and to μείωσις in emotions in *De Plac.* 240.5f De Lacy (*SVF* III.463). ἡδονή was defined by Stoics as ἄλογος ἔπαρσις, *SVF* III.391; D.L. VII.114.

ταπείνωσις: For Petersen's emendation, cf. F34.7. The opposite of αὔξησις in Arist. *PA* 689a 25; medically, the reduction of a swelling (Galen, 12.816); of humiliation, Plb. 9.33.10.

δῆξις also occurred in F34.7. It means literally 'biting', Arist. *HA* 623a 1; of physical gnawing pangs, Hipp. *VM* 19, and of mental pangs as emotions in Plu. *Mor.* 450A (*SVF* III.468).

5f Posidonius' objection to Zeno must have been not so much to the physical description of contraction and expansion as to the view that emotions supervene on judgements (F34.A.3). There is some doubt whether Zeno actually said

COMMENTARY: F153

this, because Galen himself seems uncertain (T91, F151); but on the other hand, Galen clearly conveys that Posidonius thought that Zeno held that view; F34.9, τελέως ἀπεχώρησεν ἀμφοτέρων τῶν δοξῶν.

6ff Posidonius' approval of Plato (6f) will refer to Plato's three-faculty psychology. That Posidonius could praise and yet differ from Plato can be seen e.g. from Frs. 142–6, F31. The Posidonian phraseology here lies in κινήσεις τινας (9) (cf. F153) of distinct irrational powers.

9f It is uncertain from this passage whether Posidonius also used Plato's terms, ἐπιθυμητική and θυμοειδής, but Frs. 32, 33, 34 suggest that he did on occasion.

F153 Galen, *De Placitis* v.464, p. 443.9–11 M, p. 322.12–14 De Lacy

CONTENT

Posidonius habitually applied the term 'emotional movements' (παθητικαὶ κινήσεις).

CONTEXT

In general F169. The immediate context is a discussion by Posidonius of physiognomy (320.29ff), maintaining that different physical characteristics and states produce their own peculiar 'emotional movements', i.e. emotions (πάθη). F31 follows shortly.

COMMENT

Posidonius most frequently used the term κίνησις (motion or movement) for emotions (πάθη). The motions are irrational (F168.15), in being motions of irrational faculties (F152). In

COMMENTARY: F154

other words they are peculiarly 'emotional' movements (F158, αἱ κατὰ πάθος κινήσεις, F169.115). For this Posidonius coined the technical phrase παθητικαὶ κινήσεις: also Frs. 165.118, 161, 174; Frs. 169.91, 108. This is quite different from the Zenonic συστολή/ἔπαρσις language of F152, because for Posidonius the 'emotional movements' from the irrational emotional faculties exerted an 'emotional pull' (παθητικὴ ὁλκή, clearly another term coined by Posidonius, F169.80), which in turn affected one's judgement or decision. So that emotions (πάθη), far from being rational decisions or judgements (as Chrysippus), or supervening on rational decisions or judgements (as Zeno, F152), were a factor in the movements affecting and distorting rational decisions or judgements.

For discussion: F169.80ff comm.; Kidd, *Problems* 207.

F154   Plutarch (?), *De Libidine et Aegritudine* 4–6

CONTENT

A fourfold classification of πάθη, involving both body and mind and their interplay, is ascribed to Posidonius.

CONTEXT

This is part of the first of 'Tyrwhitt's Fragments', first published by him in 1773 from *Harleianus* 5612. The authorship has been much debated. It has been widely held that it could not be Plutarch (Pohlenz, *Dissertation* 593 n. 1; Ziegler, *Studi in onore L. Castiglioni* 1135), but Sandbach (Plu. *Mor.* vol. XV (Loeb), pp. 32–5) produced parallels with extant works of Plutarch, and arguments for dating in the 1st c. A.D., possibly in relation to Plutarch's circle; and in *Rev. de Phil.* 43 (1969),

COMMENTARY: F154

211–16, he argued more positively for authorship by Plutarch himself, and this has won support.

COMMENT

The fragment addresses itself to the old question whether body or soul is responsible for πάθη. Strato assigned πάθη entirely to the soul (§4), others (Heraclides is named) to the body (§5). Posidonius (§6) had a fourfold classification:

(1) ψυχικὰ ἁπλῶς (of the soul without qualification), i.e. those having something to do with rational decisions and suppositions: desires, fears, fits of anger.

(2) σωματικὰ ἁπλῶς (of the body without qualification): fevers, chills, contractions (πυκνώσεις), opening up of the pores (ἀραιώσεις).

(3) περὶ ψυχὴν σωματικά (physical with mental effects): lethargies, madness arising from black bile, mental pangs from physical gnawing pains (δηγμούς, F34.7, F152 comm.), sense presentations (φαντασίας), feelings of relaxation (διαχύσεις, F152 comm.).

(4) περὶ σῶμα ψυχικά (mental with physical effects): tremors, pallors, that is (καὶ) changes of appearance in fear and grief.

The author goes on to mention Diodotus (of Sidon, the brother of Boethus, Strabo, XVI.2.24?; or Cicero's house-philosopher?) making a quite different classification between rational and irrational factors of soul. After examining the thesis that πάθη are not of the body nor of the soul but of the whole man (§7), the fragment ends inclining to the view that πάθη are rooted in the flesh.

The reliability of the author is not high. Some of the remarks on Strato and Heraclides in §§4–5 are puzzling. But it is not impossible that Posidonius may have devised such a classification. He was clearly interested in the interplay between physical and mental, or body and soul, e.g. F169.84ff comm.

Two things must be granted: (a) πάθος must be used in a more general sense than is usual in Posidonius, for the word must accommodate purely physical affections of the body in category (2), which would not be covered by Posidonius' definition of πάθος in F152; contrast F153. Category (2) is probably included for completeness. It is clear from the fragments of Περὶ παθῶν that Posidonius was most interested in category (1), but also in (3) and (4). (b) If the phrase (l. 13) τὰ ἐν κρίσεσι καὶ ὑπολήψεσιν in category (1) is both correct (τὸ ἐκρίσεσι *i*: τὸ κρίσεσιν *hk*; and there is an obvious lacuna shortly before these words) and to be regarded as Posidonian rather than as an interpolation of the author, it must be interpreted generously as 'in the field or area of...'; because there is precise evidence that Posidonius criticised Chrysippus and Zeno for saying that πάθη were κρίσεις or supervened on κρίσεις (F152, F34). But of course he did believe that κρίσις and ὑπόληψις were involved in πάθη (F169.77ff, comm.).

Diogenes Laertius shows that classifications of such a type were common in Stoicism; thus that of ἀγαθά in D.L. VII.95.

The problem of physical and mental interaction in πάθη arises much earlier than Posidonius, e.g. Arist. *De An.* 403a, and was a phenomenon marked earlier still by the poets, e.g. Sappho F31 LP. But it was clearly a common topic of discussion in the 1st c. B.C., as Cic. *De Off.* I.102, and in the 1st c. A.D., as Plu. *De Virt. Mor.* 450E–451A, for which see Babut, *Plutarque et le Stoïcisme, ad loc.*

F155 Lactantius, *De Ira Dei* 17.13

CONTENT

Posidonius and the definition of anger.

COMMENTARY: F155

CONTEXT

At *De Ira*, 17.12ff Lactantius is arguing that Greek philosophers (the Stoics and Peripatetics are named) did not understand that there is a just anger (which is rational) as well as unjust anger. He illustrates this from their definitions culled from Seneca's *De Ira* (F155). All this, he continues, is what above he called unjust anger, which also occurs in animals (denied by Sen. *De Ira* 1.3.3ff), but in man is to be restrained, to prevent him from dashing into any of the greatest evils through madness. Such anger does not occur in God, who cannot be hurt, but is found in man because of his weakness. Hurt results in pain, and it is pain that creates the desire for vengeance.

COMMENT

Lactantius' information comes from Seneca's *De Ira*, and the reference to Posidonius must also be derived from Seneca. The paucity of Lactantius' reading in Greek authors is discussed by Ogilvie, *The Library of Lactantius*. Unfortunately, as Lipsius was the first to notice, the Senecan original must have occurred in what is now a lacuna in the text of Seneca at 1.2.3, where several folia after 14ʳ in codex *A* have been lost. The lacuna appears to be quite extensive (Barlow, 'A Sixth-Century Epitome of Seneca, *De ira*', *TAPA* 68 (1937), 29). So we have no control over Lactantius' evidence. It is certainly compressed, for the reference to Aristotle (F155.7ff) comes in fact after the lacuna, namely in Sen. *De Ira* 1.3.2f. It also gives every sign of being garbled.

Apart from the Aristotle reference (which comes from *De An.* 403a 30, ὄρεξις ἀντιλυπήσεως), three definitions of anger are given: (a) *cupiditas ulciscendae iniuriae* (3); (b) *cupiditas puniendi eius a quo te inique putes laesum* (4f); (c) *incitatio animi ad nocendum ei qui aut nocuit aut nocere voluit* (6f). It is implied that Seneca gave (a); (c) is referred to unnamed *quidam*, and (b) is connected with Posidonius.

COMMENTARY: F155

But there is a textual variation. At line 4, codex *B* has *aut ut ait Pos.*, which would imply that (b) was the definition given by Posidonius, distinct from (a). *P* has *alii, ut ait Pos.*, which would mean that (b) is an alternative definition given by 'others', as reported by Posidonius.

Palaeographically, the difference between *aut* and *alii* is insignificant. Pohlenz has argued at length (*De Posidonii Libris* Περὶ παθῶν (Diss.), App. II, pp. 582–6; cf. 'Poseidonios' Affektenlehre und Psychologie', *NGG* (1921), 184 = *Kl. Schr.* 1.161, *Die Stoa* II.113) in favour of *alii*, mainly on the grounds that Posidonius could not himself have held definition (b) because of his distinctive psychology. Definition (b) is the stock Stoic definition where ὀργή is subsumed under ἐπιθυμία, one of the four cardinal πάθη. Pohlenz believed that Posidonius could not have referred anger to τὸ ἐπιθυμητικόν but only to τὸ θυμοειδές in the soul. Pohlenz himself considered seriously the objection to this that *cupiditas* in (b) may translate not ἐπιθυμία but ὄρεξις (as it does in the Aristotle definition, 8). But this is fruitless, because (b) clearly translates the definition given elsewhere in Greek, as *SVF* III.395, 396, 397, where the original is ἐπιθυμία. The real objection to Pohlenz is that for Posidonius the δυνάμεις of the soul are quite different from the πάθη, and there is no narrow equation between τὸ ἐπιθυμητικόν and the πάθος, ἐπιθυμία (cf. Reinhardt, *Poseidonios* 304). I see no reason why Posidonius could not also have held to the orthodox Stoic classification of πάθη. The problem is rather that (b) is conventional, and there seems to be no more reason to assign it to Posidonius in particular rather than to anyone else. If *alii* is correct, we must assume that Seneca was following one of the doxographies which seem to have been typical in Posidonius' writing; but this makes less sense in Lactantius, who is taking Seneca as his authority. In the context of Lactantius, *aut* is more plausible. Or could both *aut* and *al(ii)* be corruptions of *vel*?

Lactantius' list remains very odd. It is possible perhaps to see some distinction between (c) and the first two definitions

COMMENTARY: F155

(a) and (b), although not much. (c) is not far from Cic. *Tusc.* III.19, *proprium est enim irati cupere, a quo laesus videatur, ei quam maximum dolorem inurere . . . ex quo fit ut alieno malo gaudeat*, which is connected with Dionysius of Heraclea (ib. III.18, *SVF* I.434). But what is the difference between (a) and (b) to merit *aut* (or *vel*) in Latin? *ulcisci* and *punire* would both translate the Greek τιμωρεῖσθαι, τιμωρία. *iniuria* contains both ideas of 'injustice' and 'hurt', expressed by *inique* and *laesum* in (b). The examination and defence of Seneca's Stoic definition after the lacuna, *De Ira* I.3.1ff, could accommodate either (a) or (b). (b) certainly translates exactly the stock definitions given in D.L., Stobaeus and Andronicus (ἐπιθυμία τιμωρίας τοῦ δοκοῦντος ἠδικηκέναι οὐ προσηκόντως D.L. VII.113 = *SVF* III.396; cf. *SVF* III.395 (Stob.), 397 (Andronicus), and Cic. *Tusc.* IV.21 = *SVF* III.398: *libido poeniendi eius, qui videatur laesisse iniuria*). It is also plain that this was regarded as *the* Stoic definition, without special reference to Posidonius. The only difference is that (b) is clearly an exact, translated definition (the Latin is stilted), while (a) is a more general expression of the same notion (Cic. *Tusc.* III.11, *sic enim definitur iracundia, ulciscendi libido*). Did Seneca begin with the general statement (a), and then proceed to the formal definition (b), citing Posidonius for this, but merely as *a* Stoic authority? There is another reason for seeing why Seneca may have brought Posidonius into his discussion. After the lacuna (1.3.3ff), Seneca defends the Stoic definition from the criticism that it may be said that wild beasts become angry, although they are neither roused by injustice, nor are angry for the sake of the punishment or suffering of another. Seneca dismisses this with the orthodox Stoic denial that animals become angry or are subject to πάθη. And on this particular related point, which may well have arisen in criticism of Posidonius (see F33, F159), Seneca would be in opposition to Posidonius, and critical of his position.

In any case, Lactantius' reports emerge in such suspect form, that the evidence for Posidonius remains unclear.

COMMENTARY: F156

F156 Galen, *De Placitis* v.502, pp. 486.14–487.10 M, pp. 356.25–358.3 De Lacy

CONTEXT

At 460.9 M, 336.16 De Lacy, Galen brings an extended criticism of Chrysippus through Posidonius to an end, and turns to an examination of Plato's discussion of the parts of the soul in *Rep.* IV. At this point he has just produced *Rep.* 441a 7–c 2, with its quotation of Homer, *Od.* xx.17.

CONTENT

Chrysippus would have profited from Plato's use of quotation, by learning (a) when (ὁπηνίκα, 4) and (b) on what subjects (περὶ τίνων πραγμάτων, 4) quotations should be used.

(a) Quotations should not come at the beginning of an argument, but only when one has proved (ἀποδείξῃ, 6) what is proposed.

(b) Quotations should not be used for subjects utterly obscure (ἀδήλων παντάπασιν, 8), but for evident facts (περὶ φαινομένων ἐναργῶς), or for things the indication of which (τὴν ἔνδειξιν) lies close to sense perception (9). An example of the latter is the emotions of the soul (τὰ πάθη τῆς ψυχῆς), which do not need long arguments, or more precise apodeictic proofs (ἀποδείξεων) either, but only a reminder of what we experience (πάσχομεν) on each occasion, as Posidonius too said.

COMMENT

A. Extent of fragment

The last three lines about πάθη being recognised immediately by experience are certainly referred to Posidonius. But this is only an example of the argument on the use of quotation, Posidonius did use quotations, and the whole paragraph is a self-contained homogeneous attack on Chrysippus inserted at the end of a long passage devoted to Plato. It could all derive from Posidonius; it is at least relevant to his practice, discussed below.

B. Use of quotation in argument

See T87.

C. πάθη and ἔνδειξις

πάθη are the sort of πράγματα about which one can employ quotation, because they are φαινόμενα ἐναργῶς, or carry their own ἔνδειξις and so do not require ἀπόδειξις; we need only be reminded how we are affected.

S.E. *Adv. Math.* VIII.154 clarifies the 'indicative sign' (τὸ ἐνδεικτικὸν σημεῖον): 'It is used, directly out of its own nature and constitution, almost giving tongue, to signify that of which it is indicative' (which is a naturally non-evident object, 155) (ἀλλ' ἄντικρυς ἐκ τῆς ἰδίας φύσεως καὶ κατασκευῆς μόνον οὐχὶ φωνὴν ἀφιὲν λέγεται σημαίνειν τὸ οὗ ἐστὶν ἐνδεικτικόν). The stock example was that bodily motions are an 'indicative' sign of soul (*Adv. Math.* VIII.155). The medical Methodic School used ἔνδειξις to derive guidance directly from τῶν φαινομένων παθῶν for seemingly appropriate remedies (S.E. *Hyp.* 1.240). But Sextus distinguished the 'indicative' from τὸ ὑπομνηστικὸν σημεῖον (*Adv. Math.* VII.151ff). Is there a confusion or blurring between the two here (ἀναμνήσεως, 11)? If so, it is irrelevant. ἔνδειξις refers to the immediate recognition of fact by inspection. This is not very different from φαινόμενα ἐναργῶς, and both are very characteristic of Posidonius, well instanced in the fragments. One example will suffice: the appeal to the behaviour of children in F169 against Chrysippus (other examples at T87, T85).

COMMENTARY: F157

ἔνδειξις is opposed to ἀπόδειξις (formal apodeictic proof). At first sight this raises a difficulty with F157, where we are told that Posidonius often used ἀπόδειξις for πάθη. But Posidonius employed ἀπόδειξις to prove the cause (αἰτία) of πάθη (F157). He appealed to ἔνδειξις for the immediate recognition that πάθη occur in children, for example, or that there is an irrational emotional aspect of soul distinguishable from the rational. It is also precisely in this area that Posidonius used quotations (thus F164.50–4, comm. *F*; 56–86, comm. *H*; F165.133ff (cf. 24ff); F166.21ff, where a quotation of verses from Cleanthes, and at the *end* of the argument ((a) above), ἐναργῶς ἐνδεικνύμενα τὴν περὶ τοῦ παθητικοῦ τῆς ψυχῆς γνώμην αὐτοῦ).

F157 Galen, *De Placitis* v.430, p. 405.14f M, p. 292.25f De Lacy (and *De Placitis* IV.377–8, pp. 348.12–349.7 M, p. 248.3–13 De Lacy)

CONTENT

Much has been said by Posidonius in relation to a proof of the ancient doctrine (that emotions arise from irrational faculties, and are not judgements nor supervene on judgements).

CONTEXT

The sentence follows immediately F152, which recapitulates Posidonius' criticism embodied in *De Plac.* IV (F34) of the views of Chrysippus and Zeno on the relationship between πάθος (emotion) and κρίσις (judgement). It is followed by T62.

COMMENT

ἀπόδειξις refers to 'proof', see T83. In any case, it seems

568

virtually certain that this sentence has in mind the Posidonian proof given in F34.12–20, because

(i) The context is the same, cf. Frs. 34, 152.

(ii) In both places it is stressed that Posidonius was following 'The Ancients': κατὰ πᾶν ἀκολουθήσας τῷ παλαιῷ λόγῳ (F.34.12). 'The Ancients' in this case means Plato (F152.6ff; F34.A.3).

(iii) πολλῶν δὲ εἰρημένων echoes οὐκ ὀλιγάκις, F34.13.

The proof follows in F34.14–20, for which see F34.B.1,2.

F158 Galen, *De Placitis* IV.424, pp. 399.14–400.10 M, p. 288.8–18 De Lacy

CONTENT

The emotional aspect of soul has its own proper natural goals.

CONTEXT

The problem being discussed is why emotions diminish and cease in time; F165.

COMMENT

1–5 The argument derives a conclusion οὕτως κτλ (2ff), from an obvious (7ff) premiss (ὡς, 1), i.e. κατὰ δύναμιν ἀξιώματος (F191.32). But for the way this has arisen in the context: F165.133–150 comm.

1 The premiss is: the emotional aspect of the soul goes for its own proper goals. τὸ παθητικὸν τῆς ψυχῆς is Posidonius' phrase, see Frs. 31, 33, 166, 168. ὀρεκτῶν] ὀρεκτικῶν H^1 cannot be correct. τὸ ὀρεκτικόν would refer to the conative

569

COMMENTARY: F158

faculty (e.g. Arist. *EN* 1102b 3). ὀρεκτά are the goals of ὄρεξις or ὁρμή. Stoics appear to have confined the technical use of ὄρεξις to the rational impulse (*SVF* III.169) of the wise man (*SVF* III.441, 438), distinguishing it from ἐπιθυμία (*SVF* III.442). Posidonius may have avoided it. ὀρεκτά has a wider general use (F161, F150b). The emphasis lies on οἰκεῖα, proper goals of its own, as distinct from the goal of the rational (τὸ λογιστικόν), as F166.8, F161. The adjective is linked to the technical terms οἰκείωσις, οἰκειοῦσθαι, F160. The plural is defined, 8-10.

2-5 The conclusion: so in attaining them (the οἰκεῖα ὀρεκτά) it is satisfied, and in so doing calms down its own movement which was in control of the ὁρμή of the animal (i.e., the 'emotional movement': παθητικὴ κίνησις: Frs. 169.84, 153; 165.118, 161, 173, which produced a πλεονάζ-ουσα ὁρμή, F34) and in keeping with its nature (i.e. as an emotional 'pull', παθητικὴ ὁλκή: F169.80), was leading to whatever it was leading (the animal) astray for its own purpose (παρήγετο makes clear that although the goal is a natural one, it is not good; see F161).

4 τοῦ ζῴου: the argument includes both humans and animals, F159.

5-7: F165. By τοῖς παλαιοῖς, Plato is principally in mind; but in general see T101/102 comm.

7-11 (a) The plural natural aims (ἐφιεμένας φύσει, 9) of the emotional aspect, are now classified as two powers (δυνάμεις), aiming for pleasure, and for power and victory.

ἡδονή as a natural goal for Posidonius: Frs. 160; 161; 169.11, 19, 60;

κράτος: F161; **νίκη**: Frs. 160; 169.19, 74; 161.

These are to be seen in the other animals too, F33.

(b) The premiss is substantiated by appeal to obvious *observed* fact: οὐδὲν οὕτως ἐναργές (7f); ἐναργῶς ὁρᾶσθαι (10); cf. σαφεῖς (7). This is very characteristic of Posidonius: T85; Frs. 159; 166.20; 169.45; 156; 167 *fin*.

COMMENTARY: F159

F159 Galen, *De Placitis* v.431, pp. 406.16–407.7 M, p. 294.10–20 De Lacy

CONTEXT

F163, *s.v.* Context. Galen, in excusing the length of his attack on Chrysippus, says that there are some errors which he cannot ignore.

CONTENT

1–5 Galen and Posidonius are ashamed to acquiesce in or advocate a doctrine of Chrysippus and all other Stoics (τῶν ἄλλων Στ., 5), because (a) Chrysippus 'knocks himself down', i.e., contradicts himself (cf. F165.121; F164.87–93; F167, comm. *ad fin.*), and (b) conflicts with clearly observed fact (τοῖς ἐναργῶς φαινομένοις, 2; φανερῶς 5: F158 comm., T83, T85 comm.

5–9 The false doctrine: (a) all other Stoics (apart from Posidonius) agree that the irrational animals have no share in πάθη, because πάθη belong to the rational power (δύναμις) (*SVF* III.462; III.476; II.906; II.733; F33); (b) most Stoics do not agree that even children have a share in πάθη, because obviously children too are not yet rational (λογικά).

COMMENT

Since both Posidonius and all Stoics agreed that animals are irrational, and most Stoics and Posidonius believed that reason (λόγος) did not develop fully in children until fourteen (F31.16–18), and may not have manifested itself until the age of seven (F31 comm.), the basis of the difference lay in whether πάθη (emotions) were a manifestation of reason or not. Since Chrysippus maintained that they were, as a manifestation of the single rational ἡγεμονικόν, it followed that irrational creatures (animals and children) could not be said to experience anger or desire (ἐπιθυμία) in the full sense of the terms.

For Stoics, animals were different from plants which only had φύσις, whereas animals were ἔμψυχα and therefore had souls (*SVF* II.710; II.714; cf. M. Aur. VI.14); in general, Bonhöffer, *Epiktet und die Stoa* 67–76. It was accepted that animals possessed αἴσθησις and ὁρμή (D.L. VII.86 = *SVF* III.178), besides the consciousness of their own nature (οἰκείωσις, *conciliatio*) which all creatures possess (D.L. VII.85). But these conations remain always irrational, a natural instinct. There is no standard whereby they may be regarded as πλεονάζουσαι ὁρμαί, and so πάθη. So Sen. *De Ira* 1.3.4 says that wild beasts have impulses (*impetus*), madness (*rabiem*), fierceness (*feritatem*), aggressiveness (*incursum*), but anger (*iram*) they have no more than luxuriousness (*luxuriam*). They were even held to have a kind of instinctive sagacity, and S.E. *Hyp.* 1.69, makes fun of Chrysippus (τὸν συμπολεμοῦντα τοῖς ἀλόγοις ζῴοις) for assigning them a sort of dialectic (the fifth indemonstrable), although possessing no reason.

Pohlenz, 'Tierische und Menschliche Intelligenz bei Poseidonios' (*Hermes* 76 (1941), 1ff), building on Reinhardt (*Poseidonios* 356ff) and Jaeger (*Nemesios*), developed a theory based on Sen. *Ep.* 121, Nemesius, *De Nat. Hom.* (p. 121 Matth.), and Origen, *Contra Cels.* IV.86f, that any animal has, besides perception and impulse, a φυσικὴ σύνεσις, or inborn instinct, which is an instinct of the species, that is the same for all members of the species, without individual distinctions; and that the sharp distinction between animal and man lay in the difference between the natural instinct of φυσικὴ σύνεσις and the conscious full rationality of τέχνη in man. Pohlenz assigned this theory to Posidonius, and ultimately, through Cic. *De Off.* I.11, to Panaetius (*Antikes Führertum* 18). But while the interest in the development of τέχνη may be Posidonian (F284), it is doubtful whether any Stoic would have quar-

COMMENTARY: F160

relled with the general theory, and the recurrent illustrations from bees, spiders, ants and swallows had become stock examples (Dickerman, 'Some Stock Illustrations of Innate Sagacity of Animals', *TAPA* 42 (1911), 123ff). There is no doubt that the difference between animals and humans became a common topic of argument. A still sharper problem for the Stoa was the development of reason in children, on which opinions differed, perhaps marked by οἱ πλεῖστοι (F159.8); especially Bonhöffer, pp. 205–7. But in all this it remains consistent in the Chrysippean Stoa to deny πάθη to ἄλογα ζῷα, and to draw the sharp complete division of ἄλογα/λογικά between animals and men.

Posidonius approached from another direction, namely, that it was a matter of observed fact that children do display emotions (πάθη), although obviously they are not yet rational (F169). Therefore a theory of πάθη must accommodate their occurrence in irrational creatures as well as rational; and this leads to his different psychology. Animals and humans differ in that the latter *also* have reason, but the division is not absolute, because the irrational movements and powers of soul are similar; thus Posidonius' classification in F33. But since animals remain irrational, there is still no rational or moral interchange such as justice between humans and animals; F39. But the crucial area lay not in animals but children, in the problem of explaining how irrational babies could develop into rational moral adults.

F160 Galen, *De Placitis* v.460–1,
pp. 438.12–439.9 M,
p. 318.12–24 De Lacy

CONTENT

We have three natural affinities (οἰκειώσεων ὑπαρχουσῶν φύσει), related to each of the aspects of the soul, to pleasure through the desiring factor, to victory through the passionate factor, and to the morally good through the rational factor. Posidonius criticised Chrysippus (and Epicurus) for recognising only one of these.

CONTEXT

For the context of this fragment, and its argumentation within that context: F169, comm. *B*.

COMMENT

For the history and usage of οἰκείωσις as a technical term in Stoicism, see esp. Pohlenz, *Grundfragen* 1–47; Brink, 'Theophrastus and Zeno on Nature in Moral Theory', *Phronesis* 1 (1956), 123ff; Pembroke, 'Oikeiosis', in Long, *Problems in Stoicism* 114–49; Kerferd, 'The Search for Personal Identity in Stoic Thought', *Bull. J. Rylands Univ. Libr. Manchester* 55 (1972), 177–96.

οἰκείωσις is the perception and apprehension (ἀντίληψις) of τὸ οἰκεῖον (Plu. *De SR* 1038B = *SVF* III.724). It labels the natural affinity felt (οἰκειοῦσθαι) for a goal peculiarly one's own (οἰκεῖον), for which therefore one has a natural impulse or conation (ὁρμή or ὄρεξις). Its opposite is ἀλλοτρίωσις. It is most commonly used by Stoics (Plu. *De SR* above) to refer to the first natural impulses from birth to goals for which a creature instinctively identifies an affinity as its own, such as self-preservation (D.L. VII.85; Cic. *De Fin.* III.16, 76ff; Hierocles, *Eth. Stoich.* 7.48; Sen. *Ep.* 121.5ff; Pembroke, *Problems*). But Seneca (*Ep.* 121.15) pointed out that for Stoics each age has its own *constitutio*; children (and animals, F159) are different from adult men. Therefore it seems likely that Stoics extended the term, since ultimately the only goal to which we have a natural affinity is ἀρετή or πρὸς τὸ καλόν (3f), the goal of rational morality. Since Chrysippus, in his monolithic psychology, regarded adult man as a purely λογικὸν ζῷον, it could be maintained by the Chrysippean Stoa, that τὸ καλόν was not only peculiarly οἰκεῖον, but that this was our *only* ultimate οἰκείωσις (see Kerferd, 'The Search for Personal Identity'). Certainly at no stage did Chrysippus agree that human beings have an οἰκείωσις for pleasure (D.L. VII.85f; *SVF* I.190, I.95; III.155, 136; cf. F169).

But since Posidonius believed that we must recognise an aspect of soul independent of reason, τὸ παθητικόν (F158), which consisted of two powers (δυνάμεις), both of which accordingly had their οἰκεῖα ὀρεκτά (F158), it followed that we have three οἰκειώσεις, each with its natural goal, pleasure, power and morality. So here the three οἰκειώσεις are identified by the three δυνάμεις. This analysis leads Posidonius to identify what he regarded as the fundamental mistake of Chrysippus and Epicurus. He claims that they recognise only one of the three (Chrysippus the last, Epicurus the first), and so they not only give a lop-sided account of human nature and behaviour, but could not, in his opinion, explain ethical problems (F150, F187), and in particular emotions (πάθη, Frs. 34, 163–8) and vice (F169). Basically, it appears that Chrysippus was committed to a *succession* of *different constitutiones* (Sen. *Ep.* 121.15), between children and adults, to each of which belonged an οἰκείωσις; Posidonius insisted on a plurality of simultaneous οἰκειώσεις.

Posidonius did not mean that all the οἰκεῖα ὀρεκτά to which we οἰκειούμεθα are ἀγαθά; they are only natural (φύσει, line 1). Only the οἰκείωσις πρὸς τὸ καλόν was ἀγαθόν (cf. 7); or rather, he put it that only it was οἰκεῖον without qualification: F161; Kidd, *Problems* 205.

2 εἶδος and μόρια are Galen's imported terminology. Posidonius deliberately rejected the terms, and confined himself to δυνάμεις: Frs. 142–6.

3–4 ἐπιθυμητικόν, θυμοειδές and λογιστικόν are of course Platonic. Galen uses them. But there is sufficient evidence that they were also adopted by Posidonius, and must have been used by him here to identify the δυνάμεις, although he

COMMENTARY: F161

may have had a preference for the verbal cognates: F142. For ἡδονή and νίκη see F158 comm.

7–9 F169 comm. *B* discusses the confusion over the reference to 'the ancients'.

F161 Galen, *De Placitis* v.472, p. 452.3–10 M, p. 330.1–6 De Lacy

CONTEXT

See Frs. 187, 150b.

CONTENT

Posidonius' statement that the discovery of the cause of the emotions (τῶν παθῶν) taught us the sources (ἀρχάς) of distortion in what is to be chosen and what is to be avoided is explained. Some people are deceived into imagining that the proper goals (οἰκεῖα; F160) for the irrational powers of the soul, are proper without qualification (ἁπλῶς οἰκεῖα); they do not know that feeling pleasure and having power over one's neighbours are objects of appetition for the beast-like aspects of the soul, while wisdom and all that is good and morally fine together are the goals of the rational and divine aspect.

COMMENT

1–2 Part of a quotation from Posidonius, given a few lines before (p. 328.23–5 De L = F150b.2ff) is recapitulated. Galen recasts the section for comment to form a sentence on its own. In F150b, instead of αἱρετοῖς (F161.1), *HL* give ὁρατοῖς, corrected to ὀρεκτοῖς *Ald.*, and ὀρεκτοῖς *ed. Basil.*; and for

COMMENTARY: F161

εὑρεθεῖσα (F161.2), F150b has ὁραθεῖσα. Müller's emendation αἱρετοῖς in F150b seems almost certainly right as the normal Stoic counterpart to φευκτοῖς. It is tempting also to change ὁραθεῖσα to εὑρεθεῖσα with Müller, but Galen could easily have switched two such words in reiteration, and ὁραθεῖσα would help to explain the mistake.

It would be more interesting to know whether the explanation of the sentence (γάρ, 2–7) is taken directly from Posidonius, or is an interpretation of Galen's. It has no prefaced guarantee, such as is given in F162.3f; but the language is certainly Posidonian: οἰκεῖα (F158); ταῖς ἀλόγοις δυνάμεσιν (Frs. 148, 146); ἥδεσθαι, κρατεῖν (F158); and above all ζῳώδους, θείου (F187.4–13). Galen may have been compressing and summarising, but there is little doubt that the explanation comes from Posidonius.

2–7 The explanation is extremely important, and although brief, very clear. As we have an οἰκείωσις towards the natural goals of the irrational faculties, this 'belongs' to us as part of ourselves (οἰκεῖον), by *nature* (φύσει) (F160), but it is not οἰκεῖον without qualification (ἁπλῶς), but only to that aspect of us which we share with all other creatures. What is without qualification οἰκεῖον to us as human beings is the goal of the rational, which is the aspect we share with the divine. But we cannot ignore the οἰκεῖα of the irrational δυνάμεις, which are by experience and observation part of us, but we must bring them into the proper relationship with the ἁπλῶς οἰκεῖον (Frs. 31, 187). And they do explain how we can become distorted in our choices of good and evil (αἱρετόν and φευκτόν are associated in Stoicism with ἀγαθόν, κακόν), in that we can misunderstand the relative nature of the irrational οἰκεῖα. A more detailed exposition of how this happens, and in criticism of Chrysippean Stoicism at F169, F35, cf. Kidd, *Problems* 206f.

COMMENTARY: F162

F162 Galen, *De Placitis* v.473-4, pp. 453.11-454.7 M, p. 330.22-31 De Lacy

CONTENT

Puzzles about the impulse that arises from emotion are clarified by recognition of the cause of πάθη.

CONTEXT

F187 comm. *D* (F187.37ff).

COMMENT

This time (cf. F168), Galen quotes from Posidonius himself for the exposition (ἐπιφέρων ἐξηγεῖται, 4).

The puzzles (τὰ διαπορούμενα) seem to be:

(a) How is it that we are neither afraid nor distressed when persuaded rationally (διὰ λόγου) that an evil is with us or approaching, but are so when we get an image presentation (φαντασία) of the evils themselves? (5-7) or

(b)(i) Some fall into desire from a description (narrative, ἐκ διηγήσεως) (9f); and (ii) some people are afraid (merely) from a vivid (ἐναργῶς) injunction to run away from the charging lion, although they have not (actually) seen it (10f).

The solution is that the irrational cannot be (πῶς γὰρ ἄν, 7) moved by the rational unless it encounters in addition (προσ-, 9) a kind of vivid mental picture (ἀναζωγράφησιν, 8), similar to one you can see (αἰσθητῇ).

The examples show that this can work both ways: (a) without the mental picture we can remain unmoved by real impending misfortune, although rationally convinced; (b) we can be irrationally moved merely by the strength of our

COMMENTARY: F162

imagination. The solution depends on the recognition that πάθη are caused by the movements of the irrational aspects of soul, which are distinct from the rational aspect (F187). The form of argument is characteristic in the appeal to and recognition of observed behaviour which has to be explained.

ἀναζωγράφησις is used of a vivid mental picture. Chrysippus wrote a book Πρὸς τὰς ἀναζωγραφήσεις πρὸς Τιμώνακτα, D.L. VII.201 = *SVF* II.17, which Posidonius may have been combatting. The context (F187.60–2) suggests that Chrysippus had raised such ἀπορηθέντα, but had failed to solve them. The verb ἀναζωγραφεῖν, of creating such striking mental images, is quite common. Epictetus, II.18.16 illustrates (b)(i) above in putting aside such disturbing erotic imagination when seeing a beautiful woman: οὐδὲ τὰ ἑξῆς ἀναζωγραφῶ, παροῦσαν αὐτὴν καὶ ἀποδυομένην καὶ παρακατακλινομένην. Strabo, VIII.3.30 describes the effect of *Il.* I.528ff: προκαλεῖται τὴν διάνοιαν ὁ ποιητὴς ἀναζωγράφειν μέγαν τινα τύπον καὶ μεγάλην δύναμιν ἀξίαν τοῦ Διός . . .

This analysis is important for Posidonius' views on education (F168). The position is similar to holding that a person will not be persuaded to stop smoking by a rational argument that he is likely to fall ill with cancer, but will be emotionally motivated to stop if he has a vivid mental picture of someone (or himself) dying of cancer.

βλέπετε (5) is a favourite expression, cf. F187.12. Cf. his use of ὁρᾶν. For the recognition of the problem cf. Arist. *De An.* 403a.

4–5 If Galen is quoting Posidonius exactly, then οἶμαι ὅτι is a surprisingly early example of this construction.

COMMENTARY: F163

F163 Galen, *De Placitis* v.432–5, pp. 408.4–411.9 M, pp. 294.32–296.36 De Lacy

CONTENT

The condition of the soul of φαῦλοι, illustrated by the analogy of health and sickness.

CONTEXT
(a) General

At the end of Bk IV Galen declares his intention of continuing in Bk V to discuss Chrysippus' views on πάθη, but confines himself to contradictions in Chrysippus, to inconsistencies of his statements with observed fact (403.5–10 M), and to Posidonius' criticisms (T61). At the beginning of Bk V Galen challenges the Chrysippean contention that the heart is the seat of both πάθη and intelligence, which he thinks is due to the failure to realise that emotions and reason have different ἀρχαί. Posidonius does not agree with Chrysippus or Zeno that πάθη are judgements of the reasoning part or supervene on judgements, but holds that they are motions of irrational faculties (F152). So also Posidonius would object to the contention that πάθη do not occur in animals or children because they are irrational (F159). At 407.14 M there begins a detailed attack on Chrysippean inconsistencies which lasts until 451.2 M.

(b) Immediate

F163 is introduced by the assumption that the ancients (οἱ παλαιοί) and Chrysippus agree that: (i) πάθος is a motion of soul that is unnatural (παρὰ φύσιν) and irrational (ἄλογον); (ii) this motion does not arise in the souls of good men (τῶν

COMMENTARY: F163

ἀστείων). Disagreement occurs over the condition of souls of bad men (τῶν φαύλων), illustrated by the analogy of health and sickness. The argument after F163 in Galen shows that the background to the controversy over the analogy between mental and physical health and sickness is related to the θεράπεια or cure of sickness and emotions (Galen 411ff M; cf. *SVF* III.471).

COMMENT

A. Structure

The fragment falls into three sections: (i) 7-20, a report by Galen of criticism by Posidonius of Chrysippus' comparison (εἰκών) or analogy; the information is expressed in indirect speech throughout, but includes a snatch (17-19) of the quotation which follows in: (ii) 23-30, a literal quotation from Posidonius; (iii) 30-52, a criticism by Galen of Posidonius' position.

B. *Galen's report* (7-20)

Chrysippus (3-6) is probably paraphrased by Galen (or Posidonius) from the quotation supplied at 411.12-16 M, 298.3-7 De Lacy (*SVF* III.465): ὑπονοητέον τοίνυν τὴν μὲν τῆς ψυχῆς νόσον ὁμοιοτάτην εἶναι τῇ τοῦ σώματος πυρετώδει καταστάσει, καθ' ἣν οὐ περιοδικῶς ἀλλὰ ἀτάκτως πυρετοὶ καὶ φρῖκαι γίνονται καὶ ἄλλως ἀπὸ τῆς διαθέσεως καὶ μικρῶν ἐπιγινομένων αἰτιῶν.

If so, the substitution of πρόφασις (6) may suggest Galen; but πρόφασις was common in early use in medical contexts, and indeed occurs in the similar analogy of Pl. *Rep.* 556e 3-9.

It is impossible to say to what extent Galen is paraphrasing Posidonius. There are two criticisms: (i) against Chrysippus' statement 'from a small or chance cause' (7-12); (ii) against the application of physical sickness in the analogy (12-20).

COMMENTARY: F163

But Galen's phrase, τοῖς ἁπλῶς ὑγιαίνουσι σώμασιν (7f), is confusing. Posidonius did not want to compare souls of φαῦλοι to bodies that were healthy without qualification, because he adds the qualification τὸ εὐέμπτωτον εἰς τὴν νόσον (18, 27). But Posidonius thought (a) that Chrysippus confused a healthy condition and a diseased condition, whereas the φαῦλος was either healthy or sick (17–20, 26ff); (b) that Chrysippus was wrong to talk about proneness to disease *from a small or chance cause*. The latter phrase was irrelevant; he should have referred simply to being healthy, and within that context, to proneness or resistance to disease (εὐέμπτωτος/δύσπτωτος, 11). The argument of 7–12 seems based on (b) (εἴτε γὰρ, 8), but ἁπλῶς confuses with (a).

Although (a) derives from the quotation 23–30, and although 16–20 even verbally anticipate 26–30, Galen's report (7–20) is not simply a paraphrase of the following quotation (23–30) (although juxtaposition of paraphrase and quotation is not infrequent in ancient authors; e.g. Plu. *De SR* 21). Two points are brought out in the report which are not clear from the quotation: (i) the magnitude, and presumably the chance nature, of the external cause is irrelevant (7–12); (ii) there is no straight comparison possible between health of soul and health of body because there is no such thing as a body immune to disease, yet the soul of the wise man is ἀπαθής; and therefore the condition of the soul of the φαῦλος is more complex (12–16). This, indeed, latches on to the latter part of the quotation (16–20, 26–30). But the criticism of magnitude of cause shows that Galen must have had more of Posidonius before him than the quotation 23–30.

C. *The quotation (23–30)*

The quotation is introduced by an inference by Galen that Posidonius agrees with Chrysippus that (i) all φαῦλοι are sick in soul; and (ii) their sickness is like the aforementioned states of body. (i) follows presumably for Galen from Posidonius saying that only the soul of the wise man is ἀπαθής (15), but is also presupposed for him by (ii). He finds both (i) and (ii) substantiated (γοῦν, 23) by the quotation. The εἰρημέναι τοῦ σώματος καταστάσεις would refer in Chrysippus' case to 4, 13f and 24f; while in Posidonius' case it is τὸ εὐέμπτωτον εἰς νόσον (18, 27ff). But Galen, by putting it in this way, obscures the very point which Posidonius is trying to make, that Chrysippus confuses the issue by a straight analogy between health and sickness in soul and body. See further Galen's comment, 30ff.

Text

The text of 24–6 is uncertain. Perhaps *H* (with Cornarius) may be translated: '... the sickly bad condition of the body whereby it is swept off in such a way as to fall...'. But οἷά τ' is at the least clumsy, and copyists were clearly puzzled by it. Moreover, cf. Posidonius' phrase at F164.24: ἔδει δὲ καὶ ὑποφέρεσθαι φόβοις καὶ λύπαις περιπίπτειν μὴ μετρίαις. The text is much improved and least altered by cutting οἷά τ'. Pohlenz's lacuna derives from 411.10 M; Edelstein cut too much if Posidonius was paraphrasing the quotation from Chrysippus of 411.12–16 M (see *B* above).

Vocabulary

καχεξία (25) was used of bad physical condition by Plato (*Gorg.* 450a 6) and Aristotle (*EN* 1129a 20ff), and of mental condition as early as Diphilus (*PCG* 23). The most striking occurrence of the interplay of both uses survives in Strabo, XIV.5.14 in a quotation of Athenodorus of Tarsus, who was an admirer and possibly a pupil of Posidonius (T44 comm.). But a later quotation from Chrysippus in Galen (*De Plac.* 414.8ff M, 300.4 De Lacy; *SVF* III.471) suggests that Chrysippus also used the term. Posidonius may have chosen it here instead of Chrysippus' κατάστασις (from 411.13 M; *B* above), because it brings out his point against Chrysippus admirably. καχεξία is the opposite of εὐεξία (see both Plato and Aristotle *ad ll. cc.*, and Chrysippus, Galen 414.10 M); but either of these terms may be applied in the analogy of health to the state of souls of φαῦλοι (26–8). Chrysippus confuses proneness to disease with disease itself (28–30). The same point is made by substituting νοσώδης (24) for πυρετώδης in Chrysippus, because νοσώδης is the opposite of ὑγιεινός (e.g. Pl. *Rep.* 438e). The phrase ὑποφέρεται ... ἐμπίπτειν is probably Posidonian (cf. F164.24), and so most likely is the colourful ῥεμβώδεσιν for Chrysippus' ἀτάκτως (411.14 M; cf. Galen's τυχούσῃ, (F163.6). According to Galen (18), εὐεμπτωσία (30) is a technical term coined by Posidonius (cf. 18; F164.35. Reinhardt seems confused about this in *RE* 739). If so, the reference to it in D.L. VII.115 and Stob. *Ecl.* II.93.1 W (*SVF* III.422, 421), must derive from Posidonius, although the definitions may owe something to later graftings. Does Cicero's *proclivitas* (*Tusc.* IV.27–8) translate it?

D. *Posidonius' criticism*

(1) Chrysippus' straight analogy between psychic and physical health is impossible, because the state of perfect immunity of soul of the wise man has no counterpart in physical health (12ff).

(2) φαῦλοι may be described *either* as 'healthy' *or* 'sick'; 'healthy' if they are not experiencing πάθη, although they are liable to the disease of emotion, and so health should be qualified by proneness to sickness (εὐεμπτωσία); 'sick' if they actually are in a temper etc. Therefore Chrysippus was wrong in making a simple analogy with sickness, confusing and amalgating proneness to sickness and being sick (3–12, 23–30).

(3) Chrysippus was wrong in relating the occurrence of the sickness of πάθη to the magnitude of some fortuitous irregular external cause (3–12; cf. 411.12–16 M, *B* above). The phrase attacked at lines 5–6 cannot mean 'at the slightest excuse' which could simply apply also to Posidonius'

εὐεμπτωσία, but must refer to an *external* cause (cf. μικρῶν ἐπιγινομένων αἰτιῶν, Chrysippus 411.15 M; and cf. Pl. *Rep.* 556e 3–9); it is precisely whether the cause is external or internal which is at issue between Posidonius and Chrysippus.

Posidonius was not quibbling over words. The debate, as the sequence in Galen shows, was concerned with the cure of πάθη (*SVF* III.471). Analogies may be helpful, but they may be misleading. Chrysippus had made a straight analogy between medicine and philosophy, health and moral sanity, and therefore inferred a comparison without qualification between physical and mental cures (Galen 413.7ff M; *SVF* III.471). Posidonius saw a greater complexity in the case of φαῦλοι, who on the physical analogy were both healthy and sick. Both states required treatment, but of a different kind. In their sane/healthy periods, the cure would be directed to the logical faculty, but in emotionally sick periods to the irrational faculties (F168, F166). Most important of all, the cure cannot be related to some external cause, and the magnitude of its impression (F164). The cause is within us (F169). The inner reaction is more important than the outward experience. The understanding of the cause of πάθη is fundamental to their cure, and Chrysippus' whole psychological analysis based on 'weakness' of soul is wrong (F164).

The fragment also displays Posidonius' concern, typical of much of the later Stoa, with the facts of the common human situation. The vast majority, if not all of us, are φαῦλοι (line 39). The majority of mankind are not sick but healthy, but falling more or less easily into sickness to which we are all liable from our constitution. This is the factual position, which Chrysippus tends to ignore (T83; Galen, 403.5–10 M). While, however, this may be the normal situation, it is not the ideal 'natural' goal of the complete immunity of the wise man (F187), which is an extraordinary state, unparalleled in the physical analogy.

E. *Galen's criticism (30–52)*

It is extremely rare for Galen to criticise Posidonius, and he is only drawn to do so in two fields in which he regarded himself as an authority, medicine and mathematical proof.

(1) **30–3** Galen approves Posidonius' comparison of souls of φαῦλοι when they are free from πάθη, to healthy bodies, but objects to him calling such a state disease. This is a mistaken inference. Posidonius did not do so; see Comment above.

(2) **34–41** Galen himself lists a more detailed comparison, in line with his own classification of bodily states in *Ars Med.* 4 (1.317 K):

(a) souls of virtuous: physical immunity to disease (whether this exists or not);
(b) souls of progressors (προκόπτοντες): robust constitutions (εὐεκτικοί);
(c) souls of intermediate persons (μέτριοι): healthy without being robust;
(d) souls of the majority of φαῦλοι: bodies that become ill at a slight cause;
(e) souls of those in an affected state: bodies that are sick.

It is doubtful whether Posidonius would have disagreed with this analysis; at any rate it is not contradictory to his criticism of Chrysippus. A similar sort of progression occurs, Sen. *Ep.* 72.6–11. Galen appears to have misunderstood Posidonius' criticism of Chrysippus' use of the analogy.

(3) **41–52** Galen objects that in likening sickness of soul both to healthy bodies and to sick bodies, Posidonius commits a logical contradiction. Things that are like the same thing are also like each other. So health will be like disease. This again is a misconception (already in lines 20ff). If the term 'healthy' is used metaphorically in an absolute sense of the wise man, then all φαῦλοι will be 'sick'. But if, like Chrysippus, an exact analogy is to be made with physical

COMMENTARY: F164

health, then physical health being relative is inapplicable to the wise man; all relative degrees of health and sickness relate to φαῦλοι. And a φαῦλος will not be both 'healthy' and 'sick' at the same time. Galen mistakenly applies a modification of the first of Euclid's Common Notions against the man he respected as the most 'geometrical' of the Stoics (T83, T84).

This fragment is discussed by Kidd, 'Euemptosia', *Rutgers Studies, Arius Didymus* 107–13; in general: Cic. *Tusc.* IV.27–33; Philippson, *Hermes* 67 (1932), 285; Reinhardt, *Poseidonios* 311f; id. *RE* 739f, 752; Pohlenz, *Diss.* 630; id. *Die Stoa* II.80; Kidd, *Problems* 205ff, 214.

F164 Galen, *De Placitis* IV.397–403, pp. 369.7–376.13 M, pp. 264.9–270.8 De Lacy

CONTENT

Criticism of Chrysippus's view that the cause of emotion can be ascribed to degree of magnitude of presentations or to weakness of soul.

CONTEXT

Initiated by Chrysippus' attempted explanations of πάθος, 338.11ff M (*SVF* III.462), as involving ὁρμή, δόξα and κρίσις. Posidonius first attacked his interpretation of πλεονάζουσα ὁρμή 348.5ff M (F34); then problems related to δόξα and κρίσις are attacked. Galen debated whether a rational or irrational process was implied, whether πάθος arose simply from a mistake or error (ἁμάρτημα) or not (367f M) . He accuses Chrysippus of using κρίσις now in the sense of περίσκεψις (circumspection), now in the sense of ὁρμαί τε καὶ συγκαταθέσεις. But Chrysippus stressed κατὰ τὸ πλέον ἐκπεπτωκέναι (368.14 M), so the question arises how degree in the context of δόξα and κρίσις can cause πάθος. This is

587

COMMENTARY: F164

related to education and training, because Chrysippus' quotation at 368.12ff M involves infirmity (ἀρρωστήματα), and is taken κατὰ τὸ θεραπευτικὸν αὐτοῦ βιβλίον (368.10 M).

STRUCTURE

A series of six arguments from Posidonius is reported by Galen. Galen links all this evidence as successive items in a continuous piece (25f, 34, 38, 41f, 50ff, 52, 86f), but we do not know how much he may have omitted; he certainly omitted some material (50–2). One passage is quoted literally (57–86), and it is so vivid, clear and distinct in style, that we may wonder to what extent Galen may have compressed some of the other highly obscure reports (e.g. 38–41; 87ff, for which see below). The fragment ends with a comment of approval by Galen himself.

COMMENT

A. (1–10)

Galen is in process (368f M) of accusing Chrysippus of three contradictory statements: (a) emotion involves judgement (κρίσις); (b) emotion is irrational (ἄλογον); (c) there is no irrational faculty. A quotation from Chrysippus about people who are women-crazy and bird-crazy (γυναικομανεῖς, ὀρνιθομανεῖς) has just been dredged up at 369.2f M (*SVF* III.480). Galen seizes on madness as an obvious case of irrational emotion.

A possible objection (ἀλλὰ νὴ Δία ἴσως, 1) to Galen is now raised: madness is *not* caused by an irrational faculty (which is the thesis held by Posidonius and Galen), *but* by κρίσις and δόξα having been brought to a state beyond what is fitting. (1–3).

τὸ ἐπὶ πλέον (2) is a concept inherent in the common Stoic definition of emotion as πλεονάζουσα ὁρμή, accepted by Posidonius himself (F34; Kidd, 'Posidonius on Emotions'

588

COMMENTARY: F164

204); but Chrysippus applied it in the intellectual context of judgement, as just quoted by Galen at 368.14 M (*SVF* III.480).

The objection continues (3-10): as if it were said that infirmities of soul (ἀρρωστήματα) were *not* simply false suppositions about goods or evils, *but* thinking certain good(s) or evil(s) were the greatest (μέγιστα). An illustration is given: the δόξα of money as a good is not yet an infirmity, which only arises when one thinks it is the greatest good, so that one supposes it is not even worth living without it.

The objection stresses that emotion does not arise simply from error of judgement, but from some kind of excess in the process of judgement (κρίσις involves decision as well as judgement: Arist. *Pol.* 1275a 23), and this is interpreted in terms of magnitude (μέγιστα) of the presentation comprising the δόξα. This cannot refer to over-*valuation*, for that would be mere error of judgement, but to the effect on one's δόξα from the magnitude of the external presentation. πάθος (πάσχειν) is affection, being acted upon by an external force.

It would be dangerous to regard this objection as a 'fragment' of Chrysippus, as the indefinites of lines 1 and 11, and ὡς εἰ ... ἔλεγεν (3) show. The topic of infirmity goes back to the quotation from Chrysippus at 368.12ff M (*SVF* III.480), and Galen may be framing subsequent Stoic defences of the Chrysippean position. But it is more likely still that Galen found the whole of this controversy in Posidonius, and the 'objection' may be Posidonius' interpretation of Chrysippus (τοιούτων δὲ ὑπὸ τοῦ X. λεγομένων). It is significant that Posidonius' criticism follows the structure of the 'objection', first on degree of excess (B), then on ἀσθένεια (i.e. ἀρρωστήματα, C).

See also Cic. *Tusc.* IV.26 and Hirzel, *Untersuchungen* III.462, n. 1.

B. (11-25)

The first (13) of Posidonius' arguments against the 'objection'

COMMENTARY: F164

is based on μέγεθος τῶν φαινομένων as the cause of emotion. ἀπορίαι are raised by all arguments.

(a) 13–22 Wise men think that all moral goods are the greatest unsurpassable good, yet they are not moved effectively, nor 'desire' (in the strong sense of ἐπιθυμία, a πάθος) what they seek, nor experience excessive joy (περιχαρεῖς) when they achieve it. Yet if it were the magnitude (μέγεθος) of the apparent goods and evils (τῶν φαινομένων ἀγαθῶν καὶ κακῶν) that sets in motion the belief (νομίζειν cf. δόξα and κρίσις) that it is appropriate and in accordance with their valuation when present or at hand to be moved emotionally, and admit no reason that they be moved by them otherwise (cf. 80–2), then those who thought that what was happening to them was unsurpassably great, must have been so affected (i.e. wise men would be greatly impassioned). Which is not observed to occur.

(b) 22–5 A similar argument would apply to progressors (προκόπτοντες) if they suppose the occurrence of great harm from their vice; for they ought to be swept into experiencing *excessive* fear and distress; which doesn't occur either (in progressors). Posidonius' own explanation of this phenomenon is given in F174 and F162.

Text

19 If καί is retained, an infinitive is required before it; De Lacy supplies the sense from 14. Otherwise, delete καί (cf. 81).

22 ἤ should either be deleted, or Edelstein's ingenious supplement from F165.15 adopted.

15 χαρά (joy) as a εὔλογος ἔπαρσις (*SVF* III.431,432), is to be distinguished from ἡδονή (*laetitia*), which is marked by excess (*nimia*, Cic. *Tusc.* IV.13). χαρά is a good (*SVF* III.115), an ἐπιγέννημα (*SVF* III.76) experienced by the wise man (*SVF* III.435), who experiences emotion, but no morbid passion. But Posidonius in line 15 refers to πάθος, so all the stress is on περι- (excess); cf. μὴ μετρίαις (24f) in the parallel case of progressors.

COMMENTARY: F164

19 μηδένα λόγον προσίεσθαι, was a phrase used by Chrysippus: D, H below.

The argument is of the form: if p then q; but not-q, therefore not-p. The hypothesis that the cause of πάθη is due to the excessive force of what seems good or evil, i.e. the magnitude of the impression distorting δόξα and κρίσις, is destroyed by the necessary consequence (excessive πάθη in both wise men and progressors) not being *observed in fact*. This kind of argument is very typical of Posidonius. The phrasing in line 18 must be deliberately paradoxical: to think it καθῆκον and κατ' ἀξιάν to be emotionally disturbed and reject reason. Perhaps Posidonius is trying to bring out what he saw as the paradox of considering πάθη as δόξαι and κρίσεις, implying some kind of intellectual judgement, however erroneous. However, this point is not really developed until I below. For the moment he concentrates simply on μέγεθος as cause: A above. For this section cf. Frs. 165.19ff; 174; Philodemus, *De Ira*, col. 48, 3–13 (p. 95 Wilke); Pohlenz, *Diss.* 546, 613; id. *Hermes* 41 (1906), 333, 336; Hirzel, *Untersuchungen* III.435; Reinhardt, *Poseidonios* 278f.

C. (25–37)

Posidonius now turns to the second, infirmity (ἀρρωστήματα) section of the 'objection' (A line 4ff): if in addition to magnitude of impressions of good or evil, ἐπὶ πλέον ἢ προσῆκεν is explained also as excessive (19–20) weakness of soul, which may apply to φαῦλοι but not to wise men (i.e. argument B(a) above is countered).

Text

29–30 Something is required in the antithesis to balance ἀπηλλάχθαι τῶν παθῶν of wise men. Einarson's hypothesis of a negative lost before οὐδέ is the most economical solution.

Posidonius answers:

(a) **31–4**, this is a description of the situation in terms of

COMMENTARY: F164

sickness with which all agree; it is no explanation of how the soul is moved or moves in emotion, i.e. how πάθος is caused.

For Posidonius on the sickness analogy: F163.

(b) 34–7 In any case it is not only the excessively weak who lapse into emotion; all unwise men (including progressors) fall into emotions great and small.

Again the hypothesis is destroyed by an appeal to fact.

For εὐεμπτωσία as a Posidonian technical term: F163.18, 27–30. 'Weakness' throughout this context appears to be taken by Posidonius to mean weakness of judgement (cf. line 59f).

D. (38–41)

A very difficult and obscure sentence. I keep the reading of H, except for cutting εἶναι (38, with De Lacy; perhaps line 18 was in the copyist's mind), and changing ἐμφαίνει to ἐμφαίνειν with Bake, because I take the subject of ἐμφαίνειν to be οὕτω κεκινῆσθαι κτλ. Then translate: 'And to suppose that to be moved in accordance with valuation of what happens to one in such a way as to abandon reason reveals a great emotion (i.e. does not arise unless in a great emotion), is to suppose badly; for it occurs also through a moderate and small emotion.' But for other versions of this very uncertain sentence, see Pohlenz, *Diss.* 547 n. 1 (who can however make little of οὐ καλῶς ὑπολ. ἐστί); Reinhardt, *Poseidonios* 283 n. 1; De Lacy *ad loc.*

This still remains very obscure, and one cannot help feeling that Galen is cutting corners in his reporting. There is clearly some connection with the previous quotation (34–7). We are still on the subject of ἄφρονες, φαῦλοι and προκόπτοντες as the phrase κατ' ἀξίαν τῶν συμβεβηκότων shows, because such people proceed by external valuation (ἀξία being a technical term of 'intermediates': Kidd, *Problems* 155–6; the phrase is retained here perhaps (cf. 18) because of Chrysippus' equation of πάθη with judgements). Probably the sentence is

592

COMMENTARY: F164

an elaboration of καὶ εἰς μεγάλα πάθη καὶ εἰς μικρὰ ἐμπίπτουσι (37). Posidonius agrees with Chrysippus that πάθος involves rejection of reason, but is attacking his theories of degrees of magnitude still. Not only 'excess' of the presentation and 'excessive' weakness of judgement are inadequate explanations, but the πάθος need not be excessive either in the abandonment of reason; even here magnitude is not an indication. The facts are much more complex, as the next quotation shows. Part of the background must also be the quotations from Chrysippus at 338.11–341.2 M (*SVF* III.462), where Chrysippus equates the concepts of πάθος, ἀποστρέφεσθαι λόγον and πλεονασμός. Posidonius must also be using the term σύμμετρον (41) maliciously in the sense of 'moderate', because Chrysippus gave as a characteristic of πάθος that it ὑπερβαίνει συμμετρίαν (339.13ff M; *SVF* III.462, p. 114.1ff; 366.1 M).

E. (41–50)

This follows closely on the previous quotation (ἐχόμενα τούτων). Two persons may have the same weakness and similar presentation (φαντασία), yet one may incur emotion, the other not, one less, the other more, and the same individual may change in his reaction. The more unused a man is to a situation, the more affected he is in circumstances of fear, distress, desire and pleasure; and the more vicious, the more speedily seized by emotions.

The argument here is less compelling, because it is difficult to see how it may be subjected to the test of observation on which it appears, like the earlier arguments, to be based. But it is of importance in indicating Posidonius' stress on the individuality of the reaction of the subject rather than on the objective presentation, at least in the matter of training. General remarks are ineffective on presentations, which cannot account for the degrees of reaction, and on 'weakness', since 'sometimes the weaker of two persons, who supposes that what has befallen him is greater, is not moved' (45f).

COMMENTARY: F164

For the importance of habituation in training: F31, F165.
48f lists the four cardinal πάθη (e.g. *SVF* III.381, 378).
48 Müller's γοῦν seems necessary to avoid hiatus.
42–8 cf. Philodemus, *De Ira*, col. 47.21–7, and Praef. xxvi, Wilke.

F. (50–2)

Cf. T104. Galen now mentions (but does not quote or enumerate) that Posidonius exemplified his statements at this point with the testimony of poetical quotation and historical account. Indeed quotations from Homer are cited later (67ff, 74ff), and for the frequency of Posidonius' quotations see index. This is also clear evidence that history was used by him as an ethical tool, cf. T80.

G. (52–6)

Galen quotes the conclusion (ἄρα) with regard to habituation that follows from the examples referred to in F. It is expressed in the most general terms (neuter singulars, cf. F165.24ff): what is vicious is quickly seized by the unaccustomed, but what has been brought up in the opposite way ...

τὸ ἐναντίως ἠγμένον is the opposite of τὸ κακῶς ἠγμένον. But ἠγμένον is more suitable for the second part of the antithesis, and explains the *variatio*. For ἠγμένον cf. F169.46, and also its occurrence in the definition of τέλος (F186.15; F187.12).

χρόνῳ μετασυνεθιζόμενον. Either '(is seized) in time (opposed to ταχύ) in being changed by habituation'; or 'being changed in time by habituation ...' with a lacuna supplied of the kind suggested by Edelstein: ἢ οὐδὲ ὅλως ἐξίσταται ἢ ἐπὶ μικρόν (from F165.27f). No doubt the Posidonian theory of προενδημεῖν (F165.28ff) is in mind here, and μετασυνεθίζεσθαι is probably a word coined by Posidonius, who liked compounds. But the issue here is shaped by the context of the criticism of Chrysippus (54–6); the 'suppositions' and the 'weakness' may be the same, but the

594

COMMENTARY: F164

πάθη not equal. Therefore again δόξα and ἀσθένεια are not the explanation. Cf. also Pohlenz, *Diss.* 614f; Reinhardt, *Poseidonios* 285.

H. (56–86)

Posidonius raises certain questions (to put to Chrysippus) quoted in full: What of the case of the sleepless Agamemnon, who was extremely upset at the rout of his army, yet took counsel of Nestor (*Il.* x.17–20, 91–5)? Is not this a case of a man with a strong presentation of impending disaster, and also weak in judgement (Agamemnon was clearly cited as a stock example of this; cf. Epict. III.22.30–7), yet willing to listen to reason? Then, either (79–82) we have a case of a man in great emotion (heart pounding) who yet thinks it appropriate in evaluation of what is happening to him *not* to reject reason, which would be an argument *ad hominem* against Chrysippus, who equated πάθος and ἀποστρέφεσθαι λόγον (338.11ff M; *SVF* III.462; cf. D above); or (82–6), Agamemnon was no longer in terror, but was simply recalling to Nestor his previous emotions, when asking for advice; in which case, why did Agamemnon at one point become emotionally disturbed and reject reason, but at a later point seek it, although his supposition or presentation of the situation remained the same, and he was still the same man, equally weak in judgement? These factors then are not adequate explanations, and so Chrysippus has not given the cause of emotion in its entirety.

The writing of this passage is very lively, and is a good example of Posidonius' style; see *Structure* above.

59 The Greek would seem too compressed without the aid of a lacuna.

60 συμφράδμονας; Posidonius is using Homeric colouring (cf. *Il.* II.372).

61 διαγρυπνῶν recalls *Il.* x.1–4.

62 ἀρρήτῳ; the Homeric phrase is ἀτλήτῳ (*Il.* IX.3).

63ff cf. F165.115–22.

COMMENTARY: F164

I. (86-102)

This section is extremely obscure both in detail and argument. See also for other attempts, Pohlenz, *Diss.* 547, 613; Reinhardt, *Poseidonios* 288f; De Lacy *ad loc.*

(1) 87–90 Not only (i) to abandon reason in desires (ἐπιθυμίαι representing πάθος) as (Chrysippus) says, but also (ii) to suppose in addition that, even if not advantageous, one must have it contains a contradiction ...

But there is no apparent contradiction between (i) and (ii). In any case the ἀπορίαι of (i) have already been dealt with above. The contradiction must lie in the statement of (ii), and is indeed laid out in what follows. ὥς φησιν (i) asserts rightly that ἀποστρέφεσθαι λόγον is explicit in Chrysippus, as it is (see H above); προσυπολαμβάνειν would suggest that (ii) may not have been actually from Chrysippus but an inference by Posidonius.

(2) 90–3 The contradiction; but reading and structure are both uncertain. Two alternatives:

(i) cut τοῦ μεγέθους αὐτοῦ (92) as intrusive from the line above; read ὄφελος (93, Pohlenz, which must be right in whatever version); add καί (93, Reinhardt, to improve sense); then proposition (a) concludes with συμφέρον (91), and the contradiction lies between the following propositions (a) and (b):

(a) to be carried off as if to a great advantage;
(b) through its *greatness*, even if it is inadvantageous, think it worthy (even if it has no benefit, but actually the opposite) nevertheless even so to cling to it.

(ii) Add τε after ἄξιον (92) (Einarson), and begin proposition (b) there:

(a) to be carried off as if to a great advantage actually because of its greatness, even if it is inadvantageous;
(b) think it worthy of the greatness of the thing, even if it has no benefit ..., nevertheless even so to cling to it.

But (ii), although Einarson's emendation is ingenious and

simple, produces no contradiction; (ii)(b) simply repeats (ii)(a). Therefore (i) seems much preferable. There the contradiction is latent in 'great advantage' in (a), and brought out in (b) where the stress on 'great' is so strong that it overrides 'even thinking it inadvantageous'; which is implied by 'even so, thinking it worth . . .'.

(3) 94–6 Posidonius is prepared to consider an admission, designed to remove the contradiction of being carried off to an advantage even when you think it is inadvantageous. Even supposing three admissions (ἔστω):

(i) they (Chrysippus' supporters) reject those who say that it is not advantageous;
(ii) they think that those who profess to show that it is inadvantageous are talking nonsense;
(iii) what is pursued is pursued because of the *great* benefit.

That is (a) all pursue what seems good or advantageous, not what is inadvantageous, although they may be in error; (b) it is the degree of advantage which determines the κρίσις (not the advantage. Reinhardt may be right in deleting ὄφελος at 96, but it is doubtful whether it is necessary, since all the stress is clearly on μέγα).

(4) 96–102 But, Posidonius continues, precisely what is unconvincing is that: *because* of supposing it is a *great* good, men think that they should, even if it is a very great evil, yet grasp it; he adds as example a poetic quotation, a stock example of the utterance of a very emotionally disturbed person, that recurs in Plu. *De Virt. Mor.* 446A: let me perish; that is advantageous for me. The *cause* of *that* (πλεονάζουσα ὁρμή, 100), Posidonius maintains, cannot be the simple ὑπόληψις or δόξα: self-destruction is a great good. So once more the *cause* of πάθος or πλεονάζουσα ὁρμή cannot lie solely in the magnitude of the presentation in an intellectual context of δόξα and κρίσις. The cause is yet to seek from Chrysippus (102), who has in Posidonius' view been tangled

COMMENTARY: F165

and unclear between erroneous valuation (ἀξία), and mere degree of force of presentation.

J. (102–8)

Cf. T60. Galen can find no answer himself to Posidonius' questions, nor does he believe any will be able to counter Posidonius' difficulties, to judge from the evidence of the facts and from contemporary Stoics.

F165   Galen, *De Placitis* IV.416–27, pp. 391.3–403.5 M, pp. 280.19–190.22 De Lacy

CONTENT

Polemic against Chrysippus on the cause why emotions arise and abate in time. The explanation stresses the importance of time and habit in the treatment of emotion.

CONTEXT

After F164, Galen continued criticising quotations from Chrysippus. The beginning of F165 forms a declared transition from the general outline and character of Chrysippus' theories to Posidonius' objections (1–2).

STRUCTURE

Very complicated, because Posidonius, Galen and Chrysippus are all involved in the report, and it is not always clear who is saying what. Discussion is best confined to the details of the commentary.

COMMENT

Posidonius raises difficulties for Chrysippus over the definition of distress (λύπη).

1-13

2-5 Posidonius says (φησίν) that the definition of distress (λύπη), like many other definitions given orally by Zeno and written down by Chrysippus, clearly refutes Chrysippus' view.

This is an interesting variation of the anecdote of D.L. VII.179, that Chrysippus claimed that he wanted to be given only the doctrines, and that he would supply the proofs; but it is evidence for the belief that part at least of the Chrysippean canon was a record of the oral teaching of Zeno.

3 λύπης is an emendation by Cornarius for ἄτης *H*, which De Lacy defends because (a) we do not know Posidonius' context; (b) it may follow appositely F164.99ff. But we do know Galen's context, and the whole passage and in particular γάρ (6) surely presupposes λύπης.

6-8 Chrysippus says (φησι) that distress is fresh opinion of the presence of evil (cf. 336.11 M; *SVF* I.212; III.391, 393).

This is clearly the School definition. The rather pedantic distinctions in variation of wording may be due, as Reinhardt suggested (*Poseidonios* 291), to 'Galen, der Schulmeister'. Posidonius does not wish to challenge or reject the definition here, but to show that it creates difficulties for Chrysippus himself, because of his psychology. On the tactics of argument cf. F34.

7 ἔνιοι, Reinhardt, is tempting, but then ⟨δὲ⟩ is required.

9-13 Now on the one hand, he says that 'fresh' is 'recent in time'. Who says? Chrysippus or Posidonius? Probably Posidonius, because (a) the μέν... δέ antithesis in sense would imply that the subject is the same in both propositions; (b) other interpretations of πρόσφατος exist, e.g. Cic. *Tusc.* III.75 'as long as it retains its force'; cf. also Stob. (*SVF* III.378). This then may be a Posidonian interpretation of Chrysippus.

COMMENTARY: F165

On the other hand, he (Posidonius) asks to be told the cause why the opinion of evil, when it is fresh, contracts the soul and produces distress, but when it is prolonged, not at all or not equally. Emotion was also described by the Stoa in physical terms of contraction and expansion (ἔπαρσις): 337.12–14 M; *SVF* III.463, 468, 391, 394. The theory originated with Zeno (*SVF* I.209).

10 αὐτῷ (Einarson) is preferable to ὑπ' αὐτῶν (Müller), because the attack is *ad hominem* against Chrysippus, see below. Posidonius is saying: suppose we accept 'fresh', can it explain the cause of emotional phenomena?

13–22

Yet Chrysippus should not have accepted 'fresh', if he meant what he says, because it was rather his view that distress was an opinion, not of a fresh evil, but of a great or intolerable or unbearable evil. Galen adds that he has already reported Posidonius' attack on this latter definition, referring to F164, and particularly to the argument F164.13ff.

The implication is that πρόσφατος was Zeno's definition, accepted by Chrysippus; but Chrysippus should not have accepted it because he developed his own theory of magnitude to suit his own definition of πάθος, on all of which, F164. Cic. *Tusc.* III.25, 28 appears to combine both magnitude and freshness.

Reinhardt (*Poseidonios* 292) argued that the whole of this passage (13–22), was inserted in parenthesis by Galen. This is possible, but part at least (13–17) seems not only germane, but necessary to Posidonius' argument. The point is that in Posidonius' view, Chrysippus cannot explain πρόσφατος, because of his emphasis on magnitude of presentation, but Posidonius can.

15f Chrysippus seems to have used the word μέγα, but there is no other evidence for ἀνυπομόνητον or ἀκαρτέρητον; but καθάπερ αὐτὸς εἴωθεν ὀνομάζειν certainly declares that he did.

600

COMMENTARY: F165

22-53

22 We now return to the first definition, i.e. πρόσφατος: Posidonius asks the reason why distress is caused not by the opinion of present evil, but by the 'fresh' opinion only (i.e. returns to 10ff).

24 καί φησι διότι . . . Who says what in this highly controversial passage? The subject of φησι, and also of φησι at 28 must be Posidonius, because the theory of ἐθισμός in treating πάθη is patently his, not Chrysippus' (cf. Frs. 31; 165.172ff; 164.48; 169.116). I have little doubt that προενδη-μεῖν (28) was a metaphor coined by Posidonius, which has to be explained (29ff). Therefore the question of αἰτία which Posidonius raises at 22ff, and which Chrysippus cannot answer, Posidonius now answers first himself (24ff), adding, as he often did (cf. T104), illustrations from the poets (33-53): the reason is that (διότι, 24) anything unprepared for or strange confounds, but what is practised, familiarised or prolonged not at all or little (24-8). (For the generalising neuter singulars, cf. F164.53f.) Therefore, says Posidonius, we ought (Kühn and Cornarius are probably right that a δεῖ(ν) is missing or concealed) to live with things in advance (προ-ενδημεῖν, 28), explained as a prefiguring of what is to happen (29ff), and gradually bring about an ἐθισμός (32).

For other interpretations of this passage: Bake, 203f; Hirzel, *Untersuchungen* III.428-434; Pohlenz, *Diss.* 552f, 616f; v. Arnim, *SVF* III.482; Reinhardt, *Poseidonios* 292.

54-75

54 Galen (but the material no doubt comes from Posidonius) now quotes from Chrysippus' Περὶ παθῶν, Bk II (*SVF* III.466), to the effect that even Chrysippus (καί, 55) seems to be a witness that time makes a difference to the softening of πάθη. Chrysippus appears to relate this to relaxation of the contraction of soul (merely a redescription, 61; cf. 11), and perhaps to another supervening disposition (63). Specific

COMMENTARY: F165

Posidonian criticism of this fragment does not begin until 143–68. At this point Galen uses the passage as evidence that Chrysippus himself admitted that emotions cease (*H* corrected himself rightly above the line), although the opinion (of evil or the like) persists. Galen, fastening on Chrysippus' δυσσυλλόγιστον (63), claims that Chrysippus says it is hard to reason out the cause of this (70–3). This is a little vague, and the following sentence (73–5), referring to unspecified other like phenomena of which Chrysippus also professes ignorance of cause, is even vaguer and marked by rhetorical irony, οὐδὲ αὐτῶν δηλονότι (74). It does seem that Chrysippus may have been raising puzzles; but the point being established is that Chrysippus thinks that the cause is concealed and not susceptible to human reason (cf. *SVF* II.973; 75–102 below). The Posidonian context is clearly in the field of θεράπεια, cf. the preceding section, 24–53 above, where the poetic illustrations could be suitable for *consolationes*, or better pre-training for such situations. See also 80ff.

65 cf. 157 Either *H*'s μή must be deleted at 65, or μή inserted at 157. I now believe that μή should be deleted. If Chrysippus had written it, he would be offering another (apart from διάθεσις, 62–4) tentative explanation of the puzzle: when the underlying circumstances create unlike impressions. But it seems to me clear from 155ff that Posidonius, having dealt with 62–4, sees no additional explanation to criticise, but merely demands the cause of the phenomena.

75–102

Galen continues to contrast Posidonius and Chrysippus on aetiology, to the detriment of the latter.

Structure:

75–7 *Posidonius* (a) does not claim ignorance of causes, (b) but praises and accepts statements of earlier philosophers ('the ancients'). Cf. T101. Galen promises amplification of this, given later at 460.9–488.12 M.

COMMENTARY: F165

77-9 *Chrysippus* (a) makes no mention of 'the ancients', and (b) offers no cause of his own, but thinks the enquiry resolved if he admits ignorance of cause.

80-3 Yet the theme unifying Chrysippus' whole work on the theory and practical cure of emotions is precisely to find the causes by which they arise and cease;

83-6 because (Galen) that is the way one would prevent their arousal and stop them once aroused. For it is reasonable that the genesis and existence of things are removed with (συν-) their causes.

This would suggest that cause was regarded as material, cf. F95. οἶμαι (83, 85) shows that 83-6 is a Galenic, not a Chrysippean inference, although again it probably comes from Posidonius. The whole of 80-9 is a Galenic development.

86-9 *Chrysippus* is at a loss to give an account of this in his Περὶ παθῶν, particularly with regard to ἴασις of πάθη.

89-95 *Posidonius*

(i) praises Plato for his teaching on (a) emotions, (b) faculties of soul (c) emotions not arising at all, or once arisen stopping most quickly;
(ii) says that teaching on ἀρεταί, τέλος, and in short all teaching of ethical philosophy is bound as if by a single cord to the faculties of soul (F150a);
(iii) himself shows (a) that the emotions arise from anger and desire (i.e. Plato's τὸ θυμοειδὲς καὶ ἐπιθυμητικόν); (b) the cause of why they subside in time, even if the δόξαι and κρίσεις of an evil existing persist.

The whole section, 75-102, has the appearance of an insertion by Galen (who returns at 100ff to the point at issue at 70ff) attacking Chrysippus on general grounds, although it clearly derives from Posidonian polemic. It raises four important points which Posidonius made;

COMMENTARY: F165

(1) Chrysippus ignores earlier relevant philosophers ('the ancients'), particularly Plato.

(2) Chrysippus is willing to admit ignorance of cause (see T85, τὸ αἰτιολογικόν; cf. *SVF* II.973, 351; Kidd, *Problems* 210f).

(3) There is no philosophical guidance from Chrysippus on θεράπεια (whether παίδευσις or ἴασις); cf. F31.

(4) Chrysippus does not see that the solution derives from faculties of soul. I take it that 95-8 is a reference to Posidonius' teaching, not Plato's.

103-50

We now return to Posidonius who gives the cause of why emotions abate with time.

(a) 102-33 Posidonius uses Chrysippus as a witness for this; cf. 55 above. Maliciously he turns Chrysippus' own quotations against him (104-33), alleging a contradiction between them and Chrysippus' assumptions (121). Chrysippus' assumption is that there is only one faculty of soul (the rational); yet (i) Chrysippus illustrates from the poets satiety with emotion (104, 108, 124), and the incursion of reason when the emotional inflammation has abated (113-15); which Posidonius reinterprets as emotional movements (cf. Frs. 153, 169), and the satiety of irrational faculties (141ff); (ii) Chrysippus illustrates the *attraction* of emotion (125, 128, 133), which can only be the goal of irrational faculties (139ff).

104 Kalbfleisch is very likely right to read ἔτι δὲ καὶ τῆς λύπης ὡς...

133 Since pleasure is the point of this quotation, ἀδονάν must be right, and it is meaningless to print *H*'s ἀηδόνα with Müller, Pohlenz (*Diss.* 619) and v. Arnim.

(b) 133-50 Posidonius can call on innumerable other quotations from the poets as evidence that men are sated with grief, tears, wailing (Chrysippus' list), anger, victory, honour.

136 νίκης καὶ τιμῆς are added because they are Posidonius' goals for τὸ θυμοειδές (139ff; F158; F160; cf. F169.63), which supports by association perhaps the conjecture θυμοῦ. For Posidonius quoting the poets see T104; for Chrysippus as a quoter (especially of Eur. *Med.*), D.L. VII.180–1.

From this evidence it is not difficult to conclude or infer the cause (συλλογίζεσθαι, 138; cf. 144). The emphatic play on the word recalls Chrysippus' δυσσυλλόγιστον (63), and δυσλόγιστον (73), which suggests the Posidonian base of 54–75.

Posidonius argues thus: that which has obtained its goal is sated and so relaxes its motion and urgency (140ff, 176f); a thing is attracted by its own proper goal (139f). Therefore, if creatures find πάθη attractive, yet become sated with them, then there must be an emotional element of the soul that has them as its proper objects of desire (139f). In fact there are two such faculties, one having the natural aim of pleasure, the other of mastery and victory (147f). Nothing is plainer, and it is plain to see in all other creatures too (146, 148), or would be except for those who want to do down the earlier philosophers (145f).

For these ὀρέξεις: F158ff. They are based on the Platonic parts of soul, hence the remark about οἱ παλαιοί (146). Posidonius is to argue later that the phenomenon of satiety *is peculiar to* emotional experiences; 177ff.

τὰ ἐναργῶς φαινόμενα recur in Posidonian argument at Frs. 159, 169.45, 156, and cf. 165 below; also T85. ἐνάργεια was a concept much admired by Galen himself, who strongly approved of Posidonius' scientific respect for facts, unique in a Stoic.

151–64

151 Posidonius now returns to the criticism of the tentative suggestions made in the quotation from Chrysippus, 55ff.

(a) **152–5** 'Although the conation (ὁρμή) persists, what comes next will not comply because of another kind of supervening disposition' (see 62f above). Posidonius answers: it is impossible that the ὁρμή be present, yet its activity be

COMMENTARY: F165

hindered by some other cause. That is, Chrysippus cannot explain 'by some other cause'; there is no explanation from a monolithic structure; cf. lines 139–43 above.

(b) **155–64** So when Chrysippus says 'so men both stop weeping and weep when they don't wish to, when the underlying circumstances create like impressions' (64f above), Posidonius again at this point asks what the cause is of this common occurrence. He finds it in the emotional movements (of the irrational faculties), either pressing violently (weeping against your will), or completely at rest (cessation).

161ff is clearly Posidonius' own answer, which would be extraordinarily abrupt without an introduction like Einarson's δηλονότι.

164 αὐτῆς H^1: αὐτῶν H^{Iss}. If αὐτῆς is accepted, the subject of ἐπεγείρεσθαι (and of κρατεῖσθαι, 162) is τὰς παθητικὰς κινήσεις which can no longer be roused by the will (and so people stop weeping before they wish to, 160). If the correction αὐτῶν is read, the subject of ἐπεγείρεσθαι and κρατεῖσθαι will be 'many people' (from 159), and αὐτῶν will refer to the emotional movements.

164–72

This vindicates earlier theories of conflict between reason and emotion, and of the faculties of soul; the αἰτίαι are not ἀσυλλόγιστοι at all, but given by the earlier philosophers. Posidonius obviously included here a short doxography of the doctrine beginning with the Pythagoreans, but indicating his special debt to Plato, and to Aristotle (cf. T97, T95, T91; also Galen, *De Moribus* 26.1–5 Kraus); to Plato perhaps for psychological analysis, to Aristotle for psychology (cf. *De An.* 414b 2, 432b 4–7; see F142), causation and ἔθος. See also T101.

The vehemence of style here (οὐ μὰ Δία, 166) could reflect Posidonius, as at F168.8, F18.7.

COMMENTARY: F165

172-89

There follows a most important conclusion.

(a) Habits and time in general have the most powerful effect on emotions because (i) the irrational element gradually makes itself at home in (οἰκειοῦται, 174) habits in which it is nurtured, and (ii) in time cessation comes about of emotions through satiety of the irrational faculties.

(b) This distinguishes the irrational faculties from all rational activities like opinions, judgements, all sciences and arts, which are not subject to change and cessation like emotions. There is no question of being sated in time, and abandoning or changing one's earlier opinion that two and two are four, or that all radii in a circle are equal.

It becomes difficult to distinguish Galen and Posidonius. The former observes immediately after this fragment (T61) that he will continue in the next book (v) the discussion of Chrysippus' errors on these topics, mentioning also Posidonius' criticism. Moreover, Walzer has shown ('New Light on Galen's Moral Philosophy', *Greek into Arabic* 142-63) that there are many similarities to the above theory of habit, irrational faculties, emotions and their treatment in the Arabic summary of Galen's lost *De Moribus*. However, the progression of the argument in F165 shows that (a) and (b) above must have been Posidonius' conclusions, and formed the theoretical base of his practical teaching on what he regarded as an important category of ethics (F168), the treatment of emotion, so inadequately dealt with by Chrysippus, because of his erroneous theory. See also F31. It must remain uncertain, however, to what extent Galen may have tampered with or omitted detail. In particular the stark polarisation between 'emotional movements' and 'logical judgements' or insight into eternal verities, such as two and two are four, would have required further elaboration.

COMMENTARY: F166

F166 Galen, *De Placitis* v.474–6,
pp. 454.15–456.14 M, p. 332.5–31 De Lacy

CONTENT

How reason may gain control over emotions.

CONTEXT

This passage occurs towards the end of Galen's summary of Posidonius' ethics in Bk v, see F187. It recapitulates and adds to the more detailed account in Bk IV of the reasons why emotions abate in time, and how they may be treated. See F165. F33 follows.

COMMENT

1–7 Galen raises again the question of why emotions through time become calmer and weaker, which was dealt with at length in Bk IV, F165 above, this time giving a brief epitome of Posidonius' views. See T42 for epitomes of Posidonius. It appears from 6 that Posidonius could write at considerable length.

7–10 contain the briefest summary of Posidonius' argument that abatement of emotion is explained by the satiety of the emotional element with its proper desires; details in F165.103–50, 172–89 comm. There it is the concept of satiety which is the key (ἐμπίπλασθαι). To that, 'weariness' (κάμνει, 8) is added (διὰ ἄμφω, 9) here, enabling the rational element to gain control.

11–17 This is illustrated by the analogy of a rider gaining control of a runaway horse (once it has tired itself out, sated with its desires, 12f), which is certainly from Posidonius. The original idea no doubt came from Pl. *Phdr.* 246a 6ff, which Posidonius on another occasion adapted for his own purpose: F31.19ff with comm. For ἔκφορος (11, 16) cf. F31.22 and

608

COMMENTARY: F166

Galen, 238.16f De L (κίνησις ἔκφορος τῆς ἐπιθυμητικῆς δυνάμεως); it recurs in Stob. *Ecl.* ii.89.7-9, Arius Didymus (see Kidd, 'Euemptosia' 111). The image was a natural one for his psychology of behaviour: F187.4ff.

The comparison is strengthened by an appeal to the evidence of the training of young animals. This is legitimate evidence for Posidonius for the training of children, because he held, against Chrysippus and other Stoics, that animals were subject to emotions like humans: F33.

17-19 Chrysippus, on the other hand, could offer no explanation, because his rationalistic psychology excluded an emotional element of soul to which he might refer the cause, and so he is at variance with observed facts. T85 comm. discusses the latter and their importance for Posidonius.

19-31 Posidonius went on to show that Chrysippus was also at variance with Zeno and Cleanthes, quoting from Cleanthes' verses giving a dialogue between Anger and Reason, implying that they were two different things (ὡς ἕτερον ἑτέρῳ, 31).

It might be argued that since Posidonius had to interpret these verses as evidence that Cleanthes believed in a distinct emotional element of soul, there was no explicit statement available to him; but this would be dangerous, since the liveliness of the example may well have appealed to Posidonius, who then chose the verses for rhetorical reasons. Posidonius, who had more of Cleanthes available than we have, was in no doubt of their import (ἐναργῶς, 28), and declared that Cleanthes too asserted three faculties of soul (F32, T92). Galen clearly believed that Cleanthes adopted a kind of Platonic psychology, T91. The position of Zeno seems more obscure (T91), but Posidonius maintained that it differed from that of Chrysippus (T93).

24-7 It would have been correct Stoic usage to ally Reason to βούλεσθαι and Anger to ἐπιθυμεῖν, since βούλησις is an εὔλογος ὄρεξις, and ἐπιθυμία an ἄλογος ὄρεξις (*SVF* iii.391, 432), but the terms are not distinguished here.

COMMENTARY: F167

26 is a syllable short; guesses are in the app. crit. But βασιλικόν should be retained, perhaps (De L) reminiscent of Pl. *Gorg.* 492b.

F167   Galen, *De Placitis* v.458, p. 436.7-10 M, p. 316.12-14 De Lacy

CONTENT

Posidonius is said to be a witness for the correctness of Plato's views on treatment of emotions, and the incompetence of Chrysippus.

CONTEXT

This particular argument from Galen runs from 432.1–436.16 M (312.22–316.20 De L), and consists of an attack on Chrysippus for being unable to explain how one can heal πάθη when they occur, or prevent them from occurring, because Chrysippus held that all ἐνέργεια and πάθος occur ἐν τῷ λογιστικῷ μόνῳ (433.1-6 M). Chrysippus confuses judgement and emotion; but Galen asserts that judgements (κρίσεις) occur and πάθη arise, not through one part of the soul or through one faculty of it, as Chrysippus said, but there are a number of faculties of it different in kind (ἑτερογενεῖς) and several parts (432.5-9 M). The psychology is supported by appealing to Posidonius, Aristotle, Hippocrates and Plato (432.9-15 M = F142). F169 follows this argument.

COMMENT

Ποσειδώνιος . . . μαρτυρεῖ. It is of course Galen who cites Posidonius as a witness to the correctness of Plato against Chrysippus; and it is noticeable that the recurrence of Posidonius' name in this argument (432.11 M; F142) is also in

COMMENTARY: F167

connection with the earlier psychologies of Plato and Aristotle. But there is no reason to doubt that Posidonius in Περὶ παθῶν did in fact praise both Plato's psychology and his treatment of emotion (T97 = F165.89-95 with comm.) perhaps in a doxographical section (F31 comm.; T95). However ὀρθῶς may be misleading; in the earlier passage (F142), Galen distinguished between those positing a number of faculties (δυνάμεις, Aristotle), and those maintaining a plurality of local parts (μόρια, Plato), and Posidonius is classified with Aristotle against Plato (so also Frs. 145, 146). But no doubt here Galen offers a simple opposition between Plato and Chrysippus.

τὰς θεραπείας τῶν παθῶν: the word θεραπεία occurs only here in the fragments and may be Galen's term; in the sentence before this fragment, πάθη are classified with τὰ νοσήματα τῆς ψυχῆς. But Posidonius may well have used the term, as indeed Chrysippus did (e.g. *SVF* III.474). It is certainly in harmony with the health and sickness analogy of F163, with the treatment of πάθη recommended in Frs. 165, 166, and with the description ἡ τῶν παθῶν τῆς ψυχῆς ἴασις in F169.107. Posidonius' Περὶ παθῶν was clearly psychiatric ethics from a theoretical psychological base.

μοχθηρῶς. Galen accuses Chrysippus of (i) self-contradiction (434.3f M, 314.15ff De L), (ii) contradiction with facts (434.4f M), (iii) inadequate explanation (not stating all the causes, and admitting to being at a loss on the most important ones, 436.1of M). That all three accusations reflect Posidonius' criticism is clear from their recurrence elsewhere. Thus in related fragments, for (i), F165.121, F164.87-93; for (ii), F164.11-25 comm., F159; for (iii), F165.75-102 comm.

COMMENTARY: F168

F168 Galen, *De Placitis* v.472–3,
pp. 452.10–453.11 M, p. 330.6–21 De Lacy

CONTENT

The modes of education. Galen comments on part of a quotation from Posidonius (cf. F150b).

CONTEXT

See F187 comm. *D* (F187.37ff.).

COMMENT

The problem depends on the recognition of the cause of the πάθη.

The main educational solution that derives from Posidonius' explanation of the cause of πάθη through his psychology, is that the irrational aspect(s) of the soul cannot be trained by an appeal to reason: 'the irrational is helped and harmed by what is irrational, the rational by knowledge and ignorance' (16f). This sums up F31.1–29, esp. 28f. Cf. Frs. 169 *fin.*, 165, 164.

This passage concentrates on the training of the irrational. Following Plato's lead (in *Rep.* and *Laws*), it includes music (ῥυθμοί and ἁρμονίαι); to this is added 'practices' (ἐπιτηδεύματα), but it has the individual stamp of Posidonius. One has to know the natural characteristics of the subject, and differentiate the training for the dull, sluggish, timid character from that of the more fiery, crazily helter-skelter nature (2–8). This follows naturally from Posidonius' views on physiognomy (F169, 84ff comm.). The purpose is to mould the character by habituation so that the emotional movements can be blunted (e.g. χρηστοῖς ἐπιτηδεύμασιν ἐθισθείσας, F169.116; cf. F165.172ff) or so shaped as to bring them

612

COMMENTARY: F169

into obedience and concord with the rational aspect, as F31. The anecdote on Damon subduing a drunken party of young men which had become crazily out of hand, by making the girl who was playing the recorder change from the Phrygian to the Dorian mode (9–13), shows that the training applied to adults as well as children.

Although the comment comes from Galen, the language as well as the content indicates that a Posidonian passage is not far away. In the next exposition in this series, Galen simply uses a quotation (F162). For θυμικωτέρους (7): F169.87; ἐπιτηδεύμασι (3, 6), and ἀμβλεῖς (4): F169.116; μανικώτερον (7, 11): F164.1; ᾄττοντας (8): F169.10; ἐμπλήκτου (12): F187.52; φορᾶς (13): φέρεσθαι F187.9, ἔκφορος F166.11, 16; τὸ παθητικὸν τῆς ψυχῆς (14) and κινήσεων ἀλόγων (15f) are virtually Posidonian technical terms; and for the sudden exasperated exclamation, ἐπεὶ διὰ τί πρὸς θεῶν (8), cf. F18.7, F165.166.

The anecdote on Damon (DK, 37.A8), the 5th-century B.C. sophist and friend of Pericles, could also have come from Posidonius, because the inference from it is Posidonian (οὐ γὰρ δήπου κτλ, 13ff). For similar comment on the different effects on behaviour of the modes, in which Damon is also featured, Pl. *Laches* may be compared.

F169   Galen, *De Placitis* v.459–65,
pp. 437.1–444.11 M,
pp. 316.21–322.26 De Lacy

CONTENT

The problem of evil. The explanation of how vice arises, beginning from the behaviour of children; its constitution and the effect of physique and environment. How it may be cured.

COMMENTARY: F169

CONTEXT

F167, Context. An argument runs from 312.22–316.20 De Lacy, consisting of an attack on Chrysippus for being unable to explain, because of his mistaken psychology, how one can heal πάθη when they occur, or prevent them from occurring. Posidonius is associated with this argument: F167. F169 follows, and is followed immediately by F31.

STRUCTURE

A. (1–18)

The problem of the διοίκησις, or governing power, in children. Chrysippus cannot explain the facts of the behaviour of children (and animals), which does not follow from and is in fact contradictory to his theory.

B. (18–34)

Explanation of this behaviour by a theory of οἰκειώσεις, which comes from Posidonius, and is contrasted with Chrysippus' position.

C. (35–49)

Chrysippus accordingly cannot solve three difficulties, which are enumerated, in the problem of evil.

D. (49–77)

Chrysippus' two-fold explanation of the cause of corruption in children is criticised by Galen, who is following Posidonius.

E. (78–84)

Posidonius' explanation of the cause of vice, and how it is that children err.

F. (84–106)

Further amplification of the problems from Posidonius'

theory of physiognomy, which makes clearer another of the *aporiai* with regard to κακία, the manner of its constitution.

G. (106–17)
How vice may be cured.

COMMENT
A. (1–18)

Galen, confining himself to what is most necessary for his subject (1) begins with the problem of the governing power of children, τὸ περὶ τῆς τῶν παίδων διοικήσεως (3). διοίκησις is the noun corresponding to διοικεῖν, which is used again of irrational creatures (ζῷα) in F33.3. Cf. also Frs. 21, 102 for oral usage.

The observation of the behaviour of small children and animals is for Galen an important starting point as evidence, and recurs in the *De Sequela* (F35), and in his *De Moribus* (see Walzer, 'New Light on Galen's Moral Philosophy', *Greek into Arabic* 151ff). It was also so for Posidonius, whom Galen at least partly follows, in particular because it formed part of the base of Posidonius' attack on Chrysippus (apart from this fr., Frs. 31, 33, 35).

The argument begins with two denials aimed at Chrysippus:

(1) 'It is impossible to say that children's impulses have reason (λόγος) as their guardian (ἐπιτροπεύεσθαι), for children don't yet have reason (4f).' This is common Stoic doctrine which worked on a hebdomadal system of maturity. It was even one of the reasons why Chrysippus denied πάθη in young children.

(2) 'Nor can one say that they are not angry, feel pain and pleasure, laugh, weep and undergo countless other such πάθη; for children feel more frequent and more severe emotions than adults.' Chrysippus would not have denied that children display these feelings (44ff), but would say that

COMMENTARY: F169

they are not πάθη in his sense of the term, but that they are prepathetic.

8 But Galen maintains strongly (οὐ μὴν ... γε) that these facts, that children feel emotions, do not follow (logically, ἀκολουθεῖ, cf. ἀκόλουθος in F47.74, F49.8, and below, line 46) from Chrysippus' doctrines, just as they don't follow either from his view that there is no natural affinity (οἰκείωσις) to pleasure or alienation (ἀλλοτρίωσις) from pain. Posidonius did claim such οἰκείωσις, see below. But orthodox Stoic doctrine held that pleasure (ἡδονή) was a true ἀδιάφορον, not even προηγμένον; *SVF* I.190, 195; III.155, 136; explicitly in D.L. VII.85 (*SVF* III.178).

10ff Galen's reason (γάρ) is an appeal to fact: '*all* children rush untaught towards pleasures, avert themselves and flee from pains'.

12–18 There follows a striking passage of embroidery: 'We *see* (ὁρῶμεν) them raging, kicking, biting, wanting to win and boss other children, like some animals (ζῷα, as F33), where no other prize is on offer but victory. Such conduct is obvious in quail, cocks, partridge, ichneumon, asp, crocodile and countless others.' It is tempting to trace Posidonius here; Galen used similar language elsewhere (Walzer, 'New Light'), but the common origin could have been a striking passage in Posidonius. The very appeal to the obviousness of fact, while of course Galenic, is also very much Posidonian (φαίνεται ... ἐναργῶς as τὰ ἐναργῶς φαινόμενα, Frs. 159, 156; see F167, comm. *ad fin.*). It is a characteristic of Posidonius most admired by Galen, and possibly a reason why he called him 'most scientific', F35, comm. *B*.3, and T58.

B. (18–34)

The critical approach of *A* is followed by the positive statement of a theory of οἰκειώσεις.

18–21 A summing up of what has gone before (οὖν): 'so children too (i.e. like animals) seem to have a natural affinity (οἰκειοῦσθαι) to pleasure and victory (Posidonian: Frs. 158,

COMMENTARY: F169

160), just as at some later time they show when they grow up that they have a natural οἰκείωσις towards moral values (τὸ καλόν)'. Chrysippus only recognised the latter; the οὕτως ... ὥσπερ construction stresses the equal importance of the earlier natural affinities.

21–6 'Part proof of this (γοῦν) is that they are ashamed as they grow older of their mistakes, are glad in (χαίρει; χαρά is the emotion in the σοφός counter to ἡδονή, D.L. VII.116 = *SVF* III.431) noble actions, lay claim to justice and the other virtues and often act in accordance with their notions of these virtues, whereas before when they were still small they lived by emotion (κατὰ πάθος), having no care for the commands arising from reason (τῶν ἐκ τοῦ λόγου προσταγμάτων)'; as exactly F31.13f. This is proof only that the behaviour of small children differs from that of adults, and that the development of a rational morality comes later, none of which Chrysippus would have denied.

26–30 The theory is now stated: 'hence, since these three things to which we have an affinity (οἰκειώσεων) exist fundamentally by nature (φύσει stressed because denied by Chrysippus) corresponding to each form (εἶδος) of the parts (μορίων) of the soul, pleasure through τὸ ἐπιθυμητικόν, victory through τὸ θυμοειδές, morality (τὸ καλόν) through τὸ λογιστικόν ...'. This is Posidonius' theory (Frs. 158; 161; 165.146ff; 31), but Galen expresses it in his own words (εἶδος, μόρια of the soul, which Posidonius denied, Frs. 142–6), perhaps because he wishes to stress the Platonic base.

30–4 Since οἰκείωσις is linked to a psychology of three distinct aspects of soul, Galen can now classify the mistakes of his predecessors: (1) Epicurus fixed his gaze on the natural affinity of the worst part of the soul only (i.e. to pleasure); (2) Chrysippus concentrated solely on the best (τὸ λογιστικόν, τὸ καλόν); (3) it was only the 'ancient' philosophers who observed all three natural affinities. (Galen or Posidonius or both project the term back to ἀρχαῖοι; cf. Brink, *Phronesis* I (1956), 123ff; *Harv. Stud.* 63 (1958), 193–8). But since, as

617

COMMENTARY: F169

Galen well knew, this was also true of Posidonius, who was not for Galen an 'ancient' philosopher, this only makes sense if Galen forgot here that he was using Posidonius, *or* if this classification comes straight from Posidonius. The latter assumption is argued under *C* below. For the concept of a mistaken 'partial' view of human nature, cf. Galen, *De Sequ.* XI.814, *Scripta Min.* II.73 M; the same chapter from which F35 comes.

C. (35-49)

The base is now laid for the main theme of the fragment, that by ignoring two οἰκειώσεις, Chrysippus naturally cannot solve (ἀπορεῖ) the origin of vice. A classification is given of three questions which Chrysippus cannot answer: (1) the cause (αἰτίαν) of how vice comes to be; (2) the manner of its constitution (τρόπους τῆς συστάσεως); (3) how children err.

38f Posidonius' name is brought in for the first time: 'for *all* of which Posidonius too reasonably censures and refutes Chrysippus'. What is definite is that Posidonius attacked on all three points; but it seems likely from the analysis of the earlier part of the fragment, that Galen had been following Posidonius from the beginning.

39-49 What follows appears to carry on Posidonius' argument (γάρ, 39). It is designed to lead up to Chrysippus' account of the origin of evil.

(1) On Chrysippus' theory it cannot come from within, because if it were really true (δή, 39) that children had a natural affinity to morality right from the beginning (εὐθὺς ἐξ ἀρχῆς, 40), vice could only arise from an external source (39–42). This is garbled over-simplification, because Chrysippus did not hold that children had an οἰκείωσις πρὸς τὸ καλόν from the beginning. Children did have οἰκειώσεις, but not for pleasure (*SVF* III.178ff). Nevertheless, Chrysippus did have a problem once the οἰκείωσις πρὸς τὸ καλόν was operative.

(2) But then there is a *factual* paradox (ὁρᾶταί γε, 42),

618

COMMENTARY: F169

that we see children going wrong in any case (πάντως, 43), even if brought up in good habits.

Since Chrysippus admits this and does not dare to falsify τὰ ἐναργῶς φαινόμενα he must explain how vice can occur from an external source (44-9).

D. (49-77)

51-4 Chrysippus' explanation of the cause of corruption (τῆς διαστροφῆς τὴν αἰτίαν is two-fold (cf. D.L. VII.89): (a) from oral communication from the majority of men; (b) from the very nature of the things (τῶν πραγμάτων). It is clear from the following criticism that 'the things themselves' refer to pleasure (60), pain (62), praise, honour, censure, disgrace (63-5), all summed up by πιθανότης τῶν φαντασιῶν (70f), pleasure projecting the persuasive appearance of being good (72).

55-77 Galen (ἐγὼ δέ, 54) criticises both explanations in turn; but Posidonius is behind this, see 77. Both positions are again similarly attacked by Galen in *De Sequela*, see F35, where once more Posidonius is cited (F35, comm. *B*).

(1) 55-7 Chrysippus' first explanation is quickly dealt with; the argument is based on οἰκείωσις. There is no natural affinity for evil (as of course all Stoics would agree), therefore why should children be attracted to it merely by observing or hearing an outside example of it? Cf. *De Sequ., Scripta Min.* II.74.21-77.1 M, after which Posidonius is named.

(2) 57-77 Galen is still more surprised by Chrysippus' second explanation (57f). For this attack cf. F35 comm. *A* (*De Sequ.*). 'For what necessity (ἀνάγκη) is there that children be enticed by pleasure as a bait (δελεάζεσθαι, 60) if they have no affinity to it, or turn themselves and flee from pain if they are not naturally alienated from it too' (59-63)? There is a linguistic link with *De Sequ.* 77.6 M, where δέλεαρ is used in the same context in the sentence before F35 *q.v.* The ultimate source is Pl. *Tim.* 69d, but Posidonius is the likely intermediary. The argument is *ad hominem*, again based on οἰκείωσις.

619

COMMENTARY: F169

Chrysippus did not hold that children have an οἰκείωσις to pleasure, Posidonius did.

In fact the argument shifts to the positive aspect (63–6): 'why should children have to (τίς ἀνάγκη) fling themselves at (ἵεσθαι, 64) and delight in praise, honour etc., if it is true that (εἴπερ, 65) they actually (καὶ) do not have natural (φύσει) affinity and alienation towards these'? The implication now is that they definitely do have such an οἰκείωσις.

Indeed Galen suggests (66–9) that if Chrysippus does not actually say so, his words imply (τῇ γε δυνάμει, 67) that he recognised some kind of (τις) οἰκείωσις of this sort. Because when he says that corruption (or distortion, διαστροφή) arises through the persuasiveness of appearances (διά τε τὴν πιθανότητα τῶν φαντασιῶν, 70f), he must be asked the cause (or explanation, τὴν αἰτίαν, 72, surely Posidonian) why pleasure proffers a persuasive φαντασία of good, and pain of evil. (For a form of πιθανὴ φαντασία, see F162.) A somewhat abrupt and unexpected illustration (from Posidonius?) concludes the argument with a strong appeal to fact (73–7): 'and so why are we so readily persuaded when we hear winning at the Olympics and erection of one's statue praised and glorified by the majority as good, and defeat and disgrace as evils?' This seems to be rather an instance related to adults.

(3) 77 'Yes and these things too (καὶ ταῦθ') are criticised by Posidonius.' It is of course possible that ταῦτα refers only to the preceding sentence (73–7), but it is likely that Galen has been following Posidonius from the beginning of the argument: F35 comm. *B* (7–18). The source was Posidonius' Περὶ παθῶν, see F35.

E. (78–84)

78–80 'And Posidonius tries to show that the causes (τὰς αἰτίας) of all false suppositions (πασῶν τῶν ψευδῶν ὑπολήψεων)...' What follows is uncertain. The codices have ἐν μὲν τῷ θεωρητικῷ διὰ τῆς παθητικῆς ὁλκῆς.... This neither makes sense, nor satisfactory phrasing of the Greek, because

COMMENTARY: F169

ἐν μὲν τῷ θεωρητικῷ demands an antithesis to which διὰ τῆς παθητικῆς ὁλκῆς belongs. Pohlenz first in 1898 (in his Diss., *De Posidonii libris* Περὶ παθῶν 560–5) posited a lacuna after θεωρητικῷ (cf. *Die Stoa* II.113); this has rightly won general acceptance, and different suggestions have been made to complete the text, although Reinhardt (*Poseidonios* 315f; *RE* 740) seems eventually to have given it up. The first question to decide is the antithesis to τὸ θεωρητικόν. Pohlenz, with his eye on Plu. *De Virt., Mor.* 448A, suggested ἐν δὲ τῷ πρακτικῷ, and this was accepted by Edelstein and De Lacy, and indeed by me in volume I. It is true that Stoics seemingly differentiated between virtues which are θεωρηματικαί and those which were ἀθεώρητοι (D.L. VII.90 = *SVF* III.197), and speak of the virtuous man as θεωρητικὸς and πρακτικὸς τῶν ποιητέων (D.L. VII.125 = *SVF* III.295). Stobaeus uses the term πρακτικὴ ὁρμή (*SVF* III.169, 171, 173); the πρακτικὸς βίος is one of the three stock lives (D.L. VII.130 = *SVF* III.687); and there is even an obscure passage in Ammonius (*SVF* II.49) which refers to the πρακτικὸν μόριον of the soul. But none of this is very relevant to Posidonius here. From what follows, 81–4, and especially the subsequent antithesis in 82–4, Posidonius by τὸ θεωρητικόν appears to have in mind τὸ λογιστικόν. If this is so, the natural antithesis in Posidonian Greek is τὸ παθητικόν (τῆς ψυχῆς) (thus Frs. 148, 31, 33, and index vol. I s.v. παθητικός; cf. Plu. *Mor.* 441C). On the other hand, I agree with Edelstein (and De Lacy) that the cause of false assumptions ἐν τῷ θεωρητικῷ can only be ἀμαθία for Posidonius (as F31.24ff; F168). Therefore I would now suggest: ἐν μὲν τῷ θεωρητικῷ ⟨διὰ τῆς ἀμαθίας γινομένων, ἐν δὲ τῷ παθητικῷ⟩ διὰ τῆς παθητικῆς ὁλκῆς....

Since Galen says at this point that Posidonius was trying to explain all false ὑπολήψεις, it is natural that he should have included intellectual mistakes (ἐν τῷ θεωρητικῷ: F165.172–89, comm.); but the immediate context is the explanation of πάθος, especially beginning with children. Posidonius explains this principally by the 'emotional pull' in the

COMMENTARY: F169

irrational δυνάμεις of the soul (ἐν τῷ παθητικῷ). The term 'emotional pull' appears to have been coined by Posidonius to convey the action of his 'emotional movements' (F153). Posidonius may have derived the idea of ὁλκή from Plato (as *Laws* 644e; *Rep.* 439b; *Phdr.* 254c).

80–4 What follows seems puzzling, and may have been compressed by Galen. It is clear from Posidonius' controversy with Chrysippus and Zeno over the relationship between πάθος and κρίσις (see Frs. 34, 151, 152), that Posidonius held that πάθη were not judgements or rational decisions, nor did they result from rational decisions, but that it was the irrational movements of the 'emotional pull' that affected and distorted rational judgement, whether in children or adults. Now (80–2) he says that the 'emotional pull' is preceded by 'false beliefs' (τὰς ψευδεῖς δόξας), when the rational faculty has become weak περὶ τὴν κρίσιν. This has been thought to be inconsistent, but I do not think this is so. I take the ψευδεῖς δόξαι to be the beliefs that pleasure and winning are good, and their opposites evil, which Galen outlined above. We have a natural affinity to these (οἰκείωσις), but *simpliciter* they are ψευδεῖς δόξαι; yet this triggers a ὁρμή, which if the rational faculty is in a weak state becomes a πλεονάζουσα ὁρμή, which in turn through its 'emotional pull' demands an assent (συγκατάθεσις), and so affects a κρίσις or rational decision to a particular act. So the main αἰτία remains the 'emotional pull', although it is preceded by the ψευδεῖς δόξαι from our οἰκειώσεις and a weak λογιστικόν; see especially F164. This is further explained in 106–17. But the κρίσις is not the δόξαι, but comes at the end of the process as a result of the παθητικὴ ὁλκή. This is amplified further in *F* below, 84ff; see also F170. In general: Kerferd, 'The Origin of Evil in Stoic Thought', *Bull. of J. Rylands Univ. Libr. of Manchester* 60 (1978), 482–94.

82–4 Posidonius goes on to say, according to Galen, that a creature's (ζῴῳ, to include both children and animals as well as adults, since he held that they too had πάθη: F33)

COMMENTARY: F169

ὁρμή is born sometimes in the rational decision of the rational faculty (ἐπὶ τῇ τοῦ λογιστικοῦ κρίσει), but very often in the movement of the emotional faculty (ἐπὶ τῇ κινήσει τοῦ παθητικοῦ). This is not inconsistent either. Of course τὸ λογιστικόν has its own ὁρμή (towards τὸ καλόν, 29f) but πάθος has its ὁρμή in the irrational movements. As often in a μέν... δέ antithesis, the weight in this context is given to the δέ clause, strengthened by πολλάκις against ἐνίοτε. But both legs of the antithesis are necessary (as in 79f) to explain the first of the three *aporiai* of 35–7, namely the cause of vice. The emphasis on the δέ clause is probably related more to the third *aporia*, how children err.

F. (84–106) (Jacoby F102)

84 Posidonius reasonably (εἰκότως) attaches to this discussion the phenomena from physiognomy. Two general categories (ὅσα ... πάντα) are instanced (85–8): all broad-chested warmer creatures are more spirited by nature (φύσει), the broad-hipped and colder, more cowardly.

88–90 The theory is enlarged to include environment (κατὰ τὰς χώρας) through which men's characters (τοῖς ἤθεσι) are largely (οὐ σμικρῷ) different in cowardice or daring, love of pleasure or toil.

90–3 The grounds given (ὡς) are that the emotional movements (Posidonius' term, 102) of the soul follow always the physical state (τῇ διαθέσει τοῦ σώματος), which is altered (ἀλλοιοῦσθαι) in no small degree from the temperature (τῆς κράσεως; cf. F49.71ff) in the environment (κατὰ τὸ περιέχον).

Galen's pamphlet *De Sequela* bears the title, ὅτι ταῖς τοῦ σώματος κράσεσιν αἱ τῆς ψυχῆς δυνάμεις ἕπονται. Not only is Posidonius again referred to there, but the development of argument in ch. XI is parallel to that in F169 (see F35), which substantiates the relevance of this section *F* for Posidonius' argument. Interest in the effect of environment on character

COMMENTARY: F169

was early in Greece, cf. Hippocrates, *Airs, Waters, Places*. For Aristotle and physiognomy, cf. also *De An.* 403a.

93–6 Galen adds that Posidonius says (there is no reason to delete φησι in 95 with Müller) that even the blood in animals differs in its characteristics, a topic which Aristotle developed at length. For Aristotle refer to *Pol.* VII.6.1327b 18ff, and cf. *Problemata* XIV.1ff and *Physiognomici Scriptores*, ed. R. Foerster (Teubner), Leipzig, 1893, II. Frs. 39–62. Sandbach (*Aristotle and the Stoics*) suggested *De Part. Anim.* 647b 30–648a 13, and 650b 19–651a 19. There is some trace of physiognomy in the earlier Stoa (D.L. VII.173 = *SVF* 1.204; D.L. VII.129 = *SVF* 1.248; *SVF* 1.518 (Tertullian, *De An.* 5), but there is no sign of it in Chrysippus. Cf. also Plb. 4.21; Sen. *De Ira* II.19.1–3; Strabo, II.3.7 (F49).

96–103 Galen puts this topic off for further discussion when he turns to Hippocrates and Plato on this subject. At this point he is merely concerned with Chrysippus and his followers, who as well as their general ignorance of questions concerning emotions, do not know that different physical mixtures (or temperaments) produce their own 'emotional movements', the term usually given them by Posidonius; see F153.

103–6 But Aristotle straight out calls all such settled states (καταστάσεις) of mind in animals characters (ἤθη, adopting De Lacy's emendation in 103 for ἤδη *H*; ἤδει *L*), and explains in what way they are composed (συνίστανται) in their different mixtures.

On the face of it, this reference to Aristotle comes from Galen, and I cannot find it in our extant Aristotle. But its expression may help to explain how this whole passage on physiognomy is connected with what comes before in this fragment. It could relate to the second *aporia* listed by Posidonius in line 37, which Chrysippus failed to explain, namely τοὺς τρόπους τῆς συστάσεως (τῆς κακίας). Then indeed Posidonius συνάπτει εἰκότως τοῖς λόγοις τούτοις (84). And then the reference to Aristotle may have come from

COMMENTARY: F169

him. Certainly what remains (106-17), in spite of Galen's οἶμαι, is Posidonian in content, and F31 follows immediately.

G. (106-117)

The understanding of the τρόποι τῆς συστάσεως of vice naturally leads to the understanding of its cure (ἴασις, 107). The problem of evil is not so much a metaphysical one for Posidonius, as a psychological problem, and the important question is the practical one of psychiatry: what one does about it. See above under Context and, for θεραπεία, Frs. 163-8, F31.

There is no simple rule because:

(1) in some the cure of the πάθη of the soul is easy because (a) their 'emotional movements' are not strong, and (b) the rational is not weak by nature (φύσει, because of their physical mixture?), nor void of understanding; it is through ignorance (cf. above, 80) and bad habits that such men are compelled (ἀναγκάζεσθαι) to live by emotions (ἐμπαθῶς).

(2) But in some the cure is hard and rough, i.e. when (a) the movements of emotion which necessarily (ἀναγκαίως) occur through their physical state, are in fact big and violent, and (b) the rational is *by nature* weak and uncomprehending.

114-17 For the cure must be two-fold, if one is going to improve the man's character:

(a) the rational (τὸ λογιστικόν) aspect must grasp knowledge of the truth;

(b) the movements of emotion must be blunted by habituation (ἐθισθείσας) to good practices.

Compare Frs. 31, 165, 164.

F170 Seneca, *Epistulae* 87.31–40

CONTENT

Wealth, health and the like are not 'goods,' nor 'evils,' but 'advantages' (*commoda*).

CONTEXT

From the beginning of the *Letter*, Seneca is arguing that wealthy trappings are superfluous (*supervacua*, 1). Simple necessities are all that are needed. Precious possessions are *impedimenta*. Virtue is sufficient for the happy life (11). From § 12 a succession of Stoic syllogisms is offered to prove that riches are not a 'good'. At 28f the following syllogism is given: that which involves us in many evils, when we desire to attain it, is not a good. In desiring to attain riches, we become involved in many evils. Therefore riches are not a good. This is countered by the usual anonymous 'objector' (*inquit*), whom Seneca employs in rhetorical argument:

(a) (§28) But in desiring to attain virtue, we become involved in many evils.

(b) (§29) Anyway, if it is through wealth that we become involved in many evils, wealth is not only not a good, but is positively an evil. And yet Stoics maintain merely that it is not a good. Moreover, Stoics are accused by the 'objector' of granting that wealth is of some use (*aliquid usus*) – *inter commoda* (advantages) *illas numeratis*; but wealth cannot even be an advantage, if it is through riches that we suffer *incommoda*.

(§30) *Quidam* (i.e. certain Stoics) answer this: it is wrong to assign disadvantage (*incommoda*) to riches. Wealth harms no one; it is a man's own folly (or neighbours' wickedness) that harms him. It is not the sword that slays. Wealth does not harm just because you are harmed on account of wealth.

COMMENTARY: F170

F170 now follows, giving a better answer (*melius*), in Seneca's opinion.

STRUCTURE

A. (31–2)

Posidonius' 'better' answer explaining how wealth may be said to be a cause of evil is given in terms of a logical distinction of causes. Wealth is distinguished from 'goods' in this area.

B. (33–4)

Seneca's rhetorical objector (*inquit*) suggests that wealth then is an evil, which is countered.

C. (35)

A syllogism is specifically assigned to Posidonius, which produces the conclusion that wealth, health and the like are not goods. The syllogism is extended by Posidonius to reach the same conclusion.

D. (36–7)

Seneca's 'objector' suggests that on this reasoning they are not even 'advantages' (*commoda*). This is countered.

E. (38–40)

Posidonius reports a refutation by Antipater of a fallacious Peripatetic syllogism that wealth is not a good. Seneca comments.

At first sight this looks like a continuous argument. But whose argument is it, Posidonius' or Seneca's? The rhetorical 'objector' must come from Seneca, and cannot therefore be Posidonius. On the other hand the arguments which specifically counter the 'objections' may come from Seneca, or they may be based on Posidonius; see F90, comm. on §§24–8, and

627

Kidd, 'Philosophy and Science in Posidonius'. Each section must be examined on its own and in relation to the whole.

COMMENT

A. (§§31–2) (1–13)

(1) What is Posidonius' better answer (*melius*) addressed to? Clearly the objection raised in §29 (Context (b)), firstly, that if it is through wealth that we become involved in many evils, wealth is not only not a good, but positively an evil; and his answer is better than that given in §30 by *quidam* (Context). Posidonius' argument is that riches are a cause of evil, not because they themselves do anything, but because they rouse men to do evil (1–3). In logical terms this is a distinction betwen *causa efficiens*, which necessarily harms straight off, and *causa praecedens*, an antecedent cause (3f). As the latter, riches may swell the temper, beget pride, arouse envy (5f), and so derange the mind that a reputation for having money, even when it is harmful, delights us (6f). But, the implication is that since wealth is not a *causa efficiens*, i.e. a necessary, principal and self-sufficient cause, it is not *the* cause of evil, and so is not itself an evil. And so the objection is answered directly. Reinhardt (*Poseidonios* 339) strangely infers from this argument that for Posidonius wealth was an evil (κακόν). This is clearly false, against both sense and context; and it vitiates the whole of Reinhardt's account of the evidence of the *Letter*.

Now all this so far is certainly Posidonian. It is true that a classification of causes designed to solve the problem of determinism and free will goes back to Chrysippus (Theiler, *Phyllobolia für Peter von der Mühll*, p. 64 n. 1), who coined the terms αἰτία αὐτοτελής and προκαταρκτική, for a cause sufficient of itself, and a predisposing (or initiatory or antecedent) cause (esp. Plu. *De SR* 1056B, with Cherniss's note; Cic. *De Fato* 41–4; *SVF* II.346, 348, 351, 945, 997; Long, *Archiv für Geschichte der Philosophie* 52 (1970), 248ff). But

COMMENTARY: F170

Posidonius not only had a reputation for τὸ αἰτιολογικόν (T85), but apparently himself had an interest in classification of causes (F190), and above all applied a methodology of cause (αἰτία) to ethical problems, and particularly to the central problem for him of πάθη (F34, and the Galen frs. *passim*), and to the problem of evil (Frs. 35, 169). So the consideration of wealth as good or evil in relation to its function in the psychology of the rise of πάθη is highly characteristic. It is indeed a good instance of the category of *aetiologia*, which Posidonius pressed in admonitory or precept ethics (F176). So too is the outcome; wealth cannot be the real cause of πάθη or evil, for that lies within ourselves, in our own δυνάμεις (Frs. 35, 169). But it can be part of the pattern as an antecedent cause, in that it could provoke false beliefs (ψευδεῖς δόξαι, *fama pecuniae . . . delectet*, 7), which if the rational aspect is in a weak state (*mentem alienant*, 6; i.e. take away reason; *alienare* may also recall ἀλλοτρίωσις, the opposite of οἰκείωσις), an irrational power (δύναμις) could develop a πλεονάζουσα ὁρμή, which by its 'emotional pull' can demand an assent to an evil action (esp. F169, comm. on 80–4). But wealth is not responsible for this disturbance of our moral ὁμολογία, but our own moral intelligence (F187).

causa efficiens: *efficiens* presumably in the sense of Cic. *De fato*, 34, *quod cuique efficienter antecedat*. Cicero uses *perfectae et principales* for the Chrysippean αὐτοτελής (*De Fato* 41); and while he uses *antecedens* instead of Seneca's *praecedens* in 40, προκαταρκτική is rendered by *adiuvantes et proximae* in 41.

(2) In §32 the argument shifts to contrast the *effect* of 'goods' (*bona*) with that of wealth. Goods should be free of blame; unmixed, they do not corrupt nor disturb or seduce the mind. It is true that they elate and expand the spirit, but *sine tumore*. *fiducia* and *magnitudo animi* are produced by goods, but *audacia* and *insolentia* by wealth; and *insolentia* is nothing else than a false image of *magnitudo*.

Is this Posidonius or Seneca? The structure is still that of function within cause and effect. The terms *extollunt* and *dilatant* (9), recall the Greek Stoic technical terms ἔπαρσις and διάχυσις (F152), and the distinction, *sine tumore*, may mark the difference between ἄλογος ἔπαρσις, i.e. πάθος, and λογικαί, i.e. εὐπάθειαι (such as the wise man experiences). Hence the area of discussion is still right. But the final terms of result (10–13), *fiducia, magnitudo animi, audacia, insolentia*, look Senecan, not Posidonian (below, comm. *C*). And while the general conclusion would be that wealth is not a good, the contrast between the two is pushed further by implying that wealth corrupts, *corrumpunt* (8), which is not Posidonius' theory of διαστροφή (F169, and §31 above). Indeed the contrast between *bona* and *divitiae* is pushing the argument back to the thesis that wealth is an evil (recognised by the 'objector' in §33), which is in sharp contrast to the argument in §31.

If this is not a continuation of the Posidonian argument, but a Senecan insertion, why does it occur here? Possibly to answer the first 'objection' (a) of §28 (cf. Context above): in desiring to attain virtue, we become involved in many evils. In that case, the hypothesis would be that Posidonius had answered what appears as objection (b) of §29, while Seneca, though following Posidonius' lead, deals with objection (a).

B. (§§33–4) (13–23)

Seneca now brings his 'objector' into play (*inquit*, 13). But the objector, almost reiterating his words of §29, apparently has forgotten the Posidonian argument of §31 (1–7), which proves that wealth is not an evil. 'By that way of arguing, wealth is actually an evil, not only not a good' (13f). *isto modo* can only refer to the implications of the Senecan argument of §32, and has to be countered merely by reiterating Posidonius' distinction of cause (15–17). Even here Seneca elaborates too far; the antecedent cause not only rouses, but drags on (*adtrahentem*, 17). But for Posidonius, the power of the 'emotional pull' (it is possible that Seneca may have had in mind Posidonius' phrase (παθητικὴ ὁλκή, F169.80)) does not come from the image (*speciem boni veri similem*, 17f); that was Chrysippus' theory (F164). The problem for Posidonius lay in what made the image persuasive (*credibilem*, 18), and was answered in terms of δυνάμεις (F169.66ff comm.). The 'objector' continues (§34, 18ff): virtue too incorporates an antecedent cause, leading to envy. This clearly relates to objection (a) of §28 again. But Seneca's reply (21-3) is slightly confused: (i) it does not have this cause of itself; i.e. virtue is a *causa efficiens*, and can only of itself produce good (cf. §32). (ii) That virtue creates envy is an image which has not even a semblance of truth (*nec veri similem*, 21; cf. l. 18). More like the truth is that image of virtue which, on striking the minds of men, invites love and wonder, 22f. While (i) could be Posidonian, the stress on the power of the image in (ii) reverts to the exposition of Seneca above.

In that case, the 'objector' interlude (§§33-4), adheres closely to §32, and it looks as if 32-4 hang together as a development from Seneca. It is a development from the Posidonian base of §31, still involving cause and effect in the field of emotion, but there appear to be elements in it more characteristic of Seneca than Posidonius. If that is so, the answers to the objections should not be taken as Posidonius without further evidence. The function of 33-4 is to pull together §§31 and 32 as a combined answer to the earlier double objection (a) and (b) of §§28-9. This would be all the more necessary if §31 was Posidonius' answer to (b), and §32 Seneca's answer to (a).

C. (§35) (24-31)

If Seneca had been inserting his own development in 32-4, there would be good reason for reiterating Posidonius' name on returning to him. Seneca appears to offer a quotation: Posidonius says that we should syllogise (*interrogandum*) like this. 'Things which do not give to the mind *magnitudinem, fiduciam, securitatem* are not goods (*bona*). Riches, good health and the like produce none of these. Therefore they are not

COMMENTARY: F170

"goods".' In one aspect this is satisfactory. If we ignore 32–4, we see that this conclusion is the complement of §31. There Posidonius proved that wealth was not an evil; here he proves that it is not a good. But the content of the equation is odd. If it is a quotation, we ought to be able to translate it back into Posidonian Greek. But what is the Greek for *fiducia*? *Magnitudo animi* is μεγαλοψυχία and *securitas* could be ἀταραξία (Cic. *ND* 1.53) or εὐθυμία (Cic. *De Fin.* v.23), but none of these terms survives in the remains of Posidonian ethics. One must beware of the negative argument of omission in a fragmentary tradition, but we have positive evidence of Seneca. The three terms recur again and again as the major characteristics for Seneca of the happy life. So, *Ep.* 92.3 *quid est beata vita? securitas et perpetua tranquillitas. hanc dabit animi magnitudo, dabit constantia bene iudicati tenax*... Cf. *Ep.* 44.7: *nam cum summa vitae beatae sit solida securitas et eius inconcussa fiducia*.... In *De Const.* 10.3 *fiducia* and *magnitudo* are linked, and in 13.5, *securitas autem proprium bonum sapientis est. Securitas* is again stressed in *NQ* vi.32.4 (in general, Hadot, *Seneca* 126ff).

Now μεγαλοψυχία is a Stoic sub-virtue (D.L. vii.92f, 128). *Securitas* for Seneca is opposed to *sollicitudo* (*Ep.* 24.1–2) and means freedom from cares, worries, i.e. from πάθη. *Fiducia* means something like unshaken confidence, assurance, even courage or boldness, and in use and occurrence is not far from *constantia*: firmness, resolution, fearlessness, constancy. It is partly reminiscent of θαρραλεότης which is in the same Stoic sub-class as μεγαλοψυχία (*SVF* iii.269, 264), and Cicero can use *constantia* for εὐπάθεια (*Tusc.* iv.14). Already Cicero in *De Off.* 1.69 said that one must rid oneself of all disturbance of the mind, *ut tranquillitas animi et securitas adsit, quae affert cum constantiam tum etiam dignitatem*... (cf. ibid. 1.72). Seneca *Ep.* 92 has what looks like some echoes of Posidonius (see, however, F184).

Either (1) Seneca is reporting Posidonius correctly, and Posidonius, perhaps elaborating on Panaetius, used comparable Greek terms such as μεγαλοψυχία in his syllogism; or (2)

COMMENTARY: F170

Seneca imported his own terms into Posidonius' syllogistic form. On balance, I think that the second is more likely because (in ascending order) (a) of the lack of any kind of parallel in what remains of Posidonius; (b) *fiducia* remains untranslatable; it is a peculiarly Roman term; (c) the trinity is demonstrably Seneca's ideal. But if (2) is correct, that does not destroy the evidence that Posidonius concocted a syllogism of such a form, proving that wealth, health, etc. were not 'goods'. It would, however, then follow that Posidonius himself used some term or terms which were tampered with or freely translated by Seneca, but we cannot now know what they were. What follows (27–31) is still more peculiar. Posidonius went on to intensify (*intendit*) his syllogism still further like this: what is not productive of *magnitudo animi, fiducia* or *securitas*, but of *insolentia, tumor, arrogantia*, is evil. But we are driven to these things by chance things (*a fortuitis*). Therefore they are not 'goods'. The same class of terms is retained. *Insolentia* means want of moderation, and so could be the equivalent of ὕβρις.

But the real puzzle lies in the form of the syllogism. The major premise leads us to expect that the conclusion will be, X is evil (*malum*). But the conclusion is that *fortuita* are not 'goods' (*non bona*). And indeed if the subject is still wealth, good health, etc., an extension of the first form of the syllogism (24–7), the conclusion *must* be that they are not 'goods', but not evils either (cf. anyway the orginal Posidonian syllogism of §31, and comm. *A* (1)). On the other hand, *intendit* (28) should mean 'intensify, make more severe', perhaps 'exaggerate' or even 'strain', and this must be reflected in turning the negative form of the major premiss to the positive expression 'what is productive of *insolentia*, etc.'. The key must lie in *fortuita* (31). 'Chance things' may drive us towards *insolentia*, but *fortuita* in themselves create neither evil nor good, therefore they are not good (cf. the first Stoic syllogism at §12 involving *fortuita*). Seneca must be blamed for confusion or telescoping here, and again his *impellimur* (31) is likely to be his own exaggeration. The word seems too strong for merely setting off an appetition (cf. ὁρμῆς ... ἐκεῖνα ... κινητικά, D.L. VII.104 of προηγμένα) for which Cicero commonly uses *adpetere* (e.g. *De Fin.* III.16f). In spite of the confusion, it is abundantly clear that Posidonius argued that wealth (classified with good health, 26) was not a 'good'.

D. (§§36–7) (32–41)

In §35 Seneca had twisted the argument again to the suggestion that if wealth is not a 'good', yet it also incites to evil (although not itself an evil). So the 'objector' is brought in again to clarify: by that line of reasoning, these things (*ista*: *bona valetudo et similia* included?) will not even be advantages (*commoda*, 32). This is answered by distinguishing *commodum* and *bonum*. 'Advantage' is what has a preponderance of usefulness over distress; 'good' should be pure and totally free from harm. So what has a greater proportion of benefit is not a good; 'good' is what benefits *and nothing else* (*tantum*, 36). Also *commoda* is applied to animals, *imperfecti homines* (i.e. προκόπτοντες, or, perhaps, children) and *stulti* (i.e. φαῦλοι); *bonum* applies to the σοφός only.

Cicero (*De Fin.* III.69) used *commoda* and *incommoda* to translate εὐχρηστήματα and δυσχρηστήματα, and says that they belong to the class of *praeposita* and *reiecta* (his technical translation for προηγμένα and ἀποπροηγμένα). Certainly Stoics distinguished between εὔχρηστος which applied to the 'indifferents' (ἀδιάφορα) and ὠφέλιμος which was only applicable to 'good(s)' (e.g. Plu. *Comm. Not.* 1070A = *SVF* III.123; cf. *De SR* 1038A with Cherniss's note).

But Kilb has argued (*Ethische Grundbegriffe der alten Stoa und ihre Übertragung durch Cicero* (1939), 85f, cf. Fischer, *De usu vocabulorum apud Ciceronem et Senecam graecae philosophiae interpretes*, Freiburg im Breslau, 1914, p. 55ff) that Seneca used *commodum* for Cicero's *praepositum* (i.e. for προηγμένον); which is proved by *Ep.* 74.17, *commoda* = *producta* (i.e. προηγμένα), a passage not cited by Kilb; also *De Ben.* v.13.2; *Ep.* 92.16; *Ep.*

95.58; *De Const.* 16.2. And the definition of *commodum* here (33f, 39f), is in line with those of προηγμένον in relation to ἀξία. Cicero too sometimes (*Tusc.* v.120; *ND* 1.16) seems to come near to this; thus, *certe minus ad beatam vitam pertinet multitudo corporis commodorum* (*De Fin.* III.43).

In any case it is clear that the argument places wealth (and health, etc.) as *commodum* firmly in the category of προηγμένα, as having a preponderance of benefit, within the class of 'indifferents' (ἀδιάφορα). As such it is still radically distinguished from 'good' both in its effect, and in its application. This is orthodox Stoic doctrine: e.g. Cic. *De Fin.* III.50 (*SVF* III.129), 56 (*SVF* III.132); D.L. VII.105 (*SVF* III.126), 106 (*SVF* III.127); *SVF* III.124.

Is the *commodum* argument Seneca or Posidonius, or both? Again the sequence of argument is curious. The objector, repeating again *eadem ratione ne commodum quidem erunt* of §29, demands at this point to know why wealth and the like should not be regarded as *incommoda* (ἀποπροηγμένα). But the answer, by concentrating exclusively on the difference between *commodum* and *bonum*, ignores *incommoda*, and explains how wealth can be *commodum* although not a *bonum*. Apart from the mismatch of the argument, from the Senecan side it comes as something of a surprise that he now suddenly classifies wealth as *commodum*/προηγμένον after all his stress on the negative side of the corrupting dangers of wealth, which is an attitude abundantly common in Seneca's writing (Griffin, *Seneca* 295). Posidonius, on the other hand, proved that wealth is not an 'evil', nor a 'good'. He pairs it with good health (26); as a goal of one of our natural irrational δυνάμεις in his psychology, such *commoda* operate in the class of animals as well as in morally imperfect humans (37f) (cf. Frs. 158–160), and have relative value (F161). Where else could Posidonius put wealth on the evidence than as προηγμένον in the normal Stoic sense? Also Posidonius was brought in to answer the objection of §29, which includes the problem of *commoda*. If the Senecan fat and cosmetics are removed, the bones of Posidonius' argument emerge: wealth is not κακόν (the argument of causes); wealth, health and the like are not ἀγαθά (they do not cause ἀγαθά); such things are προηγμένα (of relative value). If this is Posidonius' position, it is completely orthodox. A different view, that Posidonius was heterodox in this matter, has often been expressed: Edelstein, *AJPh* 57 (1936), 308f; van Straaten, *Panétius* 154ff, 174ff; Laffranque, *Poseidonios* 364, 480ff; Rist, *Stoic Philosophy* 8ff; Griffin, *Seneca* p. 296 n. 5; Reinhardt, *Poseidonios* 336–42; Pohlenz, *Die Stoa* II.120; Dihle, 'Posidonius' System of Moral Philosophy', *JHS* 73 (1973), 51 n. 6; Sandbach, *The Stoics* 127; Theiler, II.383. See also comm. on Frs. 171–3.

New and distinctively Posidonian are both the approach and the method of argument (as Seneca implies): (1) An analysis of cause applied to the problem of wealth. (2) So the evaluation of wealth is based not (or not only) on ἀξία in relation to τὰ κατὰ φύσιν, but on its effect and function in moral psychology. (3) So it is linked to the problem of emotions (πάθη and εὐπάθειαι), which, as Posidonius said himself, was the starting point of all ethical problems (Frs. 30, 150).

E. (§§38–40) (42–59)

There remains a puzzling Posidonian annexure. 'One knot remains, but it is a Herculean one.' According to Macrobius (*Sat.* 1.19.16) Herculean was used for the knot joining the middle of the snakes in the caduceus. Pliny (*NH* 28.63) mentions a magical lore where the 'Herculean knot' is applied to wounds. It also describes the decoration on certain Boeotian *skyphoi* (Athen. XI.500a). Paulus, *Festi epitoma* 55.18 records it of a knot of good omen for fertility tying the belt of young married women. Above all, it was a popular feature, as the reef-knot, in hellenistic jewellery where it also had amuletic associations (Higgins, *Greek and Roman Jewellery* 155ff; cf. Plate 46). Presumably it was a magic knot, difficult to unloosen. But Seneca is probably being sarcastic.

The knot is another syllogism: good does not arise from evil; riches result from many cases of poverty; therefore riches are not a good. But this is not a Stoic syllogism. It was fabricated by Peripatetics, who also 'solve' it (46). Peripatetics of course wish to maintain that wealth is a good; so their purpose was to ape a Stoic syllogism, provide a 'solution' and so deny the conclusion, and thus show that wealth is a good. Presumably they challenged their minor premisses, probably showing that it involved the fallacy of 'the heap'. Such 'counter syllogisms' were common in the Schools (47; cf. *Ep.* 82.9f). Posidonius said that this *sophisma* was refuted by Antipater. He argued that it depended on a false notion of what 'poverty' means. It is not used *per possessionem* (καθ' ἕξιν?), but *per detractionem* (or *orbationem*) (i.e. κατὰ στέρησιν). Poverty is not what one has, but what one does not have, not the possession of little, but the non-possession of much. Wealth is created by many things, but not by many 'lacks' (Seneca apologises for not having a Latin equivalent for ἀνυπαρξία).

Edelstein (*AJPh* 57 (1936), 309) took Posidonius' approval of Antipater's refutation of the syllogism as evidence that Posidonius and Antipater by 'refuting the negation' (i.e. *not* good, in the conclusion), held that wealth was 'a good'. But it was the Peripatetics who by 'solving' the syllogism were refusing the conclusion. Antipater was attacking the minor premiss, attempting to show not that it was fallacious in a way which the Peripatetics could solve, but nonsense, hence the whole syllogism was worthless as an argument against the Stoic position. If anything can be inferred from this for Posidonius' view of wealth (which is doubtful), it could only be that Posidonius approved of Antipater's destruction of a Peripatetic attack on the Stoic dogma that wealth was *not* a good.

Nor does this support Reinhardt's theory that the main heterodox importance of this fragment lies in Posidonius' rejection of the Stoic syllogistic method of argumentation

COMMENTARY: F171

(Reinhardt, *Poseidonios* 336–42; *Kosmos und Sympathie* 401 n. 299; challenged by Pohlenz, *GGA* 184 (1922), 166). Posidonius was prepared to set up his own syllogism at §35 (*interrogandum*, 24ff), and elsewhere (F175) prepared to defend a very rickety syllogism of Zeno's.

It is not clear why Seneca brings in the Herculean knot here, unless it was a very well-known part of the debate on this subject in the schools (47), and/or he found it in the same Posidonian source as the previous arguments. Anyway, our evidence is that it was Seneca who tired of and doubted the efficacy of the dialectic of Stoic syllogisms in practical morals; thus, *Ep.* 82.19–20 on Zeno's syllogism of §9f, and the end of this *Letter*, *Ep.* 87.41, *haec satius est suadere et expugnare adfectus, non circumscribere.*

Since Seneca demurs (38f) over Antipater's refutation: 'I don't see what else poverty could be than the possession of little', the rest of the *Letter* should be Seneca and not Posidonius. It is concerned with whether it is not better to try to mitigate poverty and to relieve wealth of its arrogance, rather than quibble about words.

And yet the close of the *Letter* (41), with its plea that the Romans should return to their respect for frugality, and combat the corrupting invasion of wealth, with the final advice: *haec satius est suadere et expugnare adfectus, non circumscribere*, is hardly unlike Posidonius.

For the whole fragment, see Kidd, Fondation Hardt, *Entretiens* XXXII, with the accompanying discussion.

F171 Diogenes Laertius, VII.103

CONTENT

Posidonius says that wealth and health too are in the category of 'goods'.

COMMENTARY: F171

CONTEXT

In §102, Diogenes itemises what Stoics include under ἀγαθά, κακά, and οὐδέτερα. In §103 wealth and health, representing the species προηγμένα of the class οὐδέτερα (or ἀδιάφορα) are distinguished from ἀγαθόν, because (a) the peculiar property of good is to benefit only; wealth and health do not benefit any more than they harm; in fact they do neither (§102). (b) Both good and bad use can be made of wealth and health (1–3). The source of these arguments is given as Hecaton, Περὶ τέλους, Bk 7; Apollodorus ἐν τῇ 'Ηθικῇ, and Chrysippus. After the reference to Posidonius, Diogenes says (with specific reference to Hecaton and Chrysippus) that Stoics did not even allow pleasure to be good.

COMMENT

This statement is incompatible with Seneca, F170 comm. above. Nevertheless, Diogenes' statement has been supported by Reinhardt, *Poseidonios* 342; Edelstein, *AJPh* 57 (1936), 308f; Pohlenz, *Die Stoa* II.120; van Straaten, *Panétius* 174ff, 213ff; Laffranque, *Poseidonios* 364, 480ff; Rist, *Stoic Philosophy* 8ff; Dihle, *JHS* 73 (1973) 51 n. 6; Theiler, II.383. But against Diogenes' isolated bald statement: (a) Seneca's report is detailed and supported by argument from Posidonius himself (F170); (b) Galen's account of Posidonius' ethics in *De Placitis* supports Seneca (Kidd, *Problems* 208); (c) Cicero believed that for Posidonius virtue was the *only* good (T38); (d) it seems inconceivable that on such a fundamental break with Stoic doctrine, affecting not only the theory of Intermediates, but also the τέλος, such a stick should not have been used to beat the Stoa by such opponents as Cicero and Plutarch in their extended criticism of the School (Kidd, *Problems* 150–72).

For these reasons I think we may speculate on how such a mistake could have arisen, rather than attempt to defend the verity of Diogenes' statement. Three categories of possible confusion present themselves:

(1) Misunderstanding over the use of a term. Stoics sometimes used ἀγαθόν loosely or untechnically, no doubt on occasion in argument with opponents. Plutarch actually attests this for Chrysippus in *De SR* 1048A (cf. Plu. *De SR* ch. 15; Cic. *De Fin.* III.52). (Kidd, *Problems* 159).

(2) Misunderstanding of a Stoic argument, or the implications of opponents.
 (a) Cf. D.L. VII.105 (*SVF* III.126), where ἀξίαν δὲ τὴν μέν τινα λέγουσι σύμβλησιν πρὸς τὸν ὁμολογούμενον βίον, ἥτις ἐστὶ περὶ πᾶν ἀγαθόν, can be confused with: τὴν δὲ εἶναι μέσην τινα δύναμιν ἢ χρείαν συμβαλλομένην πρὸς τὸν κατὰ φύσιν βίον, ὅμοιον εἰπεῖν ἥντινα προσφέρεται πρὸς τὸν κατὰ φύσιν βίον πλοῦτος ἢ ὑγίεια, with the anti-Stoic argument in Alex. Aphr. *De An.* 163.4 (Bruns) = *SVF* III.192, with the false conclusion, δῆλον ὡς χρείαν ὁ σόφος ἕξει τούτων (i.e. προηγμένων). And cf. χρείαν in F173.5 (cf. Rist, *Stoic Philosophy* 9f; Kidd, *Problems* 159f).
 (b) Again debate and confusion could arise over the classification of προηγμένα into those preferred for their own sake or for the sake of something else, or both for their own sake and for the sake of something else (D.L. VII.107 = *SVF* III.135; cf. Cic. *De Fin.* III.56 = *SVF* III.134). There was a dispute on the category to which εὐδοξία (*bona fama*) belonged (Cic. *De Fin.* III.57). Wealth was usually put in the second class. Did Posidonius debate whether to transfer it to the first or third class because of his new psychology? Diogenes, according to Cic. *De Fin.* III.49, considered wealth *non eam modo vim habere ut quasi duces sint ad voluptatem et ad valetudinem bonam, sed etiam uti ea contineant; non idem facere eas in virtute neque in ceteris artibus, ad quas esse dux pecunia potest, continere autem non potest.* This shows traces of an argument in progress about the position and contribution of wealth. But if

COMMENTARY: F172

Posidonius had gone further, surely Cicero would have mentioned it.

(3) Misunderstanding of genuine innovations of Posidonius. Posidonius' new psychology recognised οἰκείωσις of irrational δυνάμεις as natural. Therefore it might be said that they were a factor in morality, and the definition of the τέλος included κατὰ μηδὲν ἀγόμενον ὑπὸ τοῦ ἀλόγου μέρους τῆς ψυχῆς (F186). But there remained a crucial difference, for although such προηγμένα as wealth were thus held to be οἰκεῖα φύσει, they were not ἁπλῶς οἰκεῖα. They still had only relative worth, they were not ἀγαθά (Frs. 160, 161, 187.4–13). The new psychological analysis was Posidonius' method of defending what he believed to be the original doctrine of the School (Kidd, *Problems* 207f).

How such a misunderstanding, once made, could develop outrageously is shown by F172. Diogenes, or his source, although mistaken on this point, was at least consistent, as is seen by F173.

F172 Epiphanius, *De Fide* 9.46

CONTENT

Posidonius of Apamea said that the greatest good among men was wealth and health.

CONTEXT

In Epiphanius' catalogue of Greek philosophers beginning with Thales and ending with Epicurus. Posidonius comes between Panaetius and Athenodorus of Tarsus.

COMMENT

This preposterous statement derives from a source such as

COMMENTARY: F173

F171. It might be argued that ἐν ἀνθρώποις is strongly emphasised, 'among men': this is what men believe, or how they behave, as if wealth and health were the greatest good, cf. Plato, *Lysis* 211e 4 for the expression. If this was the origin of the mistake, which is possible but highly doubtful, the character of Epiphanius' list shows that he believed that it was a straightforward statement about the greatest good. In general the comments of this Bishop of Salamis (b. soon after 310 A.D., d. 403 A.D.) do not inspire confidence; for example, on Chrysippus: ἔλεγε δὲ τὸ τέλος πάντων τὸ ἡδυπαθὲς εἶναι.

F173 Diogenes Laertius, VII.127–8

CONTENT

Panaetius and Posidonius say that virtue (τὴν ἀρετήν) is not self-sufficient, but they say that there is need of (χρείαν) health, resources (χορηγία) and strength (ἰσχύος).

CONTEXT

This is added as an appendix to the general statement that Stoics hold that virtue is self-sufficient for happiness, supported by reference to Zeno, Chrysippus and Hecaton (1–3).

COMMENT

This statement is consistent with D.L. VII.103, F171. Indeed they are necessarily complementary. If virtue is self-sufficient for happiness it must be the only 'good'; if there is need of other factors such as wealth and health, then virtue cannot be self-sufficient. Therefore one cannot, as Griffin, *Seneca* 296, n. 5, is inclined to do, reject F171 and accept F173. F171 is explicitly contradicted by Seneca (F170), and F173 implicitly by Cicero (T83). For additional arguments against the

COMMENTARY: F174

acceptance of both, and for suggestions as to how the misconception arose, see F171, and Kidd, Fondation Hardt, *Entretiens* xxxii with accompanying discussion.

χορηγία is an Aristotelian term and does not seem to have been used in Stoic sources; χρεία has the same ambience, and appears significantly in Alex. Aphr. *De An.* 163.4 (Bruns), for which see F171 comm. These terms may indicate that this statement arises from Peripatetic argument and criticism. ἰσχύς may refer to mental strength, e.g. Antisthenes fr. 70 (Caizzi): αὐτάρκη δὲ τὴν ἀρετὴν πρὸς εὐδαιμονίαν, μηδενὸς προσδεομένην ὅτι μὴ Σωκρατικῆς ἰσχύος (D.L. vi.11).

F174 Galen, *De Placitis* v.474, p. 454.7–15 M, pp. 330.31–332.4 De Lacy

CONTENT

A quotation from Posidonius' Περὶ παθῶν: 'And indeed "progressors" are not distressed at the thought that great evils are with them. The reason is that they are carried to this state of belief not by the irrational aspect of soul, but by the rational.'

CONTEXT

Galen adds this as an addendum to F162, to which ταῦτα (1) refers. The general context is explained in F187.37 comm.

COMMENT

The problem was raised as an ἀπορία against Chrysippus in F164.22–5, in the context of criticism of Chrysippus' theory that the cause of emotion can be ascribed to degree of magnitude of presentations. This is no doubt the passage referred to by Galen in line 3f. It recurs in F187 as one of the

643

COMMENTARY: F175

problems solved by the correct recognition of the cause of emotion.

πάθος is tied to the irrational aspect of soul, and can only be moved by the irrational, such as an irrational vivid mental picture (F162). The 'progressor on the road to virtue' (Kidd, *Problems* 164) if motivated by reason, will not experience a πάθος such as λύπη. Of course a progressor is still liable to πάθη, or he would be a wise man (σοφός). But Posidonius' point is that, if his explanation were not true, the progressor would *always* be experiencing πάθη, since he is aware that evil is with him until he achieves wisdom; and this is seen not to be the case.

This fragment is the counterpart of the position analysed in F162.

F175   Seneca, *Epistulae* 83.9–11

CONTENT

Posidonius defends the validity of a syllogism from Zeno, leading to the conclusion that the good man will not be a drunkard.

CONTEXT

Seneca's *Letter* is on the subject of drunkenness. In §8 he has been turning over in his mind what can have been meant by the most intelligent men who produced proofs that were of the lightest weight and contorted on the most important matters, proofs which may be true, but are like fallacies. This is followed by the example of Zeno's syllogism.

COMMENT

Zeno, wishing to discourage us from drunkenness, offered the following syllogism: no one entrusts a secret to a drunk man (*ebrio*). But one entrusts a secret to a good man. Therefore a good man will not be *ebrius* (drunk, 4f).

Seneca protests (6–9) that Zeno can be ridiculed by setting up a similar syllogism to face his (one out of many will do):

No one entrusts a secret to a man who is sleeping. One entrusts a secret to a good man. Therefore the good man does not sleep.

For such moves cf. *Ep.* 49.8; *Ep.* 48.

However (9–16), Posidonius pleads Zeno's case in the only way he can (*quo uno modo potest*). There is an ambiguity in the word *ebrius*. It can mean (1) one who is drunk, (2) a drunkard. Zeno meant (2). Seneca goes on to deny that (2) can apply to the syllogism. But the point is that there is a distinction *in Latin* between *ebrius* (drunk) and *ebriosus* (drunkard), which Seneca points out in §11 (cf. *De Ira* 1.4.1). But the distinction was obviously not clear *in the Greek*. Anyway, Seneca suggests, even if it did, Zeno would be guilty of equivocation (§11). But this does not seem to be correct either. Zeno would rather be guilty of lack of clarity. Seneca's real position emerges in the rest of the Letter: e.g. §12: but let us admit that Zeno meant what Posidonius says; even so it is false; people *do* entrust secrets to drunkards; and §17: *quanto satius est aperte accusare ebrietatem et vitia eius exponere*. Seneca is attempting to expose the frailty of such dialectical formulae as an effective instrument for practical morality. The logical games in the Schools which had become fashionable, such as contradictory arguments and ἐναντιώματα (as Plu. *De SR*), are merely a play on words, not moral persuasion or deterrent. Cf. also S.E. *Adv. Math.* IX.108ff.

The argument over drunkenness was clearly part of the debate whether virtue once attained can be lost (*SVF* III.237ff), no doubt pressed by opponents, but clearly argued within the Stoa itself; thus Chrysippus thought that it could be lost through drunkenness (μέθη) and madness (μελαγχολία), Cleanthes that it could not (D.L. VII.127 = *SVF* III.237). At some point in the debate on drunkenness, a distinction was

COMMENTARY: F176

made between οἴνωσις, οἰνοῦσθαι and μέθη, μεθύσκεσθαι, so that the σοφός may take wine, but not get drunk (D.L. VII.118 = *SVF* III.644, cf. *SVF* III.712. For Epictetus, Bonhöffer, *Die Ethik des Stoikers Epictet* 62f).

But this is no help for the Seneca passage, because the original Greek in Zeno must have meant 'drunk' or 'drunkard' (μεθύων covers both). So Posidonius' purpose is to defend the validity of Zeno's syllogism; he is not concerned with whether the σοφός may take a drink or not. Since for Posidonius the σοφός must have at all times the control of reason (Frs. 186, 187), his wise man must not only not be a drunkard, but not get drunk at any time.

It is no surprise that Posidonius defends Zeno; but it is interesting that he thought it worth while to defend such a syllogism from Zeno. This tells against Reinhardt's theory (*Poseidonios* 336–42, see F170 comm. *E*) that Posidonius rejected and despised the reliance of the earlier Stoa on syllogistic argument. It was Seneca who was impatient of such syllogistic dialectic (F170 comm. *E*; *Ep*. 82.19–20; *Ep*. 83.8, 17).

F176   Seneca, *Epistulae* 95.65–7

CONTENT

Posidonius gives the opinion that not only *praeceptio* is necessary, but also *suasio, consolatio* and *exhortatio*. To these he adds *aetiologia* and *ethologia*.

CONTEXT

Epp. 94 and 95 are complementary, and deal with the relative importance of *praecepta* (precepts) and *decreta* (principles). In 94 Seneca puts the case and argues against it that *praecepta* are useless for ethical training and that only *decreta* are necessary;

COMMENTARY: F176

in *Ep.* 95 he puts the opposite case, and argues against it, that *praecepta* are sufficient to make a man good. Dihle, 'Posidonius' System of Moral Philosophy', *JHS* 73 (1973), 50–7, has argued that both *Letters* are based on a work of Posidonius which introduced the *pars praeceptiva* as a sub-division of ethics, and that they reveal an original ethical standpoint on Posidonius' part. I remain unconvinced and in 'Moral Actions and Rules in Stoic Ethics', *The Stoics* (ed. Rist), 247–58, examined the *Letters* as Seneca's exposition of the common problem which existed for the Stoa at least since the time of Ariston of Chios, on the relationship in Stoic pedagogy between kathekontic and katorthomatic teaching.

COMMENT

Praecepta are moral rules or maxims or injunctions related in Stoicism to καθήκοντα (*officia*, 'appropriate acts'), that is to that intermediate section of Stoic ethics and training directed to progressors (προκόπτοντες) and the 'preferred' (προηγμένα) among the things according to nature, and so distinct from the logos philosophy, knowledge and the σοφός (e.g. Cic. *De Off.* 1.1; 1.7; II.7; III.5; III.121; Sen. *Ep.* 94.34.

In general, Kidd, 'Moral Actions and Rules' 251ff).

But there is a problem in the first three lines. Seneca clearly implies that *suasio, consolatio* and *exhortatio* are categories in addition to *praeceptio*. But at *Ep.* 95.1 he uses *praeceptiva pars* as a generic term to translate that section of ethics which the Greeks called παραινητική; and throughout the two *Letters*, *praecepta* and *decreta* (δόγματα) are used simply in contrast with each other. Reinhardt (*Poseidonios* 56f) went on to cite a tripartition of ethics in Clem. Alex. *Paed.* 1.1, where προτρεπτικός is assigned to ἤθη, ὑποθετικός to πράξεις, and παραμυθητικός to πάθη. Assuming that the Greek terms in order correspond to *exhortatio, suasio* and *consolatio*, he inferred that this is a tripartition of Posidonius, and therefore that the three are *species* of the genus *praeceptio*. Dihle ('Posidonius'

System of Moral Philosophy' 53) agreed, and points out that the tripartition ἤθη, πράξεις, πάθη is Peripatetic (as Arist. *Po.* 1447a 28), so this would be another instance of Posidonian ἀριστοτέλιζον (T85). But Marrou, in his *Introduction* p. 13 to Clem. Alex. *Paed.* in *Sources Chrétiennes*, vol. 70, had rightly been critical of the Posidonian assumption. The whole set-up and development of the Clement passage is different. There is no mention of a tripartition ἤθη, πράξεις, πάθη in Sen. *Epp.* 94, 95, nor indeed elsewhere in Posidonius, and *suasio, consolatio, exhortatio* are commonplace terms in the Stoa, Academy and Peripatos. Above all it is not what Seneca *says*; he says that *suasio* etc. are in addition to, not subdivisions of, *praeceptio*.

This brings us back then to *praeceptio*. In the first place, Seneca here uses not *praeceptiva pars* (as in *Ep.* 95.1), but *praeceptio*, and apologises for doing so. In Latin *praeceptio* is basically a legal term and is rare as a moral term; but it occurs twice in Cicero: *De Off.* 1.6 is too vague to give any clue, but in *ND* II.79 the concept is linked to law, to *eademque lex, quae est recti praeceptio pravique depulsio* to which both gods and men are subject. The word probably retained the sense of a legal edict or injunction (cf. F178). Seneca's *praecepta* are very much of this form: 'do this, don't do that' (*Ep.* 94.50; cf. 'do this if you want to be X', line 11 below). And indeed the bald opposition in *Epp.* 94, 95 is between *praecepta* and *decreta*; and *decreta* too are of the same form, rules of principle or categorical imperatives (Kidd, 'Moral Action and Rules' 253). Now such rules as *praecepta* may be only a part or sub-section of the admonitory part of ethics, the παραινετικὸς τόπος, although Seneca, fumbling for a Latin equivalent at the beginning of the *Letter*, and influenced by his concentration on *praecepta*, may translate παραινετικὸς τόπος by *praeceptiva pars*. But *consolationes*, for example, are not a kind of *praecepta* any more than *ethologia* is (although they may have the same force (*vim*), 10–14 below). Both are modes of 'admonition'. So I take *praeceptio* to be Seneca's general word for giving *praecepta* in the strict sense (which has been the centre of debate for Seneca). Posidonius said that not only *praecepta* were necessary, but also *the other* modes of admonition (well-known to the Schools both of philosophy and rhetoric) like *consolationes*.

I suspect that one of Seneca's problems may have been the fluidity of Greek terms, which did not always correspond to more precise Latin ones. *Consolatio* and παραμυθητικός are clear. But προτρεπτικός, which has been taken to be the Greek for *exhortatio*, is of course used, especially in titles (as Frs. 1–3), in a wide general sense; and ὑποθετικός (for which see also Bernays, 'Philons Hypothetika', *Gesammelte Abhandlungen* 266–71), which has been paired with *suasio* (cf. Musonius F17, p. 91.13–21 Hense), is also used as a generic term, e.g. τόν τε παραινετικὸν καὶ τὸν ὑποθετικὸν τόπον of Ariston, S.E. *Adv. Math.* VII.12 = *SVF* 1.356; cf. Stob. *Ecl.* II.41.23 W of Philo of Larissa. Dihle, who argues from the specific use in Clement, himself uses τόπος ὑποθετικός as the generic term for the whole field, Seneca's *praeceptiva pars* ('Posidonius' System of Moral Philosophy' 50). Indeed one may ask what the Greek technical term for *praecepta* was. Kerferd has suggested to me that it may have been παραγγέλματα (e.g. Stob., *SVF* 1.238; S.E. *Adv. Math.* XI.192 = *SVF* III.748; S.E. *Adv. Math.* XI.195). Themistius, *Or.* VI.81C uses the term for M. Aurelius' precepts. But uncertainty suggests fluidity of terms (perhaps also πρόσταξις, *SVF* III.519?).

Praeceptio, suasio, consolatio, exhortatio are grouped together. In spite of Seneca's concentration on precepts, Posidonius held that all forms were necessary. All were familiar τόποι in this area (cf. Sen. *Ep.* 94.39, 49; *Ep.* 94.39, *monitionum genera*) and not only in the Stoa (e.g. for Eudorus see Stob. II.44.7ff W). *Aetiologia* and *ethologia* seem to be added perhaps as being particularly characteristic of Posidonius.

Aetiologia (αἰτιολογία), no doubt Posidonius' word for *causarum inquisitio*, is adopted by Seneca with apologies. It was used already as a technical term by *grammatici* (Suet. *De Gramm.* IV.7; Quint. 1.9.3); this is different from the grammati-

COMMENTARY: F176

cal use as in 'causal' conjunctions (αἰτιολογικοὶ σύνδεσμοι, A.D. *Conj.* 231.4, 16; cf. F45), which validated its Latin form (4–6), but confuses its sense here. Of course the term was associated with Posidonius (T85). Ultimately αἰτιολογία in the strict sense was the business of the physical philosopher (F18); but the methodology of Περὶ παθῶν is characterised in Galen's report by the repeated question: 'what is the cause of...?'. Here we are in a still more restricted field, that of admonitory ethics, and it is to be regretted that Seneca did not explain exactly what Posidonius meant instead of defending his own Latinity. However, it is likely that Posidonius would have insisted even at this level not only on explanations or reasons (αἰτία in that sense) for particular actions, or for rules directed toward type situations, but also on some account of the dynamics of cause and effect in the moral psychology of practical ethics. An example of this would be the argument on the effect of wealth by distinction of causes in F170.1ff. Posidonius was certainly interested in αἰτιολογία at all levels.

Ethologia (ἠθολογία) is felt by Seneca to require more explanation, probably because it is more idiosyncratic to Posidonius than *suasio, consolatio* and the like. The term seems to have been unfamiliar in this connection. ἠθολόγος could have a slightly derogatory tone, referring to something like a pantomime actor or character (D.S. 20.63; Athen. 1.20a; Cic. *De Orat.* II.242). Here it is characterised generally as description of each virtue. Some call it *characterismos* (χαρακτηρισμός), i.e. distinguishing by a χαρακτήρ, stamp or mark; so Seneca's *signa* and *notas* by which virtues and vices are distinguished (8–10). (Cf. Plato, *Phdr.* 263b 7f: (δεῖ) καὶ εἰληφέναι τινὰ χαρακτῆρα ἑκατέρου τοῦ εἴδους....) For good measure Seneca adds a final comparison with a technical term from *publicani, iconismos* (εἰκονισμός, 14f), referring to the registered description of individuals for purposes of census (e.g. PRyl.161.15; PLond. ined. 2196, both of 1st c. A.D.; POxy 1022). εἰκονισμός also had a more general use;

COMMENTARY: F176

Plutarch (*Mor.* 54B) applies it to a verse: such a description (εἰκονισμός) is that of a parasite.

Seneca distinguishes *ethologia* from *praeceptio*. Both have the same force (*vim*), but they differ in form; first in linguistic form: a precept may be expressed as a hypothetical injunction – if you want to be self-controlled, you will do this; but ἠθολογία is couched in a descriptive statement: the self-controlled person is the man who does this, keeps off that (10–13). Secondly, they differ in logical function. The one gives precepts of virtue, the other an exemplar of virtue (13f). But *ethologia* is useful (this is stressed: *utilem*, 6; *ex usu*, 15; *utile*, 16; *utilius*, 19); it is a necessary tool of practical ethics, because in setting forward an example for praise, one will find an imitator (16). Also you will make a disastrous purchase, if you cannot recognise a fine horse when you see one (the history of this illustration goes back to Plato, *Phdr.* 260b 1ff; *cf.* Sen. *Ep.* 80.9).

Seneca goes on to give examples of *ethologia* (§§68–73), first from Vergil, *Georgics* II.75–81, and then historically of Cato. This is of great interest for Posidonius, because it gives the hint, which is borne out by the *History* that Posidonius' historical work performed the function of *ethologia*; it forms the descriptive pattern for ethics (cf. Kidd, *Antike und Abendland* 24 (1978), 14; Reinhardt, *RE* 631–3; Dihle, 'Posidonius' System of Moral Philosophy' 54 n. 20, who also compares Seneca's tragedies. A later example is Plutarch's *Lives*).

The whole group from *praeceptio* to *ethologia* is not a general classification of ethics, but an analysis of pedagogic modes relevant to the sections of ethics categorised as περὶ καθηκόντων προτροπῶν τε καὶ ἀποτροπῶν in F89, *q.v.*

COMMENTARY: F177

F177 Cicero, *De Officiis* 1.159

CONTENT

Posidonius listed actions which a philosopher would not do to save his country.

CONTEXT

At *De Off.* 1.152, Cicero, having finished the examination of his four categories of morality (*honestas*), and how *officia* are derived from them, turns to the problem of the possible conflict between two categories, a point which, he says, was completely ignored by Panaetius. *Honestas* flows from four components: (1) *cognitio* (pursuit of knowledge); (2) *communitas*, i.e. duties related to society (the category of 'justice', *officia iustitiae*, §154); (3) *magnanimitas*, 'greatness of spirit', but related to courage; (4) *moderatio*, presumably Cicero's interpretation of σωφροσύνη. Cicero goes on to argue that *communitas* (2), in being *aptior naturae* (§153), and since such duties *pertinent ad hominum utilitatem, qua nihil homini esse debet antiquius* (§154), must take precedence over *cognitio* (1). The field of argument concentrates on the responsibilities of coming to the aid of one's country. At §156 we are told that eloquence with intelligence is better than knowledge without eloquence, because *cogitatio* is introverted, eloquence embraces those with whom we are joined in society. At §157 it is also argued that *communitas* should have greater weight than *magnanimitas* (3), because even *magnitudo animi* is mere savage bloodlust without human fellowship. At §159 Cicero turns to the possible conflict between *communitas* and *moderatio* (4).

ANALYSIS AND COMMENT

It remains to consider whether duties of society (*communitas*), which are particularly in accordance with nature, are to be preferred always to duties that arise from moderation and propriety ((4) above). The answer is no. The reason is that there are some actions so vile and infamous that the wise man would not do them even to save his country. Posidonius collected a great number of these, but some instances are so foul and disgusting that it would be disgraceful even to mention them. So the philosopher will not undertake *those* for the state, *but* nor will the state even wish them to be undertaken on its behalf.

So Cicero concludes, the situation could not arise, and he finishes by reiterating that pride of place in choice of appropriate acts (*officia*) goes to those concerned with society (§160). These can be graded: to the gods, to our country, to our parents, and then in order everyone else. He finally reminds us that this problem about which is the more moral of two proposed moral actions, was omitted by Panaetius, and at least has the grace to acknowledge that his own discussion has been brief (§161); one would rather say meagre and personal.

From the context, the terms of the argument, and in particular its orientation and conclusion, it is clear that this section is Cicero and not Posidonius. The only inference that we can make with respect to Posidonius is that Cicero had heard of a compilation by him of disgraceful actions which the *sapiens* would not do to save his country. It is highly doubtful that Cicero had even set eyes on this. The excuse that they are too filthy to mention is convenient, and it is unlikely that Posidonius compiled lists without reasons or explanation. Also, Posidonius' 'compilation' is simply dismissed on the grounds that the situation could not arise: *sed haec commodius se res habet quod non potest accidere tempus, ut intersit reipublicae quidquam illorum facere sapientem.* And Cicero continues (§160) with the primacy of social appropriate acts, as if there was no real conflict between *communitas* and *moderatio.* Whatever point Posidonius was trying to make is not recoverable from Cicero; but it certainly cannot have been the moral primacy of the claims of society.

COMMENTARY: F178

Arguments are advanced in the commentary on F41 that Cicero did not know Posidonius' Περὶ καθήκοντος at first hand, and did not use it for *De Off.*

F178   Seneca, *Epistulae* 94.38

CONTENT

A quotation from Posidonius: 'I disapprove of Plato's practice of adding preambles to his laws. A law should be brief, so that the unskilled may grasp it more easily. Let it be like a voice sent from heaven; let it order, not argue. Nothing seems to be more pedantic, more pointless than a law with a preamble. Advise me, tell me what you want me to do; I am not learning, I am obeying.' Seneca disagrees with Posidonius.

CONTEXT

The general context in Seneca is significant. In *Epp.* 94 and 95, Seneca discusses the relative importance in practical ethics of *praecepta* (precepts) and *decreta* (principles), F176. *Ep.* 94 takes its orientation from the claim of Ariston of Chios that precepts are useless for ethical training, which is opposed by Seneca. Precepts are a kind of moral injunction or rules embodying an imperative, and so have a similar function to laws in a state. At §37 Ariston is represented as arguing that laws ('nothing else than precepts mixed with threats'), although they order this, order that, fail to instruct us or give us the knowledge of how we *ought* to behave. This is contested by Seneca.

COMMENT

The lead into the quotation is textually insecure, but the sense is certain. The rest of the passage gives every sign of being a literal translation; for example, *fecisse* (6) possibly represents a Greek aorist (Préchac and Noblot, Budé, p. 77 n. 1).

In Stoicism it is necessary to distinguish between (a) the πρόσταγμα of the universal natural law (*SVF* III.314, 315, 323, 332, and Plu. *Mor.* 1037cf = *SVF* III.520, although Plutarch twists the argument: Cherniss, note *ad loc.*) and (b) precept and state law. The former (a) is embodied in κατόρθωμα (right action, Plu. *Mor.* 1037cf) and is applied to the σοφός; the latter (b) is linked to καθῆκον (appropriate acts) and directed to the φαῦλος and προκόπτων: Kidd, 'Moral Actions and Rules in Stoic Ethics' in *The Stoics* 247-58; 'Stoic Intermediates' in *Problems in Stoicism* 163ff. In this distinction Philo (*SVF* III.519) notes that the σοφός has no need of προστάττειν ἢ ἀπαγορεύειν ἢ παραινεῖν. It is the φαῦλος who is in need of πρόσταξις and ἀπαγόρευσις. In Posidonius' golden age, the *officium* of the *sapientes* was to *imperare* their subjects, but in degenerate ages *opus esse legibus coepit* (F284.6f, 11-13).

Posidonius adopted a special position. Since he distinguished between rational and irrational δυνάμεις of soul, he held also that their training was different (F169.106-17, comm. *G*; F31, F168. Cf. Frs. 164-6). It is no good reasoning with the irrational; it must be helped by irrational means (F168.16). The φαῦλος has to be told what to do, the function of precept and laws (a point also made by Dihle, 'Posidonius' System of Moral Philosophy', *JHS* 73 (1973), 54, but note comm. on F176). The straightforward injunctions of laws (and precepts) should not be laced or diluted with rational explanation, which will only confuse the *imperiti* (3), because the irrational will not be affected by this. Of course Posidonius did not mean that concurrently the προκόπτων should not have his rational δύναμις instructed and taught, but that is not the function of precept and laws, but of the *logos* philosophy. Education is twofold (F169.114ff, comm.), and the two methods although complementary should not be confused, which Posidonius thought was Chrysippus' mis-

COMMENTARY: F179

take. But for the difficulties in general of this for Stoicism: Kidd, 'Moral Actions and Rules'.

For Plato's justification of his preambles to the Laws, see IV.718a–723d (also Pl. *Ep.* 3.316a, for which cf. Post, 'The Preludes to Plato's *Laws*', *TAPA* 60 (1929), 5–24, and Saunders, *Plato, The Laws* 543f). Plato's practice was followed by Cicero (*De Leg.* II.14–16) and was probably accepted by Academics and Peripatetics. Of the Stoics, Cicero singles out only Diogenes and Panaetius as having an interest in laws (*De Leg.* III.14). On this particular point Posidonius' standpoint seems to be quite distinctive. Here he differs sharply from Plato, whose psychology he admired in general, if he did not follow it in detail. Seneca also differs positively from Posidonius, and this tells against the view that the whole development of argument in *Epp.* 94 and 95 reflects an original unorthodox position derived from Posidonius (as Dihle, 'Posidonius' System of Moral Philosophy'). They are rather Seneca's presentation of a common Stoic problem (Kidd, 'Moral Actions and Rules').

F179 Seneca, *Epistulae* 78.28

CONTENT

Seneca quotes a *mot* of Posidonius: a single day for educated men spreads further than the longest lifetime for the unskilled (ignorant, untutored).

CONTEXT

Seneca's Letter is on the subject of combatting pain and illness, and this is an isolated *sententia* at the end, when he looks forward to seeing Lucilius again for however short a time. The topic of time, however, was introduced in §27. The man who has come to understand nature knows that morality (*honesta*) does not grow through time (*tempore honesta non*

COMMENTARY: F179

crescere). But, *iis necesse est videri omnem vitam brevem qui illam voluptatibus vanis et ideo infinitis metiuntur.* But this is Seneca (*De Brev. Vit.* 14f) and gives no clue to the context of Posidonius.

COMMENT

Cicero's sentence in the famous outburst in praise of philosophy at *Tusc.* v.5 has been compared: *est autem unus dies bene et ex praeceptis tuis actus peccanti immortalitati anteponendus* (so Weinreich, *Archiv für Religionswissenchaft* 21 (1922), 504ff; Reinhardt, *Kosmos und Sympathie* 160 n. 1). But there are many variations on the time theme, e.g. Sen. *De Brev. Vit.* 15.5, for the philosopher *longam illi vitam facit omnium temporum in unum conlatio.* Seneca's commentary on Heraclitus' *unus dies par omni est* in *Ep.* 12.7 adopts a different line.

The philosophical background in the Stoa for at least some of these *sententiae* was the view that knowledge, virtue, happiness were timeless, incapable of degree and not enhanced by duration (Cic. *De Fin.* III.45–8; Plutarch, *De SR* 1046c, *Comm. Not.* 1062a, *SVF* III.54); so Seneca's *tempore honesta non crescere* (§27), enlarged by Themistius (*Or.* VIII.101d = *SVF* III.54) to ταὐτὸν δύνασθαι φάσκων (sc. Chrysippus) ἀνδρὶ σπουδαίῳ μίαν ἡμέραν, μᾶλλον δὲ καὶ μίαν ὥραν πολλοῖς ἐνιαυτοῖς. Cf. Sen. *Ep.* 92.25.

Seneca uses the terms *eruditi, imperiti.* What do they translate: πεπαιδευμένοι, πολυμαθέστατοι, ἀμαθεῖς? And what do they signify? The stress may be on 'learning'. In general there was controversy on this ground between Stoics and Epicureans. Epicurus denounced learning: παιδείαν δὲ πᾶσαν, μακάριε, φεῦγε, τἀκάτιον ἀράμενος (F163 Usener; cf. F117); the Stoa supported it (cf. Zeno's exchange with Antigonus, D.L. VII.7–9). Panaetius had a reputation for being *eruditus* (Cic. *De Leg.* III.14; Hirzel, *Untersuchungen* II.257.1); Posidonius himself was πολυμαθέστατος (T48), indeed ἐπιστημονικώτατος τῶν Στωϊκῶν (T84). For the value that he put on ἐγκύκλιος παιδεία, F90.

COMMENTARY: F180

On the other hand the 'learning' may refer to moral knowledge (i.e. virtue, which was a τέχνη for Stoics, *SVF* II.96; III.95, 202, 214) or indeed to the θεωρία τῆς τῶν ὅλων ἀληθείας καὶ τάξεως (F186), thus to philosophy itself, and to the fully fledged σοφός. So even Zeno himself apparently could say τὴν παιδείαν πρὸς εὐδαιμονίαν αὐτάρκη (Sternbach, 'De gnomologio Vaticano inedito', 302, *WS* 10 (1888), 245).

Without any context, one can hardly go further, but in the case of Posidonius probably both aspects of παιδεία were in mind.

F180   Diogenes Laertius, VII.92

CONTENT

In a list of different Stoic classifications or numerations of the virtues, Posidonius is identified with the view that the virtues are four in number.

CONTEXT

D.L. VII.89–91 dealt with virtue in general. There were two allusions to Posidonius in VII.91, F29, F2. After F180, Diogenes goes on to catalogue generic and specific virtues.

COMMENT

The number of virtues depends entirely on the classification used. In another sense for Stoics virtue was one (*SVF* III.260). But at the same time they recognised that different ἀρεταί were distinct from each other (cf. F182 comm.).

It is highly probable that the same Stoic might employ different classifications according to his argument or context.

It is odd that Posidonius is singled out for a classification of

COMMENTARY: F180

four virtues, if by that is meant the primary (πρῶται) cardinal virtues. Diogenes himself goes on immediately to classify these as the traditional group φρόνησις, ἀνδρεία, δικαιοσύνη, σωφροσύνη (*SVF* III.265). And these are reproduced in our sources as a general Stoic dogma (Stob., *SVF* III.262, 264, 280; Philo, *SVF* III.263; Andronicus, *SVF* III.266; cf. Cic. *De Off.* 1.15ff), and the doctrine goes back to Zeno (Plu. *De SR* 1034C, *SVF* I.200). It is under these generic four that many other 'virtues' are subsumed (*SVF* III.264ff). To the four cardinal virtues correspond four vices (D.L. VII.93, Stob., *SVF* III.262).

Indeed Stoics also adopted a classification of four primary classes of πάθη, λύπη, φόβος, ἐπιθυμία, ἡδονή, a classification which also goes back to Zeno (D.L. VII.110 = *SVF* I.211). We cannot argue that Posidonius' original view that the explanation of πάθη held the key to all ethical problems (Frs. 30, 150), made him relate in some way the four virtues to the four πάθη. The opposite of πάθος is εὐπάθεια, which had a triple classification (*SVF* III.431, 432). But Schmekel suggested (*Die Philosophie der mittleren Stoa* 270–4) more plausibly that Posidonius' new psychology may have affected his view of the ἀρεταί; and indeed Posidonius says in F31, that the ἀρεταί of the irrational factors of the soul must be different from the ἀρετή of the rational. So Schmekel wished to assign φρόνησις as the sole ἀρετή of the rational, and allotted the remainder, ἀνδρεία, δικαιοσύνη, σωφροσύνη to the irrational as the ἀρεταί embodying the different ways in which the irrational properly followed in obedience the rational. This will not quite do, because Posidonius distinctly says that the ἀρεταί of the irrational cannot themselves be rational (or ἐπιστῆμαι); and he surely regarded δικαιοσύνη and the rest as forms of ἐπιστήμη (Frs. 2, 39). It may yet be true that Posidonius expounded a new version of the four cardinal virtues in terms of the control of the rational over the irrational. Would this approach put more weight on the four cardinal virtues? Zeller (*Die Philosophie der Griechen* III.1.244 n. 1) thought of Platonic

COMMENTARY: F181

influence, but it may have been rather a typical new defence of what Posidonius saw as the position of Zeno and the early Stoa (*SVF* 1.200) against the swarm (σμῆνος) of virtues which Chrysippus was accused of producing (Plu. *De Virt. Mor.* 441B = *SVF* III.255). But this is speculation. Diogenes' catalogue is useless without contextual reference.

The formula, οἱ περὶ Ποσειδώνιον is discussed at T45.

F181   Galen, *De Placitis* VIII.660-1, p. 662.3-8 M, p. 490.1-5 De Lacy

CONTENT

Posidonius criticised Chrysippus' four books 'On the Difference of the Virtues'.

CONTEXT

At the beginning of Bk VIII Galen explains why he attacked Chrysippus' psychology, particularly in relation to the theory of πάθη, in order to defend his own thesis that τὸ ἡγεμονικόν, as the source of the nerves, is located in the brain, τὸ παθητικόν, as the source of πάθη, in the heart, and ἐπιθυμητική in the liver. In this introductory passage Posidonius had already been mentioned with respect (T84) for his criticism of Chrysippus' psychology (F32), and for the related attack on the theory of virtues (F38). Galen blames Chrysippus' supporters for the length of his arguments (654.6ff M). Galen himself could give brief scientific proof; so he has not prolonged the discussion further for a complete exposition of Chrysippus' contradictions.

COMMENT

This is a direct reference by Galen to a work of Posidonius with which he was obviously acquainted. The content of

COMMENTARY: F182

Posidonius' arguments is indicated at F31.29-47, cf. F182 comm. The possible title of Posidonius' work is discussed in F38 comm. It is implied that Posidonius attacked a specific work of Chrysippus. It is noticeable that as in other cases where this particular Posidonian criticism is mentioned by Galen, it is coupled with an attack on πάθη (Frs. 31, 182, 38), obviously because both were based on the analysis of soul (F182).

F182 Galen, *De Placitis* VII.589, p. 584.4-10 M, p. 430.11-16 De Lacy

CONTENT

Posidonius praised the old account (τὸν παλαιὸν λόγον) in criticising Chrysippus' mistakes concerning the difference of the virtues, because all virtues except φρόνησις will be eliminated, should the soul be nothing but τὸ λογιστικόν. The criticism is analogous to that of the πάθη.

CONTEXT

At the beginning of Bk VII of *De Plac.* Galen returns to problems concerning τὸ ἡγεμονικόν pointing out that in earlier books (i.e. IV and V) he had already attacked Chrysippus on the subject of ἡγεμονικόν and πάθη. He now refers to Posidonius as a source which he had used earlier, and proceeds with criticism of Chrysippus on the difference in virtues (584.10-596.3 M), probably still following Posidonius (γάρ, 4). Cf. T64.

COMMENT

It is possible from Galen's argument, 548.10-596.3 M, when

COMMENTARY: F182

combined with F31.29-47 (446.13-448.2 M), to see Posidonius' reaction to a famous dispute in the Stoa between Chrysippus and Ariston on virtues. Chrysippus in two of his published works had attacked Ariston for stressing the essential singleness of virtue (also Plu. *De SR*, ch. 7, 1034CD). Posidonius thought that both Chrysippus and Ariston were wrong, and the argument in Galen is interesting not only for Posidonius, but also for the light it throws on a difficulty that can be traced back to Zeno, and his immediate followers and interpreters.

The argument in Galen shows:

(i) that Chrysippus believed that the ἀρεταί were distinct from each other in their οὐσίαι through a qualitative change (586 M).

(ii) In this he was following older theories: ὡς ὁ τῶν παλαιῶν ἠβούλετο λόγος (586.4 M).

(iii) This dogma was argued by Chrysippus in four books Περὶ τῆς διαφορᾶς τῶν ἀρετῶν, and particularly in a book against Ariston, Περὶ τοῦ ποιὰς εἶναι τὰς ἀρετάς (584, 585-6 M).

(iv) Chrysippus' position was clarified against Ariston, who thinking that there was one faculty of the mind inferred a single ἀρετή, ἐπιστήμη ἀγαθῶν καὶ κακῶν (591.4-7 M). νομίζει γὰρ ὁ ἀνὴρ ἐκεῖνος (Ariston) μίαν οὖσαν τὴν ἀρετὴν ὀνόμασι πλείοσι ὀνομάζεσθαι κατὰ τὴν πρός τι σχέσιν (585.15f M). (Ariston's position that justice, courage and the rest were not distinguishable in essence, but only *relatively so* (κατὰ τὴν πρός τι σχέσιν) should be distinguished from that of the Megarians who saw a difference only in nomenclature: D.L. VII.161; Plu. *De Virt. Mor.* 440Eff.).

(v) It is implied (592.1ff) that Ariston, while positing a single ἀρετή namely ἐπιστήμη ἀγαθῶν καὶ κακῶν, exampled the different relational spheres of this virtue by defining the cardinal virtues as forms of ἐπιστήμη (591.11ff M). It appears that in this he followed Zeno's definitions of the virtues,

COMMENTARY: F182

except that Zeno used the term φρόνησις throughout, not ἐπιστήμη (Plu. *De SR* 1034C with Pohlenz's emendation).

(vi) The argument concludes (586; 591ff; 447.4–448.2 M (F31.36–47)) that:

(a) Chrysippus was right but inconsistent (right in holding that there are many ἀρεταί; inconsistent in deriving them from a single psychic faculty).

(b) Ariston was wrong but consistent (wrong in positing a single ἀρετή, but consistent in deriving it from a single psychic faculty).

(c) So the critique faults Chrysippus as ἀλλοτρίας αἱρέσεως ἐπιχειρήμασι χρώμενον (586 M); οὐ μὴν τῇ γε οἰκείᾳ πρεπόντων ὑποθέσει (595 M).

(vii) The argument implies:

(a) that Ariston was the first to deny difference in essence between ἀρεταί, since it was Ariston that Chrysippus attacked, not Zeno. Also Chrysippus' argument here followed ὡς ὁ τῶν παλαιῶν ἠβούλετο λόγος (586 M);

(b) that Chrysippus was the first to maintain a single faculty of soul (τὸ λογιστικόν), because Posidonius in attacking Chrysippus on this score supported the παλαιὸς λόγος (F182.2).

It follows that Zeno maintained essential differences between virtues (as is positively stated by Plutarch, *De SR* 1034C), and did *not* press a single faculty. Therefore in Galen's view, and presumably in Posidonius', there was no contradiction or inconsistency in Zeno.

Plutarch's criticism of the Stoa on the difference of virtues (*De SR* 1034Cff) is quite independent of Posidonius, because there is no mention of the crux of the single faculty. Plutarch simply infers from the Stoic definitions of virtues that they are all relative forms of φρόνησις, ἐπιστήμη, or ἰσχὺς καὶ κράτος. Nor is there any indication of the Posidonian arguments in the doxographies (D.L. VII.90ff; Stob. *Ecl.* II.58ff W). The

COMMENTARY: F183

characteristic Posidonian elements, then, are the attack based on the psychology of a single faculty of soul, and the consequent linking of the criticism to that of the πάθη (F182, F31.29ff); typical too would be the defence of Zeno's original position by implying misinterpretation on the part of his followers Ariston and Chrysippus. It is tempting then to think that the παλαιὸς λόγος which Posidonius praised (F182.2) referred to Zeno, but it is more likely to have had a wider reference including Plato and Aristotle (cf. F183, F34.9–12). It is also characteristic that Posidonius used an accepted Stoic definition of ἀρετή (τελειότης) as a stick with which to beat Chrysippus (F31.39ff; cf. F34.12ff).

F183 Galen, *De Placitis* v.481, p. 463.1–6 M, p. 338.14–18 De Lacy

CONTENT

Posidonius, while agreeing with Plato and Aristotle in general on faculties of soul against Chrysippus, yet disagreed with them in some details on the differences in the virtues.

CONTEXT

F144 precedes; cf. T96, F143. At 460.9 M Galen embarks on an examination of part of Plato, *Rep.* IV, to prove that there are three parts or faculties of soul, and so intends to overthrow the view of Chrysippus and to establish what he claims is common doctrine to Aristotle, Plato and Posidonius.

COMMENT

οὕτω refers to F144, namely that Plato proved in *Rep.* that there were three faculties of soul different in kind.

Although Galen is talking about general agreement over

faculties of soul, the particular disagreements are referred to the differences in the virtues (F182). Galen continues (463. 6–8 M) that he will clarify this point later when he gives his detailed account of the virtues. But this he fails to do.

T96 comments on Posidonius' position in relation to Plato and Aristotle, F146 on the disagreement between the three philosophers regarding *faculties of soul*.

F184 Seneca, *Epistulae* 92.10

CONTENT

Posidonius said that flesh was suited only for the intake of food. Whether anything else should be attributed to Posidonius is uncertain.

COMMENT

There has been much speculation on the relationship of *Ep.* 92, both in part and in whole to Posidonius; in particular §§1–13 have been held to contain important evidence for Posidonius; thus Reinhardt, *Kosmos und Sympathie* 298ff; *RE* 757–60; Pohlenz, *GGA* 188 (1926), 298f = *Kleine Schriften* 1.224f; Modrze, 'Zur Ethik und Psychologie des Poseidonios', *Philologus* 87 (1932), 300–31; Husner, 'Leib und Seele in der Sprache Senecas', *Philologus Suppl.* 17 (1924), 118ff. Caution is advisable. While it is possible that Seneca may have used for his own purposes on occasion an idea from Posidonius or from other sources, and in fact he briefly quotes Posidonius in §10, as indeed he quoted Vergil just before in §9, the development of argument in the Letter is likely to be Seneca's. It would require strong evidence to maintain that Seneca is merely mirroring an argument of Posidonius, and this seems to me lacking. The question of Posidonian influence can only be approached through an analysis of §§1–13.

COMMENTARY: F184

The Letter is concerned with the self-sufficiency of virtue for the happy life, a common theme of Seneca in particular, and of Stoics in general.

§1 outlines a proportional scale of values leading to the identification of the sole supreme value. External goods are sought for the body; the body is cherished for the soul. In the soul the parts by which we move and are nourished are given to us *propter ipsum principale* (the ἡγεμονικόν). In this primary part there is something irrational and something rational. The former serves (*servit*) the latter; the latter is the only thing which is not referred to anything else, but refers everything to itself, being a part of the *divina ratio*. So (§2) the happy life depends solely on the attainment of perfect reason.

Such relative grading, where the lower forms in the scale are for the sake of the higher, is orthodox Stoicism. The division of the *principale* into irrational and rational certainly smacks of Posidonius, but the description is vague, and Hadot, *Seneca* 91, has shown how Seneca himself can vary between monistic and dualistic expression. This seems partly to arise from confusion betwen a body/soul dualism, and dualism in the soul itself (thus *Ep.* 71.27; 92.33). The dualistic expression here is probably introduced to facilitate the attack on pleasure which follows. The concept of service, obedience (*servire*) and command is also typical of Seneca (as *De Ben.* IV.2.2), and is implicit in the term ἡγεμονικόν.

The definition of the happy life which follows is very Senecan indeed. While *veritas tota perspecta* is Posidonian, it is no less characteristic of Seneca; but the main terms, *securitas, perpetua tranquillitas, magnitudo animi, constantia*, are all Senecan key terms: F170, comm. C on ll.24–31; Hadot, *Seneca* 126ff.

§5 Seneca proceeds: yet there are some (clearly Peripatetics and Academics) who hold that the *summum bonum* admits of increase, because it is scarcely full (*plenum*) when the gifts of fortune (*fortuitis*, external and physical advantages) are in opposition (*repugnantiis*). Even Antipater (the Stoic) ascribes some force to externals, although only very slight.

COMMENTARY: F184

This then is the position which Seneca attacks:

§6 If you are not content with *honestas*, it must follow that you desire *in addition*, either (1) ἀοχλησία or (2) *voluptas* (ἡδονή). Seneca at this point quickly dismisses (1). ἀοχλησία comes anyway; for the mind is free from *molestia* when it is *liber ad inspectum universi, nihilque illum avocat a contemplatione naturae*. That sounds like echoes of Posidonius, but in fact Posidonius is more positive. It does not necessarily follow for him that θεωρία brings ἀπάθεια; one has also to fight actively against being led astray by the irrational *in us* (Frs. 186, 187). As for (2), it is simply *bonum pecoris*, the good of beasts, a matter merely of *adding* the irrational to the rational.

Seneca is combatting the view that the *summum bonum* can be a *combination* of rational and irrational, virtue and pleasure, so he now has to adopt a psychology which will permit this (§8). The irrational part of the soul has two parts: (a) *animosam, ambitiosam, inpotentem, positam in adfectionibus* (i.e. in the πάθη), (b) *humilem, languidam, voluptatibus deditam*; and clearly they represent τὸ θυμοειδές and τὸ ἐπιθυμητικόν, which Posidonius, as well as Peripatetics and the Academy recognised. But the characteristics, *positam in adfectionibus* for the former, and *humilem, languidam* (cf. *De Otio* VI.2) of the latter will not suit Posidonius. Seneca dismisses (a) as neglected by philosophers, and accuses his opponents of making (b), pleasure, *necessariam beatae vitae*. He is not attacking Epicurus here; pleasure is not the *summum bonum*, but a necessary addition to it.

§9 'It is this (i.e. pleasure) that they ordered reason to serve (as it must if pleasure is a necessary part; and Seneca's theme of *servire* recurs), and made the *summum bonum* of the most noble of animals (i.e. man), abject and vulgar, and besides a monstrous mixture (*mixtum, portentumque*), and from disparate and badly suited parts (*membris*).'

To illustrate he quotes Vergil's lines on Scylla (*Aen.* III.426ff), a monster of ill-suited parts, with human face and breast but beastlike below. This image becomes the nub of the

COMMENTARY: F184

argument, and it is not Posidonian. 'To her, wild beasts were added, but they (*isti*, those who join virtue and pleasure) from what monstrous things they put together *sapientiam* (wisdom, the *summum bonum*).'

§10 Now follows the section containing the allusion to Posidonius. 'The primary part (*pars, ars* some codices) of man is virtue itself; to this is joined (*committitur*) useless flabby (*fluida*) flesh (*caro*), fitted only for the reception of food as Posidonius says. That divine virtue ends up in obscenity (*lubricum*, i.e. pleasure), and to the higher parts of man (*partibus*), worshipful and heavenly, is tacked on a sluggish languid (*marcidum*, feeble, flaccid) animal. ... What elements so inharmonious as these can be found?'

pars Q²CREWX: *ars* BQ¹D. Editors and commentators divide between these two readings. In the text of the Fragments in vol. I, I mistakenly accepted *ars*, misled by the common Stoic doctrine that virtue (or the virtues) is a τέχνη (*SVF* II.96; III.214). The phrase makes sense in itself, but the context clearly demands *pars*. The whole argument of combination of parts, the Scylla image, *committitur* and *superioribus partibus* which follow, make this certain. But if we read *pars*, the phrase is now Seneca's. There is no question of assigning to Posidonius the view that man's primary art is virtue itself (at least from this passage, as e.g. Edelstein, *AJPh* 57 (1936), 312). *Prima pars* is part of *Seneca*'s argument.

huic committitur inutilis caro at fluida. This is Seneca too, because (1) it is linked necessarily to *prima pars* etc., and (2) *caro* is Seneca's word for body representing the physical 'goods' (*Ep.* 74.16f, *Ep.* 65.21–2; Husner, 'Leib und Seele' 118ff). And the association of body, irrational and pleasure, with the resultant confusion of body/soul dualism and irrational/rational dualism seems Senecan. It is true that σάρξ is an Epicurean term (thus Frs. 410, 411, 412 Us.); but this cannot derive from a Posidonian attack on Epicurus (as Reinhardt and Pohlenz suggested) because we have the form of that in F160, where he takes the line that Epicurus τὴν τοῦ χειρίστου

COMMENTARY: F185

μορίου τῆς ψυχῆς οἰκείωσιν ἐθεάσατο μόνην. Also the analysis of Seneca's argument so far shows that the Epicureans are not his opponents here either. The target is rather the statement of Cic. *Tusc.* v.12: *non mihi videtur ad beate vivendum satis posse virtutem,* that is, Peripatetics and Academics, who *add* the irrational *fortuita* to the rational (cf. Plutarch's contortions misrepresenting Stoic attacks on Plato and Aristotle in *De SR*, ch. 15). No doubt it could be said that Epicurus is opposed *a fortiori*, but Epicurus did not produce Scylla.

§11 Seneca declared in §10 that the conjunction of pleasure and virtue would in fact destroy (*dissolvit*) the soul, so in §11 a follow-up suggestion is made: if good health, rest and freedom from pain are not going to hinder virtue at all, will you not seek them? The answer is 'yes', but not because they are goods. In other words the basis of the argument is the sole sufficiency of virtue, and the opposition to that of anything else that suggests that pleasure or any other external or physical advantage is really a good to be placed on a level and coupled with virtue; it is about the moral stature of the 'indifferents', and is good orthodox Stoicism, neither more or less Posidonius than any other Stoic, or Seneca himself.

The conclusion of the analysis is that the formative seed-core of the argument is the Scylla illustration from Vergil which cannot come from Posidonius, but which extends to the unholy union of *prima pars hominis* with *inutilis caro et fluida*. Therefore the only reference which can with certainty be attached to Posidonius lies in the four words, *receptandis tantum cibis habilis*, and there is no means of telling the context of that.

F185   Diogenes Laertius, VII.86–7

CONTENT

Zeno first said that the end was to live in harmony with

COMMENTARY: F186

nature, which is precisely to live in accordance with virtue; for nature leads us to virtue. Similarly, Cleanthes, Posidonius and Hecaton.

COMMENT

What is the extent of reference to Posidonius? Certainly the definition of end as τὸ ὁμολογουμένως τῇ φύσει ζῆν; but doubtless also are included the equation with κατ' ἀρετὴν ζῆν, and the explanation, ἄγει γὰρ ... ἡ φύσις (9), for this much would be agreed by all Stoics. Where individual Stoics differed was not in the common basic formulae, but in forms of interpretation (F186 comm.). Diogenes proceeds (87–8) with interpretations by Chrysippus and Diogenes of Babylon, with which we know that Posidonius disagreed: F187.25–37, comm.

The passage on τέλος begins with διόπερ (7), so the preceding lines (1–6) are also an explanation, outlining the various principles governing plants, animals and rational creatures (man), where in the latter reason takes over as τεχνίτης τῆς ὁρμῆς. All this is Posidonian. For the classification, see F33 comm.; and for ὁμολογία interpreted in terms of reason as a governing principle, see F187.1–22, comm., and F31.

The plural ἐν τοῖς Περὶ τελῶν suggests that the source for Posidonius (as for Hecaton) was a book entitled Περὶ τελῶν (contrast lines 7 and 10); but it may equally suggest that Hecaton's Περὶ τελῶν was in more than one book.

F186 Clement of Alexandria, *Stromateis*
II.xxi.129.1–5

CONTENT

Posidonius' definition of τέλος is given at the end of a

COMMENTARY: F186

catalogue listing definitions by individual leading Stoics beginning with Zeno.

COMMENT

A. The catalogue

Compare for other such lists, Stobaeus, *Ecl.* II.7.6ᵃ, p. 75f W; D.L. VII.87–8.

The surprising thing about Clement's list is that it omits Chrysippus, whose formula, as given by Stobaeus and D.L., is also given by Posidonius at F187.34. The order Antipater Archedemus is reversed in Stobaeus, Antipater being omitted by D.L. This is insignificant as they are near contemporaries. Apart from a chronological sequence there seems to be no significance in the grouping, τε... αὖ (8) and πρὸς τούτοις ἔτι (11) being sequence variations; so ἐπὶ πᾶσί τε (12) probably means 'on top of all'. It is after the mention of the more recent Stoics (15–17), that Clement makes a distinction by adding, with strong reservations, Ariston and Herillus. Also elsewhere, e.g. *Strom.* II.xix.101; V.xiv.95, Clement gives a blanket τέλος definition for the Stoics: τὸ ἀκολούθως τῇ φύσει ζῆν (cf. D.L. VII.88). It is clear that the catalogue is not a list of different *definitions* of τέλος, but of different clarificatory interpretations of a common accepted definition. So also Stobaeus, e.g. ὅπερ ὁ Χρύσιππος σαφέστερον βουλόμενος ποιῆσαι ... (p. 76.6f W; and D.L. VII.88). The original definition was probably τὸ ὁμολογουμένως (τῇ φύσει) ζῆν (Stob., D.L. VII.88 = *SVF* I.179), to which Posidonius like the others subscribed (see F185). The constant reformulation was no doubt forced on the Stoa by Academic criticism (Long, 'Carneades and the Stoic Telos', *Phronesis* 12 (1967), 59–90; Kidd, 'Stoic Intermediates', *Problems in Stoicism* VII). This version of Posidonius' formula occurs only here, but cf. F187.4–13.

B. The Posidonian version

'To live contemplating (θεωροῦντα) the truth (ἀλήθειαν) and order (τάξιν) of all things together (τῶν ὅλων) and helping in

COMMENTARY: F186

promoting (or establishing, or organising, συγκατασκευάζοντα) it (αὐτήν, so *L*; but Sylburg emended αὐτόν, see below), in no way being led by the irrational part of the soul.'

1 **θεωροῦντα τὴν τῶν ὅλων ἀλήθειαν καὶ τάξιν.** θεωρία is something new in Stoic versions of τέλος; and it is difficult to find any passage in the earlier Stoa where θεωρία is given such a fundamental role. It forms one of the three lives listed by D.L. VII.130 (θεωρητικός, πρακτικός, λογικός) where it is said that we should choose ὁ λογικὸς βίος, since the λογικὸν ζῷον was created by nature suitable πρὸς θεωρίαν καὶ πρᾶξιν. But that is different and of uncertain date. ἀλήθεια can refer both to truth in a logical sense (F188, and cf. ἡ τοῦ ἀκολούθου ἕνεκα θεωρία, F47.74f), but also and above all to the reality which is the object of the Stoic φυσικὸς τόπος, indeed called ἡ φυσικὴ θεωρία, F18.5. For the fundamental importance of this and the subordinate but necessary role of science, see F18 and Kidd, 'Philosophy and Science in Posidonius', *Antike und Abendland* 24 (1978), 7-15. It also can have ethical reference, F169.115. τάξις not only covers the order of the οὐρανός, which is part of the proper study of ἡ φυσικὴ θεωρία (F18.8), but the order of everything imposed by λόγος, providence and Zeus. It is because of the τάξις that Posidonius can search for causes, αἰτίαι.

If αὐτήν is the correct reading in line 14, ἀλήθειαν καὶ τάξιν form a close hendiadys. τῶν ὅλων is significant; it is neither τῶν πάντων (of all things), nor τοῦ ὅλου (of the universe), but 'of absolutely everything' and underlines neatly the distinctive Posidonian view that all knowledge is interrelated, demonstrated in the comprehensive width of his own investigations (Kidd, 'Philosophy and Science'; cf. T48). Compare ἡ τῶν ὅλων φύσις, F85.

2 **καὶ συγκατασκευάζοντα αὐτὴν κατὰ τὸ δυνατόν.** αὐτήν *L*: αὐτόν *Sylburg*. αὐτήν has been supported by Hirzel (*Untersuchungen* II.244, n. 1; 516), Pohlenz (*De Posidonii Libris* Περὶ παθῶν 562; *Die Stoa* II.121), Reinhardt (*Kosmos und Sympathie* 283; *RE* 747), Wilamowitz (*Der Glaube* II.407, n. 2);

COMMENTARY: F186

αὐτόν by Heinemann (1.67) and Edelstein (*AJPh* 57 (1936), 315). Is the object of συγκατασκευάζοντα the truth and order of all things taken together (αὐτήν), or oneself (αὐτόν)? The emendation is difficult to defend. Edelstein's translation 'and fashioning oneself as far as possible *in accordance therewith*' (my italics), is a false interpretation of συγ-; the phrase could only mean, help in establishing or organising, or join in promoting oneself as far as possible. One would have to understand by this: help the truth and order of all things together to establish such order in oneself. This is clumsy Greek, although perhaps aided by the explanation of κατὰ μηδὲν κτλ (15). Besides, κατὰ τὸ δυνατόν should not mean 'do everything one can to . . .'; it usually has a limiting effect; 'as far as is possible (for a human being)'; but Posidonius believed that we could become σοφοί. On the other hand the reading of the codex is clear and unexceptional. We can help to promote the truth and order of all things taken together, precisely because we are a part of it (cf. F85); human beings have their part to play both in the macrocosm and in the microcosm of themselves, underlined by τῶν ὅλων, but their contribution to the former is naturally limited (κατὰ τὸ δυνατόν).

The two participles, θεωροῦντα and συγκατασκευάζοντα are to be taken closely together as complementary, contemplation and action. Something like this was foreshadowed in e.g. Pl. *Tim.* 47b–c, with which Posidonius was no doubt familiar. But the Platonic view is encapsulated in ὁμοίωσις θεῷ κατὰ τὸ δυνατόν (*Theaet.* 176b), revived as Platonic and Pythagorean in the 1st c. B.C. by Eudorus (Stob. *Ecl.* II.49.8ff W; Dillon, *Middle Platonists* 122f). Posidonius' formulation is distinctively Stoic, but individual. It is only after Posidonius that we find echoes of it, e.g. Cic. *ND* II.37; *De Senect.* 77; *De Off.* I.157–8; Sen. *Ep.* 104.23; *De Otio* V.1; cf. Kidd, 'Moral Actions and Rules in Stoic Ethics', *The Stoics*, ed. J. M. Rist, esp. pp. 254–7, on Sen. *Epp.* 94, 95. But note Panaetius F108 van Str., and compare F180.

COMMENTARY: F187

3 κατὰ μηδὲν ἀγόμενον ὑπὸ τοῦ ἀλόγου μέρους τῆς ψυχῆς. This has been thought to be an addition by Clement: Pohlenz, *NGG* (1921), 192 (cf. *Die Stoa* II.121), Reinhardt, *Kosmos und Sympathie* 283 n. 2. μέρους is uncharacteristic; Posidonius preferred δύναμις (F146). μέρους may be an addition, as Galen also sometimes used μέρος for Posidonius, or Posidonius himself on occasion may have been careless, but the whole phrase is undoubtedly Posidonian (F187.12f; Philippson, *RhM* (1937), 178). It is not only highly relevant as a key explanation of the preceding (θεωροῦντα καὶ) συγκατασκευάζοντα, but is of fundamental importance for Posidonius' interpretation of the τέλος; F187.4–13 comm.

4 Finally it should be noticed that the definition unites closely all three categories of his philosophy: physics, logic and ethics. This is in tune with his organic view of the parts of philosophy expressed in F88 (Kidd, 'Posidonius and Logic', in Brunschwig, ed., *Les Stoïciens et leur logique*).

F187 Galen, *De Placitis* v.469–76, pp. 448.11–456.14 M, pp. 326.17–332.31 De Lacy

CONTENT

A quotation on the connection between the cause of emotions and goods, the end and happiness (4–13). Galen comments on the quotation (13–22). There follows another quotation from Posidonius attacking the Chrysippean explanation of the end (22–37). Posidonius' method solves other related ethical puzzles which Galen presents with quotations from Posidonius and commentary (40–67).

CONTEXT

Preceded by F31 and F30, *q.v.* At this point Galen passes from

674

COMMENTARY: F187

the connection between correct views on emotions and virtues (1-2), to the relationship between emotions (πάθη) and goods (ἀγαθά) and the end (τὸ τέλος) (3). He thus covers the three divisions of ethics enumerated in the Posidonian quotation of F30. So the first subject is on goods and on the end. Galen interpolates (παραγράψαι) a quotation from Posidonius, which is enough (ἀρκεῖ) for him (3-4).

COMMENT

A. The quotation (4-13)

'The cause (αἴτιον) of the emotions, that is of inconsistency (discord, τῆς ἀνομολογίας) and (τε . . . καί) of the unhappy life (τοῦ κακοδαίμονος βίου) is not to follow in everything the daimon in oneself (αὐτῷ HL, corr. Bake), which is akin (συγγενεῖ) and has a similar nature to the one (i.e. daimon) which governs the whole universe (κόσμον), but at times to deviate and be swept along with what is worse and beastlike. Those who have (οἱ δέ, the Chrysippeans) failed to observe this neither give the better explanation (αἰτίαν) for the emotions in these things (i.e. in the sphere of goods and the end), nor do they hold correct opinions about happiness (εὐδαιμονίας) and consistency (concord, ὁμολογίας). For they do not see that the foremost thing in it (happiness) is to be led in no way by the irrational and unhappy (κακοδαίμονος), that is (καί) what is godless in the soul.'

5 The cause of πάθη and the cause of ἀνομολογία and ὁ κακοδαίμων βίος are identified (τουτέστι); cf. 1-3 and F30.

ἀνομολογίας (5), ὁμολογίας (11): Chrysippus wrote a book Περὶ ἀνομολογίας (ἀνωμαλίας coni. Reiske), Plu. De Virt. 450c = SVF III.390. Compare ἀνομολογούμενόν ἐστι πᾶν πάθος SVF III.474. ὁμολογία is part of the Stoic definition of τέλος (e.g. SVF III.3; Cic. De Fin. III.21 = SVF III.188). ἀνομολογία is linked to (τε . . . καί, 5) the unhappy life, which is experienced by all φαῦλοι (SVF III.54).

675

COMMENTARY: F187

6–9 The αἴτιον: cf. F31.23, ἀλλὰ εἰς ἅπαν ἑτοίμων ἕπεσθαί τε καὶ πείθεσθαι τῷ λογισμῷ. δαίμων is used here following κακοδαίμονος βίου. It is clear from F31.23 and F187.13, 22 that reason is meant. So the daimon is internal (ἐν αὐτῷ, 6), and his φύσις is like that of the governing cosmic logos. Pohlenz (*Die Stoa* 1.229) tends to find much religious significance in the passage (so also Heinemann, 1.60). But what does συγγενεῖ mean?

(a) 'congenital', 'born with us', Edelstein *AJPh* 57 (1936), 314 (so also Schmekel and Norden), wishing to stress ἐν αὐτῷ;

(b) 'akin to' to be taken with τῷ . . . διοικοῦντι (Reinhardt, *RE* col. 747, who compares *cognatio* in Cic. *De Div.* 1.63, 110; further elaborated in *Kosmos und Sympathie*).

The construction, τε . . . καί linking συγγενεῖ ὄντι with τὴν ὁμοίαν φύσιν ἔχοντι, supports the sense of 'akin to', and this sense is confirmed beyond doubt by Frs. 108, 85.

Something like this occurs in D.L. VII.87–8 (= *SVF* III.4, the section dealing with τέλος), especially: εἶναι δ'αὐτὸ τοῦτο τὴν τοῦ εὐδαίμονος ἀρετὴν καὶ εὔροιαν βίου, ὅταν πάντα πράττηται κατὰ τὴν συμφωνίαν τοῦ παρ' ἑκάστῳ δαίμονος πρὸς τὴν τοῦ ὅλου διοικητοῦ βούλησιν. But this has a slightly different emphasis; the Diogenes passage seems to stress the outside agency and its will (βούλησις), the law of Zeus. Posidonius stresses the internal daimon. Both agree on the relationship.

One should also compare Pl. *Tim.* 90a: τὸ δὲ δὴ περὶ τοῦ κυριωτάτου παρ' ἡμῖν ψυχῆς εἴδους διανοεῖσθαι δεῖ τῇδε, ὡς ἄρα αὐτὸ δαίμονα θεὸς ἑκάστῳ δέδωκε, τοῦτο ὃ δή φαμεν οἰκεῖν μὲν ἡμῶν ἐπ' ἄκρῳ τῷ σώματι, πρὸς δὲ τὴν ἐν οὐρανῷ συγγένειαν ἀπὸ γῆς ἡμᾶς αἴρειν ὡς ὄντας φυτὸν οὐκ ἔγγειον ἀλλ' οὐράνιον, ὀρθότατα λέγοντες.

The whole of *Tim.* 90a–d is apposite. The συγγένειά τις θεία is also mentioned at *Laws* 899d. On the other hand, Xenocrates F81 *H*, often referred to in this connection, is rather different.

COMMENTARY: F187

It seems highly probable that Posidonius knew and had in mind the *Timaeus* passage. A development of the *Tim.* passage is also seen in Plutarch's myths in *De Facie*, *De Sera* and *De Genio*, in the last of which δαίμων is equated with νοῦς as distinct from other aspects of the soul. But the history of the use of δαίμων as a philosophical metaphor is highly complex and continued to be varied. Posidonius also perhaps owed something to Pl. *Phdr.* 246aff, but see F31 comm. for Posidonius' individual use of that passage.

The formula here, however, is distinctively Posidonian in lines **8-9: being led astray with and being swept away by the worse and animal-like** (for φέρεσθαι, cf. ἔκφορος F166.11, 16). This springs from Posidonius' psychology, and is the reason why Chrysippean Stoics, through ignoring it can neither explain πάθη nor happiness (9-13). It is for this reason that it is included as a positive factor (although expressed negatively) in Posidonius' definition of τέλος, F186. It is again emphasised and explained at line 13, where the irrational and unhappy (κακοδαίμονος), linked by τε καί, is glossed (καί) by godless. There is no question of eradicating this aspect (so κατὰ τὸ δυνατόν, F186; cf. ποτε, 8), but of relationship of subservience and obedience to the ruling (ἡγεμονικόν) rational aspect (F147). The irrational has its own natural οἰκείωσις (F160), and its own care and θεραπεία (F31, F164, F165, F166, F169), but must be brought into harmony with the rational ἡγεμονικόν (F31), in the recognition of its relative value (F161; in general, Kidd, *Problems* 209). It is this concept of harmony that is Posidonius' interpretation of the Stoic definition of ὁμολογία, see below, C. It also implies that man has a choice. It seems to me highly unlikely that we are meant to supply δαίμονι with τῷ χείρονι καὶ ζῳώδει, as Edelstein *AJPh* 57 (1936), 314 (cf. Reinhardt, *RE* 747), and κακοδαίμονος (13) is not sufficient evidence for this. Posidonius is making a sharp distinction between divine and animal, and he has only one δαίμων in mind, when he refers to *the* δαίμων within oneself (6f). The point is of importance for Posidonian physics. The contrast between divine and animal also favours 'beastlike', the aspect man shares with animals (F33), as the interpretation of ζῳῶδες (cf. F161), against Reinhardt's softer ζῷον = *animans*, *RE*, col. 748; 'dem Nur-Zoon-Artigen', *Poseidonios* 329.

10 βελτιοῦσι *HL*. There is no need to change to βλέπουσι with Reinhardt, *Poseidonios* 329, n.1; *RE* 747, 734, although I have some sympathy with the suggestion.

ἐν τούτοις: the context indicates the sphere of ἀγαθά and τέλος.

12 πρῶτόν ἐστι signifies importance, not time.

B. *Galen's comment (13-22)*

(1) The enormity of the mistake of the Chrysippean Stoa is emphasised (πηλίκον) (14).

(2) The mistake, based on psychology, involves the problem of τέλος as well as πάθη (15f).

(3) Galen refers the solution to Plato (17), not surprisingly since Galen was an Academic writing a book on 'The Doctrines of Hippocrates and Plato'. But it confuses the issue, since he is talking about the Stoic definition of τέλος: τὸ τῇ φύσει ζῆν ὁμολογουμένως (17). It also obfuscates the distinctive Posidonian view. Also Galen introduced his own Platonic term μέρους τῆς ψυχῆς. Posidonius insisted on the use of δύναμις (F146). Galen however saw correctly that Posidonius' account is his explanation of the Stoic technical term ὁμολογία, which Posidonius accepted in the standard Stoic definition of τέλος, F185.

C. *Posidonius' attack on the Chrysippean explanation of* τέλος
(22-37)

This attack is said to be clearer (ἐναργέστερον) and more forceful (23). It may be the latter, but hardly the former. Pohlenz, *Diss.* p. 625 n. 4, suspected that Galen omitted a passage between the two Posidonian quotations, on the grounds that ἃ δὴ παρέντες (25) does not latch on to F187.13. Such a lacuna may have seriously affected our understanding of the second passage.

For varying interpretations of the quotation: Pohlenz, *Diss.* 625f; *Die Stoa* II.121; Reinhardt, *Poseidonios* 330f; *RE* 749; Rieth, 'Über das Telos der Stoiker', *Hermes* 69 (1934), 13-45; Edelstein, *AJPh* 57 (1936), 313ff; Nebel, 'Zur Ethik des Poseidonios', *Hermes* 74 (1939), 51-4; *Griechischer Ursprung* (1948), 349; Long, 'Carneades and the Stoic telos', *Phronesis* 12 (1967), 84-6; Kidd, *Problems* 209f; Hirzel, *Untersuchungen* II.1.242ff; Long and Sedley, *The Hellenistic Philosophers*, vol. I.

25-31 'Some actually disregarding this, contract "living in harmony" to "doing everything possible for the sake of the first things according to nature", thereby making it similar to presenting pleasure or freedom from trouble or the like as the goal. But that exhibits a contradiction in the expression itself, and nothing morally good and pertaining to happiness. For it is a necessary consequence of the end, but is not the end.'

25 παρέντες must mean 'disregard' not 'admit'. If there was a lacuna between F187.13 and 25, one cannot be certain what ἃ δή refers to. But context makes it likely (cf. 9, οἱ δὲ τοῦτο παριδόντες) that it refers to Posidonius' definition of τέλος, i.e. his interpretation (above) of ὁμολογία or τὸ ὁμολογουμένως ζῆν (25). It cannot of course refer to Galen's platonising interpretation, although that may have supplanted some remarks by Posidonius on Plato.

ἔνιοι must include Antipater, because the following definition is his (*SVF* III, *Ant.* 58; cf. *SVF* III.195). For this, and for an examination of the general problem of Stoic rewording and reinterpretation of τὸ ὁμολογουμένως ζῆν as definition of the τέλος, see Long, *Phronesis* 12 (1967), 59-89. It is unlikely that the vague plural was used because Posidonius did not wish to attack specifically one of his teachers (T11), whom he may have admired otherwise (F170.47); more probably it is generally inclusive of the Chrysippean position, and because

COMMENTARY: F187

the view had obtained some currency in contemporary debate. It is regarded as an attack on οἱ περὶ τὸν Χρύσιππον in line 24.

Posidonius' criticism is interesting: he regards Antipater's reformulation as equivalent to raising pleasure to the status of a σκοπός. In the first place there is a contradiction in Stoic terms in regarding τὰ πρῶτα κατὰ φύσιν as the σκοπός or τέλος; and secondly, no Stoic would regard pleasure as the end or the goal, as it has no part in τὸ καλόν or εὐδαιμονία. There are clearly two points of objection. For this reason the original reading of *H*, μᾶλλον δέ . . . (30): '*or rather* nothing actually pertaining to happiness' cannot be right, since it merely offers an alternative version of the contradiction objection. *H* correctly emended to καλὸν δὲ κτλ. Posidonius is interpreting Antipater on his own Posidonian ground; it is Posidonius who regards ἡδονή as an object of οἰκείωσις (of our irrational δύναμις), not Antipater, or any other Stoic (see Frs. 158–61); but Posidonius does not thereby elevate ἡδονή to a σκοπός, or regard it as part of the τέλος (F161, F187.4ff). Long's interpretation hangs on the distinction between σκοπός and τέλος, but the context in this fragment is against this. I take it that Posidonius' answer to the running debate on and criticism of the Stoic τέλος (for which see Long) is to suggest that the criticism cannot be met by bringing τὰ κατὰ φύσιν more into prominence in the formulation of the definition. This would (on his own terms) logically end with making a Stoic an Epicurean; τὴν ἀοχλησίαν, which is an Epicurean term, is a sarcastic addition. This is the wrong way to go about it: the correct approach is his own psychological solution of the relationship between the δυνάμεις of the soul (4–13). The correct pursuit of τὰ κατὰ φύσιν may be a necessary consequent of the end, but cannot itself be the end (30f).

31–7 The rest follows from this: 'But when this too is correctly distinguished (grasped), one may use it to cut through the puzzles which the sophists bring forward, but not "to live in accordance with experience of what happens in accordance with the *whole* of nature" (i.e. without any relative differentiations), which is equivalent to saying "to live in harmony", when this tends to gaining the indifferents, but without doing so in a mean, shabby way.'

To what do τούτου and αὐτῷ in line 32 refer?

(i) Rieth and Long take the reference to be to Antipater's formula: if this is employed in the right fashion it can be used to cut through the sophistic puzzles (but not Chrysippus' formula, which follows). If my analysis above is right, this is unlikely. The attack on Antipater is basic, and his formula is regarded by Posidonius as a development of the Chrysippean position, quite distinct from his own.

(ii) τούτου refers to the distinction between end, and what follows on the end, in the previous sentence. But then αὐτῷ cannot have the same reference, because it is clear from the cast of the remainder of the sentence (μὴ μέντοι γε τῷ ..., 33f) that it should refer to a definition of τέλος; therefore αὐτῷ would have to refer to Antipater's definition. But this encounters the same objections as (i), and anyway, it would be expected that τούτου and αὐτῷ have the same reference.

(iii) Therefore, τούτου refers to τέλος, and αὐτῷ, the object of χρῆσθαι, refers to τούτου. But the 'correct grasp' (διαληφθέντος ὀρθῶς) of the τέλος is naturally in this context Posidonius' own definition: with *it*, one can cut through the opposition.

He, Posidonius, can cut the sophistic knots, not the Chrysippeans (including Antipater). This interpretation follows naturally from the analysis of 25-31.

33 τὰς ἀπορίας ἃς οἱ σοφισταί no doubt refers to the Academic and Peripatetic attack on the Stoic formulation of τέλος (Long, *Phronesis* 12 (1967), 59-89). Cf. F170.45-8.

34-7 The final formulation comes from Chrysippus, quoted by D.L. VII.87 from Chrysippus' Περὶ τελῶν Bk I (*SVF* III.4). Here Posidonius maliciously to make his point expands Chrysippus' τῶν φύσει συμβαινόντων to τῶν κατὰ τὴν ὅλην

COMMENTARY: F187

φύσιν συμβαινόντων, with the sarcastic (μικροπρεπῶς, 36) gloss that makes 'living in harmony' dependent on obtaining the 'indifferents' without meanness or shabbiness. Since the central bone of contention in this argument is τὰ κατὰ φύσιν, i.e. the 'indifferents' (with regard to τὸ τέλος), Wyttenbach's emendation ἀδιαφόρων (37) (the technical Stoic term) must be right.

Long and Sedley, *The Hellenistic Philosophers*, vol. 1.408–10, offer a different interpretation of this difficult passage.

D. (37–67)

The attack on Chrysippus, based on the Posidonian understanding of the cause of πάθη, is now widened to illustrate how Posidonius could break through not only the absurdities of Chrysippus' interpretation of the end, but also, by the same method, related ethical puzzles. This takes the form of quotation from Posidonius with commentary by Galen.

37–9 The previous quotation was perhaps enough to indicate the absurdity of Chrysippus' interpretation of the τέλος (37–9). But note that it is not the formulae of definition which are stressed, but how one *may attain* 'living in harmony with nature' (39f). Such an approach is very Posidonian, and fits exactly the method of enquiry through the πάθη (F187.4ff; F150; F30).

40–2 Galen improves the situation with another quotation, which he claims follows the previous one in Περὶ παθῶν. There is no reason to disbelieve this, and ταύτην (42) requires an antecedent. It must be Chrysippus' absurdity over the τέλος. So it was Posidonius who linked the method of explanation of τέλος with the following problems also. This is borne out by F30, F150.

42–5 Quotation: the recognition of the cause of πάθη not only solved (a) the end, but showed (b) the sources of distortion in regard to what is to be chosen and avoided (i.e. the problem of evil); (c) the modes of education; (d) the puzzles about the impulse that arises from πάθος: comm. on F150d.

The verbal aorists show that the four points are involved in the previous discussion (i.e. F187.4–13, 25–35).

Galen now comments on each in turn.

(a) 45–53 With regard to the τέλος, one is helped in understanding exactly (ἀκριβῶς, 48) what sort of thing it is 'to live in harmony with nature'. The man who lives by emotion, i.e. who follows the irrational and capricious (ἐμπλήκτῳ, as F168.12) aspect of the soul, does not live in harmony with nature; he who lives not emotionally, i.e. following the rational and divine aspect, does. This merely recapitulates 4–13.

(b) 53f The sources of corruption in choice and avoidance: F161.

(c) 54f The modes of education: F168.

(d) 55–9 The puzzles about the impulse from emotion: F162.

60–5 Galen expresses satisfaction with Posidonius' answers just given, and also with what came still next in Posidonius' exposition of all the causes of the difficulties encountered by Chrysippus, which Galen ran through at the end of the previous book (Bk IV). This is a reference back to F164 (esp. 22ff). So Galen decides to bring this discussion now to an end at this point. He adds however one more quotation from the immediate sequel in Περὶ παθῶν. The point is that 'progressors' (οἱ προκόπτοντες) are not distressed at the thought that great evils are with them, because they are carried to this belief (or condition, φέρονται . . . οὕτως), not by the irrational, but by the rational. This is the counterpart of (d) above. See F174, F164.22ff.

66f This sequence ends with F166, in which it is shown how Posidonius' explanation of the cause of emotions solves Chrysippus' difficulties about the abatement of emotion and the control of reason.

LOGIC

F188 Diogenes Laertius, VII.62

CONTENT

Posidonius defined dialectic as the science of what is true or false, or neither; Chrysippus said this was about what signifies and what is signified.

CONTEXT

This occurs in the second more detailed version of Stoic logic, which runs from 48ff (F42 Context). The account of dialectic begins at 55, and deals with language (φωνή) until 62. Immediately after our fragment Diogenes says: 'that is the kind of account given by the Stoics in their theory of language'. He then passes to the topic of τὰ πράγματα καὶ τὰ σημαινόμενα (63ff).

COMMENT

What is the relationship between the two definitions in content and authorship? 'Posidonius'' definition recurs at D.L. VII.42, that is, in the initial separate short summary of Stoic logic, and also at S.E. *Adv. Math.* XI.187. In both cases it is given as the Stoic definition without reference. We must therefore assume that it was or had become a standard Stoic definition, although Posidonius is named here. On the other hand 'Chrysippus'' version recurs, without naming, at D.L. VII.43 and at Sen. *Ep.* 89.17, also simply as Stoic. So the two versions are not in contrast but complementary. D.L. VII.42–3 shows how this is so. 'True, false or neither' is a definition of dialectic in the context of question-and-answer discussion, and is introduced to distinguish it from rhetoric (42), the other main section of Stoic logic.

'What signifies and what is signified' is a classification or division of the parts of dialectic: τὴν διαλεκτικὴν διαιρεῖσθαι εἴς τε τὸν περὶ τῶν σημαινομένων καὶ τῆς φωνῆς τόπον (D.L. VII.43; σημαίνοντα = φωνή; S.E. *Adv. Math.* VIII.11); *in duas partes dividitur, in verba et significationes* (Sen. *Ep.* 89.17; in the sentence before this, dialectic is distinguished from rhetoric by *inter respondentem et interrogantem discissa*; cf. D.L. VII.42 introducing the 'Posidonian' version).

Therefore τυγχάνει δ' αὕτη is not in contrast, but an additional clarification: 'And this...'; αὕτη may refer either to διαλεκτική or to ἐπιστήμη, or both. And the addition is the significant part of Diogenes' sentence in its context, because the two main species of dialectic having thus been established he can now say that he has dealt with the first, theory of language, and can pass on to the second, σημαινόμενα. There is no suggestion that either Posidonius or Chrysippus would not have agreed with both statements. Indeed for a Posidonian division into *vox* and *res* see F189 (i.e. πρᾶγμα = σημαινόμενον, D.L. VII.57, S.E. *Adv. Math.* VIII.12).

But why is Posidonius singled out for 'true, false or neither'? Perhaps the simplest explanation would be that Diogenes or his source, whether Diocles or another, himself used Posidonius as a source. But Chrysippus' interest in and development of σημαίνοντα καὶ σημαινόμενα was pronounced and obvious. Was Posidonius connected in some way with the other definition? What are true or false in Stoic logic are propositions (ἀξιώματα, 'statements'; D.L. VII.65, 68; S.E. *Adv. Math.* VIII.74; although this requires qualification, because Stoics also spoke of φαντασίαι as true or false: Frede, *Die Stoische Logik* 41; Kerferd, *Les Stoïciens et Leur Logique* 261). But what are neither? Diogenes immediately(VII.66, 68) defines this class as questions (ἐρωτήματα) and enquiries (πύσματα). This may merely refer to the dialectical method of question and answer; indeed in VII.42 we are told that it is because of

COMMENTARY: F189

this that Stoics also define dialectic as knowledge of what is true, false or neither (ὅθεν καὶ οὕτως αὐτὴν ὁρίζονται . . .) cf. VII.47. *fin.* Did Posidonius have a special interest in this 'neither'? He was certainly attracted to the dialectical method against Chrysippus (Galen, *De Plac. passim*); but also in the notorious controversy in mathematical logic, as to whether all propositions were theorems or problems, Posidonius went out of his way to argue that both were necessary: F195; and problems were enquiries based on the question form, as opposed to the categorical form of theorems. Cicero may have caught echoes of this in a garbled form in *Acad.* II.26, with *quaestio* and ἀπόδειξις (Kidd, 'Posidonius and Logic' 276, 281).

Without dialectic the wise man cannot be ἄπτωτος in argument, D.L. VII.47. One is reminded of Posidonius' simile of logic as bones and sinews of philosophy. It cannot be inferred from this fragment (as Theiler), that Posidonius wrote a book entitled Περὶ διαλεκτικῆς.

F189 Quintilian, *Institutio Oratoria* III.6.31–8

CONTENT

Posidonius classified *status* in rhetorical theory into two genera, *vox* and *res*, each of which was further subdivided.

CONTEXT

Quintilian devoted III.6 to the question of *status* (στάσις), that is, the crucial points of issue in a case where two opposing parties come to grips, or where the defendant makes a stand. After initial remarks on the instigator of the technical term (earlier than Hermagoras) (2f), elucidation of its reference (5ff), and of its relation to Aristotle's categories (23ff), he embarks on a historical review of theories with regard to the number and names of στάσεις. These are taken in order,

686

from theories of a single στάσις to theories of 8 (29–55). Posidonius is included in the group which recognises two στάσεις only (31–8). Q. then examines the main theories (Hermagoras) 56ff, and finishes with his own views (80ff).

COMMENT

The group

Whether Archedemus (1ff) refers to the Stoic Archedemus of Tarsus, or to a hellenistic rhetor of the same name is uncertain (Schmidt, *RE*, Supplb. XII (1970), 1388–92); but see T82 for Archedemus of Tarsus. Pamphilus (5) is still more uncertain; he cannot be the Pamphilus mentioned by Arist. *Rh.* 1400a 4, since that would be before the technical development of *status*; and there is nothing to link him to the 1st c. A.D. lexicographer of Alexandria (Wendel, *RE* XVIII.2, 349). Apollodorus of Pergamum (6) the teacher of Augustus, and Theodorus of Gadara, the teacher of Tiberius (7), headed two famous opposing schools of rhetoric, and Celsus Cornelius (12ff) was an encyclopaedist of the time of Tiberius. Since Quintilian castigated Apollodorus and Theodorus as unpractical theorists (v.13.59), he may have regarded this whole group as such.

Posidonius' theory

A. The generic classification

The classification of στάσεις into *vox* and *res* (7f) must be linked to the Stoic division of dialectic into φωνή and πράγματα (F188, comm.; D.L. VII.55–63ff). Rhetoric was a part of Stoic logic like dialectic, and Posidonius probably imported terms and classifications from the latter to the former (cf. Kroll, *RE*, Supplb. VII.1084). But what is the reference of these terms within the province of rhetoric? *vox* (φωνή) must refer to language, i.e. to the contest over words

COMMENTARY: F189

and phrases. *res* (πράγματα), on the Stoic analogy, must refer to what is signified (πρᾶγμα = σημαινόμενον, D.L. VII.57; S.E. *Adv. Math.* VIII.12; F188 comm.).

But there is another factor: a result of this classification (*unde*, 11) is another division of *scripta* and *inscripta*. Again on Stoic analogy, *inscripta* should refer to *res*, and *scripta* to *vox*; so *vox* must mean: the written law, the letter of the law. This is confirmed by Quint. III.5.4: all questions depend on (a) what is written, (b) what is not written. (a) are questions of legality (*de iure*, νομικόν); (b) are questions of fact etc. (*de re*, λογικόν). The terminology comes from Hermagoras; but Quintilian adds that those who make all questions relate to *res* and *verba* are of the same opinion. Cf. for Quintilian himself on this division, III.86ff.

B. The subdivisions

These remain in part obscure through lack of further evidence.

(*a*) *vox*, φωνή

(i) **an significet**; i.e. whether it is σημαντικόν or ἄσημος (D.L. VII.57; *SVF* II.149); in written law, presumably whether it applies or not.

(ii) **quid, τί**: what is its meaning (*quid significet*); perhaps definition of the words or legal expressions (cf. III.6 89).

(iii) **quam multa, πόσα**: perhaps covering πολυώνυμα, τὰ πολλὰ ἅμα ἔχοντα ὀνόματα (*SVF* II.150; i.e. ambiguity, ἀμφιβολία (D.L. VII.62); or perhaps referring to the extent of the law, or to the number of different laws, cf. III.6.87, and for *quam multa* referred to Arist. (*Rh.* 1416b 21?), III.6.49). Quintilian himself (III.6.90) put *quam multa* under *coniectura*, as having no connection with the complexities of the law.

(iv) **quo modo, πῶς**: in language one might think of etymology, analogy and anomaly; but perhaps in connection with written law, how the law is expressed, or how it is applied; cf. III.6.87. Quintilian earlier (III.6.23ff) had

COMMENTARY: F190

remarked that the στάσεις were often related to Aristotle's categories, and Posidonius may have been so influenced. This introduction of *significatio* into the classification of rhetorical στάσις theory seems to be peculiarly Posidonian.

(*b*) *res*, πράγματα

(i) **coniectura, στάσις στοχαστική**: refers to when the fact itself is at issue. Quintilian exemplifies this in III.6.5: 'You did it'; 'I did not'; 'Did he do it?'. Posidonius suggests that this category is κατ' αἴσθησιν, i.e. depends on sense-perception. For Posidonius and conjecture: T88.

(ii) **qualitas et finitio, ποιότης καὶ ὁρικὴ στάσις**: *et*/καί is explanatory. This refers to questions of definition of the fact, explained at III.6.5: 'You did this'; 'I did not do this'; 'What did he do?'. Posidonius claims that this is κατ' ἔννοιαν, i.e. conceptual.

(iii) **ad aliquid, πρός τι**: relation. For this cf. III.6.23 under which heading Quintilian lists *translatio* and *comparatio*. *Comparatio* deals with questions of relative terms: better/worse; greater/less. *Translatio* deals with whether the charge is competent or should be transferred (III.6.68ff, 84–6).

Posidonius' theory may have been an attack on Hermagoras (cf. F43), who was the most famous exponent of στάσις theory before his time (Kennedy, *The Art of Persuasion in Greece* 307f; Matthes, 'Hermagoras von Temnos', *Lustrum* 3 (1958), 58–214). Posidonius attacked him publicly on the question of θέσεις, F43.

F190   Galen, *De Causis Contentivis* 2.1–2

CONTENT

Athenaeus of Attaleia, the founder of the Pneumatist medical School, naturally spoke of a cohesive (*coniuncta*) cause in illness, as he based himself on the Stoic School, for he was a

689

COMMENTARY: F190

disciple of Posidonius. Athenaeus listed three primary causes: *coniunctae, antecedentes, procartarcticae*.

CONTEXT

Galen begins the introductory chapter of *De Caus. Cont.* with the claim that the first philosophers to speak of cohesive causes were the Stoics (1.1). Galen gives a physical explanation of this from Stoic physics, distinguishing in the elements fire and air as active and of fine parts (1.2), and so arriving at what the Stoics call *spiritus* (πνεῦμα) (1.3). The function of πνεῦμα is to produce cohesion (*continere*) in natural and animate bodies, and this is a cohesive cause (1.3-5). After the fragment as given (2.1-2), Galen explains Athenaeus' three causes (2.3), and gives a practical medical illustration of them (2.4-5). At 3.1 Galen turns to his own view.

COMMENT

Galen's work survives only in an Arabic version from Ḥunain ibu Isḥāq and a Latin translation from Nicolaus of Rhegium (14th c.). Both are to be found in *CMG Suppl. Or.* II; they corroborate and supplement each other satisfactorily.

1-4 See T51 for the date of Athenaeus and his relationship to Posidonius. The first sentence establishes that Athenaeus took over from Posidonius' Stoic philosophy the concept of *coniuncta causa* as the most important theory of cause.

8-12 Although Galen does not say so explicitly, it is highly probable that Athenaeus' three causes also derive from Posidonius. The Latin (and Arabic) terms are easily identifiable in Stoic Greek: *coniuncta* = αἴτιον συνεκτικόν; *antecedens* = προηγούμενον; *procatarctica* = προκαταρκτικόν.

COMMENTARY: F190

The classification

Stoic analysis of cause tended to vary according to what they were talking about. In the ultimate sphere of Stoic physical philosophy they recognised only one cause (Sen. *Ep.* 65.4; F95), the active enforming force of πνεῦμα/λόγος, which was the cause of what a thing was and how it behaved; this is the αἴτιον συνεκτικόν (cf. Frede, 'The Original Notion of Cause', *Doubt and Dogmatism* 243-9). But in the complexity of particular problems they elaborated with distinctions. For example in the question of determinism and responsibility, they distinguished usually two types: αὐτοτελής and προκαταρκτική in Plu. *De SR* 1056Bff, or the parallel classification in Cic. *De Fato* 41-4, *perfectae et principales* and *adiuvantes et proximae*. αὐτοτελές is simply another label for συνεκτικόν (Clem. Alex. *Strom.* VIII.9, *SVF* II.346, 351), so called because it is capable of producing the effect of itself independently (Clem. Alex. *SVF* II.351), and thus distinguished from the other type, which is merely initiatory (προκαταρκτικόν; for the term, Frede, 'The Original Notion of Cause' 243 n. 6; *proxima*) antecedent (*antecedens*) or assisting (*adiuvans*) cause. But in particular cases, sciences and arts, further elaboration was possible, not with the first cause (συνεκτικόν/αὐτοτελές) which remained the same and single as the perfect and principal cause (*perfecta et principalis*, and cf. F95), but with the secondary causes, so that there is evidence of two triple classifications. In one, Cicero's *adiuvantes* is subdivided into συναίτιον and συνεργόν (Galen, *Def. Med.* XIX.392f K; Clem. Alex. *SVF* II.351; Ps.-Gal. *Hist. Phil.* 19; S.E. *Hyp.* III.15. For this classification, Frede, 'The Original Notion of Cause' 237-41). In the other (as here, and in Gal. *Def. Med.* XIX.392f) the subsidiary antecedent, initiatory (*proxima*) cause is subdivided as προκαταρκτικόν and προηγούμενον (cf. Frede, 241).

Galen, *De Caus. Cont.* 2.3-5 illustrates how this works in the case of disease. The procatarctic is an external antecedent

COMMENTARY: F191

cause such as excessive heat from the sun. This may affect certain internal physical components such as the humours (χυμοί) in our bodies, the condition of which may be a predisposing cause (προηγούμενον) for disease. But the real cause is the συνεκτικὸν πνεῦμα of the individual which may or may not be affected by these preconditions.

προκαταρκτική and προηγουμένη became technical labels in medical pathology for predisposing causes, but there is a high probability that they came from Posidonius. It was Posidonius who was noted for his interest in intermediate and immediate causation in actual explanation in the sciences and particular phenomena, for which indeed he was contrasted with other Stoics who confined themselves predominantly to the ultimate cause; T85; F49.36of; F165.75–102 comm; F176; Kidd, *Problems* 210ff, *Antike und Abendland* XXIV (1978), 14ff; Frede, 'The Original Notion of Cause' 224f. It seems likely that Posidonius, with his attested involvement in the sciences, should also have had a philosophical interest (cf. F18) in such a major science as medicine with its long historical connection and parallels with philosophy. His stress on φυσιογνωμονία (F169.84 comm.) is partial evidence of this.

See also T112–14; F170.

F191 Galen, *Institutio Logica* XVIII.1–8

CONTENT

Posidonius said that the validity of relational syllogisms was due to the implied force of an axiom.

CONTEXT

Galen's treatment of relational syllogisms begins at *Inst. Log.* XVI and culminates with this fragment. Galen starts with

COMMENTARY: F191

mathematical examples, twice as much as, half as much as, and suggests that what they have in common is 'the fact that they have the cause of their structure derived from certain axioms'. What he means is: if A equals B and B equals C, A equals C because 'things equal to the same thing are also equal to one another', which he argues is the base of Euclid's first theorem. The field is widened to cover all syllogisms involving relation, including 'more' and 'better'. After some more general remarks in xvii, he returns to relational syllogisms in xviii.

COMMENT

Analysis of argument of XVIII

1-5 Relational syllogisms include syllogisms of proportion such as 'likewise', 'equally', 'similarly'. So one must enquire whether the validity (πίστις) of these too is derived from some universal axioms (ἐκ τῶν καθόλου τινῶν ἀξιωμάτων); they are all in the same case.

5-7 (§2-4) The type of argument is illustrated from Pl. *Rep.*

7-12 The form and validity of the argument can be most clearly and naturally demonstrated mathematically.

12-15 So when A:B::C:D, then if A is double B, C is double D etc.

15-18 But in arguments of this kind as well everyone understands and believes a general axiom: things which are in general in the same ratio, are also in the same particular ratio.

18-29 This is further illustrated.

29-32 Conclusion (and this is the conclusion of the whole argument on relational syllogisms): So any species of the genus relational syllogism 'is constructed by the implied force of an axiom (κατ' ἀξιώματος δύναμιν συνισταμένους), as Posidonius too says that he calls them conclusive (valid, συνακτικούς) by the implied force of an axiom'.

693

COMMENTARY: F191

The Posidonian contribution

The Posidonian reference is confined to the last four words: συνακτικούς κατὰ δύναμιν ἀξιώματος. But it is evident from the review of Galen's argument from XVI, that they form the core of his logical theory of relational syllogisms, and even in nomenclature embody the conclusion of the whole argument. Nor is Galen foisting his own language on Posidonius, because ὀνομάζειν (32) should mean that Posidonius used those particular words. It seems inescapable that Posidonius examined the logical base of relational syllogisms. Since there is no other trace of this in the rich remains of Stoic logic, Posidonius may have been the first to do so.

Since Posidonius' phrase is guaranteed by Galen, it is worth examining in detail.

ἀξίωμα in Stoic logic meant 'proposition' or 'statement', but not so here. Galen himself, anxious to avoid confusion, says so twice (*Inst. Log.* 1.5; XVII.7): 'Stoics use the word ἀξίωμα for any proposition; in this context it means a proposition which is self-evident, that carries conviction of itself to the intellect.' This ἀξίωμα is the mathematical use of axiom. It is exactly paralleled by Proclus, *In Euclid. Elem.* 76 (Friedlein), classifying Euclid's ἀρχαί. Axiom (ἀξίωμα, κοιναὶ ἔννοιαι in Euclid) is distinguished from hypothesis and postulate (αἴτημα), defined as something both known to the learner and credible in itself, and exampled by 'things equal to the same things are equal to each other'. Proclus, too (77.3 F), remarks that this is a different use of axiom from the Stoic usage for any proposition. Incidentally, Posidonius is named in the section immediately following in Proclus' Commentary (F195), and elsewhere to some purpose (Frs. 46, 47, 196, 197, 198), and one of Proclus' most frequent authorities is Geminus (T42), so Posidonian influence there too is possible. So Posidonius' ἀξίωμα that validates these syllogisms is an axiom in the mathematical–logical sense, and indeed of the form that Galen has: 'things equal to the same thing are equal

COMMENTARY: F191

to one another' or 'things which are in general in the same ratio, are also in the same particular ratio'.

κατὰ δύναμιν is usually translated 'by force of'. But there is more at stake here, as a controversy illuminated by Alexander of Aphrodisias (*In Anal. Pr.* 21.28ff Wallies) shows. Alexander takes as his base Aristotle's definition of syllogism (*A. Pr.* 24b 18ff) as consequence following from premisses without anything further requiring to be added to make the consequence necessary, and criticises the Stoics in general (*SVF* II.260) for holding that relational syllogisms 'A is greater than . . .', 'A is equal to . . .' are syllogisms. For, he argues, they can only become syllogisms if (e.g.) 'things equal to the same thing are equal to each other' is added expressly as a premiss. But according to Galen's argument, this is expressly what Posidonius was denying. Their theory maintained that the validity of the syllogisms depends on an implied axiom in the mathematical sense, which we all accept and which does not require to be expressed or included in the structure of the syllogism. That is, there are a number of universal axioms, necessarily accepted as self-evident, on which the logical validity of such syllogistic argument depends, in the same way as mathematical proof depends on a set of self-evident axioms. So κατὰ δύναμιν ἀξιώματος must mean: by the implied force of an axiom; and it is such implied axioms which validate (συνακτικούς) these syllogisms.

This theory is also of some importance for Posidonius' logic of mathematics, because his position is confirmed in his logical defence of an axiomatic mathematics against Epicurean empirical theory in Frs. 46, 47. It may be such crucial links between logic and mathematics which led Galen to admire Posidonius as the most scientific of the Stoics because of his training in mathematics (T83, T84). The evidence suggests that such axiomatic methodology was fundamental to his whole philosophy (see Kidd, 'Posidonius and Logic', *Les Stoïciens et leur logique* 273–83).

One may suspect, but cannot prove, that more of Posido-

COMMENTARY: F192

nius underlies other sections of the *Institutio Logica*. Above all, the detailed examples used by Galen in chs. XII and XIII are surprising, but all remarkable as topics especially associated with Posidonius. Again in XI, Galen's emphasis on ἔνδειξις recalls F156, but nothing else in the Stoa. Also for the treatment of the conjunctive in IV: Brunschwig, *Les Stoïciens* 75, and F45 comm., and in general cf. Kieffer, *Galen's Institutio Logica* 28–30.

F192   Apollonius Dyscolus, *De Constructione* IV.65, p. 487.3ff Uhlig

CONTENT

The causal particle ἐπεί is a synthesis of the conjunction εἰ and the preposition ἐπί.

CONTEXT

Apollonius considers (*Synt.* IV.64, 486.6ff Uhlig) the construction of prepositions (προθέσεις) with adverbs (ἐπιρρήματα), forming words like ἐπάνω, περικύκλῳ, ὑποκάτω, ἀποδίς, ἀποψέ. Earlier treatment has been inadequate. Are ἀποψέ and the like two parts of speech by juxtaposition (παράθεσις), or one by σύνθεσις?

COMMENT

A. Authorship

This fragment links closely with F45. Both have often been assigned to a different Posidonius, called 'Aristarchus' reciter' by Eustathius (T109). But see F45 comm. for arguments that Posidonius of Apamea is meant, and T109 for the absurdity of assigning it to 'Aristarchus' reciter'.

COMMENTARY: F192

B. *Apollonius' framework*

1-8 Apollonius refers to his previous argument that prepositions only have meaning by juxtaposition (κατὰ παράθεσιν) when combined with their appropriate oblique cases. With indeclinables (ἄπτωτα) they form a single formation, i.e. by *synthesis*.

8-10 Therefore it is necessary to accept the same principle in the combination of prepositions with adverbs. Adverbs are indeclinable; therefore their formation with prepositions is a single part of speech by synthesis, not a juxtaposition of two parts of speech.

10-15 The phrase δι'ὅτι does not contradict this: διά is a preposition and ὅτι is not an indeclinable conjunction, but the neuter accusative of ὅστις. So δι' ὅτι is not a *syntheton* like the causal (παρασυναπτικός) particle ἐπεί, which is a synthesis of the conjunction εἰ and the preposition ἐπί, as Posidonius too says.

C. *Posidonius*

For Posidonius' interest in conjunctions and prepositions: F45 comm. It is argued there that he advocated an original semantic theory for the conjunctions, which formed the base of Stoic propositional logic. This is confirmed by this etymology of ἐπεί, which characterises one of the major conjunctive arguments of the Stoics, the παρασυνημμένον (e.g. D.L. VII.71).

The reference no doubt came from the Περὶ συνδεσμῶν (F45).

See T89 for Posidonius' use of etymology.

COMMENTARY: F193

F193 *Etymologicum Magnum, s.v.* Ὄψις

CONTENT

Posidonius derived the etymology of ὄψις (sight) from ἅψις (ἅπτω) in the sense of 'kindling'.

COMMENT

In the Posidonian derivation, ἅψις, ἅπτω must be taken as 'kindling' for two reasons. The first is the immediate explanation which is presumably Posidonian: 'light (φῶς) being a kind of ἅψις in shining on (ἐλλάμπουσα, see below) and illuminating (καταυγάζουσα, each of the underlying objects, like fire'. The second is that it is distinguished from the etymology of some others, who derive ὄψις from ἅπτω in the sense of συνάπτω (3f), i.e. 'contact' (ψαῦσιν). Posidonius presumably had Pl. *Tim.* 45b–46c in mind, where the general account of vision involves light as internal and external fire.

2 ἐμποιοῦσα codices, is unintelligible. Perhaps Posidonius had λάμπουσα (or ἐλλάμπουσα); compare Pl. *Phdr.* 250d 1, a passage referring to ὄψις, and a work well known to Posidonius; another alternative is ἐμφαίνουσα; cf. *Tim.* 46b 1. See Arist. *De Sensu* 437a 23ff for criticism of such theories. But the fiery metaphor of *Tim.* persisted; so Plu. *De Sera* 550D, clearly referring to the later passage, *Tim.* 47b 6: καὶ τὴν ὄψιν αὐτὸς οὗτος ἀνήρ (i.e. Plato) ἀνάψαι φησὶν τὴν φύσιν ἐν ἡμῖν ὅπως ... (*Tim.* actually says ἡμῖν ἀνευρεῖν δωρήσασθαί τε ὄψιν ...); but Tim. Locr. 50 also has ἀνάψαι of this passage.

It is interesting that Posidonius is contrasted with etymologies of contact (ψαῦσις), because the latter would be identified naturally with the Chrysippean Stoic theory of vision as ἀφὴ διὰ βακτηρίας, *SVF* II.864 (Alex. Aphr.).

This is further evidence of Posidonian interest in *Tim.*; see F85.

COMMENTARY: F194-5

For Posidonius' active engagement in etymology: Frs. 24, 102, 192, 233, 272, 277a, 280, and T89, and for the Platonic base of some of this, cf. F24, T89.

F194 Aetius, *Placita* IV.13.3 (Stobaeus, *Eclogae* 1.52.11 = 1.485.1 W; *Dox. Gr.* 403.12)

CONTENT

Posidonius calls sight a natural fusion of light rays.

COMMENT

This is another clear interpretation of Plato, *Tim.* 45cf (cf. F193 and F85). Plato used συμφυές (45d 5); cf. 45c 4: συμπαγὲς γενόμενον, ἓν σῶμα οἰκειωθὲν συνέστη κτλ. There is nothing original or controversial about this interpretation, but it was probably common ground with Academics and Stoics alike. The Academic Plutarch in *Q.C.* 1.8.4, 626c referring to this passage in *Tim.*, even describes the σύμφυσις in Stoic terms: ὥσθ' ἓν ἐξ ἀμφοῖν σῶμα δι' ὅλου συμπαθὲς γενέσθαι. But the Stobaeus doxography seems to indicate that some Academics envisaged a process (*Dox. Gr.* 403.8ff).

SCIENCES

F195 Proclus, *In Euclidis Elementa*, pp. 77.7–81.4 Friedlein

CONTENT

The methodology of mathematics involves both theorems

COMMENTARY: F195

and problems, which are distinguished both in content and form.

CONTEXT

Proclus discusses the general arrangement of the propositions in the *Elements* (75.5ff). The science of geometry is based ἐξ ὑποθέσεως and its procedure is ἀπὸ ἀρχῶν ὡρισμένων τὰ ἐφεξῆς ἀποδεικνύναι (76.6ff). So he distinguishes ἀρχαί from τὰ ἑπόμενα ταῖς ἀρχαῖς (75.27ff). The ἀρχαί, distinguished here in Aristotelian terms, are: (1) axiom (in Euclid, κοιναὶ ἔννοιαι); accepted as known by the learner and credible in itself; e.g. things equal to the same thing are equal to one another; (2) hypothesis (sometimes ὅροι, definitions); not self-evident, but conceded by the student to his teacher without demonstration; e.g. a circle is a figure of such and such a sort; (3) postulate; unknown, nevertheless taken as true without the student conceding it; e.g. that all right angles are equal. Often all these ἀρχαί are just called hypotheses, as Stoics call every simple statement an axiom (77.2). Having dealt with the classification of ἀρχαί, he turns to the classification of what follows from them. He later distinguishes axioms and postulates in the same way as theorems and problems (178.9ff).

ANALYSIS

A. (1-5)

The distinction between problems and theorems. Euclid divides the things that follow from the *archai* into problems and theorems.

Problems (τὰ μέν, 2-4) comprise the constructing of figures, sections of figures, subtractions or additions to figures, and in general the characters that result from such procedures.

Theorems (τὰ δέ, 4f) demonstrate inherent properties belonging to each figure.

In the omitted lines we are told that the productive (ποιητικαί) sciences have some theory in them, while the theoretical sciences take on problems analogous to production.

B. (5-25)

A historical review of the controversy as to whether propositions were theorems or problems; cf. also Proclus, 201.

(a) 5-9 Some of the ancients, like the followers of Speusippus and Amphinomus (possibly a contemporary of Speusippus) thought it right to call all propositions theorems. Their reason was that the appellation 'theorem' is more proper for theoretical sciences than 'problems', especially since these sciences deal with eternal objects. So there is no 'coming to be' or construction of what did not previously exist; if there is any construction, it is not for making but for understanding how they exist. That is, all propositions have a theoretical not a practical import.

This is clearly a Platonist view of mathematics.

(b) 10f The mathematicians connected with Menaechmus (4th-c. B.C. pupil of Eudoxus and Plato; Heath, *A History of Greek Mathematics* 1.251ff) held that all propositions are problems. But problems are two-fold in character, i.e. are directed to two different objects: sometimes to provide something sought for, sometimes with regard to a determinate, to find out what sort it is, what quality it has, what relation it bears to something else.

In the gap (78.10–80.15), Proclus argues that both of these views are in a way right; Speusippus, because problems of geometry are different from those of mechanics, Menaechmus because discovery of theorems does not occur without recourse to matter (i.e. intelligible matter). So there are both geometrical problems and theorems. But theory is predominant: every problem has also some theory in it, but the reverse is not true. All the propositions in geometry after the first principles are obtained by demonstration, so 'theorem' is

COMMENTARY: F195

the more general term. Also not all theorems require the assistance of problems. Another distinction put forward is that every problem admits antithetical predicates in its matter, the attribute sought and its opposite, while theorem admits only a given attribute, not its antithesis also. So when it is proposed to inscribe an equilateral triangle in a circle, that is a problem, for it is possible to inscribe a triangle that is not equilateral. But proving the angles at the base of an isosceles triangle equal is a theorem, because it is not possible that they should not be equal. So if anyone proposed as a problem, to inscribe a right angle in a semicircle, he would reveal his ignorance of geometry. So all cases in which the property is universal, i.e. co-extensive with the whole of the matter, must be called theorems; but whenever the character is not universal, i.e. does not belong to the whole genus of the subject, then we are dealing with a problem.

All this is introductory to the remainder of the historical section.

(c) **12–16** Zenodotus (and his adherents) who was familiar with the teaching of Oenopides (of Chios, mid-5th c. B.C.), although he was one of the pupils of Andron, would distinguish theorem and problem. Theorem seeks what is the property (σύμπτωμα) predicated (κατηγορούμενον) of the matter in it; a problem asks the question, what is the condition for something to exist.

Zenodotus and Andron are otherwise unknown. Diels, *Die Fragmente der Vorsokratiker*, printed this under Oenopides (41.12; 1.395.6ff; cf. 1.388.8 and v. Fritz, *RE* s.n.). Tannery (*La Géométrie grecque* 89 n.1) wanted to place Zenodotus and Andron much later than Oenopides, but this is by no means certain. There is a μέν/δέ antithesis between Oenopides and Andron; the relevance of Oenopides may be that he was known to be interested in the theory of mathematical constructions (Szabó, *Beginnings of Greek Mathematics* 273ff; Heath, *History of Greek Mathematics* 1.175).

The definition of theorem is clear; cf. Proclus, 201.13 for

COMMENTARY: F195

σύμπτωμα as a subject of theorems. In the description of problem, we should more properly read: τίνος ὄντος τι ἐστίν: what is the condition for something to exist. This fits in with what follows (ὅθεν, 16), 17–18.

(d) 16–25 'Hence (ὅθεν) Posidonius and his adherents distinguished on the one hand a mathematical proposition by which what is investigated is whether a thing exists or not, and on the other hand one in which it is sought what or what sort of thing it is.'

πρότασις in mathematics means the enunciation of a mathematical proposition, question or problem.

In the second of the alternatives given, the codices have τὸ δὲ πρόβλημα πρότασιν (18). Tannery (*Mémoires scientifiques* IX.126) pointed out that the content of the first type of proposition, whether a thing exists or not, should apply to problems (cf. Proclus, 201.3ff, a passage, incidentally, in the middle of the Posidonius–Zeno controversy of Frs. 46, 47. Compare also the passage above (Proclus, 79) on the antithetical attributes of problems). Since, then, the second type of mathematical proposition must designate theorems, πρόβλημα is a false marginal insertion. I would be inclined to cut both πρόβλημα and πρότασιν.

19ff 'And they said that the theoretical proposition ought to be put in categorical form; e.g. every triangle has two sides greater than the remaining one; or, the angles at the base of every isosceles triangle are equal. But we must form the 'problematic' proposition as if it were an enquiry (ὥσπερ ζητοῦντας); e.g. is it possible on this given straight line to construct a triangle? For they said there is a difference between (a) enquiring (ζητεῖν) simply and in an undefined way whether it is possible to erect a perpendicular to a given line at a given point (i.e. a problem) and (b) contemplating (θεωρεῖν) what the perpendicular is (i.e. the nature of the perpendicular, a theorem).'

COMMENT

It would be interesting to know how much of this fragment comes from Posidonius. Introductory historical doxographies to problems seem to have been characteristic of him, and the beginnings of this one are traced to the Academy and early contemporary mathematical theory on the foundations of mathematics. And the reference to the otherwise obscure Zenodotus could also derive from him, as the Posidonian theory is linked (ὅθεν) to him. It is likely, however, that Proclus had all this filtered through Geminus. Proclus not only cites the latter frequently, but he is explicitly tied to this controversy. For later at 241.18ff, Proclus returns to the comparison of problems and theorems with Carpus of Antioch (called, 'the engineer'). Carpus held that problems are prior in rank to theorems. But Proclus says (243.21ff) that it is frivolous to criticise Geminus for saying that a theorem is more perfect than a problem. Geminus' position was also clearly the one held by Posidonius. It is quite possible that Posidonius, with his interest in the foundations of mathematics, resuscitated, if he did not inaugurate, this whole debate. Tannery argued that the terms of the controversy were comparatively late (*La Géométrie grecque* 144ff).

The expression of content distinguishing theorem and problem (17–18) shows the characteristic Posidonian relationship and overlap between the foundations of a science and natural philosophy (cf. F18). But the most interesting exposition of distinction is by dialectical form (19–23): theorem is expressed as a proposition; problem as a question. This suggests a derivation from Posidonian dialectic (rather than supposed Posidonian theology in Cic. *ND* II, as Theiler). For Posidonius defined dialectic as the science of true or false, or neither (F188, comm.). What are true or false are propositions (ἀξιώματα); 'neither' is clarified by D.L. vii.66, 68 as πύσματα and ἐρωτήματα. Compare *quaestio* and ἀπόδειξις in Cic. *Acad.* II.26, and Kidd, 'Posidonius and

COMMENTARY: F196

Logic', 276, 281. For Posidonius' interest in the logical base of mathematical methodology: Frs. 46, 47.

T45 comm. discusses the phrase οἱ περὶ τὸν Π.

F196 Proclus, *In Euclidis Elementa*, pp. 143.5–144.5 Friedlein

CONTENT

Definition of 'figure', and comparison with Euclid.

CONTEXT

The subject is Euclid, *Def.* xiv (136.18ff Fr.): 'A figure is that which is contained by any boundary or boundaries'. Proclus' lengthy commentary includes a reference to τὸ δημιουργικὸν καὶ οὐσιῶδες σχῆμα τῶν ψυχῶν of Pl. *Tim.* 36bff, followed by some general Neoplatonic discussion on the metaphysical importance of σχῆμα κατὰ τὸ Πυθαγόρειον ἀρέσκον (142.8). He then turns to Euclid as geometer.

ANALYSIS

A. (1–14)

The definitions of figure by Euclid and Posidonius are compared.

1–3 'So Euclid, calling figure the figured and that which involves matter (τὸ ἔνυλον) and coexists with quantity (τῷ ποσῷ), naturally designated it as what is contained.

3–6 Posidonius defines shape as enclosing limit, separating the definition (λόγος) of figure from quantity and making it cause (αἴτιον) of determination, limitation and containing.

6–14 For that which encloses is different from what is enclosed, and limit from what is limited.

705

COMMENTARY: F196

It seems somehow that the one (Posidonius) is concentrating on the outer enclosing boundary, the other (Euclid) on the whole of the object. So one (Euclid) will say that the circle is a figure by virtue of the whole plane surface and the outer circuit, the other (Posidonius) by virtue of the circumference. Euclid shows he is defining that which is shaped and investigated with its substratum, Posidonius that he wishes to exhibit the definition of shape itself, that which is limiting and enclosing quantity.'

B. (16–22)

An objection to Euclid's definition is answered.

The criticism of Euclid is that his definition defines genus by species, and this is countered by arguing that genera have presupposed the δυνάμεις of their species.

At first sight the counter-argument smacks of Posidonius; cf. his arguments against Zeno of Sidon in F47. But it is unlikely that Posidonius would be arguing for Euclid. It is also unlikely that the objection to Euclid comes from Posidonius, for Proclus would hardly refer to him as τις λογικὸς ἀνὴρ καὶ κομψός. So this pendent probably comes from Proclus, although he might have got the idea of the counter argument from Posidonius.

18 κατὰ γένη codices. But Grynaeus is probably right to suggest καὶ τὰ γένη; a possible alternative might be αὐτὰ τὰ γένη, Kidd.

COMMENT

The definition seems original with Posidonius. If he remembered Pl. *Meno* 76a 7, στερεοῦ πέρας σχῆμα εἶναι (cf. Bréhier, *REG* 27 (1914), 56), it is no more than reminiscence, for his own definition is Stoic-orientated. It is still unorthodox, because other Stoics, following the Aristotelian protest (*Top.* 141b 15ff), clearly alluded, when defining σχῆμα, to the whole figure: what is contained as well as the container, e.g. *SVF* II.383, 456, 455.

COMMENTARY: F197

This preoccupation with limits is also instanced by his definition of plane surface (ἐπιφάνεια) as limit of body (F16). But these mathematical concepts have close links with his natural philosophy. So limits exist in reality and are substantial (F16, F92), again against Aristotle (*Met.* 1090b 5). So Proclus is at least misleading when he suggests that Posidonius separated the definition of figure from quantity (4f). Also limit is now a generating cause (cf. Laffranque, 265ff). The *logos*, rational explanation or definition is sought in that which causes (another Stoic concept of λόγος), or that which imposes limit rather than what is limited; in the case of figure, that which causes determination, limitation and containment. Compare explanation in terms of λόγος and the αἴτιον συνεκτικόν as a bridge between logic and physics in F190. Consonant also is Posidonius' interest in the Stoic idea of soul containing body (F149; although not, of course, containing in the sense of an enveloping limit); and that he translates his comments on Plato's definition of soul in *Tim.* 35a,b into mathematical terms including limits and mathematical form (F141).

For theories arising out of this concept of limit, see esp. commentary on F16, F141.

Posidonius' definition of figure survives in Hero of Alexandria, *Def.* 23, IV.30.10 Heiberg, as an alternative definition after the usual one: λέγεται δὲ ἄλλως σχῆμα πέρας συγκλεῖον ἀπὸ τοῦ συσχηματίζοντος. The definition in Aet. *Dox. Gr.*, 312a 9f, b 12f *includes* πέρας σώματος with ἐπιφάνεια and περιγραφή.

F197 Proclus, *In Euclidis Elementa,*
p. 176.5–17 Friedlein

CONTENT

A new definition of parallel lines against Euclid.

707

COMMENTARY: F197

CONTEXT

Proclus comments on Euclid, *Def.* xxxv (*Def.* xxiii Heiberg): Parallel straight lines are straight lines which, being in the same plane and being produced indefinitely in both directions, do not meet one another in either direction. After the Posidonius fragment, Proclus protests (176.18ff) against Euclid's definition, that the absence of intersection does not always make lines parallel, and cites Geminus (176.25ff) for instances of this. He ends his comments on this Definition (and it is also the end of Bk II *On Definitions*) with: 'So much I have selected from Geminus' *Philokalia* to expound the subject before us' (177.24f).

POSIDONIUS' DEFINITION

'Posidonius says that parallel lines are lines that neither converge nor diverge on a single plane, but have all the perpendiculars equal that are drawn from points on the one line to the other. Any lines that keep causing the perpendiculars (between them) to get shorter, converge on each other. For the perpendicular can determine (ὁρίζειν) the heights of figures and the distances between lines. For this reason, when the perpendiculars are equal, the distances between the lines are equal; when they become greater or less, so the distance lessens and they converge on each other, on the side (parts, μέρη) on which the perpendiculars are shorter.'

COMMENT

The contentious base on which Euclid's definition of parallel lines relies is the notorious fifth postulate: 'that, if a straight line falling on two straight lines make the interior angles on the same side less than two right angles, the two straight lines, if produced indefinitely, meet on that side on which are the angles less than two right angles'. It seems that the definition and theory of parallels had early caused trouble, for Aristotle (*A. Pr.* 65a 4) had already accused a theory (probably a direction theory) of petitio principii. Hence Euclid based a non-intersection definition of parallel lines on a postulate of converging lines intersecting. But the work of Apollonius of Perge on conics and the hyperbola, and of Nicomedes on conchoids, raised the problem of asymptotic lines, so that the mere absence of intersection does not always make lines parallel. This is the burden of Geminus' criticism in 176.18ff, and no doubt also from Posidonius.

But the other question which troubled the ancients was what requires proof and what does not. This is immediately raised by Proclus at the beginning of the next book (III), on postulates and axioms (178ff), relying heavily still on Geminus. A postulate, he says, like an axiom, is an undemonstrated starting point; but while an axiom is known and indemonstrable, a postulate is merely assumed and not accepted without reservation. So the question arises, as with Aristotle, whether a postulate may be demonstrable. This is examined in the light of Euclid's fifth postulate (182.25ff). So Geminus said that as it is futile to try to prove the indemonstrable, like Apollonius trying to prove axioms, so it is incorrect to assume what requires proof, like Euclid's fifth postulate (183.11ff). So Geminus attempted to prove the postulate (Heath, *A History of Greek Mathematics* II.227ff for details). Geminus was followed by other attempts at proof by Ptolemy and Proclus himself (cf. 191.21ff). Al-Nayrīzī preserves an attempted proof, based on the equidistance theory, by the philosopher Aghānīs (Agapius? see Sabra, *Dictionary of Scientific Biography* x.6) which was very influential on subsequent attempts at proof in Islam. The argument continued into modern times; cf. Ivor Thomas, *Greek Mathematical Works*, Loeb, vol. 1, 442f, n. c; and Cassirer, *The Problem of Knowledge* 23, refers to Leibniz's attack on geometric intuition precisely by rejecting the fifth postulate.

There is no evidence that Posidonius made any attempt,

COMMENTARY: F198

like Geminus, to prove the fifth postulate. Instead, he offered a different kind of definition of parallel lines. By substituting for Euclid's non-intersection theory, an equidistance theory of parallels, he was able to evade the difficulty of the fifth postulate. So this may be a case where Posidonius and Geminus differed. Nevertheless, that he did so redefine shows his unease with the fifth postulate, and is further evidence of his interest in the fundamental principles of mathematics and its methodology, in what was demonstrable and what was not; cf. Frs. 46, 47.

Posidonius' definition of parallel lines was adopted by Hero of Alexandria, *Def.* 70, IV.48.5ff Heiberg. Compare the definition of σχῆμα, F196.

F198 Proclus, *In Euclidis Elementa*, pp. 169.10–171.4 Friedlein

CONTENT

Classification of quadrilaterals.

CONTEXT

On Definitions XXX–XXXIV (Def. XXII Heiberg), i.e. definitions of quadrilateral figures, square, oblong, rhombus, rhomboid, trapezia.

ANALYSIS AND COMMENT

1–3 First one ought to divide quadrilaterals into two sections:

COMMENTARY: F198

A   parallelograms   B   non-parallelograms

Λ. Parallelograms (3–10) (Fig. 16a–d)

(a)   Both right-angled and equilateral: squares

(b)   Neither right-angles nor equilateral: rhomboids

(c)   Right-angled but not equilateral: oblongs

(d)   Not right-angled but equilateral: rhombi

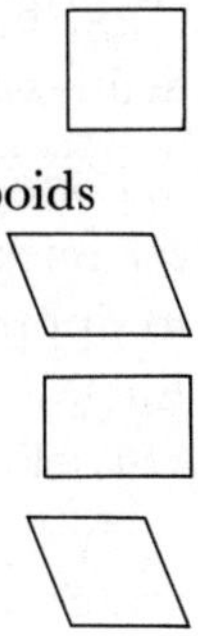

The general characteristics are summed up in 7–10.

B. Non-parallelograms (10–20)

only two sides parallel ⎫
and the other sides not ⎬ trapezia   no sides at all parallel: trapezoids

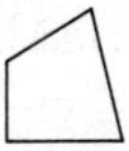

the sides joining the parallels   the sides joining the parallels
equal: isosceles trapezia   unequal: scalene trapezia

Fig. 16

Hence there is a seven-fold classification of quadrilaterals.

21–3 Posidonius has made a perfect (i.e. complete, τελείαν) division of rectilinear quadrilaterals positing these seven species, as he has done also for the triangle.

This seems to refer to p. 168.3ff Friedlein. Euclid had a six-fold division of triangles: equilateral, isosceles, scalene (i.e. based on sides); right-angled, obtuse-angled, acute-angled (based on angles). The seven-fold classification goes:

COMMENTARY: F199

(1) equilateral: one only and acute-angled;
(2, 3, 4) right-angled isosceles, obtuse-angled isosceles, acute-angled isosceles;
(5, 6, 7) right-angled scalene, obtuse-angled scalene, acute-angled scalene.

Posidonius is not named in this passage, but this must be the reference to which this fragment alludes. Proclus appears to approve of Posidonius' classification of triangles against Euclid. Compare Geminus' classification of lines, Proclus, 111.1ff.

24-7 Euclid could not make the division into parallelograms and non-parallelograms, because he had not spoken about parallel lines yet, nor instructed us about the parallelogram itself.

In fact Euclid's definition of quadrilaterals (XXII) is immediately followed by the definition of parallel lines (XXIII). It seems likely that Posidonius' interest in the problem of defining parallels (F197) led him to re-examine the classification of quadrilaterals, and achieve a more complete division than Euclid. It was approved by Proclus, and echoed in Hero of Alexandria, *Defs.* 51, 52, 53, 54, 61, 62, 63 (Frs. 196, 197 for other definitions adopted by Hero). Presumably Posidonius wished to reverse *Defs.* XXII and XXIII of Euclid.

It is most unlikely that the redefinition of quadrilaterals depends on it being hebdomadal, see F291.

See Laffranque, 256ff for speculation on Proclus' continuing remarks.

F199a Gerardus Cremonensis, *In Euclidis Opera*, Suppl. (Curtze), p. 3.23

CONTENT

Definition of point.

COMMENTARY: F199a

CONTEXT

Gerard of Cremona (*Dictionary of Scientific Biography*, Suppl. 1.173ff), the 12th-c. translator of Arabic versions of Greek science, is here translating Al-Nayrīzī's (turn of the 9/10 c.) commentary on Euclid's *Elements*. Al-Nayrīzī used extensively commentaries by Hero of Alexandria and Simplicius on the *Elements*. The comments are on Euclid, *Def.* 1: *punctum est quod partem non habet*. At p. 3.17 he adds, *praeter hanc vero multe alie diffinitiones puncto attribute fuerunt*. He gives one under the unknown name 'Herundes', and another under 'Aposedanius'.

COMMENT

The name

Names from Arabic are prone to confusion. Simplicius, for example, is rendered as Sambelichius. Aposedanius may represent the article written with the proper name as al or a. Tannery, *Mémoires scientifiques* III.40, could well be right in restoring Posidonius.

The definition

'Point is limit (extremity, *extremitas*, πέρας) without dimension, or the limit of line.'

This is Stoic, and probably Posidonian, because D.L. VII.135, immediately after F16, defines line and then: στιγμὴ δ' ἐστὶ γραμμῆς πέρας, ἥτις ἐστὶ σημεῖον ἐλάχιστον. The whole section of Diogenes is very Posidonian. Did Posidonius here consciously look back to Plato? Cf. *Meno* 75d–76a. And Aristotle, *Top.* 141b 19–22 criticised the method of those who define point as πέρας γραμμῆς as unscientific, very probably Plato or Platonists. Also Hero of Alexandria, who used other Posidonian definitions (F196, 197), includes this one in *Def.* 1:

σημεῖόν ἐστι, οὗ μέρος οὐθὲν ἢ πέρας ἀδιάστατον ἢ πέρας γραμμῆς. Proclus too, commenting on Euclid, *Def.* III, the limits of a line are points, has: ὥσπερ οὖν ἡ δυὰς ἀπὸ τῆς μονάδας ὁρίζεται καὶ τὴν ἄσχετον ἑαυτῆς τόλμαν περατοῖ κρατουμένη παρ' ἐκείνης, οὕτω δὴ καὶ ἡ γραμμὴ τοῖς σημείοις ὁρίζεται (101.8–11) ... ὅθεν δὴ καὶ ἐν ταῖς εἰκόσι τὰ σημεῖα τὸ πέρας καὶ τὴν ἀρχὴν καταλαμβάνοντα τῆς γραμμῆς ὁρίζειν αὐτὴν λέγεται. Cf. Proclus, 89.10–15.

As Posidonius defined σχῆμα as that which gives shape to a figure (F196), did he also give a causal definition of point, as what limits line? If so, he would be recognising 'punctual existence' and substantiality, as he did with other limits like plane surface (F16; so Edelstein, *AJPh* 57 (1936), 302). But this is by no means certain; see F16 comm.

F199b   Hero, *Mechanica* 1.24
(= Archimedes, II.546.4)

CONTENT

Definition of centre of gravity

CONTEXT

Hero's *Mechanics* survives only in an Arabic translation (Nix–Schmidt, II.1, p. 63). At 1.24 Hero turns to the topic of gravity and centre of gravity. He says that one speaks of gravity only in relation to bodies. But if you speak of the centre of gravity in geometric figures being a certain point, Archimedes has sufficiently explained that. Then occurs a definition of centre of gravity from Posidonius a Stoic, after which Hero continues with Archimedes.

COMMENTARY: F199b

THE FRAGMENT

'Posidonius, a Stoic, determined the point of inclination (i.e. falling centre?) and the centre of gravity in a natural (physical?) definition, and said: the falling centre and centre of gravity (κέντρον τοῦ βάρους καὶ τῆς φορᾶς?) is a point such that if the weight (βάρος?) is suspended at it, it will be divided into two equal parts (i.e. in equilibrium).' The translation goes on to say that therefore Archimedes and his followers in mechanics made a distinction between suspension point and centre of gravity.

COMMENT

There are two problems about identification:

(1) There has been some doubt about the name in Arabic (Nix–Schmidt, *Praef.* xxif). Nix–Schmidt seem confident that it represents Posidonius, but further inspection of the MS is needed.

(2) The sentence after the fragment seems to imply ('Therefore . . .') that Archimedes followed Posidonius in time. If so, it cannot be Posidonius of Apamea; so Heath (*A History of Greek Mathematics* II.222) guessed that the reference was to Posidonius of Alexandria, the pupil of Zeno of Citium (cf. Duhem, *Les Origines de la statique* II.306). This seems a real difficulty unless 'therefore' (ὅθεν?) means, 'hence it is possible for us to see that . . .'. But this is specious. On the other hand, if Hero referred to a Stoic Posidonius, one would expect it to be the great Posidonius, especially when dealing with such topics. But since the earlier Posidonius also came from Alexandria, he should perhaps not be disregarded.

However, the ambiguities of this fragment are such that little weight can be put upon it. The whole section 1.24 is somewhat garbled, see Dijksterhuis, *Archimedes* 229f, and cf. Pappas, *Collectio* VIII.5, 1030. Indeed Drachmann (*Dictionary*

COMMENTARY: F200

of Scientific Biography VI.312) thinks that this section, unlike the rest of the *Mechanics*, has the same prolix and discursive style characteristic of the introduction to the *Pneumatics*, and so may be a summary intended for students who already know the subject. Hammer–Jensen, *Hermes* 63 (1928), 34.1 thought the Posidonian reference an Arabic interpolation.

MATHEMATICAL GEOGRAPHY

F200a,b Agathemerus, *Geographiae Informatio* 1.2; Eustathius, *Commentarii ad Homeri Iliadem* VII.446

CONTENT

A doxography on the shape of the habitable world, which ends with an entry on Posidonius, who compares it to the shape of a sling.

CONTEXT

The wretched Sketch of Geography of Agathemerus was written after Ptolemy, who is followed in some sections, but elsewhere it is a hotch-potch of disconnected superficial material culled from earlier sources, for example Artemidorus (for whom see T78). This passage is in the second section of the introduction on 'The geography of the ancients'. Since it comprises a list which ends with Posidonius, it may be taken from a doxography derived from Posidonius, or from a commentator or epitome based on him. Eustathius (12th c. A.D.) simply assigns the adjective σφενδονειδής to Posidonius and couples the name Dionysius with

716

COMMENTARY: F200

him. The reference is to Dionysius Periegetes, on whose poem Περιήγησις τῆς οἰκουμένης, of the time of Hadrian, Eustathius wrote a lengthy commentary (F201). The specific reference is to Dion. *Perieg.* 7, σφενδόνῃ ἐοικυῖα (Müller, *GGM* II.105). Here, however, Eustathius was using a doxography, and the contents suggest that it was from Agathemerus, or a common source. The involvement of Dionysius and Agathemerus shows that Posidonius was still regarded as a geographical authority in the 2nd c. A.D. at least.

COMMENT

The subject of the doxography is the shape of the habitable world as represented on a map (ἔγραφον, F200a.1), and should not be confused with spherical geography or geodesy.

The doxography is organised as a whole, showing development of theories which culminate in Posidonius. The first circular maps ('the ancients', F200a.1; Homer (Eustathius); Anaximander (D.L. II.1); Hecataeus (Schol. ad Dion. Perieg., *GGM* II.428); criticised by Hdt. IV.36 and by Arist. *Meteor.* 362b 12ff) were replaced by an elongated or oblong image (προμήκης: Democritus, Dicaearchus; 'length half as much again as the breadth', F200a.5; Arist. *Meteor.* 362b 20ff mentions a ratio greater than 5:3). Then we are told that Eudoxus made the length double the breadth, but Eratosthenes more than double (Thomson, *History of Ancient Geography* 165f; this continued an established assessment, Str. 1.4.5, Gem. *Isag.* XVI.3–5). The doxography continues with overall configural images of this general ratio: semicircular (Crates), trapezoid (Hipparchus), 'shaped like a tail' (οὐροειδής, anonymous; presumably refers to 'tailing off' at an extremity; cf. μύουρος, Str. XI.11.7); finally: 'Posidonius the Stoic said that it was shaped like a sling, that is, broad in the middle from south to north but narrowing to east and west, yet with the eastern part towards India broader.' Mette's πλατυτέρα⟨ν τὰ⟩ is also possible.

717

COMMENTARY: F201

Posidonius' image is clear enough, and has an instructive additional detail. For the broader eastern end of the sling in India probably refers to his reorientation of that continent to a north–south axis, thereby widening the extremity of the map (F212).

The interesting thing about Posidonius' image is that Strabo does not use it. He has a graphic image of his own: shaped like a cloak, χλαμυδοειδής. But it is clear that Strabo has a similar, although not the same configuration in mind. At II.5.9, after mentioning that the habitable world has its length more than double its breadth, he says it is shaped like a cloak, 'for when we visit the several regions of the inhabited world, we discover a considerable contraction in its width at its extremities (πρὸς τοῖς ἄκροις), and particularly at its western extremities (καὶ μάλιστα τοῖς ἑσπερίοις)'. Compare II.5.6; II.5.14; XI.11.7. Tarbell, *CPh* 1 (1906), 283ff illustrates how a χλαμύς when spread out produces this image. See F49.305–8 comm. for Posidonius' estimate of the length of the οἰκουμένη; and in general, Berger *Erdkunde* 575f, 432f; *Eratosthenes* 219ff.

F201 Eustathius, *Commentarii in Dionysium Periegetam* 1

COMMENT

Eustathius is commenting on Dion. *Perieg.* 3–7:

ἐν γὰρ ἐκείνῳ (i.e. Ocean)
πᾶσα χθὼν ἅτε νῆσος ἀπείριτος ἐστεφάνωται·
οὐ μὴν πᾶσα διαπρὸ περίδρομος, ἀλλὰ διαμφὶς
ὀξυτέρη βεβαυῖα πρὸς ἠελίοιο κελεύθους
σφενδόνῃ εἰοικεῖα

He introduces Herodotus' objections (IV.36) to maps portraying the world as circular as if described by a pair of compasses,

COMMENTARY: F202

and surrounded by Ocean (1-3). Dionysius, he says, corrects this with: 'not completely circular throughout', but clearly extended lengthwise (or oblong, προμήκης; Sandbach may be right that Eustathius' quotation included the words, διαμφὶς ὀξυτέρη, 'sharper at either end', but perhaps it is unnecessary for sense), as will be said, like a sling. 'For the habitable world, as Posidonius thinks too, is that sort of shape,' (5f), that is, like a sling.

Eustathius is 12th c. A.D. Where did he find his information? F200b suggests that it came from Agathemerus' doxography. If so, the following information, 6-14, does not come from Posidonius, but is Eustathius' own interpretation. These lines suggest that the habitable world is divided into two κῶνοι, representing Asia and Europe, joined at the base and so broadest at the central NS axis, with one apex pointing to the east and the other to the west. There is no evidence for this in Posidonius. Anyway, Eustathius refers it to Dionysius (7, 10f), in whom κῶνοι later appear (277, 620ff). Berger takes the idea back to Eratosthenes (*Erdkunde* 432f). The fragment therefore adds nothing to F200. Bernhardy's note on Dion. *Perieg.* 7 (vol. II, p. 527) confuses cartographical shapes with sections of the earth's sphere, as in Arist. *Meteor.* 362a 32ff.

F202 Cleomedes, *De Motu Circulari* 1.10.50-2

CONTENT

Measurement of circumference of earth.

CONTEXT

There have been many opinions on the size of the earth. Cleomedes singles out the two best, those of Eratosthenes and Posidonius. Eratosthenes' proceeds by a geometrical method,

Posidonius' is simpler. Posidonius' method is described first, then that of Eratosthenes.

COMMENT

A. General

It is clear that there were indeed many guesses on the size of the earth's circumference. Aristotle, *De Caelo* 298a 16 mentions μαθηματικοί (ὅσοι τὸ μέγεθος ἀναλογίζεσθαι πειρῶνται τῆς περιφερείας) who put it at 400,000 stades. Another guess reported by Archimedes (*Sand Reckoner* 1.8) was 300,000. Strabo (II.2.2. = F49.32ff) reports a figure of Posidonius of 180,000 stades, as only one of a number of more recent (νεωτέρων) measurements after Eratosthenes, singled out because it was the smallest figure. It was the figure 180,000 stades, or 1° = 500 stades, which Ptolemy accepted from Marinus (ὅτι ταῖς ὁμολογουμέναις ἀναμετρήσεσι σύμφωνόν ἐστι *Geogr.* I.11.2; ὅπερ ἐκ τῶν ἀκριβεστέρων ἀναμετρήσεων κατελήφθη *Geogr.* VII.5.12).

B. Eratosthenes and Posidonius

Both men used a similar procedure. Choosing two places on the same meridian, they attempted to measure the difference of latitude in terms of a ratio or fraction by using the position of a celestial body in relation to the two places, then measuring the terrestrial distance between the two points, they applied the ratio to find the total circumference.

Eratosthenes chose Alexandria and Syene (Aswan), because at the latter it had been observed that at the summer solstice the sun illuminated a perpendicular well without shadow. At Alexandria the angle of shadow was measured as 1/50 (7; 12°). The distance between the two places was taken to be 5000 stades. Thus the circumference was calculated to be 5000 × 50 = 250,000 stades. At some time this figure was

COMMENTARY: F202

rounded up to 252,000 stades to give a round figure of 1° = 700 stades. This may have been due to Hipparchus converting to degrees (or 360 parts to the circle). Strabo tells us (1.4.1) that Hipparchus criticised Eratosthenes, although using his results perhaps with slight modification, Pliny (*NH* 2.247) has in addition an obscure story that Hipparchus added a little less than 26,000 stades to Eratosthenes' total (of 252,000 the Pliny context would suggest). Pliny implies that Eratosthenes' figure was universally approved in his time, no doubt for the measurement 1° = 700 stades.

Posidonius chose Alexandria and Rhodes, and used the star Canopus (α Carinae) instead of the sun. He accepted data that at Rhodes Canopus had a zero (or nearly zero, 'brushing the horizon') elevation, while at Alexandria it was 1/4 of a sign (or μέρος of the ecliptic) above the horizon, i.e. 1/48 of the ecliptic. The ecliptic was taken to be a great circle equivalent to a meridian (18f). The distance between the two cities was again taken as the round figure of 5000 stades, therefore the circumference was calculated as 5000 × 48 = 240,000 stades.

Both methods, although quite elegant in theory, were subject to the limitations of crude measurement and observation which precluded accuracy. Both assumed that Syene, Alexandria and Rhodes lay on the same meridian, whereas Syene is about 7;10° south, 3° east of Alexandria, and Rhodes about 4;50° north, 1;50° west.

There was no method by which either could accurately measure the terrestrial distances involved; that both realised this is shown by the obvious roundness of the figures adopted. Posidonius was in the more difficult position here, since it is clearly more difficult to estimate distances by sea. Indeed, he used alternatives, as shown by the circumference figure of 180,000 stades assigned to him by Strabo (II.2.2, F49.34). Eratosthenes' gnomon measurement was remarkably accurate, although Ptolemy was later to criticise the limitations of such methods for large figures. The difference was between

COMMENTARY: F202

7;12° and 7;10°. Posidonius' data for Canopus involved crude approximation. The main discrepancy lay at Rhodes, where in fact Canopus had an elevation of about $1\frac{1}{2}°$, visible for about $2\frac{1}{2}$ hours. Posidonius must have realised the limitations of accuracy here. Posidonius' result was nearer the correct figure than Eratosthenes' (who has been estimated to be *c*. 15% too large in comparison with modern measurements), and indeed his alternatives of 240,000 and 180,000 may have bracketed the correct sum more closely than any other ancient hypothesis, but the vagueness of the data (their inaccuracies tended to cancel each other out) on which they were based, is more pronounced than in Eratosthenes. Consequently Posidonius' method has been derided; but it should be realised that Eratosthenes' method was subject to the same limitations, and that it is virtually certain that Posidonius was well aware of them, and was making no pretence at numerical accuracy. This deserves further investigation.

C. *Posidonius' figures*

(1) 240,000 and 180,000

Cleomedes gives Posidonius' figure as 240,000 stades and describes in detail how and on what data this figure was reached. Strabo (II.2.2, F49.34) gives Posidonius' total as 180,000 stades, mentioned as the smallest of the more recent measurements, but he gives no indication of either method or data. Strabo must have known what he was talking about in this context; Cleomedes, although writing some four centuries later, was using a Posidonian source, and anyway the figure is internally confirmed by the rest of the data. Therefore both figures are Posidonian.

It has been argued (by Viedebantt, *Klio* 14 (1915), 207–56, and by Diller, *Klio* 27 (1934), 258–69) that the figures are in fact the same, but expressed in different standards of stade length. The distance between Alexandria and Rhodes of 5000 stades in Cleomedes is derived from the Eratosthenean stade of 1/10 of the Roman mile, while Strabo's figure involved the same distance expressed as 3750 in Philetaerian stades of 2/15 of the Roman mile. This argument was destroyed by Drabkin, *Isis* 34 (1943), 509 ff, and by Dicks, *The Geographical Fragments of Hipparchus* 150ff. It is sufficient to say here that the theory makes nonsense of the context in both Strabo and Cleomedes where Posidonius and Eratosthenes are directly compared.

Drabkin (*Isis* 34, 511) proposed another solution, that Posidonius may have reached 180,000 by a method quite different from that described by Cleomedes, and he proceeds to suggest what this might have been. But apart from the lack of any evidence (cf. Dicks, *The Geographical Fragments* 152), this solution seems highly improbable from a close reading of Cleomedes. Cleomedes makes it clear that Posidonius held to his general theory, but regarded the numerical data, in particular the distance suggested from Alexandria to Rhodes, as subject to correction. It is stated that 5000 is used as a hypothesis (15f), and the passage ends (46–9) by reaffirming 240,000, *if* the distance is 5000; if not, then the sum will be in proportion to the distance. This is strong evidence that Posidonius reached 180,000 by substituting 3750 stades as an alternative distance for Alexandria to Rhodes.

(2) 3750 and 5000

Where did 3750 come from? Strabo (II.5.24) maintains that Eratosthenes said that some sailors estimated the sea passage between Alexandria and Rhodes at 4000 stades, others at as much as 5000. These were assumptions, but he (Eratosthenes) discovered it was 3750 by using gnomons. If Strabo's account is correct, it is highly probable that Posidonius also knew this information, and therefore the possibility cannot be ignored that Posidonius simply accepted 3750 from a calculation by Eratosthenes. But if Eratosthenes arrived at that figure by gnomon measurement, the angular reading so

COMMENTARY: F202

derived could only have been used to calculate the distance in stades by using the already calculated figure for the earth's circumference. And if Posidonius knew *that*, we must ask why Posidonius would be willing to accept such a figure to calculate his own estimate of the circumference.

But Strabo's story is open to doubt. Neugebauer has expressed disbelief to me that Eratosthenes would use a gnomon measurement for such a purpose, and that 3750 is a highly suspicious figure to result. Whatever may be thought about Eratosthenes and his gnomon, the most striking fact about 3750 has nothing to do with Eratosthenes at all; it is a figure suspiciously convenient for Posidonius' calculation. By adopting it, and consequently a circumference figure of 180,000, the working unit is produced of 500 stades = 1°. This suggests that 3750 is not an exact figure at all, but a convenient approximation. The lower navigation estimate for Rhodes to Alexandria was 4000 stades. Posidonius doctored this round figure to 3750 to arrive at 500 stades = 1°, as it was suggested above that Eratosthenes' original 250,000 may have been approximated or 'doctored' to 252,000 to produce the working unit of 700 stades = 1°. It is a mistake to regard 3750 and 252,000 as exact or more accurate figures because they are not 'round'; there can be no such thing as 'exact' figures in this context. They are doctored approximations for the convenience of subsequent calculation. It is the equation of 500 stades = 1° which Ptolemy stresses (*Geogr.* I.11.2; VII.5.12), rather than the circumference figure of 180,000 (cf. Neugebauer, *HAMA* 652f). The modern average value for a degree of latitude is *c.* 111 km, or about 69 miles.

Posidonius then used 3750 as the most convenient approximation for the lower limit (ἐλαχίστην, F49.33) of calculations depending on variable estimates of the distance between Rhodes and Alexandria (F202.44–9). It would not have been surprising to find another alternative in the mean figure of 4500 for the distance, giving a circumference of 216,000 and the equation 600 stades = 1°. And in fact such an equation

COMMENTARY: F202

could be derived from Pliny *NH* 2.245 (Neugebauer, *HAMA* 654). But Posidonius appears to have been content to bracket with upper and lower limits of 240,000 and 180,000, or 5000 and 3750.

(3) Canopus

The data concerning Canopus were also approximate and probably derived from other sources known to Posidonius. The greatest discrepancy occurs at Rhodes, Posidonius' own city, where Canopus has an elevation of $1\frac{1}{2}°$, not zero. But what we know of Posidonius and Canopus does not derive from Rhodes. Strabo (II.5.14 = F204) reports that Posidonius tentatively identified a star he could just see from a high house near Gadeira as Canopus, because he connected it with observations made at Cnidus by Eudoxus from his observatory. Posidonius added that Cnidus, Rhodes and Gadeira were on the same latitude. This is very crude observational measurement, especially since refraction distorts horizon observation. But Posidonius knew about the dangers of horizon distortion (Strabo III.1.5 = F119), and yet he was content for his purposes merely to accept such supposedly scientific evidence known to him from Eudoxus.

The elevation of Canopus at Alexandria was certainly accepted from another source, and expressed in a method common at the time. The form of measurement, $\frac{1}{4}$ of a sign, i.e. 1/48 of the zodiac, shows that it was based on the form of angular measure known as 'the steps' (βαθμοί; Neugebauer, *HAMA* 669ff), expressed as fractions of the ecliptic; 'sign', 'step', 'part' (μέρος) represented 1/12, 1/24, 1/48 of the ecliptic, or, in Babylonian units, 30°, 15°, 7;30°. The limitations of this system (which was ignored by Ptolemy, who had a healthy contempt for inferior methods) are obvious, but it seems to have been used by Hipparchus and Vettius Valens, and continued to be widespread even after Ptolemy. There is a trace of it again in Posidonius in F126. This same account of Canopus at Rhodes and Alexandria is

725

COMMENTARY: F202

given by Geminus (*Isagoge* III.3.15, p. 42 Manitius) and by Pliny (*NH* 2.70).

It is very probable that Posidonius (or someone else) could calculate the elevation of Canopus at Alexandria from Hipparchus' star map. That Hipparchus had a star map is a fair inference from the information contained in his commentary on Aratus' *Phaenomena*, although the co-ordinates he used must have been different from those of Ptolemy. Canopus must have been in it. Indeed there is a reference in Hipparchus, *Ad. Arat. Phaen.* 1.11.7, which puts Canopus 38;30° from the south pole. From this it can be calculated that Hipparchus could have worked out the elevation of Canopus at Alexandria at about 8°. (It is curious that a similar calculation based on Ptolemy's star map in the *Almagest*, which was not derived from Hipparchus, reaches the same result.) Posidonius probably knew and accepted this figure, and he (or someone else) converted it into the 'step' notation, into which it conveniently fitted (allowing a little for the elevation at Rhodes) as a μέρος, or $\frac{1}{4}$ of a sign, or 7;30°. Although the final notation is still clearly an approximation, if it was derived by the method suggested, Posidonius probably had more confidence in it, in comparison with the admitted difficulty of measuring the ground distance accurately; and this attitude fits the account in Cleomedes exactly.

D. *Method and purpose*

The Cleomedes account has a marked characteristic: it stresses the hypothetical method rather than the accuracy or certainty of the figures, e.g. 5f; 18f. The figure of 5000 stades is hypothetical from the start (15f: ... εἶναι δοκεῖ. καὶ ὑποκείσθω οὕτως ἔχειν).

Perhaps no stress should be laid on the variant reading of *LN* at 27: τούτων τοίνυν οὕτως ἔχειν προϋποκειμένων, but further on at 44 we find τὸ τούτῳ τῷ τμήματι ὑποκείμενον μέρος τῆς γῆς ..., and above all the concluding words, 47–9, ἐὰν ὦσιν οἱ ἀπὸ 'Ρόδου . . . πεντακισχίλιοι· εἰ δὲ μή, πρὸς λόγον τοῦ διαστήματος.

If to this is added the conclusions argued in the last section (C), that Posidonius seems to have been content, not to attempt to establish exact data for himself, but simply to accept figures which he knew to be inexact (like 3750 and 5000), and observational measurement which he knew to be inaccurate, such as horizon observation, we must conclude that he was not primarily interested in figures or in accuracy.

This tells against the hypothesis, which I entertained at one time, that the whole operation was an *ad hominem* attack on Eratosthenes' calculation. We know from Strabo (1.4.1) that later writers thought Eratosthenes' estimate of the circumference was too large. Posidonius might have set out to show from Eratosthenes' own data (3750 and 5000, Strabo II.5.24) that even on the largest figure mentioned by Eratosthenes, the latter's circumference figure was too large.

In any case, as argued above, 3750 may have nothing to do with Eratosthenes (as used by Posidonius); but more importantly, such a hypothesis does not fit the cast of the Cleomedes account, where the figures are secondary to the method. Posidonius was interested in the method, not in the figures. Although this is now not a fashionable view, it was put forward long ago by Letronne (*Mémoires de l'institut royal de France. Académie des inscriptions et belles lettres*, tome VI, 1822, 4, p. 315) and supported by Berger (*Erdkunde* 577ff; cf. also Drabkin, *Isis* 34, 510). But it seems to me doubtful that they are correct in regarding Posidonius' motives for such a procedure merely as seeking to demonstrate a simple popular method for the benefit of the non-specialist. That Posidonius' method is simpler (ἁπλουστέρα, F202.4) is the statement of Cleomedes, and does not derive from Posidonius. We should probably look rather to his delimination of the functions of philosopher and scientist (F18). Measurement is the province of the ἀστρολόγος and other scientists like him; the physical philosopher (φυσικός) is concerned with the theories. As

COMMENTARY: F202

Posidonius was content in this instance to accept measurements, I assume that he was not trying to be a scientist, but as a philosopher demonstrating another method (like others in his works), whereby celestial and terrestrial phenomena could be related. Of course some figures were necessary, as in another context (F134.55ff) the philosopher advancing his theory of the cause of rainbows enlists the necessary aid of geometry. But it was not apparently the calculations which interested him as much as the theory.

38   Robert B. Todd reports to me that ζωδιακοῦ is only to be found in three codices of the *a* family, and he considers it a gloss. Goulet (*Cléomède* 63) reads τοῦ μεσημβρινοῦ τοῦ διὰ 'Ρόδου καὶ 'Αλεξανδρείας, *P VCN*, which may be right considering τοῦ αὐτοῦ μεσημβρινοῦ, 39.

Select Bibliography

G. Aujac, *Strabon et la Science de son Temps* 174ff; 130f (1966).
H. Berger, *Geschichte der wissenschaftlichen Erdkunde der Griechen* 577ff (1903).
E. H. Bunbury, *History of Ancient Geography* II.95f (1879).
D. R. Dicks, *The Geographical Fragments of Hipparchus* 149ff (1960).
A. Diller, 'Geographical Latitudes in Eratosthenes, Hipparchus and Posidonius', *Klio* 27 (1934), 258–69.
I. E. Drabkin, 'Posidonius and the Circumference of the Earth', *Isis* 34 (1943), 509–12.
I. Fischer 'Another look at Eratosthenes' and Posidonius' Determinations of the Earth's Circumference', *Quarterly Journal of the Royal Astronomical Society* 16, (1975), 152–67.
T. L. Heath, *A History of Greek Mathematics* II.220 (1921).
F. Jacoby, *FGrH* II c 203 (1926).
J. A. Letrone, *Mémoires de l'institut royal de France. Académie des inscriptions et belles lettres*, tome VI, 1822, 4. p. 315.
O. Neugebauer, *History of Ancient Mathematical Astronomy* 652ff (1975).
M. Pohlenz, *Die Stoa* II.109 (1949).
H. Prell, Die Vorstellungen des Altertums von der Erdumfangslänge, *Abhandlungen der Sächsischen Akademie des Wissenschaften*, Math.-Naturwiss. Klasse, 46, heft 1 (1959).
Rehm, *RE* (Kleomedes) XI.688 (1921).
K. Reinhardt, *Poseidonios* 195ff (1921).

COMMENTARY: F203

K. Reinhardt, *RE* (Poseidonios) XXII.1.669 (1953).
S. Sambursky, *The Physical World of the Greeks* 75ff (1956).
O. Viedebantt, 'Eratosthenes, Hipparchus, Posidonius', *Klio* 14 (1915), 207–56.

F203   Anonymus, *Sylloge Tacticorum* 3.2–3

CONTENT

Strabo is said to have cited Posidonius as evidence for the length of the parasang, in particular that in some cases it was put at much more than 60 stades.

CONTEXT

Chapter 3 of the *Sylloge Tacticorum* is headed 'On land measurements', and gives a table of measurements from the finger to the mile (palm, foot, cubit, pace, rod, plethron, stade), each unit in relation to the others. To these are added the parasang and the schoinos.

COMMENT

The title of this work preserved in the only surviving codex (Laur. 75.6) assigns it to the Emperor Leon VI (886–912 A.D.), but Viedebantt in *RE* XIX.17–19 referred this metrological excerpt to Julian of Ascalon. Vári, 'Die sog. Inedita Tactica Leonis', *Byz. Zeitschr.* XXVII (1927), 241–70, and Diller, 'Julian of Ascalon on Strabo and the Stade', *CPh* 45 (1950), 22–5, showed both suggestions mistaken. It appears to be the work of an unknown, probably about the time of Leon.

The table is a straightforward list until the mile. But then Eratosthenes and Strabo are cited for variations in stades to the mile, and Xenophon, Strabo and Posidonius for varia-

729

tions in the parasang. None of these sources is mentioned again in the work. In our Strabo, Polybius is cited for the stade, not Eratosthenes. At VII.7.4 Strabo says that most people reckoned 8 stades to the mile, but Polybius used $8\frac{1}{3}$ stades (Polybius again mentioned at Str. VII, F56 (Jones); see Polybius 34.12.3ff and Walbank *ad loc.*). Because of this, Diller emended τέταρτον (line 2) to τρίτον (γ'), to give the Polybian $8\frac{1}{3}$ in Strabo. The figure $8\frac{1}{4}$ does not occur elsewhere. $7\frac{1}{2}$ (line 3) recurs in the table in the third appendix to Aelian's *Tactica*. As for the parasang, Str. XI.11.5 gives the variations of 60, 30 and 40 stades, but names no sources.

Diller (*CPh* 45, p. 24) therefore accused the author of deliberate fiction in the case of Eratosthenes and Posidonius, but this seems unlikely. Either, the reference to Posidonius (13f) was in a part of Strabo now lost to us, perhaps in the missing part of Bk VII. The same may apply to the coupling of Strabo and Eratosthenes on the stade, although here it is more probable that Eratosthenes was a mistake for Polybius. Or, which seems to me more likely, our author had not referred directly to Strabo, who is not cited elsewhere, but the entry is a confused compilation from another source or sources. Although Strabo did call Posidonius πολυμαθής (15, T48), the sudden inclusion of authorities in this way in a bare list of tables smacks of intermediary sources. Also traces of Posidonius' *Tactica* no doubt filtered through a complication of later sources such as Asclepiodotus, Aelian and Arrian (Frs. 80, 81, T41), some of which our author certainly used.

Herodotus (II.6; V.53) put the parasang at 30 stades, as did Xenophon (*Anab.* II.2.6; V.5.4; VII.8.26). But this was clearly a rough estimate of a road measure, which could differ according to the nature of the country and the length of time taken to traverse it. On this problem see Bunbury, *A History of Ancient Geography* 1.359–61, who compared similar variations of farsakhs in 19th-c. Persia. Strabo's variation between 30 and 40 stades was no doubt correct. But his jump to 60 ('and still much more', 13) makes one suspect confusion at some point arising from Hdt. II.6, who gives the parasang as 30 stades, but the Egyptian schoinos as 60 stades. Strabo, XI.11.5 passed immediately from parasangs to schoinoi (for variations, Str. XVII.1,24), and the Anonymus here opines that the schoinos ('a Greek measure'!) is the equivalent of the parasang. Viedebantt, *RhM* 69 (1914), 558ff, argued for systems of 'single' and 'double' schoinoi as the basis of confusion.

On 'simple' and 'geometric' fathoms (6f), see Diller, *CPh* 45 (1950) 22–5.

F204 Strabo, II.5.14

CONTENT

Observation of Canopus near Gadeira.

CONTEXT

In Strabo's second introduction (II.5), he turns his attention (II.5.13) to the shape and size of the inhabited world as it falls on the map. After representing its general shape as a chlamys (F200 comm.), he defines the parameters of a parallelogram which contains it. Its greatest breadth lies on a line from the Cinnamon Country to the parallel through Ierne. The greatest length lies on the parallel from the Pillars, through the Sicilian Straits, Rhodes, Gulf of Issus, the Taurus and ranges to the east, to the Eastern Sea. He now goes on to mention various methods of plotting places on this parallel. Afterwards (II.5.16) he declares that with the help of these two basic climata, other latitudes and longitudes can be drawn.

COMMENTARY: F204

COMMENT

A. Strabo's report

Strabo's context lies in methods of establishing the axial Rhodian band of latitude (or klima), which runs from the Sacred Cape (Cape St Vincent), the most westerly point of the inhabited world (1f). It (actually 37°) lies approximately (πως) on the line that runs through Gadeira (36;33°), the Pillars (36°), the Sicilian Straits (38;13°) and Rhodes (the 36° parallel cuts the island, but the town is 36;21°) (2-4).

The Rhodian latitude (φ = 36°, longest daylight $14\frac{1}{2}$ hrs): there are indications that some such basic line was posited by Dicaearchus (*Agathemerus* 1.5, *GGM* II.472, Dicaearch. F110 Wehrli). What became the standard line was first defined by Eratosthenes (Strabo II.1.1) and much refined by Hipparchus, who probably corrected the most glaring errors, such as the Sicilian Straits (Str. II.5.39, but generally ignored) and Attica (Bunbury, *History of Ancient Geography* 1.629ff; Thomson, *History of Ancient Geography* 165; Berger, *Erdkunde* 415ff; Aujac, *Strabon et la science de son temps* 196f; Neugebauer, *HAMA* 234, 275, 879).

Strabo continues with four methods of establishing the line. For this he relies on a general consensus, not Posidonius: 'for they say' (5) that there is agreement in criteria. They are:
(1) τὰ ὡροσκοπεῖα (for the word, Gem. *Isag.* II.35), that is, the use of sundials and gnomons (Aujac, *Strabon et la science* 162; Neugebauer, *HAMA* VB2.2; 2.3). An example of use in fixing a latitude is Str. II.5.41: Byzantium has a ratio of index to shadow of 120: $42\frac{4}{5} \approx 19°$ from the summer tropic, or $\approx 43°$ from the equator. Pytheas gave the latitude of Marseilles thus (Str. II.5.8). But there were strange errors from such measurements, and Greeks tended to rely on calculation from a few observations.

(2) Winds. This is a puzzling non-scientific factor. The reference cannot be merely to a windrose, although Timos-

COMMENTARY: F204

thenes' compass card was based on Rhodes. The qualifying phrase (τοὺς ἑκατέρωσε φορούς; φορός means 'favourable' in Plb. 1.60.6; 31.15.8) shows that the reference is climatic rather than directional, that is to periodic winds, and derived from navigational lore, like our 'roaring forties'. So we are told that Hipparchus did not depend wholly on instruments and calculations, but for the Pillars line he trusted sailors (τοῖς πλέουσιν ἐπίστευσεν, Str. II.1.11). Such navigational sources may also explain the aberration of the Sicilian Straits on the Rhodian/Pillars line. Klimata and winds are mentioned together at Str. II.5.10.

(3) 'The length of the longest days and nights'; an inaccurate description for the measure of the longest day, or the ratio of longest to shortest day. This was the most common, indeed the standard method of establishing klimata: F205 comm.; Str. II.5.36ff; Gem. *Isag.* VI.7; VI.28; Ptol. *Alm.* II.2-3; Neugebauer, *HAMA* 40ff, 708ff; Aujac, *Strabon et la science* 163ff; Thomson, *History of Ancient Geography* 206. It is often coupled with gnomon calculation (Str. II.1.11; II.5.41). The longest day for the Rhodian clima was $14\frac{1}{2}$ hours (Neugebauer, 581), and so Groskurd's supplementation ⟨καὶ ἡμίσους ἡ⟩ at 7 is certain.

(4) Observation of stars: so, Str. II.5.35, 36, 38, 41, 42; Neugebauer, *HAMA* 335f; Aujac, *Strabon et la science* 161.

8 Ἴβηρας is clearly corrupt. The name of a star is required, and since Posidonius is brought in immediately afterwards as evidence for Canopus, an emendation which includes it is necessary. The possible variations are numerous. This is still introduced as one of Strabo's general criteria.

B. *The Posidonian fragment (9–17)*

The argument is interesting:

(1) He says that he saw from a high house in a city some 400 stades from the Gadeira coastline a star which he

COMMENTARY: F204

conjectured (τεκμαίρεσθαι, 11) was Canopus (α Carinae) itself (9–11).

(2) His conjecture *derived from* two pieces of information (ἐκ τοῦ τε..., 11):
(a) people who proceeded only a little to the south of Spain were in agreement that they saw Canopus (11–13);
(b) Eudoxus' own research at Cnidus recorded that he had seen Canopus from his observatory there, which was not much higher than the houses (13–16).

(3) Posidonius adds with regard to the evidence of (2)(b), that Cnidus Gadeira and its coastline lie on the Rhodian clima or band of latitude (16f).

This argument shows that Posidonius' context was different from Strabo's. Posidonius was not here using Canopus as a method of establishing the Pillars/Rhodes klima; on the contrary, (3) proves that the assumption of the Rhodian klima was being used as evidence that it may have been Canopus that he saw near Gadeira (1).

The figures in (1) and (2)(a) support this. Klimata (F205) were regarded rather as a band than a line parallel. Depending on the system employed and its exactness, the width of the band could vary. In a system of cardinal klimata based on longest day, the breadth could vary by several degrees (Str. 11.5.35–42). A more exact system based on calculation by degrees, such as Hipparchus' use of Eratosthenes' earth circumference figure of 252,000 stades, gives a degree difference of 700 stades. If Posidonius used his own lower circumference figure of 180,000, the distance between degrees was 500 stades (F202, comm. *C.*(2)). Also statements survive of estimated diametric limits of constant observational phenomena for such a band of latitude. Geminus *Isag.* v.58ff puts it at 400 stades. Pliny *NH* 2.182 gives between 300 and 500 stades for constant shadow readings, while Cleomedes 1.10 (98.4f Ziegler) gives 300 stades as the diameter of

COMMENTARY: F205

no noon-shadow at the summer solstice at Syene. Posidonius knew that Canopus was just visible on the Rhodian klima ((2a b); F202.28–34; F205); therefore it might possibly still be visible at the northern limits (400+ stades) of the latitudinal band.

The naive assumption that the difference in height between Eudoxus' observatory and the height of a house might have made a difference as to whether Canopus was visible above the horizon, and the uncertainty over identification of the star confirm that Posidonius was not an observational astronomer. Yet Geminus, *Isag.* III.15 repeats: οὗτος (i.e. Canopus) ἐν Ῥόδῳ δυσθεώρητός ἐστιν ἢ παντελῶς ἀφ' ὑψηλῶν τόπων ὁρᾶται. I have argued at F202 comm. C.(3) that Posidonius' use of Canopus in the measurement of the earth's circumference depended not on his own observations but on data accepted from elsewhere and calculations derived from them.

F205 Proclus, *In Timaeum* (40A–B) IV.277DE; III.124.18–125.17 Diehl

CONTENT

The elevation of Canopus at Rhodes and at Alexandria.

COMMENT

Proclus is engaged in defending Plato's theory concerning the movement of the fixed stars (*Tim.* 40a 7ff), and inveighs against the theory of precession of Ptolemy and Hipparchus, that the slow motion of precession proceeds about the pole of the ecliptic, and not about the pole of the equator (1–4; Ptol. *Alm.* VII.3; Neugebauer, *HAMA* 34, 1034). In support he cites statements from Egyptians and Chaldaeans (i.e. astrologers,

5–8, enlarged in the lacuna at 8). At 9 he adds that the phenomena are sufficient to persuade those who have eyes to see, and appeals to the phenomena of the Bear and Canopus (10–14); in particular, Canopus would no longer be seen to make a small circle above the horizon for those in the Third Klima, and shave the horizon for people in Rhodes as Posidonius says (15–17).

The information about Canopus and the comparative elevation of the star between Rhodes and Alexandria (third klima) is certainly Posidonian.

Although Strabo, in a passage defending Homer's geographical knowledge, said that Canopus was only recently named (1.1.6; it was after all not visible in mainland Greece, F202.30), it appears to have been identified by Eudoxus (Hipparch. *In Arat. Ph.* 1.11.6; F204), and was certainly named and co-ordinated on Hipparchus' star map (F202, comm.; Hipparch. 1.11.7; 38;30° from pole). But it was probably Posidonius' interest in the elevation of Canopus at Rhodes and Alexandria for the calculation of the circumference of the earth which caught subsequent notice (Vitr. *Arch.* ix.5.4; Manilius 1.216; Theon Smyrn. p.121 18ff H). The description at Rhodes here clearly derives from him; for παραξέοντα τὸν ὁρίζοντα (shaving the horizon), compare Pliny, *NH* 2.178, *a Rhodo terram quodammodo ipsam stringere*; Cleomedes in F202.33, ἐπὶ τοῦ ὁρίζοντος; Geminus (*Isag.* iii.15) simply has δυσθεώρητος, but adds, except from high places (cf. F204.14).

It has therefore been inferred (by Reinhardt and Theiler, ii.29ff) that the reference to the Third Klima (16), the Alexandrian parallel, where Canopus is visible, also comes from Posidonius, and that this is grounds for holding that Posidonius was the originator of the standard system of Seven Klimata which became popular. Neither inference is secure.

In the first place, Posidonius was more exact, naming an elevation of $\frac{1}{4}$ of a sign (7;30°) at Alexandria (Cleomedes in F202.36–8), and both elevation and place are repeated by

COMMENTARY: F205

Geminus, *Isag.* III.15. So Proclus may have given his own vaguer reference in his own words, and the Third Klima comes from him.

Secondly, the earlier historical development of klima systems remains obscure, and Neugebauer (*HAMA* 333ff, 725ff) is rightly sceptical about attempts to assign Seven Klimata to the specific authorship of Eratosthenes, Hipparchus or Posidonius.

κλίμα means inclination, and derives from the mathematical concept of the inclination of the plane of the local horizon to the earth's axis; as the earth is spherical, any such parallels to the equator will experience common phenomena in relation to the fixed stars, or length of day. Thus the commonest means of identifying a band of latitude lay in calculating the longest day (or ratio of longest to shortest day). A basic pattern came to be recognised of seven such klimata. The most frequent set was established by half-hour intervals of longest day: I 13 hrs, Meroe; II $13\frac{1}{2}$, Syene; III 14, Lower Egypt (the latitude of Alexandria); IV $14\frac{1}{2}$, Rhodes; V 15, Hellespont; VI $15\frac{1}{2}$, Mid-Pontus; VII 16, Borysthenes. The mathematical, rather than geographical original base of such sets is shown by the arithmetic progression. This one seems to have been based on Alexandria; another was based on Babylon (Neugebauer, *HAMA* 366ff); yet a different set of seven klimata is found in Pliny, *NH* 6.211–218. Although the concept of klima may possibly be traced back as far as Eudoxus (Neugebauer, *HAMA* 733, n. 28), it was developed by hellenistic–Alexandrian science from Babylonian roots. It can be argued that Eratosthenes was familiar with seven half-hour bands (Honigmann, *Die Sieben Klimata* 13; Neugebauer, *HAMA* 334 n. 8); certainly Hipparchus developed a series of klimata, and although Strabo (II.5.34–42) records ten parallels with variations between half and a quarter hours, that did not mean that Hipparchus was not also aware of a standard seven. Ptolemy used variously numbered sets, yet referred also to the seven (Neugebauer, *HAMA* 335, 725). The

COMMENTARY: F206-207

evidence shows that a variety of Sevens and a variety of variously numbered sets co-existed. There is no reason to assign the origin of any particular set to Posidonius, although it is highly likely that he knew of sets of seven, and may have used one.

It is necessary to distinguish klimata from zones, of which Posidonius recognised five, Frs. 208–10, F49.5–145.

F206, F207 Strabo, XI.1.5–6; Strabo, XVII.1.21

CONTENT

The length of the Caucasian and Suez 'isthmuses'.

CONTEXT

At Bk IX Strabo turns to Asia, dividing it from Europe by the R. Tanais (Don), and partitioning Asia itself north and south by the Taurus Mountains which he takes as stretching from the coast opposite Rhodes to the eastern boundaries of India and Scythia.

COMMENT

1–5 Strabo starts with the northern division of Asia, that is to the north of the range stretching eastwards from the Taurus mountains; and of this section he begins with the area reached by crossing the R. Tanais (Don), in other words the land mass between the Black Sea and the Caspian.

5–16 Strabo regards this area as a peninsula (5, 16), because it was thought to be bounded to the north by the Northern Ocean of which the Caspian was an inlet (8f; Str. XI.6.1). Its other boundaries are defined: on the west, the Tanais, Lake Maeotis (Sea of Azov), the Cimmerian Bospor-

COMMENTARY: F206-207

us (Straits of Kerch), and the east coast of the Black Sea (6-8); on the east, the Caspian as far as the mouths of the rivers Cyrus and Araxes (the Kura and Araks, to the south of Baku) (10-13); on the south, the river Kura to Colchis (south-east corner of Black Sea) (13-15). This includes the territory of Albania, Armenia and Iberia.

16-21 Having given his own distance of 3000 stades for the southern neck of the 'isthmus' (14), Strabo mentions for criticism Cleitarchus and Posidonius for figures which are much too small. At first sight it is surprising that Strabo does not cite Patrocles here, the Greek commander under Seleucus I and Antiochus I, who *c.* 285 B.C. explored the Caspian, and became a trusted source of Eratosthenes and Strabo (Str. II.1.2-9; XI.7.1-3; Pliny *NH* 2.167; 6.58; Berger, *Eratosthenes* 91-9, 325f; Thomson, *History of Ancient Geography* 127f). Perhaps Strabo's own figure derives from him, or from Theophanes of Mytilene. But Strabo is attacking Cleitarchus and Posidonius who may be coupled because Strabo thought that Posidonius was following a Cleitarchan tradition (cf. F272.23). Cleitarchus, the Alexander historian, writing under Ptolemy II some time after 280 B.C. was highly unreliable and had probably never been to Asia; but he was right about the low-lying coasts on the Caspian (ἐπίκλυστον, 17), especially at the mouth of the Kura, and in the north-west. No actual distance figure is given for Cleitarchus.

Posidonius

(1) The distance from Caspian to Black Sea at the southern neck is 1500 stades.

(2) It is about the distance of the isthmus from Pelusium (Port Said) to the Red Sea (?Suez); '"and I think", says he, "that from Maiotis to Ocean (the breadth of the northern finger of the Caucasian 'isthmus') does not much differ either"'.

Why is the Suez isthmus brought in at this point? Probably

because both were regarded as boundaries between Europe and Asia (Ps.-Arist. *De Mundo* 393b 25ff; Dion. *Perieg.* 20–5; probably going back to Eratosthenes), and Strabo's context also is of boundaries (4).

The distances

(1) The Causasian

The actual distance from Batumi on the Black Sea to the mouth of the Kura (or to Batu) is over 400 miles, so Posidonius' underestimate is gross. Strabo doubles (14), and Pliny *NH* 2.173 puts it at 375 Roman miles. But a tradition of the narrow neck persisted: *De Mundo* 393b 25, στενότατος ἰσθμός. The northern estimate is an admitted guess (δοκῶ, 20), recognised by Strabo (ἀδήλων, 22). An even worse mistake is the equation with the Suez isthmus which is under 100 miles.

(2) The Suez measurement

There is some geographical confusion, because Heroonpolis (F207) was to the north of Suez (Arsinoe), on the so-called Bitter Lakes (Str. XVII.1.25), from which another stretch of canal ran to the Red Sea. This might account for Posidonius' variation of 1500 stades from Pelusium (Port Said) to the Red Sea (?Suez) (F206.19f), but *less* than 1500 stades from Pelusium to the recess by Heroonpolis (F207); so Viedebantt, *RhM* 69 (1914), 558ff. Pliny too has 115 miles from the Arabian Gulf to the Egyptian Sea (*NH* 2.173), but 125 from Pelusium to Arsinoe.

Strabo's round figure of 1000 stades goes back to Hdt. II.158. But Posidonius' figure is absurdly and surprisingly too large. Viedebantt suggested that he might have been misled by a source which confused 'simple' and 'double' schoinoi, but this, even if true, would not excuse Posidonius, who evidently was not autoptic in this part of the world. There is no suggestion of confusion by Strabo or anyone else.

COMMENTARY: F206-207

Strabo's criticism (F206.22-32)

Strabo is rightly horrified.

22-4 How could one trust him περὶ τῶν ἀδήλων, when what he says περὶ τῶν φανερῶν is so irrational?

τὰ ἄδηλα refers to the region north of the Caucasus (from Maiotis to Ocean). τὰ φανερά will include the Suez isthmus but most significantly also refers to the southern cis-Caucasian measurement between the Caspian and Black Seas. This is proved by Strabo's supporting evidence (24-9), which refers to the territory of the Armenians and Iberes. Apart from earlier expeditions such as that of Patrocles, this area became familiar through Pompey's campaigns as recorded by Theophanes of Mytilene (Strabo XI.2.3-4).

24-32 But Strabo's grounds of criticism of Posidonius are weird, confused and petty.

(1) **24-9** Pompey, the commander of the famous campaign in these parts, was a friend, as shown by his respectful visit to Posidonius. But the Pompey visit cited as evidence (γοῦν, 27) was during his command against the pirates, and expressly stated as *before* the Caucasian campaign (67/6 B.C., 28). Strabo then can only imply that since Pompey was so familiar with Posidonius, he could have told him afterwards. But when was the offending measurement published? Almost certainly before the sixties, probably in *On Ocean*, which must have been published well before (Reinhardt, *RE* 662f; Schühlein, *Untersuchungen* 5; Jacoby, *Kommentar* 157; Malitz, 30f). Strabo must have been aware of this, and so his criticism is deliberately misleading. Posidonius' miscalculation may have been culpable after 65 B.C. or after Theophanes' monograph, but his friendship with Pompey can hardly be blamed if it was written before then.

(2) **29-32** Equally misleading, and still more ambiguous, is the additional (προστίθει δὲ, 29) reference to a Posidonian work supposedly relating to the subject. Whether the ἱστορία in question refers to a monograph on Pompey,

COMMENTARY: F208

which remains doubtful, or to some other book, obfuscation remains over where and when the misjudgement of distance was recorded. See F79 about the difficulties and ambiguity of τὴν περὶ αὐτόν (30f).

31 Strabo connects ἱστορία and τἀληθές at XI.5.3.

F208 Strabo, II.5.43

CONTENT

Strabo reports, clarifies and criticises the usefulness of Posidonius' classification of zones by sun shadow.

CONTEXT

Strabo concludes his second introduction (II.5) with an outline of the klimata, or belts of latitude, from the south; but not from the equator (where habitability, the concern of the geographer, was in dispute; F49, F210, F211) but from the cinnamon parallel (cf. F49) to the north (chs. 34ff). He ends (ch. 42 *fin.*) with a klima for which his reference points are confused: (a) 6300 stadia north of Byzantium, i.e. 52; 12°; (b) winter elevation of sun, 6 cubits; longest day 17 'equinoctial' (Neugebauer, *HAMA* 367) hours: i.e. 54; 11°. For this inconsistency of 2°, see Dicks, *Geographical Fragments of Hipparchus* 185ff, Aujac, Budé *ad loc.*, p. 174 n. 7. Since Strabo continues by saying that what lies beyond this parallel, as it already borders on the uninhabitable region because of cold, is no longer of use to the geographer, it appears that he is adopting the arbitrarily fixed 'arctic circle' of 54°, the circle for observers on the basic Rhodes parallel of 36° (F49 comm. on 37–43; cf. esp. II.5.8, and note on 24 below). On the other hand in the Posidonian evidence (F208.17f, 25–30) the reference is to our arctic circle of 66°. It is as well that Strabo at this point refers the reader to Hipparchus, not only for the

COMMENTARY: F208

frigid regions, but for all other astronomical information (ὅσα ἄλλα τῶν οὐρανίων); Hipparchus' treatment is of greater clarity (τρανότερα) than Strabo's present work requires. So is Posidonius' account of Periskians, Amphiskians and Heteroskians (F208.1-2).

COMMENT

Introduction (1-4)

Strabo proposes to explain Posidonius' terms nevertheless. It is clear that the terms and conceptions come from Posidonius; cf. line 22 (ἐκάλεσεν), and F49.44-8. For the names used but not defined see also Strabo II.5.37, Cleomedes, *De Motu* 1.7. It is not clear why Jacoby suggested Eratosthenes as the source; all the evidence points to Posidonius.

1 **τρανότερα** must mean in greater clarity of detail and completeness than is necessary for Strabo's purpose. Strabo's concern with the terms is limited (τό γε τοσοῦτον, 2f): *A* to clarify the conception (τὴν ἐπίνοιαν); *B* to show where they are useful and useless for geography.

A. The clarification of the conception of the terms (1-21)

4-9 establishes the method by a general explanation of how the movement of the sun casts shadows: 'Since the argument is concerned with the shadows cast by the sun, and the sun on the evidence of our senses (for πρὸς αἴσθησιν cf. τῇ αἰσθήσει II.5.5) follows a circular course parallel to that of the universe, by the conditions whereby in accordance with each revolution of the universe there comes a day and a night as the sun at one point moves above the earth and at another below it, by these conditions people whose shadow may fall on both sides (ἀμφίσκιοι) are conceived, and people with a shadow on one of two sides only (ἑτερόσκιοι).'

9-21 now gives a detailed explanation of the three key terms.

743

COMMENTARY: F208

9ff *Amphiskioi*: 'All those (ὅσοι defines the whole class) who at midday have their shadows sometimes projecting this way (ἐπὶ τάδε, 10, i.e. north) when the sun falls from the south on the vertical pointer of the sundial on the base plane, sometimes in the opposite direction when the sun changes round to the opposite side. This happens only to those who live between the tropics.' This shows that the purpose of the exercise was to define zones astronomically.

14–16 *Heteroskioi* on the other hand are defined by an exclusive alternative (ἢ . . . ἢ, reflecting ἑτερο-): *either* all whose shadow falls to the north, like us, *or* those whose shadow falls to the south (those living in the southern temperate zone).

17 'This (τοῦτο, 17; being amphiskian or heteroskian) happens for everyone whose arctic circle is less than the tropic.' Since the tropic was regarded as $\varphi = 24°$, the latitude of those whose arctic circle is the same as the tropic $\bar{\varphi}$ is 66°; therefore everyone who lives from the equator to just under 66° is either amphiskian or heteroskian. φ is the symbol for geographical latitude; $\bar{\varphi} = 90 - \varphi$, colatitude. See Neugebauer, *HAMA* 582.

18–21 'But where a person's arctic circle is the same (as the tropic, i.e. $\bar{\varphi} = 66°$) or bigger (66° +), *Periskians* begin and continue as far as those who live under the pole (i.e. at latitudes of 66° and over). For as the sun's course follows the whole revolution of the universe *above* the earth, obviously its shadow too will traverse in a circle about the gnomon; and that is the reason Posidonius gave them the name of Periskians (22).'

All this is clearly from Posidonius, and shows how his zones were fixed astronomically by the path of the sun, and in particular removed the variable factor of arctic circle as the ever-visible stars, which he criticised (F49.37ff). Although Strabo knew this and apparently approved of Posidonius' fixed arctic circle (25ff; II.2.2; F49.37ff), there is some reason to suspect that just before this (see Context, above) Strabo

COMMENTARY: F208

was thinking of the arbitrarily fixed 'arctic circle' of 54°, fixed only for observers on the Rhodes 36° latitude, primarily because he believed that latitude of 54° to be the northerly limit of the inhabited world (II.5.8).

B. *Usefulness in relation to geography (22-30)*

22f 'Periskians are of no importance in relation to geography . . .' οὐδὲν ὄντας does not mean 'do not exist' ('non-existent' Jones), but 'of no importance' in relation to (πρός).

23 'Because (γάρ) these parts are uninhabitable because of the cold.' For geography being concerned only with the habitable world: F49.81f; esp. II.5.4; II.5.34. This may be the reason why in this particular presentation of the classification Strabo concentrates on Amphiskioi and Heteroskioi, leaving Periskioi to the last. In F49.44-48, Periskioi come first, followed by Heteroskioi and Amphiskioi. At II.5.37 in his delineation of klimata, Strabo, without mention of Posidonius, adopts the terms Amphiskioi and Heteroskioi as established, but nowhere introduces Periskioi.

24 'as I said in my discussion against Pytheas'. Cf. II.5.8: Pytheas put Thule at 66° (summer tropic is arctic circle, i.e. φ = 24°, φ̄ = 66°). Strabo questions the existence of Thule, and does not believe that the inhabited world reaches the summer tropic = arctic circle (66°) latitude. He thinks that Pytheas is a liar because οἱ νῦν ἱστοροῦντες mention nothing beyond Ierne, and also there and in the northern part of Britain the population is savage and has difficulty maintaining an existence because of the cold. Stade distances show that Strabo is thinking of a latitude of about 54°, again the 'arctic circle' for observers at the basic Pillars of Hercules–Rhodes meridian of 36°; but more importantly for Strabo, he believes that that is the limit of the inhabited world in terms of *human* geography, and therefore speculation about regions still further north is useless. Strabo clearly distrusted Pytheas completely: πανταχοῦ ἀλλαχοῦ δὲ παρακρουόμενος τοὺς ἀνθρώπους ὁ Πυθέας κἀνταῦθά που διέψευσται. Cf. also II.3.5 F49.289ff; T46; II.4.1 (Πυθέαν, ὑφ' οὗ παρακρουσθῆναι πολλούς)-2 (cf. T25, comm.).

24-30 'So there is no need even to worry about the size of this uninhabited land ...'

Cf. II.5.8: τὸ δ' ἐκεῖθεν ἐπὶ τὴν Ἰέρνην οὐκέτι γνώριμον, πόσον ἄν τις θείη, οὐδ' εἰ περαιτέρω ἔτι οἰκήσιμά ἐστιν, οὐδὲ δεῖ φροντίζειν τοῖς ἐπάνω λεχθεῖσι προσέχοντας.

'... apart from accepting that those having the tropic as arctic circle (i.e. in the polar circle) fall under the circle described by the pole of the zodiac during the diurnal revolution of the universe, postulating that the interval intervening between equator and tropic is 4/60 (i.e. 24°, the generally accepted angle of the ecliptic) of the greatest circle (meridian).'

We are back to Posidonius' arctic circle of 66°, which Strabo accepts in theory, however useless for his conception of geography. But he has also dropped all reference to shadow definition.

Strabo makes clear in what way he thinks Posidonius' classification is useless for the geographer studying the habitable world: Periskian does not even, in his opinion, define the limits of habitation. But neither for that matter do Amphiskian and Heteroskian. So what aspect does Strabo find useful (πῇ χρήσιμον, 3f)?

As often, there appears to be some confusion between astronomically defined zones and zones of temperature in relation to habitable and inhabitable areas of the earth (cf. F49.71ff). Cleomedes, *De Motu* 1.7.33f, p. 62 Z uses (without acknowledgement) and explains in detail the Posidonian terms and classification (Periskioi, etc) in a chapter headed Περὶ τῶν τῆς γῆς οἰκήσεων, and beginning: ὅλης δὲ τῆς γῆς καθ' ὑπόθεσιν οἰκουμένης, τῶν οἰκήσεων αἱ μὲν περίσκιοι, αἱ δὲ ἑτερόσκιοι, αἱ δὲ ἀμφίσκιοι γενήσονται. Cf. also Achilles Tatius, *Isag.* 31, p. 66f Maass; and for recognition of the confusion, Ach. Tat. *Isag.* 31, p. 67.33-5 Maass.

The adjectives περίσκιοι κτλ may be applied to people (F208), zones (F49.44ff) or habitations (οἰκήσεις, Cleom. *De Motu* 1.7.33f). If Posidonius challenged the theory of an inhabitable equatorial zone (F210; as did others, cf. Ach. Tat. *Isag.* 29. p. 63.5 Maass), did he also challenge desert 'frigid' zones? But he did not hold that the whole of the 'torrid' zone was habitable (F49.17ff).

For some reasons for this persistent confusion, see Aujac, 'Poseidonios et les Zones Terrestres: les Raisons d'un Échec', *BAGB* 35 (1976), 74–8.

F209 Achilles Tatius, *In Aratum Isagoga* excerpta 31, p. 67.27–33 Maass

CONTENT

Posidonius is grouped with Polybius as counting six zones by dividing the torrid zone into two.

CONTEXT

The earlier part of section 31 (p. 66.28–67.26 Maass) relates the sun's shadow to the different zones of habitation. ἄσκιοι are those living on the equator when the sun is in Aries and Libra, or those living at Syene and Elephantine (which were thought to lie on the tropic) when the sun is in Cancer. After brief mention of βραχύσκιοι and μακρόσκιοι, the Posidonian terms (see F208) ἑτερόσκιοι and ἀμφίσκιοι (οἱ ὑπὸ τὸν ἰσημερινὸν κύκλον οἰκοῦντες) are introduced without any reference to Posidonius, and explained. They bracket the novel term ἀντίσκιοι (confused with ἄντοικοι?). Posidonius' third term is mentioned as a final afterthought: 'Some people (τινὲς) want there to be Periskioi who have their shadow in a circle round them.' The Posidonian influence is corrupted and much embroidered. This is however another instance of the shadow-classification linked with zones of habitation, F208 comm. and Cleom. *De Motu* 1.7.

COMMENT

1 Strabo derived the opinion that Parmenides was the instigator of the five-zone theory from Posidonius, F49.10f. A doxographical tradition also assigned five terrestrial zones to Pythagoras (Aet. *Plac.* III.14 = *Dox. Gr.* 378.20ff) and five celestial zones to Thales and Pythagoras (Aet. *Plac.* II.12 = *Dox. Gr.* 340); cf. Diels, *Proleg.* p. 181; also attributed to 'some Pythagoreans', Ps.-Galen, *Hist. Phil.*, *Dox. Gr.* 633.15ff.

2ff Strabo records Polybius' six zones (II.3.1 = F49.62ff), and Cleomedes (*De Motu* 1.6.31, p. 58.6ff Ziegler = F210.7ff) implies difference of opinion on their number, but in fact five zones became the standard number, as Cleomedes suggests; so Eratosthenes (Ach. Tat., *Isag.* 29, p. 62.22 Maass), Strabo, Pomponius Mela 1.1, Geminus, *Isag.* xv.1, Cleomedes, *De Motu* 1.2.11f.

Posidonius is wrongly grouped with Polybius here: see F49.64–118 for the criticism of Polybius' number of zones by Strabo and Posidonius, and in particular for the criticism of Polybius' division of the torrid zone into two (F49.102–18).

Posidonius supported the five-zone theory (F49.44ff). Misunderstanding and confusion could arise however from different types of classification with different criteria; for example, Posidonius argued for two narrow parched strips on the tropics (F49.49ff). Also he agreed basically with Polybius on the existence of a temperate equatorial strip, while disagreeing on detail (F49.118ff; cf. F210 comm.), which could have misled the tradition of this fragment. But even if one considered that Posidonius had more than one theory of zones, schemes of five and of seven are possible, but not of six. It is likely, however, that Posidonius on the strict subject of zones, consistently maintained five, defined astronomically

COMMENTARY: F210

by solar shadow (F218, F49.44-8). The problem of the inhabited world, climatic conditions and bands of temperature (as distinct from klimata, or bands of latitude) was different (in spite of Strabo, F49.71-92). Although there had been earlier correlations of these with zones (as in 'torrid', 'frigid' and 'temperate' zones), such a correlation could not be acceptable to Posidonius. For example, the 'torrid' zone (which is interpreted in terms of being uninhabitable) does not correspond to the central 'amphiskian' zone (F49.17ff).

F210 Cleomedes, *De Motu* 1.6.31-3

CONTENT

Cleomedes reports and criticises a theory of Posidonius that in the so-called 'torrid' zone there was a temperate and inhabited equatorial region.

CONTEXT

De Motu 1.6 examines the monthly increase or decrease of daylight between the longest and shortest day (p. 50.15ff Ziegler). The cause of the unevenness of increase (or decrease) is the obliquity of the zodiac. The sun's path crosses the equator at two signs, and touches each of the tropics at one sign (p. 52.3-7 Z). The sun crosses the equator and adjacent territory pretty well at right angles, but approaches the tropics more obliquely and with greater inclination; and so this making of an acute angle is the reason why the sun approaches and departs from the tropics more slowly (σχολαιότερον). But at the equator, the sun being more at right angles, its approach and retirement is 'all at once' (ἀθρουστέρας) (p. 52.7-17 Z). Cleomedes gives as the reason for this the eccentricity of the heliacal circle (p. 54 Z).

COMMENTARY: F210

COMMENT

A. The theory (1–10)

1–7 'Since as we said, the approach and retirement of the sun at the tropics is slower (σχολαιότερον, see Context; but for Posidonian background, also F49.125ff) and so it spends a greater period of time in their area, and since the area at the tropics is not uninhabited, nor areas still further in the interior (Syene lies on the summer tropic, Ethiopia is still further inland than that), Posidonius taking his key note from these facts, assumed that also the whole latitude at the equator was temperate.'

See F49.58–61, 125ff. Geminus, *Isag.* XVI.32ff cites only Polybius for this theory. Strabo (F49.118ff) mentions Eratosthenes and Polybius as well as Posidonius. Panaetius and Eudorus are also named in Anon. *Isag. in Arat.*, p. 97 Maass. It was clearly much debated.

7–10 'And while the natural philosophers of established reputation declared that there were five zones of the earth, he (Posidonius) declared that what they called torrid was inhabited and temperate.' According to Strabo, F49.44ff, Posidonius himself held a five-zone theory, πρὸς τὰ οὐράνια, i.e. as a φυσικός (cf. F49.65). As a human geographer (πρὸς τὰ ἀνθρώπεια, F49.49) concerned with the habitable world, he seems to have had a different classification, including two special zones at the topics (F49.49ff); in addition to these he appears to have assumed a temperate habitable zone on the equator. It is not easy to see how this approach can fit a 'physical' five-zone theory; see comm. on F49.44–145. It is possible that Posidonius distinguished at least two categories of classification.

It would be strange if τῶν εὐδοκίμων φυσικῶν (8) referred simply to 'Les Stoïciens' (Goulet, *Cléomède, théorie élémentaire*, p. 196 n. 136); cf. F209.2 comm.

COMMENTARY: F210

B. Posidonius' reasons (10–23) (γάρ, 10)

(a) **10–15** 'For whereas although the sun delays (διατρίβοντος) longer in the area of the tropics, yet the area at the tropics is not uninhabited, nor are the regions still further in the interior uninhabited, surely it was much more likely that the equatorial area was temperate, when the sun at this circle (the equator) quickly approaches and again equally quickly retires and does not delay at that latitude . . .'

This is the main Posidonian account of the argument Cleomedes summarised at 1–7. The detailed explanation about the angle of the sun is given at Cleom. 1.6, p. 52.7–17, for which see above. The wording is very similar to Cleomedes' pre-echo in 1–7. Both passages use the negative expression οὐκ . . . ἀοίκητα (11, 3) for the area at the tropic. This was probably Posidonius' form of expression, because he held the band of latitude at the tropic to be desert with a peculiar (and sparse?) ethnic population (F49.51–58). Geminus, *Isag.* XVI.32–6 assigns this argument to Polybius.

(b) **15–17** '. . . and the night is completely equal to the day here, and for that reason provides an interval long enough for cooling'. One of the main methods of establishing bands of latitude was by the proportion of longest to shortest day (Neugebauer, *HAMA* I.A.4.6; IV.D), so this feature of the equator would come readily to mind, and anyway was the initial subject of Cleom. 1.6.

(c) (i) **18–20** 'And this air (atmosphere, ἀέρος) being in the most central and deepest shadow, both rain and wind will occur capable of cooling the air.'

18 μεσαιτάτῳ: μέσος is used in astronomical texts with reference to the ecliptic or equator (LSJ *s.v.* III.6). The suggestion must be that at the equator there is not only equinoctial phenomena ((b) above), but the contrast between day and night accentuates the depth of shadow or darkness, and gives rise to rain and cooling wind.

(ii) **20–3** This is reinforced by established conditions in

Ethiopia, where continuous rain is reported in summer, and particularly at the height of summer (from which the Nile flooding is conjectured). See F222. F49.134f seems to give a different and probably garbled emphasis.

It is noteworthy that all Posidonius' reasons are theoretical, but that they involve the interplay of air, wind and rain.

C. Cleomedes' criticism of Posidonius (ὥστε οὐκ ὀρθῶς ἔοικεν ἐνταῦθα φέρεσθαι ὁ Ποσειδώνιος, 47f) (24–48)

(1) 24–7 If the equatorial area is like that, the seasons will have to come twice a year with them, since the sun too is twice overhead, making two equinoxes.

Since it would be hottest at the equinoxes, in that sense there would be two 'summers'; and since the solstices would be equidistant and so identical, there would be two 'winters'. Cf. F212.

(2) 27–34 'Those opposing this view of Posidonius say that the circumstance of the sun spending longer time at the tropics does not necessarily make Posidonius' view sound. No, the sun stays away again longer from the tropics, and so the air at the tropics is cooled longer, and these latitudes can be inhabited. Whereas the equator lies in between the tropics, and the sun is away from it for a short time and quickly wheels round to it.'

This answers directly Posidonius (a) (10–15).

(3) 35–40 'The area under the tropics receives the etesian winds from the frigid zones which both assuage the heat of the sun and cool the air. But these cannot reach the equator. And if they were to reach it, they would be hot and scorching from the length of their journey under the sun.'

This answers partly Posidonius (c)(i) (18–20).

(4) 40–4 'As for night being equal to day, that could not of itself contribute to cooling the air there, because the force of the sun is beyond expression, sending its rays perpendicularly and with intensity continually at that latitude, with hardly any inclination worth mentioning from it.'

This answers Posidonius (b) (15–17).

(5) **44–7** 'It is conjectured by the natural philosophers (τῶν φυσικῶν) that the greatest part of the great sea (i.e. Ocean) underlies this latitude, in the most central position for the sustenance of the stars.'

Who are οἱ φυσικοί? Cleanthes, Crates, Seneca? Cf. Strabo, F49.141; Cleom. F210.7f.

For this comment: see F118 comm. This passage makes explicitly clear that Cleomedes opposed Posidonius to natural philosophers who believed in an equatorial ocean, and that Macrobius (F118) and Strabo (F49.141) were confused. For details, F118 comm. Posidonius however probably believed that the heavenly bodies were nourished by moisture (F118, F10).

This detailed criticism of Posidonius by Cleomedes makes clear that he was no mere copier of Posidonius, and that his work was not simply derived from Posidonius; T57.

F211 Symeon Seth, *De Utilitate Corporum Caelestium* 44

CONTENT

A temperate equatorial climate.

CONTEXT

The date of Symeon Seth is 11th c. A.D. He reported an eclipse of the sun in the reign of Isaac Comnenus (1057–9), noted in a trip to Egypt, *Conspectus* 49. He was a dignitary of the imperial palace of Antiochus. One of his works was dedicated to Michael Ducas (1071–8), and another was commissioned by Alexis Comnenus (1081–1118); Delatte, *Anecdota Atheniensia* II.1f.

COMMENTARY: F211

The Περὶ χρείας is a work of astronomical teleology. He starts on the sun at §38, dealing with its size in 39–42. At 43 he turns to 'Why the sun moves in an ecliptic'. This rouses his religious admiration for the purpose and benefit of the obliquity of the sun's path. In the first place (πρῶτον μὲν γάρ), had it not been so, the area under its circle would have been scorched and destroyed completely. The change of path of the sun brings relief to places perpendicularly beneath it.

COMMENT

1–4 'At any rate as it is now, those living at the equator enjoy sufficiently a temperate climate through the changing path of the sun as Posidonius records and those who have come from those parts to our latitudes have narrated.'

For this Posidonian theory: see comm. on F49.118–45, and F210.

5–13 'Secondly (εἶτα answers πρῶτον μὲν γάρ of §43, see Context above) not only the country under that parallel (i.e. the equator) would have been uninhabitable but also through the excess of heat and the stationary position of the sun, the adjacent territory up to 20° or even more (the tropics were usually placed roundly at 24°). And the countries after these would have been very few and extremely narrow in width that had some little share in a temperate climate, and they would all have been useless and barren, with no winter through the retreat of the sun, nor summer through its nearness, nor spring to precede summer.'

6 τε codices links nothing, and the sense is wrong. Sandbach suggests a missing link, but a hypothetical is needed, so ἄν; cf. lines 9 and 17.

Theiler, II.75 talks of four successive zones, in the third of which there is no summer, and spring is also lacking. But if the sun were to be stationary on the equator, there would be no seasons anywhere. His reference to Arius Did. 26.462.5f is irrelevant.

COMMENTARY: F211

13 θέρος codices: θέρους Theiler, which may be right; but the accusative does occur with προηγεῖσθαι in later Greek.

13–17 'And the land next to these, such as completely... would be uninhabitable through the excess of cold, not only to humans but to all creatures as well, no better than the Cimmerians. And the whole earth would have remained uninhabitable through the excessive conditions and incongruousness deriving from such a movement.'

13 Either there is a lacuna after πάντως, or Theiler may be correct in suggesting ἂν ἦν for οἷα/οἷον of the codices.

The argument appears to be that since the path of the sun remained on the equator and did not approach the tropics, the frigid zone would come correspondingly further south (or north), leaving at most a very narrow temperate zone.

Although Posidonius mentions the Cimmerians in F272.35 in an identification theory for the Cimbri, the idea of the Cimmerians occupying the northern borders of the world was a very old and common Greek one (F272 *ad loc.*), and certainly not specifically Posidonian. Indeed it is probable that the only reference to Posidonius is the citation as an authority for a temperate equatorial zone. The argument that if the sun's path had been equatorial rather than ecliptic, not only would there not have been a temperate equatorial strip, but only a very narrow temperate habitable area squeezed in between scorched and expanded frigid zones, occurs nowhere else, and it may derive from Symeon's own characteristic religious admiration for the teleological structure of the universe. Nevertheless it is interesting that Posidonius' name crops up at this late date among the few authors cited by Symeon (cf. Delatte, *Anecdota Atheniensia* II. 127), and shows the persistence of parts of the geographical/physical/astronomical tradition.

F212, F213 Pliny, *Naturalis Historia* 6.57–8; Solinus, *Collectanea Rerum Memorabilium* 52.1–2

CONTENT

The orientation and climate of India.

CONTEXT

At 6.56 Pliny turns to India from the Himalayas. It is bordered by the Eastern Sea and the Southern Sea. The east-facing coast stretches in a straight line until it comes to a bend (presumably Cape Comorin, opposite Taprobane or Sri Lanka); from there the southerly bend of the coast stretches to the Indus, which is the western boundary of India. Pliny gives a series of conflicting measurements for coastlines and length and breadth of India, naming Eratosthenes and Agrippa. Solinus is a rehash of part of Pliny.

COMMENT

1–3 Posidonius plotted India on the map (*metatus est*) from summer rising of the sun (NE) to winter rising (SE), positioning it as facing Gaul, which he drew from summer setting (NW) to winter setting (SW).

This is a most important re-orientation of India on the map. The canonical Greek and Roman view was that India stretched in a west to east direction; so Eratosthenes followed by Strabo (Str. II.1.34; II.5.35–6; XV.1.11; Bunbury, *History of Ancient Geography* II.307; Thomson, *History of Ancient Geography* 134f); Pomponius Mela (III.68–9; Bunbury, II.365); Pliny (*NH* 6.56–7; followed by Solinus); Marinus and Ptolemy himself (Bunbury II.601f). Posidonius clearly orientated it NS. Only two others made this correct suggestion: Megasthenes, *c.* 300 B.C. (Arrian, *Indica* III.7–8), and, probably

COMMENTARY: F212-213

about 50 A.D., the author of the *Periplus Maris Rubri* (*Periplus* 50). All three were ignored and the WE projection persisted doggedly into Ptolemy's map.

2 adversam Galliam, lit.: 'positioning Gaul facing it'. Solinus (F213.4) has *adversam Galliae*; but Solinus, who was almost certainly using Pliny as his source, may have changed his construction (cf. T36, T37; Walter, op. cit. below). Solinus's *hanc* makes a difference; Pliny's *eam* is attached to *metatus est*, not to *statuens*.

4 Pliny's codices have: *totam a favonio. itaque adversum* (*adverso* R^2) *eius venti adflatu iuvari* (*adflatum iuvare z*) *Indiam salubremque fieri* ...

totam must refer to India, not to Gallia, because it would not make sense to refer significantly to Gaul with regard to the west wind, and then immediately continue: and therefore India is a healthy country because of that wind. So *adversam Galliam* ... *hibernum metabatur* (2-4) is a parenthesis. The context of the first sentence is clearly directional, the orientation of India, while the second sentence refers to climatic conditions. Therefore the reference to the west wind at the end of the first sentence (*totam a favonio*) must be directional, following the usual practice of using winds as compass points (F137). This makes perfect sense; for if Posidonius is reorientating India NS, then as a whole (the length of its coastline) it will face west (*favonius*). So the sense would be: the whole (of India) in the direction of (facing) the west wind. The climatic consequences follow. So André in Budé: 'et l'a placée tout entière du côté du Favorinus', but he is not clear on *totam*. However, I am not convinced that *totam a favonio* could mean this on its own without an additional word giving the point of view of the direction. Therefore I suggested a lacuna. But it is not easy to see how one could fill this lacuna. Theiler's *totam a favonio* ⟨*aversam*⟩ (F69a Th), referring to Gaul, is incomprehensible to me. When Latin wishes to say 'facing west', the phrase is more naturally *in favonium spectare* (e.g. Pliny *NH* 15.21) or the like. So perhaps

757

COMMENTARY: F212–213

the sentence ended, *totam ad favonium ⟨versam⟩* (cf. Pliny *NH* 37.100); but *adversus* can take a dative, so *totam favonio ⟨adversam⟩* (cf. Pliny *NH* 24.1) is possible. *versam* or *adversam* could have been omitted because of the following *advers(um, -o, -am)*. Alternatively, although in the second sentence, *adverso* (R^2) makes sense with *adflatu*, the directional point must have been made at the end of the preceding sentence where *adversam* or the like is necessary, so *adverso* may be a transpositional mistake, and could be deleted. Although it is possible to argue that corruption lies in *totam*, which might have replaced *fotam* (*a favonio*), this is unlikely because it destroys the necessary contrast between the directional thrust of the first sentence's reference to *favonius*, and the second sentence's climatic implications from *favonius*.

6–10 Pliny adds that the astronomical conditions of India are different (different aspects of the heavens, different risings of the stars), and so different climatic and agricultural conditions follow: two summers and two harvests annually, separated by a winter with etesian winds, while in our own winter time they have soft breezes and a navigable sea.

This may or may not also be Posidonius. Solinus (F213, early 3rd c. A.D.) in addition to the healthy *favonius* and the position of India opposite Gaul, also has the double summers and harvests and the etesian winds in(stead of) winter. But almost certainly Solinus was simply plundering Pliny in however garbled a form (F213.3), so this is hardly corroboration (Walter, 'Die Collectanea Rerum Memorabilium', *Hermes Einzelschr.* Heft 22 (1969); Mommsen's edition of Solinus *ad loc.*). The tradition continued in Martianus Capella, VI.694 (5th c. A.D.) and in Isidorus, *Orig.* XIV.3.6 (7th c. A.D.). Nevertheless the relationship between astronomy and climate (heavenly and terrestrial spheres) sounds Posidonian. The two summers and two winters occur also in Cleomedes' criticisms of Posidonius in F210.24ff, where they seem to be derived as an inference from Posidonian theory. But the fact that two annual harvests can be and were

COMMENTARY: F214

produced in India had already been noticed by Megasthenes and Eratosthenes (Str. xv.1.20).

See Dihle, *RhM* 105 (1962), 97ff for the earlier history of the fertile east.

TIDES, HYDROLOGY

F214   Strabo, 1.1.8–9

CONTENT

Uniform behaviour of ocean and tides. Extent of Ocean.

CONTEXT

Strabo has been explaining how Homer can be regarded as the first philosophical geographer, particularly in his account of Ocean. Ocean is represented as surrounding the inhabited world, which is thus regarded as an island. Strabo supports this view with the argument that no one has yet been stopped by land in attempts to circumnavigate the globe. F214 embodies his second argument.

ANALYSIS

A

A theory of circumambient ocean would accord with the behaviour of flood and ebb tides. Evidence to support this is that (γοῦν) everywhere there is the same basic manner of changes and particularly of highs and lows, or not much variation; and this is what one would expect to be the case if the movement were being rendered (explained?) by a single sea and from a single cause.

COMMENTARY: F214

B

Strabo does not find Hipparchus convincing when he opposes this opinion on the following grounds:

(i) Oceanus does not behave uniformly everywhere. For this statement of fact Hipparchus witnesses Seleucus.

(ii) Even if (i) were granted, it would not follow that the Atlantic flows all round in a circle.

C

But Strabo (ἡμεῖς δέ) is content to refer to Posidonius and Athenodorus for more extended arguments on Ocean and tides. They have sufficiently maintained the theory (or, the arguments) of that subject. For the moment Strabo will say only this much in reply:

(a) With regard to uniform behaviour (ὁμοιοπάθεια), it is better (βέλτιον) to believe thus.

(b) The further moisture extends round the earth, the better (more securely?, κρεῖττον) the heavenly bodies would be held together by the exhalations from it.

COMMENT

A. (1-5)

Aujac (*Strabon et la science de son temps* 1.1, p. 177 n. 4, Budé) suggests that while ἀμπώτεις and πλημμυρίδας (1-2) refer to ebb and flood tides, μεταβολῶν, αὐξήσεων and μειώσεων (3-4) are expressions referring to changing levels of sea on land, and that Strabo confused the two different phenomena. She concludes that Strabo borrows uncritically here from Eratosthenes, who was interested in changes of sea level (Strabo, 1.3.4ff), and that this is borne out by the following reference to Hipparchus' criticism. But there is no evidence for confusion in this passage. Strabo's language for changing sea levels is: μετεωρίζεσθαι, ταπεινοῦσθαι, συνεξαίρειν, συνενδιδόναι, πλεονασμός (1.3.5). He uses αὔξησις, αὔξεσθαι, μείωσις, μειοῦσθαι of high and low *tides* (III.5.8; F217.46ff). γοῦν (2)

COMMENTARY: F214

shows that the same manner of μεταβολαί, αὐξήσεις and μειώσεις is explanatory of the ebb and flood tides of line 1; and the reference to Seleucus by Hipparchus shows that the latter was here referring to tides (see Comment B). I therefore take μεταβολῶν as a general word for 'changes', further defined by 'high and low tides' (αὐξήσεων, μειώσεων). The general expression, μεταβάλλειν, can be used by Strabo of change of current in the Sicilian straits (1.3.11); and tides and ebb and flow through straits (e.g. of Messina) were connected by Eratosthenes (1.3.11; cf. 1.2.36). But even that cannot be in Strabo's mind in this passage, since he denied that there was εἷς τρόπος of currents in straits (1.3.12). There is no necessity that Strabo was 'borrowing' from anyone in this passage, although there may well have been a doxographic account of the controversy in Posidonius and Athenodorus.

The deletion of τε before μεταβολῶν (3; A. Miller, H. L. Jones (Loeb), Dicks, *Geographical Fragments of Hipparchus* 114) has no manuscript support, and is unnecessary.

B. (5-10)

Hipparchus (F4 Dicks, VIII.1 Berger) was almost certainly criticising Eratosthenes, who entertained a theory of circumambient Ocean (F8 Dicks, FII.A, 8 Berger, *Die geographischen Fragmente des Eratosthenes* 91-8, Strabo 1.3.13) and of ὁμοιοπάθεια (I.B, 16 Berger, Strabo, 1.3.11). See also Dicks, *Hipparchus* 38, 114; Berger, *Erdkunde* 395f, 461; Berger, *Die geographischen Fragmente des Hipparch* 79ff.

B.(i) (6-10) See F218 for Seleucus and his account of the diurnal tidal irregularity of the Indian Ocean. The references to Seleucus and ὁμοιοπάθεια show that Strabo here had in mind tidal phenomena only (see Comment A). Strabo agreed with Hipparchus that there was no ὁμοιοπάθεια as regards the flow of currents through straits in the Mediterranean (Str. 1.3.12). F215 comm. discusses Posidonius and this latter distinct problem.

B.(ii) (7-9) Hipparchus seems to have considered the

COMMENTARY: F214

possibility of further land masses beyond the limits of Oceanus; cf. his remark on Ceylon (Pomponius Mela III.7.7, F5 Dicks, VIII.2 Berger).

C. (10ff)

Strabo clearly regarded Posidonius and Athenodorus of Tarsus (T44) as the most up to date general authorities (ἱκανῶς διακρατήσαντας cf. F215) on tidal phenomena. Since he is content to refer to them it would follow: (i) that he was intimately acquainted with their writing on this subject (Frs. 217, 218 for the importance of this); (ii) that his own account of tides follows theirs on fundamental issues; that is, Posidonius argued for a uniform behaviour of tidal phenomena (cf. Frs. 217, 218), and held a theory of circumambient ocean (cf. Str. II.2.5, F49.229f). It does not follow that Strabo was in agreement with and simply repeated all details of their theories. Indeed this would be impossible, since on some points Posidonius and Athenodorus disagreed, as in Str. III.5.7 (see comm. on F217), and Strabo did on occasion criticise Posidonius strongly on this subject (as in Frs. 217, 49). It is therefore uncertain whether Strabo's final remarks (C.(a) (b) = 13–16) derive from Posidonius. Nevertheless it is likely that Posidonius held some such theory as C.(b) (see F10, but also F118 comm. for the difficulties of the evidence). The argument C.(a), οὕτω βέλτιον, is also not uncharacteristic of Posidonius (F18.22: ⟨ἀπὸ⟩ τοῦ ἄμεινον οὕτως ἔχειν), but is hardly peculiar to him (Plato, *Ph.* 97eff).

While Posidonius, like Strabo here and others before him (see Dicks, p. 38 for Hipparchus), may have begun his Περὶ ὠκεανοῦ with remarks on Homer's Oceanus (cf. F216), it is on the whole probable that Strabo's reference here is general, rather than a particular reminiscence of such an introductory doxography. Strabo may have been content with a reference rather than to go into details, because they were φυσικώτερα (T79b, F215, F49.359, T77).

Posidonius, as Strabo knew, was not the first to argue a

762

COMMENTARY: F215

uniform tidal theory, even a lunar theory (F138 comm.); but it was his investigations which established the theory in detail. I am inclined to believe that the consensus of manuscript readings, διακρατήσαντας, can convey this without recourse to the many emendations suggested, although I can find no exact parallel for this usage. But διαιτήσαντας Madvig, or διακριβώσαντας Meineke are attractive.

F215 Strabo, 1.3.12

CONTENT

Posidonius an authority on tidal ebb and flow.

CONTEXT

Strabo 1.3.1ff is concerned with criticism of Eratosthenes, first on the problem of inland deposits of sea shells, which leads to theories of depth of seas and changing levels. In §10 Eratosthenes is attacked for thinking that currents in straits are due to water flowing from different levels of sea bed. §11 adds a detailed lunar tidal theory of Eratosthenes for the changes of current in the Straits of Messina. In §12 Strabo leaves tidal theory to Posidonius and Athenodorus (F215), but offers criticism of Eratosthenes on currents in straits, namely: (a) it is not true that one principle can account for straits having currents; (b) even if one principle was adequate, it could not be what Eratosthenes suggests, a different level of sea bed on either side of a strait.

COMMENT

This fragment appears to be similar in function and language to F214.10–13 (F214, Comment C). However Strabo in 1.3.12 offers an antithesis: περὶ μὲν οὖν τῶν πλημμυρίδων ... in the matter of tidal ebb and flow he is content to refer to

763

COMMENTARY: F215

Posidonius and Athenodorus (presumably in answer to Eratosthenes' tidal theory described in §11, for which cf. F219); περὶ δὲ τῆς τῶν πορθμῶν παλιρροίας . . . but concerning refluent currents in straits (and with reference to the Eratosthenean theory of different levels of sea bed) Strabo himself offers the criticism outlined under Context above.

It is just possible that by the antithesis Strabo does not mean to imply that Posidonius is his authority for tidal theory but not for changing currents in straits, but only that although strait currents also (like tidal theory) involve a more scientific explanation than is suitable for his present context (ἐχόντων καὶ αὐτῶν φυσικώτερον λόγον ἢ κατὰ τὴν νῦν ὑπόθεσιν) he wishes to offer in his present work some comment on this, while leaving tides to readers of Posidonius. But on the whole this interpretation is unlikely. It is more natural to understand an antithesis between tides and strait currents, with Posidonius an authority for the former but not the latter; which exercised Greeks as a separate problem as far back as Aristotle at least (*Meteor.* II.1; see also Duhem, *Le Système du monde* II.268ff; Aujac, *Strabon et la science de son temps* 295ff, Budé Strabon I.1, p. 177). Posidonius is not mentioned in Strabo's criticism of Eratosthenes which follows, but Hipparchus is (on the straits of Byzantium). Also the refusal to accept a single principle to explain strait currents strengthens the suspicion that if Strabo had an authority in mind here it is probably Hipparchus, although no doubt in garbled fashion since Strabo seems rather muddled. See F214 and cf. also Dicks, *Geographical Fragments of Hipparchus* 116ff; Berger, *Die geographischen Fragmente des Hipparch* 83ff; id. *Die geographischen Fragmente des Eratosthenes* 60ff.

It is therefore safer to confine Strabo's evidence on Posidonius to tidal ebb and flow, on which he was accepted as an authority. This does not mean that Posidonius was silent on channel currents. Priscianus Lydus, F219.19ff, would suggest that Posidonius explained the latter also by a lunar

COMMENTARY: F216

tidal theory, which is another reason for disregarding the remainder of Strabo 1.3.12.

For Athenodorus of Tarsus: T44.

F216 Strabo, 1.1.7

CONTEXT

Strabo is engaged in praise of Homer's geographical insights. §7 is concerned with Oceanus.

ANALYSIS

A

Strabo: Homer was not ignorant of ebb and flow tides of Ocean.

Evidence:

(1) 'back-flowing Ocean' (*Il.* XVIII.399);
(2) 'three times a day she sends it up, three times a day sucks it down' (*Od.* XII.105). Strabo comments that either Homer was wrong with thrice for twice, or there is a corruption in the text.
(3) 'Soft-flowing' (*Il.* VII.422), indicates, says Strabo, that flow tides mount gently and not violently.

B

Posidonius *conjectures* (εἰκάζει) that Homer refers to flow tides

(1) when he says headlands (σκοπέλους) are sometimes covered, sometimes bared (*Od.* XII.235–43?);
(2) by calling Oceanus 'river' (as *Il.* XIV.245), its flow (τὸ ῥοῶδες αὐτοῦ) implies flow tides.

C

Strabo accepts B.(1) but not B.(2), denying that a flow tide is

COMMENTARY: F216

like a river current. He goes on to prefer the exposition of Crates of Mallos (F35a Mette, *Sphairopoiia*).

COMMENT

1 Strabo uses Posidonius (although critically) to support his views on Homer against Eratosthenes. From this it is clear that Posidonius, like Hipparchus, discussed Homer as a source of geographical information and views, although no doubt an amateur one (cf. F48), against Eratosthenes (Berger, *Erdkunde* 387f, 460; Dicks, *Geographical Fragments of Hipparchus* 38). What is more debatable is the extent of the Posidonian evidence on this question in Strabo or even in this fragment. As A.(2) and B.(1) both refer to currents in the Straits of Messina, under the guise of Scylla and Charybdis (cf. Strabo, 1.2.16; 1.2.36), it may be thought that Posidonius was the source of A as well as B. But this would be dangerous since A.(2) including the criticism of the word 'thrice' is referred to Polybius at 1.2.16, and Strabo passes in C to the remarks of Crates. Reinhardt (*RE* col. 668) pulled in the whole of 1.1.4–7 as Posidonius (also III.2.13ff; XVII.1.19). For Pohlenz (*Die Stoa* II.119), 'die Verteidigung Homers gegen Eratosthenes bei Strabon I cap. 1.2 ist wohl im ganzen in Poseidonios' Sinn gehalten'. Heinemann (*Poseidonios' Metaphysische Schriften* II.54ff) went further still. But it should be remembered that after Eratosthenes began his *Geography* with a famous attack on Homer (Berger, *Eratosthenes* 19ff), not only was he criticised by Hipparchus and Posidonius, but the Homeric Question in geography was taken up enthusiastically by Alexandrian and Pergamene scholars such as Crates (Mette, *Sphairopoiia*), Apollodorus and Agatharchides (in general, Pfeiffer, *History of Classical Scholarship* 115ff, 255ff; Fraser, *Ptolemaic Alexandria* 1.326f, 526f, 539, 548; and above all Strabo himself). *Loci communes* were bound to develop. Even the topic of Scylla and Charybdis as tidal evidence could have been discussed by anyone after Eratosthenes'

COMMENTARY: F217

speculations on tides in the Sicilian straits (Strabo, 1.3.12). It is unlikely that Strabo read or relied on only one source for his section on Homer (cf. F49.330ff). So although Posidonius may well have been implicated in other sections of the Homeric introduction, it is safest to confine fragments to express allusions by Strabo.

2 Since Eratosthenes (Berger, *Fragmente* 19ff), Hipparchus (Dicks, *Geographical Fragments of Hipparchus* 38) and Strabo (1.1.2ff) all began their geographical works with a review of Homeric evidence, it is likely that Posidonius' Περὶ ὠκεανοῦ opened with a doxographical section including Homer. No doubt Περὶ συγκρίσεως 'Ἀράτου καὶ 'Ὁμήρου περὶ τῶν μαθηματικῶν (F48) also contained Homeric material (cf. Reinhardt, *RE* col. 667); but since we know that Strabo used Περὶ ὠκεανοῦ, F216 B probably derives from it.

3 The expression of *B* is slightly illogical in that the final conjecture, τὸ ῥοῶδες αὐτοῦ ... ἐμφανίζεσθαι applies strictly to B.(2) and not to B.(1). Hence Coray cut καί before ἐκ τοῦ σκοπέλους. But the sense is clear, and it is understandable that the conclusion was framed to the nearer piece of evidence. Also Strabo may have had in mind the use of the adjective ῥοώδης with words like σκόπελος, meaning rocks exposed to strong currents (cf. Strabo, VIII.5.1; Ael. *NA* 14.24).

4 For other examples of Posidonius' use of Homeric 'evidence': Frs. 49.300ff, 137, 222, 277a. He may well have been influenced by Crates of Mallos.

5 T88 discusses Posidonius' use of εἰκάζειν.

F217   Strabo, III.5.7–8

CONTEXT

Self-contained. Strabo is giving a general account of Cadiz; he has been discussing the Pillars of Hercules (III.5.6), and

COMMENTARY: F217

whether the pillars in the Herakleion at Gadeira represented them. He proceeds to the well-known problem (F217.24f) of the spring at Herakleion.

CONTENT

From the point of view of Posidonius, this fragment falls into two distinct sections: Posidonius' criticism of previous accounts of wells at Cadiz, and his theory of tides. It is Strabo who combines the two, citing the latter as evidence against the former.

COMMENT

A. *The wells (1–30, 54–68)*

The first part (1–23) is concerned with Posidonius' criticism on the subject, the second (23–30, 54–68) with Strabo's criticism of Posidonius.

A.1 (1–11)

Polybius (34.9.1) is cited for an observed fact: the spring (κρήνη) in the Herakleion is affected inversely (ἀντιπαθεῖν) to the tides (1–4). This is followed by an explanation involving high tides blocking subterranean air passages, whereupon the air blocks the channels of the spring water (5–11). This passage must have been in Posidonius (15).

Strabo may have derived his knowledge of it from there, although he may also have known the original.

(i) Since Posidonius rejected the supposed observed fact (15ff), it seems clear that Posidonius at least did not believe that Polybius had himself witnessed the phenomena. Polybius may have derived A.1 from *Silanus* (see A.2).

(ii) ἀντιπαθεῖν (3) is used in a very Stoic sense and context, cf. ἀντιπάθεια (23). ἀντιπαθεῖν may therefore derive from Posidonius, and so strengthen the hypothesis that Strabo's

COMMENTARY: F217

knowledge of A.1 comes from Posidonius. Nevertheless, although Polybius' explanation of the spring is related to tidal phenomena, the relation seems mechanical rather than 'antipathetic' in a Stoic physical sense of natural attraction or repulsion.

A.2 (11–14)

Artemidorus criticises Polybius' theory, gives a reason of his own, and calls in Silanus the historian as support. Both are dismissed by Strabo as amateurs. For Artemidorus of Ephesus cf. F119, where again Posidonius is represented as contradicting popular tales by autopsy. For Silanus, the historian of Hannibal: *FGrH* 175. Another possible link with Artemidorus may be found at Strabo III.2.11 (cf. Silanus F7 = Pliny *NH* 4.120), where some have also seen traces of Posidonius.

This doxographical note may also have been in Posidonius, although Strabo brings in Artemidorus and Silanus merely to contrast them with Posidonius.

A.3 (14–23)

Posidonius (δέ) (i.e. an authority of weight, unlike Artemidorus and Silanus; cf. F119) says the information (i.e. of Polybius) is false. This is based on:

(a) *Observation*: there are two wells (φρέατα as distinct from κρήνη) in the Herakleion, a third in the city. The smaller of the two in the Herakleion fails within the hour if drawn continuously, but fills again if left alone. The larger can be drawn all day, although the level can fall as in all other wells; at night it fills up if no longer drawn.

(b) *Inference*: since ebb tide often coincides with the occasion of the replenishing of the well, the locals without cause (κενῶς) have been convinced of the ἀντιπάθεια.

κενῶς and ἀντιπάθεια are both emendations, but surely certain. The method of observation followed by inference is characteristic. Posidonius refuses the inductive connection between the actions of the wells and the tides, because observation shows it to be an occasional not a constant relation.

A.4 (23–5)

Strabo is puzzled by Posidonius' approach:

(a) There is no doubt that the local inhabitants believe the phenomena as reported by Polybius.

(b) Strabo himself has met the account as a notorious instance in the Paradoxa.

Strabo seems confused between the accuracy of Posidonius' *observations*, and the veracity of *reports*. His main criticism is that Posidonius did not *believe* the local inhabitants (see below). The Paradoxa presumably contained doxographic tradition. The paradoxical wells reappear in Pliny *NH* 2.219, conjoined once more with an account of tidal theory (212ff).

A.5

In the lacuna marked at line 25, Strabo continues to give his own opinion.

(a) He is inclined to believe Polybius' explanation.

(b) He suggests as an alternative a theory ascribed to Athenodorus. That the Sea is like a ζῷον (cf. Strabo, 1.3.8), and the flow and ebb tides correspond to its breathing, its exhalations (ἐκπνοή) and inhalations (εἰσπνοή); so water from such springs may be sucked in to help the exhalations (flows) of the sea.

Strabo does not explain how this hypothesis can account for the fact that the springs contained fresh water and the sea salt. It is more important to notice that the exhalation theory of tides cannot come from Posidonius because (i) it is ascribed by name to Athenodorus, and (ii) the context shows that it is advanced by Strabo against Posidonius. See T79, Frs. 214, 215. A similar theory is found in Pomponius Mela III.1 as one of three alternative theories, another being the lunar theory, the third having some affinities with Seneca *NQ* III.14.3ff (which also bears some relation to the anthropomorphic analogy). Cf. also Solinus 23.21f; Philostratus, *v.Apoll.* v.2.

A.6 (26–8)

Strabo continues the attack against Posidonius: Posidonius elsewhere reveals the Phoenicians as clever; here he accuses them of stupidity rather than recognising their sharpness.

One would expect the stupidity to refer to the inability of the Gadiretans to observe their own wells accurately. But the following explanation (μὲν γάρ, 28ff) leads into an account of Posidonius' theory of tides. This however depends in its account of annual movement on a report accepted from the inhabitants of Gadeira. So there is a long-distance reference to the greater probability that they observed diurnal movements of wells and tides accurately (see 54ff).

For Posidonius' appreciation of Phoenicians: Frs. 285, 286, but for ψεῦσμα Φοινικικόν, F246.40.

A.7 (28–30)

One day and night is a single revolution of the sun, part of the time below the earth, part above.

This appears to be the link sentence in Strabo between the wells and the tides. As such it is part of Strabo's argument, not from Posidonius; that is, he has in mind, at the beginning of his report on tides, the obvious diurnal movements of the wells, cf. 54ff, and A.6. So, there is no allusion to solar tidal force in Posidonius.

A.8 (54–68)

Strabo in the end resorts to sarcasm in attempting to expose Posidonius' sentence at lines 21–2.

(i) He seizes on πολλάκις (22). If tides occur regularly (τεταγμένως, 57) twice a day (cf. 28–30), how is it possible that it 'often' happens that the well fills at ebb tide, but not 'often' that it fails; or often, but not an equal number of times (58–60)? This argument merely exposes Strabo's ignorance of the 'regularity' of tidal cycles, and ignores altogether the possibility of a different cycle for the well.

As the tides follow the moon, and the well the sun, Posidonius' criticism is not damaged (cf. Darwin, *The Tides* 87).

(ii) Taking up πεπιστεῦσθαι κενῶς (22): How could the Gadeiritans fail to observe this daily occurrence, especially since they are credited with an annual observation of the tides (60–3, 66–8)? This factual difficulty has less interest for Strabo than the ad hominem argument confused with it, namely:

(iii) How could Posidonius trust the Gadeiritans on an annual observation, but not on a daily one (63–6, 26–8)? The answer to that presumably was that Posidonius had no alternative for the former (although he tried to check, F218.7ff), but could test the latter by personal observation.

B. The tides (30–54)

B.1

Posidonius' theory of tides as reported by Strabo.

B.1.1 Theory (30–2)

Posidonius says that the movement of ocean undergoes a cycle of a type like a heavenly body, exhibiting diurnal, monthly and annual movement in joint affinity (συμπαθῶς) with the moon.

B.1.2 Diurnal cycle (32–44)

(i) When the moon's elevation reaches one sign (of the zodiac, i.e. 30°) from the (eastern) horizon, the sea begins to swell and encroach on the land perceptibly (αἰσθητῶς) until the moon is in the meridian.

(ii) When the moon turns, the sea retreats again gradually, until the moon is one sign's elevation from sinking.

COMMENTARY: F217

(iii) Water level is stationary while the moon passes from a sign above to a sign below the horizon. Then the process continues (diagrammatically shown in Fig. 17).

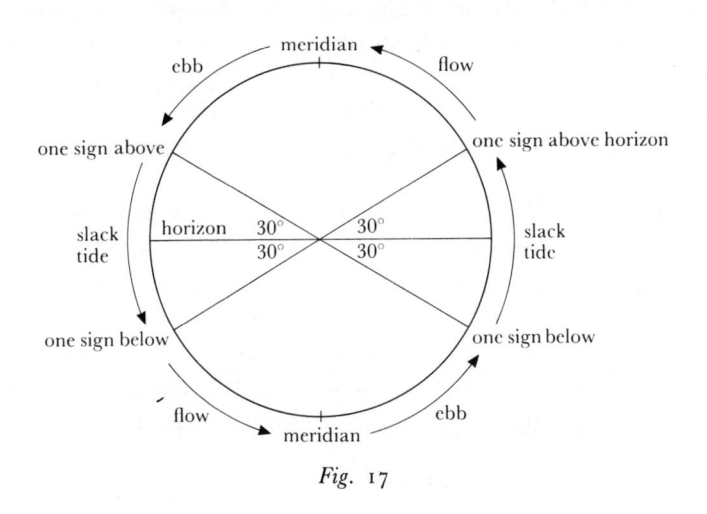

Fig. 17

B.1.3 Monthly cycle (44–9)

Posidonius' account may be shown diagrammatically in Fig. 18.

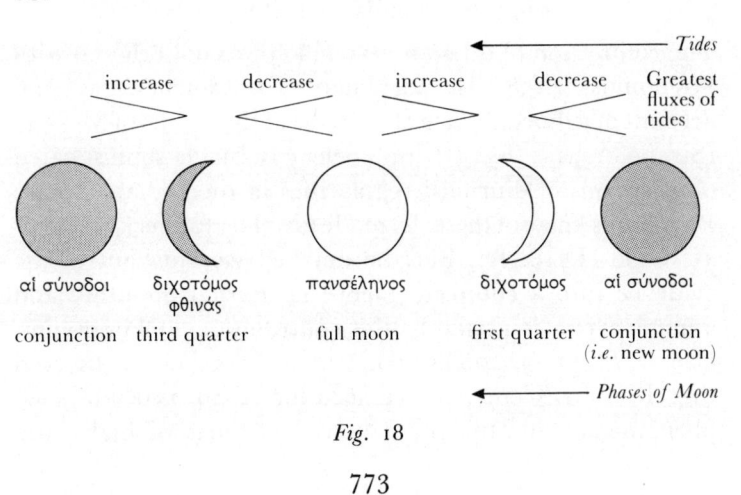

Fig. 18

Posidonius adds (48f) that between the third quarter and conjunction the increases exceed the others καὶ χρόνῳ καὶ τάχει. This rather obscure phrase probably means that the time interval between highs increases, and so consequently does the velocity of the tidal waters. Cf. Frs. 218.5; 219.46ff.

B.1.4 Annual cycle (49–54)

(i) Posidonius says that he was informed of annual movements by the Gadeiritans.

(ii) *The Gadeiritans* told him that flow and ebbs reached their maxima at the summer solstice. (This is, of course, wrong. Who made the mistake, and how? See below).

(iii) *Posidonius himself* (αὐτός) makes the conjecture (εἰκά-ζει) that the tides then decrease from summer solstice to equinox, increase from equinox to winter solstice, decrease until spring equinox, increase to summer solstice.

B.2 Strabo and Posidonius

Strabo accepts the theory and challenges no part of it, including the false account of the annual cycle. It is introduced to combat Posidonius' report on the wells (see *A*.6).

B.3 Posidonius' contribution

The connection of tides and the moon was not original with Posidonius, F138. In particular, Eratosthenes gave an account of a diurnal cycle of currents in the Straits of Messina (Strabo, 1.3.11; F215), and Seleucus made sophisticated observations of diurnal irregularities in the Indian Ocean. Posidonius knew of these; he made an effort to check Seleucus at Cadiz (F218.7ff). But the detailed working out of the evidence into a complete theory of diurnal, monthly and annual cycles is certainly the contribution of Posidonius. Caesar, *BG* VI.29, caught up in Channel flood tides, observed that Romans were not yet accustomed to associate such phenomena with the full moon; but times of highs and flooding no doubt became familiar to expeditions in the north (cf. Tacitus, *Ann.* 1.70.2). A lunar explanation of tides soon appeared in literature (Cicero, *De Div.* 11.34; Manilius 11.90ff; Lucan, *Phars.* 1.413ff), but for continuing alternative suggestions, and for Posidonius' influence, see F138.

It is of more importance to observe in this fragment Posidonius' method. The theory was based, as far as possible for him, on personal observation. He took the trouble to go to Cadiz where the phenomenon was observable. The diurnal cycle was based on autopsy (αἰσθητῶς, 34); so was the monthly cycle, for he stayed at Cadiz for thirty days (T15), and the first two cycles are carefully distinguished from the annual cycle, which depended on reported information (F217.49f), and even this he attempted to check by observation (F218.7ff). When he had to rely on reports for the annual cycle, he took some care over his informants: direct information, not through an intermediary, from men on the spot who should have known what they were talking about. In the end there is a careful distinction between autopsy, reported information, and derived theory (F217.51): an excellent example of careful observation developed by a synoptic theory (i.e. the cycle).

The account goes wrong only where it depends on hearsay. The greatest annual tides occur at the equinox, not at the solstices. Posidonius' *theory* remains correct; it is the starting point of the cycle which is wrong. Who made the mistake, the informants at Cadiz, Strabo or Posidonius?

It is difficult to think that the local inhabitants, living on the Atlantic seaboard, failed to notice excessive spring tides at the equinoxes, although this cannot be ruled out entirely (Berger, *Erdkunde* 565), if their observations on their wells were as inaccurate as Posidonius suggested. But it is unlikely. If they reported correctly, either Posidonius misunderstood them, or Strabo misunderstood Posidonius. The latter is usually assumed, on the grounds of the more remote misunderstanding. Besides, solstitial high tides do not recur in the tradition. On the contrary, in the account of the annual cycle given by writers who may be supposed to be following Posidonius (Seneca, *NQ* III.28.6; Pliny, *NH* 2.215) the maximum highs are given at the equinoxes (cf. also Tac. *Ann.* 1.70.2). Most striking of all, Priscianus Lydus, who both knows Strabo's account (F219.40), and says that he (Priscianus) is following Posidonius (F219.12ff, 77), gives the equinoctial version (F219.52ff, 110ff).

But Strabo has been dismissed too easily (as by Duhem, *Le Système du monde* II.282, and by Laffranque, *Poseidonios* 211) or ignored (Thomson, *History of Ancient Geography* 211, merely substitutes 'equinoxes' for 'solstices'). Strabo III.5.9 (F218.7ff) clearly indicates that Posidonius was looking for exceptional highs at Cadiz at the summer solstice (to check Seleucus) and that passage confirms independently that Posidonius believed in solstitial highs as reported in F217.49ff. (Posidonius recorded another high sea at the summer solstice in F227, but this time due to volcanic action.) We must therefore keep open the possibility that Posidonius misunderstood or later misremembered his informant(s) at Cadiz, perhaps because his mind was already engaged with a misinterpretation of Seleucus' observations in the Indian Ocean, which led him to expect high tides at the solstice (for the possible misinterpretation, F218). Then the mistake may have been corrected early, either by an associate or follower (Athenodorus? But then one would have expected Strabo to know. Geminus (T42, T72)? Perhaps Priscian's *Posidonius Assyrius et ei consentientes* has the vagueness of οἱ περὶ Ποσειδώνιον, T45); or even by Posidonius himself (so Lasserre, *Strabon*, tome II (Budé), p. 202, and Theiler, *Poseidonios* II.41), perhaps in the *Meteorology*, since Priscian used Geminus' Epitome, T72. This is mere conjecture, however, and in any case the problem does not detract from Posidonius' achievement, on which no real advances were made until the theory of tide-generating force expounded in Newton's *Principia*.

COMMENTARY: F218

F218 Strabo, III.5.9

CONTENT

Posidonius at Cadiz checked on accounts of tidal behaviour and theory from Seleucus. Reports on river and estuary flooding.

CONTEXT

Follows F217.

COMMENT

A. Posidonius' check on Seleucus (1–9)

Posidonius says that Seleucus from the Persian Gulf (known as the Red Sea by Posidonius) reported both a certain irregularity in these phenomena (ἐν τούτοις, i.e. the tides) and regularity in accordance with the differences of the signs of the zodiac (i.e. the different positions of the moon in the zodiac): while the moon is in the equinoctial signs the responses of the tides are regular, when in the solstitial signs, irregular both in volume and speed, and in each of the other signs proportionate to their nearness to equinoctial or solstitial. But Posidonius says that he himself at full moon at the summer solstice was in the Herakleion at Gadeira for a good many days without being able to mark the annual (ἐνιαυσίους) differences.

Seleucus the Babylonian (Str. 1.19 = F214) Chaldean astronomer (Str. XVI.1.6), mid-2nd century B.C., authority on tides, critical of Crates of Mallos and himself criticised by Hipparchus, adopted Aristarchus' axial rotation of the earth, and according to the doxographers (*Dox. Gr.* 383) suggested that because the moon's revolution resists the earth's rotation, air between the two falls as wind on the Atlantic ocean creating tidal waves (cf. F138; Neugebauer, *HAMA*

COMMENTARY: F218

610f, 697; Duhem, *Le Système du monde* II.272ff; Berger, *Erdkunde* 560ff; Dicks, *Geographical Fragments of Hipparchus* 114f; Aujac, *Strabon et la science* 289ff).

The present passage of Seleucus has been best explained by Sir George Darwin, *The Tides and Kindred Phenomena* IV.88: when the moon is in equinoxes she is on the equator; at solstices she is at her greatest north or south declination. So when the moon is on the equator there is diurnal equality (regularity) of tides, or two equal high- and low-waters a day; at solstices the regularity of this sequence is broken. Diurnal inequality is at maximum when the moon's declination is greatest, but disappears when the moon is on the equator. Whatever Seleucus' theory of tides was, Darwin remarked that this is a correct observation for the Indian Ocean, where the phenomenon of diurnal inequality is especially marked in the Gulf of Aden, presumably an area of Seleucus' observations.

It is also to Posidonius' credit that he attempted to check it by autopsy (αὐτός, 7) at Cadiz. His negative report is also correct, because diurnal inequality, while marked in the Indian Ocean, is almost unobservable in the Atlantic. But the damaging part of the report is ἐνιαυσίους (9), which implies a confusion between diurnal inequality and annual highs, by using evidence for the former to establish the latter; and this is consolidated by the evidence in F217.49–54, that Posidonius put the maximum highs in the annual cycle at the solstices instead of at the equinoxes.

Either (i) Strabo did not understand Seleucus, and put together two different statements of Posidonius;
or (ii) Posidonius did not understand that Seleucus was speaking of diurnal inequalities, and mention of equinoctial and solstitial signs led him to think of annual movements (cf. F219.110ff), perhaps fostered through misunderstanding local reports at Cadiz of annual highs (F217.49ff);

COMMENTARY: F218

or (iii) Seleucus himself confused diurnal inequalities with annual summer tides. Darwin (p. 81) observes: 'In China the diurnal inequality is such that in summer the tide rises higher in the daytime than in the night, while the converse is true in winter. I suggest that this fact affords the justification for the statement that summer tides are great.'

(ii) and (iii) seem more likely, although Strabo probably had little idea of what was going on, since he tended to sheer away from the more scientific aspects of Posidonius (T77, T79b, F49.359). Posidonius may have changed his mind about annual highs (F219.52ff, 110ff; comm. *B*.3 on F217.49-54), perhaps after cogitating on his negative observations at Cadiz.

5 **καὶ πλήθει καὶ τάχει,** cf. F217.48, F219.46ff.

B. *River and estuary flooding (9-28)*

However at the conjunction (new moon) of that month he said that he observed at Ilipa (Alcalà del Rio, 16 km north of Seville) a great change in the wave recoil of the Baitis (Guadalquivir) compared with earlier occurrences when the water level had not reached even half way up the banks; but at that time it flooded over so that soldiers drew their water where they were (Ilipa is about 700 stades (129.5 km) from the sea); and although the sea coast was covered actually to a distance inland of 30 stades (5.55 km) by the flood (πλημμυρ- ίδος, 16) so that islands even were isolated, the water mark on the base of the temple in the Herakleion and on the base of the mole that juts out in the harbour at Gadeira he says he measured at no more than 10 cubits (4.62 m). If one doubled that measure in line with rises that sometimes happened, even then one could not (⟨οὐδ'⟩ Casaubon, 21) have presented the spectacle that the size of the flood (πλημμυρίδος, 22) presents in the plains. This phenomenon is reported (ἱστορεῖται, 23) as shared round the whole circle of the sea board, but the river

779

COMMENTARY: F218

Iber, he says, is exceptional and individual. For in some places there are floods (πλημμυρεῖν, 25) quite apart from rain and snow, when the north winds strengthen. The reason is the lake through which it flows; for the standing water from the lake is driven out by the force of the winds.

This passage, which clearly refers to observations made of river and estuary flooding at the same time as he was trying unsuccessfully at Cadiz to check for high tides at the summer solstice expected from Seleucus' theory, reflects Posidonius' puzzlement. Although the tide level at Cadiz was not exceptionally high (οὐδ' ἐπὶ δέκα πήχεις, 19), there was exceptionally high river flooding on the Guadalquivir, such as could not even have been accounted for by twice the tidal water mark at Cadiz (Casaubon's οὐδ' (21) is necessary for sense). There is no clear indication how Posidonius explained this. Since he could not assign the cause simply to high tides, he could not be thinking of a tidal bore (against Aujac, *Strabon et la science* 293); and πλήμμυρις need not refer to tidal flooding, indeed cannot do so at line 25. He seems to allude to the recoil of a river full from rain or snow (25) on meeting an incoming tide (ἀνακοπῆς, 11). This is different from the explanation given earlier by Strabo III.2.4 of tidal flooding of coast and rivers through the compression of the flux between the Spanish and Moroccan coasts, a theory criticised by Posidonius as Aristotelian in F220. Philostratus, *v. Apoll.* v.6 talks of the flooding of the Baitis through wind: ἐπειδὰν γὰρ πλημμύρῃ τὸ πέλαγος, ἐπὶ τὰς πηγὰς ὁ ποταμὸς παλίρρους ἵεται, πνεύματος δήπου ἀπωθουμένου αὐτὸν τῆς θαλάττης. But we cannot be certain that this derives from Posidonius, because Philostratus earlier (v.2) adopts Athenodorus' exhalation theory of tides (cf. F217 comm. *A*.5). Compare also Onesicratus on Indian rivers (Str. xv.1.20). When Posidonius added that he was told that the phenomenon was common to the whole seaboard, he is again careful to distinguish between autopsy and hearsay (ἱστορεῖται, 23).

The reference to the exceptional river Iber is puzzling. It

would naturally refer to the Ebro in north-east Spain, far from Cadiz and the south-west. Lasserre, referring to Str. III.4.19, argues in this case for the Odiel or the Rio Tinto which empty into the Huelva basin, but he admits that neither satisfies Posidonius' description of lake flooding.

F219   Priscianus Lydus, *Solutiones ad Chosroem* VI

CONTENT

A group of problems with explanations of the behaviour and conditions of seas, straits and rivers, including the Posidonian tidal theory through the diurnal, monthly and annual cycles, with the annual highs at the equinoxes.

CONTEXT

For Priscianus Lydus: T71, T72. The *Solutiones*, or Explanations of Problems offered to King Chosroes I of Persia, consists of disconnected chapters on philosophical and scientific questions debated in the 6th c. A.D. For example, ch. I is on the soul. Ch. VI now lacks a title, but is clearly concerned with seas and rivers. Two factors inhibit interpretation: (i) the work survives only in a 9th- (?) century Latin translation of such barbarous crudity as to approach unintelligibility in places. Nevertheless, we are often helped by the literalness of translation (e.g. ἔστιν ὅτε becomes *est quando*, 2); and sometimes the translator, when stumped through ignorance of a Greek word, may simply leave it (24). (ii) Although Posidonius is named three times (14, 41, 77), the chapter is a hotch potch of views culled and jumbled from various sources. Priscianus' own bibliography in the *Prooemium* suggests that he used Strabo, Geminus' Commentary on

COMMENTARY: F219

Posidonius' *Meteor.*, and Arrian's *Meteor.* (T72), and probably Aristotle and others. But there is no clear indication that he had read Posidonius himself.

COMMENT

1-9 Two problems are posed about the Red Sea (i.e. Indian Ocean):

(i) why there is a diurnal flow and ebb, and how this varies through the moon (1-4);

(ii) why it is said that there is no increase in total volume of the sea in flood tides, nor decrease in ebb (4f).

A rider is offered for each of these:

(a) flood and ebb tides are not caused by wind or the lack of it (6f).

A wind tidal theory was popular, and may go back to Aristotle, Aetius III.17.1 (*Dox. Gr.* 382); Berger, *Erdkunde* 289f. For its history and possible Posidonian involvement: F138 comm. This is a comment on *lunaliter* (3).

(b) Although great rivers continually flow into the sea without feed back, no addition of sea water is apparent (7-9).

This also is an ἀρχαία ἀπορία which goes back to Aristotle (*Meteor.* 355b 21ff). See 134ff. Priscianus no doubt began with the Indian Ocean and Persian Gulf because his book is addressed to the King of Persia.

9-15 Priscianus states his authorities for tidal phenomena in the Red Sea, Atlantic and Mediterranean. Although there are great differences of opinion, he singles out Posidonius and those who agree with him, whose opinion has the approval of Arrian. Posidonius is called the Stoic and *Assyrius* (14, following the common confusion with *Syrius*; cf. Cic. *Tusc.* V.101). *ei consentientes* probably include Strabo and Geminus from Priscianus' bibliography (and cf. F219.40f), rather than the more general οἱ περὶ Π (T45). Arrian is the

COMMENTARY: F219

historian (Roos, *Arrianus* (Teubner) vol. II.186). Posidonius' aetiological reputation is confirmed (*causas*, i.e. αἰτίας, cf. F219.77ff, T85). Since Posidonius is cited as the main authority for this important question, one would have expected Priscianus to have read him; but the mention of *ei consentientes* and of Arrian, the plural *dicunt* (15) and the omission of Posidonius' name in the bibliography rouse grave suspicions, cf. T72. Despite the stress on the Red Sea, there is no mention of Seleucus.

15–19 The theory of the Posidonian group (*dicunt*): the outer Ocean (Atlantic) moves in relation to the cycle of the moon; the inner sea (Mediterranean) behaves in unison (*compati* = συμπάσχειν), for joined only at the Pillars of Hercules it is affected sympathetically (*compassio* = συμπάθεια) as a harbour is by the sea, and receives other special motions.

The notion of the Pillars of Hercules leading into the Mediterranean as a harbour from the Atlantic was a common idea; cf. *De Mundo* 393a 19ff, but unrelated to tides. The theory of similarity of tidal behaviour (ὁμοιοπαθεῖν) throughout the seas of the world was held by Eratosthenes and criticised by Hipparchus (Str. 1.1.8f; 1.3.11f; Berger, *Eratosthenes* 91f; Aujac, *Strabon et la science* 283ff); but the combination of tidal theory and Stoic συμπάθεια shows that this is Posidonian.

19–32 The behaviour of currents in the Straits of Messina is offered as an example of the *motus speciales* (19). There are four movements diurnally: two flows from the Tyrrhenian Sea to the Sicilian (Ionian), called κατιών (the 'descending' current), and two in the reverse direction, called ἐξιών. These are explained by the course of the moon; the κατιών occurs as the moon approaches meridian and submeridian, the ἐξιών as it approaches setting and rising (cf. F217.32–44). The problem is an old one; whose version is this? The singular *declarat* (19) should refer either to Posidonius (14) or to the approving Arrian (15). But a very similar version, complete

COMMENTARY: F219

with lunar comparison and the names of the currents is assigned by Strabo 1.3.11 to Eratosthenes. But the names of the currents were common property (Duhem, *Le Système du Monde* II.272 n.1 pointed out that still in this century the locals refer to *rema scendente* and *rema montante*); and there is a significant difference. Strabo makes Eratosthenes note the similarity (ὁμοιοπαθεῖν) of the currents to tidal behaviour, and compares the two by marking the coincidence of the currents and the position of the moon (ὁμολογεῖν δ' ὅτι καὶ κατὰ τὸν αὐτὸν καιρὸν ἄρχεταί τε καὶ παύεται καθ'ὃν αἱ πλημμυρίδες); but he, probably following a lead from Strato (Str. 1.3.5), explains the phenomenon by different levels of sea bed (Str. 1.3.11–12).

This passage offers a lunar explanation. At 1.3.12 Strabo cites Posidonius as an authority on tides rather than strait currents (F215 comm.), but he must have given an explanation for this famous problem, and it is likely to have been a lunar one like this. There are two points of detail not in Strabo: the 'descending' current is stronger 'as you would expect (*ut consequens* = ὡς εἰκός) since from the Pillars of Hercules there is a great rush of Ocean because of the narrow path, the land forcing it in' (26–8, cf. Ps.-Arist. *Mir. Ausc.* 130,843a 6f). This combats the different level of sea bed theory. Secondly, the down flow reached as far as the shore of Taormina (for the special mention of Taormina, Pliny, *NH* 2.219). At this point (24) the translator was defeated by the word Κοπρία (Dungheap, Refuseheap), which was the name given to that coast line because of the frequency of shipwrecks (Str. VI.2.3; but Pliny *NH* 2.220, Sen. *NQ* III.26.7 have a different version). In 22 the flow from the Tyrrhenian Sea is wrongly described as west to east.

32–8 It is pointed out that exactly the same happens with tides in the Atlantic, two flows and two ebbs, explained in the same way by lunar position. He also maintains that the phenomenon has been observed in gulfs, in the Red Sea (Indian Ocean), the Hyrcanian Sea (Caspian), and at Cadiz.

COMMENTARY: F219

By gulfs he may have had in mind the head of the Adriatic and Syrtis.

In the omitted lines we are told that flood tides occur not only at diurnal meridian, but on a monthly cycle at full moon and conjunction; but this is retailed in greater detail at 45ff, and at 98ff. Then some phenomena are mentioned which behave oddly for reasons other than *compassio astrorum* (for the phrase cf. ἀστροειδῆ περίοδον, F217.31). They were all notorious puzzles: the Euripus passage, which was said to change current seven times a day (Str. 1.3.12; ix.2.8; in fact now more frequently); the Hellespont (usually the Bosporus was cited, Str. 1.3.12); Arethusa, the well on Ortygia at Syracuse, which was said to change every fifth year, and so was linked to the Olympiad by a strange story that it was the Alphaeus river popping up after an undersea journey (Str. vi.2.4; Pliny *NH* 2.225; Sen. *NQ* iii.26.5).

38-45 This is a garbled version, admittedly (40f) taken from Strabo, iii.5.9 (F218.9-16 comm.), of Posidonius' account of coastal and inland flooding of the Guadalquivir basin. It adds nothing to Strabo, and makes a mistake: *septingenta* (40) probably represents Strabo's ἑπτακοσίους, the correct figure (F218.14); also *insularum* (39) may be a mistaken addition from the correctly described situation at 41-3. 44. *interim* = τέως, i.e. up to that time.

45-71 A repetitious and garbled account of the diurnal, monthly and annual cycles as given in F217.30-54, with one important difference from Strabo. After a mention of the diurnal cycle (45), he sketches the monthly (46-52) with flood tides of great volume and velocity (50f; cf. F217.48, F218.5) at full moon and conjunction, and less difference between high and low water at the quarters (*dimidiata luna* = διχοτόμος). There is a proportionate annual cycle (52-6), with highs at the equinoxes, lower tides and slower flow at the solstices. 56-66 returns to a more detailed account of the diurnal cycle, but the clear account in Strabo (F217.32-44) of the slack water period when the moon is

COMMENTARY: F219

between a sign of the zodiac (30°) above and below the horizon is sadly garbled (60–6) and does not seem to have been understood by the translator. Reference to monthly (66f) and annual (68–71) cycles is repeated; but something has gone wrong in translation in 69–71. Dübner suggested *aqua* (70), and *regredi a terra* (71). Bywater more ingeniously suspected that *terminos* (69) was a translator's confusion of ὅρους for ὁ ῥοῦς, the Greek being something like: ὥστε καὶ ὁ ῥοῦς παλιρροίας ἐνάρχεται εἰς ἑαυτὸν ἀρχόμενος ἀναρρεῖν καὶ ἐφεξῆς ἀναβαίνειν ἐπὶ γῆν.

The nugget of gold in this κοπρία is the clear assertion of annual highs at the equinoxes. It must come from Posidonius *et ei consentientes* (14); but it cannot have come from Strabo. His Posidonian source put the annual highs at the solstices (F217.49–54, confirmed by F218). Strabo almost certainly was using the Περὶ ὠκεανοῦ. Posidonius may later have changed his mind in *Meteor.*, and Priscianus could have had this from Geminus (Context, F217 comm. *B*.3, and F218.1–9 comm.). The correct Priscianus version is again given at 110ff.

71–80 Tidal action on rivers in making the natural current towards the sea flow backwards so that they seem to be flowing from the sea, is instanced by the Rhine and rivers in Spain and Britain, in particular the Thames. This again seems to be assigned to Posidonius from the following sentence (77–80): 'So Posidonius, the Stoic, seeking out the causes of these things, inasmuch as he became a personal investigator of this kind of reflux, noticed that the moon was the cause rather, not the sun.' See F218 for Posidonius' personal investigations into river flows in Spain. He certainly did not visit either Britain or the Rhine estuary, but he could well have reported stories about them. Tales of Britain had been filtering back since the time of Pytheas, and although Strabo thought him a pure romancer, Eratosthenes, Polybius and others had discussed them. More may have come from Phoenician sources, although they were secretive of the tin

COMMENTARY: F219

routes. Whether Caesar's campaigns in 55/54 B.C. were in time for Posidonian comment or not, Publius Crassus, the consul of 97 and in Spain in the nineties, had crossed to Britain (Str. III.5.11); and the mouth of the Rhine was regarded as one of the main crossings to Britain (Str. IV.5.2). The significance of *in quattuor dies* with reference to tidal flow in the Thames (75) is obscure, and probably now lost through the translation. Bywater hesitantly suggested that it was a misconstrue of ἐπὶ τὸ τεταρτημόριον.

77–80 is a hinge sentence of some importance, for it not only indicates that the whole passage of lunar tides from the last mention of Posidonius at 12 is of Posidonian origin, but also looks forward to the comparison of solar and lunar influence which follows and the recapitulation of the lunar cycles to 134.

80–134 What follows is an argument with analogy and illustration that it is the moon, not sun, which is the cause of tides. It begins in indirect speech, presumably following the reference to Posidonius.

The sun's heat is too pure, takes moisture away and destroys it (80–2). The moon's heat is weaker, being not pure (cf. F122, mixture of fire and air), and for that reason it is more fertile for earthly things (82–4); it also has greater humidity (87f). It cannot consume and destroy like the sun, but only raise moisture and make waves (84–6). Compare Pliny *NH* 2.222–3 for this contrast of solar and lunar heat.

This is illustrated by an analogy (89–91): water heated in a kettle with a small controlled weak flame, swells, but when a strong flame is applied, the water is consumed and falls. The idea goes back to Arist. *Meteor.* 355a 15f. So with the effect of sun and moon on the sea: the rise and fall of flow and ebb follows the cycle of the moon (91–5).

The pattern is demonstrated once more in the diurnal (96f), monthly (98ff) and annual (110ff) cycles. In the monthly, stress is laid on the maximum effect at full moon and conjunction, as if there were a combined effect of moon and

COMMENTARY: F219

sun (cf. Duhem *Le Système du monde* II.284f; Mieli and Brunet, *Histoire des sciences, antiquité* 657f). This may have been the origin of Pliny's *causa in sole lunaque* (*NH* 2.212, cf. 215). But for Posidonius the whole stress is on the moon; for the related problems of his theory of lunar illumination, Frs. 123, 124.

98 The curious expression *menstrualis quoque verbi gratia* probably conceals the Greek phrase μηνιαίου λόγου, cf. *annualis ratio* (68).

110ff The annual highs are again fixed at the equinoxes, this time with a precise and unmistakable reference to the equinoctial signs of Aries and Libra (111f, 118f). *Brachia* translates Χηλαί, which as the Claws of Scorpio represents Libra (cf. F126). An additional argument appears at 119ff: the greatest effect occurs at the equinoxes because then moon and atmosphere are warm and moist, whereas at the summer solstice they are hot and dry, and at winter solstice cold and moist. It may have been an argument of this kind which led to Pliny noting (*NH* 2.215) that autumnal highs were greater than spring ones. For the interaction of moon and atmosphere, cf. Cleom. *De Motu* II.3, p. 178.1–6 Z, and F138.

127–134 display the translator at his most unintelligible.

134 In the omitted lines, p. 74.6–75.22 Bywater, Priscianus raises two problems: (a) why does the sea not get bigger with large rivers pouring into it, and answers this with a theory of evaporation; (b) why is it salty (74.19ff)? In these sections Priscianus appears to be relying mainly on Aristotle, *Meteor.*, or on a source quoting or using Aristotle. For example under (a), 74.6–16 virtually quotes *Meteor.* II.355b 22–33. Under (b), 74.20f ≈ Arist. 355a 34f; 74.20–75.1 ≈ Arist. 355a 26f, 355a 32f; 75.2–7 ≈ Arist. 355b 4–12; 75.7–12 ≈ Arist. 358b 34–359a 5. Even by Aristotle's time (a) was regarded as an ἀρχαία ἀπορία (355b 21), but discussion continued unabated (Sen. *NQ* III.4), and there were different opinions on (b) (357a 5ff); and clearly the argument continued long after Aristotle (Pliny *NH* 2.222, Ps.-Arist. *Probl.* 935a 35f), and Priscianus may have been also using

COMMENTARY: F219

later sources (76.12f=Ps.-Arist. *Probl.* XXIII.37). Indeed, 75.14ff looks Stoic in tone.

136–45 Priscianus turns to saltiness in lakes, and in particular to an unspecified lake in which men and beasts float on the surface instead of sinking, that is too salt for fish, and washes clothes by shaking after submersion; it is the presence of an earthy substance which makes the water salt. All this is introduced by *declarat* (136), which on the analogy of line 19 should refer to Posidonius, or to the Posidonian source used by Priscianus. But 136–42 is clearly derived almost literally from Arist. *Meteor.* 359a 18–24. However, Priscianus immediately adds (142–5) a reference to a lake in Palestine, the Dead Sea. But it was the Dead Sea which was the subject of Aristotle's account (359a 17). It is true that *alter* (143) was supplied by G^2, but the cast of the sentence implies an addition to the previous reference. On the other hand, in later traditions lakes were confused, as Strabo, XVI.2.42 confuses the Dead Sea and Lake Sirbonis in relation to the above characteristics; and the passage is linked to Posidonius (F279). The general characteristics raised frequent comment later (e.g. Pliny *NH* 5.72; Sen. *NQ* III.25.5ff). The clothes-washing tale is revived in Ps.-Arist. *Mir.* 53, 834a 33f. of the Arcanian Lake. At 145 the Dead Sea is noted for producing bitumen. This is not in Aristotle, but a commonplace later (Pos. F279, cf. Frs. 235, 236; D.S. 2.48.6ff, 19.98; Pliny *NH* 2.226; 5.72). It seems that once again there is a confusion of sources.

146–54 Again there are brief snatches from Arist. *Meteor.* 359b 4ff: 146≈359b 4f; 148≈359b 9f. Although 150–4 is related to *Meteor.* 359b 10ff, it seems to have been filtered through later sources. The theme rose early (*Airs, Waters, Places* VII) and continued to be debated (Sen. *NQ* III.24.4).

154–8 Reference is made to an oil well in Cissia Persica. Although there is mention of such a well as early as Hdt. VI.119, at the top of the Persian Gulf near Susa, it is not in Aristotle.

COMMENTARY: F220

157f looks more like a garbled version of Pos. F236.5–9 (Str. XVI.1.15). There Posidonius distinguishes between white and black naphtha in Babylonian oil wells. He characterises 'black' naphtha as ἀσφάλτου ὑγρᾶς, ᾧ ἀντ' ἐλαίου τοὺς λύχνους κάουσι; cf. *bituminatum oleum quod vocant νάφθαν*. In 158 *aqua vero* may conceal reference to the alternative form (*vero* = δέ) of Posidonius' 'white' naphtha or liquid sulphur, θείου ὑγροῦ, where the equivalent of θεῖον is missing.

F220 Strabo, III.3.3

CONTENT

Posidonius criticised Aristotle for a tidal theory depending on recoil from a high coastline.

CONTEXT

In III.3 Strabo turns to the western part of Spain north of Cape St Vincent. At III.3.3 he is supposedly describing Lusitania north of the Tagus. Its coastline is almost all plain down to the sea (1–3).

COMMENT

Strabo's immediate context is the western seaboard north of the Tagus, i.e. from the Barbarium Promontory (Cape Espichel) to Cape Nerium (Finisterre). Posidonius' criticism clearly relates to the area between Morocco and Spain (5ff), i.e. between Cape St Vincent and Cadiz. So the low-lying nature of the more northerly coast reminded Strabo of Posidonius' attack on Aristotle.

When Strabo independently endorses Posidonius' statement (9), he too must refer to the south Atlantic coast (cf. also III.2.4). Therefore F220.3–9 is an aside, and the only part of

COMMENTARY: F220

III.3.3 of Strabo which can be safely ascribed to Posidonius.

Posidonius apparently claimed that Aristotle made the seaboard of Spain and Morocco the reason for tidal ebb and flow, in that the high rugged headlands caught the waves roughly and hurled them back. This cannot be true, because most of the coastline there has low sandy beaches (4-9).

Since Aristotle can have had no experience of marked tidal phenomena, it is doubtful whether he had any theoretical explanation for them. Posidonius' inference may have been illegitimately derived from such a passage as *Meteor.* 354a 5ff, where Aristotle says that the sea flows noticeably in narrows, where a larger area of water is contracted into a small space by the surrounding land; this is because of the frequent oscillation (ταλαντεύεσθαι) of the sea. Aristotle was referring to refluent currents in straits in the Mediterranean, and goes on to explain the general movement of water by depth of sea bed. But Posidonius may have been deceived by Aristotle's words ταλαντεύεσθαι, ταλάντωσις into thinking that Aristotle had in mind tidal movement, παλιρρεῖν (6), and transferred the supposed theory to the testing area of which he had personal experience, the Spanish coast beyond Cadiz, thereupon typically rejecting the theory as a theory on practical observational grounds. Strabo may have contracted this line of reasoning. It is just possible however that Aristotle may have heard of Atlantic tides, and that he, but much more probably the Aristotelian Problemata tradition, ventured an explanation of them. For it was apparently widely believed in antiquity that Aristotle had a theory of tides. In Aetius, *Plac.* III.17.1 (*Dox. Gr.* 382), Aristotle (coupled with Heraclitus) is assigned a theory where the sun moves winds, which push the Atlantic to create flood tides (F138).

Strabo, III.2.4 gives in greater detail his own account of tidal flooding in this area because of the low coastline. But this passage cannot be Posidonius (F17 Theiler), because the explanation is different from that given in F218 (see comm. B. 9–28).

COMMENTARY: F221

5 The codices have: τὴν παραλίαν καὶ τὴν Μαυρουσίαν. Since τὴν παραλίαν must mean the Spanish coastline, the whole phrase is probably sufficiently clear and does not require Kramer's emendations. Groskurd would require least change and be satisfactory if unnecessary. τὴν παραλίαν ⟨τὴν⟩ κατὰ τὴν M. (Corais followed by Sbordone) confuses the issue.

7 ἀκτή seems common in this sense in later Greek, so Meineke may be right.

8 τῇ Ἰβηρίᾳ destroys the sense and must be deleted. Lasserre's suggestion of a lacuna is less likely than foreshortening by Strabo.

F221   Strabo, 1.3.9

CONTENT

Depth of the Sea of Sardinia.

CONTEXT

At 1.3.4. Strabo raised Eratosthenes' problem of finding deposits of shells in the interior away from the sea. Strato's theory finds partial praise in suggesting that the Black Sea and the Mediterranean were originally lakes fed by rivers, which eventually raised the level to burst through at the Propontis and Hellespont, and at the Pillars of Hercules; at which stage the water level dropped at the outflow exposing marine phenomena higher on land. But Strabo goes on (§5ff) to criticise Strato for attempting to explain rise and fall of the sea, inundations and retirement, by a direction of flow caused by different levels of sea bed, from the shallowest in the Black Sea emptying into the deeper Aegean, and from the Mediterranean sloping into the deeper Atlantic. Strato's theory was itself derived from Arist. *Meteor.* II.1, 354a 12ff on flow caused

COMMENTARY: F221

by sea-bed level. Strabo says (§7) that this is an unscientific confusion of rivers, which flow by a sloping course, and seas, which have no slope. Strabo also attacks two details of Strato's theory: (a) that the sea bed of the Black Sea must be shallower than that of the Sea of Marmara. But, argues Strabo (§6), suppose that the bed of the Black Sea is lower than the bed of the Sea of Marmara. It could still fill up with river influx until it poured over the Propontis. So the confluence of the two seas need have nothing to do with levels of the sea bed. (b) Strato had also claimed (§5) in defence of the supposed shallowness of the Black Sea, that its bed is continually being raised by silt from rivers, and the same is happening to the Mediterranean in relation to the Atlantic. Indeed, δοκεῖν δὲ κἂν χωσθῆναι τὸν Πόντον ὅλον εἰς ὕστερον, ἂν μένωσιν αἱ ἐπιρρύσεις τοιαῦται (§4). Strabo denies such silting of the sea bed in §§7–9, which is the immediate context of F221.

COMMENT

It has been generally supposed that the whole of §§8–9 derive from Posidonius (e.g. Zimmermann, *Hermes* XIII, 104f; Schühlein, *Untersuchungen ü.d. Pos. Schr.* Π. ὠκ. 72ff; Reinhardt, *Poseidonios* 99ff; Jacoby, F91; Aujac, Budé, *ad loc.*). But this is by no means certain.

In §8 Strabo says that the αἴτιον for the silt not reaching the open sea is the refluent character of the sea. For the sea is like τοῖς ζῴοις; as living creatures inhale (ἀναπνεῖ) and exhale, so the sea had a movement that runs back and forward from and to itself. One can see this on a beach with the waves on the shore. The statement is supported by quotations from Homer. But the theory that the sea inhales and exhales like an animal is explicitly assigned to Athenodorus in III.5.7, where Strabo opposes it to Posidonius: F217, comm. A.5 (cf. Oder, *Philologus Supplb.* VII (1899) 334, n. 142). Therefore it is dangerous to ascribe it simply to Posidonius (as Reinhardt, *Poseidonios* 104; and cf. Schühlein, *Untersuchungen* 73, n. 3).

Section 9 continues: so waves have the power to expel foreign matter (τὸ ἀλλότριον). 'They call (φασί) this a sort of purging (κάθαρσίν τινα) of the sea.' Thus the sea expels dead bodies and wreckage. But the ebb is not strong enough to draw things back into the sea; so silt is deposited near the land at the mouths of rivers, and is not spread over the sea bed.

The reference to 'purging' is general (φασί), and can be taken back to Arist. *HA* VI.13.568a 4 and Theophr. *HP* VIII.3. It recurs in Pliny *NH* 2.220, and in Sen. *NQ* III.26.7–8 where there are some close parallels in language to Strabo (Schühlein, 74, n. 1). There may be a common source, but again it may be Athenodorus.

At this point F221 winds up the argument. 'Now in this way it is possible for the whole sea to be silted up, beginning from the beaches, if it has continual influx from the rivers.' At first sight this seems contradictory, because Strabo has been arguing against Strato's theory of the silting of the seas. But what Strabo attacks is that the level of the sea bed can be raised by silting. His own theory is that silting may encroach on the sea by extending the coast line into it, and it is at least conceivable (although Strabo does not really believe this, §10 *init.*), that this process could continue until the whole sea was silted up. Thus the stress is on οὕτω (1) and on ἀπὸ τῶν αἰγιαλῶν ἀρξάμενον (2). Strabo's main point, that this has nothing to do with the level of the sea bed (Strato's theory) is clarified by the next sentence. 'But this would happen even if we posit the Black Sea to be deeper than the Sea of Sardinia, which is said to be the deepest of those that have been measured, about a thousand fathoms, as Posidonius says.' Strabo here returns to his earlier supposition (§6; Context (a)) that the bed of the Black Sea may be lower than that of the Sea of Marmara. Silting, by encroachment of coast line, may cause flow from the Black Sea through the Propontis, but this is not due to the depth of the sea bed.

It is clear that not only §§8–9 are closely coherent (Schühlein, 73f), but the whole argument from §5 onwards.

COMMENTARY: F222

The argument is Strabo's, and although he was certainly using earlier works, including those of Posidonius, we cannot say how much he owes to Posidonius other than the precise reference for the depth of the Sea of Sardinia. It is likely that Posidonius acquired that information from his travels to the west. Since it is a round figure it could not have been intended to be accurate. We have no idea how it may have been calculated. 1000 ὄργυιαι were the equivalent of 10 stades, c. 1850 metres. In fact the Sea of Sardinia is more than 3000m in depth in places.

In §10 Strabo is disinclined to accept such an αἰτιολογία as is proposed at the end of §9. He prefers to tie his discussion to τῶν φανερωτέρων καὶ τῶν καθ' ἡμέραν τρόπον τινὰ ὁρωμένων; namely that movements of the sea are principally due to disturbances in the sea bed such as earthquakes and volcanic eruptions, which cause even land and islands to rise in the sea. Compare for Posidonius' interest in such phenomena, F227, F228, F49.294ff. No doubt Strabo was influenced by him.

F222 Strabo, XVII.1.5

CONTENT

A doxography from Posidonius on the course of the summer flooding of the Nile is criticised.

CONTEXT

Strabo at XVII.1.1 turns to the country round the Nile, and says that he must first set out the assertions of Eratosthenes, but after a description of the course of the Nile, he ends: Ἐρατοσθένης μὲν οὖν οὕτως (§2). Following a section on the organisation of Egypt (3), Strabo examines the Nile delta, and Egypt as the land of the river (§4). But at §5 he broaches

COMMENTARY: F222

the most famous of the ancient puzzles about the Nile, the cause of the summer flooding. He is surprisingly dogmatic: 'the ancients relying for the most part on conjecture (στοχασμῷ), but subsequently men having seen for themselves (αὐτόπται γενηθέντες), perceived that the Nile was filled with summer rains when upper Ethiopia flooded, particularly in its most distant mountains; then when the rains stopped, the river flood (πλημμυρίδα) gradually died down'. Strabo adds that this was particularly clear to those who sailed up the Arabian Gulf as far as the Cinnamon-bearing country, and to those sent on elephant-hunting expeditions by the Ptolemies (especially Philadelphus, king 283/2 B.C.ff; Raschke, 'New Studies in Roman Commerce with the East', *ANRW* II.9.2, p. 658). And if the early kings were not interested, there was still the expedition of Sesostris (Rameses II, 14th c. B.C.), and the penetration by Cambyses as far as Meroe (525 B.C.; Hdt. III.1ff). If Strabo intended these as examples of his αὐτόπται of the cause of the summer flooding, they are extremely inadequate, and it is astonishing that he expresses surprise (F222.1f) that from such a base the information about the summer rains was not perfectly clear to the men of that time. But he felt that knowledge in his day had been greatly increased by travel, and since he himself had been as far as the borders of Ethiopia, no doubt he regarded himself as something of an expert (II.5.12). Compare also the confidence of Geminus, *Isag.* XVI.24 on reports of an inhabited torrid zone.

COMMENT

The variety of conjecture and continued controversy on this subject is shown by Herodotus II.20–5; D.S. I.38–41.9; Seneca *NQ* IV.A.2.17–30 supplemented by Lydus, *De Mens.* IV.107 Wuensch; Diels, *Dox. Gr.*, Aetius, pp. 384–6; Hippolytus, *Refut.* I.8, p.22 Duncker; *Prol.* 226f; Hyde, *Ancient Greek Mariners* 274ff.

The most popular theories were (a) the action of the etesian winds, either crudely thought to drive the water back on itself and so accumulate (Thales), or in combination with an oceanic source (Euthymenes) or with a rain-cloud theory (Thrasyalces). Pliny *NH* 5.55 shows that such theories continued to hold ground. (b) The source of the Nile was Ocean itself which could cause unseasonable flooding; so Dicaearchus, Euthymenes, Egyptian priests (D.S. 1.37.7), and probably Juba (cf. Pliny *NH* 5.51; Ammianus, 22.15.8; Lucan, 10.255ff). (c) Snow on high mountains in remote Ethiopia melting in summer sun (Anaxagoras). (d) The action of the sun in some way (Herodotus). (e) Tropical rains (Thrasyalces, Aristotle, Callisthenes, Eratosthenes, Agatharchides).

Strabo dismisses (a)–(d) without mention, and entertains only (e): 'Whereas the fact that the river risings come from rain did not need investigation' (7f). He was correct in that the July–September flooding comes from the monsoon breaking in the Abyssinian highlands, but it is unclear how this was established by Strabo's αὐτόπται, and alternative theories were still being presented leaving the issue open long after Strabo's time. At least the monsoons could have been reported, and what needed continuing investigation according to Strabo, was why the rains occurred in summer and not winter, and fell in the most southerly parts (i.e. in what was thought to be the most dry and torrid zone) and not in Thebais and the area of Syene (5–7) (cf. Bunbury, *A History of Ancient Geography* II.322).

Strabo also dismisses the need for Posidonius' witnesses (8–15). They form a special kind of doxography (cf. T101) which traces the supposed stemma of a particular idea, that the cause was the summer rainstorms (10).

Callisthenes (9, *FGrH* 124, F12) was the nephew and pupil of Aristotle; for mention of him in a Posidonian context, Sen. *NQ* VI.23, F230, comm. *D.* Lydus (*De Mens.* V.107) says that he reports in his *Hellenica*, Bk IV that he took part in an expedition with Alexander, and when they came to Ethiopia they found τὸν Νεῖλον ἐξ ἀπείρων ὄμβρων κατ' ἐκείνην γενομένων καταφερόμενον.

This seems to be a different tradition from that of Strabo/Posidonius which says that Callisthenes took the idea from Aristotle (11). Aristotle wrote a book Περὶ τῆς τοῦ Νείλου ἀναβάσεως for which see Frs. 246–8 Rose, 686ff Gigon. Aristotle in turn took it from Thrasyalces (35.A.1 DK) (12), an early 'physical' philosopher from Thasus, whom we know only from Posidonius (also F137a.6) and from Lydus (*De Mens.* IV.107, probably derived ultimately from Posidonius). According to Lydus, he said that the etesian winds cause the summer flooding, because they push the rain clouds to the mountains of Ethiopia. After one more intermediary (παρ' ἄλλου, 13), the head of the stemma is reached in Homer (14f), with his use of διιπετής (fallen from Zeus, fed by rain) of the Nile in *Od.* IV.477 (cf. 581). For Strabo's own earlier interpretation of διιπετής and the Nile: 1.2.30, and for Posidonius' reference to Homer in relation to geographical evidence, F216. For the anonymous intermediary (παρ' ἄλλου, 13), Müller suggested Θαλοῦ which cannot be correct, because although Thales shared an etesian theory with Thrasyalces, he did not assign the cause in any way to rainstorms, which is the subject of the doxography. Jacoby guessed 'Ἀλκαίου, presumably from the mention of the name in Strabo, 1.2.30, but there is no other reason for preferring it to ἄλλου.

The doxography seems characteristic of Posidonius in not being merely a collection of previous opinions, but the attempt to trace the historical development of a particular explanation. It is likely that Posidonius himself inclined to the monsoon explanation (F49.134f; F210.20ff).

It is clear that Strabo does not dismiss Posidonius' witnesses because of their views, which essentially were the same as his; nor because it was unnecessary to give references at all, because he proceeds to give two of his own, contemporary

COMMENTARY: F223

accounts in Eudorus and Ariston the Peripatetic (where he suspects plagiarism between the two). It appears that he thinks there is no need of witnesses *of that sort* (τοιούτων . . . οἴους 8f). In the context the contrast should be between οἱ μὲν οὖν ἀρχαῖοι στοχασμῷ τὸ πλέον and οἱ δ' ὕστερον αὐτόπται γενηθέντες (§5 *init.*; Context). This is a case for facts recorded by autopsy rather than hereditary theoretical guesswork. However, Lydus' account of Callisthenes' first-hand experiences with Alexander in Ethiopia does not fit this interpretation, but Strabo may not have known of it, or merely followed Posidonius' statement that Callisthenes took the theory from Aristotle. There are two notable omissions from a doxography on the summer rainstorms explanation: (a) Agatharchides of Cnidos, the Peripatetic of the 2nd c. B.C., and guardian of a young Ptolemy (Soter II?). He assigned the flooding to rains in the mountains of Ethiopia, attested by the natives of the neighbouring regions; D.S. 1.41.4; *FGrH* 86, F19. (b) Eratosthenes (Arist. F246 Rose, 687 Gigon). Perhaps they did not fit in as links in Posidonius' chain; although presumably Agatharchides would have been more acceptable to Strabo. On the other hand, there is no reason to believe that Strabo's references, Eudorus and Ariston, were αὐτόπται, but they were modern and up-to-date, and not merely of historical interest in Strabo's opinion. But for Posidonius' view on when and how witnesses should be used, T87, F156.

See also F210.20ff; Capelle, 'Die Nilschwelle', *Neue Jahrb.* (1914), 317-61.

F223   Strabo, XVII.3.10

CONTENT

Paucity of rivers in Libya. Climatic differences between east and west.

CONTEXT

Strabo embarks on a description of Libya in XVII.3.1-23.

COMMENTARY: F223

Libya could be used as a general term for the continent of Africa, but Strabo here applies it to Africa apart from Egypt (xvii.1) and Ethiopia (xvii.2). In fact he virtually confines himself to the seaboard of our Morocco, Algeria, Tunisia and Libya, proceeding in that order. Maurusia (Morocco) occupies him until 3.8; 3.9, 11, 12 deal with Algeria, then at 3.13 he passes to Tunisia. So 3.10, which is a criticism of a general statement by Posidonius on the aridity of Libya (in the ancient sense) is an inserted parenthesis. Artemidorus is named three times (3.2, 3.8, 3.10), so he may have been Strabo's principal authority in this section. Up to this point Strabo had stressed the fertility and number of rivers of the seaboard (3.4, 3.6, 3.7), but the aside of 3.10 was prompted by the last sentence of 3.9, that while parts deep in the interior are mountainous and desert, 'the parts there (Algeria) near the sea consist of fertile plains, rivers and lakes'.

COMMENT

1-5 Strabo doubts Posidonius' veracity (1), when he said that Libya was irrigated by few and small rivers (2). What follows is unclear, ambiguous and doubtful Greek. τοὺς μεταξὺ ... εἴρηκε (3-4) is preserved (not added, as Jacoby F80) only in *EF*, but it is clearly right; for all the other codices containing Bks x-xvii appear to derive from an hyparchetype identified by common omissions deriving as here from *sauts du même au même* (εἴρηκε. Diller, *The Textual Tradition of Strabo's Geography* 54). But what is the subject of the second εἴρηκε? It has always been taken to be Artemidorus: for the rivers which Artemidorus spoke of, those between Linx and Carthage, he (Artemidorus) has called many and large. This is not only exceedingly clumsy Greek (see Jones' note *ad loc.*) but it verges on the incredible that the sentence began αὐτοὺς γὰρ οὓς (doubted only by Oder, *Philologus, Supplb.* vii (1899), 298, but without emendation). I suggest that Strabo wrote αὐτὸς γὰρ οὕς ... : for Posidonius himself has called those rivers

COMMENTARY: F223

Artemidorus has spoken of between L and C both many and large. Strabo is casting initial doubt on Posidonius' general statement on Libya, by suggesting an apparent self-contradiction. This is merely an introductory gambit, because correction immediately follows: it is more true to say that of the interior, namely, that it was irrigated by few and small rivers. This in turn may be either a direct statement by Strabo, or in indirect speech of Posidonius (and he said that . . .). In either case it is certainly true, and apparent from what follows, that that is what Posidonius meant, and that Strabo knew it. Linx was Artemidorus' name for Eratosthenes' Lixus (3.2; 3.8), i.e. Larasch on the north Atlantic coastline of Morocco (seemingly confused with Tangier by Strabo). So Strabo refers to the seaboard from Morocco to Algeria, hardly Libya in general.

5-9 'He (Posidonius) has said the cause of this himself: that it is not rained on in the northern parts, just as Aethiopia is not either they say. For this reason, he says, pestilences often befall through droughts, the lakes are filled with mud and locusts are prevalent.' By 'the northern parts' Posidonius could not have intended the fertile Mediterranean coastline, but the area under the tropic. F49.49-61, 118-29 (Strabo) and F210 (Cleomedes) prove that in the area between equator and tropic, Posidonius argued that there was a temperate equatorial zone to the south, but an arid subtropical zone to the north of it. Strabo, who expounded and criticised the theory, understood this perfectly well. The locality is clinched by the comparison with Aethiopia (7), for the Aethiopians were held to live *within* the two tropics (Strabo 1.2.24; F49.326ff comm.).

6 μὴ κατομβρεῖσθαι suggests that Posidonius connected the paucity of rivers with lack of rainfall (τὴν αἰτίαν, 5); cf. F49.134f; F210.20ff; F222 comm. Seneca, *NQ* III.6-7 reports this theory, but criticises it.

7 φησί: Jacoby may well be right; φησί/φασί are often confused.

COMMENTARY: F223

9-11 What follows is puzzling. Strabo adds a new separate statement from Posidonius: 'He further (ἔτι) says that eastern areas are wet, for the sun in rising passes by quickly, while the west is dry, because there the sun retires (καταστρέφειν).' As this stands, isolated from context and development, apart from the dubious assistance of Strabo, it is incomprehensible. The problem concerns (i) whether the diurnal or annual path of the sun is in question, (ii) the reference to east and west, and (iii) the theory implied. Strabo in criticism tackles each in turn.

(i) 11-13 Strabo points out that if Posidonius refers to comparative heat from the sun, that is established by the annual path of the sun through the ecliptic, and defined by klimata orientated by NS zones. Thus, even in Posidonius' theory for the klima or zone between equator and tropic, the sub-tropical arid zone is explained by the argument that the sun in its annual cycle NS on the ecliptic 'delays' longer at the 'turn' of the tropics (F49.126–129, F210.1–23). Strabo may have been confused elsewhere (F49.330ff) between annual and diurnal arguments, but the clear reference here to east and west and to the rising sun, shows that the diurnal path and EW distinctions must be meant. It is also established elsewhere that Posidonius, besides making NS latitudinal zonal distinctions of climate, also recognised EW climatic and racial distinctions between continents along the same klima (F49.326–356 comm.).

But the distorting factor now comes from Strabo. He asserts that wet and dry climates are usually explained by a combination of the factors of rain and sun (11f); so he himself (xv.1.13, 24) distinguishes Indians from Aethiopians because they ὑγροῦ κοινωνοῦσιν ἀέρος, and adds rivers and monsoon rains (cf. D.S. 2.36.1–5; 2.52.8–53.4). But so did Posidonius, e.g. ἧττον ἕψεσθαι τῇ ξηρασίᾳ τοῦ περιέχοντος of Indians in F49.329f; cf. F210.18–23; and he recognised a fertile India through factors of wind and moisture (F212). Strabo restricts Posidonius in this fragment to sun (13); but his account

802

almost certainly combined the interrelation of sun, wind and rain.

(ii) **13-21** Strabo now turns to the definition of east and west. He argues rightly that it cannot refer to particular localities, where on any given horizon it would make nonsense to apply a general rule (καθολικῶς, 17) that the eastern section had a wet climate, and the western a dry one (13-19). He admits that Posidonius could make such a statement, if at all (εἰ ἄρα, 20; Denniston, 37f), in relation to the extremities of the whole inhabited world (19-21). This indeed must have been Posidonius' context, but then it is irrelevant to introduce the sentence in relation to differences of climate within Libya.

(iii) **21-31** But even granting this, asks Strabo, what plausibility could there be in Posidonius' aetiological theory (21)? He puts his finger on the real difficulty, the force of καταστρέφειν. Strabo takes it to mean 'turn back' or 'retire' (a possible sense in the Koine, Dihle, *RhM* 105 (1962), 97 n. 1), or perhaps 'come to an end' in the sense of resting at the end of its journey, with the implication that the sun on sinking, slows down in turning back, in comparison with the speed of its rising. This seems an impossible suggestion; as Strabo says, the speed of the passage of the sun is everywhere equal. In Posidonius' argument for sub-tropical arid zones, the sun is said to remain longer in the region of the tropics since it approaches, turns and retires from them. But this is in the annual cycle of the ecliptic, and the diurnal speed remains constant (F210). Again in F49.126-9 (see comm.) an *apparent* difference of diurnal speed of the sun when at the tropics and at the equator, shown by length of daylight, is raised, but again the actual speed is constant. Neither affords any parallel for the sun's slowing down on sinking. The problem is insoluble without further evidence, and the real puzzle is that Strabo does not give it. This suggests that it was not a major argument in Περὶ ὠκεανοῦ, and that Strabo, who appears genuinely puzzled, picked it up second hand. On the analogy of the annual approach and retirement at the tropics, Posidonius may have been referring to a theory (well-known from Cleanthes) whereby the sun on sinking, turned down (καταστρέφειν) south to follow the path of the circumambient ocean, and so warmed longer the western tropical areas. But this does not seem to have been Posidonius' theory (F118) and is sheer speculation.

Strabo's second objection (23–5) attempts to turn the Posidonian criterion of clear observation of fact (ἐνάργεια, 24) against him. Iberia and Maurusia in the west are not dry, but temperate and abound in water. The mention of Iberia is irrelevant; and Posidonius himself recognised its fertility and rivers (F224). He was clearly referring to the EW differentiations of the subtropical klima. So again the mediterranean coastal strip of Morocco is out of line. Strabo himself records (XVII.3.8) that Artemidorus, criticising Eratosthenes, called the western extremities of Maurusia arid and torrid. It is noticeable that Strabo does not mention the east. He agreed with Posidonius that India was 'wet' and fertile. For the growth of the idea of the fertile east see Dihle, *RhM* 105 (1962), 97ff. Posidonius' context was clearly the intercontinental EW differences, along the single sub-tropical klima, and in particular the common problem of racial differentiations between Indians and Africans (Aethiopians/Libyans) (F49.326ff).

Finally (26–31), Strabo objects that it does not matter if the western extremity is the last point for the sun to be above, because for all places at the same latitude (klima) of the inhabited world the sun, leaving an equal interval of night, returns again and warms the earth. For the effect of night, compare F210.15–17.

27 Kramer's κατά greatly improves the Greek.

F224   Strabo, III.3.4

CONTENT

The river Bainis (Minho) in Lusitania.

CONTEXT

At III.3.1 Strabo proceeds northwards from Cape St Vincent up the Atlantic coastline of Spain. III.3.4 deals mainly with the succession of rivers in the fertile coastal strip (1f). After the Douro he mentions the Lethe, sometimes called Limaia or Belion (3f; Oblivio, Sallust, *Hist*, 3.44, Livy, *Per.* 55, hence Xylander's emendation; now the Lima). Then comes by far the biggest river in Lusitania, the Bainis, or Minios (modern Minho).

COMMENT

It is possible that the allusion to Posidonius is confined to the one sentence, 7-8 (so Jacoby, Theiler), stating that the Bainis rose in the Cantabrian Mountains to the north. The previous reference to Posidonius in III.3.3 (F220) was also in the nature of an inserted aside. Posidonius was clearly correcting a mistaken earlier view that the Bainis rose further south in the territory of the Celtiberians and Vaccaeans. This was probably Polybius from D. Iunius Brutus Callaicus, whose campaign in Lusitania in 138/7 B.C. furnished much information on the area (Plb. 3.37.10, Walbank *A Historical Commentary on Polybius, ad loc.*; Cuntz, *Polybius* 34-7; Malitz, 103, who compares D.S., 33.24-6). Brutus is mentioned again as an authority by Strabo at III.3.1 and III.3.7. If καὶ (7) is correct, Strabo must mean that Posidonius put the source of the Lethe as well in Cantabrian territory. This is rather compressed writing after the previous sentence.

Perhaps what follows may derive from Posidonius, with its

COMMENTARY: F225

interest in tidal effect on the river, and praise for the effective design of nature; compare Posidonius' praise for mines as treasure stores of nature in F239.1, 8. And it is not impossible that Posidonius mentioned Brutus, as he introduced a detail of Roman soldiers into his account of flooding in the Baitis (F218.13).

It is highly unlikely that Posidonius himself ventured into this difficult region. He would have informants at Gades.

F225   Strabo, v.1.8

CONTENT

The river Timavus.

CONTEXT

Posidonius is introduced by Strabo to contradict Polybius.

COMMENT

The question concerned the remarkable water systems at the head of the Gulf of Trieste, in the country north of Trieste and east of the river Isonzo from the Karst plateau to the sea. Because of much subsequent change, precise identification is difficult; but for a full account see Philipp, *RE, Timavus,* VIA, 1242f, *Natisco* XVI, 1807 (with map), and Nissen, *Italische Landeskunde* II.233ff. The Timavus was notorious enough to find a place in Latin poetry. Vergil (*Aen.* 1.244ff) mentions nine mouths (so also Mela II.61), its passage with a mountain's mighty roar, and its bursting out (from underground?) into a flood to the sea. Martial (IV.25.6) echoes the seven mouths or fountains of Polybius and Strabo. Pliny (*NH* 2.225) includes it in his list of underground rivers.

Polybius had said (not preserved, but see Walbank, *Comm.*

COMMENTARY: F226

III. 614f) that six of the seven fountains were salty and so connected them with the sea rather than a river, bolstering this with a local saying (4-6). Posidonius, as he had challenged Polybius over the wells at Gades (F217), countered that the Timavus was a river (hence of fresh water) rising in the mountains and disappearing underground before debouching into the sea.

The order of words at 7 stresses ποταμόν, and perhaps the Greek can mean, the *river* Timavus; otherwise ποταμόν would be predicate (the Timavus is a river), and καί would have to be supplied before ἐκ. Posidonius' information is surprisingly precise (8-9); it is possible that he may have been in the area. This is another instance of his interest in hydrology, and in particular the relationship between sea and rivers. There was a considerable mythology on underground rivers (e.g. the Alpheus and the Syracusan Arethusa, Pliny *NH* 2.225), but Posidonius was interested in facts. Strabo mentions the Timavus again at VI.2.9 in connection with a list of underground rivers. Jacoby and Theiler think that the whole section is Posidonian, but this is far from certain (F227 comm.).

F226   Athenaeus, VIII.333B-D

CONTENT

A big wave engulfed the army of Tryphon.

CONTEXT

Athenaeus is discussing fish, and at this point producing stories of when it rained fish or frogs. Posidonius had a tale about a great quantity of fish (1f).

COMMENTARY: F226

COMMENT

For this battle on the Syrian coast between Ptolemais and Tyre, fought between Tryphon, the Apamean general and contender for Syria, and Sarpedon, the general of Demetrius II Nicator: *RE*, vol. VII, *Tryphon* (1).718. The date is probably *c.* 144/3 B.C. See also Jacoby, *Kommentar* F29.

There is another account in Strabo, XVI.2.26, where there is no mention of Posidonius. Strabo's version is unclear and less detailed. He represents the battle as between 'the Ptolemaeans' and the general Sarpedon. The wave was like a flood tide (ὅμοιον πλημμυρίδι), and some of the army were swept out to sea, others left dead ἐν τοῖς κοίλοις τόποις. When the ebb (ἄμπωτις) receded, the bodies of the men were revealed all mixed up with dead fish. The story is basically the same, but Strabo is somewhat unclear as to which side won, and who was killed by the wave. Strabo's one additional detail, the comparison to a flood tide, sounds quite Posidonian, but the garbled nature of his account shows that he did not take it directly from Posidonius. Perhaps it filtered through Athenodorus (T44, T79). In contrast, the quotation in Athenaeus is precise, detailed and vivid. The last sentence shows a certain grim humour in sandwiching between the exultation of the defeated army over the bodies of their engulfed enemies and the subsequent formal sacrifice to Poseidon the Router, the picture of Sarpedon's men prudently carting off the unexpected windfall of plentiful fish supplies.

Jacoby considered the extract to come from the *History* (F29 J); Strabo introduced the tale as a παράδοξον, and it might have appeared in a collection of such natural marvels in Περὶ ὠκεανοῦ (cf. F229). Of course Posidonius may have included it in both books.

5 Casaubon suggested λειφθείς from a comparison with the Strabo passage; but since the latter is unclear, the text of Athenaeus' codices should be retained.

COMMENTARY: F227

F227 Strabo, VI.2.11

CONTENT

A volcanic eruption in the sea between the Liparaean Islands and Panarea, which occurred within the recollection of Posidonius, is described.

CONTEXT

Posidonius is cited three times before this in Bk VI: 2.1 (F249); 2.3 (F234); 2.7 (F250). VI.2.10 is concerned with the Liparean Islands, and includes some volcanic observations; Polybius is cited. VI.2.11 continues with Strongyle (Stromboli), Didyma (Salina), Ericussa (Alicudi), Phoenicussa (Filicudi), Euonymus (Panarea). 'Often flames have been seen running over the surface of the sea about these islands, when a passage has been opened up from cavities deep down and the fire forced its way to the outside.' Cf. F228. Jacoby suggested (F88 J) that sections 9 and 10 of chapter 2 are also from Posidonius; but there are no firm grounds for this.

COMMENT

1 The date is probably 126 B.C. (cf. Pliny, *NH* 2.203; Julius Obsequens 29) rather than 90/89 B.C. (cf. Pliny, *NH* 2.238). The problem is discussed in T5 comm.

2 The islands of Vulcano and Panarea are meant.

2-14 Whether from the *History* (cf. F226) or, which is more likely, from Περὶ ὠκεανοῦ, the passage is remarkable for careful detail. The timing of the eruption is recorded, at dawn about the time of the summer solstice, and the sequence and duration of the phenomena. The rising of the sea is described, and then later the flames, smoke and surfacing of volcanic mud which eventually solidified. The effects are carefully

COMMENTARY: F228

noted: the dead fish driven by the current; the sailors overpowered by the heat and the stench, with an almost clinical description of their symptoms and recovery. Finally a precise historical note is added on the measures of purification taken by the Praetor. If this was an event which Posidonius had initially heard of as a young boy (see T5), he later took considerable pains to ferret out details, whether from Panaetius (cf. F136 van Str.; Lydus, *De Mens* IV.115, p. 153 Wuensch; Grilli, *RFIC* 84 (1956), 266–72) or from other sources. The documentation is impressive, and shows the importance these descriptions had for him in his survey of such phenomena, no doubt supplying material to test his explanatory hypotheses.

14 It is very likely that the reference is to Titus Quinctius Flamininus, consul 123 B.C., praetor probably 126 B.C. (T5 comm.). Therefore Du Theil's Φλαμινῖ⟨ν⟩ον should be adopted.

14–17 Pliny *NH* 2.238 records a purificatory deputation from the senate for the eruption in 90/89 B.C. But the same procedure is likely to have been followed in 126 B.C. (T5 comm.).

F228   Seneca, *Naturales Quaestiones* II.26.4–7

CONTENT

Volcanic fire burst through the sea when an island appeared in the Aegean.

CONTEXT

See F135, Context. In chs. 21–30 Seneca is engaged with a theory of lightning and thunder which is based on Posidonius, although he is not named (see F135). At ch. 26 the question is raised how fire can arise from a moist cloud without being

810

COMMENTARY: F228

extinguished (26.1-3). F228 is an incidental parenthesis giving an example of how this can happen in another sphere, i.e. the sea, where the watery element is much more powerful (F228.12-14). *Quidni* (1) (Why not?) refers to the previous section: water may or may not put fire out. 'It depends on the amount of water; a small amount will not assist or block the force of fire.'

COMMENT

1-11 Posidonius described the rising of an island in the Aegean. The sea foamed during the day and smoke rose from the depths. Night produced intermittent fire like lightning 'as often as the heat below overcame the weight of water above' (5f). Stones and rocks were hurled up in various stages of corrosion. Finally the peak of a burned mountain emerged, which grew to the size of an island. Seneca adds that the same thing happened again in his time in the consulship of Valerius Asiaticus.

This last sentence enables us to identify both events. Seneca mentions his contemporary eruption again in connection with Thera and Therasia at *NQ* VI.21.1, for which see F230. The volcanic island which appeared in Seneca's time in 46 A.D. was Thia, between Thera and Therasia in the Santorin group of the southern Cyclades (cf. also Pliny, *NH* 2.202, who gives the date as 19 A.D.; but all Pliny's dates in this section are suspect or wrong). The emergence (and subsequent submergence) of Thia, no doubt reminded that generation of the story that was preserved (*maiorum nostrorum memoria*, 1), and which Posidonius had described, of the similar emergence of the islet Hiera in the same area at an earlier date (cf. Pliny, *loc. cit.*). It is clear from the description that this was a volcanic eruption. The ancients associated volcanic phenomena with earthquakes (e.g. F231) and with movements of the sea (F227). For Posidonius' interest in the appearance and disappearance of islands due to seismic action, cf. Strabo,

COMMENTARY: F229

11.3.6 = F49. 249–303 (the disappearance of Atlantis). The detailed account in Strabo, 1.3.16 of the emergence of a volcanic island between Thera and Therasia must, because of Strabo's dates and the reference to Rhodian thalassocracy, refer to the earlier rise of Hiera. It is similar to the Posidonian description in F228, and adds a Rhodian detail (F231 Context), but Posidonius is cited immediately afterwards for what seems to be a different event, although in part referring to the Cyclades, so there seems to be a dislocation of authority there (F231 comm.).

The date of the emergence of Hiera is usually put at 197 B.C. Pliny, 2.202 is very unreliable in his dating; but see Justin. xxx.4; Plu., *De Pyth. Orac.*, ch. 11; also Schühlein, *Untersuchungen* 53 n. 4; Wilski, *RE* v.a.2, *Thera*, 2265.

Cf. also F227.

12–14, 16–19 See Context. This shows that the Posidonian reference is brought in parenthetically *ad loc.*, to illustrate the main, quite different point at issue, namely how fire (i.e. lightning) can break out of moist clouds.

14–16 An added detail is derived from Asclepiodotus, the pupil of Posidonius, that the sea at that point was 200 feet deep, and yet fire burst through it. Therefore, (a) Asclepiodotus, although no doubt using Posidonius, was independent of him, and (b) Seneca was using more than one source for the event.

The Posidonian reference probably came from Περὶ ὠκεανοῦ.

F229 Strabo, IV.1.7

CONTENT

The explanation of the formation of the Stony Plain of la Crau.

COMMENTARY: F229

CONTEXT

Strabo is dealing with the seaboard from the Pyrenees to Massilia, and at this point is remarking on marvels (παρά-δοξα).

COMMENT

A

The subject is la Plaine de la Crau, the curious stony area to the north of the gulf of Fos, bounded to the west by the Rhone, to the north by the Alpilles, and by the Étang de Berre to the east. It was well known in antiquity as an extraordinary natural phenomenon, apparently from Aeschylus' time (F229.25ff). See also Pliny, *NH* 3.34 and Pomponius Mela, II.78.

This is by far the most detailed and accurate description of the area, and no doubt comes from Posidonius, who probably saw it himself. 100 stades (*c*. 18½ km; 4f) from the gulf of Fos takes one into the centre of the Crau. The name Λιθῶδες (6; *campi lapidei*, Pliny; *litus ignobile . . . lapideum ut vocant*, Mela; Crau itself is from a Celtic root meaning stone) comes from the stones which form its surface. Posidonius characterises these as χειροπληθῶν (7), of a size to fill a man's hand; in fact they vary from the size of an egg to a man's head. He adds that there is an undergrowth of rough grasses (ἄγρωστιν, 7) which supplied abundant pasturage (8). Pliny, *NH* 21.57 claims that wild thyme grew there and sheep were brought from distant regions to graze on it. The stony surface is in fact mixed with a proportion of fine soil, and in modern times sheep were brought down from Alpine pastures for rough grazing in the autumn. It is still an exposed and windy area (9ff), and in Posidonius' Black North wind (μελαβόρειον, 11) one can recognise the Mistral. The stories of the violence of the wind, sweeping along the stones, knocking people off their vehicles and stripping them of clothes and equipment (12–14), are repeated in *D.S.* 5.26.1.

B

However, the description is merely a prelude to explaining the phenomenon. Two accounts are given:

(i) Aristotle is credited with the theory that the stones were thrown up onto the surface by earthquakes of the kind called βράσται, and slid together into the hollow parts of the areas (15–17). In *Meteor.* II.8.368b 23ff, Aristotle distinguished horizontal and vertical shocks in types of earthquakes. In the latter type, large quantities of stones come to the surface 'like chaff in a winnowing sieve'. He maintains it was this kind of earthquake which devastated the area of Sipylos, the so-called Phlegraean plain, and the country by Liguria (presumably the Stony Plain). The plurality of his examples may have led to the plural τῶν χωρίων in line 17. Our surviving texts of Aristotle contain no mention of the term βράστης, but it is used in Ps.-Arist. *De Mundo* 4.396a 3 for Aristotle's vertical shock; F230 comm. It is the equivalent of Posidonius' βρασματίας, F12, F230.

(ii) Posidonius has a theory which is distinguished from Aristotle's (17–21). But what precisely is it?

(a) It was a lake which solidified (λίμνην οὖσαν παγῆναι; mud to stone?); and the uniformity of the stones is due to solidification happening as waves continued to lap (μετὰ κλυδασμοῦ), and so the wave ridges, become solid, were divided into a large number of stones (καὶ διὰ τοῦτο εἰς πλείονας μερισθῆναι λίθους). He compares pebbles in the beds of rivers (κάχληκας; cf. καχλάζειν, to splash or bubble) and on the shore; they are similar with regard to smoothness and uniformity of size. This is a strange theory. Pebbles in rivers and on the beach owe their smoothness and regularity to the action of the waves and force of water, not because they solidify from it.

(b) So did Posidonius also posit an initial earthquake, which threw up the rock and stones and *then*, because the area was a lake (λίμνην οὖσαν), the lava rocks were solidified and worn by the waves (παγῆναι μετὰ κλυδασμοῦ) and broken down like river and shore pebbles? But this will not do, since Strabo clearly contrasts Aristotle and Posidonius, and ἐξ ὑγροῦ παγέντας μεταβαλεῖν (23f) is decisive evidence that Strabo understood Posidonius to be saying that the Crau stones were solidified from the water of the lake, rather than thrown up by an earthquake. Therefore Steinmetz, *RhM* 105 (1962), 263, is mistaken in assigning a seismic explanation for Posidonius, and appears to confuse him with the Aristotelian explanation.

Therefore interpretation (a) must be right, although Strabo shows signs of wanting to combine the two theories. Posidonius was correct in assigning the cause to water rather than to an earthquake. Modern theories attribute the formation to a sudden inundation of the Durance river, or possibly the shingle brought down by the Durance from Alpine glaciers. The surface stones overlie a sub-soil of stones cemented into a hard mass by deposits of calcareous mud, which may have given rise to the belief of the solidification of the lake.

C

25ff The mythological interpretation from Aeschylus, complete with quotation from *Prometheus Unbound* (Fr. 199 Nauck²; 32ᵇ Mette), to the effect that Zeus thoughtfully provided the stone field as ammunition for Heracles against the Ligurians, almost certainly is culled from Posidonius, since it is followed by Posidonius' sarcastic comment (39–41); Zeus would have done better to shower the Ligurians themselves with the stones and bury the lot, rather than make Heracles need so many stones. Strabo amusingly bridles at the 'so many' (τοσούτων, 41); after all there was a large number of Ligurians, so the mythographer in this case is more plausible than the demolisher (τοῦ ἀνασκευάζοντος, i.e. Posidonius) of the myth. It is interesting to see Posidonius going out of his way to attack a mythological 'explanation' of a natural phenomenon.

D

Jacoby (*Kommentar* F90) thinks that this passage may come from Bk 23 of the *History*, which had material on Κελτοί, so Frs. 67-9, but the treatment leaves the question open that it may have come from Περὶ ὠκεανοῦ, or from a scientific work, where Posidonius gives a natural explanation of παράδοξα.

SEISMOLOGY

F230 Seneca, *Naturales Quaestiones* VI.21.2

CONTENT

Classification of earthquakes.

CONTEXT

NQ VI is devoted to earthquakes. After a review of previous theories (chs. 5-20; F12 comm.) which covers attribution of cause to water or fire or earth or air or a combination of these, Seneca at ch. 21.1 turns to himself and the Stoa (*nobis quoque placet*): it is air (*spiritus*) that is capable of such efforts. Nothing in nature is more powerful or energetic than air. It rouses fire, whips up water, scatters earth. It raises new islands in the sea, e.g. Thera and Therasia (in the Cyclades), 'and that island in our own time, born in the Aegean before our very eyes'. This probably refers to Thia in 46 A.D. (cf. Pliny, *NH* 2.202). Frs. 228 and 231 show Posidonius' interest in volcanic islands emerging in the bay of Santorini (Thera). At ch. 21.2 Seneca expands a classification of earthquakes taken from Posidonius

COMMENTARY: F230

(F230), and then proceeds (22ff) to distinguish different causes for the different kinds of earthquake.

COMMENT

A. *Seneca and Diogenes Laertius*

Seneca says: 'There are two kinds of earthquakes in Posidonius' view. Each has its own name. One is *succussio* (jolt from underneath) when the earth is shaken by an up-and-down movement. The other is *inclinatio* (tilting), whereby the earth leans to one side or the other like a ship.' Seneca himself adds to this a third, marked by their use of language: *tremor*. It is neither jolting nor tilting but vibration, and causes the least damage. On the other hand tilting is more destructive than the jolt.

Diogenes, however, has a four-fold classification for Posidonius: σεισματίας, χασματίας, κλιματίας, βρασματίας (F12.4–6).

B. *Identification of terms*

There are four other ancient sources which classify different kinds of earthquake, and are useful in identifying Posidonius' terms: Ps.-Arist. *De Mundo* 396a 1–16; Heraclitus, *Allegoriae* 38.6 (1st c. A.D.?); Ammianus Marcellinus, 17.7.13 (4th c. A.D.); Lydus, *De Ostentis* 53–4 (6th c. A.D.).

βρασματίας: the term recurs exactly in Heraclitus and Ammianus. *De Mundo* and Lydus use βράστης (from the same root, βράσσω); also F229.16. All four characterise the action of this type of quake as vertical shocks. Therefore this is Seneca's *succussio*.

κλιματίας: is a certain correction by Schneider for καιματίας or καυματίας of Diogenes' codices. κλιματίας is the form given by Heraclitus and Ammianus; *De Mundo* and Lydus prefer ἐπικλίνται. But again all four have the same descrip-

817

tion, of horizontal pressure, leaning or tilting to the side (with a wave-like action, Lydus). So this is Seneca's *inclinatio*.

χασματίας: i.e. 'gaper'. Again the term recurs in Heraclitus and Ammianus. *De Mundo* uses for this type ῥῆκται, οἱ δὲ χάσματα ἀνοίγοντες καὶ τὴν γῆν ἀναρρηγνύντες. Lydus also uses ῥῆκται with a similar description. These are 'splitters' which fissure the earth.

σεισματίας: is the only term which is difficult to identify. Heraclitus, who most exactly reproduces the Diogenes terms, simply omits it. There is no room for it in his classification, for he is maintaining that the three-pronged trident of Poseidon 'Earthshaker' represents the three kinds of earthquake which οἱ φυσικοί name. Nor does it occur in *De Mundo* or in Ammianus. It does not seem to represent *De Mundo's* παλματίαι, i.e. 'oscillators' (< παλμός, quivering), recoiling from side to side. That is like Seneca's *tremor*, which Seneca claimed as his own contribution, and denies to Posidonius. Lydus has σεισταί, which seems to be a more general term for 'shakers'. σεισματίας also looks like a more general term for a quake.

The *De Mundo* has other types not in Posidonius: ἰζηματίαι ('sinkers', also in Lydus); ὦσται ('thrusters'); παλματίαι (see above); μυκηταί ('roarers', *mycematiae* in Amm). It does not seem that *De Mundo* is following Posidonius.

C. *The classification*

Diogenes may preserve a combination of two classifications. One is based on distinguishing vertical and horizontal earthquakes. So Aristotle, *Meteor.* 368b 23ff made a two-fold classification of horizontal, like a shudder (τρόμος), and vertical, like a throb (σφυγμός). This is Seneca's *inclinatio* and *succussio*, and from the other evidence, κλιματίας (ἐπικλίντης) and βρασματίας (βράστης). *De Mundo*, Heraclitus, Ammianus and Lydus all start off their lists with these two.

Lydus may give the clue for σεισματίας and χασματίας.

COMMENTARY: F230

Having given the normal division of the *manner* of quake, ἐπικλίνται and βράσται (horizontal and vertical, p. 108.11–15 Wachsmuth), he passes to their *effect*: some are 'splitters' (ῥῆκται, i.e. χασματίαι), some 'shakers' *only* (σεισταὶ μόνον, i.e. σεισματίαι?), some 'settlers' (ἰζηματίαι) (p. 108.15ff W). Cf. P. Steinmetz, 'Zur Erdbeben-theorie des Poseidonios', *RhM* 105 (1962), 261ff.

D. *Causes of different types of earthquakes*

After the classification, Seneca maintains that since the movements of the two types of earthquake are different, their causes must be different (22.1).

Following the lead of Asclepiodotus, he suggests that the cause of *succussio* is the collapse of rock in subterranean caverns, which may happen for various reasons (22.2–4). Asclepiodotus was referred to earlier (17.3) as *auditor Posidonii* (T41), and see F228 for both Posidonius and Asclepiodotus on the volcanic rising of Hiera. But we certainly cannot assume that Asclepiodotus merely reproduced Posidonius in his Αἰτίαι Φυσικαί (Ringshausen, *Poseidonios, Asklepiodot, Seneca und ihre Auschauungen über Erdbeben und Vulkane*, Munich, 1929). Seneca adds (22.3) that underground rocks not only split off by their own weight, but also *cum flumina supra ferantur*, they may be loosened by moisture. This may or may not reflect Posidonius' interest in hydrology (cf. F225).

The cause of *inclinatio* is given as pressure of air (23). We are told that this general theory was held by a number of people (23.2). But Callisthenes (the nephew of Aristotle, whom Posidonius had cited in connection with the cause of the rise of the Nile, F222) is brought in with approval with regard to coastal disturbances (the inundation of Helice and Buris). The cause of this is that air enters earth through *occulta foramina*, even under deep sea, which then blocks its passage; hence the association of earthquakes with Neptune (Poseidon 'Earthshaker'; cf. Heraclitus, *Alleg.* 38.3ff above). Seneca

COMMENTARY: F231

(24.1–5) argues about how air enters the earth (see F12), and rejects the view that it is introduced through the surface of the earth. The analogy of the human body (24.2ff; cf. ch. 14; the analogy occurs already in Aristotle in another form, *Meteor.* 366b 15ff; but it could be Posidonian) leads to the image of air breathed into the lungs of subterranean caverns (cf. F12); that these may be deep enough to be below the sea is shown by disturbances of seas of great depth (cf. F228). Posidonius is cited (24.6 = F232) for the earthquake at Sidon on the coast of Phoenicia (cf. F231; and Frs. 226–8, F49.294–303). Clearly Posidonius was interested in such oceanic seismic phenomena.

So there are reverberations of possible Posidonian influence. But the structure of argument in chs. 22–4 comes from Seneca; e.g. he uses his own device of the anonymous objector in 24.4. It does not now seem possible to place Posidonius securely in the details of the argument (F12). Posidonius may have been one of Seneca's authorities in this passage, but to what extent he may have drawn on him remains uncertain.

There are some other similarities to this passage in *Aetna*, e.g. lines 98ff, 112ff, 158ff, 283, 307ff. But cf. the admirable caution over Posidonian influence of Goodyear, *Aetna* 55f against the overconfidence of Sudhaus, *Aetna* 59ff.

F231   Strabo, 1.3.16

CONTENT

Posidonius told how an earthquake in Phoenicia damaged Sidon, and had a widespread effect from Syria to Greece.

CONTEXT

From section 10, Strabo has been criticising Eratosthenes' theory of sea levels to explain currents in straits and

COMMENTARY: F231

inundations; F215, Context. Earthquakes can be a cause, as they can also explain the separation of Sicily from Italy. At §16 Strabo says that he will present a collection of instances illustrating inundations and the problems of the formation of Sicily, the Aeolian Islands and the Pithecussae. He is doing this to promote ἀθαυμασία, because τὸ ἄηθες disturbs the senses and shows inexperience with τὰ φύσει συμβαίνοντα. He begins with the island (Hiera) which rose through volcanic action between Thera and Therasia in the southern Cyclades in 197 B.C. This was a famous instance: Sen. *NQ* VI.21.1, Pliny, *NH* 2.202, Justin. xxx.4. It is also one that appears in Posidonius and in his pupil Asclepiodotus (Sen. *NQ* II.26.4–7 = F228). Part of Strabo's detail is a story that the Rhodians, then at the height of their sea-power, were the first to venture on the scene and to erect a temple on the new island to Apollo Asphalios. This may possibly come from Posidonius, but he is only actually cited for what follows.

COMMENT

'And in Phoenicia, says Posidonius, an earthquake engulfed a city above Sidon, and ruined about two-thirds of Sidon itself, but not all at once, so there was not much loss of life.' This suggests a real earthquake rather than inundation by seismic waves (cf. F232).

Strabo continues, τὸ δ' αὐτὸ πάθος ... διέτεινε, which implies reference to the same occasion; so we are probably still with Posidonius, although the indirect speech has been abandoned. The vivid ἐξήμεσε (vomited, 11) may have been lifted from Posidonius.

The tremor extended also over Syria, but in a somewhat mild form, crossed also to some of the Cyclades islands and to Euboea (the springs of Arethusa were cut off and many days later shot up again through another mouth); the island continued to shake in parts until a chasm opened in the Lelantine plain and vomited a river of lava. This is a most

COMMENTARY: F232

interesting and unusual observation of a whole seismic chain of disturbances. If the reference to the Cyclades is to the emergence of Hiera (see Context), the date would be 197 B.C. But in that case it would be a surprisingly offhand and obscure allusion to a famous event. Also this section from Posidonius would be attached to the detailed reference to Hiera in the previous sentences in a most maladroit fashion.

Strabo then passes in §17 to a collection of instances from Demetrius of Scepsis, and in §20 to another set from Demetrius of Callatis 'in his account of all the earthquakes that have ever occurred throughout all Greece' (*FGrH* 85, F6). Jacoby adds all this (17–20) in petit to this fragment (*FGrH* 87, F87). There is absolutely no evidence that it derives from Posidonius. Reinhardt, *Poseidonios* 87ff and Sudhaus, *Aetna* 59ff also far exceed the evidence. See also F49.294ff.

F232   Seneca, *Naturales Quaestiones* VI.24.6

CONTENT

Posidonius is cited as evidence for an earthquake disaster at Sidon.

CONTEXT

See F230. This is an isolated reference to detail.

COMMENT

Thucydides' account of the shock waves at Atalante, an island off the Opuntian–Locrian coast is much less dramatic than that of Seneca. Thucydides (III.89.3) merely says that in 426 B.C. waves created by an earthquake produced an ἐπίκλυσις, carrying away part of the Athenian fort and

COMMENTARY: F233

smashing one of two ships drawn up on the slipway. This hardly warrants Seneca's 'destruction of the whole or at least greatest part of the island'. Seneca therefore had not checked Thucydides. Did he misremember, or take the reference from someone else? He cites Posidonius only for Sidon. And that reference is extremely vague. If the event is the same as that reported by Strabo in F231, which must be the case, the details are different. Seneca's *idem* (3) ought to refer to seismic waves, but it was a genuine earthquake which appears to have done the damage in F231. Perhaps it would be more accurate to say that F231 leaves open the possibility of a combination of land earthquake and sea waves, while Seneca is innocent of any detail at all.

F233   Strabo, XI.9.1

CONTENT

An etymology of Rhagae is given from the earthquakes which Posidonius said destroyed many cities and two thousand villages in Parthia.

COMMENT

The etymology is not attributed to Posidonius (φασίν, 4), only the statement that many cities and two thousand villages in Parthia were destroyed by earthquakes. But cf. Strabo, 1.3.19 where the etymology of Rhagae is credited to Duris, ὑπὸ σεισμῶν ῥαγείσης τῆς περὶ τὰς Κασπίους πύλας γῆς, ὥστε ἀνατραπῆναι πόλεις συχνὰς καὶ κώμας καὶ ποταμοὺς ποικίλας μεταβολὰς δέξασθαι (*FGrH* 76, F54). Posidonius was interested in etymology (T89), but this guess was a common one. Strabo records a similar etymology for Rhegium in Sicily (VI.1.6), this time with reference to Aeschylus. Duris is cited only this once in Strabo; so it is possible that

COMMENTARY: F234

Strabo may have found the reference to Duris in Posidonius (cf. Rusch, *De Posidonio* 17), for the statement concerning the destruction of cities and villages is very similar in 1.3.19 and XI.9.1. Or is the Posidonian contribution merely the number of villages destroyed? Cf. also D.S. 19.44.4, and Jacoby's note on Duris F54, p. 125.27ff.

Rhagae is 12 km south of Teheran at Shahr Rey. See F282 for Parthia.

GEOLOGY, MINERALOGY

F234   Strabo, VI.2.3

CONTENT

The lava of Aetna, and the influence of volcanic ash on the soil.

CONTEXT

VI.2.1 begins Strabo's account of Sicily. Posidonius is cited at the beginning for dimensions and klimata (F249). VI.2.2–3 deals with the cities on the east coast between Messene and Syracuse. Jacoby and Theiler begin this fragment a sentence earlier with the introduction of the city of Aetna. Theiler claimed that the inclusion there of the myth of the Sicilian brothers carrying their parents on their backs to save them from the lava flow is certainly from Posidonius, because of the allusion in *De Mundo* 400b 2 and Sen. *De Ben.* 3.37.1 and 6.36.1. This is far from proof. It was a popular moral tale as Sen. *De Ben.* shows, common coin from Lycurgus, *Leocr.* 95f on, and appearing in the *Aetna* 625; Val. Max. v.4, Ext. §4 (p. 248 Kempf); Sil. Ital. XIV.197; Martial, VII.24; Pausanias, x.28.4; Hyginus, *Fab.* 154; Ps.-Arist. *Mir.* 154, 846a 9ff;

COMMENTARY: F234

Aelian, *Var. Hist.* F2 (Hercher); Solinus, 5.15 (p. 56.4 Mommsen); Ausonius XI, *Ordo Nob. Urb.* XVI.2; Claudian, *De Piis Fratr.* The brothers were even commemorated in stone and coinage. Posidonius is cited only for the scientific interest in the effect of the lava ash on the country.

COMMENT

1 The reading of the codices, ὅταν τῷ Ποσειδῶνι φαίνηται makes no sense in the sentence. I suggest that it displaced ὅταν δ', ὡς Ποσειδώνιός φησι, κινῆται . . . κινεῖσθαι is the normal word for earth tremors, Hdt. VI.98; Thuc. II.8; Arist. *Meteor.* 365b 3.

The fertility of Sicilian soil, a limestone base with a heavy coating of lava ash, was famous in antiquity (Cary, *Geographic Background of Greek and Roman History* 143ff; Frank, ed., *Economic Survey of Ancient Rome* III (Scramuzza), 253ff). Strabo, VI.2.7 apologises for even mentioning what is θρυλούμενον; it is called the ταμεῖον τῆς Ῥώμης. The ancients were well aware of the effect of different soils on the roots of vines (Vitr. VIII.3.12), but here Posidonius assigns the fertility correctly to the long-term effect of volcanic ash. Strabo (V.4.8) reasserts this for the Campanian plain and Vesuvius; and when dealing with the 'Burnt' country in Mysia (XIII.4.11), he conjectures that it would be well adapted to viticulture from its ashy soil (cf. Vitr. II.6.3).

Posidonius singles out vines and sheep. Why was grain not mentioned, although Strabo stresses it later (VI.2.7)? Did Posidonius think that the ash was particularly effective for viticulture (so Strabo, XIII.4.11; and again for minerals and viticulture, F235)? The comment on sheep is introduced by φασιν (6), and so it is possible that it did not come from the original Posidonian source. For Sicilian wine, Scramuzza, in Frank, ed., *Economic Survey* 270; Pliny *NH* 14.6.66 put it fourth best; the main centres of production were at Tauromenium and Messene. For sheep, Scramuzza, 279f; Sicily was a main

825

COMMENTARY: F235

exporter of wool. The lava soil holds the winter rainfall like a sponge and produces good summer grazing. But τὰς ῥίζας (5) is an odd expression for pasture. There is something wrong with the text at 5-6, and editors have usually followed the emendations of Corais to make τὰς ῥίζας subject of πιαίνειν τὰ πρόβατα. But ῥίζαι ought to refer to the roots of the vines; so Vitr. VIII.3.12: *quae non aliter possunt fieri, nisi, cum terrenus umor suis proprietatibus saporis in radicibus sit infusus, enutrit materiam*.... I suggest that τὰς ῥίζας goes with what precedes: ... εὐοίνου, τάς τε ῥίζας ἐκτρέφει τὰ κατατεφρωθέντα χωρία. πιαίνειν δ' ἐπὶ τοσοῦτον.... The only change is ἐκτρέφει for ἐκφέρει; the subject of πιαίνειν is τὰ κατατ. χωρία. Cf. Hdt. 1.193.1, ἡ δὲ γῆ τῶν Ἀσσυρίων ὕεται μὲν ὀλίγῳ, καὶ τὸ ἐκτρέφον τὴν ῥίζαν τοῦ σίτου ἐστὶ τοῦτο.

1, 5 κατατεφροῦν occurs already in Arist. *Meteor.* 267a 7.

4 εὐάμπελος and χρηστόκαρπος are favourite words of Strabo (e.g. III.3.1; VI.3.6; VI.4.1).

6–9 Strabo has a similar tale at III.5.4 about bleeding sheep to relieve them from choking through fatness from rich pastures. By Erythreia there, he means the island adjacent to Gades (León, now part of Cadiz). There however the recommended bleeding is within 50 days (or 30, the codices divide). Here the interval is 4 or 5 days (two late *Mixti*, *kt*, give 40 or 50). So Sicilian sheep may have been fattest of all in reputation, but manuscript transmission is notoriously suspect on figures.

9 ῥύαξ is the common word for a stream of lava (Thuc. III.116; Theophr. *Lap.* 22).

15 λίθος μυλίας: Arist. *Meteor.* 383b 11ff talks of millstones as having been calcined by fire for hardness.

F235   Strabo, VII.5.8

CONTENT

Bitumen in Apollonia, Seleucia and Rhodes.

COMMENTARY: F235

CONTEXT

At VII.5.3 Strabo starts on the Illyrian seaboard of Dalmatia from Pola southwards, and at VII.5.8 he reaches Apollonia (Vlone). Again Posidonius is cited only for mineralogical observation. But Apollonia was also well-known to mathematical geographers as lying on Hipparchus' parallel of fifteen hours as longest day (F51 Dicks).

COMMENT

2 πέτρα πῦρ ἀναδιδοῦσα. This must be some kind of seepage or burning pillar of fire from a gas-well (Forbes, *Studies in Ancient Technology* 1.24). Ps.-Arist. *Mir.* 127, 842b 15ff also notes this as a fire burning at all times in a small area 'about the size of the space occupied by five couches'. Aelian, *Var. Hist.* 13.16 on Apollonian asphalt also records an ἀθάνατον πῦρ in a confined space.

2-4 Beneath this area are warm asphaltic springs (cf. Vitr. VIII.3.8). The reason for this phenomenon is conjectured (ὡς εἰκός, by Posidonius presumably) to be burning clods of asphalt.

4 The nearby mine on a hill is not recorded elsewhere.

5-7 Detailed observation, specifically assigned to Posidonius: 'if a bit is cut, it fills out again in time, with the earth deposited in the dug hole changing into asphalt'. Ps.-Aristotle and Aelian merely say that bitumen is obtained by digging, and pitch springs up from the earth like springs of water. It is noticeable that Posidonius combines observation with aetiological theory, that bitumens were formed by earth under the influence of fire (Forbes, 1.54; cf. F279). Ps.-Aristotle and Aelian are merely concerned with natural marvels.

7-12 Posidonius' interest also lies in the interaction between mineral, soil and plant, again in this case, as in F234, viticulture. He says that 'vine-earth' (ἀμπελῖτις), i.e. bitumi-

COMMENTARY: F236

nous earth, that is mined in Seleucia in Pieria is a cure for vermin-infected vines; if the vines are smeared with it mixed with olive oil the insects are destroyed before they reach the sprouts of the roots.

Ampelitis was a technical name for a kind of bituminous earth: Pliny *NH* 35.194, *bitumini simillima est ampelitis* (Forbes, 1.5, 22, 31, 49). So γῆν ἀσφαλτώδη (7) is in apposition. Seleucia in Pieria (now Samandağ) lay at the mouth of the Orontes, below the Gulf of Iskenderun on the border between Cilicia and Syria below Mt Pieria. The area, roughly half-way between Apamea and Rhodes was presumably known to Posidonius.

He adds that similar earth (ampelitis) was discovered in Rhodes when he was prytanis (T27), but needed a greater mixture of olive oil for fluxing the bitumen. Such deposits in Cilicia in ancient times were noted elsewhere: Theophr. *Lap.* 85 remarks on earth from Cilicia which becomes viscous on boiling, and Vitr. VIII.3.8 on oil in a river at Soloi. Dioscurides, V.181 mentions ampelitis in Seleucia; see also Oribasius, Bk 13; Aetius, II.9; Galen, *De Fac. Simpl. Med.* IX.1.4 (XII.186 Kühn). There are still small deposits of asphaltites in Cilicia.

F236 Strabo, XVI.1.15

CONTENT

Classification of naphtha in Babylonia.

CONTEXT

Strabo XVI.1 is on Assyria. After dealing with towns and the geography, river systems (9–13), agriculture (14), he turns to asphalt (15). The only authorities cited before 15, are Eratosthenes, Aristobulus (the Alexander historian) and Polycleitus of Larissa.

COMMENTARY: F236

COMMENT

Ch. 15 combines a number of authorities:

(1) Eratosthenes for the distinction of liquid naphtha (petroleum) in Susis (Iran), and dry (ξηρά) bitumen which can be solidified, in Babylonia (Iraq). A well of the latter lay near the Euphrates; when the river overflowed into it, large clods of asphalt formed suitable for building.

(2) Other authorities say that liquid naphtha also is found in Babylonia.

(3) Properties of the two kinds are introduced by εἴρηται: (a) the dry bitumen is useful for building and for caulking boats; (b) the liquid naphtha is remarkably inflammable. There is a story that Alexander experimented to see whether a boy smeared with naphtha would burn; he did.

(4) Posidonius' contribution:

He classified naphtha in Babylonia into 'white' and 'black' (5f). The white consists of liquid sulphur (cf. Pliny *NH* 35.178), which is what attracts the flames; the black is liquid asphalt which they burn in lamps instead of olive oil (Pliny *NH* 35.179). Forbes, *Studies in Ancient Technology* 1.35ff notes the accuracy of observation, distinguishing the light-coloured inflammable crude oil with light petrol fractions, from the thick black fairly harmless asphaltic crude (which by evaporation yields asphaltic bitumen). A garbled form of this classification seems to occur in F219.157f.

The wells in the area of Susa and in Babylonia were known in antiquity from Hdt. VI.119 on; Pliny *NH* 6.99; 35.180; Philostratus, *Vit. Apoll.* 1.24. Pliny *NH* 2.235 also remarks on the inflammability of naphtha, and typically connects it with Medea's burning crown.

F237 Strabo, XIII.1.67

CONTENT

Floating bricks and porous clay.

CONTEXT

Strabo is dealing with Pitane on the Elaitic Gulf in Mysia, the home of Arcesilaus.

COMMENT

It is said that there are floating bricks there, and this is compared with certain earth in Tyrrhenia. Posidonius is brought in for a parallel in Iberia: bricks made from a clay with which silver-plate is moulded, when compacted, floated. On the passage, Fensterbusch, *RhM* 103 (1960), 373ff. More information comes in Vitr. II.3.4 and Pliny *NH* 35.171; both couple the Pitane bricks with those from Maxilua and Callet in Further Spain, bricks made of pumice-like earth which does not sink. It seems highly likely that Posidonius too knew of the Pitane bricks; but perhaps Strabo regarded Posidonius as the expert on Spain. Sen. *NQ* III.25.7 mentions floating pumice like stones in *Lydia*, and he cites Theophrastus.

4f Jones (Loeb) translates 'with which silver is cleaned'; but this is an unlikely rendering of ἐκμάττεται.

Either (a) the phrase refers to the cupellation of silver; in the process of separating lead from silver porous clay was used; see Forbes, *Studies in Ancient Technology* VIII.233–9. Or (b) the reference is to clay which formed moulds for silver reliefs. For ἡ ἀργυρωματικὴ γῆ in this sense, *BM Inscr.* 481, 542, 549.

COMMENTARY: F238

F238   Strabo, XVI.4.20

CONTENT

Aromatic salt in Arabia.

CONTEXT

Strabo XVI.4 is devoted to Arabia. He explicitly says that he is following Eratosthenes for 4.2-4, and Artemidorus for 4.5-19. 4.20 is introduced by saying that Artemidorus also used Eratosthenes and 'the other historians', and most of the section is occupied by Artemidorus' review of why the Red Sea was called red; Ctesias and Agatharchides are cited. This is followed by a sentence giving an unclear measurement from some anonymous writers, and a general tale (λέγεται) on emerald and beryl in the gold mines. The section ends with a specific reference to Posidonius on the occurrence of fragrant salts. At 4.22 Strabo says that much specific information on Arabia came from the expedition of Aelius Gallus (25/4 B.C.). So the Posidonian contribution is the single sentence on salt. That Diodorus' account of Arabia in 2.49-53 comes from Posidonius was first suggested by Oder, *Philologus, Suppl.* VII.324, elaborated by Reinhardt, *Poseidonios* 127ff, included in Jacoby's Appendix in petit (F114), accepted as certain and printed as F78 by Theiler, followed by Malitz, 266ff. The grounds and evidence for this are far from secure.

COMMENT

Strabo, XVII.2.2 refers to quarried salt in Arabia. The most famous area was near Gerrha (Str. XVI.3.3; Pliny, *NH* 31.78). Pliny *NH* 31.86 mentions a saffron-coloured salt quarried in Cappadocia which was very fragrant. εὐώδης almost became a stock epithet for Arabian phenomena, with their heavy trade in aromatics (Str. XVI.4.19; XVI.3.3).

831

COMMENTARY: F239

F239   Strabo, III.2.9

CONTENT

Metals and mining in Spain.

CONTEXT

Strabo begins his account of Spanish mining at III.2.8. The whole of Spain is rich in metals, but Turdetania and the adjoining territory are beyond compare. No country is so rich in gold, silver, copper and iron in the natural state both in quantity and quality (cf. Pliny *NH* 3.30). Gold is not only mined but washed down. The Spanish mines even outdo the Gallic in the Cevennes and Pyrenees. Silver-smelting furnaces occur with high chimneys. Some of the copper-mines are called gold-mines, probably because gold was earlier found there. For what follows compare the parallel passages in D.S. 5.35-8, and Athenaeus, VI.233C-E (F240a). Strabo continues in 2.10 with Polybius' version of the Spanish mines.

COMMENT

1-11   Posidonius is brought in at this point to do justice to the extravagance of nature in the πλῆθος and ἀρετή of the minerals by his own rhetorical style (1-2). In this he really lets himself go: οὐκ ἀπέχεται . . . ἀλλὰ συνενθουσιᾷ ταῖς ὑπερβολαῖς (2-3). We are to expect a purple passage; but Strabo also implies that Posidonius was usually (τῆς συνήθους, 2) rhetorical in style (T103). Posidonius says that he does not disbelieve the story (τῷ μύθῳ, 3: this is legend, not science; so Ps.-Arist. *Mir.* 87, 837a24ff; cf. Sen. *Ep.* 90.12 (F284.52ff), Lucr. V.1252-7; and see F240a.7ff comm.) that once when the forests burned the earth melted, since it was silver- and gold-earth (cf. ἀμπελῖτις, 'vine-earth', i.e. bitu-

832

COMMENTARY: F239

minous, F234), and boiled out to the surface (so again, Athenaeus F240a.9f and D.S. 5.35.3), because the whole mountain and every hill was material (ὕλην, 6; a pun?) of coin piled up by a bountiful fortune (τύχη, 6). And in general, says he, anyone looking at the area would have said that it was a treasure house of everlasting nature or an unfailing treasury of an empire. For the country was not only rich, says he, it was rich underneath, and with that lot it is not Hades who inhabits the nether regions, but Pluto. 8. We should keep the codices in the form ἀενάου (Lasserre). Posidonius was possibly playing on the famous Pythagorean oath, πηγὴν ἀενάου φύσεως ῥιζώματ' ἔχουσαν, S.E. *Adv. Math.* VII.94, DK 58.B15.

11-13 Strabo is not to be outdone himself: such were the remarks he has made about them in ripe (?, heavenly?) figurative style, as if it were from a mine that he too was drawing his speech in abundance.

12 The codices have ἐν οὐραν(ί)ῳ σχήματι, which I cannot parallel, but seems not impossible. ὡραίῳ in the margin of *A* looks like a not very successful attempt at emendation; while ῥητορικῷ in the margin of *hi* is a mere gloss. No convincing solution for the adjective has yet been found. Perhaps some rhetorical word like ἐναγωνίῳ or ἐναγωνίως τῷ σχήματι (*De Subl.* 18.2) underlies the phrase. *De Subl.* 16-29 on σχῆμα shows that the adjective need not be uncomplimentary.

13-17 In speaking of the application of the miners, he adds the *mot* of Demetrius of Phalerum (F138a, b Wehrli; *FGrH* 228, F35a): in the Attic silver mines the men dig as strenuously as if they expected to bring up Pluto himself.

This is clearly connected with the quip at line 11, and so is part of the same passage in Posidonius. So Posidonius' rhetorical flourish here is really derived from Demetrius. It occurs again in Athenaeus F240a.11ff, but it is not in Diodorus.

Πλούτων and Πλοῦτος are, as so often, identified.

COMMENTARY: F239

17-21 So in their case too (καὶ with τούτων; or, 'and in fact', καὶ ... οὖν, Denn. 445) he makes clear that their energy and dedication to work is similar, cutting their galleries aslant and deep, and for the streams that meet them in the galleries, often drawing them off with the Egyptian screw. This is still presumably from Posidonius and not an enlargement by Strabo. D.S. 5.37.3-4 gives an extended account of the screw of Archimedes (called Egyptian because it was used in Egypt for irrigation, Str. XVII.1.52, 30). It was probably introduced into the Spanish mines in the 1st c. B.C. For this see Forbes, *Studies in Ancient Technology* VII.212ff, Healy, *Mining* 95ff; for its construction, Vitr. x.6.1-4. The Archimedes screw is too late of course for Demetrius.

21-4 But the account is not the same for them (τούτοις) as for the Attic miners; no, for these (ἐκείνοις must mean 'the latter' as the run of the sentence shows and D.S. 5.37.1-2 confirms, and refer to the Attic miners; οὗτοι is kept throughout for the Spanish miners) mining is like a riddle; in their case (ἐκείνοις μέν; the Attic miners) all they took up they did not get, all they had they lost.

This is an adaptation of the Homeric riddle (*Vita Herodotea* 35. 498ff): ἄσσ' ἕλομεν λιπόμεσθα, ἃ δ'οὐχ ἕλομεν φερόμεσθα, of unsuccessful fisher boys catching lice instead; those they caught they left on the beach, those they didn't, went home with them. The Demetrian adaptation is alluded to again in Athenaeus, F240a.13-16, and is repeated in D.S. 5.37.1. Athenaeus, F240a.10-16, shows that the application of the riddle came first from Demetrius. It also shows that the context of Demetrius' remarks was an attack on greed and luxury (F240a.12-15); and the explanation of the riddle there is that by spending what you really have for what is uncertain, you get what you did not expect and throw away what you had. It is highly likely that Posidonius' context was similar (F240), which is what made him think of Demetrius. The reference must be to private speculation in mining (Richardson, *JRS* 66 (1976), 141f, n. 25). As for Demetrius' uncertainty in the operation of the silver mines at Laurium, they suffered badly towards the end of the Peloponnesian War and took a long time to recover, but again were declining towards the end of the 4th c. B.C. All this may have been present in Posidonius' mind, as the revolt of slaves *c.* 100 B.C. put an effective end to organised mining at Laurium (F262; Forbes, *Studies in Ancient Technology* VII.146; Healy, *Mining* 53, 56; Richardson, *JRS* 66 (1976), 141).

24–7 But for the Turdetanians (τούτοις δ', 24), mining is *much too* profitable. Again ὑπεράγαν (24) hints the moral background in Posidonius: it is too profitable for their good. This becomes clearer in Athenaeus, VI.233C, F240a, and D.S. 5.36. The richness of the veins is illustrated: copper workers bring up ore of which 25% is pure copper, and some private prospectors for silver pick up a Euboean talent in three days (also in D.S. 5.36.2). Spain was the most important copper-producing province of Rome, and the copper ore of Baetica was rich (Forbes, IX.101).

Str. III.2.3 mentions copper mining at Cotinae, probably near Almaden. In general the Rio Tinto ore body of the southern Sierra Morena is meant. The large deposits in NW Spain were not developed until later (Healy, *Mining* 59).

The Spanish silver mines were still more famous (Plb. 3.57.3; 34.9.8–11 (Walbank); Str. III.2.10–11; D.S. 5.35; Pliny *NH* 33.96) and brought in huge revenues (Forbes, *Studies* VII.157; VIII.226; Badian, *Publicans and Sinners* 31ff; Healy, *Mining* 56; Richardson, *JRS* 66 (1976), 141). It is clear from the remark on silver that Posidonius was describing a large number of small-scale operations, Richardson, p. 141.

27–31 Tin, he says, is not found on the surface, as the historians keep telling us (Polybius?), but is dug. It occurs in the country of the barbarians beyond Lusitania, and in the Tin Islands, and is conveyed from Britain to Massalia (so also D.S. 5.38.4–5). The tin mines of antiquity were concentrated in the north-west corner of Spain and Portugal and in Cornwall. The Cassiterides started as vague legend, Hdt.

III.115, and continued as such. Strabo, III.5.11 places them to the north of the Artabrians (i.e. north of Finisterre), but whatever he means by this, none of the islands off France or Britain contain tin (Forbes, IX.134ff; Healy, 60). Pliny *NH* 34.156f clearly describes the mining of surface alluvial tin ore, and in fact this appears to have been normal practice in Cornwall (Healy, 89; Forbes, IX.127ff). Even when dug, this may refer to buried placers (Healy, 90).

31–6 In the territory of the Artabrians (north-west corner of Spain), he says the soil effloresces (ἐξανθεῖν, 32) with silver, tin and white gold (mixed with silver) (presumably this refers to surface deposits); and the rivers bring down this soil. The women scrape it with shovels and wash it in sieves . . . What follows is corrupt. Athenaeus, F240a.5–6 completes the process with ἄγουσι ἐπὶ τὴν χώνην. So Theiler suggested πλεκτοῖς ἐπὶ τῆξιν; but ἐπὶ τῆξιν is very compressed on its own, and something more is needed like ⟨εἶτ' ἄγειν⟩ ἐπὶ τὴν χώνην of Cobet (cf. Athenaeus). εἰς κίστην Meineke (cf. ἐπὶ κίστην *B*) is very weak. The passage remains unsolved. There is nothing of this section in Diodorus.

Ore in the streams is also mentioned by Str. III.2.8 and by Ps.-Arist. *Mir.* 46, 833b 15ff. Throughout there is a distinction between metals that have to be dug, those on the surface soil, and those washed down by rivers; cf. Strabo, IV.6.12. On white (silver) gold, Pliny *NH* 33.80, Healy, 75. For the rich deposits in north-west Spain, Pliny *NH* 33.78; Healy, 48; Lewis and Jones, *JRS* 60 (1970), 169ff; *JRS* 62 (1972), 61.

The Posidonian elements in this whole account are the abundance and quality of minerals, emphasised by his extravagant language (but one must not forget that this is partly due to his handling of traditional material: Pluto, the riddle, from Demetrius), the geographical sources of the ores, the kinds of deposits and methods of mining, and a hint of the moral implications, for which see F240.

COMMENTARY: F240

F240a, b Athenaeus, VI.233D–234C; Eustathius, *Commentarii ad Homeri Odysseam* IV.89

CONTENT

The corrupting effect of gold and silver.

CONTEXT

Pontianus, a philosopher from Nicomedia in Bithynia is speaking from 231B, on the rise of gold and silver in Greece. But the immediate context begins with 233A on philosophical attitudes to silver and gold. Plato and Lycurgus ban it. Zeno of Citium puts them in the category of the 'indifferents' (233B, *SVF* I.239), for nature has not excluded such things, but made them difficult to get by burying them underground, so that it is only by laborious and painful toil that they are obtained (233C–D).

This fragment must be taken closely with F239, which shares a number of details, and also with D.S. 5.35–8.

COMMENT

1–6 Now nature gives a sample of such precious metals if it is true that at the furthest borders of the inhabited world even ordinary brooks bring down grains of gold that can be sifted by women and infirm men. For the process of rubbing, sifting, washing and smelting of alluvial ore, see F239.34–6, comm. 2–3 is repeated in Eustathius, F240b.4–5.

6–10 Evidence for this:

(a) Posidonius is cited for this happening among the Helvetii and some other Celts; F272.40ff comm. for this with moral implications.

(b) The mountains anciently called Rhipaei, later Olbian,

COMMENTARY: F240

and now Alps, when forest fires broke out spontaneously, flowed with silver. For the story, which Posidonius used in the context of the Spanish mines, F239.3–7 comm. The reference to the Rhipaean mountains (a fabulous range, ever located to the north of the known boundaries of the world of the time; Arist. *Meteor.* 350b 7ff; Kiessling, *RE, s.v.* 'Ριπαῖα Ὄρη), shows that this is indeed an ancient legend (μῦθος, F239.3), but in which Posidonius was inclined to see a factual base (F239.3, οὐ γὰρ ἀπιστεῖν). Eustathius, F240b.7, seems to imply that the identification with the Alps comes from Posidonius.

10–16 But most of it is found by deep and distressful mining as Demetrius of Phalerum says, for greed expects to bring up from the recesses of the earth Pluto himself. He wittily supports this with the Homeric riddle. All this too comes from Posidonius as the parallel passages in Strabo (F239) and D.S. 5.35–8 show. For Demetrius and the pun on Pluto, F239.11, 17 comm., and for the riddle, F239.22ff comm. βαθείαις καὶ κακοπάθοις μεταλλείαις, F240b.9; F239.19, 23; D.S. 5.36.4; 37.3; 38.1. But the moral factor of greed is stressed here, showing the context of both Demetrius and Posidonius; cf. F239.24 comm.

16–40 The ethical theme of the corrupting effect of greed for gold is continued in a series of examples given by Posidonius (17f).

(1) 16–29 The Spartans, forbidden to import gold and silver, acquired it by underhand means and so were corrupted (16–19): deposits with the Arcadians led to enmity (19–21); Lysander by introducing it was the cause of many evils (21–4); Gylippus committed suicide because of embezzling some of these funds (24–7). It was a commonly believed theme that gold and silver had been banned by Lycurgus, Xen. *Lac.* VII.6 (in general, Michell, *Sparta* 298ff). That the corruption of Sparta arose through consequent greed became a commonplace: ἁ φιλοχρᾱματία Σπάρταν ὀλεῖ, ἄλλο δέ γ' οὐδέν, Arist. F544 (Rose, 550 Gigon), D.S. 7.12.5; so in the case of Lysander, Plu. *Lys.* xvɪf, and in general, Plato, *Rep.* 548a 5ff, D.S. 7.12.8. On Spartans depositing money abroad, *IG* v.ii.159 (Buck, *Greek Dialects* 267). There is nothing elsewhere about Gylippus' suicide. This is not history as such, but moral anecdote, topped off with a gnomic generalisation (27–9).

(**2**) **29–40** The Celtic tribe, Scordistae. They will not have gold in their country (30, 38), but plunder for silver, which they accept and do many terrible things for it (39f). A note is appended: the Scordistae are the remnants of the Celts who attacked the Delphic oracle under Brennus (279 B.C.); later a leader called Bathanattus settled them on the Danube, and after him is named their route and his descendants (32–7). This is probably meant to explain the origin of why they ἀφωσιώκασι τὸν χρυσόν (38).

On the location of the Scordistae, F272.38f comm.; on the variation Σκορδίσται/Σκορδίσκοι, F277a.32; on their piratical character, D.S. 34/35.30a. Posidonius linked them with the Cimbrian invasion and its motives (F272.38), but was no doubt aware of earlier Roman expeditions against them, and particularly of the defeat of C. Porcius Cato in 114 B.C. (Livy, *Per.* 63, Malitz, *Die Historien des Poseidonios* 213).

40–5 The moral conclusion.

It is not precious metal that is the cause of such behaviour, but impiety and greed which ought to be banished, not gold; if they banished gold and silver, they would sin for bronze and iron, and if these were banned, they would fight for the bare necessities of life.

This is pure Stoicism and Posidonius. Gold is an 'indifferent'; it is lust for gold that is vice; or as Posidonius would put it, it betrays a confusion between relative and absolute natural propensities (οἰκειώσεις) in a human being (Frs. 160, 169, 170; Kidd, *Problems* 205). The general theme of the corrupting power of gold and silver and luxury became widespread: Horace, *Odes* ɪɪɪ.3.49–52; Sen. *Ep.* 94.57; *NQ* 1.17.6, v.15.3; Pliny *NH* 33.48ff, 95; Cic. *De Leg.* ɪɪ.62ff. It was

COMMENTARY: F241

clearly a major theme that runs through the whole of Posidonius' *History*, both in praiseworthy and cautionary examples, and would indeed necessarily be so, if he saw history as a descriptive sub-science to ethics.

The question remains whether the material in this fragment comes from a single source in Posidonius or from several. Jacoby, *Kommentar* 190, argued for several: the Celtic ethnology, the Iberian, the *Cimbrica*, and an unknown source for the Spartan extract. This is followed partly by Malitz, 213, 217–19. Theiler prints it as one fragment (F402 Th), from a supposititious work *On Gold and Silver*. But there is no evidence for such a work, and no need to create it. The whole fragment is not at all out of character with the *History*, which is the work of Posidonius known to Athenaeus. The whole passage hangs together through the ethical development. This may be due to Athenaeus, but it is also characteristic of Posidonius. This is historical anecdote for philosophical ethnology, and Posidonius may at one point have enlarged the theme with a diversity of examples. If this hypothesis is correct, the close relationship with F239, and in particular the enlargement of the Demetrius theme, would point to the Spanish section. But Posidonius may have repeated examples, and it could equally belong to the moral lessons of the Cimbrian invasion.

GEOGRAPHY

F241   Strabo, III.5.10

CONTENT

Remarkable trees in Spain.

CONTEXT

Follows F218.

COMMENTARY: F241

COMMENT

Posidonius gives a detailed description of a peculiar tree in Cadiz: its branches bend to the ground (1-2), it often has sword-like leaves a cubit in length but four fingers in breadth (2-3). It bears fruit (7). At the end of the passage, a further detail is reported (προσιστόρηται, 10): if a branch is broken off, it oozes milk; if a root is cut, red moisture seeps up. This has been identified as the dragon-tree (*dracaena draco*), remarkable for its resin, or dragon's blood, and still a feature of the Canary Islands. The dragon's blood actually comes from the bark, not the roots, and while the later added details of προσιστόρηται may come from Strabo, it is possible that they may derive from a distinction made by Posidonius: he had seen the tree, but only heard of the dragon's blood by report. There is another allusion to dragon's blood at Cadiz in Philostratus, *v. Apoll.* v.5, who also seems to have a reminiscence of Posidonius at v.6 (the ἀνακοπή of the Baitis, F218.11). There are other accounts of 'dragon's blood' in Pliny *NH* 33.116, Dioscurides, 5.94; see Schulten, *Iberische Landeskunde* 529f. Strabo interjects (5-7) that he himself saw a similar tree in Egypt, as far as the hanging branches went, but with dissimilar leaves and without fruit. This may have been some kind of willow (*salix Babylonica*). The comparison is not very apt, but Strabo liked to parade his knowledge of Egypt.

Posidonius also describes a tree at New Carthage (Cartagena, 3-5): it yields bark from the thorns, from which very fine woven materials are made. This is presumably the dwarf palm; the fibre from its leaf-sheaves (African hair) is used for fabric (Schulten, 529). Strabo again (8f) reports a similar low-lying fibre-producing plant in Cappadocia, which however was not a tree.

Since the extract is reported by Strabo, the source is probably *On Ocean*, but we cannot be sure, since the *History* also contained detail of natural history (F55). The fragment shows that Posidonius did not confine his visit to Spain to Cadiz; cf. T20 comm.

COMMENTARY: F242-243

F242   Athenaeus, 1.28D

The Persian King would drink only Chalybonian wine. The Persians had transplanted these vines to Damascus. Strabo, xv.3.22 is the best commentary for the context of the expensive luxurious tastes of the Persian kings: they imported their wheat from Assus in Aeolis, their wine from Syria (Strabo calls it χαλυμώνιον), and their water from the Eulaeus. The Chalybonian vines which grew also (κἄν, 2; Eustathius simply has ἐν) in Damascus, may have been the King's vineyard.

F243   Strabo, III.4.15

CONTENT

Peculiar features in Iberian fauna.

CONTEXT

At III.4.5 Strabo embarks on a short account of Iberian fauna. Before this fragment he mentions deer, wild horses, and marshes teeming with birds like swans and bustards. Theiler includes all this in Posidonius, as well as the following section 16. But Posidonius is cited only for peculiar features (ἴδιον, 2, 5). The general account most likely comes from a common stock of knowledge available to Strabo accumulated from Polybius on.

COMMENT

The organisation of this fragment is oddly disjointed. The mention of beavers in Spain (1) leads to a comparison of their castoreum with that of beavers in the Pontus (2); and it is the

COMMENTARY: F243

latter which has the medical quality peculiar to it (3). Latched on to this is the almost meaningless (in this context) generalisation, καθάπερ ἄλλοις πολλοῖς (3). It appears to be explained by the following quotation from Posidonius (ἐπεί, 4): 'For Cyprian copper *too* (καί) is alone in producing calamine, chalcanthite (copper sulphide or blue vitriol) and copper oxide' (4-5). The Posidonian connection here (ἐπεὶ καί, 4) is certainly medicinal as with castoreum, for all these by-products of Cyprian copper were used for medical therapeutic purposes (Strabo, xiv.6.5; Pliny *NH* 34.105ff, 123-7; Hipp. *Mul.* 1.104).

So far Posidonius' collection of ἴδια have little to do with Spain, but Strabo continues with another Posidonian record of peculiarity (ἴδιον, 5), which now has no medical reference, but relates to peculiar features of Spanish crows and horses. The Spanish crows are black; so all codices, but Casaubon inserted μή, followed by most editors: '⟨not⟩ black'. But Schulten, *Iberische Landeskunde* 580, pointed out that the carrion crow in Italy and Greece was ashen-coloured, with only head, wings and tail black. The Spanish crow was all black; it was remarkable to Pliny (*NH* 10.124): *cornix e Baetica primum colore mira admodum nigro*.

The peculiarity of Spanish horses is that the slightly dappled Celtiberian breed changes colour when transferred to Further Spain (7-9). Presumably he has in mind local differences between north central Spain (Celtiberia) and Asturia and Gallaecia in the north-west, and possibly also Lusitania (Pliny *NH* 8.166). ψαρός (7) seems to have meant speckled like a starling (ψάρ, Arist. *HA* 632b 19). Aristophanes, *Nubes* 1225 applied the adjective to a horse. Schulten, 582, attempted to explain the supposed colour change with reference to dun-coloured wild horses whose coat may change from a distinct dun colour in summer to a near-white in winter. Schulten's alternative was the domestic grey, which sometimes changes its youthful darker coat for an adult

COMMENTARY: F244

white. But it is not clear how this fits with ὑπόψαρος. For wild horses in Spain, *CIL* II.2660, Timotheus *CHG* II.123.5ff.

The surprising addition is made that they are like Parthian horses (9). But this probably refers not to appearance or size, because Spanish horses were thought small, Parthian, large, but to a certain smooth-stepping action. For such a comparison, see Vegetius, *Mulomedicina* 1.56.37–9; cf. Pliny *NH* 8.166; Anderson, *Ancient Greek Horsemanship* 28f and n. 32; Schulten, *Iberische Landeskunde* 582ff. So they are regarded as faster and better runners (9f).

F244 Strabo, XVI.2.17

CONTENT

A dead monster in Coele Syria.

CONTEXT

In his description of Syria (XVI.2.1ff), Strabo at XVI.2.16 reaches Coele Syria, that is the hinterland behind Tripolis to Sidon towards Damascus, or roughly, modern Lebanon. Its main feature is said to be two mountain ranges, Libanus (Jebel Liban) and Antilibanus (Jebel esh Sharqi). They enclose two plains, the Macras plain by the sea, and the Massyas plain beginning further north by Laodicea. It was in the first plain that the monster was found. See Honigmann, *RE*, *s.v.* Makras, XIV.809f.

COMMENT

The description of the δράκων is fantastic: 100 ft long, so thick that horsemen standing on either side could not see each other, jaws large enough to take a mounted man, and each flake of its scales exceeded a shield in size (4–7).

COMMENTARY: F245

What this monster was is anyone's guess. It has clearly grown in the telling. Posidonius is careful to say not that he saw it, but that it was seen (ὁραθῆναι, 4).

3 δράκων may in Greek refer either to a reptile or to a fish (e.g. the great weever in Arist. *HA* 598a 11). Since it is difficult to conceive of a reptile, even the largest of crocodiles, approaching the size of the story (but for δράκοντες in Libya, D.S. 2.51.4; and huge ones in Morocco, Str. xvii.3.4-5), the tale may have grown from a huge fish or sea animal. The ancients were full of accounts of huge sea monsters (Pliny *NH* 9.1-11). Pliny (*NH* 9.11) tells of a large whale stranded at Cadiz (cf. Arrian, *Indica* 30), and how M. Scaurus, the aedile of 58 B.C., brought to Rome the enormous skeleton of a sea monster from Jaffa, reputed to be that confronting Andromeda. Honigmann compares the story of Jonah and the whale.

6 τῆς δὲ φολίδος λεπίδα ἑκάστην may at first sight seem confusing, because strictly λεπίς was used for fishes' scales and φολίς properly referred to the horny scales of reptiles (so in Arist. *HA* and *PA*). The combination may reflect the uncertainty of the identification. But the distinction became blurred, and either could be used, for example, for flakes of metal. Whales do not have scales, but apparently some ancients thought they had. Both D.S. 17.105.5 and Arrian *Ind.* 39.5 use φολίς of a whale (but κῆτος can mean any huge sea monster).

7 θυρεός is the Greek for *scutum*, for which Polybius (6.23.2) gives the dimensions as 4ft × 2½ft.

It was fashionable to note παράδοξα or marvels (F217.24), but Posidonius' context is unknown.

F245   Strabo, XVII.3.4

CONTENT

Observation of apes on the north African coast.

845

COMMENTARY: F246

CONTEXT

XVII.3.1 begins Strabo's account of Libya, i.e. north Africa from the Atlantic to Egypt; cf. F223. This fragment is inserted in an account of the fertility of Mauretania in plants, fish and animals.

COMMENT

The nature of this encounter (2–3, T21) shows that it was not a calculated piece of research; but the recording of personal detailed and accurate observation contrasts starkly with the legendary accounts of apes in D.S. 3.35.4–6, which in turn is derived from Agatharchides, *De Mar. Eryth.* 73–5 (*GGM* 1.159f).

A personal note of Posidonius' writing is struck in mentioning his amusement at the sight (γελᾶν, 6). What stirred his mirth was apparently the resemblance to human ills and deformities: the heavy breasts of the mothers suckling their young, some males bald, others ruptured, and in general exhibiting such lesions and ailments as humans are subject to (6–8). This is much more to the point than Diodorus' τοῖς μὲν σώμασιν ἀνθρώποις δυσειδέσι παρεμφερεῖς εἰσι, ταῖς δὲ φωναῖς μυγμοὺς ἀνθρωπίνους προΐενται (3.35.5, of the dog-faced baboon).

F246 Strabo, III.5.5

CONTENTS

The founding of Gadeira, and the location and explanation of the Pillars of Heracles.

CONTEXT

At III.5.3 Strabo turns to the Pillars of Heracles and to Gadeira. Posidonius is brought in at III.5.5 in connection with

846

COMMENTARY: F246

stories on the founding of Gadeira and the identification of the Pillars. After the fragment there is a long passage of criticism from Strabo until the end of III.5.6, and Posidonius does not reappear until III.5.7 on the wells at Gadeira (F217).

COMMENT

A. The story of the local inhabitants of Gadeira (1-20)

1-4 τοιαῦτα λέγοντες μέμνηνται (1); to whom? Probably to Posidonius. Their tale is based on the story of an oracle given to the Tyrians, telling them to send a colony to the Pillars of Heracles. The story continues in indirect speech until line 20.

The Tyrians send a reconnaissance (κατασκοπῆς χάριν, 4).

(i) 4-10 When they reached the straits by Calpe, believing that the capes which formed the straits were the end of the inhabited world and so of Heracles' expedition, i.e. the στῆλαι of the oracle, they put to shore at a place inside (east) of the narrows, where the city of the Saxitani now is (Sex, between Malaca and Abdera, Str. III.4.2; its spelling varied, see *app. crit.*; it achieved fame through giving its name to a species of fish). But their sacrifices were unfavourable, so they returned home. For στῆλαι taken to be natural features marking the limits of the world with mythical reference, compare the στῆλαι Διονύσου of mountains in India in Dion. *Perieg.* 623, 1164; cf. Str. III.5.6.

(ii) 10-15 Later a second expedition went outside (i.e. through) the straits about 1500 stades to an island sacred to Heracles, situated near the city of Onoba in Spain (Huelva on the Odiel). Thinking the Στῆλαι were here, they sacrificed, but again unsuccessfully, so returned home. The grounds of identification of the Στῆλαι are not clear in this case; they may have been objects, or even pillars, believed sacred to Heracles; or they may have thought that they had reached the western limits of the world. The distance given between the Straits and Onoba is a grave overestimation, but the

COMMENTARY: F246

mistake is probably original rather than due to transmission.

(iii) **15-17** On a third expedition they founded Gadeira with a temple in the eastern part of the island and the city in the western. At this point the στῆλαι seem to have been forgotten, unless the implication is that the στῆλαι were created in the pillars of the temple (33-8). It was originally, of course, a temple of Melkart.

17-20 The three expeditions gave rise to three interpretations of the Pillars:

(a) some think they are the capes at the Straits (i);
(b) others that they are at Gadeira (iii);
(c) others that they are still further out beyond Gadeira (ii).

Here the story of the Gadeiritans and the indirect speech ends.

B. Other opinions are added, now in direct speech, dissociating them from the Gadeiretan story (20-38)

(I) 20-31 In the neighbourhood of the Straits:

(1) The rocks facing each other across the Straits, Calpe (Rock of Gibraltar) and Abilyx (Ximiera, Dschebel Musa); Eratosthenes (FIII.B.58) is mentioned here (20-2);

(2) The islets near each mountain, one of which is called Hera's island. Artemidorus is referred to (22-6). This was also the view of Euctemon of Athens (Avienus, *Or. Mar.* 350ff). These islands, which are difficult to identify (Schulten, *Iberische Landeskunde* 407), are mentioned by Strabo at III.5.3.

(3) Others (Lasserre suggested Ephorus) translate the Planctae and the Symplegades there, thinking that they are the στῆλαι which Pindar called 'gates of Gadeira' (F256, Snell), as the furthest point reached by Heracles (26-9).

This is an argument from the literary tradition. It is a combination of the island and rock theories. There was a tendency to put the Symplegades in the east, and the

848

COMMENTARY: F246

Planctae in the western Mediterranean (A.R., IV; Vian, vol. III (Budé), p. 41ff), perhaps to balance, as there were western and eastern στῆλαι or limits (above on 4-10; Campbell, *Studies in the Third Book of Apollonius Rhodius* 21).

It is rightly added (29-31) that (I) was the common Greek tradition, that the στῆλαι were natural features at the Straits themselves. Dicaearchus (F112 Wehrli), Eratosthenes (FIII.B.58, Berger, *Eratosthenes* 308f) and Polybius (34.9.4) are named, but the tradition goes much further back, e.g. Hdt. IV.8; II.33. Pindar (*P* I.19) calls Aetna κίων οὐρανία, and so does Herodotus refer to the Atlas mountain (IV.184); cf. Aeschylus, *PV* 351.

(II) 31-8 In Gadeira.

(1) 31-3 The Spaniards and Libyans say that the Pillars are in Gadeira, because the features of the Straits are not at all like στῆλαι.

(2) 33-8 Some (οἱ δέ) say that they are the eight-cubit bronze pillars in the temple of Heracles (or Melkart) at Gadeira on which are inscribed the expenses of the temple's construction. The explanation is that travellers who came to these on completion of their journey and sacrificed there to Heracles, had it noised abroad that that was the limit of land and sea.

(2) is an elaboration of (1) and furnished with a theoretical explanation or αἰτία.

C. Posidonius (38-40)

Posidonius thought II(2) was the most plausible (πιθανώτατον), and that the oracle and the many expeditions (*A*) were a Phoenician lie (ψεῦσμα Φοινικικόν).

Provenance

How much of this is Posidonius? Probably all of it for three reasons: (i) *A* is a detailed story told by the local inhabitants to someone (1f); the most likely person is Posidonius when he

COMMENTARY: F246

was at Cadiz. It is summarised by a short aetiology. (ii) B is a classified doxography of the kind known to be common in Posidonius (T102). (iii) The section finishes with the opinion of Posidonius. One may add that there follows to the end of III.5.6 a long criticism from Strabo directed against Posidonius' view. Strabo held a version of the common Greek view that the Pillars were at the Straits. He sees the term arising from attempts to mark the limits of the world, to the west in the expeditions of Heracles, to the east in those of Dionysus. They would be marked by landmarks (στῆλαι, he gives examples), the name of which when destroyed was transferred to the place (more examples). Hence the Straits are the Pillars. He is scornful of Gades as a terminal mark for the world, since it lies in the middle of a gulf; and still more scathing on the application to the pillars in the Heracleium. The originals would have been set up by commanders not merchants, and would have recorded a commemoration, not an expense account.

Posidonius

Posidonius' version is curious and interesting. He rejects the Greek view, taking the opportunity to correct, as usual, Dicaearchus Eratosthenes and Polybius, and dismisses the story of the local inhabitants as Phoenician fabrication. As to the latter, he may have been disillusioned by local information on wells and tides (F217.26–8). As a Syrian Greek, was he aware of the cult significance of the two pillars in the temple of Melkart at Tyre, reproduced by Phoenicians at Malta (*CISem* 1.122; *IG* XIV.600) and at Tigisis (Procopius, *Vand.*2.10), and so perhaps at Cadiz? And in his distrust of δεισιδαιμονία (F257), he may have set about exploding the Phoenician myth of the oracle and the Greek stories of Heracles. His explanation is practical, based on observation (he had visited the Heracleium, F218.17), and not derived from legend. It also confuses, however, the factualisation of

850

COMMENTARY: F247

legend (the Pillars of Heracles were taken to be the Straits in some form or other), with a possible theoretical explanation pointing to where the Pillars ought to be. The interesting fact that the topic had become a matter of learned discussion may reflect the conceptual complexity underlying the phrase: the marking of the limits of the world, the legend of Heracles, the cult pillars of Melkart, the Near-eastern or Egyptian tradition of the sky being held up by pillars at the edge of the world (Kahn, *Anaximander and the Origins of Greek Cosmology* 139; Campbell, *Studies in the Third Book of Apollonius Rhodius* 21; Homer, *Od.* 1.53f), the identification of natural features like mountains with 'pillars'. In general, see Schulten, *Iberische Landeskunde* 400ff.

F247 Strabo, III.4.3

CONTENT

Odysseia in Baetica and its temple.

CONTEXT

From III.4.1 Strabo proceeds up the Mediterranean coast of Spain from Calpe. Abdera (Adra) comes after Malaca, Maenaca and Sex.

COMMENT

Abdera was indeed an old Phoenician colony (Tovar, *Iberische Landeskunde* 83). Strabo himself (III.2.13) accepted that Odysseia, in the hills behind Abdera with its temple to Athene, was evidence that Odysseus' wanderings had reached Spain (cf. 1.2.11; III.4.4). Was this Posidonius' interest in the place (cf. F257.12ff), or was he in the region of Sex to check on the foundation story of Gadeira (F246)? Or

COMMENTARY: F248

was he en route to New Carthage and inspecting mining hinterland (Frs. 241, 239)? In fact Strabo takes his detail of the temple of Athene not from Posidonius, but from Asclepiades of Myrleia (in Bithynia) (*FGrH* 697, F7), a rough contemporary of Posidonius, who taught in Spain. This account could not have come through Posidonius, who saw the temple himself and had no need to refer to Asclepiades. Artemidorus was also used by Strabo here.

F248   Strabo, IV.1.14

CONTENT

The length of the 'isthmus' of Gaul.

CONTEXT

F273 precedes. The fragment is followed by a description of the river system of Gaul, and the advantages thus provided for trade.

COMMENT

Posidonius is quoted for the distance of the neck (called an isthmus) of Gaul between the Atlantic north of the Pyrenees and Narbo (Narbonne), in the middle of which Tolosa (Toulouse) stands. It is given as less than 3000 stades, a figure again mentioned by Strabo at II.5.28. It is an overestimate; it is *c.* 380 km.

Schmidt, *Kosmologische Aspekte im Geschichtswerk des Poseidonios* 80ff (and Theiler F28b Th) has argued that Strabo's whole account of the river system of Gaul (IV.1.2; IV.1.14), with the comment that the common advantages of the easy interchange of the necessities of life might lead one to find evidence for the work of providence in the regions being laid

COMMENTARY: F249

out as if with some kind of rationality, rather than at random, is Posidonius. But there is no sure or distinctive evidence to counter the natural assumption that it comes from Strabo himself. On this, compare Nash (*Britannia* 7 (1976), 117) against Tierney ('The Celtic Ethnography of Posidonius', 209). On the other hand, Posidonius is specifically cited for the detail of the length of the 'isthmus', a matter in which we know he had geographical interest (F206); as again he is specifically named in IV.1.13 on the treasure of the Tectosages (F273).

F249 Strabo, VI.2.1

CONTENT

The shape, orientation, size and position of Sicily.

CONTEXT

This is the opening of Strabo's account of Sicily.

COMMENT

A. *Shape and orientation (1–9)*

The shape is defined as usual as triangular by the three capes, which gave the island its ancient name of Trinacria: Pelorias (Cape Peloro at the Straits of Messina), Pachynus (Cape Passero), Lilybaeum (Cape Boco).

It is usually assumed that what follows (3–7 and 18–20) shows a disorientation of the axis of Sicily of > 90° anticlockwise, with Pachynus east of Pelorias instead of south, and Lilybaeum south of Pelorias instead of west. The Greek does not say this, and the matter is not so simple or clear-cut. Pelorias is defined by the Straits; Pachynus is not orientated relatively to Pelorias, but is said to project (ἐκκειμένη, 4; cf.

COMMENTARY: F249

Str. v.4.8 of the promontory of Herculaneum) to the east, washed by the Sicilian (Ionian) Sea facing towards the Peloponnese and the sea passage to Crete, which is true; and Lilybaeum is described as adjacent (προσεχής, 6) to Libya, facing both it and the winter setting (of the sun, i.e. SW, or more precisely WSW), which again is roughly true. Pliny *NH* 3.87 has much the same orientation, with Pelorias facing Italy, Pachynus Greece, and Lilybaeum Africa. These do not look like exact orientations, but general indications perhaps framed from a navigational point of view. Polybius (1.42) defines Lilybaeum exactly as here (winter setting and turned towards Libya), but Pachynus is towards the south (πρὸς μεσημβρίαν). Nevertheless, there is clearly some disorientation with Lilybaeum further south and Pachynus further east than they should be. See 18–25 below.

7–9 Two sides of the triangle are said to be concave, Lilybaeum to Pachynus (Gulf of Gela?), and Pachynus to Pelorias (Gulfs of Noto and Catania); Lilybaeum to Pelorias is described as convex, presumably thinking of the headlands from Marsala to Palermo, but ignoring the Gulf of Termini.

B. Distances (9–18)

Strabo gives three sets of distances round the coasts, which reveals the difficulty of such measurements.

(i) 9–16 Posidonius' figures are given first: the longest side, Lilybaeum to Pelorias, 1720 stades; Pelorias to Pachynus, the shortest, 1130. Since we are also given Posidonius' figure for the distance round by sea as 4400 stades, it follows that Lilybaeum to Pachynus is 1550 stades.

Strabo presents the Lilybaeum to Pelorias measurement most oddly as 1700 to which Posidonius added 20 (10f). It is a coincidence that in D.S. 5.2.2 the figures for Sicily (probably from Timaeus) are given respectively for the three coasts as 1700, 1140 and 1500 which total 4340 stades; but the total circumference is given as 4360, or 20 stades more. But

COMMENTARY: F249

Posidonius could not be correcting such a discrepancy because all his figures are different. Rather, 1700 must have been a commonly agreed figure in Strabo's Greek authorities, which Posidonius increased.

(ii) **16–18** The 'Chorography' gives longer distances and in Roman miles; details are supplied in the lacuna. Strabo refers to the Chorographer again at v.2.7, vi.1.11, vi.2.11, vi.3.10. Detlefesen, *Ursprung ... der Erdkarte Agrippas*, argued that this was the map of Agrippa (Thomson, *History of Ancient Geography* 332–4, Bunbury, *A History of Ancient Geography* ii.177), but this is far from certain (Dubois, *Géographie de Strabon* 330; Nissen, *Italische Landeskunde* 1.17), although Strabo's reference may derive from it.

(iii) In the lacuna, Strabo adds that others, like Ephorus, put it more simply: a periplous of five days and five nights. So ships had speeded up since Thucydides' time (vi.1.2) when it took not far short of eight days navigation for a merchantman.

C. Latitudinal positions (*18–25*)

Posidonius' marking off the island by klimata, puts Pelorias towards the north, Lilybaeum towards the south and Pachynus towards the east.

This is not helpful without further elaboration and context. Indeed the sentence as it stands, Ποσειδώνιός τε ... ἀφορίζων ... καὶ ... τίθησιν shows incomplete patching. It can easily be emended, but hints of a hasty additional note. Honigmann, *Die sieben Klimata* 29f is too confident of a solution, and Schmidt, *Kosmologische Aspekte* 66f builds an insupportable theory in which the supposed NS orientation of the Sicilian coastline is a continuation of the Italian, and so Sicily is regarded as a part of Italy and in the same klima with ethnological implications. There is no evidence for this.

κλίμα could mean a parallel of latitude, but more usually in Posidonius a band of latitude (F205.16, F210.7, 15, F49.320).

COMMENTARY: F249

Was Posidonius by this klima application orientating Sicily itself north and south by klima parallels, or was he attempting a more refined method of geographical location of a country than that, for example, of Polybius 3.36–8; 5.21 (criticised by Strabo, II.4.7), by locating Sicily in a particular klima or band of latitude with Pelorias towards the north of the band and Lilybaeum towards the south, the principal μέν ... δέ opposition? One cannot locate a place to the east *by* a klima, although it could be located towards the east *in* a klima. Strabo seems confused between the two, and rouses little confidence that he knows what Posidonius was about, which is our chief limitation. His criticism assumes klimata as parallelograms (21), i.e. bands, in which a slanting (διὰ τὴν λόξωσιν 24f), scalene triangle (22) such as Sicily, does not fit (ἀναρμόστως ἔχειν) since none of the sides of the triangle lies along the parallels of the parallelogram (23ff).

At least it is clear that Strabo did not think that Posidonius meant that Pachynus lay due east of Pelorias, and Lilybaeum due south (i.e. a 90° axial shift from reality), because then at least two sides of the triangle would have coincided with the parallelogram. If we need another proof to cast doubts on the 90° shift, it comes from Posidonius' own distance figures for the triangle. If Pachynus were due east and Lilybaeum due south of Pelorias, the distance from Lilybaeum to Pachynus would of necessity have been longer than that between Lilybaeum and Pelorias. If then πρὸς ἕω (20) does not mean due east, neither need πρὸς νότον (19) mean due south. We are back at the slighter distortion of 3–7 above, to which Posidonius probably subscribed (i.e. Lilybaeum facing the winter setting).

Sicily and particularly the Straits of Messina were of special historical interest in geographical orientation. Not only was the Rhodian/Pillars of Heracles axial parallel of latitude of Eratosthenes commonly supposed to pass through the Straits of Messina (falsely, F204; it passes through Algeria and Tunisia; Messina is 38.13° not 36°), but also a meridian

COMMENTARY: F250

was wrongly assumed to run from Rome, through the Straits to Carthage (attacked by Strabo himself at II.1.40); in fact Rome is 12.30°, Messina 15.33°, and Carthage 10.16°. Thus the Straits had become one of the axial key points in measurements and orientation (Str. II.4.2–3), and the distortions of klima and meridian may have affected the orientation of the whole island. Posidonius seems to have subscribed at least to the popular notion that Pachynus was further east and Lilybaeum further south than they actually were.

Such disorientation of familiar territory may seem strange, but compare the common complete disorientation of India, in this case corrected by Posidonius (F212). The Greeks perhaps tended to persist in theoretical calculation rather than to listen to their practical mariners. Corrections were often ignored (F212).

For Strabo on mapping: II.5.10; and on difficulty of longitudes: I.1.12.

F250   Strabo, VI.2.7

CONTENT

Syracuse, Eryx and Enna as Sicilian strongholds.

CONTEXT

After the initial description of Sicily (VI.2.1, F249), Strabo deals with the Pelorias to Pachynus side from Messene to Syracuse (VI.2.2–4; F234). VI.2.5 briefly accounts for the other two more sparsely inhabited coasts of the triangle. VI.2.6 deals with Enna in the interior, and Eryx with its temple of Aphrodite and some other settlements. VI.2.7 stresses the fertility of Sicily as the ταμεῖον of Rome. Our fragment is immediately followed by a reference to the

COMMENTARY: F250

devastation of Leontinine territory and their misfortunes. VI.2.8 passes to Aetna and the volcano. VI.2.9 is on water phenomena, while VI.23.10–11 turns to natural phenomena connected with the Lipari islands and the sea, in which Polybius is cited, and also Posidonius (F227). It is unsafe to assign more of this to Posidonius than the specifically named references (Frs. 249, 234, 250, 227), because it is demonstrable that Posidonius was not the only authority on which Strabo drew in this section; but he undoubtedly was an authority.

COMMENT

This is a very strange sentence in its context. Strabo is dealing at this point with the extraordinary fertility of Sicily, and suddenly throws in the remark of Posidonius that Syracuse and Eryx are two strongholds as it were (οἶον ἀκροπόλεις, 1) on the sea, and Enna is another, lying midway between them above the plains all round it. But Strabo has already dealt with Syracuse (VI.2.4), Enna and Eryx (VI.2.6, giving the lofty position). Moreover, the following sentence refers to the devastation of Leontini and its territory which is equally irrelevant, and was recommended by Siebenkees, Meineke and others for transfer after the mention of the Leontinines in VI.2.6.

The most reasonable explanation of Posidonius' context in enumerating Enna, Syracuse and Eryx as three strongholds in Sicily, derives from the two major slave revolts there in the second half of the second century, of which there are mutilated excerpts from D.S. 34–6 (see F59; Jacoby F108 (Anhang)). Enna was the centre of the first revolt (F59); and in D.S. 34/35.2.24b (*Const. Exc.* 3, pp. 206–7; F108, (h)14 Jac.), Eunus (the slave leader, Str. VI.2.6) encouraged the conspiring slaves by telling them: ὑπὸ γὰρ τῆς πεπρωμένης αὐτοῖς κεκυρῶσθαι τὴν πατρίδα τὴν Ἕνναν, οὖσαν ἀκρόπολιν ὅλης τῆς νήσου. Syracuse and the extreme west of Sicily were

COMMENTARY: F251

also focal points in the second Slave War (D.S. 36.3, 5). It is possible that the mention of the devastation of Leontinine territory also relates to the defeat of Salvius in the second revolt. Strabo's inclusion here looks like misplaced notes, which should have been introduced (and expanded) in the previous section (VI.2.6).

F251   Strabo, XVI.2.4

CONTENT

The Tetrapolis and fourfold division of satrapies in Seleucis.

CONTEXT

XVI.2 begins Strabo's account of Syria. §2 gives the major divisions: Commagene, Seleucis, Coele Syria, Phoenicia and Judaea. Starting from the north, Strabo deals with Commagene in §3, and passes to Seleucis in §4.

COMMENT

1–3   Seleucis, the best of the regions of Syria (1), is defined by its nickname of Four-Cities, and yet (ἐπεὶ, 3) it possesses a large number of them.

The Four (outstanding or distinguished, ἐξεχούσας, 3) Cities are named in the lacuna: Antiochea (Antioch on the Orontes, the capital of Seleucid Syria, XVI.2.5), its seaport (XVI.2.7), Seleucea in Pieria (founded originally by Seleucus I to be his capital), Laodicea (Latakia, a little further down the coast, XVI.2.9), and Apamea inland on the Orontes again (XVI.2.10), the birthplace of Posidonius (T48).

We are told that the four were all founded by Seleucus I, Nicator, Antiochea named after his father, Apamea after his wife and Laodicea from his mother. They were called sister

COMMENTARY: F251

cities (ἐλέγοντο ἀλλήλων ἀδελφαί) because of their concord (διὰ τὴν ὁμόνοιαν). In fact the legend ἀδελφῶν δήμων appears briefly on their coinage from 149-7 B.C., and this may have signalled an attempt at some sort of federal government during the gradual decline of Seleucid power after the death of Antiochus IV Epiphanes, perhaps suppressed by Demetrius II (Head, *Historia Numorum* 778; Will, *Histoire politique du monde hellénistique* II.318; Jones, *Cities of the Eastern Roman Provinces* 252f). The ὁμόνοια was frequently broken in the turbulent history of that area, but at least refers to the Seleucid period earlier than the 1st c. B.C.

3-6 There is now a specific reference to Posidonius: appropriately to the Tetrapolis, Seleucis was divided into four satrapies, as Posidonius says, the same number as Coele Syria, but Mesopotamia into one.

The close linking of the four satrapies to the Tetrapolis gives some grounds for thinking that the earlier information on the Four Cities may also have come from Posidonius. There is an obvious illogicality at the end of the sentence, since Mesopotamia could not be divided into a single satrapy. Perhaps a verb has disappeared from the end of the sentence, such as ⟨συνεστάλη⟩ (Honigmann, *RE* IV.1620, *s.v.* Syria); but Strabo may simply be guilty of careless writing. In addition it has been objected that in Posidonius' and Strabo's time Mesopotamia was not part of Syria (Str. XVI.1.21-2.2) and that therefore Commagene and/or Parapotamia was meant (Bake, Groskurd). But there is no warrant for this. The reference is clearly to an earlier period when Mesopotamia was part of the Seleucid Kingdom, perhaps when, through the attacks of Parthia, Mesopotamia had shrunk to a single satrapy (Honigmann, *RE* IV.1620). According to D.S. 33.28, Dionysius the Mede was satrap of Mesopotamia in the troubled reigns of Demetrius II and Antiochus VII Sidetes, about the time of the intrigues of the Apamean general Diodotus Tryphon and his attacks on Sarpedon, the satrap of Coele Syria. Posidonius was no doubt interested in this period

COMMENTARY: F252

(F226). It was certainly dealt with in his *History*, possibly in Bk XVI (Frs. 63, 64), but there is another reference in Bk XIV (F61).

It has usually been assumed from the phrase οἰκείως τῇ Τετραπόλει that the four satrapies under Seleucid rule mentioned by Posidonius were centred on the Four Cities. This has been challenged by Jones (*Cities of the Eastern Roman Provinces* 241 and 450 n. 21) on the grounds that they were too close together in only one part of Seleucis. He argues that the four satrapies were Antioch, Apamea (*OGI* 262), and then in the eastern part of Seleucis, Cyrrhestice (Str. XVI.2.8; Plu. *Demetrius* 48) and Chalcidice (or Chalcidene, from Pliny, *NH* 5.81). If this is so, οἰκείως τῇ Τετραπόλει may be faulty patching by Strabo, falsely assuming that Posidonius' four satrapies corresponded exactly to the Cities. But the Greek is itself unclear and ambiguous; οἰκείως may merely refer to the corresponsion of the four-fold division. But the relationship between the Four Cities and the four satrapies remains unclear throughout the different periods of Seleucid rule.

HISTORY

F252   Eunapius, *Excerpta de Sententiis* 36; p. 84 Boissevain

CONTENT

Posidonius said that after Alexander died the Macedonian army was like the Cyclops when blinded.

CONTEXT

The *Excerpta de Sententiis* was part of the historical anthologies

COMMENTARY: F252

compiled for Constantine VII Porphyrogenitus in the 10th c. A.D. Eunapius, the Greek sophist from Sardes, probably about the beginning of the 5th c., wrote a universal history in fourteen books of the years 270–404 A.D.

COMMENT

ἀπελθόντος Ἀλεξάνδρου: clearly in the sense of to die; cf. Eunapius, *Lives of the Philosophers and Sophists* 22.10 Boissonade, 382 Wright: Σωκράτους ἀπελθόντος βιαίως, οὐδὲν ἔτι λαμπρὸν Ἀθηναίοις ἐπράχθη.

At first sight this seems like another instance of Posidonius' vivid rhetorical turn of phrase, which was well known (T103, F239). Unfortunately Plutarch (*Galba* 1.4) assigns the *mot* to Demades, the Athenian politician and orator of the second half of the 4th c. B.C., Δημάδης μὲν γὰρ Ἀλεξάνδρου τελευτήσαντος εἴκαζε τὴν Μακεδόνων στρατιὰν ἐκτετυφλωμένῳ τῷ Κύκλωπι, πολλὰς κινουμένην ὁρῶν κινήσεις ἀτάκτους καὶ παραφόρους.

There is no reason to doubt that Plutarch was right. But obviously it was a famous quip and known to Posidonius also. Therefore Eunapius or his source found the saying in Posidonius, but lost the original ascription.

Plutarch's context is the relationship between commander and troops, or governors and governed, and his purpose is to bemoan the state of affairs in the Roman Empire after the death of Nero. He also cites Aemilius Paullus (cf. Plu. *Aemilius* XIII.4) and Plato (*Rep.* 376c). But all this is very much in Plutarch's own style, and is highly unlikely to derive from Posidonius. Nevertheless, the theme or topic may well have been common. Cicero (*De Off.* II.16) says that Panaetius recounted at great length what was self-evident: *neminem neque ducem bello nec principem domi magnas res et salutares sine hominum studiis gerere potuisse*. Panaetius cited Themistocles, Pericles, Cyrus, Agesilaus and Alexander, *quos negat sine adiumentis hominum tantas res efficere potuisse*. It is possible, but no more

COMMENTARY: F253

than that, that Posidonius' reference to Demades' *mot* occurred in the same sort of moralising historical context as in Panaetius and Plutarch. If so, it may be in tune with Posidonius' more aristocratic attitude. Jacoby (F39, *Kommentar* 189) suggested the context of the death of Marius. But we simply do not know. We also know very little about Eunapius' sources, but the omission of the reference to Demades suggests that he knew Posidonius' *History* through some intermediary source.

F253   Athenaeus, v.211D-215B

CONTENT

The account of the brief tyranny of the philosopher Athenion at Athens in the anarchic year 88 B.C. during the Mithridatic War.

CONTEXT

Masurius is speaking. Having broached the theme of kings who have been φιλόδειπνοι (210cff), referring to Posidonius for Antiochus Sidetes (210C-D; F61.b), Antiochus Grypus (210E, F72.b) and for luxury in general in Syrian cities (210E-F, F62.b), he passes to the generosity of Alexander Balas of Syria, and to his discomfiture of the Epicurean Diogenes at a dinner party (211A-D). This leads to the case of the Peripatetic philosopher Athenion (211D-215B, F253), seizing control of Athens. The speaker's intention in doing so, is explicitly to scrutinise and satirise the public, social and political pretensions of philosophers so much at variance with their doctrines (F253.7-10, 211E). Indeed the extended narrative on Athenion is followed by the Epicurean Lysias who became tyrant of Tarsus (215B-C; *FGrH* 166 F1), topped by a long and sarcastic tirade against Plato's account of

COMMENTARY: F253

Socrates (215D–220A), with an appendix on the minor Socratics (220A–221A). The context is significant (cf. Malitz, *Die Historien des Poseidonios* 341), because it shows that Athenaeus selected this particular confined extract from Posidonius' *History* not for its historical value, nor yet for its historical content, but solely for its satirical attack on a philosopher's pretence to power, thus divorcing it from its original context, which probably throws the passage out of balance on its own.

COMMENT

Discussions of this notorious and important fragment include: Niese, *RhM* 42 (1887), 574–81; Ferguson, *Klio* 4 (1904), 14ff., *Hellenistic Athens* 440ff; Wilamowitz, *S–B. Akad. Berlin*, 1923, 39–50; Jacoby, 184–8; Day, *Economic History of Athens* 113ff; Reinhardt, *RE* 636–8; Laffranque, *Poseidonios* 42–4; Candiloro, *Studi Classici e orientali* 14 (1965), 145–57; Touloumakos, *Philologus* 110 (1966), 138–42; Deininger, *Der politische Widerstand gegen Rom in Griechenland* 248ff; Desideri, *Athenaeum* 51 (1973), 249–55; Badian, 'Rome, Athens and Mithridates', in *Assimilation et résistance, VI FIEC Congress*, 501–21; Habicht, *Chiron* 6 (1976), 127ff; Tracy, *Harv. St. Class. Phil.* 83 (1979), 213–35; Malitz, 340–56; Theiler, II.125–8; Sherwin-White, *Roman Foreign Policy in the East* 135ff.

Introduction (1–12) See Context

1–5 οὐχ ὅμοιος, i.e. Athenion was neither προσηνής nor φιλόλογος. But Athenaeus would have no further information on Athenion than he found in this passage of Posidonius. So the imputation of Athenion being head of Schools in Athens, Messene and Larissa clearly embroiders on σοφιστεύσας κτλ (21f), and probably means no more than a one-man philosophical school. But he was a professional teacher of philosophy.

COMMENTARY: F253

5–7 Makes clear that we are to be given an extensive detailed literary quotation. The language of the fragment bears this out.

11 For ἀλλά ... ⟨γάρ⟩ (Meineke), see Denniston, *GP*² 98.

8 The gown and beard had come to symbolise the professional philosopher, Epict. III.1.24., but the diminutive τριβώνιον is sarcastic. The orientation and tone of attack against philosophers turned politician in this very historical context is interestingly repeated in Appian, *Mithr.* 28 in a digression related to Aristion. It sets the tone for the Posidonian fragment; cf. Context.

9–12 Malitz, 346 n. 153 suspects that the quotation from Agathon may come from Posidonius, but it fits better as the completion of Athenaeus' introduction than as the opening of the Posidonian extract.

Posidonius' preliminary sketch of Athenion's early life (*12–23*)

Athenion, an assiduous attender at the school of the Peripatetic Erymneus, bought an Egyptian slave girl with whom he had sex (ἐπεπλέκετο, 14). Her child, whether by Athenion or another (15f), also named Athenion, was brought up in the master's house (the implication is, as a slave, τῷ δεσπότῃ παρετρέφετο, 16). The boy (our Athenion) was taught to read, would help his mother prop the old man up when he went out (ἐχειραγώγει, 18), became his heir on his death, and was slipped illegally into the citizen roll (παρέγγραφος, 19) to become an Athenian citizen. He married a shapely wench (παιδισκάριον εὔμορφον, 19f) with whose help (μετὰ τούτου) he set off on the hunt (θηρεύων, 21) for young pupils in the life of a professional teacher (σοφιστεύειν, 20). Having made his pile as a sophist in Messene and Larissa in Thessaly he returned to Athens.

This is scandalous stuff, deliberately so both in language and innuendo. Posidonius manages to imply that Athenion was originally a slave boy, of doubtful parentage, who wormed his way into an inheritance and an illegal citizenship; that he did not hesitate to use his wife's charms to set himself up as a sophist, which happened not in Athens itself, but in the safer

COMMENTARY: F253

and no doubt lucrative if less literary centres of Messene and Thessaly. It is the deliberately manufactured picture of a young man on the make.

This is hardly historical objectivity, but clearly is not meant to be. It is the style of Attic oratorical invective against an opponent (Wilamowitz, 'Athenion und Aristion' 47; Reinhardt, *RE* 637).

Posidonius could not possibly have known all the facts here, and he is doing more than reporting rumour; he is manipulating rumour for his own case, which superficially is to heighten the contrast of Athenion's beginnings with his political pretensions, but more fundamentally to use this anarchic interlude in Athens as a historical demonstration of the dangers of such a character in command of a city.

Erymneus (12) is mentioned only here, but Moraux (*Der Aristotelismus bei den Griechen* 1.28 n. 68) makes a case that he was head of the Peripatetic School at Athens from the beginning of the last quarter of the 2nd c. B.C., after Diodorus of Tyre and before Andronicus. Posidonius probably knew him.

Athenion's embassy to Mithridates (23–32)

Athenion was elected ambassador by the Athenians, when affairs were turning to Mithridates. He insinuated himself into the King's good graces, became one of The Friends and gained the highest promotion. So he began to buoy up the hopes of the Athenians through letters, leading them to believe that as he had the greatest influence with the Cappadocian, not only would they be freed from their pressing debts and live in concord, but recover the democracy, and obtain huge gifts both individually and nationally. The Athenians started to brag about this, convinced that the Roman supremacy was broken.

On the embassy: Malitz, *Die Historien des Poseidonios* 347; Day, *Economic History of Athens* 113; Deininger, *Der Politische Widerstand gegen Rom* 249f; Badian, 'Rome, Athens and Mithridates' 508; Ferguson *HA* 440f, *Klio* 4 (1904) 13 n. 4, 14.

Jacoby suspected curtailment of Posidonius' account where an account of the political situation at Athens may have been cut before καὶ χειροτονηθείς ... (23), and Tarn (*Hellenistic Civilisation* 286) and others have blamed Posidonius for omitting such information altogether. Neither case seems likely. The sudden move to Athenion's embassy is a stylistic device underlining the contrast to his shady beginnings. On the other hand, Athenaeus' fragment is an extract, and there is every reason to suppose that Posidonius discussed the general situation at Athens before it began (so alternatively Jacoby *ad loc.*). Athenion did not jump into the embassy without a background of course, but there is no record of previous political office (cf. Tracy, 215ff), nor was that likely in the more recent years given his political views. But he was rich (22), well-connected to men of substance and influence (line 110 comm., and Badian, 511 ff), and clearly well-known for his political views. Furthermore the extremely volatile situation was ideal for an opportunist. All of this fits Posidonius' account.

The political circumstances at the time in Athens and the date of the embassy are both subjects of much discussion and controversy. It has often been argued that since the end of the 2nd c. B.C. the oligarchic character of the Athenian constitution strengthened considerably, finding expression in a series of crises between 106/5–89/8 (e.g. Deininger 247, Day 110ff). This used to be interpreted in terms of a continued conflict between an oligarchic pro-Roman party and a democratic party in Athens (Ferguson, *Klio* 4 (1904), 1ff; *HA* 418ff). This influential view was incisively attacked by Badian (501ff), who saw the issue as a struggle for power and status by individuals within a confined group, a view strengthened by Tracy (213ff) in his examination of *IG* II² 2336. Most likely the situation was highly complex and blurred at the edges, combining personal ambition, political groupings, and appeals to political slogans (cf. Brunt, 'Local Ruling Classes in the Roman Empire', *Assimilation et résistance VI Congress FIEC*, 172f). As far as 88 B.C. goes, the crucial factor is that Medeios of Piraeus had secured election as eponymous

COMMENTARY: F253

Archon for three years in succession (91/0–89/8), to be followed by a year (88/7) of ἀναρχία in the exact sense of the omission of an eponymous Archon in the archon list (IG II^2 1713, IG II^2 1714; Badian, 510ff; Habicht, *Chiron* 6 (1976) 127ff). It is true that the Archon was no longer an officer of chief executive power in the state (cf. line 105), although the office was sought after for honour and status (Badian, 511). But the unprecedented election to three successive Archonships argues a dangerous and extraordinary concentration of power, whether of a group or as an incipient dictatorship. In fact there was enough difference of opinion and dissatisfaction in Athens itself to appeal to the Roman senate to sort things out (95–7). Unfortunately the senate itself had too much on its hands with the Social War and political unrest to turn to Athens, and put off its investigation. It was against this highly unusual and volatile situation further sharpened by the Mithridatic war and the upset of balance of power in the east that Athenion emerged.

The exact date of Athenion's appointment cannot be determined. On the problems of chronology for 89/88: Badian, 506ff; Sherwin-White, *JRS* 1977, 74 n. 86, *Roman Foreign Policy in the East* 121ff; the issue is complicated by controversial numismatic evidence (Thompson, *The New Style Silver Coinage of Athens* 364ff; Lewis *NC* 1962, 275ff; Badian, 517ff; Habicht, *Chiron* 6 (1976), 130 n. 17). But since Athenion was with Mithridates in his Asian campaign, it must have been late 89 or possibly early 88 (Badian, 508). Posidonius says that Athenion was elected (χειροτονηθείς) by the Athenians. He cannot therefore have been an unofficial ambassador from a popular party as Day (*Economic History of Athens* 113, cf. Ferguson *HA* 440f) suggested. Nor could he have been appointed through the influence of Medeios and his associates. The appeal to Rome could not have come from Athenion and his ilk with their leanings to Mithridates; it must therefore have come from Medeios, and indicated that he expected support from Rome. So it has been assumed that

COMMENTARY: F253

Medeios had died in the interval (so Badian, 508); while possible, the assumption is unnecessary. The political situation which secured Medeios' appointment to his third Archonship could evaporate during his office. In fact Posidonius says that it did: ὅτε εἰς Μ. τὰ πράγματα μετέρρει (24). Badian (508 n. 23) castigates the phrase for unclarity; but in the context of its sentence it must refer to political opinion in Athens beginning to veer to Mithridates. Whether Rome or Mithridates was going to provide the control of stability in the Aegean had become a serious question. Posidonius makes clear the fluidity and uncertainty of the period. For the general chaos at Athens, 95-103.

25f Posidonius reports as fact Athenion's meteoric rise in the favours of the king, although with a sneer (ὑποδραμών). He received the official title of φίλος (Olshausen, *Ancient Society* 5 (1974), 166f).

26-30 We need not doubt the historical authenticity of Athenion's offers from Mithridates in his letters. Badian (504) accuses Posidonius of being 'excruciatingly unclear', especially in reference to ὀφλήματα. But Athenion's homecoming and speech leaves no doubt that he was pitching to the popular appeal of the masses, with remission of debts and gifts. ὁμόνοια (*concordia*) and 'democracy' were political slogans which could be interpreted at any level. In any case, this is precisely what Mithridates was offering elsewhere to Greek cities; after all, the creditors were likely to be Roman; cf. Appian, *Mithr.* 48, Justin, xxxviii.3.9, and esp. Nicolet, *L'Ordre équestre*, vol. 1.670f. As the sentence stands, καὶ before δωρεῶν (30) is odd; hence Wilamowitz and Jacoby changed the order.

30-2 A perfectly understandable view at the time, with Rome embarrassed in the west and seemingly crushed by Mithridates in the east. Does it also convey wishful thinking? The eventual massacres of the 'Asian Vespers', however exaggerated, betrayed a strong element of hatred for Roman dominion.

COMMENTARY: F253

Athenion's reception at Athens (32–63)

Posidonius now resorts to the power of vivid description. His purpose is patent: the portrait of a frenzied, hybristic, emotional welcome home of a supposed saviour, where the πάθη of the crowd grotesquely outrun all reason and control; as if a later historian was to highlight the welcome of an umbrella-waving Chamberlain declaring peace in our time. It is the function of a statesman and leader to control such outbursts of πάθη, as in an individual the ἡγεμονικόν of reason must discipline the emotions. But Athenion, a supposed philosopher, on the contrary sought power by fanning them with disastrous results. Posidonius deliberately uses every rhetorical device to give powerful impact to the picture, and the studied sarcasm of the language is searing. It is an exceptionally vivid and powerful piece of writing, but done for a purpose. Posidonius must have had personal accounts of these scenes: we have no reason to disbelieve them because of the underlying tone or rhetorical style.

32–6 Athenion returned to Athens when Asia had turned to the King. This is amplified by 72ff. Mithridates was by this time master of Asia and both Q. Oppius and M'. Aquillius had been captured. It was probably early summer (Badian, 509, Deininger, *Der Politische Widerstand* 250, Candiloro, *Studi classici e orientali* 14 (1965) 147). Sailing most likely from Ephesus, he was forced by a storm to put in to Carystus on the south promontory of Euboea. The Athenians, getting word of this, sent warships and a silver-footed litter to escort him home. The last sentence is heavy with rhetorical irony. The Athenians are called Κεκροπίδαι; their ancient honoured name contrasts starkly with their present fawning actions. The juxtaposition of warships and a silver-footed couch (a mark of extreme effeminate luxury, Athen. VI.255E) is sarcastically deliberate.

36–47 ἀλλ' εἰσῄειν (Kaibel; ἀλλησεισιν A) ἤδη: vivid rhetoric: 'Aye but, there he was now coming in (to the city)'.

COMMENTARY: F253

'Practically the greatest part of the city had poured out (ἐξεκέχυτο) for his reception; and running with them to join them (συνέτρεχον; the construction is chiasmic) were many other spectators (θεαταί; one is reminded of Cleon's sarcastic jibe at the Athenians in Thuc. III.38.7: ἁπλῶς τε ἀκοῆς ἡδονῇ ἡσσώμενοι καὶ σοφιστῶν θεαταῖς ἐοικότες καθημένοις μᾶλλον ἢ περὶ πόλεως βουλευομένοις) wondering at the paradox of fortune, when the illegally enrolled (cf. line 19) Athenion to Athens is conveyed (a pun on 'Ἀθηνίων and 'Ἀθηναῖος, and a rhetorical juxtaposition of 'Ἀθηνίων and 'Ἀθήνας) on a silver-footed couch with scarlet (i.e. regal) coverings (again cf. Athen. VI.255E), a man who had never seen scarlet before on his scholar's gown (τρίβωνος; there may be a side allusion to the *latus clavus*, which Polybius (10.26.1) translates as πορφύρα πλατεῖα; so leading into the next clause), when not even any single Roman (οὐδενὸς οὐδέ) had insulted Attica with such a presentation of effeminate luxury (καταχλιδῶντος). So they were running all together (συνέτρεχον οὖν is resumptive) to this spectacle, men, women, children (the asyndetic accumulation is highly rhetorical), expecting the best from Mithridates (cf. line 30; Posidonius does not forget the greedy passions of the mob), when Athenion, the pauper who had held subscription lectures (there is no contradiction to 22; the reference, for rhetorical contrast, is to his earlier days of penury), because of the King now farts his way arrogantly through town and country in escort.' The calculated use at the end of the vulgar σιληπορδῶν explodes with indignant sarcasm.

47–58 The official welcome. Or to what extent was it official? There is no word of any Athenian officials or magistrates. He was met by the Dionysiac artists. This was a powerful, ancient and highly independent guild (Ferguson, *HA* 162 n. 2, 297, 370–3; Day, *Economic History*, 92ff; Poland, *RE* 5 A, 2473ff). Besides enjoying immunities such as freedom from taxation and military service, and protection of life and property, they could vote honours, as they did for Ariarathes

V, King of Cappadocia, shortly after the mid-2nd c. B.C. (*IG* II–III² 1330). Earlier in 112 B.C. they had official support from Rome in a dispute with the Isthmian guild (*SIG* 705). That they formed the reception committee indicates the swing of opinion from Rome to Mithridates and appears to underline factually the political and social chaos claimed by Athenion in his speech, 95–103. Their welcome was extravagant, an invitation to a public dinner complete with prayers and libations, as the envoy of 'the new Dionysus'. Mithridates was in fact so called at Delos, *Inscriptions de Délos* 1562, and cf. Cic. *Flacc.* 60. Instead of going home, Athenion was then put up at the house of one of the richest men in Athens. Cod. A has the name confused (διευς), but it was almost certainly Dies (Dow, *CPh* 37 (1942), 311–14), originally from Tyre, but now an Athenian citizen, grown wealthy from business interests in Delos. For the importance of Delos both for Athenian commerce and society, see Tracy, 213–20. At first sight it seems strange that such a man, possibly earlier associated with Medeios (*Inscr. Délos* 2607) should welcome a supporter of Mithridates' policy of remission of debts and freedom of slaves (Delos was the centre of the profitable slave trade (Str. XIV.5.2)), and so Deininger (*Der Politische Widerstand* 251 n. 16) concluded that he was away, or flown from Athens. But would his house be used without his consent? It is more probable that Dies, like other rich members of the merchant class, was hedging his bets in the crisis. Posidonius returns to the rhetorical contrasts (50–5): a man who had formerly stepped out of a rented house ends up in a mansion sumptuously fitted out with rugs, paintings, statuary and silver plate, from which he exits with a brilliant cloak trailing, and wearing (chiasmus again) a gold ring on his finger engraved with the likeness of Mithridates (the insignia of a 'Friend'?). He was escorted fore and aft (rhetorical duplication but possibly also with a play on the prefixes, προ- and ἐπι-) by many attendants. In the precinct of the Artists (who still had charge of him) sacrifices were celebrated in honour of

COMMENTARY: F253

the advent of Athenion and, prefaced by solemn proclamation from the herald, thank offerings poured (a further chiasmus).

58–63 'Next day crowds came to the house to await his public appearance. The Cerameicus (i.e. the route into the Agora) was full of citizens and foreigners, and there was a spontaneous concerted rush of the masses to the Assembly.' It is clear that this was an unofficial ἐκκλησία, signalled both by αὐτόκλητος and by being held in the Agora (cf. 98).

'He came forth with difficulty, attended by a guard of those who wanted to curry the favour of the people, everyone straining to touch his garment if he could.' The innuendo of tyranny is made by δορυφορούμενος, characteristic of Greek tyrants, and by the worshipping gesture of the last phrase.

Athenion's speech (64–103)

He made it from the speaker's rostrum in front of the stoa of Attalus in the Agora. Posidonius points out that it had been built for the Roman praetors, that is, presumably used as his tribunal by the governor of Macedonia for any official business in the free city of Athens. Presumption is probably implied, but Athenion was possibly deliberately heightening anti-Roman feeling. Posidonius vividly picks out the tricks of the practised orator: 'he gazed round in a circle at the crowd, then raised his gaze and said . . .'

The speech no doubt follows, despite the cautions of Polybius (36.1), the traditional importance and function of such speeches prominent in Greek historiography. It does not pretend to be a verbatim or complete account of what was said (103f); it does not become on that account fiction. Posidonius must have had later ear-witness accounts, and we can expect that he applied no less severe canons than Thuc. 1.22.1. And yet in the context the purpose of the speech is clear, to demonstrate just how Athenion played on the πάθη of the mob. To present this effectively, no doubt he selected and because of ancient conditions phrased as best he could

873

COMMENTARY: F253

what was reported to him, but this was for him historical evidence of the psychological cause of what happened at Athens in 88. The speech itself is presented in two parts: (i) shocking the Athenians with the astounding facts of Mithridates' successes (71–92); (ii) Athenion's advice and recommendations (94–103). They are dramatically separated (92–4), and introduced rhetorically (66–70). The first part is carefully organised.

(a) **66–70** An old rhetorical trick, 'Although the situation and my country's interest are driving me to report what I know, yet the sheer scale of what is to be said, because of the incredible nature of the state of affairs, holds me back', of course eggs on his already excited audience to concerted shouts of encouragement.

(b) **71–8** The extent of Mithridates' victories. It looks as if this is the first announcement at Athens of the full scale of Mithridates' victories. Partial reports must have come in his letters, and his welcome as envoy of the new Dionysus implies a victorious Mithridates, but the completeness of the Roman defeat was dangerously exciting news, beyond all belief or dreams. Athenion spells it out in detail for full impact. Mithridates controls not only Bithynia and Upper Cappadocia, but the whole of the province of Asia as far as Pamphylia and Cilicia. The Kings of Armenia and Persia serve in his bodyguard, as do the princes of the tribes settled round Maiotis and the whole of Pontus to a circuit of 30,000 stades.

(c) **78–84** The utter defeat and disgrace of the Romans. As for the Romans, the praetor of Pamphylia, Q. Oppius, had been surrendered to him and is led a prisoner in his train; the ex-consul, M'. Aquillius, the man who won a Sicilian triumph (stressing his importance; θρίαμβον κατάγειν, Plb. 11.33.7), bound by a long chain to a seven-foot Bastarnian is dragged along on foot by a rider. Cf. App. *Mithr*. 20–1: D.S. 37.26–7; Livy, *Per*. 78; Sherwin-White, *Roman Foreign Policy* 117ff; Magie, *Roman Rule in Asia Minor* 1.215. The details vary, but Posidonius has the most graphic picture of Roman

COMMENTARY: F253

disgrace with the enormous Bastarnian cossack. Are the latter's five cubits a reminiscence of the huge skeleton reputedly found on the field of Plataea in Hdt. IX.83? Perhaps Aquillius had not yet suffered his grotesque execution of molten gold poured down his throat (App. *Mithr.* 21; but see below). His cruel death became a by-word, Cic. *Tusc.* v.14. Of the rest of the Romans, some have sought sanctuary in the temples, the rest have literally become turncoats, hastily changing from the Roman toga to the square himation of the Greeks. Badian argues (509) that this must date the speech before the notorius 'Asian Vespers' (App. *Mithr.* 22–3); possibly, but it is unlikely that Athenion would have dwelt on the discordant note of a barbaric irreligious slaughter instigated by the edict of massacre from his champion Mithridates.

(d) **85–92** The present glory of Mithridates, and evidence for his coming world domination and the annihilation of Rome.

He is met with superhuman honours and called the god-king; cf. D.S. 37.26, and line 48 above. Oracles from all sides foretell his domination of the world.

He is sending great armies into Thrace and Macedon, and all parts of Europe have changed in a body to his side. On the strategy of the future campaign in Europe, see now Sherwin-White, *Roman Foreign Policy* 132ff.

He received embassies from the Italian tribes (so D.S. 37.2.11; from the Samnites presumably, Brunt, *JRS* 55 (1965), 96) and from the Carthaginians. Since Carthage was destroyed in 146 B.C., this is either a blatant untruth to an ignorant mob with a vague memory of Rome's traditional enemy, or represents some other centre of western power. But no clear alternative presents itself. Nicolet (*Mélanges Piganiol* II.807–14) argued for Tyrian merchants. They were demanding alliance for the destruction of Rome, and the passage ends deliberately with the words, ἐπὶ τὴν τῆς Ῥώμης ἀναίρεσιν.

92–4 Such pauses have a long literary history as dramatic

COMMENTARY: F253

punctuation of speeches or arguments, as in Plato's Socratic dialogues, but we may believe Posidonius that Athenion used it as a rhetorical trick to allow the enormity of his news to sink in. It is accompanied by an oratorical gesture of rubbing his forehead, as if emphasising the anxiety of his impending advice (cf. Aeschines 2.49).

94–103 Athenion's advice is clearly an incitement to anti-Roman politics, with three sentences of prohibitions; the oratory of protest can be more incendiary than positive rational recommendation:

(i) **95–7** 'Not to put up with the anarchy which the Roman senate has made to continue until it for its part (αὐτή strongly sarcastic) makes a decision as to how we must be governed.' An official appeal must earlier have been made to Rome to settle the political confusion at Athens. Rome with the Social War and political problems of her own, had put off the investigation (see above under 23–32).

ἀναρχία is here used in the popular sense, and not in the technical sense of *IG* ii² 1713, of the lack of an eponymous Archon. ἐπισχεθῆναι (96) is hard to believe; we would expect ἐπέχειν as the usual form in this sense. Kaibel hazarded ἐπισχεθεῖν, Wyttenbach ἐπιχυθῆναι. I suggest ἐπισχύειν, cf. D.S. 5.59.3. Perhaps, ἐπισχύειν ἡμῖν. The intention of the rhetoric is to blame Rome for the present mess, which can be escaped by their own independence.

(ii) **97–100** The anarchy is detailed by the closure of the political and social centres of the state: 'Let us not stand idle while our sacred places are locked, the gymnasia squalid through disuse, the theatre without an assembly, and the courts without a voice (a succession of chiasmi), and the Pnyx, hallowed by the oracles of the gods, taken away from the Athenian people.' If this is true there was indeed dangerous and unparalleled restriction of civil liberties (cf. Day, *Economic History* 113). Athenion is also, in order to enflame the crowd, beginning to appeal to the traditional national symbols of identity and freedom. The theatre (i.e. of

876

COMMENTARY: F253

Dionysus) was where the ecclesia of the period met; but the Pnyx was its ancient hallowed home.

(iii) 100–3 The rhetoric reaches a climax, repeating μὴ περιιδῶμεν: 'and let us not stand idle, Athenian people, while the sacred voice of Iacchus is silent, and the holy shrine of the two goddesses (i.e. Demeter and Persephone at Eleusis) closed, and the schools of the philosophers without a voice'. That is, national religious processions and celebrations like the Eleusinian mysteries, and freedom of speech and criticism were banned.

Athenion's elections (103–11)

Posidonius has given enough (103) to demonstrate the cause of what inevitably followed such rabble-rousing, namely Athenion's election to power, which he describes briefly in heavy sarcasm. οἰκότριψ, literally a slave brought up in a household (cf. 14ff), has good classical antecedents, and may be a reminiscence of D. 13.24, as the phrase ἴσα βαίνων Πυθοκλεῖ (107) is taken from D. 19.314 on Aeschines, 'the ex-clerk', strutting like Pythocles (a famous phrase apparently, *De Subl.* 44.7). Both passages recall contemporary political degradation compared with earlier pride. The excited mob (ὄχλοι, 104) rushed from the agora to the theatre of Dionysus (105); since this was where official ἐκκλησίαι of the time were held, they were thus reasserting independently their civic and political rights. They promptly chose, presumably by acclamation, Athenion Hoplite General (105f). This office, the first of the ten Generals, was the most important and powerful executive position in Athens at that time (Ferguson *HA* 378, 456, 472; *Klio* (1904), 7f, Tracy, 216. It had been held by Medeios and by Sarapion at least thrice, and in Sulla's disposition it was confirmed as the chief executive office of the state). Thereupon Athenion ('our Peripatetic') strode on to the stage, thanked the Athenians and said '*Now you* (i.e. and not the Romans) command yourselves, and I am your

877

COMMENTARY: F253

commander-in-chief. If you join your strength to me, my power shall reach the combined power of all of you.' (106–10). With that statement, he appointed the rest of the archons for himself by suggesting the names of those he wanted (110f).

IG II^2 1713 labelled 88/7 as a year of ἀναρχία, i.e. without an eponymous Archon. Dow (*Hesp.* III (1934), 444ff) argued that *IG* II^2 1714, which gives a list of eight archons and the Herald of the Areopagus, was never headed by the name of the eponymous Archon, and therefore is the list for 88/7. This has been generally accepted, although doubted by Sherwin-White, *Roman Foreign Policy* 136 n. 14. Badian has shown (511f), that the names on this list include men of good political families, already distinguished by office. This would indicate that Athenion's power base was broader than mob support, which after all was only to be expected, and entirely understandable in the dangerously uncertain and volatile nature of the crisis. Then perhaps Athenion dispensed with an eponymous Archon, as *IG* II^2 1713 suggests. But Badian (510ff) and Habicht (*Chiron* 6 (1976), 128ff) argue forcibly that one was appointed but the name omitted for political reasons when the stone was struck after Sulla's capture of Athens. Badian suggested some unknown Athenian (511), but then why was he consigned to oblivion while the others remained? Habicht (130ff) plausibly argued for the name of Mithridates himself (later to become a mintmaster in 87/6). Then why did Posidonius not mention this, as he was more likely to do than a relatively obscure Athenian? But Posidonius' account is anyway infuriatingly brief and lacking detail at this point. The reason must be that in the Athenion extract, Posidonius is more interested in causes than in the details of events, concerned at least here not so much with what happened as with why it happened; so we have 103 lines on Athenion and his speech, compared with the summary of the result in 8½ lines, most of the latter still directed at Athenion's actions.

At all events it seems clear that the break with Rome and

COMMENTARY: F253

conscious siding with Mithridates occurred now. So Habicht (132), although Badian (512) argued that Athenion continued to temporise (cf. line 125). Posidonius at least with his emphasis on the anti-Roman thrust of Athenion's speech believed that this was the decisive move.

Athenion's tyranny and the reign of terror (112–44)

This passage has frequently been suspected of contamination; Wilamowitz (43) suggested importations from Aristion's later tyranny, Jacoby (187) detected conflation of doublets, Touloumakos (*Philologus* 110 (1966), 140f) referred to the clumsiness of Athenaeus as an epitomiser. Theiler (II.127) has defended the text. The intention of the passage is to give a vivid and detailed picture of the swift (μετ' οὐ πολλὰς ἡμέρας, 112) transition from supposed philosopher leader (cf. F90) to tyrant (τύραννον αὐτὸν ἀποδείξας ὁ φιλόσοφος, 112; the contrast is underlined).

112–22 The sentence betrays interpolation. It should run: ...ὁ φιλόσοφος (112) τοὺς μὲν εὖ φρονοῦντας (117) ... ἐκποδὼν εὐθὺς ἐποιήσατο ... But at 113–16 is inserted inconsequentially a side swipe at the Pythagoreans: 'displaying the doctrine of the Pythagoreans on treachery, and what was (really) meant by that philosophy introduced by the noble (sarcastic, cf. 170) Pythagoras'; this is topped by source references to Theopompus, *History of Philip* Bk 8 (*FGrH* 115, F73) and to Hermippus, a follower of Callimachus (who wrote Βίοι τῶν ἀπὸ φιλοσοφίας εἰς τυραννίδας καὶ δυναστείας μεθεστηκότων, *Academicorum Index* col. 11, p. 29 Mekler). It is necessary to remember that the ancients did not have the convenience of footnotes, so that such material could become embedded in the text. But it is difficult to believe that it appeared here in Posidonius' account. It belongs to the hostile historical tradition which accused Pythagoras and the Pythagoreans of tyranny in Croton (Burkert, *Lore and Science* 118ff). Another trace of it in parallel circumstances is in

COMMENTARY: F253

Appian's antiphilosophical digression in his account of Aristion (*Mithr.* 28). But Posidonius did not believe this (F284.16–20). More importantly, it throws the whole sentence out of joint; Posidonius is accusing Athenion of betraying the Peripatetic principles of Aristotle and Theophrastus by removing the best elements in the state (117f). Finally, εὐθέως καὶ οὗτος (117) shows patching of the clumsiest kind. The aside fits the *general* attack on philosopher–tyrants presented by Athenaeus (Context), who is probably responsible for it. I also suspect the inserted proverb, 'don't give a knife to a child' (119), which again fits the Pythagorean background better than the Peripatetic criticism.

We are now given a succession of acts illustrating Athenion's tyranny. He immediately got right-thinking citizens out of the way, but on the other hand he stationed a guard on the gates, so that many Athenians, worried for the future, escaped by letting themselves down over the walls (117–22). Cicero's remark (*Brut.* 306) about the Athenian *optimates* (τοὺς εὖ φρονοῦντας?) together with Philo, the Head of the Academy, fleeing to Rome in the Mithridatic War, may refer to this period (cf. Paus. 1.20.5). So Athenion sent cavalry after them, slew some and brought others back prisoners; he now had a large bodyguard in full armour (122–5).

125 The codices have: he called assemblies too and frequently pretended sympathy with the Roman cause. Badian (512) claimed that this shows that Athenion continued to temporise and had not yet committed himself. Habicht (132; cf. Beneden, *Philologus* 113 (1969), 153ff) maintained that he had in fact, but was playing internal politics. Neither view is possible in Posidonius' account, where the die is cast, the pro-Roman citizens proscribed, and the continuing context of the sentence deals with them. Touloumakos (*Philologus* 110 (1966) 141) restored sense by supplying ⟨τοὺς ληφθέντας⟩ after προσεποιεῖτο: he pretended that the captives were Roman sympathisers (D.S.

36.5.3 for construction), brought charges against many of them for communicating with the outlaws and attempting revolution, and kept putting them to death. Jacoby's ἀκρίτους for αὐτούς (128) is maladroit; these men were charged; ἀκρίτους comes in another context (133).

128-9 He now put permanent guards on all the city's gates (something like Jacoby's addition is necessary), preventing both exit and entrance. This is different from the earlier measure to stop fugitives, so there is no need to cut it as a doublet with Jacoby.

129 He started to confiscate the property of many, and acquired enough money to fill a large number of tanks; a graphic rhetorical exaggeration.

131-7 Again Jacoby would cut as a doublet, on the grounds that the punitive expedition into the country is a repetition. But the circumstances are different, and more sinister, from the first cavalry chase after the initial refugees (122ff). This additional (καί, 131) operation concerns secret police acting like highwaymen (ὥσπερ ὁδοιδόκους, 132; cf. Nabis, the tyrant of Sparta, Plb. 13.8.2); their victims were tortured, racked and made away with without trial (134). But many he brought to trial as traitors alleging complicity for the restoration of the exiles; some in terror escaped before the judgement, others were condemned in the courts, with Athenion casting the votes himself! (135-7).

137-9 He created in the city a shortage of even the basic necessities of life, and rationed barley and wheat.

139-43 Again wrongly thought by Jacoby to be a doublet. The picture this time (καί, 139) is of official military patrols (ὁπλίτας) on the hunt either for returned patriots who had sneaked back into the territory (for ἀνακεχωρηκότων cf. Thuc. VIII.15.1), or for any Athenian trying to cross the border. This time, anyone caught was beaten to death. What we have is not a confusion of doublets but a rhetorical *variatio*, deliberately filling out a reign of terror. This whole

COMMENTARY: F253

section from 112 is Posidonius' picture of what happened, the result of Athenion's tyranny.

143–4 Finally he imposed a curfew. Theiler's καὶ ⟨μηδὲ⟩ μετὰ λυχνοφόρου is attractive.

The expedition under Apellicon to seize Delos (145–79)

This episode is still written entirely from the point of view of Posidonius' judgement on Athenion's tyranny, namely as a catastrophic disaster caused by impious greed, superficial display and incompetence.

145–7 So no mention is made of the importance of Delos for Athens through close civic and commercial relationships (Tracy, 213ff), nor indeed as a target of Roman power, commerce and refugees in the Aegean. Rather, Athenion, not satisfied with plundering citizen property in Athens, is reaching for the god's treasure in Delos. In fact later, after Archelaus had taken Delos, Aristion was sent back to Athens with the Delos treasure (App. *Mithr.* 28).

147–57 The fiasco is illustrated by the choice of Apellicon as commander, which explains the excursus on Apellicon's career and character. Originally from Teos, now an Athenian citizen, he had led a chequered and restless career (147–9). A sometime Peripatetic, he was more of a professional and unscrupulous bibliophile than a philosopher (cf. Strabo, XIII.1.54); he had bought up Aristotle's library and many other collections (he was a wealthy man), removed and acquired ancient original decrees from the Metroon (the Athenian archive), and any other rare and ancient documents he could lay his hands on elsewhere (149–54). Caught in the act, he would have been in a dangerous position in Athens, had he not fled. He was back again not long after, through paying court to a large number of people, and signed up with Athenion as you might expect, since he shared the same philosophic sect (154.7). For Apellicon: Moraux, *Der Aristotelismus* 1.26–31, Gottschalk, *Hermes* 100 (1972), 339–42.

Posidonius dwells on his shady side, but he held the mint magistracy probably in 88/7 (Lewis, *NC* (1962), 278).

157-64 Posidonius sarcastically contrasts Athenion at home forgetting his Peripatetic principles by rationing barley to the silly (ἀνοήτοις, 159) Athenians, in quantity fit for poultry rather than human beings, while Apellicon, off with his force to Delos, behaved as if he were attending a public festival rather than a military expedition (πανηγυρικῶς μᾶλλον ἢ στρατιωτικῶς, 161, cf. D.S. 37.15.3), detailed a far too slack outpost on the Delos flank, and, above all, no guard at all for the hinterland, and without even digging in, bedded down for the night.

164-71 The Roman commander Orbius who was guarding Delos took advantage of this. Mommsen's argument (*CIL* III. Suppl. 7225, 7234) that this man was one of the merchant family of Orbii at Delos has been generally followed (Ferguson *HA* 445 n. 1, Münzer *RE s.v.* 2.879f, Jacoby, 188, Theiler, II.128). But Posidonius' description is of a Roman prefect in command of a detachment of fleet in Delian waters (Roussel, *Délos* 324; Badian, 512 n. 34; Day, *Economic History* 115 n. 363; cf. P. Orbius, propraetor in Asia in 64, Cic. *Flacc.* 76). Disembarking his men on a moonless night, he caught the Athenians asleep or drunk, cut down 600 of them like sheep (ὡς βοσκήματα, 168), and took about 400 prisoners. Our fine general (ὁ καλὸς στρατηγός) Apellicon, slipped out of Delos and fled.

171-9 This was not the end of the disaster, for Orbius noticed a mass of Athenians taking refuge in farmhouses and cremated the lot, including their siege engines together with the 'citytaker' which Apellicon had constructed on arrival in Delos. This is a strange detail. A 'citytaker' was a huge siege engine of the type invented by Demetrius Poliorcetes (D.S. 20.48). But there is evidence that Delos was only fully fortified later by the Romans (Malitz, 355f n. 243). Is this further sarcasm over Apellicon's ignorant military pretensions as well as incompetence? The Roman victory was marked by a

COMMENTARY: F253

trophy and epigram, which Posidonius may have himself seen. The epigram seems to allude to a naval engagement (177), not recorded here by Posidonius, perhaps because it did not reflect the criminal negligence of Apellicon.

Athenion and Aristion

The defeat at Delos ends the Posidonian extract. No more is heard of Athenion. In fact nothing at all is heard of Athenion apart from this passage and this raises a problem. For whenever the Athenian tyranny in the Mithridatic War is mentioned elsewhere, the only tyrant named is Aristion (App. *Mithr.* 28–9; Strabo, IX.1.20; Plu. *Sulla* 12, 13, 23, *Lucull.* 19, *Numa* 9, *Mor.* 558C, 809E; Pausanias, 1.20.5). Scholars have therefore divided over whether in fact there was only one tyrant (the Identity Thesis: Casaubon, Mommsen, Geyer (*RE s.v.* Mithridates, XV.2171), Reinhardt, Laffranque, Nicolet) or two (the Separatists: Wilamowitz, Jacoby, Ferguson, Deininger, Badian (hesitantly), Theiler, Sherwin-White). The separatist arguments have been put most powerfully by Niese, *RhM* 42 (1887), 574–8. There is no doubt about the name Aristion, as it appears on Athenian coinage of this time with Mithridates (Malitz, 342 n. 130); so on the identity thesis, Athenion must have been a nickname. Laffranque (143 n. 154) emphasised the coincidence of the slave king's name Athenion in the Sicilian revolt (D.S. 36.8–10), and pointed out that it had become a nickname used by Sulla's troops (for Fimbria, App. *Mithr.* 59) and by Cicero (*Att.* 2.12.2). But it was also a proper Athenian name (*IG* II² 1028, 151; Kirchner, *Pros. Att.* 243). Above all, Posidonius, who was an interested contemporary and had no doubt been well aware of Athenion's philosophical as well as political pretensions, details his birth and naming as his own proper name after his father (12–16). Therefore the evidence of names strongly supports the separatists, because they could not have been confused. Further, Posidonius labours the point that Athenion was a Peripatetic, Appian clearly labels

Aristion an Epicurean (*Mithr*. 28), although this in turn raises the question why Athenaeus should not have continued his attack on philosopher tyrants with Aristion, instead of with the Epicurean Lysias at Tarsus (215BC). But the clinching argument for separatism is based on comparing the narrative of Posidonius with that of Appian, *Mithr*. 28. They cannot be conflated or reconciled historically. Athenion arrived back alone in Athens after his embassy, at a time when Mithridates had just completed his military conquest of Asia. After establishing himself as tyrant at Athens, he sent the ill-fated expedition under Apellicon which failed to take Delos and its treasure. Aristion was on the coat tails of Archelaus, when he captured Delos while Mithridates was still besieging Rhodes. After the capture of Delos, he was sent back to Athens with the Delian treasure and 2,000 troops with which he then made himself tyrant of Athens. Niese's arguments remain convincing. We have two pieces of jigsaw which fit into each other giving a succession of two tyrants. They may be contaminated (Athenion's rationing of food at Athens seems more suitable for the siege of Athens when Aristion was in power, Malitz, 343), but they cannot be conflated or identical.

Three questions remain which can only be answered conjecturally; (i) Why did Athenaeus not follow Athenion with Aristion? (ii) Why does the other evidence not mention Athenion? (iii) Why did Posidonius give so much space and prominence to Athenion?

The first seems the least important. Athenaeus may well have thought that he had quite enough on that particular situation in Athens with the long Athenion extract. He liked to parade the variety and diversity of his learning. Besides, Posidonius in his *History* probably concentrated his attack on the philosopher–tyrant on Athenion, and did not repeat and dwell on this aspect in his subsequent account of Aristion and the siege and capture of Athens.

The notoriety of Ariston and obscurity of Athenion is to

some extent explained by Strabo, IX.1.20: 'The incidence of the Mithridatic War established tyrants (τυράννους, plural) over the Athenians; by far the most powerful one (τὸν δ' ἰσχύσαντα μάλιστα), Aristion, who oppressed the city, was caught and punished by Sulla after the siege'. It was Aristion whose advent overshadowed the initial bungling, who was in power through the decisive events from 88 to the fall of the city in 86, who was linked with Archelaus in the Greek campaign, and above all with Sulla. Any brief account of the Greek campaign (Appian), or of the siege of Athens (Pausanias), or of Sulla's campaigns (Plutarch), especially if from Roman sources, would concentrate entirely on Aristion. Athenion enjoyed an ephemeral tyranny of a few weeks (Wilcken, *RE s.v.* Athenion 3, II.2038f), soon forgotten because superseded by more important events.

Why then did Posidonius single him out for such a vivid historical portrait? He must have believed that it was Athenion, for all his brief and apparently unimportant because unsuccessful career, who nevertheless started off the people of Athens on a course from which by the time he was succeeded they could not withdraw; a course which inevitably was to end not only in a reign of terror, but in the eventual capture and humbling of a once proud and enlightened state. But he probably took the case of Athenion not simply as an initial antecedent cause, but as an obvious illustration and warning of the principle or governing cause of disaster, the uncontrolled πάθη in human political behaviour arising out of a combination of the silly greedy mob of Cecropids and a leader whom he regarded as a fifth-rate philosopher on the make. On the relationship between ruler and ruled, cf. F252. The deliberate overpainting in strong colours brings out a ludicrous picture of tyranny, its causes and results, as the reverse of the philosopher–king. The choice of incident and its dramatisation betrays a moralist's view of historiography, where the relation of events may for a time be sidetracked for an examination of the moral behaviour which causes them.

As such the case of Athenion was edifying; but not simply as a moral exemplar in the style of Plutarch (*Demetr.* 1.1–6). The fundamental difference between Plutarch and Posidonius, is that the latter was seeking to trace causal explanation. No doubt he then went on to give an account of Aristion, the campaign in Greece, and the taking of Athens by Sulla.

See Kidd, 'Posidonius as Philosopher-Historian', in *Philosophia Togata, Essays on Philosophy and Roman Society*, edd. J. Barnes and M. T. Griffin, Oxford, 1988.

F254 Plutarch, *Maxime cum Principibus*, *Moralia* 777A

CONTENT

Scipio sent for Panaetius when the senate sent him out 'inspecting both the outrageous behaviour and good order of men', as Posidonius says.

CONTEXT

As Plutarch's title indicates, his subject concerns the practical benefit of philosophers associating with men of power. If philosophical teaching is directed to a private individual, the benefit is limited to him, but if it affects public figures, the benefit is spread to many (1–2). Plutarch gives examples: Anaxagoras and Pericles, Plato and Dion, Pythagoras and the leading statesmen in the south of Italy, Cato and Athenagoras (Cordylion in Pergamon, Plu. *Cato Min.* 10), Panaetius and Scipio (3–5).

COMMENT

The reference is to Scipio Aemilianus' diplomatic mission to Egypt and the middle east in 140/139 or 144/3 B.C. (F58, T7,

COMMENTARY: F255

F265), accompanied by Panaetius. The passage therefore probably occurred in Bk 7 of the *History* (F58).

The quotation of *Od.* XVII.487 is repeated by Plutarch at *Mor.* 200E with reference to the same event (F58 comm.), but this time assigned to Clitomachus, the pupil of Carneades and head of the Academy from 127/6 B.C. until his death in 110/109 B.C. It is not unknown for Plutarch to misremember references, but the tag may have become common currency in connection with Scipio's embassy. Plato used it in *Soph.* 216b 3, ending with καθορᾶν.

The main codices of Plutarch have ὑφορώμενον (ἐφορῶντα *Zabu*, Plu. 200E; ἐφορῶντες Homer), and most editors have adopted Xylander's ἐφορώμενον. But the middle form of ἐφορᾶν would be very strange. It is just possible that Plutarch, or Posidonius, may have written ὑφορώμενον, inspecting covertly; according to D.S. 33.28b (F58 comm.), Scipio's party in Egypt had some problems in inspecting what they wanted to see in the face of the King's programme of lavish festivities. Or again some Homeric codices had ὑφορῶντες which may have been translated to the commoner middle form. But ἐφορῶντα (Wyttenback and Plu. 200E) is probably right.

It is clear that Posidonius' account of Scipio's visit to Egypt put some stress on the presence of Panaetius in Scipio's retinue. This is another indication that his approach to the event in the *History* was more concerned with moral than purely political analyses and comparisons. For other indications, see F58 comm. and F265.

F255   Plutarch, *Marius* 45.3-7

CONTENT

The death of Marius.

COMMENTARY: F255

CONTEXT

This account forms part of the conclusion of Plutarch's *Life*. It is followed (§§8-9) by evidence from 'a certain Gaius Piso, ἀνὴρ ἱστορικός' (printed by Jacoby F37), and by a further version from an unidentified source (τινὲς δέ, §§10-12, printed by Jacoby, and by Theiler F249).

COMMENT

A tricky fragment. Details first:

1 Marius was elected consul for the seventh time, and assumed office on 1 January 86 B.C. He was now 70 (Plu. *Mar.* 45.12), and celebrated by having Sextus Licinius thrown from the Tarpeian Rock, which was thought to be a portent for what was to follow (Plutarch). He died on 13 January (Broughton, *Magistrates* II.53).

2-9 A long vivid sentence on Marius' mental apprehensions: 'Worn out with exertions, awash as it were with anxieties (ὑπέραντλος also metaphorical in Luc. *Tim.* 18, but already in Eur. *Hipp.* 767), exhausted (κατάπονος also in Plu. *Alc.* 25; *Sull.* 29), he couldn't lift his mind, which was already quivering from his past experience of horror and weariness, in the face once again of the overwhelming thought of a new war and fresh combats and terrors, reckoning that the danger he was to face was not an Octavius or Merula as generals in charge of a flotsam band (σύγκλυς in Thuc. VII.5, Pl. *Rep.* 569a 3, but also in Str. IV.2.1) or seditious rabble, but it was the Sulla that comes against him, the man who earlier had driven him from his country (in 88 B.C.), and now had Mithridates penned in the Black Sea.' This is a fine sentence, and no doubt Posidonius could have written it, but without question Plutarch did. It is entirely in his style (Russell, *Plutarch* 132), and Plutarch was not in the habit of meekly reproducing other writers' prose. However, did he take the content and facts from Posidonius? But Carney (*Acta Classica*

COMMENTARY: F255

1 (1958), 117–32) has pointed out that the historical chronology is awry. At the opening of 86 B.C. Sulla was still fully engaged with the Mithridatic War. Athens was still uncaptured, and a Mithridatic army was threatening Greece in the north. In fact Sulla did not return to Rome until 83 B.C. Still it might be argued that Marius was morbidly preoccupied with intelligent anticipation of what was likely to happen. The stated facts are still wrong: Mithridates at this point was not penned in the Black Sea, and it is difficult to think that Posidonius, who had come recently from Rhodes which had been under siege by Mithridates (App. *Mithr.* 24–7), and anyway was contemporary with these events, can have been unaware of this. It is still possible that Plutarch was embroidering a moustache on a basic Posidonian portrait, or that Plutarch may have drawn his own picture. The interaction of physical and psychological deterioration interested Posidonius (F154), but it was a common topic in the 1st c. B.C. and afterwards. For Plutarch himself see *De Virt. Mor.* 450E–451A, and in general, F154 comm. Marius' physical exhaustion was also noted by Plutarch in 34.3 when Marius reacted positively; but that was in 88 B.C., two years before.

10–15 'Broken by such calculations, and continually fastening on visions before his eyes of his long wanderings, his flights and dangers as he was driven through land and sea, he fell into terrible distress with fears in the night and troubling dreams, for ever imagining he heard a voice saying, "Dread is the lair, though the lion is gone".' The obsession with Sulla is heightened to nightmares and delusions. Plutarch was addicted to quotations, but the untraced line is a specific detail which he could hardly have invented. It could have come from Posidonius at Rome; but the core of this picture with its stress on the importance of Sulla, 'the lion', may have originated from the Sullan annalists (as a source, Carney, *Biography of Marius* 2ff).

15–18 'As more than anything he was afraid of insomnia,

COMMENTARY: F255

he threw himself into drinking bouts, a drunkenness at all hours that fitted ill with his years, in an attempt to induce sleep as a kind of escape from his worries.' This looks like contemporary observation, and so may derive from Posidonius.

18–23 'And finally, when a messenger is come from the sea, new fears attacking him, partly apprehension for the future, partly because he could take no more of the burden of the present that weighed upon him, a little swing on top of the rest to tip the scale, he was brought down to an illness, pleurisy, as Posidonius the philosopher recounts, saying that he went in personally and conversed with him on the topics of his embassy, with Marius already ill.'

There is something wrong with this sentence. φόβοι (19) has no verb, since the only main verb is κατηνέχθη (21), and therefore the whole of the first part of the sentence is pendent. Reiske signalled a lacuna after θαλάσσης, but even if a main verb for φόβοι had occurred there, a connecting particle would still be required at 21 for κατηνέχθη. On the other hand, if κατηνέχθη is emended to κατήνεγκαν to accommodate φόβοι as subject, it demands an object which is missing. So either: θαλάσσης ⟨   ⟩ νέοι . . . παρόντων, ⟨καὶ⟩ (or ⟨ὥστε⟩) ῥοπῆς . . . (18–20), or κατήνεγκαν ⟨αὐτὸν⟩ (21). At all events, the run of the sentence makes clear that the final tip of the scale for Marius was the fears arising from this message from the sea. But this is a baffling phrase. Apart from the vividness of ἧκε, which reminded Norden (*Die Germanische Urgeschichte* 68) of the famous passage in D. 18.169 (ἧκε δ' ἀγγέλων τις), the phrase is impossibly condensed and vague. What could this mysterious message from the sea, that was the last straw, be? The run of Plutarch's context should indicate that an attack by Sulla on Marius was impending. But this is historically impossible, as an intensification of 2–9, and a translation into fact of the imaginings of 10–15 (see above).

It is noticeable that Posidonius is cited only for Marius'

COMMENTARY: F255

illness of pleurisy, with the evidence for this (21–3). This is the only secure evidence for Posidonius in this fragment; the rest is inference. Plutarch cites Posidonius from the *History* remarkably seldom in the *Lives*, and refers to him as 'the philosopher', not 'the historian'.

For Posidonius' embassy, see T28.

Section 7 is followed (§§8–9) by an account from Gaius Piso, ἀνὴρ ἱστορικός (Malitz, *Die Historien* 405, n. 386 suggested C. Calpurnius Piso, cos. 67), who merely records that one night after dinner Marius rambled on to his friends about the changing vicissitudes of his life, so that no man of sense would trust Fortune further. So he took to his bed and died a week later. This is clearly a separate account of the death, and inconsistent with §§4–7. There is no mention of pleurisy, nor of nightmares on the present situation. Why ever would Posidonius have recorded this? He saw Marius at the time, and knew he was ill. Piso's version is more in tune with D.S. 37.29.3–4: 'When he obtained his seventh consulship, he did not have the nerve to tempt Fortune further, having been taught by his great reverses about her fickleness. So foreseeing that the war from Sulla was hanging over Rome, he departed from life of his own volition.' This can hardly be a contraction or simplification of a full account from Posidonius (Malitz, 401 n. 360, 404; Jacoby, *Kommentar* 189), but a different rival version (so also Theiler, II.130).

This in turn is followed (§§10–12) by some unidentified sources (τινὲς δέ) recording a delirium in Marius' illness, which revealed his ambitious nature: he imagined he was in command in the Mithridatic War, and gave way to cries and gestures as if he were directing battles. So deeply had the lust for these events sunk into him from his love of power and envy. He grieved that he was dying ἐνδεὴς καὶ ἀτελής. This at least recognises Posidonius' report of Marius' illness, and is perhaps not altogether incompatible with §§4–7, but it is a differently slanted version (Carney, *Acta Classica* 119). The subject and content of the delirium is based on Marius' ambitions of command in the Mithridatic War, and on his envy of Sulla, not on his apprehension of an attack by Sulla; so the psychological pictures are different. Is this founded on a popular view of Marius' character? Ambition is stressed again in Plu. *Mar.* 34.6. So it may have come from a source hostile to Marius such as the Sullan annalists (cf. 10–15; Carney, *Wiener Studien* 63 (1960), 83f; *Biography of Marius* 2ff; Badian, *Historia* 11 (1962), 197f; Strasburger *JRS* 55 (1965), 41 n. 18 on the difficulty of distinguishing sources). This death scene became notorious, with different versions and traditions building up; Cicero (*Red. Quir.* 19–20) painted a very different picture.

In ch. 46 Plutarch continues by contrasting the deaths of Plato and Antipater of Tarsus counting their blessings rather than railing against Fortune. In fact this pulls together 45.8–12, and demonstrates Plutarch's customary moulding of sources. So the most likely conclusion is that chs. 45 and 46 derive from a pastiche of different sources which Plutarch fashioned into a whole for his own purposes, which is entirely what one would expect from Plutarch.

F256 Plutarch, *Brutus* 1

CONTENT

Posidonius combatted the view that the Iunii Bruti were not descended from L. Iunius Brutus, the traditional founder of the Republic and first consul.

CONTEXT

In the introduction to the Life of Brutus, the 1st-century B.C. tyrannicide, Plutarch says that there was no doubt about his mother's genealogy, but records criticism, with which he does

COMMENTARY: F256

not agree, that on the father's side the family could not have gone back to the expeller of the Tarquins, as they claimed.

COMMENT

The Iunii Bruti certainly claimed descent from the founder of the Republic, implied also in coinage (Vessberg, *Studien zur Kunstgeschichte der römischen Republik* 122–4, Pl. ii.1–4), and generally accepted (e.g. Cic. *Brut.* 53; *De Orat.* II.225; *Tusc.* IV.2; *Phil.* I.13; *Att.* 13.40.1). Modern scholars, while accepting that L. Iunius Brutus may well have been an historical figure, however encrusted with legend, are sceptical that a plebeian house such as the later Iunii Bruti could have descended from a patrician ancestor (*RE, suppl.* v.356–69; Syme, *Roman Revolution* 85). Ogilvie (*A Commentary on Livy, Books 1–5* 216) suggested that the connection may have been forged as early as D. Iunius Brutus (cos. 325) and C. Iunius Brutus (censor 307), 'who as plebeians regarded him as their "auctor nobilitatis"'. A T. Iunius Brutus was aed. pl. in 491 (Broughton, *Magistrates* 1.17).

These doubts were also raised in ancient times, and for similar reasons (7–8). Plutarch assigns them to malice rising from the tyrannicide of 44 B.C. (4), but he records that they were current in the time of Posidonius at least (8ff).

According to Plutarch, Posidonius recorded opposition to the other charge that in any case no sons of L. Iunius Brutus survived to continue the line (8–10). This is based on the common tradition that when Brutus' sons were discovered in the conspiracy of the Aquilii and Vitellii to restore the Tarquins, Brutus had them executed. Ogilvie (*Commentary on Livy, Books 1–5* 242) argued for the lateness of elements of this tale, but it was popular (Livy, 2.3–5; D.H. 5.2, 8–12; Val. Max. 5.8.1; Propert. 4.1.45; Plu. *Publ.* 3–5; see Broughton, 1.1 for other references), obviously current in Posidonius' time, and probably in Polybius (6.54.5, Walbank). It is uncertain whether Posidonius himself treated the legend seriously as historical; ὡς ἱστόρηται may simply be reproducing what has been recorded. The tradition named Titus and Tiberius, two adult sons (*adulescentes*, Livy 2.4.1; ... παῖδας ἐξ αὐτῆς πλείονας ὧν δύο τοὺς ἐν ἡλικίᾳ συγγενεῖς ὄντας ... Plu. *Publ.* 3); clearly the literary tradition permitted the survival of a younger son as Posidonius said. Perhaps Posidonius had this from Atticus' family tree of the Iunii Bruti (Nepos, *Att.* 18; Malitz, *Die Historien* 88 n. 100).

Posidonius also noted that some of the illustrious members of this house who had been born and lived in his time (καθ' αὐτόν; cf. καθ' ἡμᾶς, T6) compared the similarity of their appearance with the statue of Brutus (10–13). Family identification by physical similarities was accepted dogma at least since recognition scenes in Greek drama, but since the statue of the first Brutus on the Capitoline (Dio Cass. 43.45.3) was presumably a fictional creation of the imagination, this is a particularly audacious assertion, no less so if the statue had been modelled on some contemporary Brutus. It is more interesting to ask which Bruti he had in mind. It cannot be the tyrannicide (although he could have met him in Rhodes with Cato the Younger in 58 B.C.), because Plutarch by καθ' αὐτόν is contrasting Posidonius' Bruti with his own subject. The main contenders are: D. Iunius Brutus Callaicus, cos. 138; the M. Iunius Brutus of the end of the 2nd c. B.C. (Cic. *Brut.* 130); M. Iunius Brutus, tr. pl. 83 and father of the tyrannicide; and D. Iunius Brutus, cos. 77 B.C. (Broughton, II.88). Since Posidonius said ἐνίους (12), it could be more than one of these, or others. Perhaps the Brutus of Cicero's *Brut.* 130 is an unlikely contender, since he was a blot on the family name (*dedecus*), so hardly ἐπιφανῶν (11). The most famous, and the one most likely to have featured in Posidonius' *History* was the consul of 138, the successful general in Spain (Astin, *Scipio Aemilianus*), orator, philhellene and patron of Accius. If these remarks were occasioned in the *History* by him, they could have come from Bk 7 (F58; Theiler F129), even although the provenance of the statue remark probably fits a later date, when Posidonius was hobnobbing more freely with the Roman nobility.

We cannot assume from Plutarch's Greek that Posidonius himself argued historically from such evidence. He was more likely reporting the Brutan case, and in the story of the statue likeness, one hopes with some humour. Some coin portraits of contemporary Bruti are hardly flattering.

F257 Plutarch, *Marcellus* 20.1–11

CONTENT

The story of Nicias of Engyium in Sicily.

CONTEXT

Ch. 20 follows the account of the capture of Epipolae at Syracuse by Marcellus in 212 B.C.

COMMENT

1–10 Plutarch's praise of Marcellus' character. He was the first to show Greeks a quality of justice in the Roman character. Before that foreigners thought Romans fearsome in war, but lacking in consideration for others, humanity and social virtues in general. Marcellus' treatment of both states and individuals in Sicily was such that any unfair act was thought to be the responsibility of the sufferers rather than the perpetrator. Plutarch will give one example from many, with a story from Posidonius.

This is interesting in that it throws the impact of Roman virtue on the Greeks back into the 3rd century, before the Scipionic circle and Panaetius. But we cannot assume that it comes from Posidonius (see below). Marcellus' virtues are somewhat exaggerated, no doubt from a sympathetic (pos-

COMMENTARY: F257

sibly family) source. It was believed that he saw to it that Syracuse was granted ἐλευθερία and νόμοι by the senate, and a special relationship continued between his family and Syracuse (Plu. *Marc.* 23). And although the wholesale plunder of Syracuse was much condemned (Plb. 9.10; Livy, 25.40.2), Marcellus was personally praised for forbearance (Cic. 2 *Verr.* 2.4; 4.115–16, 120–3, 131; *Rep.* 1.21f: he took only Archimedes' *sphaera*). He was however building temples from his Sicilian spoils (Plut. *Marc.* 28), made rich dedications (F258), and compare the opposition recorded in ch. 27.

10–50 The story of Nicias of Engyium (a small town west of Aetna and north of Enna).

10–15 'There is a small town in Sicily, Engyium, very ancient and renowned for the epiphany of goddesses, called Mothers. The temple is said to be a foundation of Cretans, and they showed some spears there and bronze helmets, some bearing inscriptions of Meriones (one of the leaders of the Cretans at Troy, *Il.* II.651; he gave Odysseus his armour, *Il.* x.260ff) and Ulixes, i.e. Odysseus, who had dedicated them to the goddesses.' This introductory antiquarian section may be either Plutarch or Posidonius.

16–51 The story itself is worth quoting for the style: 'When this town was violently partisan for Carthage, Nicias, their leading citizen, tried to persuade it to change to the Roman side, speaking openly and plainly in the assemblies, and criticising the folly of his opponents. They were afraid of his power and standing, and so planned to seize him and hand him over to the Carthaginians. Nicias aware by now that he was actually being secretly watched (but καί, 21, should perhaps be deleted with Corais), began to come out openly with improper statements about the Mothers, and made great play with deprecatory scepticism about faith in their epiphany and standing – and his enemies were delighted that he was furnishing from his own lips the greatest excuse for his fate. Just as they were ready to seize him, there was an assembly of the citizens, and Nicias, right in the middle of a speech of advice to the people, suddenly threw himself to the ground, and after a moment or two, while, as you would expect, there was a stunned silence, he raised his head, twisted it round, produced a tremulous deep voice, gradually intensifying and sharpening the tone, and when he saw the theatre transfixed in a horrified silence, ripped off his coat, tore his shirt in bits, leapt up half naked and began to run for the exit of the theatre, shrieking that he was being chased by the Mothers, and no one had the nerve to put a finger on him or stand in his way through superstition, but cleared his path, and out he ran to the city gates, omitting no cry or gesture suitable for a man possessed and out of his mind. His wife, who was in the know and part of the trick with her husband, grabbed her children, first prostrated herself in supplication at the Hall of the goddesses, then pretending to look for her wandering husband, safely left the town without anyone stopping her. And so the pair escaped to Marcellus in Syracuse. However, after much violent misconduct on the part of the Engyianians, Marcellus arrived and had them all in bonds for punishment, and it was Nicias who burst into tears at his side, finally clasping him round the arms and legs and pleading for his fellow-countrymen, beginning with his enemies. Marcellus was shaken by this, let them all off, and did their town no harm; as for Nicias, he gave him a great deal of land and many gifts. Well, that's the account the philosopher Posidonius gave.'

This splendidly told tale carries the stamp of Posidonian narrative, and should be compared with the Athenion fragment (F253), with which stylistically it has much in common: vivid pictorial imagination, dramatic character, detailed description of voice and gesture, density of participles; also the relation between the crowd and the individual who can trick them into unreasonable reactions. There is also the side swipe at superstition (cf. F246 comm.), and above all a sardonic humour; Nicias' histrionic performance was as effective with Marcellus as it had been with his fellow-

COMMENTARY: F258

countrymen. The story is firmly centred on Nicias, not on Marcellus, which is a main reason for thinking that 1-10 is Plutarch. It also means that we have no secure indication of Posidonius' context. It may have been Engyium, not Marcellus.

See F86e.

For Goethe and the Mothers: Goethe, *Faust*, Part II, Act. I, Dark Gallery, 6216ff.

F258 Plutarch, *Marcellus* 30.6-9

CONTENT

Posidonius recorded that there was a statue of M. Claudius Marcellus (the sacker of Syracuse) in the temple of Athena at Lindos, and quotes the inscription.

CONTEXT

This is at the end of Plutarch's *Life*, after the account of Marcellus' death in reconnaissance near Venusia in 208 B.C., with Hannibal's reactions. For this, Plutarch refers to Cornelius Nepos, Valerius Maximus, Livy and Augustus Caesar. Posidonius is cited merely for the statue and its inscription.

COMMENT

1-3 Although there was a persistent Roman tradition that Marcellus himself took nothing from the plunder of Syracuse except Archimedes' globe (F257 comm.), the richness of his dedications here gives a slightly different picture (cf. *RE* III.2748f; Livy, 27.25.7; 29.11.13; Val. Max. 1.1.8; F257 comm.).

4-10 Posidonius would of course be personally familiar

COMMENTARY: F258

with this statue. It must mark some connection between the Claudii Marcelli and Rhodes, and it is noticeable that when Rhodes reaffirmed her treaty with Rome in 51 B.C., M. Claudius Marcellus was consul (Cic. *Fam.* 12.15.2). Whether Posidonius had anything to do with this or not (it was probably in the year of his death (T1a.4)), he may have known Marcellus, who was quaestor with the Younger Cato in 64. Another Marcellus possibly known to Posidonius was the aedile of 91 (*RE* 227) who studied at Athens (Cic. *De Or.* 1.57; Broughton, II.21), or indeed the Marcellus (*RE* 226) who was Marius' legate at Aquae Sextiae (102 B.C.), legate in 90 (Broughton, II.28), praetor before 73 (Broughton, II.114). The Claudius Marcellus (*RE* 225) who was consul for the third time in 152, appeared in the *History* in connection with the Celtiberian War in Spain (F271). But how could the 3rd-c. sacker of Syracuse appear in the *History* (see F86e)? The context is unknown.

9 ἐν Ἄρηϊ perhaps gave Posidonius the idea for his interpretation of the name Marcellus (F261).

10 This rather grim line fits uneasily with Plutarch's praise in F257.1–10, but suits Marcellus' nickname as the Sword of Rome (F259, F260).

11f Posidonius (or Plutarch) noted that the accuracy of the third line is preserved only if Marcellus' two proconsulships were added to his five consulships. Thus Plutarch's appendix (Plu. *Mar.* 45.12) to Posidonius' account of Marius' death (F255), that Marius was the first man to be elected consul for the seventh time, is preserved.

The text as given by the codices for the last line of the epigram is doubtful. καί makes little sense, and ἐγκαταχέω occurs nowhere else. Tzetzes reads: τὸν πολὺν ἀντιπάλοις ὃς κατέχευε φόνον. Other suggestions are given in the *app. crit.*

F259, F260 Plutarch, *Marcellus* 9.4–7; Plutarch, *Fabius Maximus* 19.1–4

CONTENT
Posidonius said that the Romans called Fabius their Buckler, but Marcellus their Sword.

CONTEXT
Both passages compare in general the contrasting and complementary virtues of the two men.

COMMENT
The Posidonian contribution is confined to the mot, because although the two passages are naturally similar, they lack other common features and are due to Plutarch's composition.

Posidonius does not claim the mot for himself, but says that the Romans gave their two consuls their nicknames. And indeed θυρεός is the common translation of *scutum* (Plb. 2.30.3 etc) and ξίφος of *gladius*. But although Fabius and Marcellus were often compared and so contrasted (Livy, 24.9.7–11; Cic. *Rep.* v.10, *Marcellus ut acer et pugnax, Maximus ut consideratus et lentus*) the nickname epithets do not seem to have survived elsewhere. Livy, 3.53.9 uses metaphor, but with general reference and for another occasion: *scuto vobis magis quam gladio opus est*. Florus, 2.6.27 seems to have caught an echo of it.

F261 Plutarch, *Marcellus* 1.1–3

CONTENT
Posidonius maintained that M. Claudius Marcellus (the sacker of Syracuse) was the first of his house to be called Marcellus, which means Martial (man of war).

COMMENTARY: F261

CONTEXT

The opening of Plutarch's *Life*. An explanation of the interpretation of Marcellus follows (4–10) with a brief sketch of Marcellus' character.

COMMENT

1-4 λέγουσι shows that Posidonius is only responsible for the information on the name Marcellus. Posidonius was wrong on both counts. A M. Claudius Marcellus was consul in 331 (Broughton, 1.143), and another, consul in 287 (Broughton, 1.185). He appears to have derived Marcellus fancifully from Mars. It is as well to have Posidonius identified for this sort of statement, for Plutarch was equally addicted to nomenclative etymology (*Cor.* 11; *Mar.* 1; *Ti. Gr.* 8.4f; *Pomp.* 13.7–11; *Fab. Max.* 1.2–5; *Cato Mai.* 1.2; *Sulla* 2.2; *Cic.* 1.3–5; *Publ.* 1.1, 10.9; *Aem. Paull.* 2.1). But for Posidonius see also F264. It is of course true that many Roman cognomina and agnomina were descriptive (Balsdon, *Romans and Aliens* 148).

4-10 appears to link as explanation (γάρ) with the foregoing: 'Because he was trained in warfare, strong of body, with a hammer-blow arm, a natural lover of war, actually displaying a great deal of arrogant gusto in combat, but for the rest of his character moderate, humane with a passion for Greek culture and literature to the point of holding the masters in esteem and admiration, though because of his commitments he was unable to match in himself his ambitions to work at his education.' This excellent sentence with its vivid succinctness may derive from Posidonius, perhaps embroidered or reshaped by Plutarch; but we can only be sure of lines 2–3.

COMMENTARY: F262

F262 Athenaeus, VI.272E-F

CONTENT

Revolt of the mining slaves in Attica, *c.* 100 B.C. 'The majority of these Athenian slaves in their thousands worked the mines in bonds. At any rate, Posidonius, the philosopher, whom you are continually mentioning, says that when they did revolt, they murdered the mine guards, seized the acropolis at Sunium, and for a long time plundered Attica. This crisis was at the time when also the second uprising of slaves in Sicily took place.'

CONTEXT

The topic on slaves began at 262B. F51 followed at 266E-F. After this fragment Frs. 265-7 (273A-B, 274A, 275A) occur at the end of the theme.

At 272B-D Musurius listed large numbers of slaves owned by Greeks. Larensis retorted (272D-E) that every Roman has a very large number of slaves, not for revenue, as with a Greek like Nicias, but as retinue (contrast Scipio in 273B, F265). Then comes this fragment on the Athenian slaves in the mines, for whose revolt Posidonius is referred to. This was the period of the second slave revolt in Sicily. There were many of these revolts. Caecilius, the rhetor from Caleacte, published a monograph on the slave wars (*FGrH* 183, F1). The Spartacus revolt at the time of the Mithridatic Wars is mentioned (272F-273A). F265 follows.

COMMENT

1-2 The first sentence occurs before the Posidonian reference, and probably does not derive from him, but leads into his reference. The contextual link is the preceding mention of

COMMENTARY: F262

Nicias (272E), much of whose wealth was derived from his slaves in the mines at Laurium (272C; Plu. *Nic.* 4). μυριάδες is no doubt an exaggeration to boost Nicias' holding, but it is also influenced by the large numbers owned by Romans (μυρίους καὶ δισμυρίους καὶ ἔτι πλείους, 272E), and also by the large figures for Greeks, cited from Timaeus, Ctesicles, Xenophon, Aristotle and Agatharchides (272B–D). δεδεμένοι may also be an exaggeration with μυριάδες. Compare Plu. *Nic. & Crassus* 1 (ἐνίων δεδεμένων), and in general Lauffer (*Die Bergwerkssklaven von Laureion* 51–6), who however suggested that it may reflect the influx of Roman capital and methods after the first revolt in the 130s. Malitz (163) thought that this sentence may derive from Caecilius, but it is more likely to be Athenaean linking.

2–3 Posidonius is described as the philosopher, not the historian. His frequent mention is addressed to Masurius, but no doubt reflects on Athenaeus himself (T65).

4 τοὺς ἐπὶ τῶν μετάλλων φύλακας: Lauffer (52) thought that these were special troops guarding the mines (comparing D.S. 3.12.3 on Ptolemaic mining) rather than overseers. But conditions in Egypt were different.

5 Laurium was in the district of Sunium. The slaves needed a guardable fortified base, if they were to last out; cf. the occupation of high ground by the slaves in Sicily, D.S. 36.2.6; 36.3.5; and in general Vogt, *Ancient Slavery* 75. As well as offering a controlling position both by land and sea, as a fortified acropolis, Sunium also had a number of towers, some of which may have stored silver coin and bullion (Young, *Hesperia* 25 (1956), 128ff, 142).

6–7 The Second Sicilian War is dated 102–99 B.C. (Malitz, 158). The date of the Attic revolt is controversial. Lauffer (236–240) argued unconvincingly for 104/3, possibly stretching to 102 B.C. Mattingly (*Historia* 20 (1971), 42f) would put it from the evidence of coinage at 99/8 B.C. Tracy (*Harv. St. Class. Phil.* 83 (1979), 232–4) argued a date 100/99 B.C. from inscriptional evidence. It is quite likely that there

COMMENTARY: F263

was some kind of delayed connection between the Sicilian and Attic revolts. Diodorus (34.2.19) assumed so (οὗ διαβοηθέντος; cf. 34.2.26) in the case of the first Sicilian and Attic revolts (F59). See also Vogt, *Ancient Slavery* 85-8.

This Attic revolt appears to have put an effective end to organised mining at Laurium (Forbes, *Studies in Ancient Technology* VII.146; Healy, *Mining* 53, 56; Richardson, *JRS* 66 (1976), 141; F239.21-4 comm.).

Did Diodorus' account of the second Sicilian slave war (D.S. 36.1-11) depend on Posidonius? Theiler printed Diodorus as F192a b, F194a b; Malitz uses Diodorus, but more hesitantly (158); Jacoby did not include this part of Diodorus in his *Anhang*. Since there is secure evidence that Diodorus used Posidonius for at least part of his account of the first slave war (D.S. 34.2.34; cf. F59), it is likely that he also used him for the second. But here the case for plain recognition is weaker: there is no positive link between the two authors, D.S. 36.1-11 shows little sign of Posidonian features, and there is no control to gauge any possible extent or fidelity of usage. We cannot assume that Diodorus simply reproduced Posidonius here, even although he may well have used him as a main source. Compare F59 comm.

The slave wars have also been linked to the contemporary problem of piracy (e.g. Malitz, 134-69; Strasburger, *JRS* 55 (1965), 40-53), and in this connection Strabo, XIV.5.2 has been enrolled as Posidonian (Malitz, 164ff, 430); but evidence is lacking.

There is also no evidence that Posidonius dealt with the Spartacus revolt in Italy in 73-71 B.C., and indeed that would appear to be beyond the likely terminal date of the *History* (F51).

F263   Strabo, VII.4.3

CONTENT

The number of sons of the Scythian prince Scilurus in the

COMMENTARY: F263

Taurian Chersonese at the time when Mithridates acquired the Crimea as a subject state, that is, about the end of the 2nd c. B.C.

CONTEXT

Strabo begins his description of the Taurian Chersonese (Crimea) at VII.4. When he comes to the town of Chersonesus, he gives a little of its history. As it was being plundered by the Scythians, it was forced to call in Mithridates as a protector. He gladly complied because he wanted to campaign against the barbarians as a preparatory exercise for war against the Romans. His general (Diophantus, VII.3.17) defeated the Scythian prince Scilurus and his sons, and acquired the Cimmerian Bosporus through the voluntary vassalage of its prince Pa(i)risades. From that time on the city of Chersonesus remained subject to Bithynia.

COMMENT

How much of this comes from Posidonius? It was not unusual for Greek cities hard pressed by barbarians to call in a protector. Chersonesus had already done this some seventy years before with Mithridates Eupator's great-uncle, Pharnaces I (Plb.25.2.13; Walbank, *Commentary* III.273f). But Mithridates' motives seem confused by hindsight. To his desire to campaign (στρατηγιῶντα is desiderative, cf. Str. IV.6.7) as far as the Dnieper (3f) is added, 'and as far as the Adriatic'. This hardly makes sense geographically, and if retained could only be an unintelligent throwback from the later Greek campaign of the Mithridatic War. Mithridates was more likely interested in the rich grain fields of the Crimea (Strabo, VII.4.6) and a possible recruiting area for his armies (Magie, *Roman Rule in Asia Minor* I.195), and as such possibly ἐπὶ 'Ρωμαίους παρασκευή (5). While the brief account of Mithridates' overlordship of the Crimea may have

COMMENTARY: F264

partly derived from Posidonius' *History*, we have no reason to assume so. Strabo himself came from Amisus, and had a special interest in the Black Sea area. Posidonius is cited specifically only for a small detail, the number of Scilurus' sons (50), and even here merely because there was disagreement. Apollonides put them at 80 (9). And it is interesting that in the later tradition it was Apollonides' figure which survived (Plu. *De Garr. Mor* 511c, who uses it for an anecdote on combined strength and separate weakness). Apollonides, a Greek geographer of the first half of the 1st c. B.C., wrote a Περίπλους τῆς Εὐρώπης (Σ A. R. 4.983.1174), which Strabo used for the far east (XI.14.4, snowworms in Armenia; XI.13.2, armed resources of Atropatian Media).

8 Palacus was the son in command of Scilurus' forces, VII.3.17, and had a fort named after him, VII.4.7.

11 The name is Parisades in VII.4.4; Παιρισάδου derives from numismatic evidence.

While Posidonius was interested in voluntary subjection as a proper relationship between ruler and ruled (F284), the case cited at F60 is both different and traditional.

F264   Plutarch, *Marius* 1.1–5

CONTENT

Posidonius argued that the praenomen, or first name, was the master name of Roman proper names, and not the third or cognomen.

CONTEXT

The question arises at the beginning of Plutarch's *Life* because Marius had only two names (1). Plutarch criticises Posidonius (9–12), adds illustrations of the nomen and the cognomen (12–18), but admits that the irregularity of usage gives rise to many discussions on this topic (18–19).

COMMENT

1-9 Posidonius' argument was based on Gaius Marius (ἐξ οὗ, 5); since he and others like him had no cognomen (third name), they would be left nameless if the cognomen was the master name (6-9).

In 1-5 the example of Marius is expanded by Quintus Sertorius and Lucius Mummius. Bauer (*Philologus* 47 (1889), 258-9) argued that this also comes from Posidonius, on the grounds that although Plutarch wrote a *Life* of Sertorius, he showed no interest in Mummius, whose exploits probably featured at the opening of Posidonius' *History* from where this passage could come. But Mummius' most famous exploits in defeating the Achaean Confederacy (Achaicus, 3) and sacking Corinth (Κόρινθον, 3) in 145 B.C. were dealt with by Polybius in Bk 39, and Posidonius' *History* began after Polybius (T1a.6). Also the case is elaborated by saying that although Mummius had a third name, Achaicus, this was an agnomen, not a cognomen, like Scipio Africanus and Metellus Macedonicus (3-5); but both Scipio and Metellus had also cognomina, so this rather confuses the original argument. It may all derive from Posidonius, but the additions look like embroidery by Plutarch, who was also fascinated by Roman nomenclature. Posidonius' argument was directed against the school of thought who maintained that the third name (cognomen) was the master name, such as Marcus Furius *Camillus*, the saviour and second founder of Rome after the Gallic invasion, 387/6 B.C.; Marcus Claudius *Marcellus*, the Sword of Rome and thwarter of Hannibal; Marcus Porcius *Cato*, presumably the Censor, and hammer of Carthage.

9-12 Plutarch objects that by Posidonius' own line of reasoning, Roman women would be nameless if the first name is the basic master name (κυρίως ... ὑπάρχειν, 11f), for no woman is given a praenomen (but is called, e.g. Claudia, Flavia etc).

COMMENTARY: F264

12–18 Plutarch expands by illustrating the other two Roman proper names:

(1) the second name, the nomen or gentile name (like Heraclidae or Pelopidae in Greek): Gnaeus *Pompeius*, Marcus *Manlius*, Gaius *Cornelius* (or Publius *Cornelius* Scipio) (13f);

(2) the third name, the cognomen, an appellative (προσ-ηγορικόν) or additional name (ἐξ ἐπιθέτου) given with respect to their natures, actions or bodily features or temper. The examples are: *Macrinus*, presumably derived from *macer*, 'lean' (is Pliny's friend in mind? *Ep.* III.7; III.4; if so, this would definitely be Plutarch's list); Titus Manlius *Torquatus*, supposedly from the *torques* or collar of the Celt he killed in a duel; Lucius Cornelius *Sulla*: for the interpretation by Plutarch of the name from his complexion, *Sull.* 2, *Cor.* 11; for other interpretations, Macr. *Sat.* 1.17.27, *RE* IV.1513–5 (15–18). On cognomina as descriptive: Plu. *Cor.* 11; Balsdon, *Romans and Aliens* 148. See also F261.

18–19 'Well', says Plutarch, 'the irregularity of customary usage gives rise to many discussions on this topic.' This was from a Greek in the early 2nd c. A.D., intimately familiar with many Roman houses, as indeed Posidonius had been two centuries before. The Greeks, accustomed to a single name, with if necessary a patronymic or identifying epithet, had from the first been, and continued to be, puzzled and fascinated by Roman proper names. Like Plutarch, Appian still in the 2nd c. A.D. felt the need to explain the system in his *Praefatio* 13; in general Balsdon, *Romans and Aliens* 146–60. The fluidity of development of the Roman system caused confusion. Although the Romans originally may have had a single name, the gentile nomen soon followed the praenomen, and the cognomen was then added, particularly in patrician families. Custom appeared to change again in the late Republic. By this time praenomina seem to have declined in usage, and after Sulla the praenomen ceased to be a distinguishing part of a man's name, with the official use of the cognomen (Balsdon, 147–50). In Cicero's dialogues the characters address each other by cognomina, unless a close relative or friend. Praenomen + nomen still occurs officially, but in the Empire the custom changed to nomen + cognomen (Balsdon, 155f). But there was an absence of rigid convention.

Greeks in the 2nd c. B.C. fastened in their writing on the praenomen as *the* name. This was the practice of Polybius (Schulze, *Zur Geschichte lateinischer Eigennamen* 507, Balsdon, 158), so Posidonius was simply following the Greek tradition in this argument. However, this fragment shows that he was already faced with and familiar with the changing official emphasis on the third name or cognomen during his lifetime. This however posed logical problems to his mind when faced with plebeian persons like Marius with no cognomen. He was not alone in this discussion, which engaged Roman antiquarians like the Auctor de Praenominibus and Varro, as well as later Greek writers like Plutarch and Appian. But clearly it was an intellectual discussion, not a practical problem, since in his *History* he used nomina or cognomina following contemporary convention.

F265, 266, 267   Athenaeus, VI.273A–B, 274A, 275A

CONTENT

Virtues of the old Romans.

CONTEXT

These fragments all come in an extended context in Athenaeus and consequently raise source questions. At 262B Athenaeus begins a topic on slaves, of which F51 (266E–F) forms an earlier section. At 272D he turns to Romans and slaves: many own large numbers. 272E-F (F262) is a parenthesis on the revolt of slaves in Attica. At 273A he returns to the contrast of the moderation and virtue of early Romans with regard to slave attendants in retinues.

A. 273A-B (F265)

The old Romans (ἀρχαῖοι, 1) were moderate and the best in all things. At least Scipio Africanus when sent out by the senate (140/139 B.C.) to settle the kingdoms of the world in order to put them in the hands of the proper people took only five slaves with him, as Polybius and Posidonius relate, and when one died on the journey, he bade his household buy and send him another in his place.

B. 273B-C

Other examples follow: Julius Caesar with only three personal slaves when crossing to Britain (from Aurunculeus Cotta's *Roman Constitution*) is contrasted with Smindyrides of Sybaris (from Chamaeleon) and Hestiaeus of Pontus (from Nicias of Nicaea).

273D But Scipio and Caesar ἐφύλασσον τοὺς πατρίους νόμους καὶ κεκολασμένως ἔχων τηροῦντες τὰ τῆς πολιτείας ἔθη.

C. 273E-F

So Romans in earlier times (ἐν τοῖς πάλαι χρόνοις) preserved their own ancestral ideals, but also took whatever was χρήσιμον καὶ καλόν from the different peoples they conquered (cf. D.S. 5.40; 23.2; Arsaces in D.S. 33.18). But now (νῦν δέ) they not only take what is useful from their enemies, but also τὰ μοχθηρὰ ζηλώματα.

D. 274A (F266)

For their ancestral habit, as Posidonius says, was hardihood, plain living and simple and uncomplicated use of material possessions in general, and moreover a remarkable piety with

COMMENTARY: F265-267

regard to the divinity, and justice and great care to avoid sinning against any man, together with the practice of agriculture.

E. 274A-C

This simplicity and frugality is exemplified in the Roman ancestral festivals.

F. 274C-E

The example of Quintus Mucius Scaevola, Quintus Aelius Tubero and Rutilius Rufus as the only men who observed the lex Fannia (161 B.C.). They adhered to the doctrine of the Stoa.

G. 274E-F

The first Roman who led the way in τῆς πολυτελείας τῆς νῦν ἀκμαζούσης was Lucullus from the Mithridatic Wars (from Nicolaus). Cato was disgusted (from Polybius 31.25; the context there is contrast with Scipio's moral restraint. The famous outburst of Cato against the price of a jar of Pontic pickled fish is repeated in a similar passage in D.S. 37.3.5-6; cf. 31.26.6-7, another Scipionic context. But these references go back at least to the mid-2nd century, and Cato's forebodings are as early as his censorship of 184 B.C.; Walbank, *Commentary* III.500, Brink and Walbank, *CQ* (1954) 105-7).

H. 275A (F267)

But in earlier times (πρότερον δέ) 'so sparing in their needs were the inhabitants of Italy that even in our time still (καὶ καθ' ἡμᾶς ἔτι)', says Posidonius, 'those who were very well off in their livelihood trained their sons to drink water for the most part, and to eat whatever there was. And often', says he, 'a father or mother would ask their son whether he wanted to have pears or walnuts for dinner, and when he had eaten some of them, that was enough, and he was off to bed.'

COMMENTARY: F265-267

I. 275B

But now (νῦν δέ) as Theopompus says in Bk I of the *Philippica*, everyone has an extravagant table, cooks and servants (this of course is 4th c. B.C.).

It can be seen at once that the whole of 273A-275B cannot come from Posidonius, because at least sections *B* and *G* derive from elsewhere. *C E F I* are indeterminate. *C* does not seem to be organically connected to either *B* or *D*. There are no indications of the origins of *E*. *F* could have derived from Posidonius, since he was interested in Rutilius in this connection (F78), and no doubt knew him (T13); and all three belonged to the Panaetian circle and had Scipionic connections (cf. Cic. *De Off.* III.62-3; Gruen, *The Hellenistic World* 1.258). But they were a famous trio. And indeed we must beware of thinking of Posidonius as the only, or even most obvious source for such common themes as *C E F* which were common coin from Polybius (e.g. 6.57.5; 31.25) and the mid-2nd century and continued long into the 1st c. in both Greek and Roman (e.g. Sallust) authors.

I shows the trap. Of course Posidonius could have referred to Theopompus, but Theopompus' reference to 4th-c. Greece fits ludicrously with νῦν δέ, which should refer to contemporary Rome. This as much as anything reveals Athenaeus' magpie methods. He had in any case been using Theopompus earlier on slaves (265B). Throughout the whole passage of Athenaeus there are distressing chronological ambiguities and discrepancies over the date of ancient virtues and 'present-day corruption': e.g. οἱ ἀρχαῖοι 'Ρωμαῖοι exampled by Scipio in *A* (F265.1-2); the pairing of Scipio and Caesar in *B*; νῦν δέ in *C*; in *G*, Lucullus in the Mithridatic Wars inaugurating ἡ πολυτέλεια ἡ νῦν ἀκμάζουσα, with Cato showing a disgust which must refer back at least to mid-2nd century (Walbank, *Commentary* III.500). Athenaeus appears to have had little sense of chronology (cf. T8), and what at first

913

COMMENTARY: F265-267

sight looks like a homogeneous account, is revealed as a jumble of miscellaneous pickings.

So it is safer to remain with the attested *A D H* as the Posidonian contribution. But could all three Posidonian fragments have come from the same context in the *History*? There are no book numbers, and Athenaeus' methods are rather against it. F265 could derive from the account of Scipio's embassy in Bk 7 (F58, F254), and it remains possible that the other two are from the same source (Jacoby, *Kommentar* 193), but I doubt it. Frs. 266, 267 seem to refer to an earlier period, and so Bk 1 has been suggested (Malitz, Theiler), or the introduction to the Social War (Malitz). But Frs. 266 and 267 are also disparate in that F267 is clearly a quotation, F266 looks like a compression. The *History* was a long book, and this was a common theme running through it; we do not really know where these passages occurred. For other views see Malitz, 90-4; Jacoby, *Kommentar* 193f; Theiler F81 (*D-H*), F125c (*A*).

COMMENT

F265

The event and date is Scipio's famous embassy to Egypt and the middle East dealt with by Posidonius in Bk 7 (F58, F254). If this fragment formed part of that account, it reinforces the evidence (F58, F254) that Posidonius was more concerned with moral than political interpretation of history.

1 For σωφροσύνη, cf. Plb. 31.25.2; 31.28.10 on Scipio.

οἱ ἀρχαῖοι Ῥωμαῖοι looks like Athenaeus' tampering to fit the story into his general theme; Scipio could hardly have been an illustration (γοῦν, 2) for Posidonius of the 'ancient' Romans.

3-4 This is a more positive view of the purpose of the embassy than is usually accepted (Gruen, *The Hellenistic World* 11.669 n. 265); but cf. D.S. 31.28b, for which see F58 comm.

COMMENTARY: F265-267

5 Polybius F76 Büttner-Wobst (Walbank, *Commentary* III.75f). We do not know where Polybius mentioned the embassy since it occurred after the terminal date of his *History*. There is no evidence that Polybius accompanied Scipio. As often, Athenaeus cites two sources.

6-7 As Crawford (*The Roman Republic*, 81) pointed out, Scipio may have ostentatiously been complying with the spirit of the lex Calpurnia of 149 B.C., which probably prohibited a governor from purchasing a slave except as a replacement.

F266

2-3 Examples of plain and simple living are given for Scipio on his embassy (D.S. 33.28b) in contrast to the effeminate luxury of Euergetes (F58), and for Scaevola in his command in Asia (97 B.C.) λιτότητι καὶ ἀφελείᾳ χρώμενος καὶ ἀκεραίῳ τῇ δικαιοσύνῃ (D.S. 37.5.1). Both are presumably later illustrations of a still earlier traditional simplicity. Clearly simplicity is not the same as εὐγνωμοσύνη and φιλανθρωπία (F257.1ff). Compare Harris, 66, 264f.

3 The importance of religion for the Romans in both public and private life had early impressed the Greeks, Plb. 6.56.6ff. Jocelyn (*J. Rel. Hist.* 4 (1966), 89-104) pointed out that this was beginning to degenerate also by the middle of the 2nd century.

4 The combination of piety and justice was a Greek conception going back at least to Plato, *Euth.* F257.4ff suggests that Marcellus was the first to show Greeks that the Romans could show a quality of justice, as well as being formidable and fearsome fighters.

5 The sudden addition of agriculture with its implication of the virtues of the old agricultural city state, or even stimulated by Cato's *De Agric.* or the Gracchan reforms, is understandable, but so abrupt as to suggest that Athenaeus was abbreviating or telescoping. In F284.77ff philosophy was said to have helped agricultural technology.

COMMENTARY: F268

F267

The reference of this fragment is clearly very early (1). It is also alone of the three fragments in being a genuine quotation, for it displays Posidonius' vivid descriptive style.

2 **καθ' ἡμᾶς**, i.e. in Posidonius' lifetime (see T6).

5 **κάρυα** may refer to any kind of nut, but was often used of walnuts.

F268 Strabo, v.2.1

CONTENT

The Ligurians live in hamlets, and it is rough ground that they plough and dig, or rather quarry as Posidonius puts it.

CONTEXT

Strabo has been proceeding from the north Adriatic, across country by Gallia Cispadana, this being ἡ πρώτη μέρις, or first part of his description of Italy. The second section (δευτέρα, 1), Liguria, round the gulf of Genoa, is completed in record fashion by this single sentence, whereupon he passes to the third section, Tyrrhenia or Etruria.

COMMENT

5 **λατομοῦντες** means mining or quarrying, but we must not take it literally here. Apart from the general absence of mines in Liguria (Theophrastus, *Lap.* 16–17 claimed that lignite was mined there as fuel for smiths; but even the mines in neighbouring Cispadana were running down, Str. v.1.12), the cast of the sentence shows that this was a Posidonian joke which had caught Strabo's fancy: the ground was so rough,

COMMENTARY: F269

the Ligurians did not so much plough it, as quarry it. Posidonius might well be remembering his visit to the Plain of la Crau (F229).

Although the wretchedness of Ligurian soil was well known (Cic. *De Leg. Agr.* II.95), it looks as if Diodorus was using Posidonius in Bk 5.39, for he expands the joke to literalism: οἱ δὲ τὴν γῆν ἐργαζόμενοι τὸ πλέον πέτρας λατομοῦσι διὰ τὴν ὑπερβολὴν τῆς τραχύτητος· οὐδεμίαν γὰρ βῶλον τοῖς ἐργαλείοις ἀνασπῶσιν ἄνευ λίθου. Diodorus had no sense of humour; Strabo, who had nothing to say on Liguria (3), makes a clean passage with the simple joke. There may be more diluted Posidoniana in D.S. 5.39, which Jacoby prints as F118 *Anhang*, and Theiler as F163b; Malitz, 174f.

F269   Strabo, III.4.17

CONTENT

Posidonius' story of the tough Ligurian woman, who paused to give birth while digging trenches, then quietly returned to finish her digging until discovered and paid off.

CONTEXT

Strabo is engaged with the barbaric character and customs of the Cantabrians in the north of Spain, traits they share with the Celts, Thracians and Scythians. But both men and women share the quality of courage (ἀνδρεία). As an example he gives Posidonius' story.

COMMENT

Tales of this kind became not uncommon: Varro, *R.R.* 2.10.9; Ps.-Arist. *Mir.* 91; Clem. Alex. *Strom.* IV.8.62.2. What is interesting is that Posidonius was not recounting an anecdote,

COMMENTARY: F270

but carefully recording a fact. Although he did not observe it himself, he gives first-hand evidence from his Massiliot host, Charmoleon, who had personally (αὐτός, 6) been overseer at the time.

'He said that he hired men and women together for digging, and one of the women went off from work nearby, gave birth and returned to work straightway, not to lose her pay; he personally noticed that she was labouring at the work, but at first didn't know the reason, later found out and dismissed her with her pay. She carried off the baby to a spring, washed and swaddled it with what she had, and brought it home safely.'

This is admirably succinct. Diodorus (4.20.2–3, F58b Jacoby; 4.19–20.3, F163a Th) has the same story, as an unassigned anecdote, ἴδιόν τι καὶ παράδοξον καθ' ἡμᾶς. It is told in entirely different words and some details are added: the woman retired to a thicket without fuss; after giving birth she covered the baby in leaves and hid it. She was discovered because the baby cried, and the overseer could not persuade her to stop work until finally in pity he paid her and released her from work. There is no mention of washing and swaddling the baby and going home safely. There is no means of knowing whether the additions in Diodorus are from Posidonius or natural embroidery of an anecdote. In spite of the additional details, Diodorus' presentation seems more diluted and less forceful.

F270   Scholia in Apollonium Rhodium, II.675

CONTENT

Posidonius said that the Hyperboreans existed, and inhabited the region of the Italian Alps.

COMMENTARY: F270

COMMENT

The Hyperboreans were embedded in Greek literature from Hesiod, *Cat.* F150.21 (Merkel.-West) on, and in Delphic legend entwined with fact since offerings supposedly from them arrived annually at Delphi (Hdt. IV.33). Herodotus (1-3) put a cold sceptical eye on their existence (IV.36), arguing that if there were Hyperboreans, there would have to be corresponding Hypernotians to the south, and he includes them in his scornful criticism of contemporary world maps. However, Heraclides Ponticus (*De An.*; Plu. *Cam.* 22; F102 Wehrli) appears to have alluded to the Gallic sack of Rome by Brennus as an army of Hyperboreans, much to Plutarch's disgust. The controversy was still alive in the 1st c. B.C., for Strabo (1.3.22) records Eratosthenes' criticism of Herodotus on the subject, and adds that although they occur in poetic legend, the use of the name is comprehensible as referring to the most northerly people.

Posidonius' position is interesting, and should be compared with his remarks on the Rhipaean Mountains (F240a.7-10), another legendary reference which Posidonius was inclined to identify with the Alps (F240a.7-10 comm.). In both cases Posidonius recognises the character of ancient legend, but argues for a factual base for it.

The Greek could mean that Posidonius said that the Hyperboreans still existed in his time and lived in the Alps. That is, the Delphic offerings proved the existence of the Hyperboreans, but while others placed them in various remote and imaginary locations, Posidonius dismissed such fancies and put them in a known territory. But I find it difficult to accept that Posidonius believed that the Hyperboreans were still actually there inhabiting the Italian Alps in his day. I think it possible that the remark occurred in a historical context explaining legend, and that Posidonius' opinion was that the Hyperboreans existed, i.e. were a historical fact, and used to inhabit the Italian Alps. That is,

COMMENTARY: F271

he was not assigning present location, but offering historical explanation for the origin of subsequent legend. The present infinitives of the scholiast are regrettably divorced from context.

F271   Strabo, III.4.13

CONTENT

Posidonius said that M. Marcellus exacted a tribute from Celtiberia of 600 talents (152/1 B.C.). He also made fun of Polybius for stating that Tiberius Gracchus overwhelmed 300 cities (in Spain), alleging that Polybius was pandering to Gracchus by calling forts cities, as happens in triumphal processions.

CONTEXT

At III.4.12 Strabo in his account of Spain turns to Celtiberia, the large highland country of north central Spain. At §13 he records that the Celtiberians were split into four divisions, and gives a reference to Polybius for the tribes and territory of the Iaccaeans and Celtiberians. After the Posidonian passage Strabo adds a sceptical comment on those who claim that there were more than 1000 cities in Iberia. Already in III.4.10 in his account of Iaccetania, Strabo had brought in Sertorius' war with Pompey.

COMMENT

1–4 War with the Celtiberians had broken out again in 153 B.C. M. Claudius Marcellus was elected consul for 152 (although consul 155) and sent out to deal with it (Plb. 35.1–5; App. *Iber.* 48f; Simon, *Roms Kriege in Spanien 154–133*,

COMMENTARY: F271

30–46). The circumstances of the treaty of 152/1 between Marcellus and the senate were confused, and Polybius' account is hostile to Marcellus, who returned to Rome after the treaty and set up three statues of his grandfather, father and himself with the arrogant inscription: *tres Marcelli novies consules* (Asconius, *In Pisonianam* 11).

The tribute exacted was a huge sum (Simon, 45). Nevertheless there is evidence of very considerable booty and triumphal trophies removed from Spain (Schulten, *CAH* VIII.308–12). Posidonius is the only evidence for this sum, and Strabo seems to doubt it, for the qualifying καίπερ clause in 2–4 is surely ironic and must come from him, not Posidonius: 'from which one has to infer that the Celtiberians were both populous and rich, although they lived in a pretty wretched country'. Strabo's juxtaposition of the two statements by Posidonius has little point unless he is maliciously contrasting what he suspects is a Posidonian exaggeration of the amount Marcellus managed to extract for Rome from the Celtiberians, with Posidonius making game of Polybius for exaggerating Tiberius Gracchus' triumphs. Since Polybius' account of Marcellus was hostile, Strabo may have felt that Posidonius was leaning in the other direction. At all events, after Marcellus' treaty, there was a standstill in Celtiberia until a ten-year war broke out in 143, finally ended by Scipio Aemilianus, who had been opposed to Marcellus back in 151 (Plb. 35.4), with the capitulation of Numantia in 133. Polybius, who was possibly with Scipio at Numantia, significantly regarded the Celtiberian War as a twenty-years war from 153–133, no doubt from the Scipionic point of view. Strabo probably knew both versions.

4–8 This refers to the earlier period of the first Celtiberian War of 181–179 terminated by Tiberius Gracchus (the consul of 177). His treaty was still remembered later (Plb. 35.2). Polybius is accused of bias (χαρίσασθαι), exaggerating the number of cities (πόλεις) taken by including petty strongholds (πύργοι, *castella, turres*) in the count. For the

COMMENTARY: F272

numbers, compare Livy 40.49.1; Florus 1.33.9; Oros. 4.20.32f. Walbank (*Commentary* III.270) pointed out that Polybius tended to use the word πόλις loosely in his *History* (3.18.1; 7.9.5; 10.27.3), but such a linguistic point would not help the charge. The joke about triumphs (ὥσπερ ἐν ταῖς θριαμβικαῖς πομπαῖς, 7f) has point, in that the actual models representing cities carried in the processions were no doubt exaggerated for effect (Cic. *De Off.* II.28; *In Pis.* 60).

9-10 Strabo adds that perhaps we may give Posidonius some credit in *that* (τοῦτο, 8); both generals and historians are easily swayed to such falsification in trying to embroider their events. But he probably includes Posidonius in the criticism. In fact, he says, those who claim that there are more than a thousand cities in Iberia are probably adding in larger hamlets (κῶμαι). The country is poor in soil, remote and wild, and the inhabitants scattered.

It is hardly possible to assign Posidonius' context. Strabo was combining the two statements for effect. Both refer to events which lie outside the scope of the *History* (T1a, F51 comm.). They may have been occasioned by his account in the *History* of the Celtiberian War of 143-133, or of the fall of Numantia; or they may have been part of a more general account of Celtiberia (of which D.S. 5.33-8 has been thought to be a part, F117 *Anhang* Jacoby, F89 Theiler), whether in the *History* or in Περὶ ὠκεανοῦ. A monograph on Marcellus is unlikely (F86e).

F272   Strabo, VII.2.1-2

CONTENT

The explanation of the Cimbrian migration and invasions (cf. F49.303ff). The theory that it was caused by the inundation of their peninsula by a great floodtide is dismissed (2-30), partly by arguments based on tidal action from

COMMENTARY: F272

Posidonius (31) attacking previous writers such as Ephorus and Cleitarchus (8-30). Strabo prefers (δικαίως, 31) Posidonius' conjectural explanation (εἰκάζει, 32), namely the piratical and nomadic character of the people (32f), which drove them as far as the Cimmerian Bosporus, which, Posidonius suggested, owes its name to them (34ff). Posidonius traced the cause of their incursions until their defeat by the Romans (36-47).

CONTEXT

Strabo's 7th Book is devoted to north and east Europe and the northern Balkans. In the first chapter he makes a division between (a) north of the Danube, from the Rhine to the Borysthenes (Dnieper) or Tanais (Don), and (b) south of the Danube. He begins with (a), starting with the area between Rhine and Elbe, and remarks that migration is a common feature of all the peoples in this part of the world. At ch. 2, he turns to the Cimbri.

COMMENT

A. Criticism of inundation theories of cause of migration (1-30)

1-2 There is an initial textual difficulty: on the subject of the Cimbri

(a) some things (τὰ μέν) are not well said,
(b) (i) τὰ δ' ἔχει πιθανότητας οὐ μετρίας (the consensus of the codd.), which ought to mean: others have plausibility not moderate, i.e. immoderate plausibility, that is, are extremely plausible.
This gives an excellent antithesis in itself, but we should then have to assume that τὰ μέν stretches to l.30, and the extreme plausibility only begins with

923

COMMENTARY: F272

the οὐ κακῶς εἰκάζει of Posidonius in 31ff (VII.2.2) and is perhaps continued in VII.2.3.

(ii) But it is undeniable that Strabo concentrates on extreme implausibility: οὔτε γὰρ ... ἀποδέξαιτ' ἄν τις (2f) ... ἔοικε δὲ πλάσματι (10) ... οὐκ εὖ δ' οὐδὲ (12f) ... οὐδ' (14) ... πῶς οὐκ ἀπίθανον (22) ... οὐδὲ Κλείταρχος εὖ (22f) ... So Cobet's emendation ἀπιθανότητος is attractive. The sense would then be: some things are wrong (οὐκ εὖ λέγεται), others are extremely implausible. Examples of both are given in 2–30: οὐκ εὖ δ' οὐδὲ ὁ φήσας (13) and πῶς οὐκ ἀπίθανον (22). Since then we are given plenty of examples of extreme implausibility but none of extreme plausibility, Cobet is probably right. The context favours 'extreme' qualifying implausibility. Corais's seclusion of οὐ before μετρίας solves nothing, and falls between two stools.

2–4 A general statement of the unacceptable cause or explanation (αἰτία) of why the Cimbri became migratory and predatory, namely that while inhabiting a peninsula they were driven (ἐξελασθεῖεν) from their territories by a great floodtide (μεγάλῃ πλημμυρίδι).

For the inundation theory, see also F49.303ff. comm. It reappears in Florus, 1.38.1 (III.3.1), *Cimbri Teutoni atque Tigurini* (!) *ab extremis Galliae profugi cum terras eorum inundasset oceanus, novas sedes toto orbe quaerentes* ... Verrius Flaccus in Paulus Festi 17M has a similar statement about the Ambrones, but with the additional idea of *subita inundatione maris*. Norden, *Die Germanische Urgeschichte* 468, argued that it derived from a tidal explanation by Artemidorus of Ephesus, for criticism of whom see Frs. 217, 119.

What is not being criticised is the phrase χερρόνησον οἰκοῦντες. It seems to have been commonly held that the Cimbri had territory by the northern ocean (Plu. *Mar.* XI.3.5;

COMMENTARY: F272

Tac. *Germ.* 37), between Rhine and Elbe (Strabo, VII.2.4; Aug. *R.G.* 26.4), and indeed on a peninsula (so also Pliny *NH* 2.167). This is usually taken to be Jutland, Schleswig-Holstein (Wells, *The German Policy of Augustus* 16, and n. 3 for bibliography). There remains a difficulty as to what stage they were distinguished from Celtic Galatae (Malitz, *Die Historien* 202; F73).

There now follow a series of linked criticisms of the inundation explanation.

(1) 'They occupy now the country they had before' (5); this is immediately supported by evidence: 'they sent Augustus as a gift the most sacred cauldron they had, asking for friendship and that their former offences be put out of mind; having got what they wanted, they departed' (5–8).

This is a factual historical counter, and that Cimbri still in the area of Jutland made overtures to Augustus is supported by Aug. *R.G.* 26.4. For the cauldron: Str. VII.2.3.

However, the argument does not tell against Cimbri being displaced by flooding on an earlier occasion. Also it would be equally, indeed more effective against the approved explanation of Posidonius as wanderlust in the character of the people (32ff). After all there was no denying that the migrations took place, and on a large scale (cf. Plu. *Mar.* XI.2; D.S. 37.1.5). It may have been intended as an argument against the land being generally uninhabitable because of flooding; but I think it more likely to have been directed against ἐξελασθεῖεν ἐκ τῶν τόπων (4), that they were driven from their country against their will. For Strabo continues by examining next πλημμυρίδι (4) and then μεγάλη (4). In any case, this counter must come from Strabo, not Posidonius, because of the reference to Augustus.

(2) (*8–10*) 'It is ridiculous that they departed from their area through losing their temper at a perpetual natural phenomenon that happens twice a day.' This clearly concentrates on πλημμυρίδι (4) in the sense of a floodtide. Since ταῦτα ... ἐπιτιμᾷ (31) implies that Strabo is following the

925

COMMENTARY: F272

objections of Posidonius, it is likely that these begin here. προσοργισθέντας (the compound recurs in Plu. *Mor.* 13D) is a vivid sarcasm. Posidonius' interest in and investigation of tidal phenomena (Frs. 214-20) would have led him to analyse critically a general explanation of flooding. This might have occurred either through (a) tidal flooding or (b) sudden inundation. (a) is treated here in its simplest form, that regular tidal action would be a ridiculous explanation.

(3) 'And that there at some time (ποτε) occurred an excessive (ὑπερβάλλουσαν) floodtide looks like fiction' (10f).

At this point the added element of 'excessive', looking back to μεγάλη (4), is added. The remaining counter arguments are variations of this (11-30). It is interesting that the term πλάσμα recurs at F49.298, in the context (294-305) again of the Cimbrian migrations and rise and fall of coastal levels. It may have been Posidonius' word.

(a) (11f) 'Although (μὲν) the ocean admits of increases in severity and slackenings, yet (δὲ, 12) they are ordered and regular when it is affected in this way.'

Since the insistence is on regularity of recurrence still, high equinoctial floodtides would seem to be in mind.

ἐπίτασις, intensity, is used with ὄμβρων for increase in severity by Plb. 4.39.9.

(b) (12-22)

(i) There is no approval for the statement that the Cimbri 'took up arms' (ὅπλα αἴρεσθαι) against the floodtides.

The source is not named, but the story goes back at least to Aristotle: *EE* 1229b 28f: οὔτ' εἰ γιγνώσκων ὅσος ὁ κίνδυνος, διὰ θυμόν, οἷον οἱ Κελτοὶ πρὸς τὰ κύματα ὅπλα ἀπαντῶσι λαβόντες . . . *EN* 1115b 26ff interestingly adds seismic phenomena to this: εἴη δ' ἄν τις μαινόμενος ἢ ἀνάλγητος, εἰ μηδὲν φόβοιτο, μήτε σεισμὸν μήτε κύματα, καθάπερ φασὶ τοὺς Κελτούς (cf. Berger, *Erdkunde* 236).

(ii) '. . . nor that the Celti (for the assumed relationship between Celti, Germani, Cimbri, VII.1.2) trained their fearlessness by enduring the engulfing of their homes and

COMMENTARY: F272

then rebuilding, and that their losses were greater from water than from war.'

This is expressly assigned to Ephorus (*FGrH* 70, F132), but the two stories (i and ii), even if they come from different sources, hang together, and are rebutted by the same argument (17–22). They are both instances of travellers' tales turned to ethical advantage. Whether or not they came ultimately from some common Peripatetic source, it is easy to see why Posidonius would be interested.

The rebuttal (17–22) merely expands that used at (a), namely regularity of occurrence (τάξις, 17), which must have made flooding familiar (γνώριμον). We are still dealing with tidal phenomena (πλημμυρίδων, 17), and as this occurs twice a day (19), it would be highly implausible that the Cimbri had not even once noticed that the ebb and flow (τὴν παλίρροιαν, 21) was natural and harmless, and occurred not only to them but to all living along the coast (20–2). So these stories are absurd (ταύτας τὰς ἀτοπίας, 19). παλίρροια (21) covers both ebb and flow, as shown in the metaphorical use in Plb. 1.82.3 and D.S. 18.59.

(c) (**23–30**) 'Cleitarchus (*FGrH* 137, F26) is not right either: the cavalry, seeing the onset of the sea, rode off, and were nearly cut off in their flight.' But doubt must be expressed that Cleitarchus said that of the Cimbri, because of a very similar tale in Curtius, IX.9, but of Alexander's army approaching the Indus delta. Curtius gives a graphic description of the panic in the army unfamiliar with strong tidal ebb and flow in the river delta. Alexander sent cavalry to the north to watch for the next tide, and *celeriter et equites ingenti cursu refugere et secutus est aestus* (IX.9.25).

However, this would be a very odd confusion on the part of Posidonius. It is still possible that Cleitarchus told a similar tale of Cimbri (or Celti), or that Strabo compressed a more involved account where Posidonius used a parallel example from the Indus delta. Anyway, the objection to this explanation is twofold:

(i) 'we know that the tide does not encroach so quickly, but imperceptibly' (25–7). But, of course, in certain areas this is not true.

(ii) 'What occurs daily and so (καί, 28) is familiar to the mind (ἔναυλον) of anyone about to approach the sea even before setting eyes on it, would hardly be likely to rouse terror, so that they ran away, as if it had occurred unexpectedly' (27–30).

This objection would be off the mark in relation to Alexander's army at the Indus delta, because the point made there is precisely how panic may arise through unfamiliarity with the phenomenon; but it would have force applied to a seabound nation like the Cimbri. The stress placed on the argument of familiarity, may lend support to the hypothesis that Posidonius (in a fuller version) used a Cleitarchean account of the army on the Indus, in contrast to the Cimbrian situation. It should be noticed that the criticism of 2, 3a b c, based on regularity and familiarity, is directed throughout against inundation by tidal action. But the context of F49.303ff (see comm.) suggests also the theory of sudden (cf. Verrius Flaccus in Paulus Festi 17) inundation from changing seabed or coastal level, possibly caused by seismic action. Posidonius himself recognised such phenomena (F227), and there were fabulous tales of seismic action in the Cimbrian area (Appian, *Ill.* 4). It is likely therefore that we have here only a part of Posidonius' criticism of the inundation explanation, that concerned with μεγάλη πλημμυρίς. There is also no reason to suggest that Posidonius wished to deny that the Cimbrian coastline may have suffered crippling encroachments of the sea, whether by regular tidal action, or on a particularly dangerous occasion when natural dykes burst. There was a widespread belief in flooding in the region (e.g. Pliny *NH* 16.2f). But what is clearly maintained is that Posidonius did not believe that that was the αἰτία of the migrations.

COMMENTARY: F272

B. *Posidonius' explanation and account of the Cimbrian migrations*
(*31–7*)

31 δικαίως. Strabo approves of Posidonius' criticism.

ταῦτα... ἐπιτιμᾷ, implies that the previous criticisms, that is the tidal criticisms, not *A* 1 (4–7) which must be Strabo (see above), come from Posidonius not Strabo. Posidonius criticises by an attack on previous writers (τοῖς συγγραφεῦσι); Ephorus and Cleitarchus were named. ἐπιτιμᾷ makes it clear that in Strabo's opinion Posidonius discarded these previous explanations. Therefore Jacoby's suggestion that Posidonius recognised both flooding and the character of the people at the same time as the explanation is contrary to the evidence, F49.303ff comm.

32–4 Posidonius' own explanation is not a bad conjecture (εἰκάζει, 32; cf. Plu. *Mar.* xi.7, ἀλλὰ ταῦτα μὲν εἰκασμῷ μᾶλλον ἢ κατὰ βέβαιον ἱστορίαν λέγεται, of the Cimmerian/Cimbrian identification, see below); so perhaps it was more like a hypothesis than a dogmatic statement (cf. T88), unless this is Strabo's limitation:

'It is because the Cimbri were piratical and nomadic that they made a campaign even as far as the country round Lake Maeotis (the Sea of Azov) . . .' This is a most important indication that Posidonius saw the explanation of historical events in the character of people rather than in proximate causation of occurrences.

Posidonius' theory finds echoes in Plu. *Mar.* xi.3, Κίμβρους ἐπονομάζουσι Γερμανοὶ τοὺς λῃστάς; D.S. 32.4, ζηλοῦσι γὰρ ἐκ παλαιοῦ λῃστεύειν ἐπὶ τὰς ἀλλοτρίας χώρας ἐπερχόμενοι . . .; Festus, p. 37.29 Lindsay, *Cimbri lingua Gallica latrones dicuntur*. All these could have been derived from Posidonius; if so, it would be interesting to know whether Posidonius took account of the linguistic evidence. It would not be very different from the Cimbrian/Cimmerian evidence to follow.

34–6 '. . . and the Cimmerian Bosporus (Straits of Kertch) was named after them, as it were [i.e.] "Cimbrian"

929

COMMENTARY: F272

Bosporus, as the Greeks called the Cimbrians Cimmerians.'

Diodorus 5.32.4 makes the same equation talking about the wildest of the Gauls (Γαλάται) who live beneath the Bears and on the borders of Scythia, . . . φασί τινες ἐν τοῖς παλαιοῖς χρόνοις τοὺς τὴν Ἀσίαν ἅπασαν καταδραμόντας, ὀνομαζομένους δὲ Κιμμερίους, τούτους εἶναι, βραχὺ τοῦ χρόνου τὴν λέξιν φθείραντος ἐν τῇ τῶν καλουμένων Κίμβρων προσηγορίᾳ.

Plutarch, *Mar.* XI.3–7 reveals a clash of theories of origin of the invading Cimbri. The commonest guess was that they were Germans from the northern ocean (3). Others thought Κελτική stretched to Lake Maeotis, and there Gauls mingled with Scyths, so that the invaders who struck west from that region were Κελτοσκύθαι (4–5). There was however an opposing theory that they were originally Cimmerians who had settled on the northern sea, whence they set off on their invasion of Italy, Κιμμερίων μὲν ἐξ ἀρχῆς, τότε δὲ Κίμβρων οὐκ ἀπὸ τρόπου προσαγορευομένων (5–7). This is plainly Posidonius' theory opposed to the Celtoscythian version. Plutarch leaves the question open. It seems that from early times the Greeks thought of 'Cimmerians' as occupying the northern borders of the world; cf. Homer, *Od.* XI.14ff (where Plutarch (and Posidonius?) clearly read Κιμμερίων although there were ancient variants), Hdt. 1.16. There was no clear notion where the Cimbri had come from. Their migrations and incursions no doubt extended over a considerable period. Frs. 280, 281 also show Posidonius' interest in linguistic ethnic identification.

36 φησὶ δὲ shows that we continue with Posidonius' account of the direction of the Cimbrian sweep across Europe.

36f 'He says that the Boii earlier inhabited the Hercynian Forest, and the Cimbri invaded this territory . . .'.

The Hercynian Forest is a wide vague term that could be used for the forest heights stretching from the Black Forest to the Carpathians; but very commonly it refers to the Bohe-

COMMENTARY: F272

mian Forest, which is where at least one sect of Boii had been: Caesar *BG* VI.24f; Mommsen, *Römische Geschichte* II.166 n. 2 (vol. III.176 n. 6 of reprint of 1976); Wells, *German Policy of Augustus* 18; Schulz, 'Der Wanderzüg der Kimbern zum Gebiete der Boier', *Germania* 13 (1929), 139-43; Jahn, 'Der Wanderweg der Kimbern', *Mannus* 24 (1932), 150-7.

38-9 '... repulsed by the Boii they descended (i.e. to the south) to the Ister (Danube) and the Scordiscan Galatae ...'. For the latter cf. F240a.29ff, F277a.32; D.S. 34/35.30a b. In other words, the Cimbri were now thought to be in the area of confluence between the Danube and the Savus (Morava), to the east of Sirmium, i.e. in the area of Pannonia and Illyricum (cf. F70) and Moesia (cf. F277). It is clear from F240a.27ff that Posidonius was also interested in the Skordiskoi (or Skordistae, F277a.32) because of their piratical character and natural lust for precious metals.

39-40 '... and then to the Teuristae and Taurisci, who are also Galatae ...'. The names are variants according to F277a.31ff on Ταυρίσκοι, Τευρίσκοι, Ταυρίσται. The Taurisci were a Norican tribe according to Strabo, IV.6.9; Alföldi, *Historia* 15 (1966), 224ff. Gold was found in their territory (Str. IV.6.12 from Polybius; Alföldi, *Noricum* 34ff, Bunbury, II.23). For the Cimbrian invasion of Noricum, Plu. *Mar.* xv.4.

40f '... then to the Helvetii, men rich in gold, but peaceloving'. The Helvetii were in south-west Germany (Baden Württemberg and south Hessen) as well as Switzerland (Thomson, *History of Ancient Geography* 189; Norden, *Germanische Urgeschichte* 225ff), but by this time they were probably concentrated also in Switzerland (Stähelin, *Zeitschrift für Schweizerische Geschichte* 15 (1935), 362). Mineralogists have suggested the valley of the Aare and Emmental, Solothurn as possible sources of ancient gold (Norden, 230f). Cf. also F240a.6ff.

41-4 'But seeing the gold from the robberies exceeded their own local gold, the Helvetii were roused to set out with the Cimbri, especially the Tigyrenoi and the Tōygeni among them.' Cf. Strabo, IV.3.3: φασὶ δὲ καὶ πολυχρύσους τοὺς Ἐλουηττίους μηδὲν μέντοι ἧττον ἐπὶ λῃστείαν τραπέσθαι, τὰς τῶν Κίμβρων εὐπορίας ἰδόντας· ἀφανισθῆναι δ' αὐτῶν τὰ δύο φῦλα, τριῶν ὄντων, κατὰ στρατείας. Despite the φασί, the source is clearly Posidonius. The date is *c*. 111 B.C. No doubt the corrupting effect of gold was a common topic, so also Lucian, *Cont.* 11. But Posidonius is giving another ethical αἰτία for an historical event. The Tigyreni were a *pagus* or canton of the Helvetii, Caes. *BG* 1.12.4; 1.27. The Tōygeni were presumably another, given as three in Strabo and four in Caesar. The Tōygeni have sometimes been identified with the Teutones, and connected with App. *Celt.* 13, e.g. by Hachmann, *Gnomon* 34 (1962), 59. But there is no evidence in favour of that theory. Strabo was perfectly familiar with the Τεύτονες as Γερμανοί and with their invasion with the Cimbri (IV.4.3). He could not have made the mistake of making them a *pagus* of the Helvetii.

44–7 'They were all destroyed by the Romans, both the Cimbri themselves and those who had joined their expedition, some after crossing the Alps into Italy.'

The Cimbri were finally defeated by Marius in the Po valley near Vercellae in 101 B.C. (Plu. *Mar.* XXIII–XXVII); he had already defeated the Teutones and Ambrones at Aix-en-Provence (Aquae Sextiae) in 102 B.C. (Plu. *Mar.* XVIII–XXI). Cf. in general Plu. *Mar.* XI–XXVII, but there is no control to determine how much of this may derive from Posidonius, or how accurately.

Jacoby (*FGrH* 87, F31; also 2C.179) adds to this fragment the next section, VII.2.3 which recounts how the Cimbrian priestesses sacrificed prisoners of war. But this section is introduced by the general plural διηγοῦνται, which is in sharp contrast to the preceding φησί referring to Posidonius. It is always possible that it may derive from Posidonius, but there is no evidence for this, and Strabo merely indicates plurality of sources. It is exactly the kind of anecdote which would be common currency in Rome.

COMMENTARY: F273

F273   Strabo, IV.1.13

CONTENT

The treasure of the Tectosages.

CONTEXT

Strabo in Gallia Narbonesis has been working westwards from Massilia, and reaches the Tectosages west of Narbonne, bounded by the Pyrenees to the south and the Cevennes (τὰ Κέμμενα) to the north. Their land is rich in gold. Strabo at this point is side-tracked into arguing that a tribe of the Galatians round Ancyra, also called Tectosages, came from a Celtic migration after a revolution here (so also XII.5.1; Magie, *Roman Rule* 1236f). He cannot trace the Celtic origins of the other two Galatian tribes any more than the original home of the Prausans, to whom Brennus, the invader of Delphi, was said to belong. This leads into F273, which is followed by F248.

COMMENT

The real story behind this fragment is the scandal of the *aurum Tolosanum*, whch became proverbial (Gell. 3.9.7). In 106 B.C. the Tectosages revolted, apparently in hope of support from the Cimbri (Dio, 27, F90; cf. F272). The consul of 106, Q. Servilius Caepio (Broughton, *Magistrates* 1.553), reduced Tolosa, and appropriated the wealth of the temples which was said to include treasure from the sack of Delphi by Brennus and the Gauls in 279 B.C. This booty disappeared en route to Rome under highly suspicious circumstances, and after the disaster of Arausio in 105, Caepio faced several charges including sacrilege and was forced into exile in Smyrna (Gell. 3.9.7; Dio 27, F90; Cic. *ND* III.74; Justin 32.3.9-11; Oros. 5.15.25).

1-10   Strabo in the first part (1-10), seems to be following

COMMENTARY: F273

the usual tale of the fearful results of sacrilege; cf. διὰ τοῦτο ἐν δυστυχήμασι καταστρέψαι τὸν βίον (7) with Gell. 3.9.7: *quisquis ex ea direptione aurum attigit misero cruciabilique exitu periit*. All this together with the additional information that Caepio's only children, two girls, became prostitutes, comes from Timagenes of Alexandria (6-9, *FGrH* 88, F11), the sharpness of whose tongue was well-known (*FGrH* 88, T1-3). In fact one seems to have married Q. Metellus Celer the elder, and the other M. Livius Drusus (Wiseman, *Cinna the Poet* 184). No doubt Caepio's fall was due to internal politics after Arausio rather than to outraged and superstitious piety, and Timagenes' patron, Faustus Sulla had no cause to love Caepiones (Wiseman, 186).

Strabo seems to hang this first account on the common belief (φασι, 1, 4) that the Tectosages' treasure was at least partly Delphian spoil from the temple. It was this sacrilegious note that had been embroidered by Timagenes. Timagenes came after Posidonius, having only arrived in Rome in 55 B.C. Strabo is more inclined to believe the earlier account of Posidonius (10f), who exploded that myth.

11-30 Strabo's version of Posidonius deserves careful analysis. Posidonius presented a succession of arguments: *A* to show that the treasure did not derive from Delphi: (1) it was unidentifiable; (2) there was no treasure of that kind at Delphi at the time; (3) even if there had been it could not have reached Gaul. *B* The treasure was local, shown (1) from the character of the people; and (2) from their habits.

A. *The treasure did not come from Delphi (11-20)*

(1) 11-15 It was unidentifiable. The treasure found at Tolosa, amounting to 15,000 talents, stored partly in sacred enclosures, partly in sacred lakes, was unworked gold and silver bullion. How did Posidonius know this figure if part of the treasure went missing? Had an initial inventory been made by Caepio before its despatch, or was it based on the state recovery from the lakes (25-7), or was it from local accounts which he ascertained later?

(2) **15-17** There was no such unmarked bullion left at Delphi to plunder.

The temple of Delphi by those days (15, i.e. 279 B.C. when Brennus and the Gauls sacked Delphi) was empty of treasure *of that sort*, because it had been stripped of unwrought bullion by the Phocians in the Sacred War; i.e. by Philomelus and his successors to pay for the Third Sacred War from 355 B.C. onwards, and finally pillaged by Philaecus.

(3) **17-20** Even if there had been, it could never have reached Tolosa in any bulk.

For even if there had been any left, (a) it was distributed over a large number of men (18); (b) it was not even likely that they reached their homeland safely, as they got away in miserable plight after the retreat from Delphi and scattered in different directions through dissension (18-20).

B. *Posidonius (and many others) maintained that the treasure was local (21-30)*

(1) **21-23** Evidence: (a) The country itself was rich in gold (21f). (b) The people were both superstitiously god-fearing (and so would not themselves plunder temples) and not extravagant in their way of life, and so all over Celtica treasure amassed (22f). D.S. 5.27 may be further evidence of these themes.

(2) **23-30** Their habits keep their own treasure safe.

(a) It was their lakes above all (rather than their temples) which preserved the inviolability of their treasure, for they sank great masses of gold and silver in them (23-5). Evidence for this (γοῦν, 25): when the Romans conquered the territory, they sold the lakes on the state's behalf, and many buyers found millstones of hammered silver in them (25-7).

(b) But the temple in Tolosa too was a holy place, strictly

COMMENTARY: F274

honoured by the surrounding population, and because of this the treasure multiplied, since many contributed, and no one dared to lay a finger on it (27–30).

Posidonius' historical approach as partly revealed by Strabo is of much interest, and radically opposed to the scandalous, credulous and superstitious accounts developed by Timagenes and his like from popular myth. It is the view of a rationalist, first attempting to explode by a series of critical historical arguments a legend underlying explanation of disaster through religious sacrilege. The latter is replaced on social historical grounds by an explanation of the circumstances of the treasure, based on the character of the Tectosages themselves; it was due to their god-fearing and frugal qualities, not to plunder. They were not piratical by nature like the Cimbri. This is characteristic of Posidonian historical explanation; cf. F272.

F274   Strabo, IV.4.5

CONTENT

Celtic display of decapitated enemy heads.

CONTEXT

At IV.4.1 Strabo had reached the Belgae whom he places on the coast north of the Loire, and the Veneti, in Brittany. In IV.4.2–6 he embarks on a Celtic ethnography of which Theiler prints IV.4.2, 4–6 as Frs. 33, 34 (F67 comm.). At IV.4.5 he refers to the simplicity and passionate nature of the Gauls, their silliness (τὸ ἀνόητον) and boastfulness, and love of ornamentation. Because of their volatility of character (κουφότης), they are visibly unbearable in victory, and scared out of their wits when beaten. F274 follows. The section ends with a description of human sacrifice involving

COMMENTARY: F274

divination; for this compare D.S. 5.31.3-4, but in Strabo it is distinguished from Posidonius by being introduced merely by λέγεται. F276 follows.

COMMENT

The only part of Strabo's Celtic ethnography expressly referred to Posidonius is F274.5-11, or even perhaps strictly, F274.5-7. That almost certainly came from Posidonius' Celtic ethnography in *History*, Bk 23. For the whole question of Posidonius' ethnography, and the evidence for it, see F67 comm. *A*.

1-5 Strabo introduces the barbarous Celtic custom of decapitating their enemies, taking the heads home on their horses' necks, and nailing them to the porches of their houses. He assigns this to the northern tribes (2), and quotes Posidonius for autoptic evidence. For the silliness of the Gauls (τῇ ἀνοίᾳ, 1; τὸ ἀνόητον above, Context), cf. the 'silly' Athenians in the Athenion fragment (ἀνοήτοις, F253.159).

5-7 'At all events, Posidonius says that he saw this sight himself often, and at first was disgusted, but afterwards took it lightly through familiarity.'

In spite of Strabo's reference to the northern tribes, this is not evidence that Posidonius penetrated to the north of Gaul. It is virtually certain that he did not. It is just possible, but highly unlikely, that he arranged a trip some way up the Rhone, perhaps with some of the wine transport ships (F67.28f), in the direction of the Allobroges (F67.37ff). But in fact he could have seen plenty of heads near Marseilles, where we know he stayed (F269). For head trophies have been found in Bouches-du-Rhône at Entremont on the hill to the north-west of Aix-en-Provence, and at Roquepertuse (Piggott, Daniel, McBurney (edd.), *France Before the Romans* 175 Pl. 77, 176 Pl. 80, 190, 216 Pl. 110); cf. also *Gallia* 1972, 519 for heads at Les Pennes-Mirabeau, 15 km from Marseilles. Apart from being another instance of Posidonius'

COMMENTARY: F275-276

efforts for autopsy, this snippet reveals his philosophical reflection on the experience. His emotions or πάθη were assuaged by familiarity; for the ethical principle, Frs. 165, 166.

7-9 A detail of character is added, probably by Posidonius (see below): 'They would embalm with cedar oil the heads of their distinguished enemies and display them to guests (to Posidonius himself?), and would not consider ransoming them even for their weight in gold.'

Celtic decapitation was well-known from early times: Plb. 2.28.10, 3.67.3; D.S. 14.115.5 (of the Gallic sack of Rome). Strabo's account (without the Posidonian autopsy) is paralleled in D.S. 5.29.4-5. Some details are the same, including not ransoming a distinguished head for its weight in gold, but expanded and elaborated, and the words are different. Either Diodorus was reproducing a fuller account in Posidonius, or he was embroidering (cf. Frs. 268, 269).

F275 Eustathius, *Commentarii ad Homeri Odysseam*, VIII.475

COMMENT

2-5 τὸ μηρίον . . . θανάτου reproduces literally from Athenaeus, F68.7-8.

F276 Strabo, IV.4.6

CONTENT

Rites of Samnite (Namnite) women on an island off the mouth of the Loire.

938

COMMENTARY: F276

CONTEXT

Follows F274. A couple of παράδοξα from Artemidorus follow.

COMMENT

1-3 'Posidonius says that there is a little island in the Ocean (i.e. the Atlantic) not far out to sea but lying at the mouth of the Loire outlet, inhabited by Samnite (Namnite) women.'

The codices of Strabo have Σαμνιτῶν. Caesar (*BG* III.9) followed by Pliny (*NH* 4.107) has Namnites, and Strabo himself at IV.2.1, Ναμνῖται. Ptolemy offers two distinct names, Σαμνῖται at II.8.6 and Ναμνῖται at II.8.8. Dionysius Periegetes does not commit himself with 'Αμνιτῶν, 571. Lasserre (Loeb) inclines to two distinct tribes in a similar area, but this seems an impossibly confusing coincidence. There must have been an early confusion (cf. Aly, IV.455). Caesar is most likely to have been right. The Greek for Samnite is Σαυνῖται.

4-7 'Possessed by Dionysus they propitiate the god with mystical ceremonies and other (propitiatory?, extraordinary?) rites; no man sets foot on the island, but the women sail over themselves, have sex with the men and return again.'

5 ἐξιλεουμένας is a strange addition after ἱλασκομένας. Most editors delete. Corais' ἐξηλλαγμέναις, strange, extraordinary, used with παράδοξα in Plb. 2.37.6; D.S. 1.94 is appealing.

7-9 'He says that it is their custom once a year to take off the roof of the temple and roof it again the same day before sunset, and each woman brings her load.' This is no doubt thatch, the common roofing in Gaul, Str. IV.4.3.

9-12 'The woman whose load slips is torn apart by the others; and they may not stop carrying the pieces (limbs) round the temple with holy cries until their frenzy stops.' What they carry round in their possessed Dionysiac frenzy is

939

COMMENTARY: F277a

clearly the bits of the unfortunate woman; μέρη codices may be right, but again Corais's μέλη is likely.

13 'It always happens that someone bumps into the woman who is going to suffer this' (and makes her drop her load).

The codices have τὴν τοῦτο πεισομένην, which Lasserre translates: 'Or il arrive toujours que l'une ou l'autre d'entre elles tombe et doive subire ce sort.' But ἐμπίπτειν cannot mean this and requires a dative. Jones's τῇ ... πεισομένῃ is an easy change and makes good sense.

Posidonius had not been to the mouth of the Loire. He had to take such tales from hearsay, but even so casts a cold rationalising eye on it; the rite of sacrifice was engineered, and the victim selected beforehand. Compare his attitude to popular myth in F273 (comm.). Compare also the straight reporting of παράδοξα from Artemidorus which follow, and which Strabo finds hard to swallow. The tale finds its proper niche in Dionysius Periegetes 570–9 (*GGM* II.140f), but without the details which fascinated Posidonius.

F277a Strabo, VII.3.2–7

CONTENT

The Mysians and *Iliad* XIII.3–5.

CONTEXT

At VII.3.1 Strabo turns to the country of the Getae, i.e. the lower Danube. He castigates credence that has been given through ignorance to mythical stories, such as the Rhipaean Mountains, Hyperboreans, Pytheas, the rape of Oreithyia by Boreas. But for Posidonius' serious attention to these subjects, see Frs. 240a, 270, 49.289, 208.24 and commentary. Strabo however intends to confine his narrative to what he has

COMMENTARY: F277a

gleaned from ancient and modern history (ἔκ τε τῆς παλαιᾶς ἱστορίας καὶ τῆς νῦν). Does this mean that the Posidonian contribution comes from the Ἱστορίαι rather than Περὶ ὠκεανοῦ? But perhaps we should not press ἱστορίας too far. However, what he does first is to turn to Homer.

COMMENT

Strabo's introduction (1–9)

1–3 The Greeks took the Getae to be Thracians, who settled on either side of the Danube, as did the Mysians, also Thracians, now (i.e. in Strabo's time) called Moesians.

Strabo was probably right about the Thracian origin, but there was considerable confusion in the 2nd and 1st centuries B.C. between Getae, Mysians/Moesians, and Dacians. Moesia was later to become a Roman province.

5–9 From the European Mysians came the Mysians who now (in Strabo's time, but cf. *Il.* II.858) live between the Lydians, Phrygians and Trojans. Other Asiatic nations whom Strabo takes to be originally Thracian emigrants are Phrygians (or Brigians, cf. Hdt. VII.73), Mygdonians, Berbykes, Maidobithynians, Bithynians, Thynians and possibly Mariandynians (F60). But whereas all these have completely evacuated Europe, the Mysians have remained there.

This was an old debate: Hdt. VII.20, 73, 75; Xanthus, *FGrH* 765, F14; Artemidorus, Str. XII.8.1 (cf. Str. XII.3.3, XII.4.8); *CAH* (2nd edn) II, Part 2A, 417 and Part 2B, 774, map 16; III, Part 1, 838, 849.

Posidonius' interpretation of *Il.* XIII.3–5 (9–46)

9–15 In Strabo's opinion (μοι δοκεῖ, 9f), Posidonius was right to conjecture (εἰκάζειν, 9), that Homer referred to the European Mysians in *Il.* XIII.3–5 which is quoted: 'Zeus turned back (πάλιν) his shining eyes, looking away (νόσφιν)

941

over the land of the horse-riding Thracians and the close-fighting Mysians.'

Strabo gives this as a Posidonian conjecture (εἰκάζειν), no more. On the category of conjecture in Posidonius, see T88.

16–25 The defence of this view depends on the interpretation of the two words, νόσφιν and πάλιν.

'For surely if (ἐπεὶ εἴ γε, 16) one were to understand the Asian Mysians, the argument would be dislocated (ἀπηρτημένος, 16; Porphyr. 1.183.1 has ἀδύνατον). For the idea of Zeus turning his gaze from the Trojans to the land of the Thracians, and including in it the land of the Mysians (i.e. the *Asian* Mysians, 16), when they are not "away" (νόσφιν, 19; Corais is possibly right to read ὄντων for ἐόντων, but the latter could easily have been written on the spur of the moment), but bordering on the Troad and situated both behind and on either side of it, and are separated from Thrace by a wide Hellespont, would be that of a man who confuses whole continents, and at the same time is not listening to the form of the words (i.e. νόσφιν and πάλιν). For "he turned πάλιν" means above all "behind him". And one who transfers his gaze from the Trojans to those behind *them* or on their flanks, transfers it well-forward, but certainly (πάνυ, 25) not behind him.'

This is *explication de texte*, but treated as historical evidence. In fact there was a good deal of ancient disagreement on the meaning of πάλιν, reflected in the scholia on this passage (Erbse, III.391f) and in Hesychius (*s.v.* πάλιν on Aristarchus). As to the argument, Porphyry (1.183.1) solved the puzzle in the opposite way: 'They say it is impossible; for if he turned from Ilium to Mysia with respect to the Asian tribes, it is impossible that he was looking at Thrace which lies in Europe. It is solved from the form of the words (ἐκ τῆς λέξεως); for he does not say that he was looking at Thrace, but at the land of the Thracians, from which they were emigrants, but living in Asia, Bithynians and Thynians, Thracian emigrants.' This hornet's nest in Homeric criticism

COMMENTARY: F277a

of this passage may have been started by Apollodorus (Str. VII.3.6; Thraemer, *Pergamos* 304-8), and possibly continued by Artemidorus (Str. XII.8.1). Eustathius 916.55 sided with Posidonius. In all cases it is based on critical literary interpretation of what Homer says.

25-33 Supporting evidence is supplied from the following lines in Homer (5-6), where the Mysians are linked to the Hippemolgi, Galactophagi and Abii, 'who are precisely the wagon-dwelling (i.e. nomad, νομάδας, Str. 1.1.6) Scyths and Sarmatians.' Strabo at 1.1.6 had regarded these names as not the real names of the people who lived furthest north (of whom Homer was ignorant), but nicknames by which Homer characterised their way of life (τῇ διαίτῃ): Mare-milkers, Curd-eaters, Resourceless (without fixed livelihood).

Strabo adds (28ff) that in his time these tribes, and particularly the Bastarnians (the Cossacks; F253.81), were mixed up with the Thracians on both sides of the Danube, and that there was Celtic intermingling too from the Boii, Scordisci and Taurisci. These names have variants: some call the Scordisci Scordistae, and the Taurisci Teurisci (A *in marg.*; codices have Ligyrisci) or Tauristae.

It is becoming difficult to know how much of this is Strabo, and how much Posidonius. Strabo resumes at 33 with λέγει δέ followed by reported speech, as if he were turning back to Posidonius. 16-33 may be Strabo's presentation based on Posidonius. In particular, 28-33, καὶ γὰρ νῦν ... may be an addition by Strabo; but on the other hand the Boii, Scordisci and Taurisci with their variant names turn up again in F272.38-40 (see comm.). Posidonius was interested in them because of their involvement with the Cimbrian migrations, but also through their character in relation to gold (F240a.29ff). But Strabo himself came from Pontus, and is personally knowledgeable about the north.

33-46 is couched in the syntax of reported speech from Posidonius.

33-7 Posidonius said that the Mysians abstain from any

COMMENTARY: F277a

living creature from piety, and so also from flocks and herds; they feed on honey, milk and cheese, live a peaceful life, and so are called 'god-fearing' and 'capnobatae' (37). For the vegetarian Mysians, compare Nicolaus of Damascus on the Galactophagi, *FGrH* 90, F104, and Eustathius (916.26f, on *Il.* xiii.6) who refers it to the Abii (but clearly taken from Strabo). καπνοβάται, 'smoke-treaders', makes little sense, but Eustathius 916.28 on *Il.* xiii.6, copying this passage, repeats it. Codex A *in marg.* has, 'τοὺς πιλοφόρους γέτας (the cap-wearing Getae) as others and Crito in his *Getica* say'. Is καπνοβάται a corruption for some kind of dress, like πηλοπατίδες (Hipp. *Art.* 62; πηλοβατίδες, Gal. 18 (1), 680): Mud-treaders, The Wellingtons? But conjecture becomes fanciful here. The word may be a corruption of a local name. But the name is supposed to have an explanation (διὰ τοῦτο, 36).

37–43 'He says that there are some Thracians who live segregated from women; they are called Ctistae ('Founders'; again the reason is obscure), are hallowed through the honour they are held in and live free from fear; in a word it was all these Homer called Hippemolgi, Galactophagi and Abii, most just of men (*Il.* xiii.5–6). He says that they are called Ἄβιοι precisely because they are segregated from women, thinking that a life bereft is a life half complete, just as Protesilaus' household was half-complete because it was bereft.'

We are clearly still on Homeric exegesis. Of Homer's lines, καὶ ἀγαυῶν Ἱππημολγῶν/γαλακτοφάγων, Ἀβίων τε δικαιοτάτων ἀνθρώπων, Posidonius seems to have taken γαλακτοφάγων as a proper name, or at least Strabo understood it so (26f). There was much ancient discussion with various solutions over all four words ἀγαυῶν, ἱππημολγῶν, γαλακτοφάγων, ἀβίων as to which were proper names and which adjectival descriptive epithets, e.g. scholia *ad loc.*; Eustathius 916.9; Nic. Dam. *FGrH* 90, F104; see Erbse, iii.392ff for the collected evidence. Posidonius takes ἄβιος as 'non-life',

COMMENTARY: F277a

because of the segregation from women, and produces a Homeric parallel of the δόμος ἡμιτελής on Protesilaus' death from *Il.* II.701. But Homeric interpretation is linked to Posidonian ethnography (T89, F280), because the elucidation of Ἄβιοι depends on his story of the Thracian celibate monks, which only appears again in Eustathius' copy (916.26f, on *Il.* XIII.6), ὁ δὲ γεωγράφος φησὶν ὅτι παρ᾽ Ὁμήρῳ Ἄβιοι οὕτω λέγονται διὰ τὸ χωρὶς εἶναι γυναικῶν. But Eustathius adds other explanations, such as Strabo's ἀνέστιοι and ἀμάξοικοι (50f), and other elements such as women and children in common, which appears to come from Nic. Dam. *FGrH* 90, F104 (Eustath. 916.12ff).

43-6 'And he said that the Mysians were called "close-combat" because they were unsacked like brave warriors; and that in Bk XIII we ought to emend "close-combat Mysians" to "close-combat Moesians".'

46 Μοισῶν τ᾽ ἀγχεμάχων is an addition by Kramer and Corais, adopted by all editors, for it is necessary for grammar and sense.

45 ⟨τρισκαι⟩δεκάτῳ Corais. Our divisions of the books of Homer appear to be the product of the 3rd c. B.C. (West, *The Ptolemaic Papyri of Homer* 18ff; Campbell, *Mnem.* 36 (1983), 154f). But it is very unusual, indeed unparalleled both in the Posidonius fragments and in Strabo, for Homer to be cited by book number. Perhaps Posidonius wished to confine this interpretation to this one reference to Mysians in Homer, to distinguish it from the other Mysian references in *Iliad* which undoubtedly refer to the Asian Mysians (II.858; X.430; XIV.512; XXIV.278). Also the title of Bk XIII, μάχη ἐπὶ ταῖς ναῦσιν, was not remarkable enough to distinguish it.

Strabo's criticism of Posidonius (47-63)

47-59 (1) Perhaps it is excessive to disturb a reading sanctioned for many years (47f). Compare F280.4f.

(2) It is much more credible that the original name was

COMMENTARY: F277a

Mysian, and changed to the present Moesian (48f). Compare F280.5ff.

(3) Strabo himself resorts to etymology and textual exegesis. For the Ἄβιοι, one could accept 'without hearth' (ἀνεστίους, 50), or 'wagon-living' (ἁμαξοίκους, 51; again in Eustathius on *Il.* XIII.6), i.e. nomad, as much as 'bereft' (χήρους, 50) (cf. Str. VII.1.3). Strabo is interpreting ἄβιος as 'without livelihood', as he explains (51–4): acts of injustice arise from contracts and a high value on property, so people who live cheaply from little (as nomads do) could reasonably be called 'most just'. This cockeyed argument supports his interpretation of Ἀβίων from the accompanying adjective, δικαιοτάτων. This in turn is supported (a) with the philosophical parallel of philosophers who couple justice with self-sufficiency in frugality, like Cynics (54–7), and (b) from the literary base of denying that Homer gives any such significance to living apart from women, especially with the Thracians and the Getae in particular (57–9). In the lacuna (59) Strabo continues with lengthy evidence in support of this from Menander. Again there is a confusion between literary and historical evidence.

59–63 Strabo concludes that we should not believe the celibate theory, but stick to the account of their zeal for religion, and abstinence from living things through piety, that comes from both Posidonius and from the rest of our historical accounts. In other words it is the special celibate sect theory which is peculiarly Posidonian, and which Strabo rejects. For still other explanations of Ἄβιοι, see Nic. Dam. *FGrH* 90, F104.

62 καὶ ἐμψύχων . . . εὐσέβειαν is extremely awkward, splitting ἔκ τε ὧν εἶπε Π and καὶ ἐκ τῆς ἄλλης ἱστορίας, and is probably a gloss as Kramer suggested.

Strabo, VII.3.5 concerns Zalmoxis (a notorious legendary figure, and a god of the Getae, Hdt. IV.94–6) supposedly establishing a powerful political priesthood among the Getae (really Dacians), which Strabo claims persisted to his own

COMMENTARY: F277b

day. Theiler prints all this as F135, taking it as an explanatory development (γάρ, VII.3.5 *init.*) of lines 60–3. But this is insecure because it is introduced by λέγεται, an indefinite which goes better with ἐκ τῆς ἄλλης ἱστορίας (63) than with the previous definite references from Posidonius. Secondly, Strabo illustrates his present-day situation by Byrebistas, King of the Dacians, and his priest Decaeneus, against whom Julius Caesar was preparing an expedition. But this was in 44 B.C. just before Caesar's death. Theiler omits this section, but the whole passage leads up to it. We should allow Strabo his head, especially in this area of special interest to him. Strabo does not allude to the campaign of C. Scribonius Curio in 75 B.C., and in any case even that falls outside the scope of Posidonius' *History*.

In VII.3.6 Strabo attacks at length Apollodorus' work *On the Catalogue of Ships in Homer*, and Eratosthenes for their scornful criticism of Homer's geographical ignorance. He continues this argument to the end of VII.3.10. Strabo had established his own position of respect for Homer as a 'geographer' against Eratosthenes and others at the beginning of his work, 1.1.2ff (cf. T77). But it is interesting that he groups Posidonius with himself, against the opposing camp of Eratosthenes and Apollodorus (63–7).

For the lively Homeric Question in geography, and for Posidonius' use of Homer, see e.g. F216 comm. This fits with his preparedness to look for a historical basis in legendary or poetic material (F270, Hyperboreans; F240a, the Rhipaean Mountains), and with his use of doxographies (T102).

F277b Eustathius, *Commentarii ad Homeri Iliadem* XIII.6

CONTENT

Germans eat roasted joints for luncheon and drink their wine undiluted. Compare F73.

COMMENTARY: F278

CONTEXT AND COMMENT

Eustathius, commenting on Abii in *Il.* XIII.6, clearly refers to Strabo VII.3.2–7 (F277a) in a passage beginning ὁ δὲ γεωγράφος φησίν . . . (916.25ff), in which Posidonius is echoed, but not by name (F277a comm.). But in the middle of this passage is inserted this reference to Posidonius on Germani, and to Pindar, F166f (Bergk), on the Centaurs giving up milk for wine. The Posidonius passage partly reproduces Athen. IV.153E (F73), but omits the statement that the Germani drank milk. The Pindar fragment is also quoted by Athenaeus elsewhere (XI.476B). Milk-drinking nomads are very much in the context because of γαλακτο-φάγων (*Il.* XIII.6). The question arises whether Eustathius found this reference to Germani in the same Posidonian context as his interpretation of the Mysians/Moesians of F277a. For the possible consequences for Germani, see F73 comm.

F278 Josephus, *Contra Apionem* II.7.79–96

CONTENT

Posidonius is accused of scandalous calumnies against Jewish worship and their temple in Jerusalem.

CONTEXT

Apion of Alexandria, pupil of Didymus and of Theon, the head of the Alexandrian school, moved later to Rome, where he was active under Claudius (Fraser, *Ptolemaic Alexandria* 1.475; *FGrH* 616). In *c. Ap.* II Josephus attacked him for his criticism of the Jews (a) on the exodus from Egypt (8–32), (b) on the Jews of Alexandria (33–78), and now (79ff) for scandalous stories of the temple at Jerusalem.

COMMENTARY: F278

COMMENT

For *c. Ap.* 11.52–113 the original Greek text is missing, and we have to rely on the Latin version made for Cassiodorus in the 6th c. A.D. Sometimes it looks as if the translator did not entirely understand his Greek original.

1–8 (§79) Josephus is astonished also at those who supplied Apion with tinder of this kind, namely Posidonius and Apollonius Molon (Molon was the name of Apollonius' father; he is usually called Apollonius Molon, so *Molonem*, Reinach, but sometimes 'of, i.e. son of, Molon', as here). The charges are twofold: (a) they blame Jews for not worshipping the same gods as other people; (b) they tell lies and invent absurd defamatory statements about the temple. (a) could presumably apply to Posidonius, and (b) might be charged against him by a Jewish apologist (if, for example, D.S. 34/35.1 derives from Posidonius).

The first story (9–13, §80)

However, Josephus proceeds to a specific example from Apion, the story of the worship of a golden ass's head in the temple at Jerusalem; an item disclosed, according to Apion, on the occasion of the entry and looting of the temple by Antiochus IV Epiphanes in 169 B.C. It is highly doubtful that this came, at least in that form, from Posidonius. Josephus himself says (§84) that it is not in Polybius, Strabo, Nicolaus of Damascus, Timagenes, Castor or Apollodorus. Moreover Diodorus (34/35.1), who carries a detailed account of Epiphanes' entry in order to contrast it with that of Antiochus VII Sidetes, relates that he found a marble statue of a heavily bearded man, whom he took to be Moses, seated on an ass. That is more likely to be derived from Posidonius, especially as it is linked to the main account of Sidetes. If Josephus is still thinking of sources for Apion, Molon is the more likely candidate. The story persisted (Tac. *Hist.* v.3f). Josephus (*c. Ap.* 11.112ff) added an embellishment of a supposed theft of the ass's head, but he attributes that to Mnaseas.

COMMENTARY: F278

In §§81–88 Josephus counters the story.

At §89 Josephus adds a second story from Apion in which he says that the authors are more concerned to defend a sacrilegious king (Epiphanes) than to give a fair and truthful account of Jewish rites and their temple (90–1). This again is hardly apposite for Posidonius, who would hardly have defended Epiphanes' actions in the temple. The events themselves (in 169 B.C.) fall outside the scope of Posidonius' *History*, and if mentioned at all must have been in comparison with Sidetes' invasion of Judaea and his taking of and visit to the temple in 134–2 B.C. (F61 comm.). But again, the account in Diodorus (34/35.1) which may derive from Posidonius, gives a favourable reaction to Sidetes' restraint and fairness, *in contrast to* Epiphanes' actions.

The second story (16–43, §§91–6)

Again Apion is said to be *propheta aliorum*, i.e. an expounder (προφήτης?) of others. The tale, in considerable detail, is that Epiphanes found in the temple a kidnapped Greek who was being fattened up for sacrifice in a year's time. There is no hint of this wild tale elsewhere, certainly not in D.S. 34/35.1. Later Josephus varies (II.109–11) between the indefinite plural of authors and the singular of Apion (*hominis autem Graeci compraehensionem finxit . . .*).

Molon is mentioned several times elsewhere (*c. Ap.* II.16, 145, 148, 236, 255, 258, 262, 270, 295), but this is the only time that Posidonius' name occurs in the whole of Josephus. There is no sign that he had read the *History*. It is more probable that anything from it came second-hand through Strabo or Nicolaus of Damascus (Schürer–Vermes–Miller, *History of the Jewish People* 1.21). But they were acquitted of these tales (*c. Ap.* II.84). Furthermore, the only main surviving evidence which is likely to have derived from Posidonius (D.S. 34/35.1) does not support Josephus' insinuations. Therefore we should disregard this as evidence for Posidonius, or at most confine it to the vague generalisations

COMMENTARY: F279

of §79 (1-6), which carry little weight; so Theiler F131b against Jacoby F69.

But how did Posidonius' name arise? Apollonius Molon, originally from Alabanda in Caria, settled, like Posidonius, in Rhodes, and taught rhetoric there. Like Posidonius, he instructed Cicero (*Brut.* 307, 312, 316), and even went on an embassy to Rome, as Posidonius had done (T28). The names of the two men were clearly associated in some contexts, and may have been mistakenly so here by Josephus. Apion's father was also named Posidonius (*FGrH* 616. T3).

F279   Strabo, XVI.2.42-3

CONTENT

The solidification of asphalt in the Dead Sea.

CONTEXT

XVI.2.34 starts on Judaea. After a general geographical introduction, Strabo embarks on a long and rather wordy excursus and homily on Moses, his successors and the Jewish religion (35-9). This is followed by a section on Pompey's reduction of Judaea and the taking of Jerusalem (40), and then a section (41) on the local flora. At 42 he turns to the most remarkable phenomenon, the Dead Sea. The whole of this has been fathered on Posidonius: Norden, *Festgabe von Harnack* (1921), 292ff; Jacoby prints 34-45, but almost all in petit; Reinhardt (originally in *Poseidonios über Ursprung und Entartung* 6ff) *RE* 639f included 35-9 in Posidonius' supposed monograph on Pompey (F79 comm.); Theiler prints 35-9 as a fragment (F133), and this is followed by Malitz, 315ff. Aly, *Strabonis Geographica* Bd. 4, 191-207, in a review section, argued that this is far from proven. Caution is certainly needed. Posidonius is mentioned only for a specific point in 43

COMMENTARY: F279

with regard to the asphalt in the Dead Sea. There is nothing to link 35–9 with the citation of Posidonius in 43; indeed Reinhardt (followed by Theiler) regarded the latter as from *On Ocean* and quite separate from the 'Moses fragment'; and this leaves the question where the latter came from (cf. F79). There is nothing else explicitly to connect the Moses fragment with Posidonius. If it displays some Greek learning and tinges of general Stoicism, there is nothing characteristically Posidonian in it, and we should perhaps remember that Strabo was a Stoic. More evidence is required for any firm conclusion.

COMMENT

At 42, in spite of an initial confusion between Lake Sirbonis and the Dead Sea, Strabo gives a remarkably clear account of the asphalt blown to the surface from the depths of the sea at irregular intervals, with bubbles rising as though the water were boiling. This is a good description of an oil seepage emitting hydrogen sulphide containing gases (Forbes, *Studies in Ancient Technology* 1.28). The peculiar properties of the Dead Sea and its asphalt fisheries were well-known, and recorded by D.S. 19.98.2, Josephus *BJ* 4.476ff, Pliny *NH* 35.178, Tacitus *Hist.* v.6 (Forbes, 1.28, 45, 55). They are all descriptive. What seems to be peculiarly Posidonian is an aetiological theory that bitumens were formed from earth under the influence of fire (F279.1), and then solidified by cold water when blown to the surface of the lake (2–4). This is also the theory underlying F235, and is the basis of Strabo's continuation of F279, where he remarks that it is reasonable that the phenomenon should occur in the middle of the lake, because the source of the fire and asphalt is at the middle of it.

Here, however, Posidonius is cited for a specific criticism in defence of his theory (9–12). In reality (τὸ μὲν οὖν συμβαῖνον τοιοῦτον, 9), it is the cold water peculiar to this lake that makes the asphalt solid (2–4), but the people pretend that by pouring urine and the like over it with incantations they

COMMENTARY: F280-281

make it solid (9-12). This is the protest of science against superstitious magic (γόητας, 9; σκήπτεσθαι ἐπῳδάς, 10).

Strabo goes on to wonder whether perhaps urine might have such a property (12-15). It is possible, although less likely, that this is still Posidonius, distinguishing the ἐπιτηδειότης of urine from ἐπῳδαί. In fact Tac. *Hist.* v.6 has the theory that bitumen coagulates with the application of vinegar, and Pliny *NH* 16.22.53 holds the same view for pitch.

11 Corais was probably right to delete ἅ.

F280, 281a, b Strabo, 1.2.34; Strabo, XVI.4.27; Eustathius, *Commentarii ad Homeri Iliadem* II.783

CONTENT

The Erembians of Homer, *Od.* IV.84, and the Aramaeans.

CONTEXT

(a) F280

In 1.2.3 Strabo's criticism of Eratosthenes' attitude to poetry leads to a long defence of Homer, who he claims shows a wide range of knowledge, and in particular of geography. At 1.2.31 he turns to the account of Menelaus' wanderings in *Od.* IV.81-5, and to the lines: Κύπρον Φοινίκην τε καὶ Αἰγυπτίους ἐπαληθείς,/Αἰθίοπάς θ' ἱκόμην καὶ Σιδονίους καὶ 'Ερεμβοὺς/ καὶ Λιβύην. They were notorious. Aristonicus, the Alexandrian grammarian, wrote a whole book *On the Wanderings of Menelaus*; Strabo will be brief. He examines the problems of Ethiopians, citing Crates, Eratosthenes and Homer himself. At §33 he turns to the Sidonians, and then in §34 to the puzzle of Erembians.

COMMENTARY: F280-281

(b) F281a

Strabo, XVI.4 is concerned with Arabia.

COMMENT

F280

Strabo's introduction (1-8)

There was much controversy over the Erembians (1). Aristonicus of Alexandria no doubt discussed it thoroughly in his *Wanderings of Menelaus* (Str. 1.2.31).

But clearly the argument was much older, since Zeno of Citium wanted to emend to Ἀραβάς τε (2-4, cf. F281a.10f). But Strabo (4-8) is conservative in textual criticism: (a) it is an old reading (cf. F277a.47f); (b) it is better to see the explanation in the variation of name, which is frequent and obvious in all nations (cf. F277a.48f, 31-3); for instance some actually do this by changing a letter (F281a.11ff).

Posidonius' explanation (8-24)

8-9 Strabo approves of Posidonius' opinion best. He does it 'by etymologising from the kinship and common element of the peoples' (9). Strabo implies that this is a frequent practice of Posidonius (κἀνταῦθα, 8; T89). At first sight the phrase seems to combine two distinct features, etymology of the name, and a common ethnology. But as the sequel shows, the etymology derives from the kinship which is reflected in the common or allied names of the peoples.

9-19 The common features of the Mesopotamian peoples. The Armenians, Syrians and Arabians show common features of race in language, way of life and physical characteristics, particularly in so far as they border each other. There may be greater differences between north and south because of latitude (παρὰ τὰ κλίματα, 15), but the common element is predominant. In 17-19 the Assyrians are added, and a people called Ἀριμάνιοι. From now on in this fragment and in F281a, whenever Aramaean, or some version of the name appears, the codices show considerable confusion. But here it is just possible that a specific sect was intended, like Ptolemy's Γαραμαῖοι (1.15.5; VI.1.2; Schwartz, *Philologus* 86 (1931), 391f; Honigman, *RE*).

19-24 Posidonius' hypothesis (εἰκάζει, 19, cf. T88) follows: the nomenclature of these tribes too is similar, because the people we call Syrians were called by the Syrians themselves (Armenians or) Aramaeans.

The first of these names is reported by the codices as Armenians, which makes no sense. It is either a corruption of another form of Aramaean like 'Αριμαίους (Friedmann; cf. F281a.26), or a silly gloss, or an intrusion from τοὺς 'Αρμενίους in line 22. τούτῳ (22) suggests one name. Posidonius was himself a Syrian Greek.

He said that (22) the names Armenians, Arabians and Erembians are like it (Aramaeans), perhaps because the ancient Greeks so called the Arabians. τάχα (23) perhaps reinforces εἰκάζει (19). For the early influx and diffusion of the Aramaeans into Mesopotamia, Assyria, Babylonia and Syria: *CAH* II².529ff; III².248ff, 297ff, 494f.

Posidonius' theory is now clear. The 'true interpretation' (etymology) of the word Erembian is found from the ethnology of the Mesopotamian peoples. Their common features are reflected in their similar names. Therefore Erembian is a variation or corruption of the common root forms Aram-, Arab-, Arm-, Aramb-. Thus historical etymology is not divined from possible interpretations of the elements of the name, but grasped from ethnographical similarities of nomenclature (see also T89 comm.).

24-9 It follows that the remainder of this fragment is not Posidonius at all but Strabo; i.e. the etymology of Erembian as εἰς τὴν ἔραν ἐμβαίνειν (to go into the earth), a popular (οἱ πολλοί, 26) identification of Erembians with Troglodytes (Cave-dwellers), and so with Arabians. Strabo actually tags this on in the middle of a sentence on Posidonius (24f: ἅμα καὶ

COMMENTARY: F280-281

τοῦ ἐτύμου συνεργοῦντος πρὸς τοῦτο. ἀπὸ γὰρ τοῦ . . .), which reveals the caution required in interpreting Posidonian sources.

F281a

All this is confirmed by F281a when Strabo returns to the question in XVI.4.27.

Again the difficulty of Erembians is stressed (7), where the Troglodyte etymology forcing (βιαζόμενοι) an interpretation of εἰς τὴν ἔραν ἐμβαίνειν (7-10), is explicitly contrasted with Posidonius (11ff).

This time Strabo adds that Posidonius slightly emended Homer's text (τῷ παρὰ μικρὸν ἀλλάξαι, 12; cf. F280.7) to καὶ Σιδονίους καὶ 'Αραμβούς. The codices have 'Ερεμβούς, which is not an emendation. The grounds for this is that Homer was calling the Arabians by the common name of his time. This emendation is contrasted with Zeno's Ἄραβάς τε, who was probably following the linguistic etymology, rather than the ethnic.

15-21 Posidonius' reasons are again developed: the Arabians consisted of three tribes, Armenians, Aramaeans and Arambians (again variations in the codices), basically homogeneous, but the difference in κλίματα or latitudes explains the variation of name. This is similar to F280.9-19, but indicates that Posidonius had a sizeable excursus or ethnography on the subject from which Strabo extracted and abbreviated. Posidonius may have dealt with the subject both in Περὶ ὠκεανοῦ (κλίματα), and in the *History*, which could also explain variations. Here Arabians are the focal point; in F280.20f it appears to be Syrians; but cf. F280.23f.

21-30 Strabo adds further examples of variation of nomenclature, among which he cites Posidonius again (22-7) for 'Αρίμοις in *Il.* II.783. Posidonius took this as another variation of Aramaean, and so the reference should be to Syria, 'for the people in Syria are Aramaeans, and perhaps the Greeks called them 'Αριμαῖοι or Ἄριμοι'.

COMMENTARY: F282

This last passage is referred to and partially reproduced in Eustathius (347.1-3) in his commentary on *Il.* II.782, in a long discussion on various opinions on the whereabouts of the Arimi. Unfortunately he substitutes ἡ Τυρία for ἡ Συρία. Compare also Strabo, XIII.4.6.

F282 Strabo, XI.9.3

CONTENT

Posidonius said that the Parthian senate was twofold, one part of Kinsmen, the other of Wise Men and Magi; in accordance with the advice of both of these it appoints the kings.

CONTEXT

In Bk XI Strabo proceeds east from the Tanais (Don), and at XI.9 arrives at Parthia. He points out correctly that originally Parthia was not large, but in his time extended west past Rhagae (12 km south of Teheran at Shahr Rey; F233) and the Caspian Gates (XI.9.1). He mentions the possession of Parthia by Arsaces (*c.* 250 B.C.) the first of the Arsacid dynasty, a Scyth from the nomad Dahae or Aparni (or Sparni or Apartani, Justin, 41.1.10), east of the Caspian Sea (cf. Str. XI.7.1; 8.2), then records their growth of power from the Euphrates to Bactria until they rivalled Rome in power. αἴτιος δ' ὁ βίος αὐτῶν καὶ τὰ ἔθη . . . (XI.9.2). However he declines to repeat his former excursus on Parthian νόμιμα which he had made in his *Historical Sketches* (F282.1-4; *FGrH* 91, F1), except for an added note from Posidonius on the Parthian senate.

COMMENT

The context thus helps to explain this strange inclusion of an

COMMENTARY: F282

isolated reference from Posidonius. Strabo has committed himself to an explanation for the growth of the Parthian empire from their natural character. This sounds very Posidonian, but it must be Strabo himself, for he refers the reader to his own historical work for its expansion, and the added note might suggest that he had not consulted Posidonius on this subject when he wrote it. The Posidonian sentence is no more than an additional footnote, but since the ancients did not employ the device of footnotes it is incorporated in the text. Theiler argued (F48 Th) that it must come from Π. ὠκεανοῦ, since Strabo would have read Posidonius' *History* for his own historical work, and now supplements from Π. ὠκεανοῦ which he used for the *Geography*. But this is an uncertain argument. It is true that ethnographical material could occur in both, as Strabo himself demonstrates, but the composition and powers of the senate sound more historical, and other surviving Parthian evidence comes from the *History* (Frs. 57, 64). Jacoby would connect the reference with the war of Demetrius Nicator, king of Syria, against the Parthians in 141 B.C. (F71, F5 Jac.; *FGrH* 91, F1); but this is a long shot. Such an isolated footnote gives few clues of origin or context.

There is a difficulty of reading in line 7. The codices have καθίστησιν, already in the Palimpsest (Π); the Epitome (E) alone offers καθίστασθαι; Casaubon suggested καθιστᾶσιν. καθίστησιν is defensible. The subject would be τὸ συνέδριον, and the sense that the senate as a whole, according to the advice of both its sections, appoints the kings (so Aly, *Strabonis Geographica* IV.425f). This authority of appointment by the senate is borne out by Justin (Trogus) (42.1.1; 42.4.16; 42.5.1). The situation in the Arsacid succession was complicated. The king seems to have had a voice during his lifetime in the appointment of his successor (Justin, 42.4.14), but the senate could make its own choice from the Arsacid family. So the regal house had a right to the throne, but no individual had. The senate could also depose a king as it did Mithridates

COMMENTARY: F283

(Justin, 42.4.1). See Widengren *ANRW* II.9.1, 237-9. The double composition of the senate is reported only here. The Kinsmen clearly included the royal family and relations, but seemingly also philarsacid nobles (Str. XVI.1.28; Colledge, *The Parthians* 61); the second section comprised priests, judges, intellectuals. Since a royal candidate could not come from the latter, ἐξ ὧν ἀμφοῖν (6) must mean, 'in accordance with the advice of both sections'.

See also Frs. 57, 64.

F283 Athenaeus, II.45F

CONTENT

Friendship toasts among the Carmani.

CONTEXT

Athenaeus' discussion is on drinking. The special topic of προπινεῖν or drinking toasts was broached at 45D in a medical context on the bad digestive effect of too many toasts (cf. Wellmann, *Hermes* 35 (1900), 364f). The fragment is followed by a quotation from Alexis on the benefits to health of inhaling perfume. It is however extremely unlikely that Posidonius' context was medicinal.

COMMENT

2-5 'As marks of friendship in their cups, they open facial veins, mix the dripping blood in their drink and quaff it off in the belief that to taste each other's blood is the ultimate in friendship.' Posidonius condemned the custom (1), probably not for medical reasons, but as a barbaric practice, which no doubt revolted him in the same way as Gallic head trophies had done (F274).

COMMENTARY: F284

5–8 The following sentence has been suspected as not from Posidonius because of the following link with Alexis (Context; Jacoby F72; Theiler F116); but Athenaeus continues in indirect quotation, and there is no need to doubt Posidonius' interest in the added detail: 'After swallowing, they anoint their heads with rose perfume preferably, (otherwise with quince perfume) otherwise with iris perfume (orris) or nard to repel the effects from the potion and avoid harm from the fumes of the wine.'

6 There appears to be a doublet of εἰ δὲ μή. Sandbach would cut the first group, and Desrousseaux and Astruc transfer the second from the end of the sentence. Perhaps the simplest solution would be: εἰ δε μή, μηλίνῳ [εἰ δὲ μ]ἢ ἰρίνῳ ἢ ναρδίνῳ. All three were recognised bases for perfumes; Theophr. *Od.* 26 for μύρον μήλινον.

Carmania (Kirmān) was the south-eastern part of Iran, its coastline straddling the Strait of Hormuz from about Qeys in the Persian Gulf eastwards originally to about Ra's al Kūh on the Gulf of Oman, but expanding to Ra's Jaddī; it was a large province stretching well north between Persis and Gedrosia (Str. xv.2.14). It was well known from the Alexander historians, Nearchus (Arr. *Ind.* 27, 32–8, 43; *FGrH* 133, F1) and Onesicritus (Str. xv.2.14; *FGrH* 134, F24); see also Arr. *An.* vi.27f. Posidonius must have included some remarks on it in his eastern ethnographies, probably in the early Bks 3–5 (Frs. 54–7). But Athenaeus has left no clue for its context.

F284 Seneca, *Epistulae* 90.5–13; 20–5; 30–2

CONTENT

The Golden Age; the political and cultural development of man.

CONTEXT

Seneca's Letter is a paean to philosophy and its ultimate

COMMENTARY: F284

importance for human beings as the culminating aim of human endeavour. He argues (§§1-4) that our debt to philosophy is even greater than our debt to the gods; to the latter we owe life, but to the former, the good life (§1). Philosophy is not given to all, but it is available to all; so it is independent of chance, and more valued in that we ourselves have to work for it (§2). All the virtues and religion are its companions. It teaches worship of the divine and love of the human. Human fellowship (*consortium*) remained inviolate until avarice destroyed and impoverished it (§3; a very Senecan theme). The earliest human generations followed nature and had leader and law in one. *Potioribus deteriora summittere* is a natural law (for this, F60 comm.). With humans what is best ranks highest. So the leader was chosen for his mind (*animo*). Those races were happiest where a man could not be more powerful unless he was better. There is no danger in a man having as much power as he likes, when he thinks that he has power to do only what he thinks he ought to do (§4). This leads to Posidonius on the 'philosophers' of the Golden Age.

COMMENT

A. *The Golden Age in a philosophy of political and social development (1-19)*

(i) Posidonius' Golden Age (1-11, §5)

'Therefore (*ergo*; presumably from Seneca; see Context) in the era which people call 'golden', Posidonius holds that sovereignty was in the power of philosophers (*sapientes*). They held men's hands in check, protected the weak from the strong, persuaded and dissuaded (i.e. used argument, not force), pointed out advantage and disadvantage (*utilia*, συμφέρον; i.e. the canon of conduct for the ordinary man). It was their wisdom (*prudentia*) that saw for their people's needs, their courage that warded off danger, their beneficence that

COMMENTARY: F284

advanced and distinguished their subjects. For them command was a duty, not an attribute of power.'

It is difficult to know how close this is to the original; it has a Latin rhetorical ring of expression and style.

'No one made trial of his powers against those who had first given him the power, nor did anyone have inclination or cause for wrong-doing, since good commander implies good subject, and the king could make no greater threat to malcontents than his own abdication.'

This is very Platonic, but for the Posidonian application, see F60.

(ii) The second stage of development (11–19, §6)

When kingship turned to tyranny through the inroads of vice (in Seneca this would be avarice and luxury, cf. Context and below), then there was need of laws, but these too at first wise men (philosophers, *sapientes*) brought forward (cf. Cic. *Tusc.* v.5, *tu inventrix legum*). This is substantiated by actual examples: Solon (one of the Seven Wise Men; F49.299), Lycurgus (cf. Cic. *Tusc.* v.7), Zaleucus and Charondas (Arist. *Pol.* 1274a 22) who learned their legal justice in the quiet holy retreat of Pythagoras (cf. T91, T95; but contrast F253.115), rather than in public forum and legal office.

But we have now passed from 'Golden Age' to historical account. Does that mean that Posidonius regarded his Golden Age also as historical, or saw no difficulty in passing from myth to history? Versions of the Golden Age run from Hesiod, *Op.* 109ff through the whole of Classical literature and thought. Of the earlier Greek versions, the most relevant are Plato's myth in *Politicus* 271a–272b on the γηγενὲς γένος which Posidonius in effect changed from supervision by gods to supervision by philosophers; and that of Dicaearchus (F49 Wehrli), whose socio-political account of τοὺς παλαιούς, ἐγγὺς θεῶν ... γεγονότας βελτίστους τε ὄντας φύσει καὶ τὸν ἄριστον ἐξηκότας βίον, is marked by absence of war and internal strife and antedates the advent of the τέχναι. But there is also considerable evidence of the theory of a Golden Age of primeval man in the Roman world of the 1st centuries B.C. and A.D., where it was applied to the actual development of Rome. The conjunction is recognised and deliberate in Cicero *Rep.* II.21-2, but simply stated elsewhere as an initial golden age under the first kings of Rome with the introduction of law when this broke down (Cic. *De Off.* II.41-2; Lucr. V.1105-44; Tac. *Ann.* III.26). In a passage of Lactantius (*Inst. Div.* 7.15.4) assigned to Seneca himself (on authenticity, Griffin, *JRS* 62 (1972), 19), the six ages of man are imposed on the history of Rome, beginning with the education of infant innocence under Romulus, followed by a legal system after the tyranny (in general, Griffin, *Seneca* 194-201).

B. Philosophy of cultural development (20-130)

(1) General objections to Posidonius (20-47)

19ff So far Seneca agrees with Posidonius (but not completely, see below), but not with his view that philosophy invented the arts and sciences of everyday life. Seneca will not claim for philosophy the honour of the workshop of the artisan. Seneca by *fabricae* (22) deliberately depreciates the claim.

22-4 Quotation from Posidonius (§7): 'It was philosophy which taught men, who before had been sheltered in caves or by some undermined rock or in the trunk of a hollow tree, to erect roofed houses.' *Sparsos* (22) has point: philosophy is the author of civilisation, which involved society, which entails living together. So Cicero, *Tusc.* v.5: *Tu urbes peperisti, tu* DISSIPATOS *homines in societatem vitae convocasti, tu eos inter se primo domiciliis... iunxisti.* Cf. *Tusc.* 1.62, and the myth of Protagoras in Plato, *Prot.* 320dff.

24-47 (§§7-10) Seneca's objections.
Philosophy did not think out these devices of piling storey on storey, or city elbowing city, or fish farms for the luxury of the gourmet, nor locks and bolts and beetling dangerous

COMMENTARY: F284

garrets. This is the work of avarice. *Luxuria* (28) and *avaritia* (31) are keynotes of Seneca, who is using the rhetorical device of excess. Blessed was the era before architects. He goes on to contrast (§§9–10) early simplicity and peace of mind (*securi*, 45; cf. §§17, 38, 41) with the luxury created by the arts. But Posidonius clearly did not have in mind technological luxury, but the rise of a cultural civilisation through the arts. He countered the popular mythology of a Prometheus or divine dispensation as in Protagoras, with a purely human progression sprung from rationality.

(2) A series of objections in detail to Posidonius
(47–60, §§11–13)

(i) **47–52** (§11) Seneca disagrees with Posidonius that tradesmen's tools were devised by wise men. Seneca jibes: did they then devise snares and traps (quoting Vergil, *G* 1.139f)? No, says Seneca, that was *sagacitas* (cleverness) not *sapientia* (wisdom); compare Dicaearchus in D.L. 1.40 (F30 Wehrli): the Seven Wise Men were not philosophers, συνετούς δέ τινας καὶ νομοθετικούς. But where did Posidonius say or imply this, and in what context? Is Seneca perhaps deliberately interpreting him literally?

(ii) **52–6** (§12) 'Philosophers discovered iron and copper mines, when the earth, burnt by forest fires in molten form cast surface veins of ore.' Seneca objects that rather they were discovered by entrepreneurs (55f).

But he gives himself away by his semi-quotation. For Posidonius on the story of molten earth from forest fires becoming minerals: F239.3ff, F240a.9f and comm. It is of course nonsense to say that philosophers 'invented' mines. Frs. 239, 240 show that Posidonius as a philosopher was interested in the origin and explanation of metals and was willing to examine critically the old story that they were formed from molten earth. Also Posidonius' context (F240) seems to be an ethical one about the effect of such wealth on human beings. And lastly, this particular passage was

COMMENTARY: F284

probably raised in an ethnography in the *History*, so that Seneca is plucking supposed evidence for his criticism from various sources in this Letter, not from one passage on 'The Golden Age'. This section is a warning that we should treat other sections in this Letter with some reserve.

(iii) 56-60 (§13) The nice question whether the hammer or the tongs came first worries Seneca less that Posidonius. Both were invented by someone with a talent that was nimble and sharp rather than great and sublime.

Is this a rhetorical joke by Seneca, or was there some remark in Posidonius about the smith's tools, the σφῦρα and θερμαστρίς? In fact the smith's tools are used as an analogy (ὥσπερ ἐν τῇ χαλκευτικῇ ἡ σφῦρα καὶ ὁ ἄκμων) for the instrumental cause of πνεῦμα in nature by Arist. *GA* 789b 11. The example may have persisted in argument. But there was also a popular fashion of assigning mythical inventors for the arts and sciences (e.g. Pliny *NH* 7.191ff). Pliny (195) made Cinyras, the mythical hero of Cyprus, the inventor of tiles, mining, tongs, hammer, crowbar and anvil. Posidonius may have countered such amiable nonsense by a more philosophical analysis. But this is speculation, and it may simply be a case of Senecan rhetorical scorn.

§§14-19 Seneca contrasts philosophers and artisans, in which again is the contrast between natural simplicity of the satisfaction of necessary needs, and luxury which presses the ingenuity of the arts into the service of the vices by creating the superfluous and the injurious as fodder for lust and desire. So Seneca sees the *artes* as the fomentors of luxury, greed and vice, and so hardly the creation of philosophy. Posidonius sees them as the necessary tools of the philosopher (F90).

(3) Individual arts (62-100, §§20-3)

62-4 'It is hard to believe how easily the charms of eloquence lead even great men from the truth.' Seneca himself has hardly been sparing his rhetorical efforts. 'Look at

COMMENTARY: F284

Posidonius, in my judgement one of those who have contributed most to philosophy' on weaving.

(a) 65–77 (§20) *Weaving*

Posidonius describing the intricacies of weaving (65–70) 'says that the art of weaving too was discovered by philosophers' (70). Seneca says that such artistic intricacy was a later discovery. Later than what? Philosophy is not confined to the Golden Age, although Seneca implies that Posidonius thought so (125).

74–7 contain typically irrelevant Senecan argument. What would have happened if Posidonius had seen the shameless see-through garments of Seneca's own day? But did Posidonius actually say that philosophers 'invented' weaving, or that the most efficient operation to the desired end was ultimately endorsed through philosophy?

(b) 77–83 (§21) *Farming*

78 nec minus facunde: Seneca keeps implying that Posidonius only gets away with his absurd position through his eloquence. Posidonius describes the proper method of ploughing, sowing and weeding (78–81). This too he assigns as the job of the philosopher, as if even today agriculturalists were not inventing new devices to increase the yield (81f). But did Posidonius actually say that this was the *opus* of the philosopher, or that it was an ἔργον or function of philosophy to discriminate the best method for the end? The argument from improvement again assumes that Posidonius meant a once-for-all 'invention' in the 'Golden Age'.

(c) 84–99 (§§22–3) *Baking*

Here we supposedly have a quotation from Posidonius on how the philosopher will have started to make bread through imitating nature (86–99): 'Grain is crushed in the mouth between hard teeth meeting together; whatever escapes is brought back by the tongue to the teeth again; then it is

COMMENTARY: F284

mixed together by the saliva to enable it more easily to pass through the mucous passage of the throat. When it comes into the stomach it undergoes coction by the even heat in it; then at last it is assimilated to the body. Taking this as a model, someone put one rough stone on another to copy teeth, which work by one stationary set waiting for the movement of the other set; then the grain is crushed by the grinding of the two, and is returned again and again until it is reduced to a fine powder by the constant grinding. Then he sprinkled water on the flour, and working it thoroughly by continual kneading fashioned a loaf, which in the first place was cooked in a glowing hot earthenware pot by ashes, and subsequently by the gradual discovery of ovens and other appliances whose heat was more subject to control.'

Seneca's comment on this interesting passage is to remark that Posidonius will be assigning the discovery of shoemaking to philosophers next, a remark on a par with some of Socrates' interlocutors. The first part (87–91) has a more detailed parallel in Cicero *ND* II.134–6, where the natural disposition and function of the human organs for digestion are seen as a mark of providence in the organisation of nature. In general for learning from nature, Vitr. II.1; and for innumerable arts discovered through the teaching of nature, Cicero, *Leg.* 1.26.

There are medical undertones here, particularly the concept of digestion as coction (90). Aristotle in *Meteor.* IV.2–3 related natural processes of coction and forms of cooking; μιμεῖται γὰρ ἡ τέχνη τὴν φύσιν (381b 6). Earlier still in the 5th c. B.C. the medical tract *Ancient Medicine* (chs. IIIff) argued that the ἀρχή of the science of medicine was grounded in the natural processes of human diet. This is the more interesting in that the author appears to confuse and use ἀρχή both as philosophical starting point or explanatory principle and as historical starting point of how medicine actually began to form. This type of confusion persisted in ancient accounts. Was Protagoras' myth of the growth of human society and justice, or that of Plato in *Plt.* 271df, an historical account or

COMMENTARY: F284

merely a mythical explanation? The argument over Plato's *Timaeus* was notorious. The same problems are inherent in any 'Golden Age' theories (see above, 11–19). Did Posidonius believe in this as an historical account or as a rational aetiological analysis of philosophy? It may have been both.

100–10 (§§24–5) Seneca objects that all this is the product of reason (*ratio*), but not of *recta ratio* (ὀρθὸς λόγος), the function of the *sapiens* or philosopher (cf. Dicaearchus, F30 Wehrli), any more than the art of nautical steering, rationally imitated from fish. But he quotes Posidonius again: 'All these things the philosopher indeed discovered, but handed over to his humbler agents what was too insignificant for him to deal with himself.' No, replies Seneca; they were thought out by none other than those who attend to them today.

Seneca's *sordidioribus ministris* (109) points to Posidonius' real basic position. In F90.21ff Posidonius was careful to distinguish between philosophy and the arts and sciences, but regarded the latter as the necessary tools of the former: *aliquod nobis praestat geometria ministerium: sic philosophiae necessaria est quomodo ipsi faber, sed nec hic geometriae pars est nec illa philosophiae* (F90.23–26; cf. F134.57ff; Kidd, *A & A* 24 (1978), 7–15). Yet philosophy was also in turn necessary for the arts and sciences (F18).

§§25–9 Seneca gives examples of recent inventions, the discoveries *vilissimorum mancipiorum*, not of philosophers. Philosophy trains the mind, not the hand. *Non est, inquam, instrumentorum ad usus necessarios opifex* (§27); but is this a travesty of F90.23ff? He then proceeds to a description of philosophy (§§27–9), with which Posidonius would not disagree.

111–14 (§30) 'The philosopher has not withdrawn, say I (i.e. Seneca), as Posidonius thinks, from these arts; he never approached them at all.'

This is the nub of disagreement between Seneca and Posidonius. Seneca, whose subject after all in this Letter was a panegyric of philosophy itself, wishes to draw a sharp and excluding line between philosophy and the arts and sciences; Posidonius, while distinguishing them, wanted to emphasise their natural and necessary relationship. This is borne out, not only by Frs. 18 and 90, but by his whole philosophy, with its organic interests in the sciences and history, and with his aetiological analyses traced from top to bottom. But since Seneca presses his attack to rhetorical limits, the lengths to which Posidonius was prepared to go in details are not entirely clear.

(4) Philosopher inventors (114–30, §§31–2)

(i) **114–25 (§31)** 'Anacharsis, he says, invented the potter's wheel, by the circular motion of which vessels are shaped.'

Anacharsis was a 6th-c. B.C. Scythian prince, early renowned for his wisdom (Hdt. IV.76f), later added to the Seven Sages (Str. VII.3.9; D.L. I.13). In hellenistic literature he became a noble savage of Cynic hue (e.g. Str. VII.3.8), with a corpus of invented *Letters*, one of which is translated by Cicero, *Tusc.* V.90.

But Seneca goes on to say: 'Then because the potter's wheel is found in Homer (*Il.* XVIII.600f), they prefer (*malunt*) to think that the verses are spurious, not the story.' This is somewhat suspicious. Strabo (VII.3.9) had said that it was Ephorus who declared that Anacharsis invented the potter's wheel; and Strabo at once says that this is impossible because Homer knew of it, quoting *Il.* XVIII.600. Strabo has no mention of Posidonius, although the context includes Ephorus' interpretation of *Il.*XIII.3–6, of which Strabo had just given Posidonius' account (F277). Did Seneca confuse Ephorus and Posidonius? Or did he mean that Posidonius accepted Ephorus' statement, and so rejected *Il.* XVIII.600 as spurious (cf. F292 comm.)? But *malunt* (117) is plural, not singular. Editors emend to *maluit*. Perhaps this is right; it seems to have been a well-known crux. But doubts remain; Posidonius tends to defend Homer.

Seneca does not believe the story, but even if Anacharsis

had invented the wheel, it would not have been because he was a philosopher. If a philosopher wins a race, he does so *qua* being fast, not *qua* philosopher. This is a fair point. His other point (125), that inventions have taken place after the Golden Age, depends on the assumption that Posidonius thought that philosophers existed only in the Golden Age, but not subsequently (*postquam sapientem invenire desimus*), which can hardly be true, and can be no more than a rhetorical attempt to score a point.

(ii) 126–30 (§32) 'Democritus, he says, is said to have discovered the arch so that the gradual curvature of inward leaning stones be held fast by the keystone.'

This is vague (*invenisse dicitur*, 126) and there is no mention elsewhere of it. Seneca's unsubstantiated counter of curved arches before Democritus is followed by a sneering riposte (§33) that Posidonius has forgotten to mention that Democritus discovered how to make ivory pliant and how to melt down a pebble and turn it into an emerald. This seems to come from the Bolus literature attributed to Democritus, to which level Seneca is trying to reduce the attribution to Posidonius (DK, *Vors.* 68, 300, 14).

Seneca finishes the *Letter* with his own views in opposition to Posidonius (§§34–46). Philosophy is concerned with higher things than the arts: truth, nature, the law of life, a true scale of relative values with moral virtue as the only good (§§34–5). In the primeval era before the arts and sciences there was no philosophy either but humans learned by experience. It is true that this was the most admirable and happy era because men simply followed nature before the corrupting influences of avarice and luxury began (§§36–43). Their happiness was the happiness of innocence and ignorance, not of philosophy, their conduct a similitude of virtue, not virtue itself which is not bestowed by nature, but like goodness and philosophy has to be worked for like an art (§§44–6). This again seems to posit an historical picture of the Golden Age, and to assume this in Posidonius, that there was indeed a primeval Golden Age of

COMMENTARY: F285-286

philosophers, followed by degeneration, including that of philosophy itself. But even if it were a theoretical picture, Seneca is assuming what he claims to be a contradictory direction to Posidonius. For him philosophy is the final end to which human kind progresses, while he thinks that for Posidonius it is the beginning from which all else flows. But the directions need not be contradictory unless and only unless the account is intended as historical. For Plato had already argued for both the upward and downward paths; and in this Posidonius probably agreed with Plato.

Part of the trouble may lie in the interpretation of *sapiens* (philosopher). Sextus (*Adv. Math.* IX.28) in a passage which seems to refer to Posidonius says: 'Some of the later Stoics declare that the first men, the earth-born, greatly surpassed the men of today in intelligence (συνέσει: Seneca's *sagacitas*), as one can learn from the comparison of ourselves with the ancients, and that those heroes possessed an extra organ as it were of perception, and apprehended divine nature and discerned certain powers of the gods (i.e. philosophers?).'

HISTORY OF PHILOSOPHY

F285, F286   Strabo, XVI.2.24; Sextus
Empiricus, *Adversus Mathematicos*
IX.359–64

CONTENT

Posidonius said that the doctrine of atoms was ancient and derived from Mochus, a man from Sidon, who was born before the Trojan period.

COMMENTARY: F285-286

CONTEXT

At XVI.2.22 Strabo passed from Coele Syria to Phoenicia. §23 is concerned with Tyre. The Sextus passage is in his concise doxography of theories of the fundamental στοιχεῖα in the section Περὶ σώματος.

COMMENT

A. *The extent of the Posidonian fragment*

Besides the parenthesis on Mochus, the ascription of astronomy and arithmetic to the Sidonians (F285.1-5) has been thought to be Posidonian (Theiler, F57a, II.65). This is unlikely from the context. Strabo lists the traditional (παραδέδονται, F285.1) accomplishments of the people of Sidon, first, in arts and crafts (1) for which he evidences Homer (ὁ ποιητής, 2); presumably *Il.* XXIII.743, the silver mixing-bowl as the prize for the foot race, ἐπεὶ Σιδόνες πολυδαίδαλοι εὖ ἤσκησαν. 'In addition, they had an old reputation as philosophers (φιλόσοφοι, 3) in astronomy and science of numbers, arising from calculation and sailing at night (3-4, chiasmus); for each is germane to trade and shipping (4-5); just as geometry is said to be an invention of the Egyptians from measuring the land, rendered necessary from the Nile confusing the boundaries by its rising (5-7). So people are convinced that geometry came to the Greeks from Egyptians, but astronomy and science of numbers from Phoenicians (8-9).' But Strabo repeats this same theory about the origins of geometry and arithmetic in XVII.1.3, although he confines there the contribution of the Phoenicians to λογιστική and ἀριθμητική. So far then this section is likely to be Strabo, not Posidonius. But further, Strabo now turns from past history to the present day, νυνὶ δέ (9): 'but in present times it is possible to get the very greatest abundance of all the rest of philosophy too (πάσης καὶ τῆς ἄλλης φιλοσοφίας) from these cities

972

(9-11)'. It is here that the parenthesis from Posidonius is inserted: 'but even here (i.e. in philosophy in the proper or more restricted sense) if Posidonius is to be believed, the doctrine of atoms is an ancient one from Mochus of Sidon, born before the Trojan period (11-13)'. But Strabo dismisses this: well, so much for ancient history (τὰ μὲν οὖν παλαιὰ ἐάσθω), and returns to his personal modern experience of present day famous philosophers from Sidon, citing his own teacher Boethus, Boethus' brother Diodotus, Antipater of Tyre, and Apollonius, the cataloguer of Stoic philosophers, who was a little before his time. This shows that only the parenthesis comes from Posidonius.

This is born out by the doublet in F286. Sextus classifies theories of στοιχεῖα as σώματα or ἀσώματα (F286.1-3). Under the former, Democritus and Epicurus are credited with the atomic theory, 'unless one should make this theory somewhat more ancient as derived from Mochus, a Phoenician, as Posidonius the Stoic said'.

B. *Mochus and atom theory*

Mochus is named in Josephus (*AJ* 1.107) in a list of historians as one of οἱ τὰ Φοινικικὰ συγγραψάμενοι; and similarly in Athenaeus, III.126A where he is coupled with Sanchuniathon as οἱ τὰ Φοινικικὰ συγγεγραφότες, fellow citizens of Ulpian of Tyre. Diogenes Laertius in the *Prologue* at the opening of Bk I.1, refers to some who say that the business of philosophy started from the barbarians, citing the Magi, the Chaldeans, the Gymnosophists and the Druids. He adds that they say that ⟨M⟩ochus (Ochus also in the Suda *s.v.*, probably from D.L.) was a Phoenician, Zalmoxis a Thracian, and Atlas a Libyan. Not surprisingly then Mochus turns up in the Neoplatonist tradition in Damascius (*De Princ.* 125c, 1.323,6 Ruelle) and Iamblichus (*VP* 14). See *FGrH* 784. Tatian (*Ad Graec.* 37; Euseb, *Praep. Evang.* x.11; *FGrH* 784, T1, F1) says that he was translated into Greek by Λαῖτος (for Laetus compare Plu. *Aet. Phys.* 911F, 913E).

COMMENTARY: F285-286

Mochus and Sanchuniathon are parallel cases. The latter too was translated into Greek by Herennius Philo of Byblos (64–141 A.D.) and was said to have lived before the Trojan War (Euseb. *Praep. Evang.* 1.9.20–1.10.53; *FGrH* 790, F1; West, *Theogony* 24ff; Miller, *JRS* 61 (1971), 5f). The 'translations' of Laetus and Philo were thought to be mere forgeries until the Ugarit finds at Ras Shamra proved a genuine Phoenician mythological literature older than the Trojan War. The main existing evidence for both Mochus and Sanchuniathon is of this mythical cosmogonical nature (Damascius, *FGrH* 784, F4; Eusebius *FGrH* 790, F1), but Posidonius must have read something in the literature which he took to be an early foreshadowing of an atomic theory. Schmidt (*Philologus* 122 (1978), 137–43) argued that Nonnus, *Dion.* 41.51–8 may derive from the Mochus literature. The lines deal with the primeval people of Berytus, and mention a mingling of atoms in four-fold combination linked to the four elements, which may reflect an early, more Indian orientated atom theory.

Although the Mochus/Sanchuniathon literature may ultimately trace back to pre-Trojan Phoenician cosmogonies, we have no means of control over the date of Mochus or Sanchuniathon, or of the works translated by Laetus and Philo, or indeed of the fidelity of the translations. No doubt they underwent changes and accretions, and perhaps some hellenistic doctoring. See also Eissfeldt, *Ras Schamra und Sanchuniathon*; Diels, *Hermes* 40 (1905), 315; Zeller, 1. 1048; DK, *Vors.* 68.A55. The reference shows Posidonius' interest in foreign literatures, whether he read Mochus in the Laetus translation or not, and is another instance of his habit of seeing philosophy as a continuous development and improvement of the theories of the ancients (T101–2). It possibly occurred in a doxography. There are no grounds for regarding it as a sneer against Epicurean atom theory (Hirzel, *Untersuchungen* 1.34.1; Rudberg, *Forschungen zu Poseidonios* 31).

COMMENTARY: F287

Fragments showing Posidonius' ambivalent attitude to the Phoenicians are: 217.26-8; 246.40.

F287 Diogenes Laertius, IX.68

CONTENT

An anecdote on Pyrrho.

CONTEXT

The chapter on Pyrrho begins at IX.61, and this passage occurs in the first section of the Life, dealing with Pyrrho's character, disposition and way of life. Up to IX.67, Diogenes, or his source, may have been relying at least to some extent on Antigonus of Carystus (62). Timon and Eratosthenes (66) are also quoted.

COMMENT

1 'Posidonius relates something of this sort about him.'
τοιοῦτόν τι: just before this we have been told, on the authority of Philo of Athens, that Pyrrho admired Homer, and would quote anything that related εἰς τὸ ἀβέβαιον καὶ κενόσπουδον ἅμα καὶ παιδαριῶδες τῶν ἀνθρώπων. Animal stories occurred: Pyrrho once washed a pig ὑπ' ἀδιαφορίας (66). He admired Homer because he likened men to wasps, flies and birds (67).

2-5 'When his fellow-passengers in a storm were showing the strain, he remained calm (γαληνός) and stiffened the spirit by pointing to a piglet in the boat continuing to feed and said that the wise man ought to be in such a settled unperturbed state (ἀταραξίᾳ).' The language is Sceptic rather than Stoic: S.E. *Hyp.* 1.10, ἀταραξία δέ ἐστι ψυχῆς ἀοχλησία καὶ γαληνότης. Neither ἀταραξία nor γαληνός recurs in Posidonius.

COMMENTARY: F288

The anecdote resurfaces in Plutarch, *Quomodo quis, Mor.* 82F, unascribed and recast in Plutarch's own words: Πύρρωνα δέ φασι πλέοντα καὶ κινδυνεύοντα χειμῶνος δελφάκιόν τι δεῖξαι χρώμενον ἀσμένως κριθαῖς παρεγκεχυμέναις, καὶ πρὸς τοὺς ἑταίρους εἰπεῖν ὅτι τοιαύτην ἀπάθειαν παρασκευαστέον ἐκ λόγου καὶ φιλοσοφίας τὸν ὑπὸ τῶν προστυγχανόντων ταράττεσθαι μὴ βουλόμενον. So it had passed into the general anecdotal tradition. It is surprising that Diogenes quotes Posidonius here. Apart from the frequent references in the Stoic Bk vII, Posidonius is only referred to here by Diogenes, and in F288, a vaguer and more understandable allusion. Presumably it did not occur in the earlier literature such as Antigonus of Carystus (62), and Posidonius picked it up from 2nd- or 1st-century B.C. anecdotal discussion. He probably used it as an illustration in an ethical work, which shows his willingness to use such material from another school for his own purposes, and to recognise what was good and useful from earlier philosophers for the development of his own philosophy (T101-2). It was certainly quoted with approval, not hostility.

F288 Diogenes Laertius, x.3-4

CONTENT

Posidonius (and his followers) are grouped with the tradition hostile to Epicurus.

CONTEXT

The passage occurs in the opening sections of the Life of Epicurus.

COMMENT

'The Stoic Diotimus, being hostile to him (i.e. Epicurus), has

976

COMMENTARY: F288

slandered him most bitterly, producing fifty scandalous letters as written by Epicurus; so too the man who edited as Epicurean the notelets commonly attributed to Chrysippus; but also Posidonius the Stoic (and his group) and Nicolaus and Sotion in the twelve books (twelfth book?) of those entitled *Dioclean Refutations*, which are . . ., and Dionysius of Halicarnassus.'

Posidonius' hostility to Epicurus and Epicureanism is apparent from the fragments: Frs. 22, 46, 47, 149, 160, 187.28f. Malitz hesitantly included also as Posidonian the anti-Epicurean story of Diogenes of Seleucea at the court of Alexander Balas, sandwiched in Athen. v.211A–D in between Frs. 61b, 72b, 62b and F253 (F253 context; Malitz, 9 n. 42, 272). Of course Epicurean ethics and physics were so fundamentally opposed to Stoic philosophy that even Posidonius with his penchant for discovering cogent antecedents in earlier philosophers of other Schools, hardly surprisingly never attempts this with Epicurus. Indeed this reference and the other evidence goes much further than this. Posidonius is singled out among Stoics for animosity (although οἱ περὶ Π. could mean Posidonius and his followers, it almost certainly refers here to Posidonius himself, T45). This must have been notorious. Evidence for the stinging virulence of his attack may be found especially in Frs. 46, 47 (see comm. *ad loc.*, and Kidd, 'Posidonius and Logic' 280; in general, Rudberg, *Forschungen zu Poseidonios* 30ff; Crönert, *Kolotes* 177, 115 n. 516).

What Posidonius, Nicolaus, Sotion and Dionysius of Halicarnassus are being accused of is not entirely clear, since their nominatives hang pendent. It is just possibly implied that they regarded as genuine the scandalous forgeries of Diotimus, but it is more likely that we should simply supply πικρότατα αὐτὸν διαβεβλήκασι from line 2.

Athenaeus, XIII.611B has a similar story about Diotimus (he is called there Theotimus), citing Demetrius of Magnesia (the friend of Atticus) for the reference, and adds that

COMMENTARY: F289

Diotimus/Theotimus was convicted of forgery on the accusation of Zeno of Sidon and put to death (cf. Crönert, *Kolotes* 22, 175). Posidonius must have known the case and may well have been partisan, since he attacked Zeno indignantly on other matters (Frs. 46, 47). But the hostile doxography can hardly come from him, since other names in the group are slightly later. See F51 comm. for Nicolaus of Damascus. Sotion is probably not the author of the *Compendium of Philosophers* (early 2nd c. B.C.?) used elsewhere by Diogenes (F42); he may have been Seneca's teacher (*Ep.* 49.2; 108.17, 20).

6-7 The textual cruces have not been solved. Since one would expect τῶν . . . ἐλέγχων to be partitive, Gassendi's τῷ δωδεκάτῳ for τοῖς δώδεκα (PF) is tempting; B has τοῖς δωδεκάτω.

The following phrase: ἅ ἐστι περὶ τοῖς κ̄δ̄ is clearly corrupt. Some editors see a reference to additional numbers: δ' πρὸς τοῖς κ' Bignone; πρὸς τοῖς εἴκοσι τέσσαρα Arrighetti; but this makes poor sense. Most adopt ἅ ἐστι περὶ τῆς εἰκάδος (Hübner) supposing presumably the subject to be the common dines of the Epicurean School held on the twentieth day of each month as laid down in Epicurus' will (D.L. x.18; Cic. *De Fin.* II.101). But this is more ingenious than convincing. Non solvitur aenigma.

F289   Athenaeus, VII.279D-E

CONTENT

Posidonius made some remarks about other hedonistic sects of philosophers besides the Epicureans.

CONTEXT

At 278D Archestratus was mentioned. This is presumably the 4th-c. B.C. author of the gastronomical Ἡδυπάθεια, or Γαστρολογία, called by Athenaeus (VII.310A) the Hesiod or Theognis of gourmets. This led to a reference from Chrysip-

COMMENTARY: F290

pus that Archestratus was the forerunner of Epicurus and those who adopted his doctrines of pleasure (278E; cf. III.104B; *SVF* III.709), which in turn develops into a discourse on Epicurus.

COMMENT

Little can be gleaned from this fragment because of the state of the text. There must be a lacuna in line 2. But Kaibel's καὶ ⟨οἱ⟩ Μνησιστράτειοι δὲ καλούμενοι will not do, because of the following δέ. There must be another proper name missing, but this is difficult to supply, since we know nothing about Μνησιστράτειοι. Two Μνησίστρατοι are known (Jacoby, *Kommentar* 206): the Mnesistratus at the court of Ptolemy Philopator who accused Sphaerus of denying that Ptolemy was a king (D.L. VII.177; *SVF* I, Sphaerus, 625); and the Mnesistratus of Thasos cited by Sabinus for making Demosthenes a pupil of Plato (D.L. III.47); hence Capps suggested καὶ ⟨οἱ Θάσιοι⟩ Μνησιστράτειοι δὲ καλούμενοι. There are no grounds for thinking that either is or is not meant here. μέν and syntax indicate another lacuna in line 3, where a δέ clause balancing 3ῆν μὲν ἡδέως is missing. Theiler (F290c) suggested 3ῆν μὲν ἡδέως ⟨βούλονται, ἅμα δὲ τῷ ἀοχλήτως⟩ χαίρουσι. But this is guesswork.

There is nothing to suggest that this comes from the *History* (as Malitz, 68 n. 76; Jacoby F106). It was more likely part of a doxographical review of early hedonistic theory and the origins of Epicureanism. Compare Frs. 285, 286.

F290   Hermias Alexandrinus, *In Platonis Phaedrum Scholia*, ad 245C

CONTENT

In the interpretation of ψυχὴ πᾶσα ἀθάνατος in the

COMMENTARY: F290

immortality argument of Pl. *Phdr.* 245c 5, Posidonius held that πᾶσα referred to the world soul only.

COMMENT

Posidonius is singled out as the representative of the group who interpret ψυχὴ πᾶσα as world soul only, while Harpocration represents the other group believing that the phrase refers to all individual souls including those of ants and flies. Since this was a notorious controversy, the parallel choice of Posidonius and Harpocration is extraordinary. Harpocration was a lexicographer obviously accessible to Hermias. But what source made Posidonius so prominent for him? One possible answer could be that Posidonius had written a Commentary on *Phaedrus*, known to Hermias (so Zeller, III.599 n. 3; but see F86c comm.).

There are two possible ways of looking at the Posidonian evidence:

(a) This is an example of simple exegesis, where Posidonius is merely trying to clarify Plato's meaning without any motive of reinterpretation for his own philosophy. This appears to be supported by Posidonius' argument for his interpretation, which is based on consistency in Plato by citing another passage from Plato's argument: ἢ πάντα τε οὐρανὸν πᾶσάν τε γένεσιν κτλ (245 δ 8f). In that case some form of commentary is likely, and nothing can be derived as to Posidonius' own views; Hoven, *Stoïcisme et Stoïciens face au problème de l'au-delà* 62.

(b) Posidonius introduced his interpretation of Plato as world soul, because he himself believed that only the world soul was immortal (Hirzel, *Untersuchungen* I.237ff; Reinhardt, *Kosmos und Sympathie* 90f; Edelstein, *AJPh* 57.300; Theiler, II.326). This may be true, but it cannot be derived with certainty from this passage, although Posidonius may well have sought the support of Plato for his own theory (Hirzel, 239). In that case the passage may have come from Περὶ

COMMENTARY: F291

ψυχῆς or elsewhere. In fact Posidonius did believe in the sole immortality of the world soul (F139), and in the destruction of the cosmos (F13, F97), unlike Panaetius. But then he was merely in line with well-known orthodox Stoic theory, and it remains difficult to see why he was singled out by Hermias. See also F86c comm.

F291 Theo Smyrnaeus, *Expositio Rerum Mathematicarum ad Legendum Platonem Utilium* 103.16–104.1 Hiller

CONTENT

Commenting on Plato's *Timaeus* where the soul is constructed from seven numbers, Posidonius said that he was following nature, because day and night have the nature of even and odd, and a month is completed by four sevens marked by the phases of the moon.

CONTEXT

Theo of Smyrna was a Platonist of the first half of the 2nd c. A.D., and his surviving work on elementary arithmetic was written as an aid to reading Plato. He used Thrasyllus, the astrologer of the 1st c. B.C./A.D.

At p. 93 (Hiller) he proceeds to discuss the various tetractyes, the second of which is relevant to the fragment. After going through eleven tetractyes, he starts on each number beginning with 1. At p. 103 he embarks on 7, which has remarkable power and is unique in the decad in its characteristics. After the fragment he gives other examples of sevens, quoting Empedocles for the growth of foetuses, and Herophilus, the 3rd-c. B.C. physician, for the length of the human gut as being four sevens.

COMMENTARY: F291

COMMENT

The first sentence refers to the seven numbers constituent of soul in Pl. *Tim.* 35b f, later commonly schematised as shown in Fig. 19, and known as the second tetractys, or double

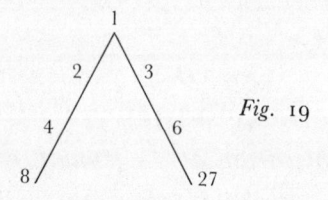

```
        1
       / \
      2   3
     /     \
    4       6     Fig. 19
   /         \
  8           27
```

tetractys of odd and even (Theo, 94ff). The relevance of Posidonius' explanation as given here is obscure and has been much debated.

Theo is clearly deep into the popular game of arithmology, and this has led commentators to speculate that Posidonius too engaged extensively in such fancies. Parallel arithmological passages have been pointed out in Varro, Philo, Ps.-Hipp. *Sevens*, Nicomachus, Censorinus, Macrobius and Sextus (Schmekel, *Die Philosophie* 405ff; Robbins, *CPh* 15 (1920), 309ff; De Folco, *Riv. indo-greco-ital.* 6 (1922), fasc. 3-4, 51ff; Burkert, *Lore and Science* 54ff; Mansfeld, *The Pseudo-Hippocratic Tract* Περὶ Ἑβδομάδων 156ff), and Mansfeld has argued a case not only for Posidonius as a source for all this literature, but that the reference here to the hebdomad in lunar months parallel to the psychic hebdomad may reflect an actual expression for Posidonius' own philosophy of the comprehensibility of sensibilia (esp. Mansfeld, 196ff; but see F85 comm.). Now it is true that for Posidonius mathematics and logic were closely allied, and that logic was concerned with the structure of nature and reality (Kidd, *Les Stoïciens et leur logique* 273-83). It is also the case that mathematical limits were substantial for him (F16, F92), that shape was the containing limit (F196), the cause of definiteness, and that he toyed with a mathematical definition of soul (F141). But still

COMMENTARY: F292

the evidence for Posidonius for the kind of arithmology in which Theo engages is exiguous.

It must be remembered that the three key passages in Posidonius (F85, F141, F291) are all comments on Pl. *Tim.* And in fact in *Tim.* the creation of soul is closely followed and linked to the creation of time as days, nights months, through the creation of sun, moon and planets (*Tim.* 37dff, 39c). It is possible that Posidonius was merely commenting on this with reference to the hebdomad. Posidonius seems to be justifying the psychic double tetractys given by Plato in *Tim.* by an appeal to nature. The characteristic of the double tetractys is the number seven, and the combination of odd and even. Nature reveals a hebdomadal pattern in time marked by the lunar month, and also by the unit of time, day, which displays the characteristic of both odd and even. For day is also two (day and night), and as the unit of time, is in any case odd and even (Theo, 22.5–10; Arist. *Met.* 986a 19). So Plato in his picture of the structure of the soul is following nature, ἑπόμενος τῇ φύσει (1). So Posidonius is merely using *Tim.* itself to comment on the Platonic structure of soul, although in terms also appropriate to Posidonian physics (cf. F290). It need be no more than that.

See also F85.

MISCELLANEOUS

F292 Athenaeus, xiv.635c–d

CONTENT

The magadis in Anacreon.

CONTEXT AND COMMENT

The interpretation of this fragment depends on the context of

COMMENTARY: F292

the development of Athenaeus' argument, as Reinhardt (*Poseidonios über Ursprung und Entartung* 48 n. 2) was the first to see.

After some initial discussion on whether the magadis belonged to the αὐλός or κιθάρα family of musical instruments (634C–E), Masurius, relying on the quotation of Anacreon, *PMG* 374 Page, 96 Gentili, maintains that the magadis is certainly an instrument played like a harp, and was an invention of the Lydians (634F). He adds that according to Euphorion the magadis is very old, but its construction was latterly altered, and its name changed to sambuca. References to Menaechmus (4th c. B.C.: it was the same as the πηκτίς, which was invented by Sappho), Aristoxenus (4th c. B.C.) and Pindar (in the Scolion to Hieron) follow (635B).

Now the fragment:

1–4 'But some people are puzzled at the mention of the magadis in Anacreon, "With my magadis I play with twenty strings, Leucaspis" (*PMG* 374, repeated from 634F), for they say that instruments with many strings came on the scene at a late date (2).'

4–9 'And Posidonius says that he (i.e. Anacreon) was making mention of three modes, the Phrygian, ⟨Dorian⟩ and Lydian (for these were the only ones used by Anacreon); since, said he, each of these is encompassed by seven strings, he naturally said he was playing with twenty strings, rounding off to an even number by deleting one.'

9–12 Athenaeus/Masurius now rebuts this: 'But Posidonius is not aware that the magadis is an ancient instrument, with Pindar clearly saying that Terpander invented the barbitos antiphonal to the pectis used by the Lydians.' He goes on to quote Pindar, *PLG* 1.440 (F110 Bowra), and says again that the pectis and magadis are the same instrument (Aristoxenus and Menaechmus), and that the pectis was first used by Sappho; both she and Terpander were earlier than Anacreon (635E). The argument continues to 637B, citing on the way Alcman (F99 Diehl) and Telestes (F3.2 Diehl).

COMMENTARY: F292

It is clear from this discussion that Athenaeus and Posidonius are in opposition. Athenaeus supports the reading of μάγαδις in Anacreon's text. It does not make sense to suggest (Reinhardt, *Poseidonios über Ursprung*; Malitz, 290 n. 243) that μάγαδιν ἔχων is an addition of Athenaeus. It is the text of Anacreon which is in question, so μάγαδιν ἔχων (also in the earlier use of the quotation at 634F) is an old reading (whether it is actually correct or not does not concern us here) accepted by Athenaeus. Posidonius was in the group (ἔνιοι, 1) who doubted it (διαποροῦσι, 1), because of the belief (2, mistaken in Athenaeus' opinion from the evidence, 9ff) that the magadis was a much later invention. So it appears that Posidonius wished to excise the word magadis from the text of Anacreon, explaining that by 'playing with twenty strings' Anacreon was simply referring to the three different musical modes he employed, each of which separately in its turn required seven different scale strings; but this did not of course necessarily imply that he used a single twenty-stringed instrument.

The argument shows Posidonius' readiness to emend poetical texts for what he believed to be historical reasons of anachronism. Another example of this may occur in F284.114-25 (comm.).

In line 1 a negative has clearly fallen out. Jacoby suggested οὐκέτι but οὔπω (Reinhardt, Peppink) is demanded from the argument. I would read: ὅπως ⟨οὔπω⟩ τῆς μαγάδιδος οὔσης κ. Ἀν.

The μάγαδις was a development of the harp class of instruments with an increased number of strings. This may incidentally have permitted scales comprehending more than one mode (Winnington-Ingram, *Modes in Ancient Greek Music* 49), but its function appears rather designed for playing in octaves. The verb μαγαδίζειν occurs in Arist. *Probl.* 921a 12, 918b 40 in the sense of doubling a vocal part at the octave (cf. Aristoxenus, F99 Wehrli). But arguments over its identity and use go back to Aristoxenus Περὶ ὀργάνων (Frs. 98-101

985

COMMENTARY: F293

Wehrli; all from Athenaeus). Whether Posidonius regarded it as a sign of later decadence (Reinhardt) is unclear. He objected rather to musical instruments in the wrong place and time (in army baggage on active service, F54), or to excessive indulgence in continuous loud music (F62). But he seems to have been interested in musical instruments (F62a.11). μάγαδις also occurs in Strabo's list of musical instruments at x.3.17.

F293 Scholia in Apollonium Rhodium, II.105–6

CONTENT

On the meaning of λάξ in Homer.

COMMENT

The lemma αὐτὸς (i.e. Polydeuces) δ' 'Ιτυμονῆα refers to A.R. II.105f: Polydeuces slew huge Itymoneus and Mimas, τὸν μὲν ὑπὸ στέρνοιο θοῷ ποδὶ λὰξ ἐπορούσας/πλῆξε.... Faced with the pleonasm ποδὶ λάξ the scholiast first suggests that λάξ refers to sound (ψόφος) or the slap made by the toes of the foot against the solar plexus. Alternatively, it properly refers to the part under the toes of the foot (i.e. the sole). That is the way Posidonius rendered Homer *Il.* x.158, λὰξ ποδὶ κινήσας. This is the passage where Nestor rouses the sleeping Diomedes by prodding him with (the sole of) his foot. Posidonius' suggestion also found its way into the Homeric scholia: Erbse K 158c, τῷ ὑποκάτω τῶν δακτύλων μέρει. Many contexts of λάξ indeed favour an interpretation of *under* foot.

There is no reason to foist the authorship of this suggestion on to Aristarchus' reciter (see T109, 110) as Susemihl

986

COMMENTARY: F293

(*Geschichte der griechischen Literatur* II.160 n. 83) and Theiler (II.414) do. Posidonius' interest in Homeric interpretation is well attested (e.g. Frs. 277a, 281), and so is his interest in the exact meaning of single words (Frs. 170.46ff; 175; 261; 277a).

REFERENCES

This is not intended to be a bibliography of Posidonius. It is a key to works cited in more abbreviated form in the Commentary.

Abel, K., 'Zu Poseidonios' schriftstellerischem Nachlass', *RhM* 107 (1964), 371-3.
Alföldi, G., 'Tauriski und Norici', *Historia* 15 (1966), 225-41.
  Noricum, London/Boston, 1974.
Aly, W., *Strabon von Amaseia. Untersuchungen über Text, Aufbau und Quellen der Geographika (Strabonis Geographica*, vol. IV), Bonn, 1957.
Anderson, J. K., *Ancient Greek Horsemanship*, Los Angeles, 1961.
André, J., *L'alimentation et la cuisine à Rome*, Paris, 1961.
Arnim, H. von, *Stoicorum Veterum Fragmenta (SVF)*, Leipzig, 1903-24.
Ascher, E. J., 'Graeco-Roman Nautical Technology', *Journal of Tropical Geography* 31 (1970), 10-26.
  'Timetables of the Periplus and Pliny's Voyage to India', *Journal of Tropical Geography* 34 (1972), 1-7.
Astin, A. E., 'The date of the Embassy to the East of Scipio Aemilianus', *CPh* 54 (1959), 221-7.
  Scipio Aemilianus, Oxford, 1967.
Aujac, G., *Strabon et la science de son temps*, Paris, 1966.
  Géminos, Paris, 1975.
  'Poseidonios et les zones terrestres', *Bull. de L'Ass. G. Budé* 35 (1976), 74-8.
Axelson, B., *Senecastudien, Kritische Bemerkungen zu Senecas Naturales quaestiones*, Lund, 1933.

Babut, D., *Plutarque et le Stoïcisme*, Paris, 1969.
Badian, E., 'Harpalus', *JHS* 81 (1961), 16-43.
  'From the Gracchi to Sulla', *Historia* 11 (1962), 197-245.
  Roman Imperialism in the Late Republic, Cornell, 1968.
  'Quaestiones Variae', *Historia* 18 (1969), 447-91.
  Publicans and Sinners, Oxford, 1972.
  'Rome, Athens and Mithridates', *Assimilation et résistance, VI Congress FIEC*, 1976, 501-21 = *AJAH* 1 (1976), 105-28.
Baeumker, C., *Das Problem der Materie in der griechischen Philosophie*, Münster, 1890.
Bake, I., *Posidonii Rhodii Reliquiae Doctrinae*, Leiden, 1810.
Balsdon, J. P. V. D., *Romans and Aliens*, London, 1979.

REFERENCES

Baltes, M., *Timaios Lokros, Über die Natur des Kosmos und der Seele*, Leiden, 1972.

'Die Zuordnung der Elemente zu den Sinnen bei Poseidonios und ihre Herkunft aus der Alten Akademie', *Philologus* 122 (1978), 183-96.

Bar-Kochva, B., *The Seleucid Army*, Cambridge, 1976.

Barlow, C. W., 'A sixth-century Epitome of Seneca, *De ira*', *TAPA* 68 (1937), 26-42.

Bauer, A., 'Poseidonios und Plutarch über die römischen Eigennamen', *Philologus* 47 (1889), 242-73.

Beare, J. I., *Greek Theories of Elementary Cognition*, Oxford, 1906.

Bellinger, A. R., 'The end of the Seleucids', *Trans. of the Connecticut Acad. of Arts and Sciences*, 38 (1949), 41-102.

Beneden, P. van, 'Poseidonios von Apameà, F36 (Jac)', *Philologus* 113 (1969), 151-6.

Berger, H., *Die geographischen Fragmente des Hipparch*, Leipzig, 1869.

Die geographischen Fragmente des Eratosthenes, Leipzig, 1880.

Geschichte der wissenschaftlichen Erdkunde der Griechen, Leipzig, 1903.

Berger, L., 'Poseidonios Fragment 18. Ein Beitrag zur Deutung der spätkeltischen Vierecksschanzen?', *SP* 27 (1963), 26-8.

Bergson, H. L., *Time and Free Will*, trs. F. L. Pogson, London, 1913.

Bernays, J., 'Philons Hypothetika', *Gesammelte Abhandlungen*, ed. H. Usener, 266-71, Berlin, 1885.

Bevan, E. R., *The House of Seleucus*, London, 1902.

Boll, F., 'Studien über Claudius Ptolemäus', *Jahrb. f. class. Philol.*, *Supplb.* 21, Leipzig, 1894.

'Die Erforschung der antiken Astrologie', *N. Jahrb.* 1908 = *Kleine Schriften* 1 ff.

Bonhöffer, A., *Die Ethik des Stoikers Epiktet*, Stuttgart, 1894.

Bouché-Leclerq, A., *Histoire de la divination dans l'antiquité*, Paris, 1879-82.

L'astrologie grecque, Paris, 1899.

Histoire des Lagides, Brussels, 1963 (1903).

Boyancé, P., *Études sur le songe de Scipion*, Paris, 1936.

Braund, D., 'Royal Wills and Rome', *Papers of the British School at Rome* 51 (1983), 16-57.

Bréhier, E., 'La théorie des incorporels dans l'ancien stoïcisme', *Arch. f. Gesch. d. Phil.* 22 (1909), 114-25.

Histoire de la Philosophie, Paris, 1928-34.

'Posidonius d'Apamée. Théoricien de la géométrie', *REG* 27 (1914), 44-58 = *Études de philosophie antique* 117-30, Paris, 1955.

Bringmann, K., 'Weltherrschaft und innere Krise Roms im Spiegel der Geschichtsschreibung des zweiten und ersten Jahrhunderts v. Chr.' *A & A* 23 (1977), 28-49.

REFERENCES

'Geschichte und Psychologie bei Poseidonios', in Fondation Hardt, *Entretiens* 32 (1986), 29-66.
Brink, C. O., 'Theophrastus and Zeno on Nature in Moral Theory', *Phronesis* 1 (1956), 123ff.
Horace on Poetry, Cambridge, 1963, 1971, 1982.
Brink, C. O. and Walbank, F. W., 'The construction of the Sixth Book of Polybius', *CQ* N.S. 4 (1954), 97-122.
Brock, S., *The Syriac Versions of the Pseudo-Nonnos Mythological Scholia*, Cambridge, 1971.
Brockelmann, C., *Geschichte der Arabischen Litteratur*, Leiden, 1898; *Supplement*, Leiden, 1937.
Broughton, T. R. S., *The Magistrates of the Roman Republic*, New York, 1951-2.
Brunschwig, J., ed., *Les Stoïciens et leur logique*, Paris, 1978.
'Le modèle conjonctif', in *Les Stoïciens et leur logique* 59-86.
Brunt, P. A., 'Italian aims at the time of the Social War', *JRS* 55 (1965), 90-109.
'The Romanisation of the local ruling classes in the Roman Empire', in *Assimilation et résistance, VI Congress FIEC*, 1976, 161-73.
Buck, C. D., *The Greek Dialects*,[4] Chicago/London, 1968.
Bunbury, Sir Edward H., *A History of Ancient Geography among the Greeks and Romans from the Earliest Ages till the Fall of the Roman Empire*, London, 1879.
Burkert, W., *Weisheit und Wissenschaft*, Nürnberg, 1962 = *Lore and Science in Ancient Pythagoreanism*, tr. E. L. Minar, Jr., Cambridge, Mass., 1972.
Busolt, G., *Griechische Staatskunde*,[3] Munich, 1920, 1926.
Cambridge History of Iran III (1) and (2), ed. E. Yarshater, Cambridge, 1983.
Cameron, A., 'The date and identity of Macrobius', *JRS* 56 (1966), 25-38.
Campbell, M., *Studies in the Third Book of Apollonius Rhodius' Argonautica*, Hildesheim, 1983.
'Apollonian and Homeric book division', *Mnem.* 36 (1983), 154-5.
Candiloro, E., 'Politica e cultura in Atene da Pidna alla guerra mitridatica', *Studi classici e orientali* 14 (1965), 134-76.
Capelle, W., 'Der Physiker Arrian und Poseidonios', *Hermes* 40 (1905), 614-35.
'Die Schrift von der Welt', *Neue Jahrbücher für das klassische Altertum* 15 (1905), 529-68.
'Erdbeben in Altertum', *Neue Jahrb.* 21 (1908), 603-33.
'Zur Geschichte der meteorologischen Litteratur', *Hermes* 48 (1913), 321-58.
'Die Nilschwelle', *Neue Jahrb.* 1914, 317-61.
'Berges- und Wolkenhöhen bei griechischen Physikern', *Stoicheia* 5 (1916).

REFERENCES

'Griechische Ethik und römischer Imperialismus', *Klio* 25 (1932), 86–113.
Carcopino, J., *Le Maroc antique*, Paris, 1948.
Carney, T. F., 'The death of Marius', *Acta Classica* 1 (1958), 117–22.
'Cicero's picture of Marius', *W. St.* 63 (1960), 83–122.
A Biography of C. Marius, Assen, 1961.
Cary, M., *The Geographic Background of Greek and Roman History*, Oxford, 1967.
Cary, M. and Warmington, E. H., *The Ancient Explorers*, London, 1929.
Cassirer, E., *The Problem of Knowledge*, trs. W. H. Woglom and C. W. Hendel, New Haven, 1950.
Casson, L., *Travel in the Ancient World*, London, 1974.
Cherniss, H., 'Galen and Posidonius' Theory of Vision (from notes of R. M. Jones)', *AJPh* 54 (1933), 154–61.
ed. Plutarch, *De facie*, Loeb *Mor.* vol. XII, Cambridge, Mass./London, 1957.
ed. *Plutarch's Moralia*, vol. XIII, Parts I and II, Loeb edn., Cambridge Mass./London, 1976.
Christ, W.–Schmidt, W.–Stählin, O., *Geschichte der griechischen Literatur, Die nachklassische Periode* (in *Handbuch der Altertumswissenschaft* VII.II.1–2), Munich, 1920–4.
Colledge, M. A. R., *The Parthians*, London, 1967.
Corpus Hippiatricorum Graecorum, edd. E. Oder and C. Hoppe, Teubner, 1924, 1927.
Courcelle, P., *Les lettres grecques en occident*, Paris, 1943.
Coutant, V. and Eichenlaub, Val. L., *Theophrastus, De ventis*, Notre Dame, 1975.
Crawford, M. H., *The Roman Republic*, New Jersey, 1978.
Crönert, W., *Kolotes und Menedemos. Studien zur Palaeographie und Papyruskunde VI*, Leipzig, 1906.
Cumont, F. V. M., *La Théologie solaire du paganisme romain*, Paris, 1909.
Cuntz, O., *Polybius und sein Werk*, Leipzig, 1902.

Darwin, Sir George H., *The Tides and Kindred Phenomena in the Solar System*, London, 1898; 3rd edn, 1911.
Day, J., *An Economic History of Athens under Roman Domination*, New York, 1942.
Debevoise, N. C., *A Political History of Parthia*, New York, 1968.
Deininger, J., *Der politische Widerstand gegen Rom in Griechenland 217–86 v. Chr.*, Berlin, 1971.
De Lacy, P. and E. A., *Philodemus: on Methods of Inference*, Philadelphia, 1941.

REFERENCES

De Lacy, P., 'The logical structure of the Ethics of Epictetus', *CPh* 38 (1943), 112–25.

'Galen and the Greek poets', *Greek, Roman & Byzantine Studies* 7 (1966), 259–66.

Del Corno, D., *Graecorum de re onirocritica scriptorum reliquiae, Testi e Documenti per lo studio dell' Antichità*, 26, Milan, 1969.

Desideri, P., 'Posidonio e la guerra mitridatica', *Athenaeum* 51 (1973), 3–29, 237–69.

Detlefesen, S. D. F., *Ursprung, Einrichtung und Bedeutung der Erdkarte Agrippas*, Berlin, 1906.

Dickerman, S. O., 'Some stock illustrations of animal intelligence in Greek psychology', *TAPA* 42 (1911), 123–30.

Dicks, D. R., *The Geographical Fragments of Hipparchus*, London, 1960.

Diels, H., *Doxographi Graeci*, Berlin, 1879.

'Aristotelica', *Hermes* 40 (1905), 301–16.

Die Fragmente der Vorsokratiker, Berlin, 6th edn, 1951.

Dihle, A., 'Der fruchtbare Osten', *RhM* 105 (1962), 97–110.

'Zur hellenistischen Ethnographie', in Fondation Hardt, *Entretiens* VIII (1962), 207–32.

'Posidonius' system of moral philosophy', *JHS* 73 (1973), 50–7.

'Die Entdeckungsgeschichtlichen Voraussetzungen des Indienhandels der römischer Kaiserzeit', in *Aufstieg u. Niedergang d. r. Welt* II.9.2, 546–80, Berlin/New York, 1978.

Dijksterhuis, E. J., *Archimedes*, Copenhagen, 1956.

Diller, A., 'Geographical latitudes in Eratosthenes, Hipparchus and Posidonius', *Klio* 27 (1934), 258–69.

'Julian of Ascalon on Strabo and the Stade', *CPh* 45 (1950) 22–5.

The Textual Tradition of Strabo's Geography, Amsterdam, 1975.

Dillon, J., *The Middle Platonists*, London, 1977.

Dodds, E. R., *The Greeks and the Irrational*, Berkeley, 1951.

Dörrie, H., 'Der Begriff "Pronoia" in Stoa und Platonismus', *Freiburger Zeitschr. f. Philos. u. Theol.* 24 (1977), 60–87.

Douglas, A. E., *M. Tulli Ciceronis Brutus*, Oxford, 1966.

Dow, S., 'The lists of Athenian archontes', *Hesperia* 3 (1934), 140–90.

Drabkin, I. E., 'Posidonius and the circumference of the earth', *Isis* 34 (1942–43), 509–12.

Dragona-Monachou, M., 'Posidonius' "Hierarchy" between God, Fate and Nature', *Philosophia* 4 (1974), 286–301.

The Stoic Arguments for the Existence and the Providence of the Gods, Athens, 1976.

Dreyer, J. L. E., *History of the Planetary Systems from Thales to Kepler*, Cambridge, 1906, revised W. H. Stahl, New York, 1953.

REFERENCES

Dubois, M., *Examen de la géographie de Strabon*, Paris, 1891.
Duhem, P., *Les origines de la statique*, Paris, 1905-6.
Le système du monde, Paris, 1914.
Dyroff, A., *Die Ethik der alten Stoa*, Berlin, 1897.

Edelstein, L., 'The Philosophical System of Posidonius', *AJPh* 57 (1936), 286-325.
The Meaning of Stoicism, Harvard, 1966.
Eissfeldt, O., 'Ras Schamra und Sanchuniathon', *Beitr. z. Religionsgeschichte des Altertums*, Heft 4, Halle, 1939.
Erbse, H., *Scholia graeca in Homeri Iliadem*, Berlin, 1969-77.

Faust, A., *Der Möglichkeitsgedanke*, Heidelberg, 1931-2.
Fensterbusch, C., 'Schwimmende Ziegel - schwimmende Inseln', *RhM* 103 (1960), 373-7.
Ferguson, W. S., 'The oligarchic revolution at Athens', *Klio*, 4 (1904), 14ff.
Hellenistic Athens, London, 1911.
Festugière, A. M. J., *La révélation d'Hermès Trismégiste: l'astrologie et les sciences occultes*, Paris, 1944-54.
Finley, M. I., *Ancient Sicily*, London, 1979.
Fischer, I., 'Another look at Eratosthenes' and Posidonius' determinations of the earth's circumference, *Quart. Journal of the Royal Astronomical Society* 16 (1975), 152-67.
Fischer, R., *De usu vocabulorum apud Ciceronem et Senecam graecae philosophiae interpretes*, Freiburg i.B., 1914.
Fischer, T., 'Zu Tryphon', *Chiron* 2 (1972), 201-13.
Flamant, J., *Macrobe et le Néo-platonisme latin à la fin du IVe siècle*, Leiden, 1977.
Flashar, H., *Melancholia und Melancholiker in den medizinischen Theorien der Antike*, Berlin, 1966.
Forbes, R. J., *Studies in Ancient Technology*, Leiden, 1958-66. I *Bitumen and Petroleum, Water Supply*, 2nd edn, 1964; II *Irrigation, Drainage, Power, Transport*, 2nd edn, 1965; III *Cosmetics, Perfumes, Food, Beverages, Crushing, Salts, Pigments*, 2nd edn, 1965; IV *Textiles*, 2nd edn, 1964; V *Leather, Honey and Sugar, Glass*, 2nd edn, 1966; VI *Heat, Cold, Light*, 1958; VII *Geology and Mining*, 1963; VIII *Metallurgy, Gold, Silver, Lead, Zinc, Brass*, 1964; IX *Copper, Bronze, Tin, Antimony, Arsenic, Iron*, 1964.
Forschner, M., *Die stoische Ethik*, Stuttgart, 1981.
Frank, E., *Platon und die sogennanten Pythagoreer*, Halle, 1923.
Frank, T., ed., *Economic Survey of Ancient Rome*, Baltimore, 1933.
Fraser, P. M., *Ptolemaic Alexandria*, Oxford, 1972.
Frede, M., *Die stoische Logik*, Göttingen, 1974.

REFERENCES

'Principles of Stoic grammar', in *The Stoics*, ed. J. M. Rist, Berkeley, 1978.

'The original notion of cause', in *Doubt and Dogmatism* 217–49, edd. M. Schofield, M. Burnyeat, J. Barnes, Oxford, 1980.

French, R. and Greenaway, F., *Science in the Early Roman Empire: Pliny the Elder, his Sources and Influence*, London, 1986.

Fritz, K. von., 'Poseidonios als Historiker', in *Historiographia Antiqua. Commentationes Lovanienses in honorem W. Peremans septuagenarii editae*, Leuven, 1977.

Fuchs, H., 'Enkyklios Paideia', in *Reallexikon für Antike und Christentum* 5 (1962).

Gärtner, H. A., *Cicero und Panaitios (Beobachtungen zu Ciceros De Officiis)*, Sitzb. d. Heidelberger Ak. d. Wissensch., Phil.-hist. Kl., 1974.

Gauger, J-D., 'Eine missverstandene Strabonstelle', *Historia* 28 (1979), 211–24.

Gelder, H. van, *Geschichte der alten Rhodier*, Haag, 1900.

Gercke, A., 'War der Schwiegersohn des Poseidonios ein Schüler Aristarchs?' *RhM* 62 (1907), 116–22.

Gerhäusser, W., *Der Protreptikos des Poseidonios*, Diss. Heidelberg, 1912.

Gigon, O., rev. of Pease, *Cicero, De natura deorum*, *Gnomon* 34 (1962), 662–76.

'Der Historiker Poseidonios', in *Festgabe Hans von Greyerz*, 83–99, Bern, 1967.

'Posidoniana, Ciceroniana, Lactantiana', in *Romanitas et Christianitas, Studia I. H. Waszink*, Amsterdam/Leiden, 1973.

'Theorie und Praxis bei Platon und Aristoteles' (Part II), *MH* 30 (1973), 144–65.

Gilbert, O., *Griechische Meteorologie*, Leipzig, 1907.

Giusta, M., *I Dossographi di Etica*, Turin, 1964.

Goldschmidt, V., *Le Système stoïcien et l'idée de temps*, Paris, 1953.

Goodyear, F. D. R., *Incerti auctoris Aetna*, Cambridge, 1965.

Görgemanns, H., *Untersuchungen zu Plutarchs Dialog De facie in orbe lunae*, Heidelberg, 1970.

Gottschalk, H. B., 'Notes on the wills of the Peripatetic scholarchs', *Hermes* 100 (1972), 314–42.

Goulet, R., *Cléomède, théorie élémentaire*, Paris, 1980.

Graeser, A., *Plotinus and the Stoics*, Leiden, 1972.

Zenon von Kition, Berlin, 1975.

'Ein unstoischer Beweisgang in Cicero, *De Fin.* 3.27?', *Hermes* 100 (1972), 492ff.

Grenfell, B. P.–Hunt, A. S., *The Hibeh Papyri*, London, 1906.

Griffin, Miriam T., 'The Elder Seneca and Spain', *JRS* 62 (1972), 1–19.

Seneca, A Philosopher in Politics, Oxford, 1976.

REFERENCES

Griffiths, J. G., *Plutarch's De Iside et Osiride*, Univ. of Wales, 1970.
Grilli, A., 'Il frammento 136 v. Str. di Panezio', *RFIC* 34 (1956), 266-72.
Gruen, E. S., *The Hellenistic World and the Coming of Rome*, Univ. of California, 1984.
Gsell, S., *Histoire ancienne de l'Afrique du Nord*, Paris, 1914-28.
Habicht, C., 'Zur Geschichte Athens in der Zeit Mithridates VI', *Chiron* 6 (1976), 127-42.
Hackl, U., 'Poseidonios und das Jahr 146 v. Christ als Epochendatum in der antiken Historiographie', *Gymnasium* 87 (1980), 151-66.
Hadot, I., *Seneca und die griechisch-römische Tradition der Seelenleitung. Quellen und Studien zur Geschichte der Philosophie* XIII, Berlin, 1969.
Hagendahl, H., *Augustine and the Latin Classics*, Göteborg, 1967.
Halleux, R., *Le Problème des métaux dans la science antique. Bibliothèque de la Faculté de Philosophie et Lettres de l'Université de Liège, Fasc.* 209, 1974.
Hammer-Jensen, I., 'Die Heronische Frage', *Hermes* 63 (1928), 34-47.
Harmatta, J., 'Poseidonios über die römische Urgeschichte', *Acta Classica Universitatis Scientiarum Debreceniensis*, Tom. 7 (1971), 21-5.
Harris, W. V., *War and Imperialism in Republican Rome 327-70 B.C.*, Oxford, 1979.
Hawkes, C. F. C., *Pytheas: Europe and the Greek Explorers*, The Eighth J. L. Myres Memorial Lecture, Oxford, 1977.
Head, B. V., *Historia Numorum*, Oxford, 1911.
Healy, J. F., *Mining and Metallurgy in the Greek and Roman World*, London, 1978.
Heath, Sir Thomas, *Aristarchus of Samos*, Oxford, 1913.
A History of Greek Mathematics, Oxford, 1921.
Heidel, W. A., *The Frame of Ancient Greek Maps*, New York, 1937.
Heinemann, I., *Poseidonios' Metaphysische Schriften*, Breslau, 1921.
Higgins, R. A., *Greek and Roman Jewellery*, London, 2nd edn, 1980.
Hirzel, R., *Untersuchungen zu Ciceros Philosophischen Schriften*, Leipzig, 1882.
Holler, E., *Seneca und die Seelenteilungslehre und Affektpsychologie der Mittelstoa*, Kallmünz, 1934.
Holm, A., *Geschichte Siciliens im Altertum*, Leipzig, 1870-98.
Honigmann, E., *Die Sieben Klimata*, Heidelberg, 1929.
Hourani, G. F., *Arab Seafaring in the Indian Ocean in Ancient and Early Mediaeval Times*, Princeton/Oxford, 1951.
Hoven, R., *Stoïcisme et stoïciens face au problème de l'au-delà*, Paris, 1971.
Hultsch, F., *Poseidonios über die Grosse und Entfernung der Sonne*, Berlin, 1897.
Husner, F., 'Leib und Seele in der Sprache Senecas', *Philologus Supplb.* 17 (1924), 118ff.
Hyde, W. W., *Ancient Greek Mariners*, New York, 1947.

REFERENCES

Ilberg, J., 'Über die Schriftstellerei des Klaudios Galenos', *RhM* 44 (1889), 207-39.
Inwood, B., *Ethics and Human Action in Early Stoicism*, Oxford, 1985.

Jacobsthal, P., *Early Celtic Art*, Oxford, 1944.
Jacoby, F., *Die Fragmente der griechischen Historiker (FGrH)*, zweiter Teil: A 87, *Poseidonios von Apameia*, Leiden, 1961.
c *Kommentar*, Leiden, 1963.
Jadaane, F., *L'influence du stoïcisme sur la pensée musulmane*, Beirut, 1968.
Jaeger, W., *Nemesios von Emesa*, Berlin, 1914.
Jahn, M., 'Der Wanderweg der Kimbern', *Mannus* 24 (1932), 150-7.
Jaki, S. L., 'The Milky Way before Galileo', *Journal for the History of Astronomy* 2 (1971), 161-7.
James, W., *Principles of Psychology*, London, 1890, New York, 1950.
Jocelyn, H. D., 'The Roman nobility and the religion of the republican state', *Journal of Religious History* 4 (1966), 89-104.
Jones, A. H. M., *The Cities of the Eastern Roman Provinces*, 2nd edn, Oxford, 1971.
Jones, R. M., 'The Ideas as the thoughts of God', *CPh* 21 (1926), 317-26.
'Posidonius and solar eschatology', *CPh* 27 (1932), 113-35.
Joret, C., 'Le Πέρσειον de Posidonius', *REG* 12 (1899), 43-7.
Jullian, C., *Histoire de la Gaule*, Paris, 1908-26.

Kahn, C. H., *Anaximander and the Origins of Greek Cosmology*, New York, 1960.
Kaibel, G., 'Antike Windrosen', *Hermes* 20 (1885), 579-624.
Keller, R. E., *The German Language*, London, 1978.
Kennedy, G., *The Art of Persuasion in Greece*, London, 1963.
Kerferd, G. B., 'The search for personal identity in Stoic thought, *Bull. J. Rylands Univ. Libr. Manchester* 55 (1972), 177-96.
'Origin of evil in Stoic thought, *Bull. J. Rylands Univ. Libr. Manchester* 60 (1978), 482-94.
'The problem of Synkatathesis and Katalepsis in Stoic doctrine', in *Les Stoïciens et leur logique*, ed. J. Brunschwig, 251-72, Paris 1978.
Kidd, I. G., 'Stoic intermediates and the end for man', *CQ* N.S. 5 (1955), 181-94, and in *Problems in Stoicism*, ed. A. A. Long, 150-72, London, 1971.
'Posidonius on emotions', in *Problems in Stoicism* 200-15.
'Moral actions and rules in Stoic ethics', in *The Stoics*, ed. J. M. Rist, 247-58, Berkeley/London, 1978.
'Philosophy and science in Posidonius', *Antike & Abendland* 24 (1978), 7-15.

REFERENCES

'Posidonius and Logic', in *Les Stoïciens et leur logique*, ed. J. Brunschwig, 273–83, Paris, 1978.
'Euemptosia – proneness to disease', in *On Stoic and Peripatetic Ethics; The Work of Arius Didymus*, Rutgers Univ. Studies in Classical Humanities, vol. 1, ed. W. W. Fortenbaugh, 107–13, New Brunswick/London, 1983.
'Posidonian methodology and the self-sufficiency of virtue', in Fondation Hardt, *Entretiens* XXXII, *Aspects de la philosophie hellénistique* (1986), 1–28.
'Orthos Logos as a criterion of truth in the Stoa', in *The Criterion of Truth*, edd. P. M. Huby and G. C. Neal, Liverpool Univ. 1988.
Kieffer, J. S., *Galen's Institutio Logica*, Baltimore, 1964.
Kilb, G., *Ethische Grundbegriffe der alten Stoa und ihre Übertragung durch Cicero im dritten Buch De finibus bonorum et malorum*, Freiburg i.B., 1939.
Kirchner, J., *Prosopographia Attica*, Berlin, 1901–3.
Kneale, W. and M., *The Development of Logic*, Oxford, 1963.
Kraft, K., 'Tougener und Teutonen', *Hermes* 85 (1957), 367–78.
Kroll, W., *Die Kosmologie des Plinius*, Breslau, 1930.
Die Kultur der ciceronischen Zeit, Breslau, 1933.
Kudlien, F., 'Poseidonios und die Aerzteschule der Pneumatiker', *Hermes* 90 (1962), 419–29.
Kühner, R.–Gerth, B., *Ausfürliche Grammatik der griechischen Sprache*,[3] II.1–2, Hanover/Leipzig, 1898, 1904.

Laffranque, M., 'Poseidonios d'Apamée et les mines d'Ibérie', *Pallas* 5 (1957), 17–25.
'Poseidonios historien. Un épisode significatif de la première guerre de Mithridate', *Pallas* 11 (1962), 103–13.
'Poseidonios, Eudoxe de Cyzique et la circumnavigation de l'Afrique', *Rev. Philos.* 153 (1963), 199–222.
Poseidonios d'Apamée. Essai de mise au point, Paris, 1964.
Lasserre, F., 'Abrégé inédit du Commentaire de Posidonios au Timée de Platon (PGen inv. 203)', *Accademia Toscana di Scienze e Lettere "La Columbaria" Studi* 83, 71–127, Firenze, 1986.
Lauffer, S., *Die Bergwerkssklaven von Laureion*, Akad. d. Wiss. Mainz geistes- und sozialwiss. Kl., 1955, No. 12; 1956, No. 11.
Leo, F., *Die griechisch-römische Biographie nach ihrer litterarischen Form*, Leipzig, 1901.
Letronne, A. J. *Mémoires de l'institut royal de France; Académie des inscript. et belles lettres*, tome VI, section cinquième: 'Des deux mesures de la terre attribuées à Posidonius', pp. 313–23, Paris, 1822.
Oeuvres choisies de A-J. Letronne, Paris, 1881–3.

REFERENCES

Lewis, D. M., 'The chronology of the Athenian new style coinage', *NC* 2 (1962), 175-300.
Lewis, P. R. and Jones, G. D. B., 'Roman gold-mining in north-west Spain', *JRS* 60 (1970), 169-85; *JRS* 62 (1972), 61-74.
Long, A. A., 'Carneades and the Stoic telos', *Phronesis* 12 (1967), 59-90.
'Stoic Determinism and Alexander of Aphrodisias De Fato I-XIV', *Arch. f. Gesch. d. Phil.* 52 (1970), 247-68.
ed., *Problems in Stoicism*, London, 1971.
'Language and thought in Stoicism', in *Problems in Stoicism*, 89-93.
Hellenistic Philosophy, London, 1974.
Long, A. A. and Sedley, D., *The Hellenistic Philosophers*, vol. 1, Cambridge, 1987.
Lörcher, A., *De compositione et fonte libri Ciceronis qui est de fato*, Diss. phil. Halenses, vol. 17, 1907.
Luschnat, O., 'Das Problem des ethischen Fortschritts in der alten Stoa', *Philologus* 102 (1958), 178-214.

Maass, E. W. T., *Aratea, Philol. Unters.* 12, Berlin, 1892.
Magie, D., *Roman Rule in Asia Minor*, Princeton, 1950.
Malitz, J., *Die Historien des Poseidonios*, Zetemata 79, München, 1983.
Mansfeld, J., *The Pseudo-Hippocratic Tract* Περὶ Ἑβδομάδων, Assen, 1971.
'Zeno of Citium', *Mnem.* 31 (1978), 134-78.
'Providence and the destruction of the universe in early Stoic thought', in *Studies in Hellenistic Religions*, ed. M. J. Vermaseren (*Études preliminaires aux religions orientales dans l'empire romain*, vol.78), 129-88, Leiden, 1979.
'Diogenes Laertius on Stoic philosophy', *Elenchos* 7 (1986), 297-382.
Marrou, H. I., *Histoire de l'éducation dans l'antiquité*, Paris, 1948.
Mates, B., *Stoic Logic*, Berkeley, 1961.
Matthes, D., 'Hermagoras von Temnos', *Lustrum* 3 (1958), 58-214.
Mattingly, H. B., 'Some problems in second-century Attic prosopography', *Historia* 20 (1971), 26-46.
'Scipio Aemilianus' Eastern Embassy', *CQ* 36 (1986), 491-5.
Mejer, J., 'Diogenes Laertius and his hellenistic background', *Hermes, Einzelschr.* 40, Wiesbaden, 1978.
Merlan, P., *From Platonism to Neoplatonism*, The Hague, 1953.
Merritt, B. D., 'Athenian Archons, 347/6-48/7 B.C.', *Historia* 26 (1977), 161-91.
Mette, H J., *Sphairopoiia (Untersuchungen zur Kosmologie des Krates von Pergamon)*, München, 1936.
Pytheas von Massalia (Kleine Texte für Vorlesungen und Übungen), Berlin, 1952.
Michell, H., *Sparta*, Cambridge, 1952.

REFERENCES

Mieli, A. and Brunet, P., *Histoire des sciences; antiquité*, Paris, 1935.
Miller, F., 'Paul of Samosata, Zenobia and Aurelian'. *JRS* 61 (1971), 1-17.
Modrze, A., 'Zur Ethik und Psychologie des Poseidonios', *Philologus* 87 (1932), 300-31.
Momigliano, A., *Alien Wisdom. The Limits of Hellenization*, Cambridge, 1975.
Mommsen, T., *Römische Geschichte*, Berlin, 1902-4.
Moraux, P., *Der Aristotelismus bei den Griechen von Andronikos bis Alexander von Aphrodisias*, Berlin, 1973.
Moreau, J., 'Ariston et le Stoïcisme', *REG* 50 (1948), 27-48.
Mühl, M., 'Poseidonios und der plutarchische Marcellus', *Klass. Phil. Stud.* ed. Jacoby, IV, Berlin, 1925.
Müllenhoff, K., *Deutsche Altertumskunde*, Berlin, 1870/77.
Müller, C., *Geographi Graeci Minores (GGM)*, Paris, 1882.

Nash, D., 'Reconstructing Poseidonios' Celtic Ethnography', *Britannia* 7 (1976), 111-26.
Nebel, G., 'Zur Ethik des Poseidonios', *Hermes* 74 (1939), 34-57.
Griechischer Ursprung, Wuppertal, 1948.
Neugebauer, O., *A History of Ancient Mathematical Astronomy (HAMA)*, Berlin, 1975.
Neugebauer, O. and Heusen, H. B. van, *Greek Horoscopes*, Philadelphia, 1959.
Nicolet, C., 'Mithridate et les ambassadeurs de Carthage (et Posidonius fr. 41)', in *Mélanges A. Piganiol*, II. 807-14, Paris, 1966.
L'ordre équestre, Paris, 1966, 1974.
Rome et la conquête du monde méditerranéen, Paris, 1977, 1978.
Nielsen, K., 'Remarques sur les noms des vents et des régions du ciel', *C & M* 7 (1945), 1-113.
Niese, B., 'Straboniana', *RhM* 42 (1887), 574-81.
Ninck, M. H., *Die Entdeckung von Europa durch die Griechen*, Basel, 1945.
Nissen, H., *Italische Landeskunde*, Berlin, 1883-1902.
Nock, A. D., 'Posidonius', *JRS* 49 (1959), 1-15.
Norden, E., 'Jahve und Moses in hellenistischer Theologie', *Festgabe von Fachgenossen und Freunden A. von Harnack zum siebzigsten Geburtstag dargebracht*, Tübingen, 1921 = *Kleine Schriften* 276-85.
Die Germanische Urgeschichte in Tacitus' Germania, Stuttgart, 3rd edn, 1923.

Oder, E., 'Quellensucher im Altertum', *Philologus, Supplb.* 7 (1899), 231-84.
Ogilvie, R. M., *A Commentary on Livy, Books 1-5*, Oxford, 1965.
The Library of Lactantius, Oxford, 1978.

REFERENCES

Olshausen, E., 'Zum Hellenisierungsprozess am pontischen Königshof', *Ancient Society* 5 (1974), 153-70.
O'Meara, D. J., *Structures hiérarchiques dans la pensée de Plotin*, Leiden, 1975.
Oost, S. I., 'Cyrene 96-74 B.C.', *CPh* 58 (1963), 11-25.
Otto, W. and Bengtson, H., *Zur Geschichte des Niedergangs des Ptolemäerreiches*, Abh. Bayr. Akad. N.F. 17, München, 1938.
Parete, M. I., 'χρόνος ἐπινοούμενος *e* χρόνος οὐ νοούμενος', *Parola del Passato* 31 (1976), 168-75.
Pearson, A. C., *The Fragments of Zeno and Cleanthes*, London, 1891.
Pease, A. S., M. *Tulli Ciceronis De natura deorum libri*, Cambridge, 1955.
Pembroke, S. G., 'Oikeiosis', in *Problems in Stoicism*, ed. A. A. Long, 114-49, London, 1971.
Pépin, J., *Idées grecques sur l'homme et sur Dieu*, Paris, 1971.
Pfeiffer, E., *Studien zum antiken Sternglauben, Stoicheia* II, 1916.
Pfligersdorffer, G., *Studien zu Poseidonios*, Sitz. d. Osterr. Akad. d. Wiss., Phil.-hist. Kl., Bd. 232, Abh. 5, Wien, 1959.
Philippson, R., 'Panaetiana', *RhM* 78 (1929), 337-60.
'Das dritte und vierte Buch der Tusculanen', *Hermes* 67 (1932), 245-94.
'Des Akademikers Kritik der epikureischen Theologie im ersten Buche der Tusculanen Ciceros', *Symb. Osl.* 20 (1940), 21-44.
Piggott, S., Daniel, G. and McBurney, C., edd., *France before the Romans*, London, 1974.
Pohlenz, M., *De Posidonii libris* περὶ παθῶν, (Diss.), Fleckeisens Jahrb. Supplb. 24, 1898.
'Das dritte und vierte Buch der Tusculanen', *Hermes* 41 (1906), 321-55.
'Poseidonios' Affektenlehre und Psychologie', *NGG* Phil.-hist. Kl., 1921, 163-94.
'Stoa und Semitismus', *Neue Jahrb. f. Wissenschaft und Jugendbildung* 2 (1926), 257-69.
'Antikes Führertum. Cicero de officiis und das Lebensideal des Panaitios', *Neue Wege z. Antike* II. 3, Leipzig, 1934.
'Cicero De Officiis III', *NGG* I.1 (1934) = *Kleine Schriften* I.253ff.
'Zenon und Chrysipp', *NGG* II.9 (1938).
Grundfragen der stoischen Philosophie, Abh. Gött. Ges., phil.-hist. Kl., 3 Folge 26, 1940.
'Tierische und menschliche Intelligenz bei Poseidonios', *Hermes* 76 (1941), 1ff.
Die Stoa, Göttingen, 1948-9.
Stoa und Stoiker, Zurich, 1950.
Kleine Schriften, Hildesheim, 1965.
Porter, B.-Moss, R. L. B., *Topographical Bibliography of Ancient Egyptian Hieroglyphic Texts, Reliefs and Paintings*, Oxford, 1927.

REFERENCES

Post, L. A., 'The Preludes to Plato's *Laws*', *TAPA* 60 (1929), 5-24.
Pozzi, E., 'Sopra il termine estremo della storia di Posidonio di Apamea', *RFIC* 41 (1913), 58-67.
Prell, H., *Die Vorstellungen des Altertums von der Erdumfangslänge*, Abh. d. Sächsischen Akad. d. Wiss., Math.-Naturwiss. Kl., 46, Heft 1, Berlin, 1959.

Raschke, M. G., 'New studies in Roman commerce with the East', in *Aufstieg u. Niedergang d. römischen Welt* II.9.2, 604-1378, Berlin/New York, 1978.
Rehm, A., *Griechische Windrosen*, Sitz. d. Königl. Bayer. Akad. d. Wiss., Abh. 3, Munich, 1916.
Das siebente Buch der Naturales Quaestiones des Seneca und die Kometentheorie des Poseidonios, Sitz. d. Bayer. Akad. d. Wiss., Phil.-Hist. Kl. 1921.
Reinhardt, K., *Poseidonios*, München, 1921.
Kosmos und Sympathie, München, 1926.
Poseidonios über Ursprung und Entartung, Orient und Antike 6, Heidelberg, 1928.
Poseidonios von Apameia, *RE*. XXII.1, 558-826, 1953.
'Philosophy and history among the Greeks', *G & R*, 2nd ser. 1 (1954), 82-90.
Parmenides,[2] Frankfurt-am-Mein, 1959.
Reitzenstein, R., *Die hellenistischen Mysterienreligion*, Leipzig/Berlin, 1910.
Richardson, J. S., 'The Spanish mines and the development of provincial taxation in the second century B.C.', *JRS* 66 (1976), 139-52.
Rieth, O., 'Über das Telos der Stoiker', *Hermes* 69 (1934), 13-45.
Ringshausen, K. W., *Poseidonios, Asklepiodot, Seneca und ihre Anschauungen über Erdbeben und Vulkane*, Borna-Leipzig, 1929.
Rist, J. M., *Stoic Philosophy*, Cambridge, 1969.
ed. *The Stoics*, Berkeley, 1978.
'Zeno and the origins of Stoic logic', in *Les Stoïciens et leur logique*, ed. J. Brunschwig, Paris 1978.
Robbins, F. E., 'Posidonius and the sources of Pythagorean arithmology', *CPh* 15 (1920), 309-22.
Rose, V., *Aristoteles Pseudepigraphus*, Lipsiae, 1863.
Rougé, J., *Recherches sur l'organisation du commerce maritime en Méditerranée sous l'empire romain*, Paris, 1966.
Roussel, P., *Délos*, Paris, 1925.
Rudberg, G., *Forschungen zu Poseidonios*, Uppsala, 1918.
Rusch, P., *De Posidonio Lucreti Cari auctore in carmine de rerum natura VI*, Diss., Griefswald, 1882.

REFERENCES

Russell, D. A., *Plutarch*, London, 1973.
'Longinus' On the Sublime, Oxford, 1964.

Sabra, A. I., 'Al-Nayrīzī' in *Dictionary of Scientific Biography* x.6, ed. C. C. Gillispie, New York, 1970-80.
Salvestroni, L., 'Sulle orme di Posidonio', *RSF* 3 (1948), 1-7.
Sambursky, S., *The Physical World of the Greeks*, London, 1956.
Physics of the Stoics, London, 1959.
Samuel, A. E., *Ptolemaic Chronology*, Münchener Beiträge zur Papyrusforschung und antiken Rechtgeschichte, Heft 43, München, 1962.
Sandbach, F. H., 'Phantasia Kataleptike', in *Problems in Stoicism*, ed. A. A. Long, 9-21, London, 1971.
'Ennoia and Prolepsis in the Stoic theory of knowledge', in *Problems in Stoicism* 22-37, London, 1971.
The Stoics, London, 1975.
Aristotle and the Stoics, Cambridge Philological Society, Suppl. vol. 10, Cambridge, 1985.
Saunders, T., *Plato, The Laws*, Penguin Books, 1970.
Schedler, P. M., *Die Philosophie des Macrobius und ihr Einfluss auf die Wissenschaft des christlichen Mittelalters*, Beitr. z. Gesch. d. Phil. des Mittelalters, Bd. 13, Hft. 1, Münster, 1916.
Scheppig, R., *De Posidonio Apamensi rerum gentium terrarum scriptore*, Diss. Halle, 1869.
Schindler, K., *Die stoische Lehre von den Seelenteilen u. Seelenvermögen insb. bei Panaitios u. Poseidonios u. ihre Verwendung bei Cicero*, Diss. München, 1934.
Schmekel, A., *Die Philosophie der mittleren Stoa in ihrem geschichtlichen zusammenhange dargestellt*, Berlin, 1892.
Die positive Philosophie in ihrer geschichtlichen Entwicklung, published by J. Schmekel, Berlin, 1938.
Schmidt, E. G., 'Atome bei Mochus, Nonnos und Demokrit', *Philologus* 122 (1978), 137-43.
Schmidt, K., *Kosmologische Aspekte im Geschichtswerk des Poseidonios*, Hypomnemata 63, Göttingen, 1980.
Schmidt, R., *Stoicorum Grammatica*, Halle, 1839, Amsterdam, 1967.
Schnabel, P., *Berossos und die babylonisch-hellenistische Literatur*, Leipzig, 1923.
Schofield, M., 'The retrenchable present', in *The Bounds of Being: Studies in Hellenistic Metaphysics*, edd. J. Barnes and M. Mignucci, Naples, *Elenchos* (forthcoming).
Schühlein, F., *Studien zu Posidonius Rhodius*, Programm Freising, 1885/86.
Zu Posidonius Rhodius, Programm Freising 1890/91.

REFERENCES

Untersuchungen über des Posidonius Schrift Περὶ ὠκεανοῦ, Freising, 1901.
Schulten, A., *Iberische Landeskunde*, Strasbourg, 1955–57.
Schulz, W., 'Der Wanderzug der Kimbern zum Gebiete der Boier', *Germania* 13 (1929), 139–43.
Schulze, W., *Zur Geschichte lateinischer Eigennamen*, Berlin, 1904.
Schumacher, W., *Untersuchungen zur Datierung des Astronomen Kleomedes*, Diss. Köln, 1975.
Schürer, E. (revised G. Vermes and F. Miller), *The History of the Jewish People in the Age of Jesus Christ*, vol. 1, Edinburgh, 1973.
Schwartz, E., 'Einiges über Assyrien, Syrien, Koilesyrien', *Philologus* 86 (1931), 373–99.
Scramuzza, V. M., 'Roman Sicily', in *Economic Survey of Ancient Rome*, ed. T. Frank, III.225–377, Baltimore, 1937.
Shackleton Bailey, D. R., *Cicero's Letters to Atticus*, Cambridge, 1965.
Sherwin-White, A. N., *Roman Foreign Policy in the East*, London, 1984.
Simon, H., *Roms Kriege in Spanien 154–133 v. Chr.*, Frankfurt, 1962.
Skeat, T. C., *The Reigns of the Ptolemies*, Münch. Beitr. z. Papyrus-forschung u. Antiken Rechtsgeschichte, 39, Munich, 1954.
Solmsen, F., *Cleanthes or Posidonius? The Basis of Stoic Physics*, Mededelingen der Koninklijke Nederlandse Akademie van Wetenschappen, Afd. Letterkunde, N.R. 24 no. 9, 265–89, Amsterdam, 1961.
Sorabji, R., *Time, Creation, and the Continuum*, London, 1983.
Spoerri, W., *Späthellenistische Berichte über Welt, Kultur, und Götter: Untersuchungen zu Diodor von Sicilien*, Schweiz. Beitr. z. Altertumswiss. 9, Basel, 1959.
'Zu Diodor von Sizilien 1.7–8', *Mus. Helv.* 18 (1961), 63–82.
Stähelin, F., 'Die vorrömische Schweiz im Lichte geschichtlicher Zeugnisse und sprachlicher Tatsachen', *Zeitschr. f. Schweiz. Gesch.* 15 (1935), 337–68.
Stahl, W. H., 'Astronomy and geography in Macrobius', *TAPA* 1942, 232–58.
Macrobius' Commentary on the Dream of Scipio, New York, 1952.
Stein, L., *Die Psychologie der Stoa*, Berlin, 1886/88.
Steinmetz, F-A., 'Die Freundschaftslehre des Panaitios', *Palingenesia* III (1967).
Steinmetz, H., *De ventorum descriptionibus apud Graecos Romanosque*, Göttingen, 1907.
Steinmetz, P., 'Zu Erdbebentheorie des Poseidonios', *RhM* 105 (1962), 261–63.
Straaten, M. van, *Panétius*, Amsterdam, 1946.
Panaetii Rhodii Fragmenta, 3rd edn, Leiden, 1962.
Strack, M. E. D. L., *Die Dynastie der Ptolemäer*, Berlin, 1897.

REFERENCES

Strasburger, H., 'Poseidonios on problems of the Roman Empire', *JRS* 55 (1965), 40–53.
Straume-Zimmermann, L., *Ciceros Hortensius*, Bern & Frankfurt, 1976.
Strohm, H., 'Studien zur Schrift von der Welt', *Mus. Helv.* 9 (1952), 137–75.
'Theophrast und Poseidonios', *Hermes* 81 (1953), 278–95.
Stückelberger, A., *Senecas 88 Brief*, Heidelberg, 1965.
Sudhaus, S., *Aetna*, Leipzig, 1898.
Susemihl, F., *Geschichte der griechischen Literatur in der Alexandrinerzeit*, Leipzig, 1891.
Swerdlow, N., 'Hipparchus on the distance of the sun', *Centaurus* 14 (1969), 287–305.
Syme, Sir Ronald, *The Roman Revolution*, Oxford, 1939.
Szabó, Á., *The Beginnings of Greek Mathematics*, Holland, 1978.

Tannery, P., *La géométrie grecque*, Paris, 1887, repr. New York, 1976.
'Sur Héraclide du Pont', *REG* 12 (1899), 305–11.
Mémoires scientifiques, Paris, 1912–50.
Tarán, L., *Parmenides*, Princeton, 1965.
Tarbell, F. B., 'The form of the chlamys', *CPh* 1 (1906), 283–9.
Tarn, W. W., *Hellenistic Civilisation*, London, 1927; revised with G. T. Griffith, 1966.
The Greeks in Bactria and India, Cambridge, 1938, 2nd edn, 1951 (1966).
Taylor, A. E., *A Commentary on Plato's Timaeus*, Oxford, 1928.
Tchernia, A., *Le vin de l'Italie romaine*, Ecole française de Rome, 1986.
Thalamas, A., *La géographie d'Eratosthène*, Versailles, 1921.
Theiler, W., 'Tacitus und die antike Schicksalslehre', in *Phyllobolia für P. von der Mühll*, 35–90, Basel, 1946.
Poseidonios, Die Fragmente, Berlin, 1982.
Thévenaz, P., *L'Âme du monde, le devenir, et la matière chez Plutarque*, Paris, 1938.
Thiel, J. H., *Eudoxus van Cyzicus*, Amsterdam, 1939 = *Eudoxus of Cyzicus*, trans. by A. M. de Bruin-Cousins, Groningen, 1966.
Thompson, D'Arcy, 'The Greek winds', *CR* 32 (1918), 49–56.
Thomson, J. O., *History of Ancient Geography*, Cambridge, 1948.
Thomson, M., *The New Style Silver Coinage of Athens*, New York, 1961.
Thraemer, E., *Pergamos*, Leipzig, 1888.
Tierney, J. J., 'The Celtic ethnography of Posidonius', *Proc. Royal Irish Acad.* 60 (1960), no. 5, pp. 189–275; repr. 1985.
Todd, R. B., 'The Stoic common notions', *Symb. Osloenses* 48 (1973), 47–75.
Alexander of Aphrodisias on Stoic Physics (Philosophia Antiqua 28), Leiden, 1976.

REFERENCES

Toepelmann, P., *De Posidonio Rhodio rerum scriptore*, Diss. Bonn, 1867.
Touloumakos, J., 'Zu Poseidonios Fr. 36 (Jac)', *Philologus* 110 (1966), 138–42.
Tovar, A., *Iberische Landeskunde*, Baden-Baden, 1976.
Tozer, H. F., *A History of Ancient Geography*, Cambridge, 1897.
Tracy, S. V., 'Athens in 100 B.C.', *Harv. St. in Class. Phil.* 83 (1979), 213–35.
Trüdinger, K., *Studien zur Geschichte der griechisch-römischen Ethnographie*, Diss. Basel, 1918.
Tsekourakis, D., 'Studies in the terminology of early Stoic ethics, *Hermes*, Einzelschr. 32 (1974).
Turcan, R., 'Mithras Platonicus: recherches sur l'hellénisation philosophique de Mithra', *Études préliminaires aux religions orientales dans l'empire romain*, 47, Leiden, 1975.

Ueberweg, F.–Flashar, H., *Grundriss der Geschichte der Philosophie*, Band 3, Basel/Stuttgart, 1983.
Unger, G. F., 'Umfang und Anordnung der Geschichte des Poseidonios', *Philologus* 55 (1896), 73–122; 245–56.

Vári, R., 'Die sog. Inedita Tactica Leonis', *Byz. Zeitschr.* 27 (1927), 241–70.
Vessberg, O., *Studien zur Kunstgeschichte der römischen Republik*, Lund, 1941.
Viedebantt, O., 'Antike Messungen der Landenge von Suez', *RhM* 69 (1914), 558–64.
'Eratosthenes, Hipparchus, Posidonius', *Klio* 14 (1915), 207–56.
Vlastos, G., 'Zeno of Sidon as a critic of Euclid', in *The Classical Tradition; Literary and Historical Studies in Honor of Harry Caplan*, ed. L. Wallach, Cornell, 1966.
Vogt, J., *Sklaverei und Humanität*, 2nd edn, Wiesbaden, 1972 = *Ancient Slavery and the Ideal of Man*, trans. T. Wiedemann, Oxford, 1974.

Walbank, F. W., *A Historical Commentary on Polybius*, Oxford, 1957, 1967, 1978.
Polybius, Berkeley, 1972.
Walter, H., *Die Collectanea Rerum Memorabilium, Hermes Einzelschr.* 22 (1969).
Walzer, R., *Greek into Arabic: Essays on Islamic philosophy* (Oriental Studies 1), Oxford, 1962.
Waszink, J. H., *Tertullian, De anima*, Amsterdam, 1947.
Watson, G., *The Stoic Theory of Knowledge*, Belfast, 1966.
Weinreich, O., 'Ciceros Gebet an die Philosophie', *Archiv für Religionswissenschaft* 21 (1922), 504–6.
Wellmann, M., *Die pneumatische Schule bis auf Archigenes, Phil. Unters.* 14 (1895).

REFERENCES

'Zur Geschichte der Medicin im Altertum', *Hermes* 35 (1900), 349-84.
Wells, C. W., *The German Policy of Augustus*, Oxford, 1972.
Wendland, P., *Die hellenistisch-römische Kultur in ihren Beziehungen zu Judentum und Christentum*, Tübingen, 1907-12.
Wendling, E., 'Zu Posidonius und Varro', *Hermes* 28 (1893), 335-53.
West, M. L., *Hesiod, Theogony*, Oxford, 1966.
West, S., *The Ptolemaic Papyri of Homer*, Köln, 1967.
Whittacker, T., *Macrobius, or Philosophy, Science and Letters in the Year 400*, Cambridge, 1923.
Widengren, G., 'Iran, der grosse Gegner Roms: Königsgewalt, Feudalismus, Militärwesen', in *Aufstieg u. Niedergang d. römischen Welt*, (*ANRW*), II.9.1, 219-306, Berlin/New York, 1976.
Wilamowitz-Moellendorff, U. von, 'Asianismus und Atticismus', *Hermes* 35 (1900), 1-52.
'Athenion und Aristion', *Sitzb. Akad. Berl.* (1923), 39-50.
Der Glaube der Hellenen, 3rd edn, Darmstadt, 1959.
Will, E., *Histoire politique du monde hellénistique*, Nancy, 1979.
Winnington-Ingram, R., *Mode in Ancient Greek Music*, Cambridge, 1936.
Wiseman, T. P., *Cinna the Poet and other Roman Essays*, Leicester, 1974.
Wright, F. A., *A History of Later Greek Literature*, London, 1932.

Young, J. H., 'Studies in South Attica: country estates at Sounion', *Hesperia* 25 (1956), 122-46.

Zeller, E., *Die Philosophie der Griechen in ihrer geschichtlichen Entwicklung*, Leipzig, 4-6 edn, 1919-22.
Ziegler, K., in *Studi in onore di L. Castiglioni*, Florence, 1960.
Zimmermann, R., 'Posidonius und Strabo', *Hermes* 23 (1888), 103-30.

INDICES

The indices refer to the *Commentary*. They should therefore be used in combination with the indices of volume 1, which refer to the text. The references are to testimonia and fragment numbers. Testimonia are prefixed by the letter T (e.g. T18). Fragments have no prefix, and longer fragments whose commentary is subdivided in a classificatory system are further defined by subsection and where necessary by line number as given in the *Commentary*. Thus, 49B(2)(a), 10–13 means F49 under subsection B(2)(a) lines 10–13 as tabulated in the commentary on that fragment. 219, 1–9 means F219 in the commentary on lines 1–9.

INDEX OF PASSAGES CITED OR DISCUSSED

ACHILLES TATIUS
In Aratum Isagoga excerpta
Isag. 2, p. 30.20ff Maass   18
Isag. 8, p. 38 M   97
Isag. 14, p. 41.13ff M   127/128
Isag. 24, p. 55.17ff M   129/130
Isag. 26, p. 59–60 M   49B(2)(b), 37–43
Isag. 29, p. 62ff M   49B(1), 5–9; 49B(4)(b)(iv), 118–25; 209
Isag. 31, p. 66f M   49B(2)(a), 10–13
Isag. 31, p. 67.27 M   49B(2)(a), 10–13

AELIANUS, CLAUDIUS
Varia Historia
13.16   235
F2 (Hercher)   234

AELIANUS
Tactica
App. 3   203

AETIUS
Placita
I.14, *Dox. Gr.* 312a 9f, b 12f   16; 196
II.12, *Dox. Gr.* 340.7ff   49B(2)(a), 10–13; 209
II.20.4, *Dox. Gr.* 349   118A
II.20.16, *Dox. Gr.* 351   118A
II.22.5, *Dox. Gr.* 352.9f   117
II.23.5, *Dox. Gr.* 353   118B
II.29.4, *Dox. Gr.* 360a 3–8, b 5–11   124
III.1, *Dox. Gr.*   129/130
III.1, *Dox. Gr.* 364.19–366.3
III.2, *Dox. Gr.* 366.5–367.18   131; 132
III.3, *Dox. Gr.* 367.20–370.22   135
III.4, *Dox. Gr.* 370.25–371.26   136
III.5, *Dox. Gr.* 371.28ff   134B(3)(5)
III.5.11, *Dox. Gr.* 373.28ff   121
III.6, *Dox. Gr.* 374.10ff   121
III.11.4, *Dox. Gr.* 377.18f   49B(2)(a), 10–13
III.14.1, *Dox. Gr.* 378.21ff   49B(2)(a), 10–13; 209
III.17, *Dox. Gr.* 382.15–383.25   138; 219.1–9; 220
III.17.9, *Dox. Gr.* 383.26ff   218A
III.18, *Dox. Gr.* 384.1–14   133
IV.1, *Dox. Gr.* 384–6   222
IV.13, *Dox. Gr.* 403   194

AETIUS MEDICUS
II.9   235

AETNA
625   230D; 234;

AGATHARCHIDES
De mari Erythraeo
73–75, *GGM* I.159f   245

INDEX OF PASSAGES CITED OR DISCUSSED

AGATHEMERUS
1.5, *GGM* II.472   204A
II.6–7, *GGM* II.473   137

ALEXANDER APHRODISIENSIS
De anima
p. 163.4 Bruns   171
In Aristotelis Analyticorum Priorum librum I commentarium
21.28ff Wallies   191
24b 18ff Wallies   191
In Aristotelis Meteorologicorum libros commentaria
16.12ff H   120
72.18–22; 73.1–9 H   118A

AMMIANUS MARCELLINUS
15.9   67; 69
17.7.13   230B
22.15.8   222

AMMONIUS
In Aristotelis Analyticorum Priorum librum I commentarium
8.20ff Wal.   88

ANONYMUS I
Isagoga in Arati Phaenomena
6, p.97.1 Maass   49B(2)(a),
32–6; 49B(4)(b)(iv),
118–25; 118B; 210

ANONYMUS II
Isagoga in Arati Phaenomena
8, p. 127 Maass   11; 135; 136

APICIUS
II.2.6   52
III.13.1, 2   70
III.113–15   70
IV.2.3   70

APOLLONIUS DYSCOLUS
De Adverbiis
154.28ff   45

De Conjunctionibus
243.11–25   45
244.6ff   45
De Syntaxi
376f, 382, 388.9ff, 436.10ff,   45
444.9ff, 485

APOLLONIUS RHODIUS
Bk IV   246B(I)(3)

APPIANUS
Praefatio
13   264.18–19
Bella Civilia
BC IV.66.282   T27
Κελτική
   Celt. 12   67D; 69
   13   272B, 41–4
Ἰβηρική
   Iber. 48f   271
Ἰλλυρική
   Ill. 4   73
   11   70
Μιθριδάτειος
   Mithr. 20–3   253.78–84
   24–27   255.2–9
   28   253.8, 112ff, 145–7
   28–9   253 *fin.*
   48   253.26–30
   55   51
   59   253 *fin.*
Συριακή
   Syr. 67   54; 64
   68   61; 63
   68–9   72

ARATUS
Phaenomena
148–59   121

ARCHIMEDES
Sand-reckoner   115A(b);
   115K; 115L
1.8   202A

INDEX OF PASSAGES CITED OR DISCUSSED

ARISTARCHUS
On Sizes and Distances   9; 115; 122B; 125

ARISTOTLE
Analytica Priora
24b 18ff	191
65a 4	197

Analytica Posteriora
90a 15ff	125
93a 23ff	125

De Anima
403a	154; 155; 162; 169F
404b 8ff	85
411b 6	149
414b 2	165.164ff
432b 4–7	165.164ff

De Caelo
279a 11f	97
286b 10–287b 21	116
291b 11–23	116
291b 20ff	122D
292a 4	122D
298a 10ff	49E, 305–8
298a 16	202A
310ab	93

Categoriae   189B(a)

Ethica Eudemia
1229b 28f   272A3(b)(i), 12–22

Ethica Nicomachea
1115b 26ff   272A3(b)(i), 12–22

De Generatione Animalium
777b 21f	122D
789b 11	284.56–60

De Generatione et Corruptione
314ab	96
317b 34f	96
324a 24ff	95

Historia Animalium
544a 18–21	106
568a 4	221
598a 11	244
632b 19	243

Metaphysica
Z3	92
1090b 5	196

Meteorologica
I.3, 340ab	120
I.4, 341b 1–342a 33	131; 132
I.5, 342b 5ff	119C
I.6–7, 342b 35–345a 10	131; 132
I.8, 345a 11–346b 15	129/130
I.8, 345b 1–9	9
I.9–12, 346b 16–349a 11	136
I.11–12, 347b 12–349a 12	136
I.11, 347b 23	11
I.13, 350b 7ff	240.6–10
II.1, 354a 5ff	215; 220; 221
II.2, 354b 35ff	118A
II.2, 355ab	219.134
II.2, 355a 15f	219.80–134
II.2, 355b 21ff	219.1–9
II.3, 358b 34ff	219.134
II.3, 359a 17ff	219.136–45
II.3, 359b 4ff	219.146–54
II.4–6, 359b 27–365a 14	137
II.4, 360a 10	135
II.5, 362a 32ff	49B(2)(a), 14–17; 201
II.5, 362b 12ff	49E, 305–8; 200
II.7, 365a 14ff	12; 135
II.8, 366b 15ff	230D
II.8, 368b 23ff	229B(i); 230C
II.9, 369a 10–370a 34	135
III.1, 370b 5ff	135
III.2–6, 371b 18–378b 9	121
III.3, 372b 12–373a 32	133
III.4–5, 373a 32–377a 28	134
III.4, 373b 13f	114; 119C
III.6, 377b 24ff	121
IV.2–3, 379b 10–381b 22	284.84–99

De Nobilitate   86a

De Partibus Animalium
647b 30–648a 13	169F
650b 19–651a 19	169F
680a 31–4	106

Physica
B2	18
206a 17	97
206b 20ff	97

INDEX OF PASSAGES CITED OR DISCUSSED

207a 8ff	97	395b 14ff	131A4
212b 8	97	395b 30ff	12
213b 31	97	396a 1–16	230B
Δ10–14, 217b 29–224a 16	98	396a 3	229B(i)
Poetica		399a 26	95
1456b 38ff	45	400b 2	234
Politica		400b 12	101
1264a 12–35	60	*Problemata*	
1274a 22	284.11–19	14.1ff	169F
1327b 18ff	169F	19.24	106
De Respiratione		20.21	106
193b 23ff	18	33, 35, 37	219.134
Rhetorica			
1416b 21	189B(a)(iii)	ARISTOXENUS	
De Sensu		Frs. 98–101 Wehrli	292
437a 23ff	193		
437b 11ff	85	ARIUS DIDYMUS	
Topica		F14, *Dox. Gr.* 454f	121
141b 15ff	196	*Dox. Gr.* 455.15f	15;
Fragmenta			134B(2)(5)
F92 Rose³, 69 Gigon	T12	F20, *Dox. Gr.* 457	96
F210, 738 Gigon	125	F25, *Dox. Gr.* 460f	97
Frs. 246–8, 686 ff Gigon	222	F26, *Dox. Gr.* 461	98
F544, 550 Gigon 240.16–29		F29, *Dox. Gr.* 464	99
		F30, *Dox. Gr.* 465	102
		F33, *Dox. Gr.* 467	126
		F35, *Dox. Gr.* 468	136B
PS.-ARISTOTLE		Stobaeus, *Ecl.* II.57–116 W	89
De Mirabilibus Auscultationibus			
46, 833b 15ff	239.31–6	ARRIAN	
53, 834a 33f	219.136–45	*Indica*	
87, 837a 24ff	239	3.7–8	212/213
91, 837b 20ff	269	29	49B(3)(b), 49–61
127, 842b 15ff	235	30	244
130, 843a 6f	219.19–32	39.5	244
154, 846a 9ff	234		
De Mundo		ASCLEPIADES OF MYRLEIA	
391b 9f	14	*FGrH* 697, F7	247
392b 20ff	49C, 229ff		
393a 19ff	219.15–19	ASCONIUS	
393b 22	49E, 305–8	*In Pisonianam* 11	271.1–4
393b 25ff	206		
394a 33ff	11; 136	ATHENAEUS	
394b 20ff	137	*Deipnosophistae*	
395a 11ff	135	III.126A	285B
395a 33ff	15; 134B(2)(5)		

INDEX OF PASSAGES CITED OR DISCUSSED

Deipnosophistae (cont.)
V.211A–C	56; 288
VI.255E	253.32–6
VI.272D–275B	265–7 Context
VI.274C–E	78
XIII.611B	288

ATTICUS
F8, 814Aff	21

AUGUSTINUS
Confessiones
XI.10–28	98

De Civitate Dei
VIII.22–4	108B(2)

AUSONIUS
Ordo Nobilium Urbium
XVI.2	234

AVIENUS
Ora Maritima
350ff	246BI(2)

CAECILIUS
FGrH 183, F1	262

CAESAR, GAIUS JULIUS
De Bello Gallico
I.1	73
I.12.4	272B41–4
I.27	272B41–4
II.3–4	73
III.9	276
IV.29	217B3
VI.11–28	67
VI.13–16	69
VI.14	68
VI.24f	272B36f

CICERO
Academicae Quaestiones
1.19	87
2.5	58
2.26	188; 195

Brutus
53	256
130	256
306	253.112ff
307	278 *fin.*
312	T28; 278 *fin.*
316	T29; 278 *fin.*
317–33	T33

De Consolatione 37
De Divinatione
Bk 1	7; 26; 107; 109
1.6	107
1.9–10	108
1.11–64	107
1.12	106; 108
1.15	106
1.34	110
1.35	106
1.63	187A
1.71	104D; 106
1.82–3	107
1.86	106
1.109	106
1.110	106; 107; 187A
1.117–20	107
1.118	106
1.120	106
1.124–5	106
1.125–8	25; 107
1.125–30	107; 110
II.27	110
II.34	217B3
II.46–7	109
II.90	111

Epistulae ad Atticum
1.12.4	T109/110
II.12.2	253 *fin.*
XIII.40.1	256

Epistulae ad Familiares
12.15.2	258

Epistulae ad Q. Fratrem
1.1.37	36

De Fato
41–4	170A(1); 190

De Finibus
III.16ff	89; 160

INDEX OF PASSAGES CITED OR DISCUSSED

III.21	187A	III.37	118A; 118B		
III.43	170D	III.74	273		
III.45-8	179	*De Officiis*			
III.49, 56, 57	171	I.1.7	176		
III.50, 56	170D	I.11	159		
III.52	171	I.15ff	180		
III.69	170D	I.69, 72	170C		
III.76ff	160	I.90	T9/10		
IV.4	87	I.102	154		
V.23	170C	I.157-8	186B		
De Inventione Rhetorica		II.2	176		
I.8	43	II.16	252		
De Legibus		II.28	271.4-8		
I.26	284.84-99	II.41-2	284.11-19		
II.14-16	178	III.5	176		
II.62ff	240.40-5	III.8	T9/10		
III.14	178; 179	III.34	41		
De Lege Agraria		III.121	176		
2.95	268	*De Oratore*			
De Natura Deorum		1.45	T9/10		
1.16	170D	1.57	258		
1.37	20	2.225	256		
1.53	170C	*Philippicae*			
1.85	22	1.13	256		
1.93	87	*In Pisonem*			
Bk II	85B	60	271.4-8		
II.14	121	*Post Reditum ad Quirites*			
II.18	99a	19-20	255 *fin.*		
II.21	99a	*De Re Publica*			
II.23ff	93	1.10.15	121		
II.24	118A	1.21f	T86; 257		
II.37	186B	2.21-2	284.11-19		
II.39-40	118A; 127/128	3.9.16	67.28-30		
II.40	9; 17	5.10	259/260		
II.54	127/128	6.11	58		
II.58	101	*De Senectute*			
II.71	100	77	186B		
II.79	176	*Tusculanae Disputationes*			
II.81-88	T85	1.62	284.22-4		
II.85	99b	III.11	155		
II.103	122B	III.18-19	155		
II.115ff	8	III.25	165		
II.118	13; 99b	IV.2	256		
II.134-6	284.84-99	IV.10	T91		
II.136	T111				

1015

INDEX OF PASSAGES CITED OR DISCUSSED

Tusculanae Disputationes (cont.)
IV.14	170C
IV.21	155
IV.26	164A
IV.27-33	163CE; 165
V.5	179; 284.11-19, 22-4
V.7	284.11-19
V.12	184
V.14	253.78-84
V.101	219.9-15
V.120	170D

In Verrem
II.4	257
IV.62	76
IV.115-16, 120-3, 131	257

CLAUDIAN
De Piis Fratribus   234

CLEMENS ALEXANDRINUS
Paedagogus
1.1	176

Stromateis
II.19.101	186
IV.8.62.2	269
V.14.95	186
VIII.9	95; 190

CLEOMEDES
De Motu Circulari Corporum Caelestium
I.1.1, p. 2.9f Z	14
I.1.2-8, p. 4.10-16.12 Z	97
I.1.7, p. 14.2 Z	16
I.1.9, p. 16f Z	8
I.2.11f, p. 20f Z	209
I.4, p. 34.23-36.1 Z	126
I.5.21ff, p. 38.25ff Z	49B(2)(b), 37-43
I.6, p. 50ff Z	49B(4)(b)(iv), 118-25; 209; 210
I.6.31-2	118B
I.7, p. 62ff Z	49B(3)(a), 44-8; 208; 209
I.7.35, p. 64 Z	49B(2)(b), 37-43
I.10.53, p. 98.4f Z	115Ab; 204B
II.1, p. 120.7-	T57; 9; 19

168.10 Z	
II.1.75, p. 136.24ff Z	115K
II.1.76, p. 140.7ff Z	115Ab
II.1.80-2,	115F-X; 116
p. 146.18-150.23 Z	
II.1.80, p. 146.18-27 Z	122B
II.1.85, p. 156.10-16 Z	138
II.1. 89, p. 162.14ff Z	119E
II.2, p. 168.13-170.27 Z	9
II.2.94, p. 170.11-27 Z	115G; 116
II.3.95, p. 172.9ff Z	125
II.3.98, p. 178.1-5 Z	138; 219.80-134
p. 178.2 Z	9
p. 178.10ff Z	122B
p. 178.13-24 Z	125
II.3.99, p. 178.26-180.20 Z	10
p. 180.4ff Z	122A
II.4.100-105,	123; 125
p. 180.23-190.16 Z	
II.4.100, p. 180.26-182.7 Z	122D
II.4.104, p. 188.8ff Z	134A
II.4.106, p. 192.14-20 Z	125
II.6.24, p. 224 Z	121

COLUMELLA
2.22ff	70
5.5.15	T22

CORPUS INSCRIPTIONUM LATINARUM
CIL II.2660	243

CORPUS INSCRIPTIONUM SEMITICARUM
CISem I.122	246

CRATES
F34f Mette	49F(3), 326ff

CURTIUS
XI.9	272A3(c)

DEMOCRITUS
68.300,14 DK	284.126-30

1016

INDEX OF PASSAGES CITED OR DISCUSSED

DEMOSTHENES
13.24	253.103ff
19.314	253.103ff

DICAEARCHUS
F30 Wehrli	284.47–52
F49 Wehrli	284.11–19
F110 Wehrli	204A
F112 Wehrli	246B(1)(3)

DIO CASSIUS
27, F90	273
45.17.5	121
47.40.2	121

DIODORUS SICULUS
1.38–41.9	222
2.36.1–5	223
2.48.6ff	219.136–45
2.49–53	238
2.51.4	244
2.52.8–53.4	223
3.15ff	49B(3)(b), 49–61
3.35.4–6	245
4.19–20	269
5.2.2	249B
5.23.2	265–7 Context
5.25–32	67
5.26.1	229A
5.27	273.21–30
5.28	67
5.29.4–5	274
5.31	69
5.31.3–4	274 Context
5.32.1–5	73
5.32.4	272B32–4, 34–6
5.33–8	271 fin.
5.35–8	239/240
5.39	268
5.40	265–7 Context
5.40.3	53
5.59.3	253.95–7
7.12.5, 8	240.16–29
14.115.5	274.7–9
17.105.5	244
19.44.4	233
19.98	219.136–45
19.98.2	279
20.48	253.171ff
31.26.6–7	265–7 Context
33.4a	54
33.6, 12–13, 22–3	58
33.18	57
33.22	56
33.24–6	224
33.28	251
33.28b	58; 266
34/5.1	61; 278
34/5.2	59; 262
34/5.2.24b	250
34/5.15–17	63
34/5.21	65
34/5.22, 28	72
34/5.30a b	240.29–40; 272B38f
34/5.31	78
34/5.34	66
36.1–11	262
36.3.5	250
36.5.3	253.125
36.8–10	253 fin.
37.1.5	272.2–4
37.2.11	253.85–92
37.3.5–6	265–7 Context
37.5.1	266
37.15.3	253.157ff
37.26–7	253.78–84
37.29.3–4	255 fin.

DIOGENES LAERTIUS
Vitae Philosophorum
I.1	285B
I.6	69
I.40	284.47–52
III.67	139; 141A
VII.7–9	179
32	90
40	88
41	89
41–83	42
42–3	188
47	188

INDEX OF PASSAGES CITED OR DISCUSSED

Vitae Philosophorum (cont.)

49–53	42	173	169F
55–63	189	179	165.2–5
57	188; 189	201	161
58	45	VIII.32	108B(2)
65	188	48	49B(2)(a), 10–13
66	188	XI.21	49B(2)(a), 10–13
68	188		
71f	45; 192		
84	89		
85–6	159; 160; 169A		
87–8	186; 187A		
88	101; 102		
89–91	180; 182		
92f	170C		
93	180		
95	154		
105–6	170D; 171		
107	171		
110	147; 180		
111	152		
113	155		
114	152		
115	163C		
118	175		
127	175		
128	170C		
129	90; 169F		
130	186B		
132–3	18; 89; 90		
135	199a		
136	92		
137	93; 101; 127/128		
138	20		
139	21		
140	97		
141	98		
147	102		
148–9	103; 107		
150	92		
151	108B(2)		
152	131A4; 132B		
153	135		
156f	139		
157	147		
161	182		

DIONYSIUS OF HALICARNASSUS
Antiquitates Romanae

1.5.2	60
5.2, 8–12	256

De Compositione Verborum

II.70.15ff Roberts	45
IV.96.12ff Roberts	45
VI.108.15ff Roberts	45

DIONYSIUS PERIEGETES

3–7	201
7	200
20–5	206
623, 1164	246A(i)

DIONYSIUS THRAX

93 Uhlig	45

DIOSCURIDES

3.52 W	70
5.94 W	241
5.181 W	235

DURIS

F54	233

EMPEDOCLES

F109 DK	85

EPHORUS

FGrH 70, F132	272A3(b)(ii)

EPICTETUS

2.18.16	162
3.2.1ff	89
3.22.30–7	164H

EPICURUS

F163 Us.	179

INDEX OF PASSAGES CITED OR DISCUSSED

ERATOSTHENES
FIII B 58 Berger   246B(1)(3)

EUCLID
Def. I   199a
Def. XIV   196
Defs. XXX–XXXIV
  (XXII Heiberg)   198
Def. XXXV (XXIII Heiberg)   197

EUSEBIUS
Praeparatio Evangelica
XV.14.1   95

EUSTATHIUS
916.9   277.37–43
916.28   277.33–7
916.55   277.16–25

FESTUS
p. 37.29 Lindsay   272B32–4
p. 94 Lindsay   104.14ff
p. 332 Lindsay   104.14ff

FLORUS
1.33.9   271.4–8
1.37.5   67D
1.38.1   272.2–4
2.6.27   259/260

GALEN
De Alimentorum Facultate
2.65   70
De Causis Contentivis
1–2   190
Definitiones Medicinales
Def. Med. XIX.392 Kühn   190
De Simplicium Medicamentorum Temperamentis ac Facultatibus
*De Fac. Simpl. Med.*ix.1.4
  (XII.186 Kühn)   235
Institutio Logica
I.5   191
IV   191

XI–XIII   191
XVI–XVIII   191
In Hippocratis de Humoribus
XVI, p. 396ff Kühn   137
De Moribus   165.164ff, 172ff;
       169 Context
De Placitis Hippocratis et Platonis
IV.1.16, p. 238.16f De Lacy   166
IV.2.4–7, p. 240.1–10 De L   34A2
IV.2.8–18,   34B2(a)
  p. 240.10–242.11 De L
IV.2.29ff,   34B2(b)
  p. 244.14ff De L
VII.1.10–2.17,   182
  p. 430.17–438.23 De L
VII.5.41–6.1,   85
  p. 460.28–462.24 De L
VII.7.16ff, p. 472ff De L   85
VIII.1.19ff, p. 484.17 De L   T83/84
VIII.3.13, p. 498.6f De L   45
De Sequela
III.36.21ff M   92
XI.73 M   169B
XI.74.21–77 M   169D
XI.75.21ff M   35B; 169D
XI.77.6 M   169D

PS.-GALEN
Historia Philosopha
16, Dox. Gr. 609.1f   101
19, Dox. Gr. 611.5ff   190
85, Dox. Gr. 633.15ff   209
88, Dox. Gr. 634.10ff   138

GARGILIUS MARTIALIS
Medicinae
34   70

GELLIUS, AULUS
2.22   137
3.9.7   273
9.7   106
14.1   111
20.8.4   106

INDEX OF PASSAGES CITED OR DISCUSSED

GEMINUS
Isagoge
III.15	202C(3); 204B; 205
V.45f	49B(2)(b), 37–43
V.58ff	204B
V.66	115Ab
VI.7	204A
VI.9	119E
VI.28	204A
VIII.20–24	T42
IX.1–2	123
XI.5–12	122D
X.1	125
XI	126
XV.1–3	49B(1), 5–9; 49B(3)(a), 44–8; 209
XVI.3–5	200
XVI.7	49B(2)(a), 18–36
XVI.10f	49B(2)(b), 37–43
XVI.16	115Ab
XVI.21ff	118B
XVI.24	49B(2)(a), 18–36; 222
XVI.25ff	49B(4)(b)(iv), 118–25
XVI.32ff	210
XVII.15	127/128
XVII.47	133
XVII. p. 180 M	120

HERACLIDES PONTICUS
F102 Wehrli	270
F116 Wehrli	132B

HERACLITUS
Quaestiones Homericae (Allegoriae)
38.6	230B
45–6	9

HERMIPPUS
Acad. Ind. col. 11, p. 29 Mekler	253.112ff

HERO OF ALEXANDRIA
Def. 1	199a
Def. 23, IV.30.10 Heiberg	196
Defs. 51–4, 61–3	198
Def. 70, IV.48.5ff Heiberg	197

HERODOTUS
I.16	272B, 34–6
II.6	203
II.20–5	222
II.33	246BI(3)
II.158	206
III.1ff	222
III.19	49B(3)(b), 49–61
III.106	49F(3), 326ff
III.115	239.27–31
IV.8	246BI(3)
IV.33	270
IV.36	200; 270
IV.42–4	49
IV.152	T22
V.53	203
VI.119	236
VII.20, 73, 75	277.5–9
IX.83	253.78–84

HESIOD
Opera et Dies
109ff	284.11–19
Catalogue of Women, F150.21 Merkel.-West	270

HIEROCLES
Ἠθικὴ Στοιχείωσις	160

HIPPARCHUS
In Arati Phaenomena
1.11.6	205
1.11.7	202C(3); 205

HIPPOCRATES
Airs, Waters, Places
5, 7, 12	49F(3), 326ff
Ancient Medicine	
3ff	284.84–99
Περὶ καρδίης	
Cord. 2	T111
Ἐπιδημίαι	
Epid. 1.20	111

INDEX OF PASSAGES CITED OR DISCUSSED

Γυναικεῖα
Mul. 1.104   243

PS.-HIPPOCRATES
Sevens 3   137

HIPPOLYTUS
Refutatio Omnium Haeresium
1.8, p. 22 Duncker   222
IV.8, p. 66 Duncker   115M

HOMER
Iliad
VI.511   T109
VII.422   216
IX.5   137
X.17–20, 91–5   164H
X.158   293
XII.1–33   49D(1), 297ff
XIII.3–5   277
XIV.245   216
XVII.75   T110
XVIII.399   216
XVIII.600F   284.114–25
XX.225   137
XXII.325   T111
XXIII.743   285
Odyssey
I.23–4   49F(3), 326ff
IV.84   280/281
IV.477   222
V.295f   137
XI.14ff   272B34–6
XII.105   216
XII.235ff   216
XVII.487   254

HORACE
Odes
III.3.49–52   240.40–5

HYGINUS
Fabellae
154   234

IAMBLICHUS
De Communi Mathematica Scientia
p. 4 of Feste   141A
De Mysteriis
3.2   108B(3)
Περὶ ψυχῆς
Stob. *Ecl.* I, p. 364ff W   141A

IBN ABĪ UṢAIBIʿAH
ʿ*Uyūn al-Anbāʾ fī Ṭabaqāt al-Aṭibbā*   T114

INSCRIPTIONES GRAECAE   T1
II²1028   253 *fin.*
II.²1713, 1714   253.23–32, 103ff
v.ii.159   240.16–29
XIV.600   246

ISIDORUS
Origenes
XIV.iii.6   212/213

ISOCRATES
1.3   3

JOSEPHUS
Antiquitates Judaicae
1.107   285B
13.131ff   54
13.184–6   64
13.223–246   61
13.249–53   63
13.267ff   72
13.365   75
14.114–18   51
Bellum Judaicum
IV.476ff   279
1 Maccabees
14.1–3   64
15–16   61

JULIUS OBSEQUENS
29   T5; 227

JUSTIN
30.4   228; 231

1021

INDEX OF PASSAGES CITED OR DISCUSSED

JUSTIN (cont.)
32.3.9–11   273
36.1.2–6   64
38.3.9   253.23–32
38.8.8–10   58
38.9.2–3   64
38.10   63; 64
39.1.4ff   72
39.1.6   63
39.5.1   77
42.1.1   282
42.1.3   65
42.4.1, 14, 16   282

LACTANTIUS
Institutiones Divinae
7.15.4   184.11–19

LIVY
1.7   53
2.3–5   256
3.53.9   259/260
10.23.2   53
22.1.10   121
24.9.7–11   259/260
25.40.2   257
27.25.7   258
28.11.3   121
29.11.13   258
29.14.3   121
40.49.1   271.4–8
42.45.4   T27
Periochae
57   61
61   67D
63   240.29–40
78   253.78–84
97   73

PS.-LONGINUS
De Sublimitate
44.7   253.103ff

LUCAN
Pharsalia
1.412–17   138; 217B3

VII.155   132B
X.255ff   222
X.258   118A

LUCRETIUS
5.523–6   118B
5.1105–44   284.11–19
5.1252–7   239.1–11

LYCURGUS
In Leocratem
95f   234

LYDUS
De Mensibus
IV.107 W   222
IV.115, p. 153 W   T5; 227
De Ostentis
53–4   230B

MACROBIUS
Saturnalia
I.17.27   264.12–18
I.19.6   170E
I.23.1–9   118B
VII.14.16   115Ab
Somnium Scipionis
I.12.1   129/130
I.15.18   115Ab
I.19.10–13   123
I.21.9ff   115K
II.9   49C, 229ff
II.10.10   118B

MANILIUS
Astronomica
I.216   205
I.246   49C, 229ff
I.718–57   129/130
I.841   132B
II.89–92   138; 217B3
IV.711–43   49F *fin.*
IV.724ff   49F(3), 326ff

INDEX OF PASSAGES CITED OR DISCUSSED

MARCUS AURELIUS
II.13 108B(2)
V.27 99; 108
VI.14 159
IX.40 40

MARTIAL
IV.25.6 225
VII.24 234

MARTIANUS CAPELLA
VI.595 115Ab
VI.694 212/213
VIII.860 115K

NEMESIUS
De Natura Hominis
1, p. 41 Matth. 33
2, p. 121 Matth. 159
6–7, p. 171ff Matth. 85
26, p. 249ff Matth. 147

NEPOS, CORNELIUS
Atticus 18 256

NICOLAUS OF DAMASCUS
FGrH 90, F104 277.33–7,
  37–43, 59–63

NONNUS
Dionysiaca
41.51–8 285B

OLYMPIODORUS
In Aristotelis Meteora Commentaria
II.1, p. 130 S 118A
III.2, p. 210.15ff 133
III.2, p. 210.22ff 121

ORIENTIS GRAECI INSCRIPTIONES
SELECTAE
OGI.262 251.3–6

ORIGEN
Contra Celsum

IV.86f 159
De Oratione
vol. II p. 368 Koe 92
De Principiis
II.3.6 49C, 229ff

OROSIUS
4.20.32f 271.4–8
5.14.1 67D
5.15.25 273

PANAETIUS
F71 van Str. 107
F73 van Str. 107
F135 van Str. 49B(4)(b)(iv), 118–25

PAPYRI
P Berl. 5883, 5853 49C(1)(c),
  170–90
P Gen. inv. 203 85
P Herc. 1413 98
P Oslo. 73 115K

PAUSANIAS
1.9.3 77
1.20.5 253 *fin.*
X.28.4 234

PERIPLUS MARIS RUBRI
2 49B(3)(b), 49–61
49 49C(1)(d), 191ff
50 212/213
57 49C(2)(c), 289–93

PHILO
De Aeternitate Mundi
78ff 96
De Providentia
II.64 118B
De Somniis
1.134 108B(2)

PHILODEMUS
col. 47.21–7 164E
col. 48.3–13 164B

1023

INDEX OF PASSAGES CITED OR DISCUSSED

PHILOPONUS
In Aristotelis Meteorologicorum Librum Primum Commentarium
p. 28.27ff H   120

PHILOSTRATUS
Vita Apollonii
I.24   236
V.2   217A5
V.5   241
V.6   218B

PINDAR
Pythian 1.19   246BI(3)

PLATO
Cratylus
398b 5–c 4   24
401d   95
Critias
108e   49D(1).297ff
Laws
653b 1ff   31A
674b 5f   31A
718a–723d   178
776d   60
789a 8ff   31A
899d   187A
Meno
75d–76a   199a
76a   16; 196
Phaedo
97d   49B(2)(a), 10–13
Phaedrus
245c5   290
246a 6ff   31D; 86c; 166; 187A
246bc   102
246e 4–247a 2   24; 86c
250d 1   193
253c–254a   146
Politicus
271a–272b   284.11–19
Protagoras
320dff   284.22–4

Republic
IV.   142; 143; 144; T96
VI.508b 3   121
VI.509a 1   121
VIII.548a 5ff   240.16–29
VIII.556e 3–9   163B
IX.588c 6–d 8   146
X.597e   103
X.607a 4ff   44
Sophist
216b 3   254
Theaetetus
176b   186B
Timaeus
24e–26e   49D(1), 297f
30b   99
31b   4
35ab   85; 141
35b f   291
36bff   196
37dff   291
40c 9–12   112
44b   31D
44d   146
45   85
45b   17
45b–46c   193; 194
47bc   186B
53cff   16
69d   35A; 169D
69d 7–70a 7   146
70e   33
71d–72b   108
73b   28
77b   33
87b7   31D
90a–d   187A

PLINY
Historia Naturalis
2.46   118A
2.49   122B
2.51   9; 115G
2.70   202C(3)
2.97   138
2.98   133

INDEX OF PASSAGES CITED OR DISCUSSED

2.99	121	9.1–11	244
2.100	132B	10.124	243
2.108	106	11.196	106
2.109	106	14.6.66	234
2.119	137	16.2f	272A3(c)
2.127	T22	16.193	106
2.150	134B(5)	18.227	106
2.167	272.2–4; 206	19.4	T22
2.167–71	49C(1)(f), 229ff	19.146	52
2.168	49C(2)(b), 237–88	21.57	229A
2.169	49C(1)(a), 146–50; 49C(1)(f), 227–32	28.63	170E
		29.59	106
2.173	206	31.78	237
2.178	205	31.86	237
2.182	115Ab; 204B	33.48ff	240.40–5
2.189–90	49F fin.	33.78, 80	239.31–6
2.202	228; 230; 231	33.95	240.40–5
2.203	T5; 227	33.96	239.24–7
2.212–20	138; 217A4; 217B3; 219.19–32, 80–134; 221	33.116	241
		34.33	53
2.221	106	34.105ff, 123–7	242
2.222–3	219.80–134	34.156f	239.27–31
2.225	219.32–8; 225	35.19	53
2.226	219.136–45	35.171	237
2.235	236	35.178	279
2.238	T5; 227	35.180	236
2.242	49E, 305–8	35.194	235
2.247	202B		
3.12.6	T22	**PLINY, THE YOUNGER**	
3.30	239	*Epistulae*	
3.34	229A	II.7	264.12–18
3.87	249A	III.4	264.12–18
4.107	276		
4.120	217A2		
5.5.15	T22	**PLOTINUS**	
5.51	222	*Enneads*	
5.55	222	VI.1.25–8	92
5.72	219.136–45		
5.81	251		
6.56–7	212/213	**PLUTARCH**	
6.58	206	*Vitae*	
6.99	236	*Aemilius Paullus* 2.1	261
6.211–18	205	*Camillus* 22	270
7.191ff	284.56–60	*Cato maior* 1.2	261
8.166	243	*Cicero*	
8.217	52	1.3–5	261

1025

INDEX OF PASSAGES CITED OR DISCUSSED

Vitae (cont.)
3.1	T31
4.1	T29
Coriolanus 11	261; 264.12–18
Crassus 9.7	73
Demetrius	
1.1–6	253 *fin.*
48	251
Fabius Maximus 1.2–5	261
Galba 1.4	252
Lucullus	
2.3–4	51
19	253 *fin.*
Lysander 16f	240.16–29
Marcellus	
19.6	T86
23	257
28	257
Marius	
1	261
11–27	272B44–7
11.2	272A2–4
11.3–7	272B34–6
11.3.5	272A2–4; 272B32–4
15.4	272B39f
34.3	255.2–9
34.6	255 *fin.*
45–6	255 *fin.*
45.8–12	255
Nicias 4	262
Nicias and Crassus 1	262
Numa 9	253 *fin.*
Pompeius 13.7–11	261
Publicola	
1.1	261
3–5	256
Sulla	
2.2	261; 264.12–18
12, 13, 23	253 *fin.*
Tiberius Gracchus 8.4f	261

Moralia
Quomodo quis suos in virt. sentiat profectus
82F	287

Regum et Imperatorum Apophthegmata
200EF	58; 254

Mulierum Virtutes
255E–257E	51

De Iside et Osiride
358F	134B(5)
367E	118A

De Pythiae Oraculis
399Bff	228

De Virtute Morali
440Eff	182
441B	180
441C	169E
441E	T91
446A	164I
450A	152
450C	187A
450E–451A	154; 255.2–9
451C	35C

De Garrulitate
511C	263

De Sera Numinis Vindicta
550D	193
558C	253 *fin.*
564B	152

De Genio Socratis
590F	129/130

Quaestiones Conviviales
626C	194
670B	106

Amatorius
765E–F	134B(5)

Praecepta Gerendae Reipublicae
809E	253 *fin.*
816C	53

De Facie
921A	134B(5)
921D	18
921F	122A
922A	122A
922D	85
923B	115FG; 122B
928CD	127/128
929B–D	124; 122D
930F–931	124
932E	9; 115G
940C	17; 122B
940D	10

INDEX OF PASSAGES CITED OR DISCUSSED

De Sollertia Animalium		**POLYAENUS**	
980Bf	33	VIII.38	51
De Animae Procreatione in Timaeo			
1023Dff	141AB		
1028D	115F	**POLYBIUS**	
De Stoicorum Repugnantiis		1.42	249A
1034C	180	2.28.10	274.7–9
1034CD	182	2.30.3	259/260
1035A–E	91; 150	3.36–8	249C
1035F	93	3.37.59	49F(1), 309
1037Cf	178	3.38.1	49B(4)(b)(iv), 141;
1038A	170D		49C, 229ff
1038B	160	3.57.3	239.24–7
1046C	179	3.67.3	274.7–9
1048A	171	4.21	169F
1048E	29	5.21	249C
1051E	22	6.54.5	256
1052B	22	6.57.5	265–7 Context
1053A	17; 118A	9.10	257
1053EF	93	10.26.1	253.36–47
1054B	93	12.3.10	52
1054E	8	13.8.2	253.131ff
1056B	170A(1); 190	25.2.13	263
De Communibus Notitiis		27.7.2	T27
1062A	179	31.25	265–7 Context
1070A	170D	31.28.10	265
1073E	5; 92	34–7	224
1075E	22	34.9.1	217A
1076B	29	34.9.4	246B(1)(3)
1076E	101	34.9.8–11	239.24–7
1077Df	92	34.12.3ff	203
1078E	16	35.1–5	271
1080E	16	36.1	253.64–103
1081Cff	98	F76 Büttner-Wobst	265
1083A–1084A	96		
1084E	118A		
1085B–1086B	92; 101	**POMPONIUS MELA**	
1085C	93	I.1	209
1085D	149	II.61	225
		II.78	229A
		III.1	217A5
		III.7.7	214B
PS.-PLUTARCH		III.9.89ff	49C(1)(f), 229ff
De Placitis		III.9.90	49C(1)(f), 227ff
1.6, *Dox. Gr.* 292a 23–293a 1	101	III.68–9	212/213

INDEX OF PASSAGES CITED OR DISCUSSED

PORPHYRY
De Antro Nympharum
11 118A
28 129/130
Quaestionum Homericarum ad Iliadem Pertinentium Reliquiae
1.183.1 277.16-25
FGrH 260
F2.8 77
F32 63; 64

PROCLUS
In Primum Euclidis Librum Commentarii
75ff Friedlein 195
76-7 F 191
89 F 141A
89.10-15 F 199a
101.8ff F 199a
111.1ff F 198
136.18ff F 196
168.3ff F 198
201.3ff F 195B(c)(d)
Hypotyposis Astronomicarum Positionum
IV.73-5 115K
IV.80-6 115K
De Sphaera 11, 12 115Ab

PROCOPIUS
De Bello Vandalico
2.10 246

PROPERTIUS
4.1.45 256

PTOLEMY
Almagest
II.2-3 204A
IV.9 115F, K
V.11 115M
V.14 115K
Tetrabiblos
I.5.1 93
II.2 49F(1), 311, 313; 49F(3), 326ff; 49F *fin*; 115K

Geographia
I.11.2 202A, C(2)
II.1.6 49F(1), 309
II.8.6, 8 276
IV.5.13 49F(1), 309
VII.5.12 202A, C(2)

QUINTILIAN
1.4.18f 45
III.6 189

RES GESTAE DIVI AUGUSTI
RG 26.4 272.2-4

SCHOLIA IN ARATUM
811, p. 488.14ff Maass 121
811, p. 488.21ff Maass 133

SENECA
De Beneficiis
III.37.1 234
IV.2.2 184
V.13.2 170D
VI.36.1 234
De Brevitate Vitae
15.5 179
De Constantia
10.3 170C
13.5 170C
16.2 170D
Epistulae
12.7 179
24.1-2 170C
31.5, 8 40
44.7 170C
48 175
49.8 175
49.11 2
58.12 95
65.2 101
65.2-14 95; 190
65.21-2 184
71.27 184
72.6-11 163E
74.16f 184; 105

1028

INDEX OF PASSAGES CITED OR DISCUSSED

74.17		170D	VI.5–25		12
74.19		105	VI.16		118B
82.19–20		170E; 175	VI.21.1		228; 231
83.8, 17		175	VI.23		222
87.41		170E	VI.32.4		170C
89.9ff		87	VII		131; 132
89.17		188	VII.21.2		118B
92		170C; 184	*De Otio*		
92.1		147	V.1		186B
92.3		170C	VI.2		184
92.16		170D			
92.25		179	SEXTUS EMPIRICUS		
92.33		184	*Hypotyposes*		
94–95		176; 178	Hyp. I.69		159
94.57		240.40–5	Hyp. III.15		190
95.58		170D	Hyp. III.38–9		16
104.23		186B	*Adversus Mathematicos*		
121		159	III.93		46
121.15		160	V.1–105		111
De Ira			VII.2–23		87; 89
I.2.3ff		155	VII.12		176
I.3.4		159	VII.22–3		91
II.19.1–3		169F	VII.89–140		85
Quaestiones Naturales			VII.94		239.1–11
I.2		133	VII.150ff		42
I.2–13		121	VII.227ff		42
I.6.5		119FG	VIII.11–12		188; 189
I.15.6f		121	VIII.74		188
I.17.6		240.40–5	VIII.151–5		156
II.5		118A	IX.13		29
II.12–53		135	IX.20–2		108B(1)
III.4		219.134	IX.28		284 *fin.*
III.6–7		223	IX.71–4		149
III.14.3ff		217A5	IX.72–4		108B(2)
III.24.4		219.146–54	IX.79		106
III.25.5		219.136–45	IX.88		99
III.25.7		237	IX.104		99
III.26.5		219.32–8	IX.108ff		175
III.26.7–8		219.19–23; 221	IX.196		95
III.28.6		138; 217B3	X.121, 169		98
IV.A.2.17–30		222	X.123–41		98
IV.B.3.5		136	X.197ff		98
V.10		T22	X.189ff, 200ff		98
V.15–16		137	X.218ff		98
V.15.3		240.40–5	X.313–18		147

1029

INDEX OF PASSAGES CITED OR DISCUSSED

Adversus Mathematicos (cont.)
XI.187	188
XI.192, 195	176

SILIUS ITALICUS
XIV.197	234

SIMPLICIUS
In Aristotelis de Caelo Commentaria
p. 32.29ff Heiberg	18

In Aristotelis Physica Commentaria
p. 786.12f Diels	98

SOLINUS
5.15	234
23.21f	217A5

SPEUSIPPUS
F40 Lang	141A

STOBAEUS
I.229f W	131; 132
I.235 W	135
I.247 W	11; 136
I.317.21ff W	31D
I.364 W	141A
II.41.23 W	176
II.57–116 W	89
II.58ff W	182
II.75f W	186
II.87.7–9 W	31D

STOICORUM VETERUM FRAGMENTA
I.85	5
86	92
87	92
88	100
93	98
95	97
97	4
98	5; 103
102	13; 103
106	13
111–14	21; 99
115	20
120	122A; 17
121	118A
134–5	99
136	139
137	139
145	139
153	101
154	23; 100
155, 157	100
158	21; 28; 100; 103
160–1	100
163	14
165	127/128
176	103
179	186
190, 195	160; 169A
209	165.9–13
211	180
238	176
275	280.1–8
333	3
349–50	90
356	176
434	155
435	3
449	105
459	99
481	3
499	118A
501	17
506	122A
508	122C
518	169F
530	100; 127/128
533	100
537	35C
551	103
659	118A
677	122C
II.35	T81; 87
39, 40	88
42	87
49	88
92	127/128
96	2; 179
120	1
149	189B(a)(i)
150	189B(a)(iii)
229	5; 92

INDEX OF PASSAGES CITED OR DISCUSSED

260	191	579	13
283	196	590	14
301	92	594	13
305	5	609–10	97
II.306–9	92	613	127/128
310	5; 100; 101	619	97
311, 313	92	620	4
317, 318	92	624	14
320	101	634	23
323, 325, 326	92	638	14
336–49	95	650	118A
346	170A(1); 190	652	17; 118A
348	170A(1)	652–4	117
351	T85; 95; 170A(1); 190	655	17
354–5	95	655–6	118A
357–8	16	666	115G; 122B
368	21	667	117
378	93	669	122A
387	139	674	122A
393	93	677	10; 122A
395	96	681	8; 117
413	17; 122A; 13	682	127/128
414	100	688	127/128
418	93	692	132B
430–1	93	701	11; 136
439–40	93; 149; 21	703, 705	12
447–8	8	708	33
455–6	196	710	33; 159
458	21; 33; 28	714	159
471	96; 139	733	159
472–3	96	773	139
475	100	774	99
482	16	779–80	139
488	16; 141A	786–7	139
494	96	788	127/128
502–5	97	790–801	139
509–10	98	827–30	147
522, 524, 525	97	841	100
526	101	864	193
527	8; 14	906	159
528	4; 8; 99; 101	913	103
533	4; 8	917–18	103
534–6	8; 97; 104	928, 931	103
542	4	937	103; 101
546–7	8; 117	945	21; 103; 170A(1)
550	8	949	T85

INDEX OF PASSAGES CITED OR DISCUSSED

STOICORUM VETERUM FRAGMENTA	
(cont.)	
965-7	105
970-1	105
973	T85
976	103
988	139
997	170A(1)
1009	117; 127/128
1012	22
1013	8; 21; 28
1015	21
1021	100
1022	14
1024	103
1027	100; 101; 127/128
1033, 1035	100
1042, 1051	100
1053, 1057	101
1059	22
1059-60	101
1064	5
1076	102
1143	8; 117
1207-16	110
III.3	187A
4	101
52	105
54	179; 187A
95	179
124	170D
125	169E
136	160; 169A
155	160; 169A
169	158; 169E
171, 173	169E
188	187A
192	171
197	169E
202	179
214	2; 179
237ff	175
255	180
260, 262-6	180
264, 269	170C
280	180
305	139
390	187A
391	152; 165.9-13
395-8	155
421-2	163C
438	158
441-2	158
456	34A2
461	34A1
462	34B2; 159; 164DH
463	152; 165.9-13
466	165.54-75
468	152; 165.9-13
471	163CD
474	167; 187A
476	159
482	165.22-53
574	T38
604	40
687	169E
712	175
724	160
748	176
IV. Apoll. 9	8
VI. Boeth. 10	139

STRABO
Geographica

1.1.4-7	216
1.6	205
1.8f	219.15-19
1.9	49C, 229ff
1.20-1	49B(1), 5-9; 49B(4)(b)(iv), 141
1.21	137
2.6	44
2.11	247
2.16	216
2.20	137
2.24	49F(3), 326ff; 49B(4)(b)(iv), 141; 118B
2.25, 26, 28	49F(1), 309; 49F(3), 326ff
2.27-8	118B
2.28	49C(2)(b), 237 ff
2.36	214A

INDEX OF PASSAGES CITED OR DISCUSSED

3.1	T46; 49C(2)(a)	5.24	202C(2), D
3.4	49D; 214A	5.28	248
3.5	49D; 219.19–32	5.33, 37	49B(3)(b), 49–61
3.8	217A5; 221	5.34	T76; 208B
3.10	49D	5.34–42	205
3.11	138; 214A; 217B3; 219.15–19; 219.19–32	5.35	204A
		5.35–6	212/213
3.12	214A; 219.32–8	5.36ff	204A
3.13	49C, 229ff	5.37	208
3.16–21	49D	5.39	204A
3.16	228; 231	5.41–2	204A
3.17–20	231	5.42	119F
3.19	233	5.43	49B(3)(a), 17–36
3.22	270	5.53	49B(3)(b), 49–61
4.1	49B(2); 202BD	III.2.3	239.24–27
4.5–6	49E, 305–8; 200	2.4	218B; 220
II.1.1	204A	2.6	T24; 49C(1)(d), 191ff; 52
1.2–9	206		
1.11	204A	2.8	239.31–6
1.18	119F	2.10–11	239.24–7
1.34	212/213	2.11	217A2
1.35	115Ab	2.13ff	216
1.37	49A, 1–5	3.1	224
1.40	249C	3.7	224
2.2	208A	4.2	246
2.7	249C	4.4	T25; 247
3.5	208B	4.5ff	243
4.1–2	T25; T46; 49C(1)(f), 229ff; 49C(2)(a), 233–7; 49C(2)(c), 289ff	4.10–11	T8
		5.2	52
		5.3–6	246
4.1	208B	5.4	234
4.2–3	249C	5.8	214A
5	208	5.11	219.71–80; 239.27–31
5.2	18; 90	IV.1.2	248
5.3	49B(1), 5–9; 49B(3)(a), 44–8	1.14	248
		2.1	276
5.4	49B(4)(b)(iv), 130–5; 208B	3.3	272B, 41–4
		4.1–5	274
5.5	49B(4)(b)(iv), 130–5	4.2–6	67
5.6	49E, 305–8; 200	4.2	73
5.7	49B(2)(a), 17–36	4.3	272B, 41–4
5.8	49C(2)(c), 289ff; 208AB	4.4	68; 69
5.9	200	5.2	219.71–80
5.10	204A	6.9	272B, 39f
5.12	49C(2)(c), 289ff; 222	6.12	239.31–6; 272B, 39f
5.14	200	V.1.2	268

1033

INDEX OF PASSAGES CITED OR DISCUSSED

Geographica (cont.)

2.7	249B(ii)	2.10	54
4.6	49C(1)(d), 191ff	2.24	T48
4.8	234; 249A	2.26	226
VI.1.6	233	2.34–43	279 Context
1.11	249B(ii)	2.42	219.136–45
2.1–11	250	3.3	237
2.3	219.19–32	4.4	49C(2)(b)
2.4	219.32–8	4.19	237
2.7	234	XVII.1.3	285
2.11	249B(ii)	1.12–13	49C(2)(c)
3.10	249B(ii)	1.19	216
VII.1.2	73	1.24	203
2.3–4	272.2–4; 272 *fin.*	1.25	206
3.5	277.62	1.52	239.17–21
3.9	284.114–25	2.2	237
3.30	162	3.2	49C(1)(c), 183ff
4.4–7	263	3.4–5	244
7.4	203	3.7	49C(1)(d), 199ff
F56 Jones	203	3.22–23	49B(3)(b)
IX.1.20	253 *fin.*		
2.8	219.32–8	**TACITUS**	
XI.2.3–4	206	*Annales*	
6.1	206	1.70.2	217B3
11.5	203	3.26	284.11–19
11.7	200; 206	*Germania*	
XII.3.4	60	2.5	73
XIII.1.36	49D(1), 297ff	37	272.2–4
1.54	253.147ff	45.1	119E
4.11	234	*Historia*	
XIV.1.41	56	V.3f	278
2.5	T2/3; T27	V.6	279
5.2	253.47–58; 262		
5.14	163C	**THEMISTIUS**	
6.5	243	*Orationes*	
XV.1.11	212/213	VIII.101d	179
1.13	223		
1.20	212/213; 218B	**THEON OF ALEXANDRIA**	
1.24	223	*Commentary to the Handy Tables*	
3.22	242	Halma HT I, p. 54, 55.16	126
XVI.1.6	218A		
1.21–2.2	251	**THEON OF SMYRNA**	
2.5	251	121.18ff Hiller	205
2.7	251	166.4–10 Hiller	18
2.8	251	199.9ff Hiller	18
2.9–10	251		

INDEX OF PASSAGES CITED OR DISCUSSED

THEOPHRASTUS
Historia Plantarum
V.1.3 — 106
VII.4.3 — 70
VIII.3 — 221
De Lapidibus
16–17 — 268
85 — 235
De Signis Tempestatum
56 — 122D
F6.1.22 W — 121

THEOPOMPUS
History of Philip
Bk 1 — 265–7 Context
Bk 8, *FGrH* 115, F73 — 253.112ff

THUCYDIDES
III.38.7 — 253.36–47
III.89.3 — 232

TIMAGENES
FGrH 88, F2 — 67; 69
F11 — 273

TROGUS
Prologi
39 — 66; 75
42 — 65

VALERIUS MAXIMUS
I.1.8 — 258
I.8.8 — 104
I.8.9 — 104
I.8.16 — 104
V.4, Ext. §4 — 234
V.8.1 — 256
IX.6.3 — 67D

VARRO
De Re Rustica
2.10.9 — 269
3.12.6–7 — 52
apud Sen. *NQ* v.15–16 — 137

VEGETIUS
Mulomedicina
1.56.37–9 — 243

VERGIL
Aeneid
I.244ff — 225
III.426ff — 184

VETTIUS VALENS
1.18, p. 31 Kroll — 126
III.4, p. 140.4–28 Kroll — 126

VITRUVIUS
De Architectura
1.6.4ff — 137
II.1 — 284.84–99
II.3.4 — 237
II.6.3 — 234
V.3 — 133
VI.1.1–12 — T50; 49F *fin.*
VIII.3.1–19 — T50
VIII.3.8 — 235
VIII.3.12 — 234
VIII.3.28 — 93
IX — T50
IX.5.4 — 205
X.6.1–4 — 239.17–21

XANTHUS
FGrH 765, F14 — 277.5–9

XENOCRATES
F81 H — 187A

XENOPHON
Anabasis
II.2.6 — 203
V.5.4 — 203
VII.8.26 — 203
Memorabilia
I.4.8 — 99
Respublica Lacedaemoniorum
VII.6 — 240.16–40

1035

INDEX OF PROPER NAMES

A PERSONS

Academics: Old Academy, 85 *fin.*, 87; definition of soul, 141A; sight, 194.
Achilles Tatius: use of Posidonius, 129/130, 149
Aenesidemus: 147
Agatharchides: 50; 216; 222
Agathemerus: and Posidonius, 200; 201
Agrippa: geographical comm., 212/213; map, 249B(ii)
Alexander (the Great): 222; 236; 252; 272A3(c)
Alexander Balas: 54; 56; 253 Context
Alexander Polyhistor: 108B(2)
Alexander II Zabinas: 72
'Alī b. Riḍwān: T114
Allobroges: 67D
Al-Nayrīzī: 197; 199a
Amphinomus: 195B(a)
Anacharsis: 284.114–25
Anaxagoras: on comets, 131A3, 132; on thunderstorms, 135; on hail, 136B; Nile flooding, 222
Anaximander: thunderstorms, 135; map, 200
Anaximenes: thunderstorms, 135
Andron: theories of mathematics, 195B(c)
Andronicus, the Peripatetic: 253.12–23
Antiochus of Ascalon: T31
Antiochus I: 206
Antiochus IV Epiphanes: 251; 278
Antiochus VI Epiphanes: 54
Antiochus VII Sidetes: 61; 63; 64; 251; 278
Antiochus VIII Grypus: 66; 71; 72; 74; 75
Antiochus IX Cyzicenus: 66; 72

Antiochus X: 75
Antiochus XI: 75
Antipater of Sidon: 104
Antipater of Tarsus: T11; 8; 107; 139; 170E; formulation of τέλος criticised, 187C
Antipater of Tyre: 285
Antiphanes of Berge: T46; 49C(2)(a), 233–7; 49C(2)(c), 289–93
Antisthenes: 3; 29
Apameans: Posidonius' attitude to, 54
Apellicon: 253.147–57
Apicius (Roman knight): 78
Apion of Alexandria: 278
Apollodorus of Athens: 87; 277.16–25; 277 *fin.*
Apollodorus of Pergamum: 189; 216
Apollodorus of Seleucea: 87
Apollonides: 263
Apollonius of Citium: T112
Apollonius Molon: T28; T29; 278
Apollonius of Myndus: 132
Apollonius of Perge: 115M; 197
Apollonius of Tyre: 185
Aquillius, M': 253.78–84
Arabians: 280
Aramaeans: 280/281
Arambians: 281
Aratus: 48; 49F(3), 346ff
Arcadians: 240.16–40
Arcesilaus: 42
Archedemus of Tarsus: T82; 189
Archelaus: 135
Archestratus: 289 Context
Archigenes of Apamea: T114
Archimedes: T86; 115; 199b; 239.17–21; 257
Aristarchus: 49F(3), 326ff; 115; 122B; 125

1036

INDEX OF PROPER NAMES

Aristion: and Athenion, 253 *fin*.
Ariston of Alexandria, Peripatetic: 222
Ariston of Chios: 3; 90; 91; 176; 178; on plurality of virtues, 182
Aristonicus of Alexandria: 280.1-8
Aristonicus of Pergamum: 59
Aristotle: influence on Posidonius, T100, 165.164ff, 167, 183; possible source, 49D(1), 297ff; faculties of soul, 142, 143, 144, 145, 146; virtues, 183; on physiognomy, 169F; compass card, 137; on tides, 138, 220, 219.1-9; on refluent currents in straits, 220; on the Nile flooding, 222; on the Stony Plain, 229B(i); Aristotle's library, 253.147ff; 153. 112ff
Arius Didymus: 89
Armenians: 280/281
Arrian: 219.9-15; use of Posidonius, 81
Arsaces VI (Mithridates I): 57; 64
Arsaces, Phraates II: 61; 63; 64; 65
Arsacids: dynasty and succession, 282
Artabrians: 239.27-36
Artemidorus of Ephesus: T78; 50; 246; 247; 272.2-4; criticised from Posidonian evidence, 119; length of inhabited world, 49E, 305-8; on wells at Gadeira, 217A; on Libya, 223; on Arabia, 237; on Mysians, 277.5-9, 16-25
Artemidorus of Parium: 134A, B(5)
Artephila of Cyrene: 51
Asclepiades of Myrleia: 247
Asclepiodotus: T41; use of Posidonius, 80, 81, 228, 230D; on thunderstorms, 135; on earthquakes, 230D
Athenaeus: T8; use of Posidonius, T65, 61, 71; methods of composition, 265-7 Context
Athenaeus Attaleus: T51; T114; 190
Athenians: satirised, 253.32-63
Athenion: 253; and Aristion, 253 *fin*.

Athenodorus of Tarsus (Calvus): T44; T79; 7; 41; 163C; 214C; 215; 226; exhalation theory of tides, 217A5, 221
Attalus III: 59
Augustine: sources and knowledge of Posidonius, T69, T74, 111; criticism of Posidonius, 111
Averni: 67D

Bastarnians: 253.81; 277.25-33
Bathanattus: 240.29-40
Berenice: 77
Berossus: 48; 123
Bion of Abdera: 137
Bituitus: 67D
Boethius: T74; knowledge of Posidonius, T70
Boethus of Sidon: 99b; 109; 285
Bogus: 49C(1)(d), 199ff
Boii: 272B, 36ff; 277.25-33
Brennus: 240.29-40; 270; 273
Bruti, Iunii: 256; statue of Brutus on Capitoline, 256
Brutus, D. Iunius Callaicus: 224; 256
Byrebistas, king of Dacians: 277a *fin*.

Caepio, Q. Servilius: 273
Caesar, Julius: use of Posidonius, 67; on Channel flood tides, 217B3, 219.71-80; moderation in slaves, 265-7 Context
Callisthenes: 222; 230D
Cambyses: 222
Carneades: 42
Carpus of Antioch: 195
Carthaginians: 49C(1)(a)(i), 147; 257
Cato, M. Porcius: name, 264.1-9
Cato, Gaius Porcius, *cos.* 114 B.C.: 240.29-40
Cato, Marcus Porcius Uticensis: 256
Celsus Cornelius: 189
Celti: 73; 272A3(b)(ii); ethnography, 67, 68, 69, 73, 274; eating and drinking habits, 67; duels, 68;

1037

INDEX OF PROPER NAMES

parasites, Bards, and Druids, 69; attack Delphic oracle, 240.29-40; plunder for silver, 240.29-40; migration, 273 Context; head trophies, 274
Celtiberians: 224; Celtiberian wars, 271
Celtoscyths: 272B, 34-6
Charmoleon of Massilia: 269
Charondas: 284.11-19
Chians: enslaved 86BC, 51
Chorographer, The: 249B(ii)
Chrysippeans: 187A
Chrysippus: attacked, 31, 32, 34, 42, 146, 148, 150, 151, 159, 163, 164, 165, 167, 169, 182, 187; conflict with observed fact, 159, 167, 164.11ff; inadequate explanation, 165.75ff, 167; self-contradiction, 159, 165.103ff, 167; psychology, 160; on faculties of soul, 144; division of soul, 147; on substance of soul, 146; on souls, 139; theory of emotions, 151; plurality of virtues, 180-2; on τέλος, 187; formulation of τέλος criticised, 187C; definition of dialectic, 188; theory of vision, 193; divination, 107; on thunder, 135; on hail, 136
Cicero: T29-34; T107; use of Posidonius, 41, 100, 107, 118A; criticism of Posidonius, 104, 106, 109
Cimbri: 73; Cimbrian invasion, 240.29-40, 272B, 36ff; cause of migration, 49D(2), 272; original territory, 272A, 2-4; defeat by Romans, 272B, 44-7
Cimmerians: 211; 272B, 34-6
Claudius, Appius, *cos.* 143 B.C.: 53
Cleanthes: 3; 91; 100; 121; sun nourished by ocean, 118A; sun's path on ecliptic explained by equatorial ocean, 118B, 223; on souls, 139; theory of emotions, 151, 166, T92, 32, T91
Cleitarchus (Alexander historian): 206; 272A(c)

Cleomedes: T57; 19; report of Posidonius, 114; use of Posidonius, 115; criticism of Posidonius, 210
Cleopatra III, wife of Ptolemy IX Euergetes II Physcon: 49C(1)(c), 170-90; 49C(1)(f), 227-32; 77
Cleopatra Thea: 72
Clidemus: 135
Clitomachus: 254
Crassus, Publius, *cos.* 97 B.C.: 219.71-80
Crates of Mallos: 49C, 229ff; 102; 118B; 200; 216

Damon: 168
Damophilus: 59
Daphitas: 104
Darius: 49C(1)(a), 146-50
Demades: 252
Demetrius II, Nicator: 54; 61; 63; 64; 72; 226; 251
Demetrius III: 75
Demetrius of Callatis: 49D, 294ff; 231
Demetrius of Phalerum: on miners, 239/240
Demetrius of Scepsis: 49D, 294ff; 231
Democritus: on comets, 131A3, 132; shape of inhabited world, 200; discovery of the arch, 284.126-30
Dercyllides: 18D
Descartes: 133
Dicaearchus: T25; 49E, 305-8; 200; 204A; 222
Dies: 253.47-58
Diocles of Magnesia: 42; 99
Diodorus of Alexandria: 18; 128; 149
Diodorus Siculus: use of Posidonius, 53 (Bk 5), 67 (Bk 5), 58 (Bk 33), 59 (Bk 34), 268, 269, 274.7-9
Diodorus of Tyre (Peripatetic): 253.12-23
Diodotus of Sidon: 285
Diodotus Tryphon: 54; 61; 226; 251
Diogenes of Babylon: 99b; 107; 111; 132A(b); 178
Diogenes the Cynic: 29
Diogenes the Epicurean: 253 Context

1038

INDEX OF PROPER NAMES

Diogenes Laertius: sources: T66, 4, 5, 6, 11, 13, 21, 99, 199a, 287; misunderstanding of Posidonius, 171
Dionysiac Artists: 253.47–58
Dionysius of Cyrene: 48
Dionysius the Mede: 251
Dionysius Periegetes: 200; 201
Dioscurides of Anazarbus: T113
Dioscurides Phakas: T113
Diotimus: slanderer of Epicurus, 288
Drimacus of Chios: 51
Duris: 233

Empedocles: thunder, 135
Ephorus: 246BI(3); 249B(iii); 272A3(b)(ii); 284.114–25
Epicurus: criticism of, 22, 46, 47, 149, 160, 288, 289, 114, 115, 149, 160, 169B; and learning, 179; in criticism of the Stoic τέλος, 187C
Epigenes: 132
Eratosthenes: T47; 49; 49A; 49B(2)(a),10–13; 49B(4)(b)(iv), 118–25; 49C,229ff; 49D,294ff; length of inhabited world, 49E, 305–8; shape of inhabited world, 200, 201; circumference of earth, 115H; measurement of circumference of earth, 202B; boundaries of continents, 206; zones, 209; equatorial zone, 210; klimata, 205; latitudinal approximation, 115Ab; on Rhodian band of latitude, 204A; measurement for stades and mile, 203; size of sun, 116; on winds, 137; moon and tides and currents, 217B3; tidal unison, 219.15–19; currents, 138, 214A, 215, 219.19–32; sea levels, 221, 231; on Nile flooding, 222; on India, 212/213; on Arabia, 237; naphtha wells, 236; Pillars of Heracles, 246; criticism of Homer, 216, 277 fin., 280 Context; criticism of Herodotus, 270
Erembi: 280/281

Erymneus (Peripatetic): 253.12–23
Ethiopians: 49C(1)(d), 199ff; on same latitude but different from Indians, 49F(3), 326ff
Etruscans: banquets, 53
Euclid: and the fifth postulate, 197
Euctemon of Athens: 246
Eudorus: 48; 49B(4)(b)(iv), 118–25; 85; 89; 118B; 141A1; 149; 176; 186B; 210; 222
Eudoxus of Cnidus: 48; 49B(2)(a), 10–13; 200; 202C(3); 204B; 205
Eudoxus of Cyzicus: 49C
Euhemerus of Messene: T46; 49C(2)(c), 289–93
Eunapius: use of Posidonius, 252
Eusebius Hieronymus: knowledge of Posidonius, T67
Eustathius: and Posidonius, 201
Euthymenes of Marseilles: 138; 222

Fabius Maximus (*RE* 116): nickname, 259/260
Firmicus Maternus, Julius: 112
Fisheaters: 49B(3)(b), 49–61
Flaminius, Titus Quinctius, *cos.* 123 B.C.: T5; 227

Gadiretans: 217A; 217B,1.4; 246
Galatae: 73
Galen: use and valuation of Posidonius, T58–64, 146, 163, 187; criticism of Posidonius, 163E
Gallus, Aelius: 49C(2)(c); 238
Geminus: T42; use of Posidonius, 118B, 197; and Proclus, 195; and the fifth postulate of Euclid, 197; classification of lines, 198
Germani: 73; 272B, 34–6; 277b
Getae: 277.1–3
Gracchus, Tiberius (*RE*53, *cos.* 177 B.C.): 271
Gylippus: 240.16–40

Harpalus: 66
Harpocration: 290

1039

INDEX OF PROPER NAMES

Hecataeus: map, 200
Helvetii: and Cimbri, 272B, 40ff
Heracleon of Beroea: 75
Heraclides Ponticus: 18; 49C(1)(a)(ii), 148; 110
Heraclitus: 135
Hercules: temple at Rome, 53
Hermagoras of Temnos: 43; 189
Hero of Alexandria: and Posidonius, 196, 197, 198, 199a, 199b
Hierax of Antioch: 56
Himerus: viceroy of Babylonia, 65
Hipparchus: T47; 18; 48; 49; 49A; 49C,229ff; 202B; breadth of inhabited world, 49E,305–8; shape of inhabited world, 200; klimata, 205; on Rhodian band of latitude, 204A; degrees, 204B; step measurement, 202C(3); earth shadow, 115F; on tides, 138, 214A, 219.15–19; star map, 202C(3); channel currents, 215; on Sri Lanka, 214B; criticism of Eratosthenes, 216
Hippasus: 49C(2)(c)
Hippocrates: 131A2; faculties of soul, 142, 143
Homer: 28; Posidonian interpretation of, 277, 280/281, 293; for geographical evidence, 137, 214, 216, 49, 222, 277 *fin.*; as a scientific source, 48; on tides, 216; on Nile flooding, 222; map, 200; books of, 277.43–6
Hyperboreans: 270; 277a Context
Hyspaosines of Charax: 65

Icadius: 104
Indians: on same latitude, but different from African Ethiopians, 49F(3), 326ff, 223

Jews: 61; 278
Josephus: use of Posidonius, 278
Juba: 222

Lactantius: use of Posidonius, 155
Lucullus, Lucius Licinius (*RE*104): expedition to Cyrene, 86 B.C., 51; luxury, 265–7 Context
Luvernius: 67D
Lycurgus: 284.11–19
Lydus, J: on Nile flooding, 222
Lynceus: 114
Lysander: 240.16–40
Lysias, tyrant of Tarsus: 253 Context

Macrinus: name, 264.12–18
Macrobius: 49C, 229ff; sources, T68; use of Posidonius, 118B, 129/130
Manilius: use of Posidonius, 129/130
Manlius Torquatus, Titus: name, 264.12–18
Manlius, M: name, 264.12–18
Marcellus, M. Claudius (*RE*218): 261
Marcellus, M. Claudius (*RE*219): 261
Marcellus, M. Claudius, the conqueror of Syracuse (*RE*220): 86e; 261; and Nicias of Engyium, 257; statue, 258; name, 259/60, 264.1–9
Marcellus, M. Claudius (*RE*225, *cos.* 152 B.C.): 258; 271
Marcellus, M. Claudius (*RE*226): T1a.4; 258
Marcellus, M. Claudius (*RE*227, *aed.* 91 B.C.): 258
Marcellus, M. Claudius (*RE*229, *cos.* 51 B.C.): T1a; 258
Mariandynians: 60; 227.5–9
Marius, Gaius: name, 264; defeat of Cimbri, 272B, 44–7; death, 255
Medeios of Piraeus: 253.23–32
Megasthenes: and India, 212/213
Melkart: 246.15–17
Menaechmus: theory of mathematics, 195B(b)
Metellus Macedonicus, Quintus Caecilius: name, 264.1–9
Mithridates VI Eupator: 51; 253; 255; 263

1040

INDEX OF PROPER NAMES

Mnesistrateans: 289
Mochus of Sidon: 285/286
Moderatus: 141A
Moses: 278.9-13; 279 Context
Mothers, The; goddesses, 257
Mummius Achaicus, L: 53
Mummius, Lucius: 264.1-9
Mysians: 277

Namnitae: 276
Nearchus: 49B(3)(b), 49-61; 138; 283
Necho: 49C(1)(a)(i), 147
Nicias of Athens: 262
Nicias of Engyium: 257
Nicolaus of Damascus: 51; 56; 277.33-7; 278; 288
Nicomedes: 197
Nymphodorus of Syracuse: 51

Odysseus: and Spain, 247
Oenopides of Chios: theories of mathematics, 195B(c)
Onesicratus: 138; 283
Oppius, Q.: praetor of Pamphylia, 253.78-84
Orbius: 253.164ff

Panaetius: T1; T7; T8; T9/10; T12; 7; 41; 58; 99b; 107; 118B; 159; 178; 179; 210; 227; 252; 254
Parmenides: and zones, 49B(2)(a), 10ff, 209
Patrocles: 206
Peripatetics: fabricate Stoic syllogisms, 170E; distortion, 173
Persians: Chalybonian wine drunk by Persian kings, 242
Pharnaces I: 263
Philip of Macedon: 104
Philippus I: 75
Philon of Larissa: T31; 176
Phoenicians: 49C(1)(a),147; Posidonius' attitude to, 217A6, 246C, 285B
Phylax: 50

Piso, Gaius: 255
Plato: faculties of soul, 142, 143, 144, 145, 146, 160, 165.164ff; theory of emotions, 151, 167; virtues, 183; interpretation of, 85, 141, 290, 291
Pliny: use of Posidonius, T56, 120
Plutarch: use of sources and Posidonius, 141, 252, 255
Polybius: T25; T47; T77; T78; 49B(4); 49C,229ff; on measurement, 203; zones, 209; equatorial zone, 210; strait currents, 216; Spanish mining, 239; criticised by Posidonius, 271, 217A, 225
Pompeius, Gnaeus: T35-39; monograph on, 79; campaigns in Caucasus, 206; command against pirates, 206; name, 264.12-18
Pomponius Mela: 49C, 229ff; 217A5(b)
Posidonii: T1
Posidonius of Alexandria: T1; 199b
Posidonius of Apamea: dates, T4; Grand Tour, T14-18, T22, T23, T25, T26; date of journey to west, 49C(1)(f), 227ff; embassy, T28, 255; friendship with Romans, T32, T35; historical sense of development of philosophy, T101/102; argues from School definitions, 34, 165; interest in Pythagoreans, 151; approval of Plato, 152, 165.89ff, 165.164ff, 167, 183; approval of Aristotle, 165.164ff, 167, 183; criticism of Epicurus, 22, 46, 47, 149, 160, 288, 289, 114, 115, 169B; criticism of Chrysippus, 146, 150, 160, 167, 182, 183; criticism of Polybius, 217A, 225, 271; orthodoxy, 13, 20, 21, 23, 101, 107, 127/128, 139, 170D; unorthodoxy, 35BC, 115G, 144, 146, 150, 160, 196; interpretation of Plato, 85, 141, 290, 291; history of ideas, 151; criticism of popular lore, 119; influence, 134B(5); style, T103-6, T34, 239

1041

INDEX OF PROPER NAMES

Posidonius of Olbia: T1
Priscianus Lydus: sources, T71–2, 219
Proclus: use of Posidonius, 195, 198; and Geminus, 197
Ptolemy Apion: 51
Ptolemy, Claudius: 49C, 229ff; 115; and the fifth postulate of Euclid, 197
Ptolemy II Philadelphus: 206; 222
Ptolemy VI Philometor: 54; 56
Ptolemy VII: 58
Ptolemy VIII, Euergetes II, Physcon: 49C(1)(a)(ii), 150; 49C(1)(b), 151ff; 49C(1)(f), 227ff; 77; his will, 51; his parasite, 56; physical deterioration, 58
Ptolemy IX, Soter II, Lathyrus: 49C(1)(c), 170ff; 49C(1)(f), 227ff; 51
Ptolemy X, Alexander I: 49C(1)(f), 227ff; 51; deterioration and grossness, 77
Ptolemy XI, Alexander II: 51; 77
Ptolemy XII, Auletes: 51
Pyrrho: 287
Pythagoreans: T91; T95; 49B(2)(a), 10–13; 117; 253.112ff; 284.11–19; on soul, 141A; psychology, 151, 165.164ff; zones, 209; comets, 131, 132
Pytheas: T25; T46; 49C(2)(a), 233–7; 49C(2)(c), 289–93; 119E; 138; 208B; 219.71–80; 277a Context

Rufus of Ephesus: T113
Rutilius Rufus, P.: T13; 41; 78; 265–7 Context

Samnites: 253.85–92
Sanchuniathon: 285B
Sarpedon: 226; 251
Sataspes: 49C(1)(a), 146–50
Scaevola, Q. Mucius: 78; 265–7 Context; 266
Scaurus, Marcus Aem. (*aed.* 58 B.C.): 244

Scilurus: Scythian prince, 263
Scipio Aemilianus Africanus, Publius Cornelius: name, 264.1–9; moderation, 265; triumph in 146 B.C., 53; tour to the east, 58, 254, 265; in Spain, 271; and Antiochus Sidetes, 61
Scordistae, Scordisci: 272B,38f; 277.25–33; and silver, 240.29–40
Scythians: 263
Seleucus the Babylonian, of the Red Sea: on tides, 138, 214B, 217B3, 218A
Seleucus I Nicator: 206; 251
Seleucus, son of Antiochus VII Sidetes: 63; 64
Seleucus V, son of Demetrius and Cleopatra: 64; 72
Seleucus VI: 75
Seneca: valuation and use of Posidonius, T41, T52–5, 12, 132B, 135, 136, 155, 170, 175, 176, 230D, 105, 284.52–6
Sertorius, Quintus: 264.1–9; 271 Context
Sesostris (Rameses II): 222
Seven Sages, The: 284.11–19, 17–52, 114–25
Severus, the Platonist: 141A
Silanus, the historian: on wells at Gadeira, 217A
Simplicius: T73
Socrates: T81; 29; 253 Context
Solon: 284.11–19
Soranus: 147
Spartacus: 73; 262
Spartans: on gold and silver, 240.16–29
Speusippus: definition of soul, 141A; theory of mathematics, 195B(a)
Stoics: theory of comets, 132; rainbow, 134B(5); thunder, 135; definition of soul, 139; division of soul, 147; on limits, 141A; on animals and children, 159; syllogisms, 170E, 175; definitions of anger,

1042

INDEX OF PROPER NAMES

155; definitions of end, 186, 187C; definitions of dialectic, 188; definition of figure, 196; classification of virtues, 180; classification of cause, 190

Strabo: 263; valuation and use of Posidonius, T46–49, 49G, 67, 119, 137, 206, 214C, 217B2, 250, 272B, 277.25–33, 277 *fin.*, 280.24–9, 282; criticism of Posidonius, 49, 49C(2), 49F, 49G, 217A8, 222, 223, 239, 271, 277.47–63; and Posidonius, 49 Structure, 49A; acquaintance with Posidonius, T8; on geography and philosophy, T75; use of ethnology, 282; circumfluent ocean, 49C, 229ff

Strato: emotions, 154; currents, 219.19–32; sea levels, 221

Sulla, L. Cornelius: name, 264.12–18; siege of Athens, 253 *fin.*; and Marius, 255

Symeon Seth: 211

Syrians: 280

Taurisci: 272B, 39f; 277.25–33
Tectosages: their treasure, 273
Tertullian: use of Posidonius, 147
Thales: 49B(2)(a), 10–13; 209; 222
Theodorus of Gadara: 189
Theophanes of Mytilene: 79; 206
Theophrastus: 237; 253.112ff
Thracians: 277; celibate monks, 277.37–43
Thrasyalces of Thasos: 137; 222
Tigyrenoi: 272B, 41–4
Timagenes of Alexandria: 273
Timosthenes of Rhodes: compass card, 137
Tōygeni: 272B, 41–4
Tryphon: see Diodotus Tryphon
Tubero, L. Aelius: T12
Tubero, Quintus Aelius: 78; 265–7 Context
Tyrians: 246

Vaccaeans: 224
Valerius Asiaticus: 228
Varro: 52; 137
Vettius Valens: step measurement, 202C(3)
Vitruvius: T50

Xenarchus: 18
Xenocrates: 28; 141AB
Xerxes: 49C(1)(a), 146–50

Zaleucus: 284.11–19
Zeno of Citium: ambiguity of evidence, T91, T99, 166; verbal teaching, 165; defended by Posidonius, 175; on god, 100; on eclipses, 126; on thunder, 135; on soul, 139; theory of emotions, 151, 166; on emotions and judgement, 34,152; verbal definition of distress, 165; on drunkenness, 175; and learning, 179; on virtues and mental faculties, 182; emends Homer, 280.1–4, 281
Zeno of Sidon: 46; 47; 288
Zeno of Tarsus: 99b
Zenodotus: theory of mathematics, 195B(c)
Zopyrus: T112

B GEOGRAPHICAL

Abdera (Adra): 247
Aetna: scene of the brothers saving their parents from lava flow, 234
Albania: 206
Alexandria: 202B
Alps: 240a, 7–10; 270
Antioch (Syria): 54; 56; 72; 251
Apamea: T2/3; 251
Apollonia (Vlone): 235
Arabia: salt, 238
Araxes, R. (Araks): 206
Arcanian Lake: 219.136–45
Arethusa: 219.32–8
Armenia: 206
Arsinoe (Suez): 206

INDEX OF PROPER NAMES

Athens: political situation after end of 2nd c. B.C., and chronological problems of 88–87 B.C., 253.23–32; archonships, 253; political coup of Athenion, 253; taken by Sulla in 86 B.C., 51, 253 *fin.*
Atlantic ocean: 219.15–19; 221
Atlantis: 49D(1), 297–303

Babylonia (Iraq): naphtha wells, 236
Baetica: copper mines, 239.24–7
Bainis, R. (Minho): 224
Baitis, R. (Guadalquivir): wave recoil and flooding, 218B
Barbarium, Promontory (C. Espichel): 220
Bitter Lakes: 206
Black Sea: 206; 221
Byzantium: straits of, 215

Callet (Further Spain): 237
Calpe: 246
Canaries: 49C(1)(d), 209ff
Canopus: elevation, 202B,C(3), 205; observation near Gadeira, 204; history of, 205
Cantabria: 224
Carmania (Kirmān): 283
Carthage: 223; 253.85–92
Caspian Sea: 206; 219.32–8
Cassiterides (Tin Islands): 239.27–31
Caucasian 'isthmus': measurement of, 206
Chalcidice (Chalcidene): 251
Chersonesus: 263
Cilicia: 235
Cimmerian Bosporus (Straits of Kerch): 206; 263; 272B, 34–6
Cinnamon-bearing country: 222
Cissia Persica: 219.154–8
Cnidus: on the Rhodes-Gadeira latitude, 202C(3), 204
Coele Syria: 244; 251
Colchis: 206
Comorin, Cape: 212/213
Cornwall: tin mines, 239.27–31

Crau, Plaine de la: 229; 268
Crimea: 262
Cyprus: 243
Cyrenaica: bequeathed to Rome, 51; wars, 51; Ptolemy Euergetes, 58
Cyrrhestice: 251
Cyrus, R. (Kura): 205

Dalmatia: 70
Damascus: 242
Danube: 240.29–40; 272B, 38f
Daphne: royal park, 72
Dead Sea: 219.136–45; asphalt in, 279
Delos: 253
Delphi: Delphic oracle, 240.29–40, 270; treasure stolen by Brennus, 273
Dicaearcheia (Puteoli): T24; 49C(1)(d), 191ff; 52
Dnieper, R.: 263

Egypt: willow tree, 241
Engyium (Sicily): 257
Enna: 250
Eryx: 250
Ethiopia: climate, 210B; summer rains, 222; drought, 223
Euboia: 231
Euripus: 219.32–8

Fos, Gulf of: 229

Gadeira: T15; 49C(1)(f); 49C(2)(c); 217B3; on Rhodes band of latitude, 202C(3), 204; behaviour of wells in Heracleium, 217A; dragon tree, 241; founding of, 246; temple of Heracles, 246
Gallia Narbonensis: T19
Gaul: 212/213
Gedrosia: 49B(3)(b), 49–61
Germania: 73
Gerrha (Arabia): 238
Guardafui, Cape: 49C(2)(b), 237–88
Gymnasiae (Balearic Islands): plagued with rabbits, 52

INDEX OF PROPER NAMES

Hellespont: 219.32-8
Heraclea: 60
Heracleium: at Gadeira, 217A
Hercynian Forest: 272B, 36f
Heroonpolis: 207
Hiera, Isl. (in Cyclades): 228; 231
Hiera Hephaesti, Isl. (Vulcano): 227
Hyrcanian Sea (Caspian): 219.32-8

Iber, R.: 218B
Iberia (Georgia): 206
Iberia (Spain; *see also* Spain): 223: floating bricks and silver, 237; metals and mining, 239
Ierne: 208B,24
Ilipa (Alcalà del Rio): 218B
Illyria: 235
Illyricum: 272B,38f
India: sailing west to, 49E; orientation and climate of, 212/213, 223
Indian Ocean (called Red Sea): tidal phenomena, 218A, 219.1-9, 219.32-8
Indus, R.: 212/213; 272A3(c)
Ister, R. (Danube): 272B, 38f; 240.29-40
Isthmus: of Caucasus, 49F(1), 309

Jerusalem: the temple, 278
Jutland: 272.2-4

Laodicea: 251
Larissa (Syria): 54
Larissa (Thessaly): 253.1-23
Laurium: silver mines, 239.21-4, 262
Lelantine Plain: 231
Leontini: 250
Lethe, R.: 224
Libya: 223
Liguria: 229; 268; toughness of women, 269
Lilybaeum (C. Boco): 249A
Lindos: temple of Athena, 258
Linx (Larasch, Lixus): 223
Liparaean Islands: 227
Lixus, R.: 49C(1)(c), 183ff

Loire, R.: rites at mouth of, 276
Lusitania: 224
Lydia: 237

Maeotis, Lake (Sea of Azov): 206; 272B, 32-4
Malta: 246
Marmara, Sea of: 221
Massilia: 269
Mauretania: 49C(1)(d), 199ff, 209ff
Maxilua (Further Spain): 237
Mediterranean: and Atlantic ocean, 219.15-19, 221
Meroe: 49B(2)(a), 17-36
Mesopotamia: 251; 280.19-24
Messene: 234; 253.1-12
Messina, Straits of: 138; 214A; 215; 216; 219.19-32; axis on Rhodes–Pillars of Heracles parallel, and on meridian through Rome and Carthage, 249C
Moesia: 272B, 38f; 277
Morocco: 220; 223
Myos Hormos: 49C(2)(c), 289-93

Narbo (Narbonne): 248
Nerium, Cape (Finisterre): 220
Nesis (Nisida): 52
New Carthage: 247; dwarf palm, 241
Nile; continental division, 49F(1), 309; explanation of summer flooding, 222; exploration of, 49C(1)(b), 150-70
Noricum: 272B, 39f
Numantia: 271
Numidia: 49C(1)(d), 209ff

Pachinus, Cape (C. Passero): 249A
Panarea (Euonymus): 227
Pannonia: 272B, 38f
Parthia: 57; 64; 251; senate, 282; earthquakes, 233
Pelorias, Cape (C. Peloro): 249A
Pelusium (Port Said): 206
Persian Gulf: 219.154-8
Phasis, R.: 49F(1), 309

INDEX OF PROPER NAMES

Phoenicia: earthquake in, 231
Pillars of Heracles: 204A; 219.15–32; explanation of, 246
Pitane (Iberia): 237
Planctae: 246
Pontus: 243

Red Sea (*see also* Indian Ocean): length, 49C(2)(b), 237–88, 206; continental division, 49F(1), 309
Rhagae (Shahr Rey): etymology, 233
Rhine, R.: tidal action on, 219.71–80
Rhipaean Mountains: 240.6–10; 270; 277a Context
Rhodes: T2/3; 202B; 228; 231; 235; band of latitude, 202C(3), 204
Rhone, R.: 274
Rio Tinto: copper mining, 239.24–7

Sacred Cape (C. St Vincent): 204A; 220
Sardinia, Sea of: depth, 221
Savus, R. (Morava): 272B, 38f
Seleucia in Pieria (Samandag): 235; 251
Seleucis: the Tetrapolis, 251
Sex: 246; 247
Sicily: 250; shape, orientation, size and position, 249; fertility of soil, 234, 250; first slave war, 59; Engyium, 257; Lindos, 258

Sidon: 285/286; earthquake, 231, 232
Sirbonis, Lake: confused with Dead Sea, 219.136–45
Spain (*see also* Iberia): T14–18; T20
Stony Plain: 229
Suez: 206
Susa: 219.154–8; 236
Syene (Aswan): 49B(1)(a), 17–36; 115; 202B; 222
Symplegades: 246
Syracuse: 219.32–8; 250; 257

Tanais, R. (Don): 49F(1), 309; 206
Taormina: 219.19–32
Taprobane (Sri Lanka): 212/213
Taurian Chersonese (Crimea): 262
Tauromenium: 234
Thames, R.: tidal action on, 219.71–80
Thebais: 222
Thera, Isl.: 228; 230; 231
Thia, Isl.: 228
Thule: 208B
Timavus, R.: 225
Tolosa (Toulouse): 248; 273
Trieste, Gulf of: 225
Turdetania: plagued with rabbits, 52; mining, 239
Tyrrhenia: 237

Vesuvius: 234

SUBJECT INDEX

Although for the reader's convenience I have subdivided this index into (A) Philosophy (B) History, Sciences, Geography (C) Style and Miscellaneous, it is sometimes difficult to compartmentalise a topic since Posidonius regarded all his work as organically related, and therefore there may be occasions when the reader will wish to check more than one section.

A PHILOSOPHY

abatement: of emotions, 165
advantage (συμφέρον, commodum): 164I; 184; defined as opposed to 'good', 170D; wealth, health, 170; applied to animals, progressors and bad men, 170D
aetiology: T85; 18; 34B; 109; 138; 165.75–102; 186B; 190; 219.9–15; 221; 223; 229B; 246BII(2); applied to ethical problems, 170A(1); part of admonitory ethics, 176; historical explanation, 253 fin., 270, 272.32–4, 41–4, 273 fin., 280.19–24; aetiology of formation of bitumens, 279
agreement (ὁμολογία, consistency, concord, harmony): 185; interpretation of in definition of the end, 187ABC
alteration (ἀλλοίωσις): 96
anger: definition, 155
animals: T82; 33; 39; 158; 187A; and emotions, 159, 166, 169A; natural impulse, 185
animate (ζῷον): 99; 127/128; 149
'antipathy': 217A1(ii)
apodeictic proof (ἀπόδειξις): 34; 156; 157
appropriate acts (καθήκοντα): 176; possible conflict between, 177; related to society, 177

arts: liberal arts, 90; classification of, 90; relation to philosophy, 90, 284.100–14; development of artistic and cultural civilisation, 284.20ff; imitate nature, 284.84–99
avarice; 239/240; 284.11–19; 284.24–47
axiom: 191; axiomatic methodology, 46, 47, 191; in mathematics, 195

beastlike (ζῷωδες): 161; 187A
belief (δόξα, opinion): with respect to emotion, 164ABGI, 165; in definition of distress, 165; false belief, 169E, 170A(1)
blood: differs in characteristics in animals, 169F
body (σῶμα): contained by soul, 149; and emotions, 154

cause: T85; definition, 95; analysis and classification of causes, 170A(1), 190; of emotions, 161, 162, 163D, 165.22–53, 169E; of why emotions abate with time, 165.103ff; ignorance of, 165.75–102; of vice, 169; of false suppositions, 169E; limit, 196, 199a
chance: 104; 105
children: T82; 31D; 33; and emotions, 159, 166, 169AB; without

1047

SUBJECT INDEX

reason, 169A; how err, 169C
choice and avoidance: 150; 161; 187D(b)
cohesion (ἕξις): 21; 28
conation (ὄρεξις, ὀρεκτόν): 158; 160; 161; 165.133ff
conjunctions: 45; 191; 192; conjunctive argument, 45, 192
consolation: 176
contemplation (θεωρία): 186B
corruption (διαστροφή, distortion): 170A(2); cause of, 161, 169D; explained by recognition of cause of emotions, 187D(b); through gold and silver, 240.16–40; through pleasure, denied, 35A
cosmos: 4; 6; 8; 13; 14; 20; 21; 23; 99a
courage: 180
criterion (of truth): 42; 85
cure (θεράπεια, ἴασις): of mental and physical sickness, and treatment, 163; of distress, 165; of emotions, 167; psychiatric, 169G, 31; twofold, knowledge and habituation, 169G

daimones: 24; 108; the daimon in oneself, 187A; the one governing the whole universe, 187A; philosophical metaphor, 187A
decadence/degeneration (see also corruption): 58; 62; 65; 77; 78
definitions: School definitions, 34B, 165.6ff, 182 fin., 31.39ff
desire (ἐπιθυμία): 155; 164I; desiring faculty, 160, 169B
dialectic: 44; definition of, 188; classification of φωνή and πράγματα, 189; and mathematics, 46, 47, 191, 195
dismemberment (διαίρεσις): 96
dissolution (ἀνάλυσις): 96
divination: T74; 7; 86b; 103; science, 104; scientific, 106; natural, 110; justification of, 107; dreams, 108;
prognostics, portents, 109; augury, 113
divine (θεῖος): 161; 187A
dreams: classification of divinatory dreams, 108
drunkenness: 63; and the good man, 175

education: 162; 163D; 178; two-fold, 169G; modes of education and cause of emotions, 168, 187D(c)
ekpyrosis: 5; 13; 92; 97; 99b; 139
elements: 5; 13; 100; natural places, 93
emotions (πάθη): definition, 34, 163, 164A; classification, 180; mental and physical classification, 154; physical description of, 34; physical description in terms of contraction and expansion, 152, 165.9–13, 170A(2); the emotional aspect (τὸ παθητικόν), 31, 33, 158, 166, 168, 160; emotional pull (ὁλκή), 158, 169E, 170B; relationship to moral questions, 30; explains ethical puzzles, 187D; relationship to faculties of soul, 150; explanation of in relation to theories of others, 151; cause of, 161, 164, 168, 187A; external cause of, 163CD; emotional movement, 153, 158; that is unnatural and irrational, 163, 168, 169EF; only moved by irrational, 162, 174, 178; as mental illness, 163; and belief, 164; and reason, 164H, 165.164ff; relationship to judgement or rational decision, 34, 152; explanation of why rise and abate, 165, 166; satiety of, 165.133ff; weariness of, 166; cure of, 165, 167; controlled by reason, 166; anger, 155; of the crowd, 253
end (τέλος): definition, 185, 186; interpretation of definition, and criticism of Chrysippus, 187;

1048

SUBJECT INDEX

explained by cause of emotions, 187D(a)
environment: 49B(4)(a)(ii), 89-92; influence on character, 169F
ethics: subdivisions of, 89, 150; and psychology, 150; hortatory and admonitory ethics, 176
ethology: part of practical ethics, 176; relation to history, 176
evil: problem of, 169; cause of evil internal, 35C; explained by cause of emotions, 187D(b); opinion or belief of, 165
extension: 141A

faculties (δυνάμεις, powers): 32; of soul, 142, 143, 144, 145, 150, 158, 159, 166, 178; irrational, 31, 142-6, 147, 148, 34, 160, 161, 166, 169; cause of emotions, 150; and plurality of virtues, 182
fate (εἱμαρμένη): 25; 103; 104; 105; 106
fear: 162
flesh: 184
form: in definition of soul, 140, 141 (mathematical), 146, 160, 169B
fusion (σύγχυσις): 96

generation and destruction: 13; classification, 96
genus/species: in definition, 196
goal (σκοπός): 187C
god(s): 20; 23; 100; 101; and divination, 108
golden age: 284
good: 161; 184; apparent goods, 164BI, 169D; effect of goods, 170A(2); applied only to wise man, 170D
good men: 163
governing principle (ἡγεμονικόν): 23; 147; 159; 184
grammar: 45; 192

habituation: 31; 164EG; 165.22-53, 172ff; 168; 169G; 274

happiness (εὐδαιμονία): 187AC: timeless, 179
health: mental and physical, 163; not a good, 170; in category of goods (misunderstanding of D.L.), 171; necessary for virtue (Peripatetic distortion), 173
heart: 146
heaven (οὐρανός): 20; 23
human geography: 49B(3)(b), 44-61; 49F, 309-56
hypostasis (ὑπόστασις, substance, reality): 16; 92; 96; 121; 129/130; 131; 132; 141A

ignorance (ἀμαθία): 169E; 31; 168
imagination: 162
impulse (ὁρμή): 34; 150; 158; 159; 160; 164; 165.151ff; 169E; 'excessive' impulse (emotion), 34, 169E; rational, 169E; in animals and in rational beings, 185; from emotion, 162, 187D(d)
inconsistency (ἀνομολογία): 187A
indication (ἔνδειξις): T87; 156; 191
indifferents (ἀδιάφορα): 187C
inferior men (φαῦλοι): condition of soul, 163; 164D; 178
infinite/finite: 97; 98
infirmity (ἀρρώστημα): of soul, 164AC
'intermediates': 105; 164D; not goods, 170C
irrational (ἄλογον): faculties, 31, 34, 142-8, 161, 162, 159, 164A, 165.103ff, 172ff, 166, 169, 184, 187C; unmoved by rational, 162, 31, 168; part of soul, 186B, 187A

judgement (κρίσις, rational decision): and emotions, 34, 152, 154, 164AI, 169E
justice: 180

knowledge: of truth, 169G; timeless, 179

1049

SUBJECT INDEX

law: natural, precept and state law, 178; does not need preambles, 178
learning (παιδεία): 179; T48; T84; 90
limit (πέρας): 141A; 149; 196; 16; 92; 199a
logic: role of, 88; and mathematics, 191, 46, 47; and physics, 190, 196
logical concept: 92
luck: 105
luxury: 53; 58; 59; 61; 62; 65; 67D; 72; 77; 78; 136B(1); 239/240; 242; 253.36-47; 284.11-19

madness: 164A
mathematicals (τὰ μαθηματικά): 141A
matter: 92; 141A
meaning: 44; 45
mental picture (ἀναζωγράφησις): 162
methodology: T83/T84; T85; 18; 47; axiomatic methodology, 47, 191; in psychology and ethics, 150; of mathematics, 195; *see also* 'hypothesis' in science index
mistakes: intellectual, 169E
moral (καλόν): 161
morality (τὸ καλόν, honestas): and end, 187C; and time, 179
motion (κίνησις): emotional movement, 153, 158, 168, 169EF
music: in education, 168; sign of decadence, 54, 62; instruments: flute, recorder, 54; lyre, 62; magadis, 292

natural affinity (οἰκείωσις, οἰκεῖον): 158; 159; 160; 161; 165.133ff; 169ABD; 171; 187C; 240.40-5
natural constitution (constitutio): T82
natural law: 104D
natural philosophy: and science, 18, 202D; and logic, 190, 196
nature (φύσις): 103; and divination, 110; and end, 185; the things according to nature (τὰ κατὰ φύσιν) and the end, 187C; arts learn from nature, 284.84-99
now: 98
number (ἀριθμός): 141A

order (τάξις): 186B

pain (λύπη, distress): 162; definition, 165
passionate: faculty of soul (θυμοειδές), 160
pedagogy: pedagogic modes of ethics, 176
Peripatetic distortion: 173; 171
philosophers: associating with men of power, 254
philosopher tyrants: 253
philosophy: divisions of, 87; similes for, 88; parts of, 88, 186B; organism, 88, 186B; relation to arts and sciences, 18, 90, 284; order of teaching, 91; function in political, social, artistic and technological development, 284; as author of civilisation, 284.20ff
philosophy of language: 45
physiognomy: 36; 111; 168; 169F
place (τόπος): 97
pleasure: 184; as corrupting force denied, 35A, 169D; natural goal, 158, 160, 161, 169ABD; but not the end, 187C
pneuma: 100; 101; 139; 149; 190
poverty: 170E
power (κράτος): as a natural goal, 158, 160, 161, 169B
prayer: 40
precepts (praecepta): 176
'preferred' (προηγμένον): 170D; 176
prefixes: 45
prepositions: 45; 192
present (time): 98
presentation (φαντασία): of evil, 162; and magnitude, 164AEHI; of good, 169D; persuasive presen-

1050

SUBJECT INDEX

tation, 169D, 170B; true or false, 188
principles (ἀρχαί): 5; 92; mathematical, 195
prognostics: 109
progression (προκοπή): 29
progressor (προκόπτων): 176; 178; and emotion, 164BCD, 174, 187D
proof: T33/34; 2; 7; 29; 34; 156; 157; 164B; 197
prophecy: 108
propositional logic: 45; 192; 191
propositions (ἀξιώματα): 188; 191; propositions theorems or problems in mathematics, 195B; mathematical proposition (πρότασις), 195B(d)
protreptics: 3
providence: 104D; 106; 186B
psychology: and ethics, 150; classification of psychological theories, 169B; of animals and children, 159, 166, 169AB; of vice, 169E

questions: dialectical classification of, 188, 195

rational element (λογικόν, λογιστικόν): 147; faculty of soul, 160, 161, 165.172ff, 169BE
reason (λόγος, λογισμός): and emotion, 164H; controls emotion, 166; natural artificer of impulse, 184; and order, 186B; daimon, 187A
rhetoric: T39; 44; 45; θέσεις, 43; 'status' in rhetorical theory, 189; part of logic, 189; rhetorical style, 239.1-11; rhetorical devices, 253.32-103
rules: moral, 176, 178

satiety: of emotions, 165.133ff, 172ff
saving the phenomena: 18
shape (σχῆμα): 141A; 149
sickness: mental and physical, 163
sight (ὄψις): 193; 194

signification (σημαίνειν, significatio): in dialectic, 188; in rhetorical 'status' theory, 189B(a)
solar theology: 23
soul: 16; 21; 28; definition, 139, 140, 141; substance and localisation, 146; division of, 147; contains body, 149, 196; faculties, 142, 143, 144, 145, 146, 158; 'parts' of soul, 146, 160, 169B, 186B; natural affinities, 160; and emotions, 154; emotional aspect, 31, 33, 158, 166, 168; condition of soul of inferior men, 163; infirmity of, 164A; kinship with gods, immortal daimones, 108; world soul, 290; tetractys constituent of soul, 291
space (χώρα): 97
starting point (ἀρχή): of emotions and reason, 163
'Status' (στάσις): in rhetorical theory, 189; classification of vox and res, 189
substance (οὐσία): 20; 92; 96; 100; 141A; of soul, 146
supposition (ὑπόληψις): and emotions, 154, 164AGHI; cause of false suppositions, 169E
surface: 16
syllogism: 170C; 170E; 175; relational syllogisms, 191
'sympathy' (συμπάθεια, natural cosmic interactive affection): 104; and divination, 106; tidal, 219.15-19
synthesis (σύνθεσις): grammatical, 192

temperament: 169F
tetractys: 291
theory of knowledge: 42
thought and reality: 16; 92
time: 98; with respect to emotion, 165; and morality, 179
training: 31; 150; 162; 163D; 164E; 165.22-53, 89ff, 172ff; 168; 169G; 178

SUBJECT INDEX

true and false: 188
truth (ἀλήθεια): 186B; criterion of truth, 42, 85
unhappy life (κακοδαίμων βίος): 187A

value (ἀξία): 164DHI
vice (κακία): constitution of, 169C; psychology of, 169E; cause of, 169C; internal, 35, 169; cause not external, 169D; no natural affinity for, 169D
virtue(s): 29; 38; 150; 181; classification of, 4; cardinal, 180; incapable of degree and timeless, 179; moral knowledge, 179; techne, 179; and psychology, 180; plurality and faculties, 31E, 182; differences in virtues, 182, 183; self-sufficiency of, 184; related to end, 185; whether it can be lost, 175; teachable, 2; dispute between Chrysippus and Ariston, 182; requires health, wealth (Peripatetic distortion), 173; Roman virtues, 257, 265-7
vision: theories of, 193
void: 6; 84; 97

weakness (ἀσθένεια): of soul, 164ACEGH; of rational faculty, 169E
wealth: analysis of cause, 170; not a good, 170C; not an evil, 170A(1); but an antecedent cause of evil, 170A(1); provokes false belief, 170A(1); effect of, 170A(2); relative value (προηγμένον), 170D; effect and function in moral psychology, 170D; in category of good (misunderstanding of D.L.), 171; greatest good, 172; necessary for virtue (Peripatetic distortion), 173
wisdom (σοφία): 161
wise man: 29; 40; 164BC; 177; 178; 284; free from emotion, 163; and drunkenness, 175; and time, 179; and dialectic, 188

Zeus: 103; etymology, 102

B HISTORY, SCIENCES, GEOGRAPHY

agriculture: importance in older Roman way of life, 266; and philosophy, 284.77-83
air: on equator, 210B; and earthquakes, 230D; marsh air, 94
apes: 245
architecture: invention of the arch, 284.126-30
archonship: at Athens, and the ἀναρχία of 88/7 B.C., 253.23-32, 103ff
arctic circle: 49B(2)(a), 14-17; 49B(2)(b), 37-43; 208; as tropic, 208B
arithmetic: assigned to Phoenicians, 285
arithmology: 291
Arsacid dynasty and succession: 282
ash: fertility of volcanic ash, 234
asparagus: 52
asphalt: 235; 236; in the Dead Sea, 279
astrology: T74; 112; 126; astrological explanation, 111
astronomy: 18; astronomical conditions for India, 212/213; ascribed to Phoenicians, 285
atmosphere: at equator, 210B
atom theory: origin of, 285/286
augury: 113; T1a
axiom: 46; 47; 191; 195

Babylonian measurement: 126; 202C(3)
baking: 284.84-99
banquets: Roman, 53; Etruscan, 53; Syrian, 61, 72, 75; Parthian, 64; Celtic, 67
barbaric customs: 274; 283
bards: 67D; 69
beavers: 243

1052

SUBJECT INDEX

beer: 67
bitumen: in Dead Sea, 219.136-45, 279; in Apollonia, Seleucia and Rhodes, 235
boats: λέμβος, 49C(1)(d), 209ff

camels: 72
carrots: 70
celestial projection: 49B(3)(a), 44-8; 49B(4)(a)(i), 67-70
Celtic ethnography: 67; 68; 69; 73; 274
cinnamon parallel: 49B(2)(a), 10-36; 208
circumference of earth: 49B(2)(a), 10-36; 202
circumnavigation of Africa: 49C
climate: 49F(3); of India, 212/213; of Libya, 223; *see* zones
cloud: 121; distance of cloud belt from earth, 120; and rainbows, 134; and thunder, 135; and hail, 136
coction: 284.84-99
comets: theory of, 131, 132; classification of, 131; doxography of, 131, 132
compass cards: 137
concord (ἁρμονία): mathematical, 141A
conluminous combustion: 123; 124
continents: division and boundaries of, 49F(1), 206/207; intercontinental racial differentiation, 223
copper: mining in Spain, 239.24-7; medicinal by-products, 243
crows: 243
cups: 76
currents: explanation of refluent currents in straits, 214A, 215, 216, 219.19-32, 220

day: longest day ratio in establishing latitudes, 204A, 205, 210B
degrees: of latitude, 202C(2), 204B;
Babylonian sexagesimal measurement, 202C(3)
disorientation: of Sicily, 249A; of India, 212
druids: 68; 69

earth: circumference of earth, 49E,305-8; measurement of circumference, 202; length of inhabited world, 49E, 305-8; shadow, 115F, 9; 'vine-earth', 234, 239.1-11; 'silver- and gold-earth', 239.1-11; *see also* 'habitable world'
earthquakes: 12; 229B; terms, 230B; classification, 230C; cause of, 230D; oceanic, 230D; seismic chain, 231; in Sidon, 231; in Parthia, 233
ecclesia: Athenian, 253.97ff
eclipse: lunar, 115D, 116, 123, 126; solar, 123, 124, 125
ecliptic: 49B(2)(a),10-13; angle of, 208B; fractions of, 126; intersection with milky way, 129/130
Eleusinian mysteries: 253.100ff
environment: 49B(4)(a)(ii), 80-92
Epicurean mathematics: 47
equator: temperate and inhabited, 209, 210
equatorial ocean: 49B(4)(b)(iv), 136-45; 118B; 210C
ethnography: T80; 49B(3)(b); 49C(1)(d), 199ff; 49F, 309-56; 283; explanatory, 49F *fin.*, 67, 277, 280/281; linguistic ethnic identification, 272B,34-36, 280/281; and Homeric interpretation, 277.37-43, 280/281; Roman and Italian ethnography, 53; Celtic ethnography, 67, 68, 69, 73, 274; Syrian and Arabian ethnography, 280/281
Euclidean geometry: 47
exploration: of Nile, 49C(1)(b), 150-70

1053

SUBJECT INDEX

figure (σχῆμα): mathematical definition of, 196
flooding: river, estuary and coastal, 218B, 219.38-45
frugality: virtue of Romans, 58, 265-7

genealogy: of Iunii Bruti, 256
geography: T75-9; concerned with habitable world, 208B; and zones, 208B; human geography, 49F, 309-56, 49B(3)(b), 44-61
gnomons: 115Ab; 202B, C(2); 204A
gold: 240; white gold, 239.31-6; mining, 240.1-16; corrupting effect of, 240.16-40, 272B, 40ff; an 'indifferent', 240.40-5
gravity: 199b
guilds: Dionysiac Artists, 253.47-58

habitable world (οἰκουμένη): 208; shape, 200; northern limits of, 208A; geography concerned with, 208B; see also 'earth'
hail: theory of, 136
halo: theory of, 133
hares: 52
history: termination date of Posidonius' *History*, 51, T1; historical explanation, 253 *fin.*, 270, 272B, 32-4, 41-4, 273 *fin.*, 280.19-24; and philosophy, T8, 253, 265; and ethnology, 176; as sub-science to ethics, 240.40-5; as an ethical tool, 164F; concerned with moral analyses and comparisons, 254
hoplite general: at Athens, 253.103ff
horizon distortion: 119
horoscopes: 111
horses: 243
human geography: 49B(3)(b), 44-61
hypothetical method: 18; 115; 202D; 272B, 32-4; 280.19-24; alternative hypotheses, 18, 49, 138, 210, 219; in mathematics, 195

ice: 136B(1)
iced water: 136B(1)
inventions: 284.114-30
isthmuses: Caucasian and Suez, 206, 207; or 'neck' of Gaul, 248

kingship: 57; 58; 60; 66; 67D; 252; 263; 284
klimata (latitudes): 49F(1); 208; 210; 223; 249C; seven klimata, 205; definition, 205; methods of establishing, 204A, 205; Rhodes-Pillars of Heracles parallel, 49E, 305-8, 204, 249C; approximations of, 115Ab, 204B(3); Strabo on, 208; in mapping Sicily, 249C; in ethnology, 280/281

lakes: salt, 219.136-45
latitudes: *see* klimata
lava: 231; of Aetna and fertility of soil, 234
lex Calpurnia: 265
lex Fannia: 78; 265-7
lightning: theory of, 135
line: definition of, 199a
locusts: 223
lunar eclipse: 115F; 116; 123; 126
lunar illumination: 123; 124
lunar latitude: 126

maps: 200; 201; of Agrippa, 249B(ii)
marvels (παράδοξα): 244; explained scientifically, 229D
mathematics: logic of, 46, 47, 191; mathematical postulates and hypotheses, 47; mathematical proof, 134; mathematical definition, 141A; mathematical methodology, 195; mathematical reality, 16, 98, 141A, 199a
measurement: of land and sea distances, 202B, 249B(iii); by gnomon, 202B, C(2); by 'step', 202C(3); Babylonian sexagesimal, 202C(3), 126; table of measure-

1054

SUBJECT INDEX

ment of stade, mile, parasang, schoinos, 203; of 'isthmus' of Gaul, 248; of coastline of Sicily, 249B
medicine: T51; T111-14; 190
meridians: 202B; 208B
methodology: *see* Philosophy Index
milky way: 129/130
mining and miners: T20; 239/240; private speculation in Spain, 239.21-4; in Athens, 262; in Egypt, 262; lack of in Liguria, 268; 'discovered' by philosophers, 284.52-6
mistral: 229A
monsoon: trade routes, 49C(2)(c), 293; and Nile flooding, 222
monsters: 244
moon: 10; 115F; star, 125, 127; composition, 122A; size, 122B; shape, 122C; density, 123, 124; diameter of, 115JK; phases, 122D, 217B; radius of orbit of, 115LM, 120; lunar illumination, 123, 124; eclipse, 126; latitude, 126; and tides, 217B; and strait currents, 219.19-32; nourished by fresh water, 118A; heat, and atmosphere, 219.80-134
music: *see* Philosophy Index

naphtha: white and black, 219.154-8; classification and uses from Babylonian wells, 236
nicknames: T1; 259/260; 277.25-33
nomenclature: 261; Roman proper names, 264

ocean: equatorial ocean, 49B(4)(b)(iv), 139-45, 118B, 210C; northern ocean, 206; circumambient ocean, 49C(1)(a)(i)(d), 147, 49C(1)(f), 229ff, 118B, 214A; scope and orientation of Posidonius' *On Ocean*, 49 Structure, 49 F *fin*.
oil wells: in Cissia Persica, 219.154-8; Babylonian, 219.154-8

optical phenomena: 131; 132; 133; 134
ore: alluvial, 239.34-6; 240.1-6

paradoxa: 217A4; 244
parallax: 115G
parallel lines: definition, 197; and the fifth postulate of Euclid, 197
parasites: Syrian, 56, 74; Parthian, 57; Celtic, 69
parhelion: 121
part (μέρος): as measurement, 126, 202C(3)
Parthian history: 57; 61; 63; 64
pathology: medical, 190
perfume: 71; 238; 283
periegesis: 50
periplus: 50, 263
philosopher tyrants: 253
piety: of older Roman way of life, 266
pillars (στῆλαι): as landmarks, 246
piracy: 262
pistachios: 55
plane surface: 16
planetaria: T86
planets: 127/128; 131; 132; equal velocity of, 115N
plants: 159; and natural principle, 185
point: 16; 98; definition of, 199a; punctual existence, 199a, 16
political and social development: 284.1-19
popular lore: 106; criticised, 119
portents: 109; 121; 132B; 133
postulate: mathematical, 195; the fifth postulate of Euclid and proof, 196
pottery: invention of the potter's wheel, 284.114-25
precession: 205
precious stones: 49C(1)(b), 151-70
problems: in mathematics, 195
purification: 227

quadrilaterals: classification, 198

SUBJECT INDEX

rabbits: 52
race: differentiation, 223
rain: 136; at equator and in Ethiopia, 210B, 222; and climate, 223
rainbow: definition, 15; theory of, 134
reflection (ἔμφασις, ἀνάκλασις): 121; 123; 124; 133; 134
refluent currents: T79
refraction: 119C; 133
rites: of sacrifice explained, 176
rivers: and seas, 219.1–9, 225; tidal action on, 218B, 219.71–80, 224; flooding, 218B; silting, 221; in Libya, 223; underground, 225
rods (ῥάβδοι): 121
Roman luxury: 78
Roman virtues: 257
ruler/ruled: *see* 'kingship'

sacrilege: 273
salt: aromatic in Arabia, 238
science(s): and philosophy, T73–4; 18; 90; 134; 186B; 202D
screw of Archimedes (or Egyptian): 239.17–21
sea: and rivers, 219.1–9, 219.134; depth of sea bed, 220, 221; change of sea bed through earthquake and volcanic eruption, 221; changes of sea level, 214A, 215, 219.19–32, 221; saltiness, 219.134; silting, 221; exhalation theory, 221
seismology (*see also* 'earthquakes'): changes in earth or sea bed levels, 49D, 294–6, 12
senate: Roman, 253.95ff; Parthian, 282
sheep: in Sicily, 234
sign of zodiac (ζῴδιον): as measurement, 126, 202C(3), 217B
silver: mines in Attica, 239/240; mines in Spain, 239; silver plating and floating bricks in Further Spain, 237; corrupting effect of, 240.29–40

simplicity: of older Roman way of life, 266–7
slavery and slaves: 51; 60; 265
slave revolts: first Sicilian, 59; first and second Sicilian, 250, 262; Aristonicus' revolt, 59; Attic mining revolt, 239.21–4, 262; Spartacus' revolt, 262
snow: 11; 136
solar declination: 126
solar eclipse: 123; 124; 125
spice trade: 49C(1)(c)
stade: lengths, 202C(1)
stars: definition, 127, 128; characteristics of, 127, 128; nourished by earth moisture, 118A; in establishing latitudes, 204A; positive influence in astrology, 112, 111; moon, 125; Canopus, 202B,C(3), 204, 205; ever-visible stars, 208A
'steps' (βαθμοί): as form of measurement, 126, 202C(3)
subjection: 60; 263; 284
sun: 9; 17; 19; apparent size and distance, 114; size and method of measurement, 115, 116; diameter, 115K; diameter of sun, circumference and radius of orbit of sun, 115A–E, N–T; shape, 117; star, 127; ζῷον, 118A; distance of sun from earth, 120, 115; nourished by vapour from ocean, 118A; path on ecliptic explained by equatorial ocean, 118B; inclination of, 210; delay at tropic, 210; on equator, 210; sunset phenomena, 119; and rainbows, 134; summer/winter rising/setting as orientation, 212/213; diurnal and annual path, 223, 49F(3), 49B(4)(a)(iv)(α); not cause of tides, 219.80–134; and climate, 223
superstition: distrust of, 246, 257, 273, 276, 279
Syrian history: 54; 56; 61; 63; 64; 66; 72; 75

SUBJECT INDEX

tactics: 80; 81
technology: development and relation to philosophy, 284.20ff
temperate equatorial zone: 49B(4)(b)(iv), 118ff; 223
temperate zones: 208A
temperature: 49B(4)(a)(i)(β), 71–80
temples: of Heracles at Gadeira, 246; of Athena at Odysseia, 247
theorems: mathematical, 195
thunder: theory of thunderstorms, 135; classification, 135; doxography, 135
tides: T79; 106; 226; Posidonius an authority on, 214, 215; theory of tides and cycles, 217B, 219; exhalation theory, 217A5(b), 221; Aristotelian theory of recoil criticised, 220; uniformity from circumambient ocean, 214A; equinoctial and solstitial tides, 217B, 218; annual highs, 217B, 219.45-71, 218, 219.80-134; moon and not sun cause of, 219.80-134; moved by wind, 138; diurnal inequality, 218A; in Indian Ocean, 218A, 219.1-9; in Atlantic and Mediterranean, 219.15-19; and straits currents, 219.19-32; tidal action on rivers, 218B, 219.71-80, 224; tidal action as cause of Cimbrian migration dismissed, 272.2-4
tin: 239.27-31
tools: of artisans, 284.56-60
torrid zone: 49B(2)(a), 10-36
trees: dragon-tree; willow; dwarf palm; 241
triangles: classification, 198
triumphs: celebration of Roman triumphs, 53
tropic: 49B(2)(a), 10-36; 115; regarded as 24°, 208AB; area between the tropics, 208A; approach of sun to, 210
turnips: 70
twilight: 119B

twins: 111
tyranny: 253.58-63, 112-44; 284.11-19

vates: 69
vines: in Sicily, 234; vine-earth, 235; Chalybonian, 242
volcanic eruption: in sea, 227, 228; volcanic ash, 234

waterclocks: 115K
wave: big wave, 226; shock wave inundation, 232; solidification in Stony Plain, 229B(ii)
weather signs: 109; 121; 133
weaving: 284.65-77
wells: behaviour of wells in Heracleium at Gadeira, 217A; asphaltic and gas, 235
wind: compass cards, 137; systems in western Mediterranean, T22; regional winds, 137; etesian winds at tropics, 210C; etesian winds and Nile flooding, 222; in India, 212/213; *favonius* as direction, 212/213; and climate, 223; relation to moon and tides, 138, 219.1-9; establishing latitude, 204A
wine: Sicilian, 234; Chalybonian, 242; vintage marks, 136B2(i)
wool: 234

zodiac: 126; 129/130; 131; 132; 149; 202C(3); 219.80-134; obliquity of, 210
zones: 49B; 49F(1),313; 208; classification of with technical terms, 208; defined astronomically, 208A; in relation to geography, 208B; confusion and non-correspsion between astronomically defined zones and zones of temperature, 208B, 209; different classifications as scientist and human geographer, 210; number of, 209; frigid, temperate and torrid zones, 208B,

1057

SUBJECT INDEX

209; parched on tropics, 209, 210, 223; temperate habitable equatorial zone, 209, 210, 211, 223

C STYLE AND MISCELLANEOUS
analogy: 21; 163; 166
ancients, the: T101; T102; 34; 157; 158; 160; 163; 165.75-102, 133ff; 169B; 182
anecdote: 168; 269; 287
asyndeton: 253.36-47
autopsy: 217B3; 218A; 274

chiasmus: 253.36-47
coinage: of new words or technical phrases, 153; 163C; 164C; 165.22-53; 169E
commentaries: supposed, on Plato's *Timaeus*, 85, 141, 291; on Plato's *Phaedrus*, 86c, 290; on Plato's *Parmenides*, 86d; on Marcellus, 86e
common τόποι: in argument, 36, 159; as instances, 104, 111, 164HI; in geography, 216
conjecture: T88; 49D(2); 216; 272B,32-34; 277.9-15; 280.19-24

diminutives: 54
disgusting instances: 177
doxographies: T101/102; 31B; 42; 49C(1)(a); 87; 91; 118B; 129/130; 131B(b); 135; 139; 149; 155; 165.164ff; 195; 200; 216; 217A2; 222; 246; 285/286 *fin.*

equivocation: 175
etymology: T89; 24; 102; 103; 192; 233; 261; 272; 277a; 280; 280/281

Homeric criticism and interpretation: 277; 280/281; 293

invective: 54; 57; 58; 59; 253.12-23

legend: interpreted with factual base, 239.1-11; 240.6-10; 256; 270

metaphor: 31A; 35C; 163; 105
monograph: supposed, on Pompey, 79
mythological explanation: attacked, 229C, 273, 276

observation of fact: T85; T87; 223; 269; used in empirical argument, 2, 7, 29, 33, 115, 119, 150, 156, 158, 159, 164BC, 165.133, 169A, 217A, 217B3, 218A, 246; deceptive, 114; of zoological or botanical detail, 52, 245
οἱ περὶ Π.: T45; 8; 29; 117; 141A1; 180; 195

personification: 105
puns: 58; 239.1-11; 240.10-16

quotation: T87; T104; 156; 164F; 165

Rhodian examples: 104; 108
riddles: 239.21-4; 240.10-16

sarcasm: 54; 253; 257; 272.2-4
satire: 253
sententiae: 179
simile: T105; 31D; 88; 114; 149; 150
speeches: 253.64-103
style: T103-7; 54; 55; 61; 253; 257

textual emendation: 281.13; 284. 114-25; 292
textual exegesis: 277a; 280/281; 293
triads: 87; 95; 103

vivid or pictorial detail: 54; 57; 61; 71; 72; 77; 226; 227; 253; 257; 267; 274.7-9

1058